MALT
WHISKY
YEARBOOK
2017

First published in Great Britain in 2016 by
MagDig Media Limited

© MagDig Media Limited 2016

ISBN 978-0-9576553-3-1

MagDig Media Limited
1 Brassey Road
Old Potts Way, Shrewsbury
Shropshire SY3 7FA
ENGLAND

E-mail: info@maltwhiskyyearbook.com
www.maltwhiskyyearbook.com

Previous editions

Introduction

Looking back at the first Malt Whisky Yearbook, published in 2005, I wrote in the introduction "the usually turbulent world of malt whiskies can currently be said to be more turbulent than ever". At that time, it did indeed seem turbulent, not least with the big deal of Pernod Ricard taking over Allied Domecq and all their distilleries. Yet at the same time, sales of Scotch whisky were increasing steadily, we didn't debate whether or not a whisky should have an age statement on the label and most of us could afford to buy a thirty year old whisky from a closed distillery without mortgaging our house.

Things have changed since then and the whisky world continues to be turbulent as you can see when you go through this, the latest edition of the Malt Whisky Yearbook. One way of highlighting this was to examine the State of Scotch by asking seven key whisky people some burning questions. Check out their answers to see if you agree.

And again, my excellent team of whisky writers have excelled themselves this year and have contributed with some fascinating articles;

Grain whisky is vital for all the big blends but is there more to it than that? Gavin D Smith widens the perspective when he sees a bright future for single grain as a perfect dram.

What does it take to understand the Millenials and how do they want their whisky? Neil Ridley examines one ot the most important consumer groups today.

Gone are the days when whisky production was restricted to a handful of countries. Becky Paskin met with world distillers trying to define themselves.

Fascinated about stills and what they can do, Jonny McCormick believes that you cannot claim to truly know a distillery until you have set foot inside the stillhouse.

Diageo, the world's largest spirits company, celebrates it´s 20th anniversary next year. Charles MacLean examines the first two decades of a global giant.

The price of whisky - debated amongst whisky enthusiasts but considered by the industry as the elephant in the room. Ian Buxton wants to know why.

A number of new distilleries are opening up in Japan. Nicholas Coldicott and Stefan Van Eycken tell the story of a whisky category on the move.

In Malt Whisky Yearbook 2017 you will also find the unique, detailed and much appreciated section on Scottish malt whisky distilleries. It has been thoroughly revised and updated, not just in text, but also including numerous, new pictures, new distilleries and tasting notes for all the core brands. The chapter on Japanese whisky is completely revised and the presentation of distilleries from the rest of the world has been expanded. You will also find a list of more than 150 of the best whisky shops in the world with their full details and suggestions where to find more information on the internet. The Whisky Year That Was provides a summary of all the signficant events during the year. Finally, the very latest statistics gives you all the answers to your questions on production and consumption.

Thank you for buying Malt Whisky Yearbook 2017. I hope that you will have many enjoyable moments reading it and I can assure you that I will be back with a new edition next year.

Malt Whisky Yearbook 2018 will be published in October 2017.
To make sure you will be able to order it directly, please register at
www.maltwhiskyyearbook.com.

If you need any of the previous eleven volumes of Malt Whisky Yearbook,
some of them are available for purchase (in limited numbers) from the website
www.maltwhiskyyearbook.com

Contents

Acknowledgments

First of all I wish to thank the writers who have shared their great specialist knowledge on the subject in a brilliant and entertaining way – Ian Buxton, Nicholas Coldicott, Stefan Van Eycken, Charles MacLean, Jonny McCormick, Betty Paskin, Neil Ridley and Gavin D. Smith.

A special thanks goes to Gavin who put in a lot of effort nosing, tasting and writing notes for more than 100 different whiskies. Thanks also to Suzanne Redmond for the tasting notes for independent bottlings and to Nicholas and Stefan for the Japanese notes. I am also grateful to Philippe Jugé for his input on French distilleries.

The following persons have also made important photographic or editorial contributions and I am grateful to all of them:

Kevin Abrook, Iain Allan, Stephanie Allison, Alasdair Anderson, Russel Anderson, Nuno Antunes, Paul Aston, Duncan Baldwin, Jan Beckers, Herman Beckley, Georgie Bell, Bartley Blume, Keith Brian, Ross Bremner, Andrew Brown, Earl Brown, Graham Brown, James Brown, Alex Bruce, Gordon Bruce, Simon Buley, Stephen Burnett, Chris Byrne, Pär Caldenby, Neil Cameron, Nathan Campbell, Peter Campbell, Andy Cant, Daniel Cant, Jim Casey, Robert Cassell, Ian Chang, Oliver Chilton, Ashok Chokalingam, Stewart Christine, Claire Clark, Dudley Clark, Gordon Clark, Suzanne Clark, Margaret Mary Clarke, Doug Clement, Willie Cochrane, Zach Cohen, Shelagh Considine, Mike Cotherman, Graham Coull, Jason Craig, Georgie Crawford, Andrew Crook, Keith Cruickshank, Gloria Cummins, Kirsty Dagnan, Susie Davidson, Natasha DeHart, Paul Dempsey, Scott Dickson, Ludo Ducrocq, Will Edwards, Winston Edwards, Lucie Ellis, Craig Engelhorn, Simon Erlanger, Graham Eunson, Patrick Evans, Andy Fiske, Robert Fleming, Callum Fraser, John Gavin, Ewan George, Alison Gibb, Gillian Gibson, Jonathan Gibson, John Glaser, John Glass, Kenny Grant, Jason Grossmiller, Jim Harrelson, Wendy Harries Jones, Stuart Harrington, Steve Hawley, Mickey Heads, Joe Helle, Russell Horn, Liam Hughes, Robbie Hughes, Kathy Humphrey, Jill Inglis, Kevin Innes, Louise Jack, Helen Jagger, Sandy Jameson, Jemma Jamieson, Tom Jensen, Valero Jimenez, Michael John, Jason Jorgensen, Rhona Kallman, Woody Kane, Steven Kearsley, Lena Klopp, Roy Kroeze, Chad Larrabee, Roar Larsen, Nico Liu, Mark Lochhead, Allan Logan, Ian Logan, Polly Logan, Alistair Longwell, Eddie Ludlow, Bill Lumsden, Horst Lüning, Iain MacAllister, Graeme Macaloney, Lauren McArthur, Des McCagherty, Alan McConnochie, Alistair McDonald, Andy Macdonald, John MacDonald, William McHenry, Sandy Macintyre, Alistair Mackenzie, Bruce Mackenzie, Jaclyn McKie, Ian MacMillan, Sarah McNaught, Ian McWilliam, Dennis Malcolm, Derrick Mancini, Martin Markvardsen, Jennifer Masson, Eric Michaud, Santiago Mignone, Leah Miller, Glen Moore, Celine Moran, Carol More, Nick Morgan, Keren Mosessco Kariel, Jake Mountain, Ollie Mulligan, Jari Mämmi, Andrew Nairn, Andrew Nelstrop, Hasse Nilsson, Ingemar Nordblom, Stephen Notman, Nathan Nye, Tim Obert, Jason O'Donnell, Ewan Ogilvie, Linny Oliphant, Ian Palmer, Chieh-Chang Pan, John Pastor, Sean Phillips, Tony Reeman-Clark, Nicol van Rijbroek, Jackie Robertson, James Robertson, Stuart Robertson, Brian Robinson, Karen Robinson-Stark, Darren Rook, Caroline Rylance, Colette Savage, Kirsty Saville, Ernst Scheiner, Ian Schmidt, Lorien Schramm, Jacqui Seargeant, Mike Selberg, Nestor Serenelli, Andrew Shand, Euan Shand, Nicholas Sikorski, Sam Simmons, Sukhinder Singh, Matthieu Smakman, Daniel Smith, Alison Spowart, Greig Stables, Marie Stanton, Karen Stewart, John Stirling, Katie Stirling, Reto Stoeckli, Steven Stone, Gordon Sustins, Duncan Tait, Arttu Taponen, Elizabeth Teape, Phil Thompson, Simon Thompson, David Thomson, Roselyn Thomson, Trent Tilton, Louise Towers, Cordelia Toy, Jon Tregenna, Zac Triemert, Jennifer Turkington, David Turner, Sandrine Tyrbas de Chamberet, Stuart Urquhart, Sean Venus, Brandon Voorhees, Stewart Walker, Heather Wall, Grace Waller, Arch Watkins, Jennifer Watson, Ranald Watson, Mark Watt, Iain Weir, Desiree Whitaker, Nick White, Ronald Whiteford, Anthony Wills, Alan Winchester, Ellie Winters, Stephen Woodcock, Allison B Young.

Finally, to my wife Pernilla and our daughter Alice, thank you for your patience and your love and to Vilda, our labrador and my faithful companion in the office during long working hours.

Ingvar Ronde
Editor
Malt Whisky Yearbook

Girvan grain distillery

Going with the Grain

by Gavin D Smith

Writing in 1969, David Daiches (Scotch whisky), declared that grain whisky was "…not a whisky to drink by itself, nor can it compare as a drink with pot-still malt whisky but it is clearly not just 'silent spirit'; indeed it is rather noisy."

Traditionally, grain spirit has been the ugly duckling of the Scotch whisky world, compared to the single malt swans. Grain whisky is comparatively cheap to produce, and essential to the rise to global dominance of blended Scotch, but glamorous and individualistic it was not. Then, little more than a handful of years ago, a few discerning consumers discovered what blenders had known all along, namely that grain whiskies were by no means characterless and interchangeable, and that without the addition of malt they could even be enjoyed in their own right.

But we are getting way ahead of ourselves. Firstly, we need to examine the evolution of grain whisky. Although Aeneas Coffey rightly gets much of the credit for developing stills that could produce large quantities of relatively inexpensive whisky from unmalted grains, it was in fact Robert Stein who first came up with the idea that the alcohol in fermented wash could be driven off by the use of steam. He patented a still using this principle in 1826.

The Steins intermarried with the Haig family, and together they were almost Scotch whisky royalty during the 18th and early 19th centuries. Robert Stein operated the vast Kilbagie distillery in Clackmannanshire and having installed a 'continuous' still

Aeneas Coffey - inventor of the Coffey still

malted barley converts the starch into sugar, just as in the malt whisky mashing process. Subsequently, the fermented wash – at around 7.5% – is pumped into the stills, which consist of two large, connected, parallel columns, known as the analyser and the rectifier. The wash enters the top of the analyser, and is met by live steam as it flows downward, being slowed in its descent by a series of perforated copper or stainless steel plates. When the wash meets the steam, the alcohol is stripped out, and it enters the rectifier at between 10 and 20% abv. There, the same principle produces a vapour which is condensed into liquid form at approximately 94% abv.

The Scotch Whisky Regulations 2009 define "Single Grain Scotch Whisky" as "…a Scotch Whisky distilled at a single distillery but which, in addition to water and malted barley, may also be produced from whole grains of other malted or unmalted cereals." Like malt whisky, grain whisky must be matured for a minimum of three years in oak casks.

Today Scotland boasts seven grain distilleries, namely William Grant & Sons Ltd's Girvan distillery in Ayrshire, Diageo's Fife Cameronbridge facility, North British in Edinburgh, Chivas Brothers' Strathclyde plant in Glasgow, The Loch Lomond Group's malt and grain distillery at Alexandria in West Dunbartonshire, La Martiniquaise's Starlaw facility near Bathgate in West Lothian, and Whyte & Mackay's Invergordon distillery in the Highlands. Of these, Cameronbridge is the oldest, dating back to 1824 and also Scotland's largest, with a post-expansion capacity in excess of 100 million lpa. The newest of the country's grain distilleries is Starlaw, built to supply grain spirit for French company La Martiniquaise's best-selling Label 5 and Sir Edward's brands.

there, his cousin John Haig soon followed suit at his Cameronbridge distillery in Fife. Stein's design was improved up on by Aeneas Coffey, a former Inspector-General of Excise in Ireland, who patented his Coffey still in 1831. Interestingly, both Stein and Coffey carried out some of their research at Port Ellen distillery on Islay. The development of grain whisky distillation during the 19th century ultimately led to the large-scale blending industry we know today, as it was discovered that when grain spirit was blended with a quantity of malt whisky, the result was a palatable, consistent product. This had a far more widespread appeal than the sometimes fiery and unpredictable output of the pot stills of the Highlands and islands.

One of the principal advantages of producing grain whisky in Coffey, column, continuous or 'patent' stills as they are variously known, is that much larger quantities of spirit can be produced over a given time than is possible in pot stills. For example, during 2014, seven Scottish grain distilleries made 350 mla, while 106 malt distilleries between them turned out 305.7 lpa. Additionally, the unmalted wheat or maize usually used in grain whisky production in Scotland are also considerably cheaper than malted barley, although a percentage of malted barley – usually 10 to 15% – is also required in the 'mash bill'.

When making grain whisky, the unmalted wheat or barley is first cooked in converters under steam pressure in order to release the starch, and the residue after cooking is transferred into the mash tun, where malted barley is added. The diastase in the

Different styles

We have already implied that there is a significant degree of stylistic difference between many grain whiskies, and this informs their use by Scotch whisky blenders. William Grant & Sons' Master Blender Brian Kinsman says that "What we have at Girvan is called a multi-pressure apparatus. We can change the conditions in the first column. The still operates under a slight vacuum, which means a lower boiling temperature. The main reason for this is that it's more efficient, and from a quality point of view you get a clearer spirit, with no degradation of the cereal, that can sometimes give a sulphur-like note when you work at higher temperatures. Our spirit is cleaner and sweeter."

He makes the point that "If you use the same malt whisky components overlaid on different grain bases

Brian Kinsman - Master Blender for William Grant & Sons

then you will get different styles of blend. When I'm working on a new blend, I do the grains and malts separately in the very early stages – I make a blended grain and a blended malt, as it were. The fundamental style of blends is often defined by the grains used, excepting smokiness. Generally, Girvan grain reflects the style of our house blends, such as Grant's Family Reserve – light, fruity and floral."

In terms of where the various grain whiskies fit into the overall stylistic spectrum, Kinsman says that "You have Girvan at one end, and work right through to the big cerealy, sulphury grains. Invergordon stands alone, with a buttery, oily, grassy note, and you have North British and Port Dundas [closed by Diageo in 2011] at the opposite extreme to Girvan. North British is a more robust grain than Girvan, with a slight note of sulphur. In the middle you've got Cameronbridge, which is actually not a million miles from Girvan in style, while Strathclyde is in the middle ground, and Starlaw is quite light."

Sandy Hyslop is Master Blender for Chivas Brothers, owners of Strathclyde grain distillery in Glasgow's Gorbals district, and he declares that "Strathclyde grain is light, delicate and sweet. Personally, I find it like old-fashioned bubble gum. You're looking for light, sweet, 'pink' flavours. For

Sandy Hyslop - Ballantine's Master Blender

Girvan grain distillery

me, it stands shoulder to shoulder with Girvan. It's perfect for the soft, sweet Ballantine's blends and for the big, sweet fruity character of Chivas Regal. It complements malts very well. I will usually use four different grains in a 'standard' blend, but up to seven in Ballantine's 30 or Chivas 25 year old."

Hyslop makes the interesting point that "Single grain is hugely versatile. You can play all sorts of tricks in the cask too, as it picks up cask influence very easily. I like to use grains from second and third-fill casks because I think first-fill casks overwhelm the grain."

Until its closure in 2002 and subsequent demolition, Chivas Brothers predecessors Allied Domecq also owned the large Dumbarton grain distillery, located some 15 miles from Glasgow. Clearly Dumbarton grain whisky still plays a part in the blends produced by Sandy Hyslop, as he points out that "We have large inventories of old Dumbarton grain. Stylistically, it was very different to Strathclyde, but when we closed Dumbarton we adjusted the equipment at Strathclyde to produce spirit closer in character to Dumbarton. We fine-tuned it a little. Strathclyde used to be a little more sulphury.

"I'm a big believer in the use of sacrificial copper

[copper surfaces inserted into the stainless steel still]. Copper contact is important to get a lighter spirit, and you can draw off spirit at seven or eight different places on the still. If you draw higher, you get lighter, cleaner spirit. Fermentation acidity is another factor you can play around with. If the wash is more acidic then the spirit is likely to be heavier in style."

The choice of grain

As already noted, North British sits at the opposite end of the grains spectrum to the likes of Girvan and Strathclyde, and Production Director Tommy Leigh explains some of the reasons why this is the case. "We still use maize at present, rather than wheat," he notes. "The costs were comparable a few years ago because even though maize was more expensive, you get a much higher yield from it due to it having more starch than wheat and being less energy-intensive. It gives you a different quality of spirit, too.

"Over the last few years maize has actually been cheaper than wheat, and for a time Invergordon and Starlaw were also using maize as well as us. But for the next few years wheat is going to be significantly

Loch Lomond grain distillery

cheaper, and they've switched back. We continue using maize because of the ease of processing it through our particular plant, though we are currently doing wheat trials to see how it goes.

"To me, North British has more vanilla and toffee on the nose than other grains, and more vanilla character. It's a heavier-bodied spirit than some, and more complex than wheat-based spirit. It has more sweetness, which might appeal to younger drinkers; and blenders like that quality if they are aiming at the younger market."

Apart from the choice of grain, what other features influence the style of spirit being produced in grain distilleries, in the opinion of Tommy Leigh? "The key differences between various grains include the malt inclusion rate, and at North British we use green malt, which nobody else does.

"North British has a high inclusion of green malt, and we do our own malting on site", he says. Green malt is germinated barley before it is dried by kilning, and at North British, part of the distinctive character of the spirit is due to the fact that the amount of green malt in the mash bill is as high as 16%. Other grain distilleries use smaller amounts of malted barley rather than green malt, and Leigh

explains that "We believe it is part of the character of North British, and there is also a monetary factor in that we avoid the high energy input costs incurred by drying the malt".

Leigh adds that fermentation times are also a factor, pointing out that "Maize takes much longer than wheat – always 75 hours plus, whereas wheat would usually have a maximum fermentation time of 65 hours. There are differences from distillery to distillery. You can also adjust temperatures to affect flavour, but in my opinion this really makes only a very slight difference."

Unique among Scotland's distilleries is Loch Lomond, located in the West Dunbartonshire town of Alexandria. Loch Lomond produces both malt and grain spirit, and Loch Lomond Group's Master Blender Michael Henry notes that "We have two styles of grain whisky: the first, based on wheat, is the standard style of grain whisky which would be closest in flavour profile to Girvan. The second style, unique to Loch Lomond, in Scotland is based on 100% malted barley and is closer to a single malt in flavour profile."

Henry adds that "We use smaller column stills than other grain distilleries in Scotland, and they are effectively less efficient in flavour separation, which means you get butterscotch notes coming over. We also use a relatively low mash temperature, compared with somewhere like North British. Their high temperature mashing releases some sulphur, which they are looking for in their spirit.

"As well as the standard grain spirit made from wheat, we also distil 100% malted barley in a separate column still. We take that off at 85% rather than the 94% we would normally use. You get lots more flavour in the wash, and collecting at 85% keeps more flavour in. It's a malt, and we use it with our 'standard' grain and our malt in some blends. This frees up more of our malt spirit for bottling as single malt."

In terms of operational flexibility, Henry adds that "You can have flexibility in the character of the malted grain by varying temperatures, to give a more fruity style, and we can take spirit off at various points on the column. There are eight 'plates' where you can take spirit off – nearer the bottom is a heavier style."

"Each grain distillery has different types of equipment, and the older ones like Invergordon have higher temperature mashing. In general it's the equipment and the way it is set up that dictates how you run it. There's not much flexibility. In most column stills there is just one take-off point to collect spirit, and you can only change the strength a little, certainly not much. Grain stills need to be set up to run as efficiently as possible, due to the cost of production and the volumes being processed."

The rise of a new category

Having explored some of the stylistic differences between grain whiskies and how those differences are created, it is time to return to our starting point, and the relatively recent discovery of the virtues of grain whisky by consumers. For many years, the only proprietary brand of single grain Scotch whisky on the market was Old Cameron Brig, distilled at Cameronbridge, though other producers experimented with single grain releases for a time before quietly dropping them due to lack of interest.

However, independent bottlers such as Douglas Laing & Co and the Scotch Malt Whisky Society championed single grains, and John Glaser's Compass Box Whisky Co launched the first 'vatted' or 'blended' grain in the shape of Hedonism during 2000.

John Glaser is on record as saying that grain whiskies are "…the elegant, almost feminine alter ego to Scotland's malt whiskies. Most people think of them as the 'filler' whiskies in the well-known, com-

mercial blends, but this is far from the whole story. Each grain whisky distillery in Scotland makes a distinctive spirit. And the best grain whiskies – from great casks – are some of the silkiest, sweetest, most mouth-wateringly delicious whiskies in the world. I believe that great grain whiskies from well-chosen casks are the undiscovered treasures of Scotland's whisky kingdom".

Glaser explains that "Hedonism represents a style that we are meticulous about. It is based on two key things: using Scottish grain whisky distilleries which produce what we call a 'sweet' style, (e.g. Cameron Bridge distillery); and aging only in 'first fill' American oak barrels."

The expression shares a welcome degree of transparency with other Compass Box whiskies. Bottle batch label details can be explored at the Compass Box website to give unprecedented transparency regarding composition.

Different styles of grain whisky

For example, batch MMXIV - B was blended from three Scotch grain whiskies, with the youngest whisky being distilled in 1997. According to Compass Box "The majority of the recipe (58%) is from a Fife distillery and all the casks used were first fill American oak barrels. Next, 26% of this batch comes from a Glaswegian distillery, grain whiskies aged in first fill American casks. Finally, the remainder of this recipe is grain whisky from a South Ayrshire distillery, and the casks used were all first fill American oak barrels. This batch of Hedonism was created by blending a total of 19 casks…"

Eventually some of the major distillers began to think that there might just be something in this grain whisky notion, most significantly William Grant & Sons and Diageo. In 2013 Grant's announced the release of Girvan 25 year old, the first bottling in a new Girvan Patent Still range, and followed it up with Girvan No. 4 Apps' and Girvan 30 year old. The No. 4 Apps was the first, non-age statement whisky to be released by the brand, and the name 'Apps' is a distillery term for 'Apparatus.' No.4 Apps has been producing Girvan's unique 'vacuum distilled' spirit since 1992.

Brian Kinsman notes that "Girvan single grain releases have all been matured in American oak, as it accentuates the style of the grain. We're looking for something sweet, with a hint of fruitiness. It's an additive maturation, as there's nothing to clean up, as it were. Over the years we will augment the existing range as we're very pleased by the reception so far. There is definitely more we can do with it. Grain is still continually overlooked – I think there's room for a really high volume single grain that could compete with Bourbon. It has an easy taste profile and is incredibly versatile."

Not to be outdone, Diageo launched Haig Club during 2014 in association with David Beckham and entrepreneur Simon Fuller. Haig Club is a single grain whisky from Cameronbridge, and according to Dr Nick Morgan, Diageo's Head of Whisky Outreach "Haig Club has been crafted using a unique process that combines grain whisky from three cask types – refill, American Oak and rejuvenated (largely ex-Bourbon). The refill casks (both barrels and hogsheads), express distillery character (creamy, toffee, butterscotch flavours), while the fresh Bourbon casks add toffee, butterscotch, coconut and Brazil nut nuances. And finally we added whisky that had been matured in rejuvenated oak casks, adding a unique measure of peppery spicy rich wood flavour."

2015 saw Douglas Laing & Co start to take grain whiskies even more seriously than they previously had when the firm launched its range of Old Particular Single Cask Single Grain Whiskies, which initially issued Cameronbridge 25 years old, Girvan 25 years old, North British 21 years old and Strathclyde 27 years old bottlings.

According to Managing Director Fred Laing, "Over the last five to six years we have softly promoted, and gently educated the malt community with the 'surprise' quality of old grain Scotch whiskies, and we have been rewarded with sustained growth. Douglas Laing & Co certainly believes the time is now right to give this long under-rated sector far greater kudos. So within our Old Particular Single Cask flagship brand, we will now release selected antique stocks of different grain Scotch whiskies."

Laing's release of such old grain whiskies – many distilled from maize rather than wheat – begs the question as to whether the cereal in question has affected their style. William Grant's Master Blender Brian Kinsman declares that "We've got old stocks of grain from pretty much every grain distillery in Scotland, and many of the old ones will have been distilled from maize, not wheat. However, the differences between the two are not that great. When you sample grains that are 30 years and older there's no obvious step change between the use of maize and the use of wheat."

Douglas Laing's veteran 'sipping' single grains are obviously targeting a different market to those of Girvan and Haig Club, but the momentum behind the grain whisky sector is clearly growing, and on an international basis, with other major Scotch whisky distillers such as Chivas Brothers almost certainly planning to enter the fray at some point in the not too distant future.

Taking it out of context, David Daiches' comment about grain whisky being "rather noisy" has nonetheless proved rather apt!

Gavin D Smith is one of Scotland's leading whisky writers and Contributing Editor to www.whisky-pages.com. He regularly undertakes writing commissions for leading drinks companies and produces articles for a wide range of publications, including Whisky Magazine, Whisky Advocate, Whiskeria and Drinks International. He is the author of more than 20 books and collaborated with Dominic Roskrow to produce a new edition of the Michael Jackson's Malt Whisky Companion in 2010. His latest books are The Whisky Opus, co-written with Dominic Roskrow and Let Me Tell You About Whisky, co-written with Neil Ridley.

Watch Out!
The Millenials Are Coming

by Neil Ridley

Neil Ridley examines the whisky industry's
latest buzz word and attempts to understand its impact on a
new generation of whisky drinkers.

Why Must I Be A Teenager In Love? Are you familiar with the names Doc Pomus and Mort Shuman? No? Then again, why should you be. How about Dion & The Belmonts? Getting warmer? The two gentlemen in question were successful American songwriters in the 1950s. As the decade drew to a close, a chance songwriting session saw the duo pen arguably one of the most defining moments in pop culture: A Teenager In Love. With vocal group Dion & The Belmonts as their vehicle to perform the song, Pomus and Shuman launched an assault on the charts, which saw Teenager hit the top 5 on both sides of the Atlantic and become an enduring classic in the canon of dreamy doo-wop Americana.

The song had another huge influence too, perhaps almost vicariously. Despite not being able to lay claim to being the first use of the word Teenager it effectively gave birth to the concept of youth marketing; a discovery of a demographic that really didn't exist until the end of the 50's. The word Teenager was a dream come true for the Mad Men. A new hook to sell-in to corporations who produced tooth-rotting fizzy drinks; a sweet, chunky wedge of the pie chart, ripe for exploitation and overexposure of mass-produced action figures, fashion lines and junk food. Four decades later, another tantalisingly delicious marketing term emerged. In 1991, Canadian author Douglas Coupland released Generation X – Tales For An Accelerated Culture which, helped coin the description of a previously untitled demographic. Loosely speaking, Gen X spanned anyone born between 1961 and 1981.

Now I'd put money on it now that most of you reading this probably fall into this group. I certainly do. Here's the question though. How does it feel to be herded together – all right into the centre of the venn diagram?

It's an issue that has once again reared up over the last few years and especially so within the marketing of whisky. I remember hearing the word Millennial for the first time back in 2013, in the boardroom of a well known Scotch whisky company. I was immediately suspicious. I suspected that some clever marketing bod had come up with a internal company term to describe the next generation of drinkers. For a second, I felt isolated, outdated and if I'm honest, quite old. But as I listened, I grew more enlightened about just how this new term was going to effectively change the landscape of the spirit, whether I liked it or not.

For those who aren't familiar with the phrase, a Millennial can be anyone born between the very late 1970's (yes, there's a slight crossover with Gen X) and the year 2000. They also masquerade as Generation Y for logical reasons that I don't need to mention here. The term undoubtedly has its fans (mostly those in front of a whiteboard with power-point presentation beaning straight onto it,) but also its critics.

"Millennial is an overused catch-all phrase for digitally adept younger people, which has crept into the everyday vernacular of the marketing community," thinks Jason Craig, Brand Director for Highland Park. "The opportunities for this target are the same as they have been for decades: recruiting younger people into the whisky category – the challenge is how to do that into the future. The label is simply just a new label."

"I don't like the word Millennial," explains Daryl Haldane, Global Brand Advocate for The Macallan. "We talk about this hugely diverse and complex group of people as if they are one person or a homogeneous group of people. In fact, they are often spoken about as if they are not even people, rather they are outlandish beings that landed from a far flung planet that we never even knew existed until 3 years ago."

"That being said," he continues, "I am aware that we have a younger and more curious consumer - aka 'The Millennials' - enjoying whisky. They have a thirst for information and experiences. For a single malt whisky brand, I believe this offers a huge opportunity to be more creative in terms of production, innovation and most importantly, the moment when our consumers actually enjoy our products – we must be very open-minded."

Jason Craig, Brand Director for Highland Park

Haldane raises a salient point here, with two words that will keep cropping up a few times during this article: Information and Experiences. Both words have become insightful into the mindset of the Millennial, along with Authenticity and Craftsmanship. Together, they have shaped whisky marketing strategies and crucially, have also played a big part in the new product development (NPD) of whisky.

Allow me to turn to my long standing colleague and friend, drinks writer Joel Harrison, who whether he likes it or not, is probably classed as a Millennial, albeit only just, being born in November, 1979. He recently wrote an excellent commentary on the Rise Of The Millennial for a drinks industry website, which raises the tricky job of trying to define the behaviour of Millennials and their slightly flighty consumption habits.

"The Millennial consumer lives their life as something of a juxtaposition and drinks companies need to be very aware of the consequences of getting this wrong," he explains. "There's a phrase here that seems to apply very succinctly: You really wouldn't want to buy a watch made by the same people who make your pants. This may sound vaguely cryptic," he continues, "but the sentiment is sound. Millennials are equally as happy extolling the virtues of

The succesful Haig Club campaign

why the single malt they're drinking is hand crafted in small batches, dating back to 1877 or whenever, but they're equally adept at telling you why it's cool to use a cheap, mass market white rum when making the best Daiquiri cocktail."

Focused on quality

By way of example of the above, consider the recent Haig Club campaign. To some, this represents a liberation of whisky; a spirit with purported heritage dating back to the 1700's, but maverick in its approach to its suggested serve and brand positioning. Potentially, very appealing to our new group of drinkers then. To others however, it lacks the authenticity that Millennials crave, simply because it is backed by a man who has his own successful line of underwear. The internet savvy consumer isn't fooled one bit by glossy campaigns any more and marketeers are becoming increasingly aware of the pitfalls.

"Millennials are focused on quality, a good story that has merit – (i.e you can't make things up so easily nowadays, as if you do, and it gets out on social media, you risk damaging your brand) and variety," explains Alywnne Gwilt, former whisky writer and blogger, now Whisky Specialist at William Grant & Sons UK - and a Millennial to boot.

"Scotch already has very solid foundations in its history, and very good quality. The key is in creating variety, without undermining either of those things. Creating a fancily packaged product that's rubbish will only be successful in the short term. The other important aspect is finding a way to communicate these virtues through the right medium, such as Instagram and Twitter, where you see a large number of Millennials interacting. It's about creating a quality product that wows without 'selling out', because that will be seen through more easily.'

For Georgie Bell, Global Brand Ambassador at Dewar's/Bacardi (and another Millennial), the word 'experience' is central to the understanding of the Millennial mindset. "We now live in a 'glocalised' world – where global has become local," she explains, "and we want to experience all of that, to have access to all of that physically, and digitally with the rise – and increased importance placed on social media. What we want is new, true, honest experiences."

"Everything for us is experiential," she continues: "from the ritual, to the surroundings, to the bragging rights - and we want education! We want to learn, as much as we can, to become those 'in the know' to be able to share that knowledge with others."

Georgie Bell – Global Brand Ambassador for Dewar´s

So how does a whisky company begin to plan out promoting a traditionally parochial drink to a younger Millennial audience?

"The opportunities are endless," thinks Bell, but we're wise – we can see through gimmicks – we don't mind spending money – in fact, most of us live outside our means but we want to spend it on quality, rather than quantity, and often this spending is tied to a past experience of first trying it, or buying to create a shared experience in the future with friends."

From a global spirit perspective, what learnings are there to be had for Scotch whisky, when it comes to enticing millennials to take a sip? American Rye and Bourbon, Irish and Japanese whisky all seem to have successfully spoken to this emerging generation, in a vernacular that inspires a confidence to seek out new flavours but also to respect heritage and authenticity when it is delivered truthfully. Yes, there are numerous examples, particularly in American whiskey, where dubious stories of false provenance have been exposed – for very good reason, but as a spirit, it appears to be bullet proof – and winning more fans over by the second.

"I saw an online promo video recently for a well-known Scotch single malt whisky brand, which was achingly trying to appeal to Bourbon drinkers, which made it feel almost surreal at times," laughs Joel Harrison. "You simply can't carry a bottle of single malt into a party, or in this instance, a summer barbecue and expect it to perform, or be as openly consumable and widely accepted as an American whiskey. No matter how you dress Scotch up, it just doesn't have the same cultural DNA as a Bourbon, which is somewhat ironic, given the actual liquid DNA that both spirits share! Irish whiskey on the other hand," he continues, "is fortunately blessed with an imagery that has never taken itself too seriously and therefore isn't saddled with the same fundamental issues that lie at the heart of Scotch. Brands like Jameson have consistently invested in Millennials and now Teeling are doing the same thing, making very appealing, approachable whiskeys for younger palates."

The parochial image

I'm taken back to something that Georgie Bell mentioned earlier, the intriguing portmanteau that is 'glocalisation' and the fact that younger generations are so far more adept at communicating with their international peers than ever before, which is a fundamental trait of the Millennial. In some respects, particularly in mature markets closer to home, Scotch will always struggle to shake its parochial image, despite being given a craft makeover that is clearly appealing to Millennials. But travel further afield and things are definitely different.

Stephen Notman, (you've guessed it…a Millennial)

Shaking The World Of Whisky

Stephen Notman

whisky consultant and founder of a number of highly successful experiential Whisky L events across China – and more recently in Taiwan – thinks that despite similarities in the way South East Asian Millennials are as tech savvy and information hungry as those living in Europe and North America, they aren't saddled with the same negative preoccupations about whisky.

"One of the things we've always had here is that it isn't seen as your father's drink. It is definitely a lifestyle choice and because we're in the early stages, it hasn't had an opportunity to become stagnant," he explains. "There's a lot that the west can really adopt here which has resonated well with Millennial drinkers in China."

One of Notman's recent successes involved a live streaming event programme for World Whisky Day, via WeChat, the phenomenally successful Chinese social media app. Shaking The World Of Whisky saw 80,000 people watch live streamed tastings conducted by Notman and some key bartenders in six coordinated bars across Shanghai. "It was a crazy experience," he smiles. "Like a food show but with all these questions being texted in from the viewers, during the tastings. The interaction was incredible. Where once, we would walk into a bar and look at what they stocked behind it for inspiration, these new drinkers are looking at their phones to guide them on what to drink."

So where are the other inspirational hotspots where the Millennial consumer is being best understood?

"One of my top markets would be Australia," responds Georgie Bell. "The experiential side of activating whisky in Australia – across brands and styles – really taps into the Millennial lifestyle and desires. I've seen a lot of great collaborative work with designers, award shows, music festivals, boating weekends, street-food pop ups…things that are actually cool – that influential lifestyle magazines like VICE, Munchies and Concrete [who are notoriously difficult to pitch 'whisky' stories to in the first place] would write about. With Dewar's and our malt whiskies we have started to run some exciting experiential activations aimed directly at Millennial lifestyle, our amazing Scotch Egg Club events [which bring together whisky cocktails, live music,

Dewar´s Scotch Egg Club events bring together whisky cocktails, cuisine and live music

cuisine and other experiential activities] have been a lot of fun in Madrid, Berlin and Beirut.”

"For me," continues Jason Craig, "it was a couple of years ago, whilst I was Brand Director on Cutty Sark in Spain, Portugal and Greece, as I watched younger men and women actively consuming blended Scotch in long mixed serves. They were consuming Scotch because they wanted to: it has appeal, tastes great and it enhanced their own personal brand. That made me confident that the hundreds of years of development, brand equity building and most importantly, trust in our world class whiskies will last the test of time.”

The danger here is that seemingly brands are becoming totally fixated on the romanticism of younger Millennial drinkers and what they potentially bring to the world of whisky, from a cultural reference point, besides an ever increasing bottom line on the balance sheet. In doing so, are they potentially focusing all their attentions and crucially messaging and NPD on a volatile, highly unproven demographic, rather than servicing those from Generation X, who not only have the existing interest, but also the regular disposable income to spend on premium

whisky. Yes, the business needs to progress and can only do so by forecasting and becoming more appealing to future generations, but let's not throw all our Scotch eggs into one hand crafted, Millennial-shaped basket.

"I think you simply have to make the best whisky you possibly can, be completely clear on what you stand for and what you do not stand for, have a purpose and a clear communication message," argues Jason Craig. "This will ensure you can last through fashions and fads to have longevity – then your brand will last. If you are short term and chase fads, then Scotch whisky is the wrong business to be in. However, there is always the opportunity to be creative, innovative and ensure that you do not rest on your laurels: packaging, new finishes, storytelling and remembering our Scottish sense of humour.”

"The whisky world is one that lives on future predictions," adds Alwynne Gwilt: "how many casks should I be setting aside for 10 or 12 years from now? What will the future drinker want? Yes, you can potentially use that stock to create new releases that respond to market demand of the time, but the industry is based on a lot of forecasting. Therefore,

The Centennials prefer a healthy lifestyle

even more reliant on online technology to communicate, consume and develop personal experiences. They are more risk averse than Millennials, likely to be highly influenced by peer-to-peer opinion, and more likely to 'curate' their possessions, rather than be influenced by disposable fads and fashions.

From the perspective of whisky brands, despite Centennials being clearly under the legal drinking age at the moment, the two latter findings bode well, especially given the industry's increased focus on world-of-mouth reputation building, authenticity, experience and the balance between information and education. However, dig a little deeper and perhaps the most worrying aspect for the drinks industry to get its collective head around is that Centennials are far less likely to be interested in consuming alcohol when the time presents itself, preferring to get their kicks from much more holistic, healthy lifestyle choices, including more nutritious eating habits, exercise and abstinence. Such is the lack of excitement for this new cohort that some studies have already labelled it 'Generation Yawn'. As a demographic, Centennials are much more likely to do the exact opposite to what their parents and grand parents did – and do, which is a scary thought, considering the huge emphasis whisky companies are placing on those very people.

"Oh no – please no Generation Yawn!" laughs Georgie Bell. "However, you touch on a very relevant point and this does cover Millennials too. The 'sugar' fear – mindfulness – fitness – Ironman/triathlon obsessives. Not all are like this, but it is relevant and should be considered by whisky companies. I do believe that we can learn from what we're doing from a marketing/experiential/innovation perspective, and refine it even further for future generations. Brands need to look outside of whisky – what's trending from a lifestyle perspective, and how can they fit within that."

I think it is important to be considering this because even if a Millennial may not be drinking Scotch today, they may be in one, two or eight years time and it's vital to understand how your potential market shifts and develops. It shouldn't be a 'worry' but very much a consideration."

Next up – Generation Z

Speaking of forecasting, shouldn't the industry be looking a bit further round the corner to a generation beyond the hallowed Millennials? That's right folks. Hot on the heels of the already tech savvy, information-hungry would-be whisky drinkers is something much more terrifying altogether.

I recently read a fascinating piece of research by Futures Company, a London-based global research forecasting agency, which pointed to the rise of the Centennials; Generation Z by any other name, who were born into a post-2000 world. Already dealing with issues that were faced by Millennials much later into their lives, Centennials, who currently make up over 25% of the population of the USA, are potentially a more responsible, savvy generation,

Maybe in my advancing years I should become a songwriter… just think of the marketing possibilities I could potentially influence…

Neil Ridley writes regularly about whisky for a wide range of drinks and lifestyle publications. He is the Editor-at-Large for Whisky Magazine, Spirits & Cocktail Columnist for the Sunday Telegraph, Deputy Editor for Whisky Quarterly, as well as presenting a regular drinks feature on the popular TV show, Channel 4 Sunday Brunch. He is also one of the authors (together with Gavin D Smith) of Let Me Tell You About Whisky and in 2014, his latest book, Distilled (written together with Joel Harrison) was published, winning the Fortnum & Mason Drink Book Of The Year in 2015.

Matt Hofmann - Master Distiller at Westland Distillery

Malts
of no nation

by Becky Paskin

Gone are the days when whisky production was restricted
to a handful of countries. These days you find distilleries in all
corners of the world. Innovators and craftsmen are making high quality
whisky but many of them also feel there is a need for regulations.
Defining what constitutes a malt whisky in their country,
can prove to be a unique selling point.

Love them or loathe them, the Scotch Whisky Association (SWA) has been fighting battles in the name of defending Scotch from fraudsters, imitators and rogue distillers since 1912. The spirit's regulations – which are protected by the EU – may be considered overly strict by the more innovative distillers, but they have also helped Scotch become the most respected and popular whisky in the world.

It's not just the Scottish who are protective of their whisky and its heritage; as demand for global single malts has increased in recent years, so has an aspiration from some distillers to establish legally binding regulations governing their own production practices. Distillers in the world's emerging malt-producing regions have, over time, developed their own philosophies about what single malt from their patch of the earth should be: minimum age requirements, use of local water and barley, non-chill-filtra-

Garryana - the latest innovation from Westland Distillery in Seattle

tion, prohibiting the addition of caramel colouring, even permitting column distilling. The specifications are varied, and although most are largely based on Scotch whisky's regulations, many believe their own definition of single malt to be an improvement.

While some individual distillers are considered renegade in their approach and are flying solo, those that share similar sentiments and postal codes are banding together to form cohesive alliances. The more local distilleries that share the same views and production processes, the greater the perceived necessity for their whisky to be regulated. And, just like Scotch, that need is driven by both a desire to protect the style of whisky produced, as well as promote its unique qualities. After all, these are mostly small distilleries from emerging malt markets with no established definition of single malt whisky. Individually they are small – the malts of no nation – that are struggling on the global market to make their voices heard above the roar of Scotch, Bourbon and Irish whiskey. But together they represent a new movement that will change the single malt status quo forever.

A new category in the USA

There needn't be an established history or tradition of making single malt for a region's whiskies to gain protection. In the US, where the advent of single malt whisky can be linked to the recent evolution of

craft distilling, a movement to establish a nationwide definition is gathering pace.

"One of the challenges we all face is the fact that it has never been done before in the US," says Matt Hofmann, master distiller of Westland Distillers, a member of the American Single Malt Whiskey Commission (ASMWC), which is leading a campaign to define American single malt whiskey for the first time. "There's no history of single malt here, so there's no official category definition under the TTB and therefore there's no best practise in the way it's positioned on shelves, simply because it hasn't existed before."

Up until recently the ASMWC was a collective of 10 distilleries across the US that shared a common vision of American single malt's definition. Now that collective has reached 20 distilleries, and Hofmann hopes to have doubled that figure by the time the TTB opens its rare public consultation in the summer. "It's important that the people in this country who are making single malt have a say in how we're going to categorise it," he says. "It shouldn't just be Westland; we should be as open and inclusive as possible."

The definition itself is strikingly parallel to Scotch whisky, the only dissimilarity being that single malt can also be distilled in column stills up to 80% abv – a provision disallowed in Scotland. American single malt is also not tied to the requirement to

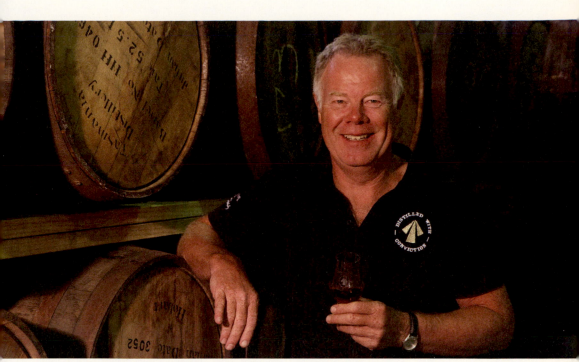

Patrick McGuire – distiller and president of the Tasmanian Whisky Producer's Association

be matured in 'traditional' oak casks, allowing for innovation in ways Scottish distillers are forbidden from exploring.

"There are all these cultural traditions in Scottish whisky making that they follow very tightly, whereas the way we use those same ingredients can manifest itself differently," Hofmann explains. "As far as the definition goes, we want to be sure to keep it wide enough to allow for us to continue that innovation you're already seeing in single malt, and that's what makes American single malt whisky different, and unique from Scotland, aside from the fact it's made in the US."

If approved by the TTB, the regulation will also pave the way for producers across the US to establish regional variants, centred around water source and oak provenance, and subcategories could very well be established in the future.

Hofmann hopes that through defining American single malt, the category will be given greater prominence in stores, leading to better consumer education and ultimately an opportunity for the category to compete with the likes of Scotch whisky.

As the ASMWC mission statement declares: "In the end, the goal is to better compete with other regional single malt brands and categories around the globe based on the merits of our product instead of competing against a lack of knowledge."

Tasmanian whisky

A similar movement is gaining momentum Down Under, only this time Tasmanian distillers are more concerned with protecting the style of whisky they create from confusion with the product made in the rest of Australia. In Tasmania, a temperate seasonal microclimate means provenance is king – single malt is made using barley grown on the island, the whisky cut with water gleaned from its rivers, and all bottling completed before the whisky sees sight of a ship. Rather than settle for being labelled 'Australian whisky', a catch-all for whisky matured through the south's changeable seasons, the tropical climate of Queensland, or even the arid plains of Northern Territory, the Tasmanian Whisky Producers' Association (TWPA) wants an appellation of its own.

Patrick McGuire, president of the TWPA and master distiller at Sullivan's Cove, says: "We have everything we need to make the bones of a really good product. That's not to say the other parts of Australia can't do the same; some places are beautiful and their location is great but in Tasmania we've been doing it the longest, we have a better skill set than the others at this stage, and we've better maturation."

In the country's island state producers are under no illusion that they'll be able to compete with the might of Scotch, Bourbon or Irish whiskey anytime soon. The annual output of Tasmania's largest distillery – Hellyer's Road near Devonport – is insignificant even compared to Scotland's smallest distillery, and although plans for major expansion are rumbling on, it will be some time before Tasmania establishes itself as a whisky powerhouse. It's unfortunate considering the number of global accolades bestowed upon the region's whiskies.

The TWPA's own definition of single malt is exactly the same as Scotch, although due to the warmer climate, it need only be matured for a minimum of two years. The group has already run its proposal past the Tasmanian government – which McGuire says has offered its full support – and is due to meet with Brand Tasmania, the same government-funded organisation that helped put Tasmanian wine on the map.

McGuire adds that the success of the proposal so far has hinged on the collaborative effort of all the island's 12 distilleries. "If we'd been only one or two distilleries and we didn't work together we wouldn't be in the position we are now," he explains. "We are all too small to do this alone, so by banding together and building a name for the Tasmanian whisky brand rather than naming any individual brand, we'll get a lot further."

Single malt appellations

The total agreement and collaboration between a region's distilleries is a more powerful gift than you'd imagine. One need only turn back toward Europe and examine the fractious impact the introduction of France's two whisky appellations has had to realise they only really work when distilleries function together.

Since January 2016, 44 French whisky producers and bottlers have united under the Fédération du Whisky de France, a trade association designed to protect and promote whisky produced entirely in the country. Although the association is officially recognised by the French government, its whisky as a whole does not carry an appellation.

However, in 2015 the government granted protected status for whisky produced in Alsace and Brittany (Whisky Breton) to certain specifications. Not every distillery welcomed the news. Almost immediately Jean Donnay, owner of Glann ar Mor distillery announced the closure of his Brittany distillery as its production set-up did not comply with the new regulations for Whisky Breton. He later changed his mind and succumbed to the new rules, though is forbidden from referring to Brittany as a place of origin on his bottles.

It was difficult for Brittany's five whisky distilleries to agree on a definition – not all of them made whisky in the same way, as although the region has a long history of brewing and brandy distillation, its first single malt was only released in 1997.

At first the definition of Whisky Breton was created to also include unaged spirit, a description soon removed following a challenge from the SWA – staunch defenders of Scotch and single malt as a whisky. As the region's Distillerie des Menhirs has produced a whisky made from buckwheat since 2002, Brittany was granted permission to be the only protected whisky region in Europe to make grain whisky from a pseudo-grain.

The same issues plagued Alsace. Its nine distilleries found it impossible to reach an agreement on how single malt produced in the region should be defined. As blending German grain with French malt is so rife in Alsace, blended whisky was omitted from the regulations. The region now has a definition for single malt only, that just three of the 12 distilleries takes advantage of.

"They decided to create a complicated regulation, to over-protect the whisky," explains whisky expert Philippe Jugé. "The other nine decided not to join the association that protects the whisky, so they can't have the label. The regulation is too difficult to adhere to."

Alsatian single malt must be distilled in pot stills smaller than 250 litres, and made from ingredients sourced within the region. Its most unique regulation is that while the whisky must be matured in oak casks for its first three years, any combination of alternative wood can be used for further maturation afterward, including hickory acacia and larch.

What's the use of a protected appellation if only a quarter of distilleries want to make use of it? "There was no point in defining such a regulation if a vast

French whisky expert Philippe Jugé

Box distillery in Sweden is looking for cooperation with craft distillers around the world

majority of distillers are not included," shrugs Jugé. "Of course the geographical origin is very important when you talk about food, but it's less important for spirit. In the world we live in now, and especially in the spirits world, it's more about brands than regulation or category."

Distillers of the world unite

An appellation or protected status can give regional distillers a much louder presence on the global stage than on their own, though forcing a regional definition through without the support of all parties or a solid code is futile. The reality is all too true for Box distillery in Sweden, which is attempting to establish an appellation for Swedish whisky defined as non-chill-filtered and containing zero caramel colouring or anti-foam, to no avail. "I'm not too optimistic that all of Sweden's distilleries will agree on a definition," says Jan Groth, brand manager for Box. "The document is there, the only problem is only two of us agree on all the points. With up to eight of us making whisky, only two agreeing doesn't say very much."

Faced with an impossible task of talking round six headstrong Swedes, Box is eyeing up a different solution. "If we had the opportunity to meet other craft distilleries around the globe they would probably agree on all our points," he explains. "We can do something global about this." Box's idea is to create a marque that defines a craft distillery, one that would unite similar-minded distillers around the world under one common label. Products car-

rying the marque would notify consumers that the whisky is made to a certain specification, one that is not bound by geographical borders but by a shared global ethos.

"We are the same family but we're not working together," says Groth. "At the end of the day we want to earn money but we have to help each other to develop rather than only compete, and it's what we have to do, particularly in the future, to survive."

The establishment of varying regional single malt styles and even global definitions united by a craft philosophy will certainly provide clarity for consumers on an individual basis, but ultimately they will break down the existing globally accepted definition of single malt whisky.

There is no one approach anymore – gone are the days when single malt was another term for Scotch whisky. As consumers we will be seeing far more innovation within the single malt category outside Scotland, and quite probably even the rise of new single malt nations.

Becky Paskin is editor of new digital magazine Scotchwhisky.com, the world's most authoritative online guide to Scotch whisky. She is the only journalist to gain a General Certificate in Distillation with the Institute of Brewing and Distilling – a qualification usually reserved for distillery operators. The former editor of The Spirits Business magazine, Becky is an expert in all manner of spirits and regularly presents educational whisky seminars at global drinks shows including Tales of the Cocktail in New Orleans and The Whisky Show in London.

Swan Neck Vapour Trails

journeys through the copper pot still

by Jonny McCormick

The copper pot still epitomizes the Scotch whisky industry. I am of the opinion that you cannot claim to truly know a distillery until you have set foot inside the stillhouse. Hasten past the mashtun and washbacks: mere appetizers, nothing more than pine and steel preliminaries before the main event. Lead on, my friend, I am impatient.

Enter the stillhouse and marvel at the glory of it all. Watch, listen, and above all, remember to keep breathing. Polished copper Goliaths occupy the room, orbicular kettles of distillation fashioned like lanterns, pears, or onions. Elegant necks are bent over and angled into sturdy condensers. Against the constant operational thrum, you can detect the frothing creamy wash slapping the viewing window and the scrape of work boots over steel gratings. With a sultry, radiant heat sticking your shirt to your back, peer in at the nodding tongue of the spirit safe's spout as the clear spirit gurgles into the collecting bowl.

Fine details are set against the stills' overwhelming presence: quivering needles on dials and gauges, worn engravings on brass handles, streams of numbers written diligently into the stillman's ledger, and the swollen scarlet bulb and tapering stem of a hydrometer slouched against the sampling chamber. It's a breath-taking panorama to behold. Yet look beyond the aesthetic beauty of the curvaceous stills, and study context, form, and function. Their dimensions, silhouettes, and adornments are far from accidental. When we stare up in wonder at the reflective lacquer of the stills, can we begin to decode their secrets?

The peaks of the Black Cuillins look forbidding and wintery as I leave Carbost and drive southeast towards the Armadale ferry for my first visit to

Hamish Fraser at Torabhaig distillery

Torabhaig distillery. When Mossburn Distillers Ltd open it to the public in 2017, it will be the second operational distillery on the Isle of Skye and the closest whisky production facility for visitors to reach by road or ferry from the mainland. With idyllic views past Knock Castle over the bay, I can tell this is going to be a popular place to hang out and drink whisky. Back in late April 2016 however, it's home to a large construction crew who are transforming the old farm steading into a working distillery, café, and shop based around a sunny courtyard. I pull on a hi-vis jacket and safety helmet and follow Hamish Fraser, the site supervisor, for a tour of the works, treading on scaffolding boards, past pallets of stacked bricks, and skirting round the caterpillar treads of the heavy excavator.

With a mighty sense of anticipation, I hear that they have recently taken delivery of the distillation apparatus; I spot a shrink-wrapped copper-topped mashtun, the next room is crammed with towering wooden washbacks that seem to scrape the ceiling, and then I get my first glimpse of the Torabhaig stills. The upper floor has yet to be built, so they can be inspected top to bottom in all their glory. Above the belly of the modest-sized stills sits a golden crown of rivets, topped with a squat doughnut of a

boil ball leading to a finely tapering neck stretching up into the roof space. At present, the swan neck looks strangely amputated; the lyne arms and virgin condensers lie on the floor suffocated in polythene and sealed with Forsyth's branded sticky tape.

I'm fascinated. How will they perform? How will they run them? Why will it be the end of the next decade before we can taste a Torabhaig 12 year old single malt Island whisky (or read all about it in the Malt Whisky Yearbook 2030)? Trying to quell my impatience, I recall a visit I made to another island distillery a few months earlier just as they were about to commission a set of brand new stills.

The Social Distillery

The Isle of Harris Distillery, known as 'The Social Distillery', opened in October 2015 in the coastal community of Tarbert, the home of Harris Tweed. It became the second licensed working distillery in the Outer Hebrides. Their aspiration is to make a whisky called 'The Hearach' named for a native to the island in the same fashion as Ileachs and Diurachs hail from Islay and Jura respectively. Hearach is pronounced like 'Eric' with an H in front. The enterprise has employed a lot of local people from surrounding

Harris distillery

areas, not least, those serving up the delicious home baking in the busy distillery café.

Over the first month, they were making (and selling out of) batches of Isle of Harris gin as fast as they could produce it in their tidy gin still. By November 2015, it was time to begin whisky production. Frilli were the company chosen to make their stills in their facility in Monteriggioni, near Siena, Italy. Rumour has it the Italian company has a 'pipe artist' whose sole job is to make the stills and pipework aesthetically pleasing. Having admired the beautiful stills for myself, I can tell you they have done a fine job.

"We're looking at the second mash going in right now," says Kenny Maclean excitedly. Kenny has a background in electrical and electronic engineering, and brings experience in management and technical skills to his new job as the production manager at the Isle of Harris Distillery. He's relishing the task, but this is a critical week, "There's a time pressure on everybody. We're trying to schedule all the commissioning to be seamless, which is very difficult because the pipework isn't quite complete. The company that are commissioning the mashtun this week will need to come back to train us again when the pipework is finished."

The Italian gentlemen from Frilli are expected to arrive soon to help with the efforts and the adjustments. Kenny gives an example of how the spirit safes had to be lowered slightly from their original position to head height for health and safety reasons when it was recognised that the stillmen would need to go up a ladder to reach the top of the spirit safe.

New stills can be used straight away, unlike equipment in other stages of whisky production, "They don't need seasoned like the washbacks, where a culture will develop," explains Kenny. "Copper does not need treated because we want it to be as clean as possible. We want the spirit to have really good copper contact." He has 72 hours left before their inaugural run, "At the minute, our plan is to mash on Thursdays and Fridays, and then we will distil on Mondays and Tuesdays over the next three weeks. That gives us a day to fix any issues in-between plus the weekend. Also, it helps with our training as we're concentrating on mashing for two days and then distilling for two days."

The spirit cuts are pre-designed to create the character of The Hearach, developed to reflect the rugged and elemental landscape combined with the warmth of the people and the island's position in the Gulf Stream. They don't need to use the early runs to determine the cuts. That's the time for the team to fine tune the production process designated by leading industry consultants, as Kenny explains, "We'll increase or decrease the temperature here a bit, we'll run a bit quicker, or grind a bit finer to get the flavours we want."

Nor will they be filling their first casks too quickly either, "At the beginning of the process, we don't have any heads or tails to put in to build up the strength. At the end of our first distillation it is only going to be at about 20%, so all of that liquid will go back into the tank again. It will take four or five mashes and distillations to get us up to strength. We can discard any spirit that we don't want and segregate it from the spirit that we want to put into casks. We're going to wait until we've got the spirit just right before we try keeping it."

Once satisfied with the set-up, full production can get underway. Double distillation in copper pot stills distinguishes single malt scotch whisky from the process of continuous column still distillation for grain whisky. Distillation exploits the different volatility of alcohol, water, and other substances. Evaporation and condensation concentrates the alcohol portion of the resulting liquid. Let's take a copper-bottomed excursion through the stills and follow the transformation from creamy wash to wispy vapours and into crystal clear new make spirit. While they tinker with the stills on Harris, I'm heading back to the mainland as I have a birthday party to attend.

Birthday party in Fife

Kingsbarns distillery, the first distillery owned by Wemyss Malts, are throwing a party to celebrate their first year of whisky production. A splendid cake has been sliced up and offered to the local dignitaries. Songs are sung, heartfelt speeches are made, and glasses are raised to toast the success of their future. Stepping away from the end of the celebrations in the visitor centre, Peter Holroyd, the distillery manager, takes me inside the distillery to view the pair of stills for a detailed examination of distillation.

We start at the wash still. To begin with, fermented worts are pumped into the pot from the wash charger to 'charge the still'. The charging line can usually be spotted entering the sweeping curved copper surface around the height of the manhole cover, and the still is charged until the level is just lipping the bottom of the door. Peter talks me through the set-up for their 8,000 litre Forsyths's stills.

"We fill it through a manual valve to 7,500 litres, pumped from the bottom of a washback," he begins, telling me that it takes fifteen minutes to charge the still. "We rinse out the washback for any remaining

yeast. It's probably a good flavour contributor if nothing else, and it all goes in too."

Direct firing of stills in Scotland was mostly phased out in the 1960s and 1970s. An external heat exchanger is used to heat the Kingsbarns wash still: countercurrent heat exchange works with steam going one way through the plates while the wash increases in temperature as it's pumped in the opposite direction.

"We heat it up quite slowly because you don't want a high temperature differential between the wash going into the heat exchanger and coming out." That could cause 'burn on' whereby any yeasts or solids burnt by the steam can cause a build up of charcoal and foul up the heat exchanger. That is why direct-fired stills have motor-driven rummagers to agitate the contents in the base of the pot to avoid the same problem.

It takes 60-90 minutes before anything comes through the spirit safe, at which point they knock back the steam to maintain a steady flow rate. "We have a temperature probe inside the still, and a thermometer inside the spirit safe, so we can determine the strength our low wines," shares Peter. "As those more volatile compounds burn off, you've got to push it a little bit harder to maintain that steady flow rate."

Once the alcohol strength has dropped down to 1.5% after four or five hours, they stop distilling with the distilled contents safely collected in the low wines receiver. Chasing the residual alcohol further would be energy inefficient at that stage. The first distillation will have taken six hours from starting the charge to discharging the still.

Wash stills have two easily identifiable features; pipework and manhole covers are usually painted red (for contrast, spirit still paintwork is blue), and they typically have a viewing window that bears a passing resemblance to a rivet-studded porthole in the hull of a ship. Spirit stills do not require viewing windows, though you will find some stills have them if you look. Where a window is used, the stillman can spot the boiling wash bubbling up against the viewing window and reduce the heat. The danger is that if the contents were to boil up higher and spill over into the lyne arm, it could cause a foul distillation. A lot depends on the malt itself; some malt is fierier than others. Some stillmen will boil it hard and break it early, others will control their heat, but they must always make sure that the froth doesn't get too high as that window mists up.

At Kingsbarns, the heat from the pot ale, the residue left after distillation in the wash still, is recovered to provide under floor heating in their visitor

Peter Holroyd - distillery manager at Kingsbarns distillery

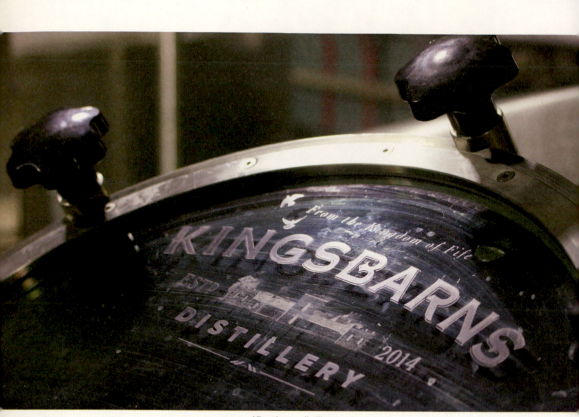

Kingsbarns distillery

centre. The wash still requires cleaning every week by being filled with a caustic solution. This cleans the still, rinses the route through all the pipework, and gives the distiller a fresh layer of copper for the next run.

A distillery's spirit still need not be the same shape or design as the wash still, though many are similar. Shape, height, capacity, and heating can all vary. At Kingsbarns, their spirit still is filled to a consistent volume of 7,500L and heated by a steam coil, a serpentine spiral of piping in the base of the pot. Alternatively, some stills are fitted with radiators or annular heaters (known as 'pans'), a connected ring system of five steam-heated cylindrical tubes, which are easier to clean than steam coils due to their smooth surfaces. "After the wash still run, we are left with 4,500 litres to charge the spirit still," says Peter, explaining how the remainder of the spirit charge is made up with feints and foreshots from previous distillations, making it around 28% alcohol in the final liquid.

"For the foreshots, you can really ramp the steam up until you start to see it run into the spirit safe," describes Peter. "Once that happens, we turn it down to a set point on the valve for consistency and run the spirit still on foreshots for eight minutes. Then we switch on to spirit. When it comes out, it's at

74-75% alcohol. You don't want it coming into the spirit safe too hot, as you could be losing vapours, which means you are losing alcohol, losing yield, and losing important flavour compounds. That's detrimental to spirit character in the end."

The Kingsbarns distillery production target for 2016 was 140,000 lpa, based on a program of mashing and distilling five times a week. As a Lowland distillery, they take a fine cut, as they are looking for a light, floral, fruity character. They run it on spirit slowly, at four litres per minute for four hours, and then take the second cut at 69%. Whatever the distillery or still shape, the rate of distillation is critical to the final spirit character. "Once you're back on to feints, you can ramp it back up again," encourages Peter.

The spirit collected at Kingsbarns distillery amounts to around 800-850 bulk litres at a final alcohol content of 73% (equating to 600-650 litres of pure alcohol). "We want to leave any heavier characteristics behind in the feints. That means you get a faster maturing spirit because you don't have any feints to mature out." The rising vapours will change depending on how hard the still is run: a faster distillation will allow heavier components to rise with less copper contact. As more evaporates from the pot, the available surface area of copper

Shiny pot still at Kingsbarns

"At Kingsbarns, we were not allowed to build any higher than the existing roof structure of the doocot as this is a listed building." A doocot is the Scottish name for a dovecot, and Fife is rich in these historic structures. "We had to compromise: we run the spirit still very slowly, we have relatively long lyne arms, and shell and tube condensers to try to maximize copper contact."

Stills with smaller capacity means a better surface area to liquid volume ratio for copper contact. Sulphur compounds and other undesirable congeners are removed by copper contact, and the dissolving copper acts as a catalyst to improve the flavour profile of the spirit. Air rests between runs helps to oxidize the copper surface, enabling it to better perform this role (or these reactions can be minimised if a more pungent spirit is sought). Peter is very happy with the Kingsbarns new make spirit which is fruity, bursting with citrus, lime, and grapefruit.

The Kingsbarns stills should last at least 20-25 years. During maintenance, ultrasound is the modern method used to measure the thickness of the copper, targeting areas that have experienced the greatest wear. "These stills have only been running since January 2015. We are running them five days a week, so they are not getting heavy use. If we increase production, that will bring down the lifespan of the stills. It all depends on how hard you run them."

There are several hundred pot stills distributed across Scotland's distilleries, and happily, new ones like the stills at Torabhaig and Isle of Harris are coming on stream every year. Every still has its own idiosyncrasies. These burnished cuprous vessels are intrinsically responsible for the origin of the spirit, and every stillman appreciates the familiarity and individuality of their pot stills. As blessed whisky aficionados basking in the cathedral-like glory of a still room, we can imagine ourselves as vapournauts, running with the hot gases, twisting and somersaulting upwards, and funnelling through dark, elongated copper tunnels, inexorably heading for the light until the spirit is safely received. Amen.

Follow those swan neck vapour trails, for they lead to enlightenment.

will increase. Phenolic compounds increase in proportion as the strength drops, so the second cut point is lower for peaty whiskies to allow those flavours to carry over.

"Batch to batch, some washes have higher alcohol in them and run slightly longer, but we're looking for consistency to make the highest quality spirit we can," says Peter. About two weeks' worth of distillation are blended together in the Spirit Receiver Warehouse Vessel (SRWV) before they do a cask filling. They always keep some contents in the SWRV for consistency, while the spirit for filling is brought down in strength to an industry standard 63.5%.

"Originally, we would have liked to have gone for taller stills," confesses Peter. "Glenmorangie produce a very light spirit, it's the reason for having the tall stills. The vapours have got to travel up higher, so the heavier compounds stay in the pot and you'll get more reflux." Swan neck shape, height, cross sectional dimensions, flat tops, and boil balls all contribute to the degree of reflux, as does the temperature, the lyne arm angle, and the presence of purifiers. As the vapours condense, the use of spiralling worm tubs or the copper dense surfaces inside a shell and tube condenser add a further substantial influence on the nature of the spirit produced.

Whisky writer, author, and photographer Jonny McCormick has written hundreds of whisky articles for publications including Whisky Advocate, Whisky Magazine, Wine Spectator and the Malt Whisky Yearbook. McCormick created the Whisky Magazine Index and the Whisky Advocate Auction Index to track trading and value in the secondary market. He is a Keeper of the Quaich and he has led presentations about whisky in Europe, Asia, and North America.

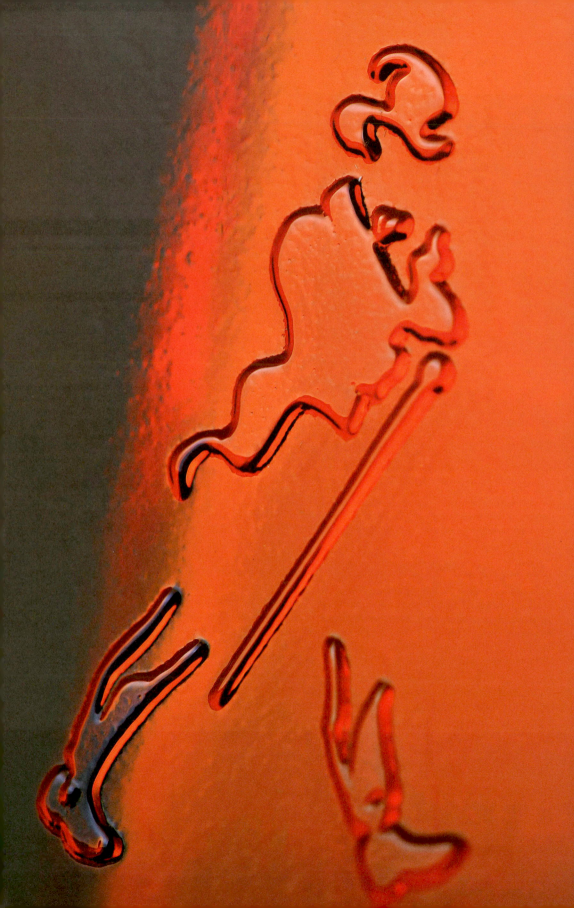

Global Giant
Diageo – the first 20 years
by Charles MacLean

The world's largest spirits company adopted the name 'Diageo' twenty years ago and has since played a key role in the success of Scotch whisky today. Charles MacLean explores two key aspects of this, in relation to the company's approach to malt whiskies and the renaissance of Johnnie Walker.

In May 1997, the City of London awoke to the news that Grand Metropolitan and Guinness had agreed to merge. Grand Met began as an hotel group, owned the massive American food corporation, Pillsbury (which itself owned Burger King, Jolly Green Giant, Häagen-Dazs, etc.) and moved into drinks in 1973 by acquiring Watney Mann Brewers and its subsidiary International Distillers and Vintners (IDV), which owned J & B (the second best-selling Scotch in the world) and Gilbey's gin. It also held the European rights to Smirnoff vodka. Guinness had become the major player in the Scotch whisky industry in 1985, when it acquired Arthur Bell & Sons and the leading brand of blended Scotch in the UK market. Next year it raised its sights and took over the Distillers Company Limited (DCL), far and away the world's largest whisky company.

DCL had its origins in the amalgamation of six grain whisky distilleries in 1877, became involved with malt distilling in 1894, and increased this area of activity following the sharp downturn in the Scotch whisky industry after 1900, when many companies left the trade and sold their distilleries, brands and stock to the DCL. The 'Big Amalgamation' of 1925 brought John Walker & Sons, John Dewar & Sons and James Buchanan & Company – the largest blending houses, known as 'The Big Three' – under the DCL umbrella.

Until the early 1960s, the company controlled around 75% of the UK market for Scotch and slightly more of the export market, but during the 1970s the position changed drastically and by 1984 the company's home sales were down to 16%. Worldwide market share had fallen from 48% (1973) to 35%, and although Johnnie Walker Red Label was still the best selling Scotch in the world, with 10% of the global market, it was being challenged. In his book *Takeover*, the financial journalist Ivan Fallon

The six Classic Malts on the equally classic plinth

describes the DCL in 1984 as "one of the most traditional and conservative companies in Britain…also among the most badly managed… the average age of the board was 60." It was a clear target for takeover.

The merged company was originally to be named GMG Brands (i.e. Grand Met Guinness), with United Distillers & Vintners (UDV) as its trading division. The CEOs of both companies, George Bull and Anthony Greener, became joint Chairmen. Later in 1997 the holding company was changed to Diageo – a name devised by the company's branding consultants, Wolff Olins, for a substantial fee. The new name was an uncomfortable mix of Latin and Greek, alluding to the fact that every day (Dia) the company operated all round the world (Geo). In 2000 the corporate structure was simplified so that Diageo replaced UDV as the trading entity.

In his Scotch Whisky Industry Review 1997, Alan Gray remarked: "The new name was greeted with not inconsiderable amusement by the public at large, commentators and the whisky industry generally. However, although the shareholders at the meeting to approve the new name voted against it on a show of hands, the block postal votes delivered the requisite number and Diageo came into being."

The new entity was the largest spirits company in the world: the brands it owned included the world's leading and number two Scotch whiskies (Johnnie Walker and J&B), the world's best selling gin and vodka (Gordon's and Smirnoff) and the world's leading liqueur (Bailey's Irish Cream). It was also the seventh largest Food and Drinks Group in the world, and although spirits accounted for 59% of its business at the time of the merger, it was only after Pillsbury was sold in 2000 (and Burger King in 2002), followed by the acquisition of the bulk of Seagram's non-Scotch brands in 2001, that the focus was directed on spirits. These brands included Cap-

tain Morgan rum, Crown Royal Canadian whisky, 7 Crown American blended whiskey and Don Julio tequila, and also the best selling Scotch in Korea, Windsor Premier. The bulk of Seagram's Scotch whisky interests were acquired by Pernod Ricard.

Within the spirits category, the focus was also to be on Scotch, and on Scotland. Chairman Tony Greener acknowledged Scotch as being the the bedrock of the business and reported to shareholders in 1998: "The company's vision for Scotch is based on promoting Scotland not only as the home of Scotch Whisky… but also as the source of heritage and knowledge increasingly sought by the company's customers and consumers world-wide". In spite of these bold words, the company had not yet made its mind up about this. It was only by 2000 that they really understood how important Scotch was to future growth – and began the process of divestment from non-drinks businesses.

Global Malts Team is formed

The change of focus was significant. Indeed, it might be argued that had Diageo continued as a diversified food and beverage company, the Scotch whisky category would be nowhere near its current position.

However, in 1997 a Global Malts Team was established under the direction of Jonathan Driver and Dr. Nicholas Morgan to promote the company's malt whiskies, to develop the category.

The 'Classic Malts' range, which had been introduced in 1988/89 – six malts chosen to represent 'regional differences' in flavour – had been phenomenally successful in this regard. The range had been expanded shortly before the merger – reluctantly, but by popular demand – to include expressions of each of the six 'Classics' (Glenkinchie, Dalwhinnie, Cragganmore, Oban, Talisker and Lagavulin) finished in sherry or wine casks. These were named the 'Distillers Editions', and soon the range itself was doubled: Clynelish, Caol Ila, Knockando, Cardhu, Glen Elgin and Royal Lochnagar joining the original six. The Singleton of Auchroisk, inherited from IDV, and the infamous Loch Dhu, introduced in the early 1990s, were quietly ditched.

The 'Rare Malts' series of limited edition bottlings from uncommon, often closed, distilleries at venerable age and at cask strength had been begun in 1995. At the time, Diageo was the only major distiller to offer bottlings from all their distilleries, and now the range was extended and replaced after 2001 (although the Rare Malts continued in parallel until 2005) by annual 'Special Releases' of selected malts, the first being a Port Ellen 1979.

These initiatives have done much to raise the profile of malt whisky generally, expand the market for 'collectable' malts and to support the growing interest in investing in rare whiskies. Unfortunately for those of us who are consumers rather than collectors, the result has been to drive up prices. The recommended retail price of the first edition of Port Ellen was £95; the 2015 release was £2,300. In truth, Diageo underpriced the earlier releases, which began to appear on the secondary market (at auctions, etc.) at two or even three times the purchase price, within

days of being released. Understandably, in recent years the company has pegged the RRP to the likely secondary market prices. While this has reduced secondary market sales, this market will soon catch up.

Industry commentators like Alan Gray, quoted above, had long been urging the Scotch whisky industry to do more in relation to attracting visitors to distilleries: "Over a million people visit distilleries annually and it is important that they depart as potential ambassadors for Scotch. This can only be done if the centres, staff and ambience conspire to make an unforgettable experience." Beginning with Glenfiddich and Glenturret in the 1960s, by 1997 around forty distilleries were welcoming visitors, including those of the Classic Malts, Blair Athol, Knockando and Cardhu, but historically Diageo's predecessor, the Distillers Company Limited, was deeply secretive and the idea of allowing members of the public or even the press on site was anathema.

Now the company set about up-grading its existing visitor centres and creating new facilities at Caol Ila, Cardhu, Clynelish and Royal Lochnagar, with the latter (the smallest distillery in Diageo's estate) becoming 'Malts Brand Home'. Lochnagar was also chosen to be the base for the company's Malt Advocate's Course, devised by the Malts Group and introduced in 1998. Tutored by senior chemists and external experts, and embracing distillery visits on Speyside, Islay and Skye, this week-long course explores in considerable detail 'where flavour comes from in malt whisky'. The inspiration for the course was to bring together production and marketing personnel, so that each gained a greater understanding of the other's role, and over the years many hundreds of Diageo employees and suppliers have benefitted from participating – senior management, distillery and visitor centre managers, advertising and design agencies, overseas marketing teams and members of the press.

In the USA, Diageo introduced the Masters of Whisky Programme, a team of (ultimately) twenty-four ambassadors, many of whom had attended the Malt Advocates Course and all of whom were required to earn a General Certificate in Distillation from Heriot Watt University. Spread widley across the States, these highly trained and passionate ambassadors engaged with 'key influencers' – bar tenders, retailers, consumer groups – in talks and tastings, to enthuse, educate and inform them about whisky. And they weren't just talking about Diageo brands; they were helping to develop the entire category. In 2015 alone they mentored over 120,000 people.

So it came as a shock when Diageo America announced, in August 2016, that it was changing

One of many sought-after bottlings in the Rare Malts Selection

Cardhu Pure Malt was one release that backfired...

its marketing agency, abandoning the Masters of Whisky Programme and replacing it with sales-orientated 'luxury experiences'.

This is misguided. As Dave Broom wrote on www.scotchwhisky.com: "The diminishing of the importance of education removes everything special about Scotch (and, by extension, all whiskies and premium spirits). It rejects the importance of people, place, provenance and pride, and replaces them all with one word – profit. It is a decision that says: 'Actually, we don't care how it is made, where it is made, or who makes it, as long as it sells'… The luxury experiences might be fun – look at the balloons, listen to the cane rapping on the ground, eat the jelly, marvel at the dancers, sip the whisky – but it is no more than a tawdry facade."

The Malt Advocates Course and Masters of Whisky Programme inspired other whisky companies to develop educational programmes for their staff, supliers and marketing people, and has had an important influence on the way malt whisky is analysed and talked about by consumers generally. Diageo's decision to wind down the former and abandon the latter is surprising, and regretable.

The pure mistake

During the years immediately following the merger, Spain became a significant market for both J&B Rare and Cardhu 12 year old single malt. Both were former IDV brands, and the Diageo representatives in this market were largely drawn from former Grand Metropolitan employees. At the time, Spain was the largest market for Scotch whisky in the world (by volume). By 2002, the success of Cardhu was creating a serious inventory problem: there was simply not enough of the malt to meet the demand.

To address this, Diageo resolved to replace Cardhu Single Malt with a blended malt, named Cardhu Pure Malt, a vatting of Cardhu and Glendullan – the latter was the company's largest distillery at the time, with a very similar flavour profile to Cardhu. This was perfectly legal and was agreed to by the Scotch Whisky Association. Only when the new expression had been released in Spain did Diageo's competitors, particularly William Grant & Sons, realise what a threat this was to their own brands, particularly Glenfiddich – far and away the best-selling malt whisky in the world.

Grants orchestrated a storm of protest, maintaining that consumers were being tricked and the high reputation of single malt Scotch whisky would be damaged. There was some truth in this, since Cardhu Pure Malt was presented in the same bottle as Cardhu Single Malt, with a very similar label, although stating 'Pure Malt' in small print and explaining the concept on the bottle's carton. The press had a field day – "Industry Giant challenged by family

...while The Singleton has become the biggest sales success amongst Scotch in the last decade

company" – in spite of the fact that it was a trade dispute in a foreign market. Questions were asked at Holyrood and Westminster. Shocked by the furore, Diageo was obliged to withdraw the product.

The affair led to the Scotch Whisky Association setting up a committee to look into "the production, labelling, advertising and packaging of Scotch Whisky", tightening the definition of Scotch, banning the use of the words 'Pure Malt' (henceforward it must be 'Blended Malt') and extending previous legislation with The Scotch Whisky Regulations, which became law by Statutory Instrument in November 2009.

Smarting from the Cardhu experience and conscious of the potential problem of supplying demand in the event of a single malt whisky taking off in a big way, in 2006 Diageo launched a series of three malts which they named 'The Singleton'. The first was The Singleton of Glen Ord, which would be directed to Asian markets; The Singleton of Dufftown would be available in Europe and The Singleton of Glendullan in North America. The bottle shape and labelling are all very similar, as are the whiskies' flavour profiles, so they can support each other in the event of success in their respective markets.

The Singleton malts currently stand at number five in world sales. Glen Ord is the fastest growing single malt in the world and recently topped The Macallan

as the best selling malt in Taiwan, which is itself the third largest malt whisky market, just behind France, with the USA as the leader.

The re-birth of Johnnie Walker

In 1998, Johnnie Walker was on red alert. Although it was the best-selling Scotch in the world, it was loosing market share fast – between 1996 and 1999 sales had dropped by 14%. Stephen Morely, Global Brand Director, admitted: "Johnnie Walker was all over the place: it was a mess. In Europe it was open fires and comfy slippers, in Latin America a spirit for mixing at parties, in the US a premium brand and a status symbol in Asia"

The brief Diageo gave to the leading London advertising agency Bartle, Bogle, Hegarty (BBH) was: "To reverse the immediate fortunes of the brand in terms of sales, and to develop a future-proof, global communications strategy that would ensure sustained growth in all Johnnie Walker's markets and much-needed focus internally." The solution had to be appropriate to all Walker expressions, from Red Label (£20) to Blue Label (£120) and to appeal to a very broad constituency, with consumer profiles varying in terms of age, mind-set, cultural diversity and economic prosperity.

The campaign that BBH masterminded has become the stuff of legend.

The "Keep Walking" line, coined more than 15 years ago is still in focus, like here in Bangkok last year

"Global qualitative research was commissioned to understand the nature of masculine success at the dawn of the 21st century", writes Steve Mustardé of BBH. "We found an emerging trend – to men all around the world, success was no longer about material wealth or ostentatious displays of status. It was now an internal quality, about becoming a better man, having an unquenchable thirst for self-improvement. A man was judged a success not by where he was, but where he was going. The most powerful expression of masculine success in the 21st Century was 'progress'… The brand's key benefit, its statement of intent, became 'Johnnie Walker Inspires Personal Progress'".

Next, the brand needed an icon. The answer to this lay in the familiar image of the 'Striding Man', which had originally been drawn on the back of a restaurant menu in 1908, and represented the pionee-ring and entrepreneurial zeal of three generations of the Walker family. It carried the strength of heritage but was inherently dynamic. Only problem was, he was perceived as walking into the past, rather then the future. BBH turned him round and added the simple line 'Keep Walking'.

The 'global communications strategy' demanded by Diageo had to be simple if it was to be effective across very varied markets, and all media. Also, BBH determined that the execution of the adverti-sing associated with a global brand must represent fundamental human values that unite, rather then try to reflect local market idiosyncrasies.

The TV campaign was based on individual 'walks' – stories of personal progress from celebrities and other inspiring individuals, beginning with Harvey Keitel recalling stage fright in his early days as an actor and overcoming his fears. The print advertise-ments featured inspiring quotations from a diversity of writers, relating to journeys/progress.

A number of significant measures were taken to develop and support the brand. First were line exten-sions. The traditional Red and Black Label expres-sions had been joined by the de-luxe Blue Label in 1990 (replacing Johnnie Walker Oldest, which had been introduced in 1988). In the late/mid 1990s they were complimented by Gold and Green Label – the latter a blended malt – and after 2010 by Double Black and Platinum. A number of limited, super-de luxe expressions were also introduced (King George V, Odyssey, The John Walker and, since 2014, an annual Private Collection release). For Travel Retail, the Travel Retail Explorers' Club range of four expressions was introduced in 2013.

Luxurious 'Johnnie Walker Houses' were opened in Beijing and Shanghai (and more recently at Schiphol Airport, Amsterdam). Described as 'exclusive embassies for luxury Scotch whisky', these are private clubs (not Schiphol), designed to 'immerse members and their guests in the history, provenance and pioneering spirit of Johnnie Walker'.

Diageo's brief to BBH targeted 'a return to aggressive growth'. In 1999, when the Keep Walking campaign was launched, Johnnie Walker was selling 10.2 million 9 litre cases. By 2007 the brand was selling 15.1 million cases, an increase of 48%. Today the figure is in excess of 20 million cases. Volume growth was accompanied by value growth from $2.35bn to $4.56bn between 1999 and 2007 – an increase of 94%.

Unfortunately, the brand's success was tarnished in 2012 by Diageo's decision to close the company's packaging plant in Kilmarnock, Johnnie Walker's home since 1820, in order to save £42 million per annum and consolidate bottling and packaging in Leven, Fife, where £86 million would be invested. 700 jobs were lost, and although 300 of these were relocated to Fife, it was a disaster for Kilmarnock, where Diageo was the largest employer.

Politicians and the press had a field day. One SMP described the closure as the equivalent of the ravens leaving the Tower of London; demonstrations were held in Glasgow, with an estimated 20,000 marchers. Led by its First Minister, Alex Salmond, the Scottish National Party government offered to support the scaling down and relocating of the Kilmarnock operation, but the company's reponse was that this did not address the 'basic economics' of the business.

Paul Walsh, Diageo's CEO, wrote on the company's website: "Bear in mind that a lot of the restructuring efforts we've announced over time will help gross margin". In the Scottish Parliament his attitude was described as 'shocking'. The SNP leader of East Ayrshire Council said: "It confirms my impression that Paul Walsh is this kind of alpha male whizzkid in braces from the 1980s, who can't be seen to be wrong ... It's capitalism at its worst."

The same year that the Kilmarnock plant closed, Diageo announced plans to invest over £1 billion in malt and grain distilling over a five year period, leading to a substantial increase in capacity at Cameronbridge, Teaninich, Glen Ord, Caol Ila and Clynelish Distilleries. Plans to double the size of Mortlach

and build another mega-distillery on an undisclosed site are currently on hold.

In fact, expansion had begun in 2008 with the opening of a new mega-distillery at Roseisle, capable of producing 12 million litres of pure alcohol per annum – second only to Glenfiddich as the largest malt distillery in Scotland.

Roseisle is not only large, it employs an ingenious range of recyling procedure to reduce the distillery's environmental impact and increase efficiency. It is also capable of producing a range of spirit characters – broadly speaking 'light' and 'heavy' – made possible by equipping the seven spirit stills with interchangeable condensers, one made of copper (for light spirit), the other of stainless steel (for heavy spirit). This led some commentators to speculate that it would pave the way for the closure of smaller, less efficient distilleries.

Notwithstanding the criticisms leveled against Diageo during its twenty years of existence, the success of Johnnie Walker and many of other brands – not least The Buchanan Blend, which is the fastest growing blended Scotch in the USA – combined with the company's premiumisation of malt whisky, has made a massive contribution to the global success of Scotch whisky in recent years.

Charles MacLean has spent the past twenty-five years researching and writing about Scotch whisky and is one of the leading authorities. He spends his time sharing his knowledge around the world, in articles and publications, lectures and tastings, and on TV and radio. His first book (Scotch Whisky) was published in 1993 and since then he has published nine books on the subject. He was elected a Keeper of the Quaich in 1992, in 1997 Malt Whisky won the Glenfiddich Award and in 2003 A Liquid History won 'Best Drinks Book' in the James Beard Awards. In 2012 he also starred in Ken Loach's film The Angel's Share.

Whisky Pricing
the elephant in the room

by Ian Buxton

It's the elephant in the room;
the 800 pound gorilla; the mad aunt in the attic – the topic no one
wants to mention in polite company.

The normally loquacious PR spokesmen and women deflected my enquiries with their usual charm; the talkative marketing types went silent and I thought for some time I was never going to get anyone in the industry to talk on the record about whisky pricing. Then, as we shall see, my persistence paid off and a few brave souls – all credit to them – shared their thoughts. But, as it turned out, consumers were not nearly so coy and the blogosphere had plenty to say. Canadian blogger Curt Robinson of www.allthingswhisky.com has been commenting on whisky since 2010. He summed up the situation pretty trenchantly.

"I think there is a feeling of betrayal. I don't imagine for a minute that names like A'bunadh or Uigeadail would resonate nearly as loud without the swell of voices from the whisky writers, bloggers, vloggers, commenters and forum participants. In essence, I think we've helped push these brands [to] heights not imagined in a world of pure commercial marketing. It has been the groundswell populace that has helped create 'cult' status."

"Those of us that have been enjoying whisky for years now have helped in our own tangible ways to build these brands and have been somewhat responsible for helping to elevate many to their current status of reverence. In turn, prices have soared and those same individuals who supported by way of

Whisky bargains are getting harder to find

voice and buying power have in many cases, unfortunately, been priced out of the market."

I feel he's got a point. I entered this industry as a marketing guy and I know that not many products, save perhaps some car marques and a few fashion brands, enjoy the level of engagement and interest amongst consumers – especially those elusive young male consumers – that whisky has luxuriated in for the last two decades. Frankly, the average consumer goods marketing exec wouldn't know how to handle such committed, well-informed consumers. And I also know that they weren't always there, and that you ignore or leave them behind at your peril: there are other things that they can move on to if they start feeling, to use a word, 'betrayed'.

But that is a serious charge. Is there anything to substantiate it, other than a broad feeling, shared across many social media channels, that prices have risen unjustifiably? Well, again, Robinson claims to have the data, for Canada at least, and has the following to prove his point.

"Locally (here in Canada) we've witnessed Highland Park 18 jump by about $60 a bottle to $180. Laphroaig 25 soared from $450 to $650. Talisker 25 was launched here at $225 and is now at $425 or

more. Old favourite Bunnahabhain 18 has crept to just shy of $150. Glenfarclas 40 went from sub $500 just over a year ago to $1200 this year. GlenDronach 21 from $120 jumped to $185. Hell...GlenDronach 15 soared from $77 to $110. Springbank and Longrow 18s? $150-170 each now. Lagavulin 12 went from about $120 to $175."

Those are certainly substantial increases, but perhaps they're just a local, Canadian phenomenon. However, as it happens I made extensive notes on typical UK prices in specialist whisky retailers during 2010 as part of the research for my book *101 Whiskies to Try Before You Die* and, fortuitously enough, had cause to revisit those very recently as I prepared its 3rd edition (sorry to plug my books but it's important you understand the data source and its limitations – this is more than anecdotal but equally it's not a comprehensive market survey).

There were, I'm sorry to say, some nasty surprises. Take Speyburn 25, for example. I recommended it in 2010 as a bargain at around £70, which I described as "just silly". I should have kept quiet. That same whisky, albeit now in snazzy new packaging and a smart box with two dram cups, is £250. Sorry about that. There wasn't a single cask, cask strength version to compare back in 2010 but if you want one

One of the reasons for higher prices is the scarcity of old whisky in the Scottish warehouses

today it will set you back £350. I do like Speyburn but that feels like a lot of money.

Speyburn is far from alone. Going through the book I found a number of examples: Aberlour a'Bunadh has moved from £35 to about £47 (still a relative bargain, I feel); Highland Park 18, £58 to £105; Lagavulin 16 has crept up from £43 to £55 but, as commentators weren't slow to observe, the 'limited edition' 8 years old to commemorate 200 years of official distilling was released at just a pound or so less. Of the sister 25 years old expression, perhaps the less said the better. Oh, OK, it was priced at £799.

On whiskyrover.blogspot Jason Julier took this to task, contrasting it with the pricing of Lagavulin's 2016 Feis Ile release (18 years old; £125) suggesting that the older whisky would "have to be the greatest whisky of the modern age to justify such a price tag. Think about it for a moment after reading the review of this 18 year old and ask can a whisky be worth six times the price of this and frankly deliver an equivalent experience?" It's a fair question….

Are we running out of whisky?

Before we discover what the industry have to say,

it's only fair to observe that it isn't all bad news. Talisker 10, for example was £32 in 2010, and if you take a moment to look around is no more than £34 today. That's a 6.25% increase at a time when the UK's retail price index grew at more than twice that rate over the comparable period. Remarkably, Green Spot from Ireland (about £36) is around 20% cheaper than when I first wrote about it, and it was a bargain then. Better grab some fast.

But so far, I've written only about malts and, fascinating though they are, they are less than 10% of global sales. Blends, lest we forget, are what drive the whisky market. And behind blends there is the question of stock and the recent media-driven scare story that the world was running out of whisky (and hence, by implication, the price rises).

Nonsense, say the industry. Diageo's Dr Nick Morgan, who refreshingly was happy to talk to me and go on the record, was quick to scorn the idea.

"Remember that the vast majority of whisky sold round the world will be 5 to 10 years old," he emphasised. "In fact, if you manage your inventory properly you will never have 'old' whisky – there was no interest at all in 'old' whisky until [very] recently and if there isn't a shortage of 'old' whisky there's something wrong [with industry planning]. With over eight million casks in our warehouses, we're not going to suddenly run out of stock."

For Chivas Brothers, Strategy & Development Director, Leslie Fitzell made much the same point.

"We can't comment on the activity or stock levels of our competitors," he told me. "However, Chivas Brothers continuously reviews its production capacity capabilities as a matter of course to keep the business ahead of current and anticipated trends. Chivas Brothers currently has in excess of six million casks maturing in more than 300 warehouses across Scotland and is committed to spending £60m per annum to increase and enhance distillation capacity and production facilities. Sustained investment allows us to continue to respond effectively as the global Scotch whisky market grows and shifts and is in line with our confidence in the long-term prospects of the category."

It's not just the larger producers who dismiss the idea that the world will run out of whisky. At Glenfarclas, Sales Director George Grant was happy to share the news that they are constructing five new warehouses to hold the casks they are currently producing "at record levels".

Yet he was swift to emphasise that while costs have risen and accept that whisky prices "have definitely increased, whisky has been historically underpriced."

It's a point that Nick Morgan also made forcefully, going on to suggest, provocatively I think, that "a standard blend should arguably be more expensive than the equivalent aged 'standard' single malt as there is more work in it for the distiller". While we might argue that at some length it's difficult to see why a bottle of non-aged vodka, Ciroc for example, should retail at £34.

Of course, we now have no age statement (NAS) whiskies and for Highland Park, Brand Director Jason Craig was candid enough to spill the beans on pricing, accepting that "Scotch has become relatively expensive as many distilleries have used up much of their aged stock and are turning to NAS in the short to middle term. This has put a price premium on some of the older Scotch whiskies with a genuine age, provenance and limited release packaging."

So there you have it. At least part of the story is driven by production variations. According to the Scotch Whisky Association Databank and the Scotch Whisky Industry Review 2015 these are the definitive figures for production since the turn of the Millennium in millions of original litres of pure alcohol (lpa).

Year	Single Malt	Single Grain	Total
2000	144.7	215.3	360.0
2001	145.8	216.7	362.5
2002	157.7	228.5	386.2
2003	153.2	238.7	391.9
2004	152.0	224.2	376.2
2005	165.3	243.5	408.8
2006	178.4	273.6	452.0
2007	213.5	306.2	519.7
2008	240.7	310.8	551.5
2009	223.2	261.3	484.5
2010	208.3	252.7	461.0
2011	239.3	316.4	555.7
2012	272.8	337.0	609.8
2013	294.9	363.6	658.5
2014	305.7	350.0	655.7
2015 Est.	280.0	320.0	600.0

Source: Scotch Whisky Industry Review, 2015.

As you can see, production of both malt and grain was relatively stable from 2000 to 2004. That was followed by a substantial increase from 2005 to 2008 and then lowered again in 2009 and 2010 after the financial crisis. From 2011 to 2014 there were further increases with malt production growing by some 25%. One might be tempted to ask if there will there be a good supply of aged stock in 5 to 10 years from now and does that mean that prices on aged whiskies will once again decrease?

I suspect not. Faced with this very question Chivas Brothers' Fitzell concurred that while "There will be a good supply of mature Scotch whisky in five to ten years, just as there is in the Chivas Brothers inventory today due largely to our expert production team and sophisticated forecasting modelling, Scotch Whisky continues to be aspirational for consumers around the world and to command a significant price premium vs most local spirit categories"

In fact, he went on "Despite recent political and economic instability in some regions, the growth of the middle classes in emerging markets in general has been a key trend over the past ten years and is forecast to continue over the next three years. This development brings with it an opportunity for Chivas Brothers' Scotch whisky portfolio to increase its global footprint as consumers move from the consumption of domestic spirits to global brands – the category is in a leading position for this transition due to its international prestige, a product of the sector's unrivalled quality and rich heritage."

I think, in short, that the answer is 'no'. As we've

I can still remember when Scotch was cheap

insanity" and making bitter jokes about the product they once loved perhaps it's time to sit up and pay attention.

For my part, I believe this move to NAS expressions from brands previously shackled to age definitions is part of a wider process of dramatic change and needs to be seen in that context.

If I am correct we are living, in fact, through a process of fundamental reorientation, a "sea change" if you will in Scotch whisky's relationship with the world which has to be understood as a long term transformative change. If the industry succeeds in persuading the consumer to accept this, then over the next two or three decades Scotch whisky will be very different – perhaps unrecognisable – from the product we know today.

As a consequence, the last 'golden age' of whisky – one exclusively the preserve of Western consumers now in their 50s and 60s who have enjoyed an unparalleled availability of exceptional whiskies at prices which will never be repeated – has just come to an end. While that group may not have realised their good fortune at the time, it is certainly becoming clear that their privileges have been swept away.

seen, the industry has turned to NAS whiskies as a way out of this dilemma. That, of course, has been controversial to say the least and generated much heat on social media. Robinson again told me that "..even NAS whiskies have reached a point of incomprehensive insanity. These options have historically been a somewhat affordable alternative to age-stated older quality malts. Again though... A'bunadh jumped from $77 to $136 in the last two years. The beloved Laphroaig Quarter Cask from $40 to $60. Corryvreckan from just over $100 to $120-130. Others simply get launched at sky high prices, such as Highland Park's Dark Origins at over $100, Laphroaig Lore at $190 and BenRiach Cask Strength at $120. The days of blind purchasing are behind us. It is simply too expensive to take a risk on that sort of cash outlay without knowing what we're getting for our money."

And Jason Julier warmed to this theme regarding Lagavulin: "The classic Lagavulin 16 year old will set you back around £47 and is bottled at a slightly lower strength [than the 8 year old]. It's been priced at this level for some time now and is viewed – and rightly so – as a classic premium malt. This 8 year old doesn't necessarily compute a 50% reduction in price (if only that was the case folks) but it should in theory constitute a lesser asking price to the consumer. Funny how we can use history to inspire a whisky yet not when it comes to price."

I don't really think he found it funny. Remember what I said at the beginning about an industry losing touch with its core consumers, with the true believers? When they start referring to "incomprehensive

As Curt Robinson ruefully acknowledged, "At the end of the day, though, we love whisky. We cry foul over these situations not because it's enjoyable to be the dissenter, but because we feel like something we love is being eroded and taken from us. What we should have acknowledged all along is that it never belonged to us."

And that's a rather more elegant epitaph than my blunt conclusion on whisky pricing: simply suck it up or move on.

Ian Buxton has close to 30 years whisky experience. He runs his own strategic marketing consultancy and regularly lectures, presents, holds tastings, and writes regular columns for several trade and consumer magazines. As well as several corporate histories, Ian has written three titles in the bestselling 101 Whiskies series and has enjoyed great success with the companion 101 Gins To Try Before You Die. His most recent work is a new edition, fully annotated and with period illustrations, of the classic Whisky by Aeneas MacDonald. A third, fully revised 101 Whiskies To Try Before You Die will appear in November 2016. He is currently working on a book on Scotland's Island Distilleries.

Royal Brackla Distillery

Malt distilleries

Including the subsections:
Scottish distilleries | New distilleries | Closed distilleries
Japanese distilleries | Distilleries around the globe

Explanations

Owner: Name of the owning company, sometimes with the parent company within brackets.

Region/district: There are four formal malt whisky regions in Scotland today; the Highlands, the Lowlands, Islay and Campbeltown. Where useful we mention a location within a region e.g. Speyside, Orkney, Northern Highlands etc.

Founded: The year in which the distillery was founded is usually considered as when construction began. The year is rarely the same year in which the distillery was licensed.

Status: The status of the distillery's production. Active, mothballed (temporarily closed), closed (but most of the equipment still present), dismantled (the equipment is gone but part of or all of the buildings remain even if they are used for other purposes) and demolished.

Visitor centre: The letters (vc) after status indicate that the distillery has a visitor centre. Many distilleries accept visitors despite not having a visitor centre. It can be worthwhile making an enquiry.

Address: The distillery's address.

Tel: This is generally to the visitor centre, but can also be to the main office.

Website: The distillery's (or in some cases the owner's) website.

Capacity: The current production capacity expressed in litres of pure alcohol (LPA).

History: The chronology focuses on the official history of the distillery and independent bottlings are only listed in exceptional cases.

Tasting notes: For all the Scottish distilleries that are not permanently closed we present tasting notes of what, in most cases, can be called the core expression (mainly their best selling 10 or 12 year old).

We have tried to provide notes for official bottlings but in those cases where we have not been able to obtain them, we have turned to independent bottlers.

The whiskies have been tasted by Gavin D Smith (GS), a well-known and eperienced whisky profile and author of 20 books on the subject.

There are also tasting notes for Japanese malts and these have been written by Nicholas Coldicott.

All notes have been prepared especially for Malt Whisky Yearbook 2017.

Aberfeldy

[ah•bur•fell•dee]

Owner:
John Dewar & Sons
(Bacardi)

Region/district:
Southern Highlands

Founded: **Status:**   **Capacity:**
1896   Active (vc)   3 500 000 litres

Address: Aberfeldy, Perthshire PH15 2EB

Website: **Tel:**
aberfeldy.com   01887 822010 (vc)

The story of Aberfeldy is also the story of Dewar's, ever since the distillery was founded by the family in the late 1800s.

The foundation of this reputable family company was already laid in 1846 by John Dewar, but it was his two sons who would make the company one of the most successful in the history of whisky. After their father had died in 1880, the two brothers divided the responsibilities in an efficient way. John Alexander was responsible for the blending, while Tommy took care of the sales. The combined work of the two was the key to its success, but it was Tommy´s use of unorthodox and energetic sales methods, not least during his two tours to all the corners of the world, which were spoken about most. During his visit to Canada, there was an ongoing debate whether or not prohibition would be imposed in the country. Tommy made a classic interjection to the debate when he, using statistics, showed that "total abstainers" had a two year shorter life span than the "habitual drunkard".

The Dewar brothers were assisted by the master blender, Alexander Cameron. He had introduced a new way of creating the whisky when he mixed different malt and grain whiskies separately and allowed them to marry before blending them. This was then followed by yet another period of marrying. This technique is still used at Dewar´s today.

The equipment at Aberfeldy consists of a 7.5 ton stainless steel mash tun, eight washbacks made of Siberian larch and three made of stainless steel with an average fermentation time of 70 hours and four stills. With the additional washback, production has now escalated to 23 mashes per week and 3.4 million litres of alcohol. The owners have also invested £1.2m in a biomass boiler that will reduce greenhouse gas emissions by up to 90%.

Since 2014, the core range from Aberfeldy is **12, 16** and **21 year old** and they have also introduced the first Aberfeldy duty free exclusive expression – an **18 year old**. There are also rumours of a limited **30 year old** to be released in the future.

History:

1896   John and Tommy Dewar embark on the construction of the distillery, a stone's throw from the old Pitilie distillery which was active from 1825 to 1867. Their objective is to produce a single malt for their blended whisky - White Label.

1898   Production starts in November.

1917   The distillery closes.

1919   The distillery re-opens.

1925   Distillers Company Limited (DCL) takes over.

1972   Reconstruction takes place, the floor maltings is closed and the two stills are increased to four.

1991   The first official bottling is a 15 year old in the Flora & Fauna series.

1998   Bacardi buys John Dewar & Sons from Diageo at a price of £1,150 million.

2000   A visitor centre opens and a 25 year old is released.

2005   A 21 year old is launched in October, replacing the 25 year old.

2009   Two 18 year old single casks are released.

2010   A 19 year old single cask, exclusive to France, is released.

2011   A 14 year old single cask is released.

2014   The whole range is revamped and an 18 year old for duty free is released.

2015   A 16 year old is released.

Tasting notes Aberfeldy 12 years old:

GS – Sweet, with honeycombs, breakfast cereal and stewed fruits on the nose. Inviting and warming. Mouth-coating and full-bodied on the palate. Sweet, malty, balanced and elegant. The finish is long and complex, becoming progressively more spicy and drying.

12 years old

Aberlour

[ah•bur•<u>lower</u>]

Owner:
Chivas Brothers Ltd
(Pernod Ricard)

Region/district:
Speyside

Founded: **Status:** **Capacity:**
1879 Active (vc) 3 800 000 litres

Address: Aberlour, Banffshire AB38 9PJ

Website: **Tel:**
aberlour.com 01340 881249

The two dominant companies within Scotch whisky today, are Diageo and Pernod Ricard with a combined market share of almost 60%. The first distillery that the French acquired was Aberlour in 1974.

It would later show that this was a brilliant move. Aberlour single malt has been established as one of the big sellers and with the exception of 2009, when basically all the whisky brands lost ground due to the financial crash, the sales of Aberlour single malt has increased steadily every year. Over the past five years alone the increase is an incredible 53%! With 3.8 million bottles sold during 2015, it makes Aberlour the world's sixth most sold single malt today. France has been the key market since way back, and in 2008 Aberlour managed to surpass Glenfiddich as the most sold single malt in the country.

The distillery is equipped with a 12 ton semi-lauter mash tun, six stainless steel washbacks and two pairs of stills. Aberlour was one of the first distilleries to tailor its distillery tours for the discerning whisky aficionados, rather than for large groups of tourists. The basic tour lasts for two hours and includes a tasting of no less than six expressions. One can also add on an additional tasting (Casks of the Past) of bottlings that are no longer available for purchase.

The core range of Aberlour includes **12, 16** and **18 year olds** – all being matured in a combination of ex-bourbon and ex-sherry casks. Another core expression is **Aberlour a'bunadh,** matured in ex-Oloroso casks. It is always bottled at cask strength and up to 56 different batches have been released by July 2016. Four bottlings have been released for the French consumers (but are available in other selected markets as well). These include **10 year old, 12 year old un chill-filtered, 15 year old Select Cask Reserve** and **White Oak Millennium 2004**. Two exclusives are available for duty free – a **12 year old Sherry Cask** and a **15 year old Double Cask**. There are also two cask strength bottlings from the new Distillery Reserve Collection which are available at all Chivas´ visitor centres – a **17 year old bourbon cask matured,** as well as a **25 year old single cask.**

History:

1879 The local banker James Fleming founds the distillery.

1892 The distillery is sold to Robert Thorne & Sons Ltd who expands it.

1898 Another fire rages and almost totally destroys the distillery. The architect Charles Doig is called in to design the new facilities.

1921 Robert Thorne & Sons Ltd sells Aberlour to a brewery, W. H. Holt & Sons.

1945 S. Campbell & Sons Ltd buys the distillery.

1962 Aberlour terminates floor malting.

1973 Number of stills are increased from two to four.

1974 Pernod Ricard buys Campbell Distilleries.

2000 Aberlour a´bunadh is launched.

2001 Pernod Ricard buys Chivas Brothers and merges Chivas Brothers and Campbell Distilleries under the brand Chivas Brothers.

2002 A new, modernized visitor centre is inaugurated in August.

2008 The 18 year old is also introduced outside France.

2013 Aberlour 2001 White Oak is released.

2014 White Oak Millenium 2004 is released.

12 years old

Tasting notes Aberlour 12 year old:

GS – The nose offers brown sugar, honey and sherry, with a hint of grapefruit citrus. The palate is sweet, with buttery caramel, maple syrup and eating apples. Liquorice, peppery oak and mild smoke in the finish.

Allt-a-Bhainne

[alt a•vain]

Owner:	**Region/district:**
Chivas Brothers Ltd	Speyside
(Pernod Ricard)	

Founded:	**Status:**	**Capacity:**
1975	Active	4 000 000 litres

Address: Glenrinnes, Dufftown, Banffshire AB55 4DB

Website:	**Tel:**
-	01542 783200

One could argue that Scotch whisky has seen three golden eras; the first in the late 1800s which ended with the Pattison crash, then from the late 1950s to the late 1970s and finally the one we´re in now which started at the end of the 1990s.

During the second era it was the big blends that took the world by storm. The Second World War had ended and many countries had experienced a strong economic growth. Blends such as Johnnie Walker, Ballantines, and Bells showed increasing sales figures from year to year and on the American market J&B and Cutty Sark had reaped great rewards. In that same market, Chivas Regal was one of the biggest premium blends but Chivas Brothers and the owners, Seagram's, had lacked a top selling standard whisky. They decided to launch a completely new brand and in 1966, 100 Pipers was introduced. Its success was undeniable and in the mid 1970s, Seagram's realised that they needed more stock of malt whisky. Allt-a-Bhainne was built and has ever since been one of the most important ingredients in 100 Pipers. The brand´s popularity has decreased with time, but about 18 million bottles are still sold annually.

Since the distillery was founded it has been equipped with a traditional mash tun with rakes and ploughs. In summer 2015, however, a new, modern lauter mash gear was fitted into the existing tun. The rest of the equipment consists of eight stainless steel washbacks and two pairs of stills. The distillery is currently a busy place working 7 days a week with 25 mashes resulting in four million litres of alcohol per year. Chivas Brothers has no distillery on Islay so, to cover their need of peated whisky for their blends, they need to resort to other solutions. During the last few years, 50% of the production at Allt-a-Bhainne has therefore been peated spirit with a phenol content in the malted barley of 10ppm.

There are no official bottlings of Allt-a-Bhainne single malt but it has been used for bottlings of the Deerstalker brand from time to time. A limited 18 year old, bottled at cask strength, was released in summer 2015.

History:

1975 The distillery is founded by Chivas Brothers, a subsidiary of Seagrams, in order to secure malt whisky for its blended whiskies. The total cost amounts to £2.7 million.

1989 Production has doubled.

2001 Pernod Ricard takes over Chivas Brothers from Seagrams.

2002 Mothballed in October.

2005 Production restarts in May.

Deerstalker 18 years old

Tasting notes Deerstalker 18 year old:

GS – Honey, icing sugar, lanolin; becoming buttery. Soft fruits, and finally toffee bonbons. Silky mouth-feel, slightly oily, vanilla, white pepper and tangerines. Relatively long finish and persistently spicy.

Ardbeg

[ard•beg]

Owner:
The Glenmorangie Co
(Moët Hennessy)

Region/district:
Islay

Founded: **Status:** **Capacity:**
1815 Active (vc) 1 300 000 litres

Address: Port Ellen, Islay, Argyll PA42 7EA

Website: **Tel:**
ardbeg.com 01496 302244 (vc)

It is every blender´s dream to work with a distillery that has had a consistent production during a long period of time. Anything to the contrary could be a challenge even for such an experienced master blender as Bill Lumsden.

In the case of Ardbeg, Lumsden has over the years been working with whiskies which have been produced during three different epochs under three different ownerships. The first was from 1974, when Hiram Walker came into the picture, until 1981. The distillery was in full production during that time and until 1977, most of the malt was provided from the distillery´s own maltings which has given the whisky a special character. The distillery was then silent between 1981 and 1989 under the ownership of Allied Distillers. They re-opened it in 1989 but until 1996 it only produced for two months at a time. All the malt that was used was bought from Port Ellen maltings. As a result of the intermittent production, the quality of whisky that hailed from this period of time was also varied. The third epoch was initiated when the current owner, Glenmorangie, bought Ardbeg in 1997 and, since then, the distillery has been producing 100% of its production capacity.

With such varying quality and small quantities of certain ages, Lumsden has had to muster creativity, as well as innovation with new bottlings in order to please the distillery's many fans. This has led to the fact that the core range only consists of three expressions, of which the most recent (Corryvreckan) was launched as far back as in 2009. Lumsden has, instead, regularly created limited editions where a combination of different ages and wood, as well as finishing techniques have been in the focus. This has been proved successful and in 2015 sales exceeded 1 million bottles for the first time, which means that Ardbeg is the fourth biggest seller on Islay, after Laphroaig, Lagavulin and Bowmore.

The distillery is equipped with a 5 ton stainless steel semilauter mash tun, six washbacks made of Oregon pine with a fermentation time of 56-57 hours and one pair of stills. A purifier is connected to the spirit still to help create the special, fruity character of the spirit. In 2016 they will be making 16-17 mashes per week, thereby accounting for 1.3 million litres of pure alcohol – the highest production level ever.

The core range, all non chill-filtered, consists of the **10 year old**, a mix of first and re-fill bourbon casks, **Uigeadail**, a marriage of bourbon and sherry casks and bottled at cask strength and **Corryvreckan**, also a cask strength and a combination of bourbon casks and new French oak. Recent, limited releases have included **Kildalton**, **Perpetuum** and the fifth and final bottling of **Supernova**. The new expression for Ardbeg Day during Feis Ile 2016 was **Dark Cove**, which had partly matured in "dark sherry casks". It was bottled at 46.5% while a committee version which was released a couple of months earlier was bottled at 55%. Finally, a very special treat for Ardbeg Committee members appeared end of September when a **21 year old**, bottled at 46%, was released.

History:

1794 First record of a distillery at Ardbeg. It was founded by Alexander Stewart.

1798 The MacDougalls, later to become licensees of Ardbeg, are active on the site through Duncan MacDougall.

1815 The current distillery is founded by John MacDougall, son of Duncan MacDougall.

1853 Alexander MacDougall, John's son, dies and sisters Margaret and Flora MacDougall, assisted by Colin Hay, continue the running of the distillery. Colin Hay takes over the licence when the sisters die.

1888 Colin Elliot Hay and Alexander Wilson Gray Buchanan renew their license.

1900 Colin Hay's son takes over the license.

1959 Ardbeg Distillery Ltd is founded.

1973 Hiram Walker and Distillers Company Ltd jointly purchase the distillery for £300,000 through Ardbeg Distillery Trust.

1974 Widely considered as the last vintage of 'old, peaty' Ardbeg. Malt which has not been produced in the distillery´s own maltings is used in increasingly larger shares after this year.

1977 Hiram Walker assumes single control of the distillery. Ardbeg closes its maltings.

1979 Kildalton, a less peated malt, is produced over a number of years.

1981 The distillery closes in March.

1987 Allied Lyons takes over Hiram Walker and thereby Ardbeg.

1989 Production is restored. All malt is taken from Port Ellen.

1996 The distillery closes in July and Allied Distillers decides to put it up for sale.

History continued:

1997 Glenmorangie plc buys the distillery for £7 million. Ardbeg 17 years old and Provenance are launched

1998 A new visitor centre opens.

2000 Ardbeg 10 years is introduced and the Ardbeg Committee is launched.

2001 Lord of the Isles 25 years and Ardbeg 1977 are launched.

2002 Ardbeg Committee Reserve and Ardbeg 1974 are launched.

2003 Uigeadail is launched.

2004 Very Young Ardbeg (6 years) and a limited edition of Ardbeg Kildalton (1300 bottles) are launched. The latter is an un-peated cask strength from 1980.

2005 Serendipity is launched.

2006 Ardbeg 1965 and Still Young are launched. Almost There (9 years old) and Airigh Nam Beist are released.

2007 Ardbeg Mor, a 10 year old in 4.5 litre bottles is released.

2008 The new 10 year old, Corryvreckan, Rennaissance, Blasda and Mor II are released.

2009 Supernova is released, the peatiest expression from Ardbeg ever.

2010 Rollercoaster and Supernova 2010 are released.

2011 Ardbeg Alligator is released.

2012 Ardbeg Day and Galileo are released.

2013 Ardbog is released.

2014 Auriverdes and Kildalton are released.

2015 Perpetuum and Supernova 2015 are released.

2016 Dark Cove and a 21 year old are relased.

Corryvreckan   21 years old   Dark Cove

Tasting notes Ardbeg 10 year old:

GS – Quite sweet on the nose, with soft peat, carbolic soap and Arbroath smokies. Burning peats and dried fruit, followed by sweeter notes of malt and a touch of liquorice in the mouth. Extremely long and smoky in the finish, with a fine balance of cereal sweetness and dry peat notes.

10 years old   Uigeadail

Ardmore

[ard•moor]

Owner: **Region/district:**
Beam Suntory   Highland

Founded: **Status:**   **Capacity:**
1898   Active   5 550 000 litres

Address: Kennethmont, Aberdeenshire AB54 4NH

Website: **Tel:**
ardmorewhisky.com   01464 831213

Many producers have, during the last few years, started looking at their distilleries in a new light. Some of them have more or less exclusively been making whisky for blends over the years, but will now get more and more attention even as single malts.

This is not to be seen as a coincidence. Since 2011, the value of Scotch blend exports has fallen by almost 18%, while the corresponding figure for malts shows an increase of 23%! While blends may still form the backbone of the industry, there is a lot of money to be earned in the single malt business nowadays. Ardmore is a brilliant example of this new strategy. It has been the signature malt in Teacher´s since the late 1800s, but lately the Ardmore single malt range has been largely expanded and sales have since, more than tripled.

The distillery is equipped with a large (12.5 tonnes) cast iron, semilauter mash tun with a copper dome, 14 Douglas fir washbacks (4 large and 10 smaller ones) with a fermentation time of 55 hours, as well as four pairs of stills. At the moment, Ardmore is working a 7-day week with 23 mashes per week resulting in 4.5 million litres of alcohol. Traditionally, Ardmore has been the only distillery in the region consistently producing peated whisky with a phenol specification in the barley of 12-14 ppm. For blending purposes, they also produce the unpeated Ardlair (around 40% of the yearly output) since 2002. A £2m investment was made in 2015 when the distillery was equipped with a membrane bio reactor and an effluent treatment plant which is able to return all the waste liquids into the water in an environmentally friendly way.

The core expression is **Legacy**, a mix of 80% peated and 20% unpeated malt. In summer 2015, **Tradition** was released as an exclusive for duty free. Simultaneously, **Triple Wood** without age statement and matured in bourbon barrels, quarter casks and sherry puncheons, was launched. Finally, in October 2015, yet another core bottling appeared; a **12 year old port finish** with 7 years in sherry puncheons, previously used to mature Ardmore spirit and a second maturation of 5 years in port pipes.

History:

1898 Adam Teacher, son of William Teacher, starts the construction of Ardmore Distillery which eventually becomes William Teacher & Sons´ first distillery. Adam Teacher passes away before it is completed.

1955 Stills are increased from two to four.

1974 Another four stills are added, increasing the total to eight.

1976 Allied Breweries takes over William Teacher & Sons and thereby also Ardmore. The own maltings (Saladin box) is terminated.

1999 A 12 year old is released to commemorate the distillery's 100th anniversary. A 21 year old is launched in a limited edition.

2002 Ardmore is one of the last distilleries to abandon direct heating (by coal) of the stills in favour of indirect heating through steam.

2005 Jim Beam Brands becomes new owner when it takes over some 20 spirits and wine brands from Allied Domecq for five billion dollars.

2007 Ardmore Traditional Cask is launched.

2008 A 25 and a 30 year old are launched.

2014 Beam and Suntory merge. Legacy is released.

2015 Traditional is re-launched as Tradition and a Triple Wood and a 12 year old port finish are released.

Legacy

Tasting notes Ardmore Legacy:

GS – Vanilla, caramel and sweet peat smoke on the nose, while on the palate vanilla and honey contrast with quite dry peat notes, plus ginger and dark berries. The finish is medium to long, spicy, with persistently drying smoke.

Arran

[ar•ran]

Owner: **Region/district:**
Isle of Arran Distillers   Islands (Arran)

Founded: **Status:**   **Capacity:**
1993   Active (vc)   1 200 000 litres

Address: Lochranza, Isle of Arran KA27 8HJ

Website: **Tel:**
arranwhisky.com   01770 830264

The success of the Arran distillery and the huge number of visitors, have encouraged the owners to build yet another distillery on the island and, this time, on the southern part in Lagg.

The original Lagg distillery closed in 1837 and it was the last legal distillery operating on Arran until 1995. A building application was registered in May 2016 and, if all goes according to plans, work could start in September, with production starting by the end of 2018. The distillery will be equipped with two pairs of stills and there will also be a visitor centre and warehouses.

Arran distillery is currently equipped with a 2.5 ton semi-lauter mash tun with a copper canopy, six Oregon pine washbacks with an average fermentation time of 60 hours and two stills. The total production capacity is 750,000 litres but, with the installation of another two stills in October 2016, the capacity will increase to 1.2 million litres. Since 2004, the distillery has been producing its fair share of peated spirit every year. The phenol specification of the malt is 20ppm and, since 2012, they also produce heavily peated spirit (50ppm).

The core range consists of **10 year old, 12 year old cask strength, 14 year old, Robert Burns Malt** and **Lochranza Reserve**. In spring 2015, an **18 year old**, was also released in limited numbers, but this has now become a permanent member of the core range. Also included is the peated expression **Machrie Moor** (with a 7th edition being launched in 2016). There are also four cask finishes; **amarone, port, sauternes** and, new since 2016, **madeira**. Furthermore, a number of limited releases have been launched in 2015/2016; **The Bothy Quarter Cask** bottled at cask strength, the second edition of **Machrie Moor cask strength** and **The Illicit Stills**, which is a cask strength vatting of port pipes, sherry hogsheads and bourbon barrels spiced up with young, peated whisky. This is the first release in a series called Smuggler's Edition and which reflects on the island's history of illicit distilling. A second release is due in 2016. A limited bottling in September which will celebrate the distillery's 21st anniversary has also been announced.

History:

1993 Harold Currie founds the distillery.

1995 Production starts in full on 17th August.

1998 The first release is a 3 year old.

1999 The Arran 4 years old is released.

2002 Single Cask 1995 is launched.

2003 Single Cask 1997, non-chill filtered and Calvados finish is launched.

2004 Cognac finish, Marsala finish, Port finish and Arran First Distillation 1995 are launched.

2005 Arran 1996 and two finishes, Ch. Margaux and Grand Cru Champagne, are launched.

2006 After an unofficial launch in 2005, Arran 10 years old is released as well as a couple of new wood finishes.

2007 Four new wood finishes and Gordon's Dram are released.

2008 The first 12 year old is released as well as four new wood finishes.

2009 Peated single casks, two wood finishes and 1996 Vintage are released.

2010 A 14 year old, Rowan Tree, three cask finishes and Machrie Moor (peated) are released.

2011 The Westie, Sleeping Warrior and a 12 year old cask strength are released.

2012 The Eagle and The Devil's Punch Bowl are released.

2013 A 16 year old and a new edition of Machrie Moor and released.

2014 A 17 year old and Machrie Moor cask strength are released.

2015 A 18 year old and The Illicit Stills are released.

2016 Bothy Quarter Cask is released and the distillery is expanded with two more stills.

14 years old

Tasting notes Arran 14 year old:

GS – Very fragrant and perfumed on the nose, with peaches, brandy and ginger snaps. Smooth and creamy on the palate, with spicy summer fruits, apricots and nuts. The lingering finish is nutty and slowly drying.

Auchentoshan

[ock•en•tosh•en]

Owner:
Morrison Bowmore (Suntory)

Region/district:
Lowlands

Founded: 1823
Status: Active (vc)
Capacity: 2 000 000 litres

Address: Dalmuir, Clydebank, Glasgow G81 4SJ

Website:
auchentoshan.com

Tel:
01389 878561

A twenty minute drive to the west of Glasgow city centre lays Clydebank, a town famous since the late 1800s for its ship yards.

During the Second World War, this industry was of huge importance to the war efforts and this was, of course, also recognised by the Germans. On the 13th and 14th of March 1941, Clydebank was targeted for a blitz bombing by the German Luftwaffe and only seven buildings remained unharmed. Auchentoshan distillery was one of them (although three adjacent warehouses were damaged). As a reminder of the bombings, a huge crater behind the distillery now hosts the dam for the distillery´s cooling water.

Auchentoshan is the only distillery in the entire Scotland doing 100% triple distillation. This means, among other things, having a very narrow spirit cut. They start collecting the middle cut at 82% and stop at 80%, long before any other distillery starts collecting. The equipment consists of a semilauter mash tun with a 6.8 ton mash charge, four Oregon pine washbacks and three made of stainless steel, all with a fermentation time of 50 to 120 hours, and three stills. On site are also three dunnage and two racked warehouses which can hold about 20,000 casks. The plan is to do 9 mashes per week and 1 million litres of alcohol in 2016.

The core range consists of **American Oak**, a first fill bourbon maturation without age statement but typically around six years, **12 years, Three Woods, 18 years** and **21 years**. The last couple of years, the duty free range has comprised of six expressions; Springwood, Heartwood, Solera, Cooper´s Reserve, Silveroak and Vintage 1975. Each of them has now been replaced with two new ones, launched in autumn 2015. **Blood Oak**, without age statement, has been matured in a combination of bourbon and red wine casks, while the 24 year old **Noble Oak**, bottled at cask strength, is a vatting of bourbon and oloroso casks. There is also a **Distillery Cask** to be found exclusively at the visitor centre, the most recent being a 2004 oloroso single cask. Recent limited bottlings include **Auchentoshan Virgin Oak**, fully matured in charred oak casks that have held neither bourbon nor sherry before and a **1988 Bordeaux finish**.

History:

1817 First mention of the distillery Duntocher, which may be identical to Auchentoshan.

1823 The distillery is founded by John Bulloch.

1823 The distillery is sold to Alexander Filshie.

1878 C.H. Curtis & Co. takes over.

1903 The distillery is purchased by John Maclachlan.

1941 The distillery is severely damaged by a German bomb raid.

1960 Maclachlans Ltd is purchased by the brewery J. & R. Tennant Brewers.

1969 Auchentoshan is bought by Eadie Cairns Ltd who starts major modernizations.

1984 Stanley P. Morrison, eventually becoming Morrison Bowmore, becomes new owner.

1994 Suntory buys Morrison Bowmore.

2002 Auchentoshan Three Wood is launched.

2004 More than a £1 million is spent on a new, refurbished visitor centre. The oldest Auchentoshan ever, 42 years, is released.

2006 Auchentoshan 18 year old is released.

2007 A 40 year old and a 1976 30 year old are released.

2008 New packaging as well as new expressions - Classic, 18 year old and 1988.

2010 Two vintages, 1977 and 1998, are released.

2011 Two vintages, 1975 and 1999, and Valinch are released.

2012 Six new expressions are launched for the Duty Free market.

2013 Virgin Oak is released.

2014 American Oak replaces Classic.

2015 Blood Oak and Noble Oak are released for duty free.

American Oak

Tasting notes Auchentoshan American Oak:

GS – An initial note of rose water, then Madeira, vanilla, developing musky peaches and icing sugar. Spicy fresh fruit on the palate, chilli notes and more Madeira and vanilla. The finish is medium in length, and spicy to the end.

Auchroisk

[ar•thrusk]

Owner:	**Region/district:**
Diageo	Speyside
Founded: **Status:**	**Capacity:**
1974 Active	5 900 000 litres

Address: Mulben, Banffshire AB55 6XS

Website:	**Tel:**
malts.com	01542 885000

The character of the new make spirit will reveal a lot about the flavour of the matured whisky. Even though the time spent in the cask will add many more nuances and enhance the flavours, the foundation has been laid once the distillation process has finished.

In whisky production, you try to group newmakes into a number of styles; of which green/grassy, fruity/floral, nutty and sulphury are the most common. Over the last few years, Auchroisk has been a producer of nutty newmake, in keeping with fellow Diageo distilleries such as Knockando and Blair Athol. But having a nutty newmake can also further be divided into two sub categories – spicy and malty. When it comes to Auchroisk, the newmake can definitely be described as malty. The cloudy wort and short fermentation will give the spirit notes of cereals. When matured, this type of malt whisky is very useful in certain blends and, in the case of Auchroisk, it happens to be J&B.

Auchroisk is a big distillery with an unusually large number of warehouses. The equipment consists of a 12 ton stainless steel semilauter mash tun, eight stainless steel washbacks with a fermentation time of 53 hours and four pairs of stills. The spacious still house was a role model for the still house of Diageo´s latest distillery, Roseisle. In 2015 Auchroisk was closed for five months due to a substantial upgrade, which included an automated control system. It is now back to full production, which means 5.8 million litres of alcohol.

The first, widely available release of Auchroisk single malt was in 1986 under the name Singleton, as the Scottish name was deemed unpronounceable by the consumers. In 2001, it was replaced by a **10 year old** in the Flora & Fauna range. Recent, limited bottlings include a **20 year old** from 1990 and a **30 year old**, both launched as part of the Special Releases. In October 2016, it was time for the next limited Auchroisk in the Special Releases series; a **25 year old**, distilled in 1990 and bottled at 51.2%. A total of 3,954 bottles were released.

History:

1972 Building of the distillery commences by Justerini & Brooks (which, together with W. A. Gilbey, make up the group IDV) in order to produce blending whisky. In February the same year IDV is purchased by the brewery Watney Mann which, in July, merges into Grand Metropolitan.

1974 The distillery is completed and, despite the intention of producing malt for blending, the first year's production is sold 12 years later as single malt thanks to the high quality.

1986 The first whisky is marketed under the name Singleton.

1997 Grand Metropolitan and Guinness merge into the conglomerate Diageo. Simultaneously, the subsidiaries United Distillers (to Guinness) and International Distillers & Vintners (to Grand Metropolitan) form the new company United Distillers & Vintners (UDV).

2001 The name Singleton is abandoned and the whisky is now marketed under the name of Auchroisk in the Flora & Fauna series.

2003 Apart from the 10 year old in the Flora & Fauna series, a 28 year old from 1974, the distillery's first year, is launched in the Rare Malt series.

2010 A Manager´s Choice single cask and a limited 20 year old are released.

2012 A 30 year old from 1982 is released.

2016 A 25 year old from 1990 is released.

10 years old

Tasting notes Auchroisk 10 year old:
GS – Malt and spice on the light nose, with developing nuts and floral notes. Quite voluptuous on the palate, with fresh fruit and milk chocolate. Raisins in the finish.

Aultmore

[ault•moor]

Owner:
John Dewar & Sons
(Bacardi)

Region/district:
Speyside

Founded: 1896
Status: Active
Capacity: 3 200 000 litres

Address: Keith, Banffshire AB55 6QY

Website: aultmore.com
Tel: 01542 881800

Bacardi, the largest privately held spirits company in the world, is the owner of Aultmore and four other distilleries in Scotland. Since 1998 when they first stepped onto the Scotch whisky scene, that part of the business has become more and more important.

Not only do they own five distilleries but, more importantly, they are the third biggest seller of blended Scotch in the world after the two giants, Diageo and Pernod Ricard. Their two brands, William Lawson's and Dewar's, are number 6 and 9 on the Top 10 list and have sold a total of 67 million bottles in 2015. The rapid expansion forced the owners to look for a new blending centre and in 2008 they started building a plant south of Glasgow in Poniel, South Lanarkshire. The construction was done in stages and, when officially opened in autumn 2015, there were 18 ware-houses holding a total of 1.3 million casks, as well as a state-of-the-art blending facility.

Aultmore was completely rebuilt at the beginning of the 1970s and nothing is left of the old buildings from 1896. The distillery is equipped with a 10 ton Steinecker full lauter mash tun, six washbacks made of larch with a minimum fermentation time of 56 hours and two pairs of stills. Since 2008 production has been running seven days a week which, for 2016, means 16 mashes per week and 2.8 million litres of alcohol.

Most of the output from Aultmore is used in Dewar's blended whiskies. Until 2014, a 12 year old which was launched in 2004 was the only official bottling available. Through the launch of the Last Great Malts in autumn 2014 there is now a new **12 year old**, as well a **25 year old** for domestic markets. At the same time a **21 year old** has been reserved for duty free. The range was further expanded to include an **18 year old** in spring 2015 and there have been talks of releasing a **30 year old** in the foreseeable future. All the new bottlings are un chill-filtered, without colouring and bottled at 46%.

History:

1896 Alexander Edward, owner of Benrinnes and co-founder of Craigellachie Distillery, builds Aultmore.

1897 Production starts.

1898 Production is doubled; the company Oban & Aultmore Glenlivet Distilleries Ltd manages Aultmore.

1923 Alexander Edward sells Aultmore for £20,000 to John Dewar & Sons.

1925 Dewar's becomes part of Distillers Company Limited (DCL).

1930 The administration is transferred to Scottish Malt Distillers (SMD).

1971 The stills are increased from two to four.

1991 UDV launches a 12-year old Aultmore in the Flora & Fauna series.

1996 A 21 year old cask strength is marketed as a Rare Malt.

1998 Diageo sells Dewar's and Bombay Gin to Bacardi for £1,150 million.

2004 A new official bottling is launched (12 years old).

2014 Three new expression are released – 12, 25 and 21 year old for duty free.

2015 An 18 year old is released.

Aultmore 12 years old:

GS – A nose of peaches and lemonade, freshly-mown grass, linseed and milky coffee. Very fruity on the palate, mildly herbal, with toffee and light spices. The finish is medium in length, with lingering spices, fudge, and finally more milky coffee.

12 years old

Balblair

[bal•blair]

Owner:
Inver House Distillers
(Thai Beverages plc)

Region/district:
Northern Highlands

Founded: 1790   **Status:** Active (vc)   **Capacity:** 1 800 000 litres

Address: Edderton, Tain, Ross-shire IV19 1LB

Website:
balblair.com

Tel:
01862 821273

Balblair was acquired by Inver House Distillers twenty years ago and that heralded the beginning of a new and brighter future for this lesser-known distillery on the Dornoch Firth, north of Inverness.

The new owners released the first official bottlings from the distillery in 2000 and seven years later, they relaunched the whole core range of whiskies as vintages, together with Glenrothes being the only distillery to do so. Four years ago an excellent visitor centre was opened which contributed to additional attention for one of the oldest distilleries in Scotland. The last couple of years, Inver House have reduced bulk whisky sales in favour of single malts. New markets have since been explored and in 2015 Balblair, together with Old Pulteney and Speyburn, were introduced in the emerging Indian market. The concentration on single malts has paid off well for Inver House which in 2014 showed a 20% profit jump. A major investment on the maturation side has also been made with another 12 warehouses being built at their head office in North Lanarkshire.

The distillery is equipped with a stainless steel, 4.75 ton full lauter mash tun, six Oregon pine washbacks with a fermentation time of 56 hours and one pair of stills. The production target for 2016 is 21 mashes per week which translates to 1.75 million litres of alcohol. In 2011 and 2012, part of the production was heavily peated spirit with a phenol specification of 52ppm in the barley. Since then, however, there has been no peated production. Last year, the distillery converted from using heavy fuel oil to gas, thereby reducing the emission of greenhouse gases significantly.

The current core range consists of four vintages – **1983, 1990, 1999** and, released in January 2016, **2005**. For the duty free market, three new expressions were released in 2014; a **1999** and two versions of **2004** matured in **bourbon** and **sherry** casks respectively. The oldest vintage available from the distillery at the moment is **1969**. For visitors to the distillery there is also the opportunity to bottle a single cask Balblair, from a selected cask which is replaced as it becomes depleted.

History:

1790 The distillery is founded by James McKeddy.

1790 John Ross takes over

1836 John Ross dies and his son Andrew Ross takes over with the help of his sons.

1872 New buildings replace the old.

1873 Andrew Ross dies and his son James takes over.

1894 Alexander Cowan builds a new distillery, a few kilometres from the old.

1911 Cowan is forced to cease payments and the distillery closes.

1941 The distillery is put up for sale.

1948 Robert Cumming buys Balblair for £48,000.

1949 Production restarts.

1970 Cumming sells Balblair to Hiram Walker.

1988 Allied Distillers becomes the new owner through the merger between Hiram Walker and Allied Vintners.

1996 The distillery is sold to Inver House Distillers.

2000 Balblair Elements and the first version of Balblair 33 years are launched.

2001 Thai company Pacific Spirits (part of the Great Oriole Group) takes over Inver House.

2004 Balblair 38 years is launched.

2005 12 year old Peaty Cask, 1979 (26 years) and 1970 (35 years) are launched.

2006 International Beverage Holdings acquires Pacific Spirits UK.

2007 Three new vintages replace the former range.

2008 Vintage 1975 and 1965 are released.

2009 Vintage 1991 and 1990 are released.

2010 Vintage 1978 and 2000 are released.

2011 Vintage 1995 and 1993 are released.

2012 Vintage 1975, 2001 and 2002 are released. A visitor centre is opened.

2013 Vintage 1983, 1990 and 2003 are released.

2014 Vintage 1999 and 2004 are released for duty free.

2016 Vintage 2005 is released.

Tasting notes Balblair 2005:

GS – Chocolate-flavoured ice cream, vanilla and a hint of ozone on the nose. The palate is full and oily, with big spice notes, honey, soft toffee and citrus fruit. The finish is medium in length, with malt and enduring spice.

Vintage 2005

Balmenach

[bal•may•nack]

Owner:
Inver House Distillers
(Thai Beverages plc)

Region/district:
Speyside

Founded: 1824
Status: Active
Capacity: 2 800 000 litres

Address: Cromdale, Moray PH26 3PF

Website: inverhouse.com
Tel: 01479 872569

Balmenach is one of five distilleries owned by Inver House and definitely the least known one. No official bottlings have been released by the owners and the malt goes into their many blends instead.

Starting in May 2016, however, the distillery has suddenly been opened up to visitors but they won´t be guided around to see the whisky production. Instead, the product in focus is gin! Apart from a few of the newest craft distilleries, Balmenach is one of two established whisky distilleries in Scotland (Bruichladdich being the other) which also produces gin. It all started in 2009 and after only six years, their brand, Caorunn, had become the third biggest super-premium gin in the UK. Today it is also sold worldwide. The 16 botanicals that are used to create the flavour include rowan berries, bog myrtle and Coul Blush apple. The gin tour at Balmenach includes a look at the production, as well as a tutored nosing and tasting session.

The distillery´s old cast iron mash tun was replaced in 2014 with an 8 ton stainless steel semi-lauter tun, but the old copper canopy was fitted to the new tun. There are six washbacks made of Douglas fir with a 52 hour fermentation period, and three pairs of stills connected to worm tubs where each worm is 94 metres long. In 2016, the distillery will be doing a combination of 16 to 21 mashes per week which translates to 2.7 million litres of alcohol for the year. Since 2012, a part of the production (of up to 400,000 litres) has been heavily peated (50ppm), but during 2016 they are taking a break and there will be no peated production. The three dunnage warehouses currently hold 9,500 casks.

There is no official bottling of Balemanch single malt. Aberko in Glasgow though, has been working with the distillery for a long time and, over the years, has released Balmenach under the name Deerstalker. The current expression is a 12 year old.

History:

1824 The distillery is licensed to James MacGregor who operated a small farm distillery by the name of Balminoch.

1897 Balmenach Glenlivet Distillery Company is founded.

1922 The MacGregor family sells to a consortium consisting of MacDonald Green, Peter Dawson and James Watson.

1925 The consortium becomes part of Distillers Company Limited (DCL).

1930 Production is transferred to Scottish Malt Distillers (SMD).

1962 The number of stills is increased to six.

1964 Floor maltings replaced with Saladin box.

1992 The first official bottling is a 12 year old.

1993 The distillery is mothballed in May.

1997 Inver House Distillers buys Balmenach from United Distillers.

1998 Production recommences.

2001 Thai company Pacific Spirits takes over Inver House at the price of £56 million. The new owner launches a 27 and a 28 year old.

2002 To commemorate the Queen's Golden Jubilee a 25-year old Balmenach is launched.

2006 International Beverage Holdings acquires Pacific Spirits UK.

2009 Gin production commences.

Tasting notes Deerstalker 12 years old:

GS – The nose is sweet and fruity, with sherry and chilli. Faintly savoury. Fruity and very spicy on the palate, with black pepper and hints of sherry. More chilli in the finish, plus plain chocolate-coated raisins.

Deerstalker 12 years old

Balvenie

[bal•ven•ee]

Owner:　　　　　　　　　　**Region/district:**
William Grant & Sons　　　　Speyside

Founded:　**Status:**　　**Capacity:**
1892　　　　Active (vc)　　6 800 000 litres

Address: Dufftown, Keith, Banffshire AB55 4DH

Website:　　　　　　　　**Tel:**
thebalvenie.com　　　　　　01340 820373

One of the people who have contributed the most to the huge success for Balvenie single malt in recent decades is the Malt Master, David Stewart, who already started his career with W. Grant in 1962.

Having been responsible for the company´s entire range of whiskies for many years, he has since 2009 devoted his time to Balvenie. In recognition of his services to the whisky industry, Stewart was presented with an MBE by the Queen in July 2016. Sales of Balvenie have increased by 46% during the last five years and in 2015 it was the 9th most sold single malt in the world with 3.2 million bottles.

The distillery is equipped with an 11.8 ton full lauter mash tun, nine wooden and five stainless steel washbacks with a fermentation time of 68 hours, five wash stills and six spirit stills. Balvenie is one of few distilleries still doing some of their own maltings and there is also a coppersmith and a cooperage on site. For 2015, the production plan is to do 30 mashes per week and 6.8 million litres of alcohol. The main part is unpeated but each year a smaller part is produced from peated barley (20-40 ppm).

The core range consists of **Doublewood 12 years, Doublewood 17 years, Caribbean Cask 14 years, Single Barrel 12 years First Fill, Single Barrel 15 years Sherry Cask, Single Barrel 25 years Traditional Oak, Portwood 21 years, 30 years, 40 years** and the extremely rare **50 years old**. Recent limited releases include **Tun 1509** with batch 3 having been released in July 2016 and **Tun 1858** which has been reserved for Asia. Chapter number one of **The Balvenie DCS Compendium** was launched in autumn 2015. The first five expressions, all single casks and bottled at cask strength, were from **1968, 1978, 1985, 1997** and **2005**. Chapter two of five is due for release in autumn 2016. For Duty Free there is the **Triple Cask** series (**12, 16** and **25 years old**) which are vattings of first-fill ex-bourbon barrels, refill American oak casks and first-fill ex-sherry butts. In spring 2016, a **21 year old madeira finish** was included in the Triple Cask range.

History:

1892　William Grant rebuilds Balvenie New House to Balvenie Distillery (Glen Gordon was the name originally intended). Part of the equipment is brought in from Lagavulin and Glen Albyn.

1893　The first distillation takes place in May.

1957　The two stills are increased by another two.

1965　Two new stills are installed.

1971　Another two stills are installed and eight stills are now running.

1973　The first official bottling appears.

1982　Founder's Reserve is launched.

1990　A new distillery, Kininvie, is opened on the premises.

1996　Two vintage bottlings and a Port wood finish are launched.

2001　The Balvenie Islay Cask, with 17 years in bourbon casks and six months in Islay casks, is released.

2002　A 50 year old is released.

2004　The Balvenie Thirty is released.

2005　The Balvenie Rum Wood Finish 14 years old is released.

2006　The Balvenie New Wood 17 years old, Roasted Malt 14 years old and Portwood 1993 are released.

2007　Vintage Cask 1974 and Sherry Oak 17 years old are released.

2008　Signature, Vintage 1976, Balvenie Rose and Rum Cask 17 year old are released.

2009　Vintage 1978, 17 year old Madeira finish, 14 year old rum finish and Golden Cask 14 years old are released.

2010　A 40 year old, Peated Cask and Carribean Cask are released.

2011　Second batch of Tun 1401 is released.

2012　A 50 year old and Doublewood 17 years old are released.

2013　Triple Cask 12, 16 and 25 years are launched for duty free.

2014　Single Barrel 15 and 25 years, Tun 1509 and two new 50 year olds are launched.

2015　The Balvenie DCS Compendium is launched.

2016　A 21 year old madeira finish and batch 3 of Tun 1509 are released.

Tasting notes Balvenie Doublewood 12 years:

GS – Nuts and spicy malt on the nose, full-bodied, with soft fruit, vanilla, sherry and a hint of peat. Dry and spicy in a luxurious, lengthy finish.

Doublewood 12 years old

Ben Nevis

[ben nev•iss]

Owner:
Ben Nevis Distillery Ltd
(Nikka, Asahi Breweries)

Region/district:
Western Highlands

Founded: 1825
Status: Active (vc)
Capacity: 2 000 000 litres

Address: Lochy Bridge, Fort William PH33 6TJ

Website:
bennevisdistillery.com

Tel:
01397 702476

Towards the end of the 1800s there were three working distilleries in Fort William. Two of them, Ben Nevis and its sister distillery Nevis, were of such a magnitude that their joint production far exceeded distilleries such as Macallan and Glenlivet.

The reason for this can be ascribed to the success of the blend Dew of Ben Nevis, which was introduced by the legendary distillery owner, "Long" John MacDonald. In the 1940s and 50s, when the distillery was owned by the eccentric millionaire, Joseph Hobbs, the distillery became a centre for experimentation with concrete washbacks and a Coffey still. The distillery was eventually sold to the giant brewing company, Whitbread. When almost all the producers had closed some of their distilleries in the early 1980s, Whitbread went against the current and had invested more than £2m in refurbishing the distillery. In spite of this, the distillery was forced to close down and was subsequently sold to Nikka in 1990. Since then, production has been uninterrupted under the supervision of long-time distillery manager, Colin Ross.

Ben Nevis is equipped with one lauter mash tun, six stainless steel washbacks and two made of Oregon pine and two pairs of stills. The plan for 2016 is to do 2 million litres. A small part of this will be heavily peated. Ben Nevis is an important supplier of whisky for the owner´s (Nikka) blends and every year, around 50% of the newmake is sent to Japan, primarily to be part of the blend, Nikka Black.

The core range consists of the **10 year old** and the peated **MacDonald´s Traditional Ben Nevis**. A new range of limited releases, called Forgotten Bottlings, was introduced in 2014. The manager since 1989, Colin Ross, had discovered stocks of bottles that for some or other reason hadn´t been claimed by customers. One of the latest releases in the series is a **40 year old "Blended at Birth"** single blend which was first released 13 years ago. Other recent limited bottlings include a **12 year old single white port cask**, a **15 year old sherry cask**, a **21 year old** with 8 years of second maturation in a ruby port bodega butt, as well as a **25 year old first fill sherry cask**.

History:

1825 The distillery is founded by 'Long' John McDonald.

1856 Long John dies and his son Donald P. McDonald takes over.

1878 Demand is so great that another distillery, Nevis Distillery, is built nearby.

1908 Both distilleries merge into one.

1941 D. P. McDonald & Sons sells the distillery to Ben Nevis Distillery Ltd headed by the Canadian millionaire Joseph W. Hobbs.

1955 Hobbs installs a Coffey still which makes it possible to produce both grain and malt whisky.

1964 Joseph Hobbs dies.

1978 Production is stopped.

1981 Joseph Hobbs Jr sells the distillery back to Long John Distillers and Whitbread.

1984 After restoration and reconstruction totalling £2 million, Ben Nevis opens up again.

1986 The distillery closes again.

1989 Whitbread sells the distillery to Nikka Whisky Distilling Company Ltd.

1990 The distillery opens up again.

1991 A visitor centre is inaugurated.

1996 Ben Nevis 10 years old is launched.

2006 A 13 year old port finish is released.

2010 A 25 year old is released.

2011 McDonald´s Traditional Ben Nevis is released.

2014 Forgotten Bottlings are introduced.

2015 A 40 year old "Blended at Birth" single blend is released.

Tasting notes Ben Nevis 10 years old:

GS – The nose is initially quite green, with developing nutty, orange notes. Coffee, brittle toffee and peat are present on the slightly oily palate, along with chewy oak, which persists to the finish, together with more coffee and a hint of dark chocolate.

10 years old

Benriach

[ben•ree•ack]

Owner:		Region/district:
BenRiach Distillery Company (Brown Forman)		Speyside

Founded:	Status:	Capacity:
1897	Active	2 800 000 litres

Address: Longmorn, Elgin, Morayshire IV30 8SJ

Website:	Tel:
benriachdistillery.co.uk	01343 862888

When the former Burn Stewart director, Billy Walker, together with two South African partners, bought BenRiach in 2004, he embarked on a journey that would arouse admiration in the whisky world.

Over the past ten years, two more distilleries were added to the portfolio, GlenDronach and Glenglassaugh. To complement that, a modern bottling plant which was opened in Newbridge in 2010 and a large stock of maturing whiskies and it thus comes as no surprise that such a company would attract many suitors. Billy Walker has received several bids over the years and in April 2016 he accepted one from the American spirits giant, Brown Forman. They offered to pay no less than £285m for the company, a deal which gives the Brown Forman access to the increasingly important Scotch single malt market.

BenRiach distillery is equipped with a traditional cast iron mash tun with a stainless steel shell, eight washbacks made of stainless steel and two pairs of stills. The production for 2016 will be 2.35 million litres of alcohol (which includes 150,000 litres of peated spirit at 35ppm). In 2013, the owners revamped the malting floor which hadn't been used since 1998. It has, since, been used sporadically, the last time being in November 2014.

The core range of BenRiach is **Heart of Speyside** (no age), **10, 16, 20, 25** and **35 years old** in what the distillery calls Classic Speyside style. Added to that range in March 2016, was **Cask Strength** batch 1. Peated varieties include **Birnie Moss, Curiositas 10 year old, Septendecim 17 year old, Authenticus 25 year old** and the new **Peated Quarter Cask**. The latter carries no age statement but has been matured in quarter casks for around 8 years. There used to be four different wood finishes in the Classic Speyside style but the only remaining is the **12 year old Sherry Wood**. Three 18 year old, limited peated wood finishes were released in 2015 - **Dunder** (dark rum), **Albariza** (PX sherry) and **Latada** (madeira). They will all be replaced by new expressions late in 2016. Finally, every year a number of **single cask** bottlings are released and **batch number 13** was launched in June 2016.

History:

1897 John Duff & Co founds the distillery.

1900 The distillery is closed.

1965 The distillery is reopened by the new owner, The Glenlivet Distillers Ltd.

1978 Seagram Distillers takes over.

1983 Production of peated Benriach starts.

1985 The number of stills is increased to four.

1998 The maltings is decommissioned.

2002 The distillery is mothballed in October.

2004 Intra Trading, buys Benriach together with the former Director at Burn Stewart, Billy Walker.

2004 Standard, Curiositas and 12, 16 and 20 year olds are released.

2005 Four different vintages are released.

2006 Sixteen new releases, i.a. a 25 year old, a 30 year old and 8 different vintages.

2007 A 40 year old and three new heavily peated expressions are released.

2008 New expressions include a peated Madeira finish, a 15 year old Sauternes finish and nine single casks.

2009 Two wood finishes (Moscatel and Gaja Barolo) and nine single casks are released.

2010 Triple distilled Horizons and heavily peated Solstice are released.

2011 A 45 year old and 12 vintages are released.

2012 Septendecim 17 years is released.

2013 Vestige 46 years is released. The maltings are working again.

2015 Dunder, Albariza, Latada and a 10 year old are released.

2016 Brown Forman buys the company. BenRiach cask strength and Peated Quarter Cask are launched

Tasting notes BenRiach 10 year old:

GS – Earthy and nutty on the early nose, with apples, ginger and vanilla. Smooth and rounded on the palate, with oranges, apricots, mild spice and hazelnuts. The finish is medium in length, nutty and spicy.

10 years old

Benrinnes

[ben rin•ess]

Owner:	**Region/district:**
Diageo	Speyside
Founded: **Status:**	**Capacity:**
1826 Active	3 500 000 litres

Address: Aberlour, Banffshire AB38 9NN

Website:	**Tel:**
malts.com	01340 872600

When distilleries around Scotland closed their own floor maltings during the first half of the 20th century, most of them went straight on to buying directly from commercial maltsters, but not Benrinnes.

In 1964 they installed a so called Saladin box, named after Charles Saladin who invented it in the 1890s. A Saladin box is a long concrete box with revolving rakes. The barley is steeped and turned by the rakes and air circulates through perforated floors to keep the temperature under control. To dry, the green malt goes into a kiln, which is very different to traditional ones. It is simply a large, self-filling and self-emptying box with air blowing through it. Benrinnes closed their maltings in 1984 and until 2011, Tamdhu was the only remaining distillery using a Saladin box. Now, also that has been taken out of use.

Benrinnes was completely rebuilt in the 1950s and none of the original buildings remain. A major upgrade was made in autumn 2012 which included a full automation of the process, as well as a new control room where one operator can handle all the work. The equipment consists of an 8.5 ton semilauter mash tun, eight washbacks made of Oregon pine with a fermentation time of 65 hours and six stills. The composition of stills is rare, in that there are two wash stills and four spirit stills and, until a few years ago, they were run three and three with a partial triple distillation. This system has since been abandoned and one wash still will now serve two spirit stills. The spirit vapours are cooled using cast iron worm tubs which contribute to the character of Benrinnes newmake, which is light sulphury. The wide spirit cut (73%-58%) also plays its part in creating a robust and meaty spirit. For 2016, the distillery will be working a 5-day week which translates to 2.5 million litres of alcohol per year.

Most of the production goes into blended whiskies – J&B, Johnnie Walker and Crawford´s 3 Star – and there is currently only one official single malt, the **Flora & Fauna 15 year old**. In 2010 a **Manager´s Choice** from **1996** was released and in autumn 2014 it was time for a **21 year old** Special Release bottled at 57%.

History:

1826 Lyne of Ruthrie distillery is built at Whitehouse Farm by Peter McKenzie.

1829 A flood destroys the distillery and a new distillery is constructed by John Innes a few kilometres from the first one.

1834 John Innes files for bankruptcy and William Smith & Co takes over.

1864 William Smith & Co goes bankrupt and David Edward becomes the new owner.

1896 Benrinnes is ravaged by fire which prompts major refurbishment. Alexander Edward takes over.

1922 John Dewar & Sons takes over ownership.

1925 John Dewar & Sons becomes part of Distillers Company Limited (DCL).

1956 The distillery is completely rebuilt.

1964 Floor maltings is replaced by a Saladin box.

1966 The number of stills doubles to six.

1984 The Saladin box is taken out of service and the malt is purchased centrally.

1991 The first official bottling from Benrinnes is a 15 year old in the Flora & Fauna series.

1996 United Distillers releases a 21 year old cask strength in their Rare Malts series.

2009 A 23 year old is launched as a part of this year´s Special Releases.

2010 A Manager´s Choice 1996 is released.

2014 A limited 21 year old is released.

Tasting notes Benrinnes 15 years old:

GS – A brief flash of caramel shortcake on the initial nose, soon becoming more peppery and leathery, with some sherry. Ultimately savoury and burnt rubber notes. Big-bodied, viscous, with gravy, dark chocolate and more pepper. A medium-length finish features mild smoke and lively spices.

15 years old

Benromach

[ben•ro•mack]

Owner:	**Region/district:**
Gordon & MacPhail	Speyside
Founded: **Status:**	**Capacity:**
1898　　Active (vc)	700 000 litres

Address: Invererne Road, Forres,
Morayshire IV36 3EB

Website:	**Tel:**
benromach.com	01309 675968

Benromach distillery will be a busier place than usual during 2016. Due to the success of the brand in recent years, the owners have decided to increase its production capacity.

Gordon & MacPhail have installed no less than an additional nine new washbacks, which means that its capacity will increase by 40% to 700,000 litres. However, the actual production, once the new washbacks are in place, will probably only be around 400,000 litres. The total number of washbacks (14) also indicates that, with a possible future increase in mashing and distillation capacity, the volumes could go even higher. Work on the distillery has also included an extended visitor centre, as well as three new tasting rooms.

The goal at Benromach is to produce a Speyside whisky, just like it used to taste back in the 1950s and 1960s. This is achieved by predominantly using medium peated barley (12ppm). Benromach is equipped with a 1.5 ton semi-lauter mash tun with a copper dome, four washbacks (soon to be 14) made of larch and one pair of stills. Almost the entire production is destined to be sold as single malt. New warehouses have lately been added, which now totals five, all dunnage and holding 18,000 casks.

In 2014, most of the bottles in the range received a new look and new expressions were added. The core range now consists of a **5 year old**, a **10 year old**, a **15 year old** (launched in spring 2015) and the **100 Proof** (bottled at 57% thus replacing the Cask Strength). Limited releases include a **35 year old** released in February 2016, a **1974 single cask** launched in summer 2016 and **Classic 55 year old**. There are also special editions; **Organic**, the first single malt to be fully certified organic by the Soil Association and currently from 2010 and **Peatsmoke**, produced by using heavily peated barley and distilled in 2006. Every year wood finishes are released in limited quantities with **Hermitage** and **Sassicaia 2007** (launched in March 2016) being the latest. Finally, a duty free bottling called **Traveller´s Edition**, was released in 2014.

History:

1898　Benromach Distillery Company starts the distillery.

1911　Harvey McNair & Co buys the distillery.

1919　John Joseph Calder buys Benromach and sells it to recently founded Benromach Distillery Ltd owned by several breweries.

1931　Benromach is mothballed.

1937　The distillery reopens.

1938　Joseph Hobbs buys Benromach and sells it on to National Distillers of America (NDA).

1953　NDA sells Benromach to Distillers Company Limited (DCL).

1966　The distillery is refurbished.

1968　Floor maltings is abolished.

1983　Benromach is mothballed.

1993　Gordon & McPhail buys Benromach from United Distillers.

1998　The distillery is once again in operation.

1999　A visitor centre is opened.

2004　The first bottle distilled by the new owner is released under the name 'Benromach Traditional'.

2005　A Port Wood finish (22 years old) and a Vintage 1968 are released together with the Benromach Classic 55 years.

2006　Benromach Organic is released.

2007　Peat Smoke, the first heavily peated whisky from the distillery, is released.

2008　Benromach Origins Golden Promise is released.

2009　Benromach 10 years old is released.

2010　New batches of Peatsmoke and Origins are released.

2011　New edition of Peatsmoke, a 2001 Hermitage finish and a 30 year old are released.

2013　A Sassicaia Wood Finish is released.

2014　Three new bottlings are launched; a 5 year old, 100 Proof and Traveller´s Edition.

2015　A 15 year old and two wood finishes (Hermitage and Sassicaia) are released.

2016　A 35 year old and 1974 single cask are released.

Tasting notes Benromach 10 year old:

GS – A nose that is initially quite smoky, with wet grass, butter, ginger and brittle toffee. Mouth-coating, spicy, malty and nutty on the palate, with developing citrus fruits, raisins and soft wood smoke. The finish is warming, with lingering barbecue notes.

10 years old

Bladnoch

[blad•nock]

Owner:
David Prior

Region/district:
Lowlands

Founded: 1817

Status: Mothballed

Capacity: 1 500 000 litres

Address: Bladnoch, Wigtown, Wigtonshire DG8 9AB

Website: bladnoch.com

Tel: 01988 402605

Bladnoch distillery has experienced a chequered history of ownership changes, as well as periods of no production. The man, who resuscitated the distillery after it had been mothballed in 1993, was Raymond Armstrong, an entrepreneur from Northern Ireland.

He started the production anew in 2000, but then stopped again in 2009. But in the meanwhile, he kept up the business of releasing whiskies from both the old and the new production. In 2014, however, Armstrong and his brother (who was a co-owner) failed to agree on the future of the distillery and the company was forced into liquidation. Rumours of possible buyers started doing the rounds and it wasn't until July 2015 that Bladnoch was sold to an Australian businessman, David Prior, who had sold his successful yoghurt company five:am for $80m during the previous year. Prior also managed to involve the Master Blender and Distilleries Director of Burn Stewart, Ian MacMillan, who joined the team as distillery manager.

When the new owners took over, they found that both the distillery and the warehouses were in a poor condition. After the warehouses had been attended to, distillery manager Ian MacMillan rummaged through the rest of the equipment and found that the only piece that could be used was the mill. A new 5 ton stainless steel semi-lauter will be installed, as well as six Douglas fir washbacks. There will also be two pairs of stills as opposed to the one pair in the old distillery. The capacity will be 1.5 million litres of alcohol and the goal is to have the distillery up and running by May of 2017.

In the last two years before liquidation, a number of official bottlings were released, ranging from 12 to 22 years old. When the new owners took over, the deal included several thousand casks of Bladnoch whisky dating back to the 1980s, a stock which was examined cask by cask by Ian MacMillan. Where needed, MacMillan re-filled whiskies from inferior casks into new quality casks and the idea is to release a number of whiskies by the end of 2016 and then again in 2017 to celebrate the distillery's 200th anniversary.

History:

1817 Brothers Thomas and John McClelland found the distillery.

1825 The McClelland brothers obtain a licence.

1878 John McClelland's son Charlie reconstructs and refurbishes the distillery.

1905 Production stops.

1911 Dunville & Co. from Ireland buys T. & A. McClelland Ltd for £10,775. Production is intermittent until 1936.

1937 Dunville & Co. is liquidated and Bladnoch is wound up. Ross & Coulter from Glasgow buys the distillery after the war. The equipment is dismantled and shipped to Sweden.

1956 A. B. Grant (Bladnoch Distillery Ltd.) takes over and restarts production with four new stills.

1964 McGown and Cameron becomes new owners.

1966 The number of stills is increased to four.

1973 Inver House Distillers buys Bladnoch.

1983 Arthur Bell and Sons take over.

1985 Guiness Group buys Arthur Bell & Sons which, from 1989, are included in United Distillers.

1988 A visitor centre is built.

1993 United Distillers mothballs Bladnoch in June.

1994 Raymond Armstrong buys Bladnoch in October.

2000 Production commences in December.

2003 The first bottles from Raymond Armstrong are launched, a 15 year old cask strength from UD casks.

2004 New varieties follow suit: e. g. 13 year olds 40% and 55%.

2008 First release of whisky produced after the takeover in 2000 - three 6 year olds.

2009 An 8 year old of own production and a 19 year old are released.

2014 The distillery is liquidated.

2015 The distillery is bought by David Prior.

8 years old

Tasting notes Bladnoch 8 year old:

GS – Bright, fresh and citric, with lemon, cereal, soft toffee and nuts on the nose. Medium in body, the palate is gingery and very lively, with vanilla, hot spices and hazelnuts. The finish offers persistently fruity spice.

Blair Athol

[blair ath•ull]

Owner: Diageo	**Region/district:** Eastern Highlands

Founded: 1798	**Status:** Active (vc)	**Capacity:** 2 800 000 litres

Address: Perth Road, Pitlochry, Perthshire PH16 5LY

Website: malts.com	**Tel:** 01796 482003

When whisky blending took off in the late 1800s, a group of companies soon took the lead; John Walker, Dewar's, Buchanan, White Horse and Haig. They were called the Big Five. Arthur Bell & Sons were regarded too small to play any significant part.

But while the Big Five all had been absorbed into the mighty Distillers Company Ltd. (DCL) by 1927, Bell's was still an independent, family run business gamely struggling on building its reputation, not only domestically, but also in such remote places such as South Africa and Australia. The assiduous work paid off and between 1970 and 1980, sales in the UK alone increased from £20m to £159m which had transformed Bell's to a superior market leader domestically. Since then, that position has been lost to Famous Grouse.

Right from the start, Blair Athol was the most important malt in the blend and in 1933, Bell's bought the distillery to secure whisky for its growing brand. Today, the distillery is the spiritual home of Bell's blended whisky with a magnificent visitor centre attracting 35,000 people every year.

The equipment of Blair Athol distillery consists of an 8 ton semi-lauter mash tun, six washbacks made of stainless steel and two pairs of stills. The part of the spirit which goes into Bell's is matured mainly in bourbon casks, while the rest is matured in sherry casks. For 2016, the distillery has gone from a 7-day week to a 5-day week with 12 mashes per week and 1.9 million litres of alcohol. This also means that a scheme of short (46 hours) and long (104 hours) fermentations has now been implemented. A very cloudy wort gives Blair Athol newmake a nutty and malty character.

The output today is still used for Bell's whisky and the only official bottling used to be the **12 year old Flora & Fauna**. In autumn 2016, however, a **distillery exclusive** without age statement was released.

History:

1798 John Stewart and Robert Robertson found Aldour Distillery, the predecessor to Blair Athol. The name is taken from the adjacent river Allt Dour.

1825 The distillery is expanded by John Robertson and takes the name Blair Athol Distillery.

1826 The Duke of Atholl leases the distillery to Alexander Connacher & Co.

1860 Elizabeth Connacher runs the distillery.

1882 Peter Mackenzie & Company Distillers Ltd of Edinburgh (future founder of Dufftown Distillery) buys Blair Athol and expands it.

1932 The distillery is mothballed.

1933 Arthur Bell & Sons takes over by acquiring Peter Mackenzie & Company.

1949 Production restarts.

1973 Stills are expanded from two to four.

1985 Guinness Group buys Arthur Bell & Sons.

1987 A visitor centre is built.

2003 A 27 year old cask strength from 1975 is launched in Diageo's Rare Malts series.

2010 A distillery exclusive with no age statement and a single cask from 1995 are released.

2016 A distillery exclusive without age statement is released.

12 years old

Tasting notes Blair Athol 12 years old:

GS – The nose is mellow and sherried, with brittle toffee. Sweet and fragrant. Relatively rich on the palate, with malt, raisins, sultanas and sherry. The finish is lengthy, elegant and slowly drying.

Bowmore

[bow•moor]

Owner:		Region/district:
Morrison Bowmore (Suntory)		Islay

Founded:	Status:	Capacity:
1779	Active (vc)	2 000 000 litres

Address: School Street, Bowmore, Islay, Argyll PA43 7GS

Website:	Tel:
bowmore.com	01496 810441

During the last two years, three of the famous Islay distilleries have celebrated their 200th anniversaries. Bowmore, on the other hand, can look forward to its 240th jubilee in just three years, making it the oldest distillery on the island by far.

Bowmore has always been known for making a whisky which is less smoky than those from the three Kildalton cousins. This has probably been one of the reasons for the success amongst consumers who like peat "but not too much of it". The sales figures peaked in 2012, but have since declined by 8% to 1.9 million bottles sold in 2015.

The distillery is one of only a few Scottish distilleries with its own malting floor, with 30% of the malt requirement being produced in-house. The remaining part is bought from Simpson´s. Both parts have a phenol specification of 25ppm and are always mixed according to the proportions, 2 ton in-house malt and 6 ton malt from Simpson´s before mashing. The distillery has an eight ton stainless steel semi-lauter mash tun, six washbacks of Oregon pine with both short (48 hours) and long (100 hours) fermentations and two pairs of stills. The 27,000 casks are stored in two dunnage and one racked warehouse. Vault No. 1, closest to the sea and dating back to the 1700s, is probably the oldest whisky warehouse still in use in Scotland. In 2016, they will be doing 11 mashes per week, which amounts to 1.3 million litres of alcohol.

The core range for domestic markets includes **Small Batch Reserve** (bourbon matured and with no age statement), **12 years, Darkest 15 years, 18 years** and **25 years**. The duty free line-up consists of **Springtide** (matured in Oloroso casks), **Black Rock** (predominantly matured in first-fill sherry casks), **Gold Reef** (mostly from first-fill bourbon casks), **White Sands** (a 17 year old matured in 100% ex-bourbon casks) and **Vintage 1984**. Recent limited releases include the sixth release of **Tempest** (a 10 year old cask strength from first fill bourbon casks) and a further 50 bottles of the **50 year old** which was first released in 2013. A surprise release in 2015 was the **Mizunara Cask Finish**. Having Japanese owners, Bowmore has easier access to the rare casks made of the Japanese mizunara oak. Parts of the content came from three casks that had been filled with 12 year old Bowmore malt a couple of years ago. A limited release was made in autumn 2016, highlighting the influence from Vault No. 1 where some of the warehouse walls are actually found below sea level. The new expression, bottled at 51.5% is called **Bowmore Vault Edit1on** with the added "Atlantic Sea Salt". Autumn 2016 also saw the release of a new, oloroso-matured **9 year old** core bottling as well as a **10 year old**, matured in sherry casks and red wine barriques and destined for travel retail. There were two bottlings for Feis Ile 2016; one **unaged** where four casks of American virgin oak had been vatted together with a first fill Oloroso sherry butt and a **25 year old** which had received a second maturation for twelve years in French wine casks.

History:

1779 Bowmore Distillery is founded by David Simpson and becomes the oldest Islay distillery.

1837 The distillery is sold to James and William Mutter of Glasgow.

1892 After additional construction, the distillery is sold to Bowmore Distillery Company Ltd, a consortium of English businessmen.

1925 J. B. Sheriff and Company takes over.

1929 Distillers Company Limited (DCL) takes over.

1950 William Grigor & Son takes over.

1963 Stanley P. Morrison buys the distillery for £117,000 and forms Morrison Bowmore Distillers Ltd.

1989 Japanese Suntory buys a 35% stake in Morrison Bowmore.

1993 The legendary Black Bowmore is launched. Another two versions are released 1994 and 1995.

1994 Suntory now controls all of Morrison Bowmore.

1996 A Bowmore 1957 (38 years) is bottled at 40.1% but is not released until 2000.

1999 Bowmore Darkest with three years finish on Oloroso barrels is launched.

2000 Bowmore Dusk with two years finish in Bordeaux barrels is launched.

2001 Bowmore Dawn with two years finish on Port pipes is launched.

2002 A 37 year old Bowmore from 1964 and matured in fino casks is launched in a limited edition of 300 bottles (recommended price £1,500).

2003 Another two expressions complete the wood trilogy which started with 1964 Fino - 1964 Bourbon and 1964 Oloroso.

History continued:

2004 Morrison Bowmore buys one of the most out standing collections of Bowmore Single Malt from the private collector Hans Sommer. It totals more than 200 bottles and includes a number of Black Bowmore.

2005 Bowmore 1989 Bourbon (16 years) and 1971 (34 years) are launched.

2006 Bowmore 1990 Oloroso (16 years) and 1968 (37 years) are launched. A new and upgraded visitor centre is opened.

2007 An 18 year old is introduced. New packaging for the whole range. 1991 (16yo) Port and Black Bowmore are released.

2008 White Bowmore and a 1992 Vintage with Bour-deaux finish are launched.

2009 Gold Bowmore, Maltmen´s Selection, Laimrig and Bowmore Tempest are released.

2010 A 40 year old and Vintage 1981 are released.

2011 Vintage 1982 and new batches of Tempest and Laimrig are released.

2012 100 Degrees Proof, Springtide and Vintage 1983 are released for duty free.

2013 The Devil´s Casks, a 23 year old Port Cask Matured and Vintage 1984 are released.

2014 Black Rock, Gold Reef and White Sands are released for duty free.

2015 New editions of Devil´s Cask, Tempest and the 50 year old are released as well as Mizunara Cask Finish.

2016 A 9 year old, a 10 year old travel retail exclusive and Bowmore Vault Edit1on are released.

Tasting notes Bowmore 12 year old:

GS – An enticing nose of lemon and gentle brine leads into a smoky, citric palate, with notes of cocoa and boiled sweets appearing in the lengthy, complex finish.

10 years old

Springtide

9 years old

12 years old

Small Batch

15 years old

Braeval

[bre•vaal]

Owner:		Region/district:
Chivas Brothers (Pernod Ricard)		Speyside

Founded:	Status:	Capacity:
1973	Active	4 000 000 litres

Address: Chapeltown of Glenlivet, Ballindalloch, Banffshire AB37 9JS

Website:	Tel:
-	01542 783042

Braeval is one of those distilleries where the drive to reach it and the surroundings play as big a role, as experiencing the distillery itself. Situated in the isolated Braes south of Glenlivet, it is not a distillery you stumble across by accident.

When you drive on the B9008, you reach the small hamlet, Auchnarrow, which is just a mile south of Tamnavulin. From there you follow the narrow road east towards Chapeltown and drive until the road ends. Set in an idyllic and pastoral environment, lies the impressive and surprisingly beautiful Braeval (considering that it was built in 1973 as a working distillery). This area was regarded as a haven for illicit distillers from the 1780s to the early 1800s and the whisky was smuggled out of the valley along narrow paths. At one time over 200 illicit stills were operating in this wild and beautiful part of the glen. Today there are three marked trails (called Smuggler's Trails) which are open to hikers.

Braeval and its sister distillery, Allt-a-Bhainne, which is a 20 minute drive to the north, both have contrasting features as regards their exterior, yet both were built in the mid 1970s when Chivas Brothers was still owned by the Canadian drinks giant Seagram's. Both were also mothballed in 2002 by the new owners Pernod Ricard, just before today's Scotch whisky boom took off. Subsequently, when new markets got interested in Scotch, the distilleries were re-opened – Allt-a-Bhainne in 2005 and Braeval three years later.

The equipment consists of a 9 ton stainless steel mash tun with traditional rakes, but this may be converted to a more modern full lauter tun in keeping with Allt-a-Bhainne which was converted last year. Furthermore, there are 13 stainless steel washbacks with a fermentation time of 70 hours and six stills. There are two wash stills with aftercoolers and four spirit stills, and with the possibility of doing 26 mashes per week, the distillery can now produce 4 million litres per year.

Braeval single malt is used for many of Chivas Brothers' blends. There are no official bottlings but, from time to time, it has been used for the bottling of Deerstalker.

History:

1973 The distillery is founded by Chivas Brothers (Seagram's) and production starts in October.

1975 Three stills are increased to five.

1978 Five stills are further expanded to six.

1994 The distillery changes name to Braeval.

2001 Pernod Ricard takes over Chivas Brothers.

2002 Braeval is mothballed in October.

2008 The distillery starts producing again in July.

Tasting notes Deerstalker 20 year old:

GS – Newsprint, herbal notes, fleeting green apples, sawdust and burgeoning vanilla on the nose. Mouth-coating, initially fruity – apricots and peaches, with an edge of chilli. Spicy, lengthy finish, with a hint of oak.

Deerstalker 20 years old

The State of Scotch

six burning questions

John Glaser,
Owner and Chairman,
Compass Box Whisky

1. The Millenials are often referred to as perhaps the most Important consumer demographic today. Do you think Scotch whisky appeals to that category and what can the producers do to attract them and keep them interested?

While we're familiar with the term 'Millennial' we don't tend to categorise people that way ourselves – when we think about the whiskies we make or who will be interested in them. But in terms of engaging with people that value craftsmanship, substance provenance I would say that Scotch whisky – as a category – has not been traditionally strong but is getting better. In the past Scotch was about guarded traditions and 'the way it's always been done', which doesn't play well for an audience interested in craftsmanship, innovation and provenance. We've always advocated sharing as much information with our audience as regulations permit us to (more on that later) and that has probably helped us engage more with this type of audience than a lot of other brands. There is a fantastic provenance story behind every quality Scotch whisky – the Scotch category has maybe been poor at sharing those in the past but the stories are there and today we see more and more brands taking ever more open stances and sharing ever more information. It's a good thing for the industry and for the consumer.

2. Several Scotch whisky producers have recently questioned the rules what can and can´t be said on the label about the whisky. Should the legislation be changed, allowing more transparency?

Yes. It is inconceivable in the 21st Century to have a regulatory system that actively prohibits producers from sharing complete and accurate information about what goes into the whiskies they produce. Can you imagine if the same regulations applied to fast-food restaurants – preventing them from sharing ingredients lists or calorie information? There would be a consumer backlash. We have been very vocal on this issue and have gone so far as proposing specific changes to the existing regulations to address the concerns we have – and to date over 8,000 whisky enthusiasts around the world have signed our Statement of Beliefs to indicate their support for our position. There is a way to provide greater transparency with no down-side for the industry or the consumer. It is incumbent on us as an industry to make that happen.

3. We see more and more Scotch whiskies being bottled without an age statement. Will that trend continue and, from a consumer point of view, is that all bad?

Almost every release in the history of Compass Box has been a NAS whisky so we have no issue with NAS per se. For us, it has always been about using different ages of whisky to create additional layers of complexity in a blend – and we have (until we were recently prevented from doing so) shared details of the age of every parcel of whisky that's gone into the blend so that consumers can understand more about what each element brings and make up their own mind about value. That said, whenever we can, we try to tell consumers not to obsess about age. For some, it can become (like colour or category) a cognitive short-cut for quality or value, when such a direct correlation simply doesn't exist. Put a fantastic new-make spirit in a bad or tired cask for 25 years and it will taste infinitely inferior to the same new-make aged for just half that time in quality oak.

4. Not a new discussion but one that does resurface from time to time. Does the quality of a whisky suffer from chill-filtration and colouring?

Yes, the quality suffers and the character of the whisky changes. We have in the past helped illustrate this for visitors to our blending room by adding tiny amounts of caramel colouring to our whiskies and completing blind tastings – the impact on mouthfeel is not hard to detect. It deadens the mouthfeel somewhat, strips back the character but increases the perceived 'smoothness' of the blend – this has been consistent feedback. Chill-filtering has a negative effect on mouthfeel for similar reasons. We've never used either approach and we don't intend to in the future. Scotch whisky is a natural product with very few component ingredients – why would you want to strip any of the natural character away or add anything additional?

5. In the steps of flavoured vodka, flavoured whisky has become increasingly popular. Mostly bourbon and Irish whiskey but also Scotch. What are the benefits and downsides of this new trend?

What's important in these matters is transparency – if it's not Scotch, consumers need to be made aware of that. In this respect, the Scotch market has in fact been more stringently regulated than other whiskies around the world (American, Canadian, Irish), however there is still (in our opinion) potential for consumer confusion with several flavoured Scotch products that are currently on the market. If consumers understand what it is they're drinking they can make an informed decision about what they want to drink next (more of the same or progression onto an unflavoured spirit). If they believe they're drinking Scotch or Bourbon or Rye when they're actually drinking a honey spirit infusion then they will be in for a shock when they move on to try an unflavoured whisky – and that doesn't do anyone any good.

6. Scotch whisky exports have declined in the last couple of years. Is the position of Scotch under threat and if so, what can be done to change the trend?

American whisky is very strong at the moment and certain world whisky producers are creating excellent spirits too – notably in East Asia (Taiwan, India – not just Japan). They are evolving quickly, they are using local climatic conditions to create styles of whisky that can't be created in Scotland. We have always believed that innovation and the pursuit of quality is the key for Scotch to maintain its position as the world's leading whisky. We have pushed at the edges of what is acceptable in the past by experimenting with different types of oak, different maturation techniques, flavour profiles that haven't been seen before. Today, there is a growing spirit of experimentation within Scotch (especially within the new wave of craft distillers). It feels like an exciting time in the industry – things are changing and the combination of a growing culture of innovation with a strong regulatory system to uphold standards suggests Scotch will be in a good position in years to come.

Bruichladdich

[brook•lad•dee]

Owner:	**Region/district:**
Rémy Cointreau	Islay
Founded: **Status:**	**Capacity:**
1881 Active (vc)	1 500 000 litres

Address: Bruichladdich, Islay, Argyll PA49 7UN

Website:	**Tel:**
bruichladdich.com	01496 850221

Ever since Bruichladdich was taken over in 2001 by Mark Reynier and fellow investors, the barley being used for the production has been in focus. All the time, the company has shown a strong belief in the role the barley plays for its whisky flavour.

This approach is not only limited to the sorts used but, perhaps even more so, where the barley has been grown. Bruichladdich has been experimenting with different varieties from different parts of Scotland, but all the while, one part of their operation has been lacking – their own maltings. It was in 1961 that the malting floors had closed, but now it seems that there is a chance that they can rebuild it. There are plans to revive it in two steps, first for barley to be grown on Islay and then, later, it will be time for Scottish-grown barley, but no time table for commencement of the work has been presented.

With Rèmy Cointreau as new owners since 2012, the increase in sales for Bruichladdich has been healthy, to say the least. During 2014/2015, sales have doubled and the latest report indicates that the trend has continued. Increased volumes have resulted in a new bottling line being opened, new warehouses having been constructed and the distillery now employs around 80 people on the island. The distillery is equipped with a cast iron, open mash tun with rakes, dating back to 1881 when the distillery was founded. There are six washbacks of Oregon pine and two pairs of stills. All whisky produced is based on Scottish barley, 40% of which comes from Islay. During 2016, they will be doing 12 mashes per week, resulting in 1.5 million litres of alcohol per year. The breakdown of the three whisky varieties are 60% Bruichladdich, 20% Port Charlotte and 20% Octomore.

Bruichladdich single malt was unpeated between 1962 and 1994 but, today, there are three main lines in the distillery´s production; unpeated **Bruichladdich**, heavily peated **Port Charlotte** and the ultra-heavily peated **Octomore**. The core expressions for each of the three varieties are **Scottish Barley** and **Islay Barley**. For Bruichladdich there are four duty free exclusives – **Organic Barley, Bere Barley, Black Art 4** (with a maturation in American oak and various wine casks) and, since spring 2016, **The Laddie Eight**. The duty free expressions for Port Charlotte are the **PC11** and **PC12**, both bottled at cask strength, as well as the new **2007 CC: 01** with a full maturation in Eau de Vie casks. For Octomore it is **7.2**, which is a vatting of whiskies matured in American oak and syrah casks. During spring of 2016, Octomore **7.4** was released where 25% of the whisky has been matured in French virgin oak, while the rest is a combination of ex bourbon casks and virgin oak. There were three special bottlings for Feis Ile 2016; a 15 year old, lightly peated Bruichladdich named **2016-1881-135**, which is a vatting of bourbon casks and wine casks and finished in virgin oak and two bottlings from **2006** and **2008** respectively. The aged expressions (**Laddie Ten, the 16** and the **22 year old**) have been withdrawn from all markets, but are still available at the distillery.

History:

1881 Barnett Harvey builds the distillery with money left by his brother William III to his three sons William IV, Robert and John Gourlay.

1886 Bruichladdich Distillery Company Ltd is founded and reconstruction commences.

1889 William Harvey becomes Manager and remains on that post until his death in 1937.

1929 Temporary closure.

1936 The distillery reopens.

1938 Joseph Hobbs, Hatim Attari and Alexander Tolmie purchase the distillery through the company Train & McIntyre.

1938 Operations are moved to Associated Scottish Distillers.

1952 The distillery is sold to Ross & Coulter from Glasgow.

1960 A. B. Grant buys Ross & Coulter.

1961 Own maltings ceases and malt is brought in from Port Ellen.

1968 Invergordon Distillers take over.

1975 The number of stills increases to four.

1983 Temporary closure.

1993 Whyte & Mackay buys Invergordon Distillers.

1995 The distillery is mothballed in January.

1998 In production again for a few months, and then mothballed.

2000 Murray McDavid buys the distillery from JBB Greater Europe for £6.5 million.

2001 The first distillation (Port Charlotte) is on 29th May and the first distillation of Bruichladdich starts in July. In September the owners' first bottlings from the old casks are released, 10, 15 and 20 years old.

2002 The world's most heavily peated whisky is produced on 23rd October when Octomore (80ppm) is distilled.

History continued:

2004 Second edition of the 20 year old (nick-named Flirtation) and 3D, also called The Peat Proposal, are launched.

2005 Infinity, Rocks, Legacy Series IV, The Yellow Submarine and The Twenty 'Islands' are launched.

2006 The first official bottling of Port Charlotte; PC5.

2007 New releases include Redder Still, Legacy 6, PC6 and an 18 year old.

2008 More than 20 new expressions including the first Octomore, Bruichladdich 2001, PC7, Golder Still and two sherry matured from 1998.

2009 New releases include Classic, Organic, Black Art, Infinity 3, PC8, Octomore 2 and X4+3 - the first quadruple distilled single malt.

2010 PC Multi Vintage, Organic MV, Octomore/3_152, Bruichladdich 40 year old are released.

2011 The first 10 year old from own production is released as well as PC9 and Octomore 4_167.

2012 Ten year old versions of Port Charlotte and Octomore are released as well as Laddie 16 and 22, Bere Barley 2006, Black Art 3 and DNA4. Rémy Cointreau buys the distillery.

2013 Scottish Barley, Islay Barley Rockside Farm, Bere Barley 2nd edition, Black Art 4, Port Charlotte Scottish Barley, Octomore 06.1 and 06.2 are released.

2014 PC11 and Octomore Scottish Barley are released.

2015 PC12, Octomore 7.1 and High Noon 134 are released.

2016 The Laddie Eight, Octomore 7.4 and Port Charlotte 2007 CC:01 are released.

Tasting notes Bruichladdich Scottish Barley:

GS – Mildly metallic on the early nose, then cooked apple aromas develop, with a touch of linseed. Initially very fruity on the gently oily palate. Ripe peaches and apricots, with vanilla, brittle toffee, lots of spice and sea salt. The finish is drying, with breakfast tea.

Tasting notes Port Charlotte Scottish Barley:

GS – Wood smoke and contrasting bonbons on the nose. Warm Tarmac develops, with white pepper. Finally, fragrant pipe tobacco. Peppery peat and treacle toffee on the palate, with a maritime note. Long in the finish, with black pepper and oak.

Tasting notes Octomore Scottish Barley:

GS – A big hit of sweet peat on the nose; ozone and rock pools, supple leather, damp tweed. Peat on the palate is balanced by allspice, vanilla and fruitiness. Very long in the finish, with chilli, dry roasted nuts and bonfire smoke.

Black Art 4

Bruichladdich The Laddie Eight

Bruichladdich Islay Barley 2009

Port Charlotte PC12

The Classic Laddie Scottish Barley

Port Charlotte 2007 CC:01

Bunnahabhain

[buh•nah•hav•enn]

Owner:
Burn Stewart Distillers
(Distell Group Ltd)

Region/district:
Islay

Founded: | **Status:** | **Capacity:**
1881 | Active (vc) | 2 700 000 litres

Address: Port Askaig, Islay, Argyll PA46 7RP

Website:
bunnahabhain.com

Tel:
01496 840646

The whiskies from Islay are always expected to have a smoky flavour and, indeed, some of the really peaty ones come from that island. Bunnahabhain, on the other hand, has often been described as the one going against the current.

It has, however, not always been that way. One is uncertain about the early days but, at least until 1963, most of the Bunnahabhain single malt was peated. Then there came a period from 1963 until 1997 when Bunnahabhain was an atypical, unpeated Islay malt, with the exception of a few runs in the 1990s. The first peated Bunnahabhain single malt in modern days was released as a 6 year old in 2004.

The distillery is equipped with a 12.5 ton traditional stainless steel mash tun, six washbacks made of Oregon pine and two pairs of stills. The fermentation time varies between 48 and 110 hours. The production for 2016 will be 6-8 mashes per week and around 1.4 million litres, of which 15% will be peated (35-40ppm). In 2014 the old malting floors were converted into another warehouse, holding 1,500 casks.

The core range consists of **12, 18** and **25 year old**, as well as two peated versions – the 10 year old **Toiteach** and **Ceobanach** without age statement. The difference between the two is that, while Toiteach is a blend of younger, peated and some older, unpeated whisky, Ceobanach is 100% peated Bunnahabhain, aged for a minimum of 10 years in bourbon casks. Recent limited releases include a new batch of the **40 year old** which from now on will be a part of the core range. There are also two travel retail exclusives – **Cruach-Mhòna** which comprises of young, heavily peated Bunnahabhain matured in ex bourbon casks along with 20-21 years old matured in ex sherry butts, as well as **Eirigh Na Greine**, a vatting of whisky from bourbon and sherry casks, and also red wine casks from France and Italy. For Feis Ile 2016, there were two releases; the peated **Moine 12 year old** with a 3 year finish in PX casks and a **16 year old** with an additional six years in amontillado casks.

History:

1881 William Robertson of Robertson & Baxter, founds the distillery together with the brothers William and James Greenless, owners of Islay Distillers Company Ltd.

1883 Production starts in earnest in January.

1887 Islay Distillers Company Ltd merges with William Grant & Co. in order to form Highland Distilleries Company Limited.

1963 The two stills are augmented by two more.

1982 The distillery closes.

1984 The distillery reopens. A 21 year old is released to commemorate the 100th anniversary.

1999 Edrington takes over Highland Distillers and mothballs Bunnahabhain but allows for a few weeks of production a year.

2001 A 35 year old from 1965 is released during Islay Whisky Festival.

2002 A 35 year old from 1965 is released during Islay Whisky Festival. Auld Acquaintance 1968 is launched at the Islay Jazz Festival.

2003 Edrington sells Bunnahabhain and Black Bottle to Burn Stewart Distilleries for £10 million. A 40 year old from 1963 is launched.

2004 The first limited edition of the peated version is a 6 year old called Moine.

2005 Three limited editions are released - 34 years old,18 years old and 25 years old.

2006 14 year old Pedro Ximenez and 35 years old are launched.

2008 Darach Ur is released for the travel retail market and Toiteach (a peated 10 year old) is launched on a few selected markets.

2009 Moine Cask Strength is released.

2010 The peated Cruach-Mhòna and a limited 30 year old are released.

2013 A 40 year old is released.

2014 Eirigh Na Greine and Ceobanach are released.

12 years old

Tasting notes Bunnahabhain 12 years old:

GS – The nose is fresh, with light peat and discreet smoke. More overt peat on the nutty and fruity palate, but still restrained for an Islay. The finish is full-bodied and lingering, with a hint of vanilla and some smoke.

Caol Ila

[cull•eel•a]

Owner:
Diageo

Region/district:
Islay

Founded:
1846

Status:
Active (vc)

Capacity:
6 500 000 litres

Address: Port Askaig, Islay, Argyll PA46 7RL

Website:
malts.com

Tel:
01496 302760

For many years, an Islay single malt was synonymous with either Lagavulin, Laphroaig or Bowmore. But then, Glenmorangie bought Ardbeg in the late 1990s and a fourth brand started to build its fan base. The biggest distillery on the island, however, was still in the shadows.

At least since 1972, when the old distillery from 1846 was replaced by a new one, has Caol Ila been the number one Islay distillery in terms of capacity and with the most recent expansion in 2011, it currently produces almost as much as the other four put together. The owners were for a long time reluctant to release anything else other than a single Flora & Fauna 15 year old bottling. In 2002, however, encouraged by the success of the Classic Malts, Diageo decided to create yet another range called Hidden Malts. The backbone of the series comprised of three expressions of Caol Ila, supplemented by one each from Clynelish, Glen Elgin and Glen Ord. The Hidden Malts were later abandoned and the brands were absorbed into the expanded Classic Malts but this had ignited the start of a new life for Caol Ila single malt which now sells around 560,000 bottles each year.

Caol Ila is equipped with a 13.5 ton full lauter mash tun, eight wooden washbacks and two made of stainless steel and three pairs of stills. The fermentation time is 60 hours, except for the unpeated version when it is increased to 80 hours. During 2016 the distillery will be doing 26 mashes per week which amounts to 6.5 million litres of alcohol. Caol Ila is known for its peated whisky but, since 1999, an increasingly bigger part of unpeated, nutty newmake has been produced.

The core range consists of **Moch** without age statement, **12, 18** and **25 year old**, **Distiller's Edition** with a moscatel finish and **Cask Strength**. The release for Islay Festival 2016 was a **12 year old** bottled at 56.2% and matured in refill American oak and European ex-bodega sherry butts. In October 2016, a **15 year old** unpeated Caol Ila, bottled at 61.5%, was launched as a part of this year's Special Releases.

History:

1846 Hector Henderson founds Caol Ila.

1852 Henderson, Lamont & Co. is subjected to financial difficulties and Henderson is forced to sell Caol Ila to Norman Buchanan.

1863 Norman Buchanan sells to the blending company Bulloch, Lade & Co. from Glasgow.

1879 The distillery is rebuilt and expanded.

1920 Bulloch, Lade & Co. is liquidated and the distillery is taken over by Caol Ila Distillery.

1927 DCL becomes sole owners.

1972 All the buildings, except for the warehouses, are demolished and rebuilt.

1974 The renovation, which totals £1 million, is complete and six new stills are installed.

1999 Experiments with unpeated malt.

2002 The first official bottlings since Flora & Fauna/ Rare Malt appear; 12 years, 18 years and Cask Strength (c. 10 years).

2003 A 25 year old cask strength is released.

2006 Unpeated 8 year old and 1993 Moscatel finish are released.

2007 Second edition of unpeated 8 year old.

2008 Third edition of unpeated 8 year old.

2009 The fourth edition of the unpeated version (10 year old) is released.

2010 A 25 year old, a 1999 Feis Isle bottling and a 1997 Manager's Choice are released.

2011 An unpeated 12 year old and the unaged Moch are released.

2012 An unpeated 14 year old is released.

2013 Unpeated Stitchell Reserve is released.

2014 A 15 year old unpeated and a 30 year old are released.

2016 A 15 year old unpeated is released.

12 years old

Tasting notes Caol Ila 12 year old:

GS — Iodine, fresh fish and smoked bacon feature on the nose, along with more delicate, floral notes. Smoke, malt, lemon and peat on the slightly oily palate. Peppery peat in the drying finish.

Cardhu

[car•doo]

Owner: **Region/district:**
Diageo   Speyside

Founded: **Status:**   **Capacity:**
1824   Active (vc)   3 400 000 litres

Address: Knockando, Aberlour, Moray AB38 7RY

Website: **Tel:**
malts.com   01479 874635

The majority of Diageo's 28 malt distilleries are workhorses where the main task is to produce malt whisky for blends. The yearly maintenance is executed to ensure a safe and efficient production and rarely does the aesthetics come into focus.

But there are exceptions and Cardhu is one of them. This was the first distillery acquired by John Walker & Sons and for a long time it has been the brand home of Johnnie Walker. This means a lot of corporate visits, as well as tourists, and the distillery is kept meticulously neat. Last October, all the copper work in the still house was cleaned and lacquered and three of the warehouses had the stonework refurbished and new hardwood doors were fitted. Located in the old kiln with the two pagoda roofs, is a stylish Johnnie Walker Brand Home used for corporate events.

Cardhu distillery is equipped with an 8 ton stainless steel full lauter mash tun with a copper dome, ten washbacks (four made of Scottish larch, two of stainless steel and four of Douglas fir), all with a fermentation time of 75 hours and three pairs of stills. In 2016, Cardhu will be working a 7-day week with 21 mashes per week and a production of 3.4 million litres of alcohol. In 2016, Cardhu and three nearby distilleries (Dalmunach, Tamdhu and Knockando) were connected to Scotland's gas network by way of an eight-mile pipeline. A similar construction was made in 2014 when another four Speyside distilleries shifted from fuel oil to gas, in order to reduce carbon emissions.

Even though Cardhu single malt is one of the most important components of Johnnie Walker, at the same time, it is one of the Top Ten single malt brands in the world with 2.3 million bottles sold in 2015.

The core range from the distillery is **12, 15** and **18 year old** and, released in 2014, two expressions without age statement – **Amber Rock** and **Gold Reserve**, both bottled at 40%. There is also a **Special Cask Reserve** matured in rejuvenated bourbon casks and in 2016, a **distillery exclusive** was released.

History:

1824 John Cumming applies for and obtains a licence for Cardhu Distillery.

1846 John Cumming dies and his wife Helen and son Lewis takes over.

1872 Lewis dies and his wife Elizabeth takes over.

1884 A new distillery is built to replace the old.

1893 John Walker & Sons purchases Cardhu for £20,500.

1908 The name reverts to Cardow.

1960 Reconstruction and expansion of stills from four to six.

1981 The name changes to Cardhu.

1998 A visitor centre is constructed.

2002 Diageo changes Cardhu single malt to a vatted malt with contributions from other distilleries in it.

2003 The whisky industry protests sharply against Diageo's plans.

2004 Diageo withdraws Cardhu Pure Malt.

2005 The 12 year old Cardhu Single Malt is relaunched and a 22 year old is released.

2009 Cardhu 1997, a single cask in the new Manager's Choice range is released.

2011 A 15 year old and an 18 year old are released.

2013 A 21 year old is released.

2014 Amber Rock and Gold Reserve are launched.

2016 A distillery exclusive is released.

Amber Rock

Tasting notes Cardhu 12 years old:

GS – The nose is relatively light and floral, quite sweet, with pears, nuts and a whiff of distant peat. Medium-bodied, malty and sweet in the mouth. Medium-length in the finish, with sweet smoke, malt and a hint of peat.

Websites to watch

scotchwhisky.com
Without a doubt the best whiskysite there is! It covers every possible angle of the subject in an absolutely brilliant way.

whiskyfun.com
Serge Valentin, one of the Malt Maniacs, is almost always first with well written tasting notes on new releases.

whiskyreviews.blogspot.com
Ralfy does this video blog with tastings and field reports in an educational yet easy-going and entertaining way.

maltmadness.com
Our all-time favourite with something for everyone. Managed by the founder of Malt Maniacs, Johannes van den Heuvel.

whiskyadvocateblog.com
A first class blog on every aspect of whisky by Whisky Advocate´s John Hansell and others.

edinburghwhiskyblog.com
Lucas, Chris and company review new releases, interview industry people and cover news from the whisky world.

whiskycast.com
The best whisky-related podcast on the internet and one that sets the standard for podcasts in other genres as well.

nonjatta.com
An excellent blog with a wealth of interesting information on Japanese whisky and Japanese culture.

whiskyintelligence.com
The best site on all kinds of whisky news. The first whisky website you should log into every morning!

whisky-news.com
Apart from daily news, this site contains tasting notes, distillery portraits, lists of retailers, events etc.

thewhiskylady.net
Anne-Sophie Bigot´s mission is "to remove the dusty cliché that whisky is only an old man´s drink" and she does it so well!

whisky-emporium.com
Keith Wood has created a treasure trove for whisky geeks with more than 1,000 tasting notes.

meleklerinpayi.com
I don´t read Turkish but, since Burkay Adalig´s blog is the 7th most visited whisky blog in the world (!), a lot of people do.

whisky-pages.com
Top class whisky site with features, directories, tasting notes, book reviews, whisky news, glossary and a forum.

whiskynotes.be
This blog is almost entirely about tasting notes (and lots of them, not least independent bottlings) plus some news.

whiskyforeveryone.com
Educational site, perfect for beginners, with a blog where both new releases and affordable standards are reviewed.

blog.thewhiskyexchange.com
A knowledgeable team from The Whisky Exchange write about new bottlings and the whisky industry in general.

recenteats.blogspot.com
Steve Ury serves tasty bits of information (and entertainment) from the world of whisky and other spirits.

whiskymarketplace.com
This is divided into three parts - well written tasting notes, whisky price comparison site and Whisky Marketplace TV.

whisky-distilleries.net
Ernie Scheiner describes more than 130 distilleries in both text and photos and we are talking lots of great images!

connosr.com
This whisky social networking community is a virtual smorgasbord for any whisky lover!

jewmalt.com
An excellent blog by Joshua Hatton who also acts as an independent bottler, check out www.singlecasknation.com.

canadianwhisky.org
Davin de Kergommeaux presents reviews, news and views on all things Canadian whisky. High quality content.

whiskyisrael.co.il
Gal Granov is definitely one of the most active of all bloggers. Well worth checking out daily!

spiritsjournal.klwines.com
Reviews about whiskies and the whisky industry in general by David Driscoll from the US retailer K&L Wines.

thewhiskywire.com
Steve Rush mixes reviews of the latest bottlings with presentations of classics plus news, interviews etc.

bestshotwhiskyreviews.com
Jan van den Ende presents his honest opinions on everything from cheap blends to rare single cask bottlings.

whisky-discovery.blogspot.com
An entertaining blog with tasting notes and event reports from Dave Worthington and his daughter Kat.

whiskiesrus.blogspot.com
Clint Anesbury delivers tasting notes and current reports from the world of Japanese whisky.

scotch-whisky.org.uk
The official site of SWA (Scotch Whisky Association) with i.a. press releases and publications about the industry.

misswhisky.com
Filled with great tasting notes and well-written stories, interviews, event reports and accounts on distillery visits.

whiskysaga.com
Brilliant blog by Norwegian whisky enthusiast Thomas Öhrbom - not least on every detail relating to Nordic whiskies.

Clynelish

[cline•leash]

Owner: Diageo

Region/district: Northern Highlands

Founded: 1967

Status: Active (vc)

Capacity: 4 800 000 litres

Address: Brora, Sutherland KW9 6LR

Website: malts.com

Tel: 01408 623003 (vc)

The Clynelish name dates back to 1819 when the first distillery on the site was built. This lasted until 1967 when a second distillery was opened and named Clynelish.

The old distillery was re-named Brora, a name that makes the heart skip a beat among whisky enthusiasts. The whisky from the old plant (closed in 1983) has attained a type of cult status and new official bottlings will cost around £1,500. The remaining distillery has an important task in the Diageo emporium - namely to produce single malt for Johnnie Walker blends and the Gold version, in particular. Clynelish single malt is so important that it was announced two years ago that the capacity would be expanded. Decreasing sales of Scotch whisky overall got the owners to put the plans on hold. The existing distillery, on the other hand, still needs refurbishing and will be closed from May 2016 to April 2017, in order to complete the work.

The existing cast iron mash tun, with its beautiful copper canopy, will be replaced by one made of stainless steel. The distillery is also equipped with 8 wooden washbacks and two made of stainless steel. The still room, with its three pairs of stills, has stunning views towards the village of Brora and the North Sea. When in production, Clynelish will be working a 7-day week, producing some 4.8 million litres of alcohol. Approximately 6,000 casks of Clynelish are stored in the two old Brora warehouses next door, but most of the production is matured elsewhere. There is also one cask of Brora single malt which was brought back to the distillery for visitors to see during the tour. Most of the old Brora equipment (stills, washbacks and mashtun) is still left in the listed buildings.

Official bottlings include a **14 year old** and a **Distiller's Edition**, with an Oloroso Seco finish. There is also an **American oak cask strength** exclusively available at the distillery shop. For two years in a row now, **Clynelish Select Reserve** has been launched as part of the annual Special Releases. None of them have carried any age statement, but the selected casks were at least 15 years old and comprises of a mix of American and European oak.

History:

1819 The 1st Duke of Sutherland founds a distillery called Clynelish Distillery.

1827 The first licensed distiller, James Harper, files for bankruptcy and John Matheson takes over.

1846 George Lawson & Sons become new licensees.

1896 James Ainslie & Heilbron takes over.

1912 James Ainslie & Co. narrowly escapes bankruptcy and Distillers Company Limited (DCL) takes over together with James Risk.

1916 John Walker & Sons buys a stake of James Risk's stocks.

1931 The distillery is mothballed.

1939 Production restarts.

1960 The distillery becomes electrified.

1967 A new distillery, also named Clynelish, is built adjacent to the first one.

1968 'Old' Clynelish is mothballed in August.

1969 'Old' Clynelish is reopened as Brora and starts using a very peaty malt.

1983 Brora is closed in March.

2002 A 14 year old is released.

2006 A Distiller's Edition 1991 finished in Oloroso casks is released.

2009 A 12 year old is released for Friends of the Classic Malts.

2010 A 1997 Manager's Choice single cask is released.

2014 Clynelish Select Reserve is released.

2015 Second version of Clynelish Select Reserve is released

14 years old

Tasting notes Clynelish 14 year old:

GS – A nose that is fragrant, spicy and complex, with candle wax, malt and a whiff of smoke. Notably smooth in the mouth, with honey and contrasting citric notes, plus spicy peat, before a brine and tropical fruit finish.

Cragganmore

[crag•an•moor]

Owner:	**Region/district:**
Diageo	Speyside

Founded:	**Status:**	**Capacity:**
1869	Active (vc)	2 200 000 litres

Address: Ballindalloch, Moray AB37 9AB

Website:	**Tel:**
malts.com	01479 874700

When Cragganmore was founded in 1869, it was on land that belonged to Ballindalloch Estate. The Macpherson-Grant family, who had owned the castle and the estate for more than 500 years, granted John Smith a lease to build the distillery.

In time, the distillery was taken over by John's son, Gordon, and in 1923 his widow, Mary Jane, sold the distillery to the Cragganmore-Glenlivet Distillery Co., which was owned equally by Peter Mackie from White Horse and Ballindalloch Estate. Mackie soon sold his share to DCL but the Macpherson-Grant family had continued with its ownership of 50% of the distillery right up to 1965 – an unusual arrangement at a time where all distilleries were being drawn in to the big companies. Today, the Macpherson-Grants are back in the distillery business through Ballindalloch distillery they opened in 2014.

The distillery is equipped with a 6.8 ton stainless steel full lauter mash tun with a copper canopy and six washbacks made of Oregon pine with a 60 hour fermentation time. There are two large wash stills with sharply descending lyne arms and two considerably smaller spirit stills with boil balls and long, slightly descending lyne arms. For 2016, the distillery will be working a 5-day week which translates to 1.65 million litres of alcohol.

Cragganmore is one of Diageo's original six Classic Malts and, even though it is not a big seller, devoted fans consider it one of the best examples of a classic Speysider. Cragganmore single malt is also a key contributor to the Old Parr blend, first launched in 1909 and with Latin America as its biggest market.

The core range of single malts is made up of a **12 year old** and a **Distiller's Edition** with a finish in Port pipes. In 2014, a **25 year old** appeared as a Special Release and in 2015, the oldest Cragganmore ever, a **43 year old**, was released as an exclusive to Dubai Duty Free with only 474 bottles available. Finally, in autumn 2016, a **distillery exclusive** without age statement was launched as well as a **special vatting** as part of the Special Releases.

History:

1869 John Smith, who already runs Glenfarclas distillery, founds Cragganmore.

1886 John Smith dies and his brother George takes over operations.

1893 John's son Gordon, at 21, is old enough to assume responsibility for operations.

1901 The distillery is refurbished and modernized with help of the famous architect Charles Doig.

1912 Gordon Smith dies and his widow Mary Jane supervises operations.

1917 The distillery closes.

1918 The distillery reopens and Mary Jane installs electric lighting.

1923 The distillery is sold to the newly formed Cragganmore-Glenlivet Distillery Co. where Mackie & Co. and Sir George Macpherson-Grant of Ballindalloch Estate share ownership.

1927 White Horse Distillers is bought by DCL which thus obtains 50% of Cragganmore.

1964 The number of stills is increased from two to four.

1965 DCL buys the remainder of Cragganmore.

1988 Cragganmore 12 years becomes one of six selected for United Distillers' Classic Malts.

1998 Cragganmore Distillers Edition Double Matured (port) is launched for the first time.

2002 A visitor centre opens in May.

2006 A 17 year old from 1988 is released.

2010 Manager's Choice single cask 1997 and a limited 21 year old are released.

2014 A 25 year old is released.

2016 A Special Releases vatting without age statement and a distillery exclusive are released.

12 years old

Tasting notes Cragganmore 12 years old:

GS – A nose of sherry, brittle toffee, nuts, mild wood smoke, angelica and mixed peel. Elegant on the malty palate, with herbal and fruit notes, notably orange. Medium in length, with a drying, slightly smoky finish.

Craigellachie

[craig•ell•ack•ee]

Owner: **Region/district:**
John Dewar & Sons   Speyside
(Bacardi)

Founded: **Status:**   **Capacity:**
1891   Active   4 100 000 litres

Address: Aberlour, Banffshire AB38 9ST

Website: **Tel:**
craigellachie.com   01340 872971

White Horse is one of those legendary blends that has been around for ages, and for many years, Craigellachie single malt was a key component.

The White Horse blend peaked in terms of sales in the 1950s and 1960s and is no longer among the top 10 selling blends. During the last decade, however, the brand has made an impressive comeback, tripling the sales and the whisky has strongholds all over the world, for instance in Japan, Brazil, Greece, South Africa and the USA. Due to changes in ownership, Craigellachie has now become more important to one of the world's biggest blended Scotch – Dewar's – which is the most sold Scotch whisky in the USA.

Craigellachie was refurbished in 1964 under the supervision of Leslie Darge who was Chief Architect of Scottish Malt Distillers (SMD). During 28 years, he was in charge of the building or refurbishing of no less than 46 distilleries. His trademark was most notably the glazed curtain walls of the still houses. For many of the visitors, this is a great and novice way to view the stills from the outside, but the practical use was dissipating the heat and more significantly that the pot stills could be replaced without removing the roof.

The distillery is equipped with a modern Steinecker full lauter mash tun, installed in 2001, which replaced the old, open cast iron mash tun. There are also eight washbacks made of larch with a fermentation time of 56-60 hours and two pairs of stills. Both stills are attached to worm tubs. The old cast iron tubs were exchanged for stainless steel in 2014 and the existing copper worms were moved to the new tubs. Production during 2016 will be 21 mashes per week and 4.1 million litres of alcohol.

Apart from a 14 year old, which at times could be hard to get hold of, there was no official bottling of Craigellachie until 2014, when the brand was completely re-launched. No less than three new expressions (**13, 17** and **23 year old**) were released for selected domestic markets and a **19 year old** was launched for duty free. This was followed in 2015 by a limited **31 year old**.

History:

1890 The distillery is built by Craigellachie–Glenlivet Distillery Company which has Alexander Edward and Peter Mackie as part-owners.

1891 Production starts.

1916 Mackie & Company Distillers Ltd takes over.

1924 Peter Mackie dies and Mackie & Company changes name to White Horse Distillers.

1927 White Horse Distillers are bought by Distillers Company Limited (DCL).

1930 Administration is transferred to Scottish Malt Distillers (SMD), a subsidiary of DCL.

1964 Refurbishing takes place and two new stills are bought, increasing the number to four.

1998 United Distillers & Vintners (UDV) sells Craigellachie together with Aberfeldy, Brackla and Aultmore and the blending company John Dewar & Sons to Bacardi Martini.

2004 The first bottlings from the new owners are a new 14 year old which replaces UDV's Flora & Fauna and a 21 year old cask strength from 1982 produced for Craigellachie Hotel.

2014 Three new bottlings for domestic markets (13, 17 and 23 years) and one for duty free (19 years) are released.

2015 A 31 year old is released.

13 years old

Tasting notes Craigellachie 13 years old:

GS – Savoury on the early nose, with spent matches, green apples and mixed nuts. Malt join the nuts and apples on the palate, with sawdust and very faint smoke. Drying, with cranberries, spice and more subtle smoke.

Dailuaine

[dall•yoo•an]

Owner:	**Region/district:**
Diageo	Speyside
Founded: **Status:**	**Capacity:**
1852 Active	5 200 000 litres

Address: Carron, Banffshire AB38 7RE

Website:	**Tel:**
malts.com	01340 872500

With 32% of the malt whisky production capacity in Scotland, Diageo owns most of the distilleries, 28 to be exact. From only three of these, the entire output of whisky is destined to be bottled as single malt.

The exceptions are Lagavulin and Talisker due to the increased popularity of the brands and Oban, for the same reason, but also due to its small capacity. Included in the remaining 25 distilleries are those who sell huge volumes of single malt, such as Cardhu, the three Singletons and Dalwhinnie, but they are also important to many blends. The third category of about 15 distilleries, of which Dailuaine is one, exists only to make malt for blends. For many years it was impossible to find bottlings from these work horses, but that changed in 1991 when Diageo (or UDV at the time) decided to bottle single malts from all its distilleries. The range didn´t have a name, but was later nicknamed Flora & Fauna by the whisky writer, Michael Jackson, and since then the name has stuck.

Dailuaine distillery is equipped with a stainless steel, 11.2 ton full lauter mash tun, eight washbacks made of larch, plus two stainless steel ones placed outside, all with a fermentation time of 85 hours and three pairs of stills. Last year, the fermentation time was changed to help achieve a more waxy character to the spirit. The reason for the change was that Clynelish distillery has been closed for refurbishing. That is the only Diageo distillery so far that has accounted for this style which is so important for some blends. During 2016, the distillery will be doing 12 mashes per week which translates to 2.6 million litres of alcohol. On site also lies a dark grains plant processing draff and pot ale into cattle feed. To help power the plant and the distillery, Diageo recently invested £6m in a ground breaking bio-energy plant. Through anaerobic digestion, spent lees and waste water from the distillation are converted into biogas, which provides 40% of the electrical demand for the entire site.

The only core bottling is the **16 year old Flora & Fauna** release. In autumn 2015, a **34 year old** from 1980 was launched as part of the Special Releases.

History:

1852 The distillery is founded by William Mackenzie.

1865 William Mackenzie dies and his widow leases the distillery to James Fleming, a banker from Aberlour.

1879 William Mackenzie's son forms Mackenzie and Company with Fleming.

1891 Dailuaine-Glenlivet Distillery Ltd is founded.

1898 Dailuaine-Glenlivet Distillery Ltd merges with Talisker Distillery Ltd and forms Dailuaine-Talisker Distilleries Ltd.

1915 Thomas Mackenzie dies without heirs.

1916 Dailuaine-Talisker Company Ltd is bought by the previous customers John Dewar & Sons, John Walker & Sons and James Buchanan & Co.

1917 A fire rages and the pagoda roof collapses. The distillery is forced to close.

1920 The distillery reopens.

1925 Distillers Company Limited (DCL) takes over.

1960 Refurbishing. The stills increase from four to six and a Saladin box replaces the floor maltings.

1965 Indirect still heating through steam is installed.

1983 On site maltings is closed down and malt is purchased centrally.

1991 The first official bottling, a 16 year old, is launched in the Flora & Fauna series.

1996 A 22 year old cask strength from 1973 is released as a Rare Malt.

1997 A cask strength version of the 16 year old is launched.

2000 A 17 year old Manager´s Dram matured in sherry casks is launched.

2010 A single cask from 1997 is released.

2012 The production capacity is increased by 25%.

2015 A 34 year old is launched as part of the Special Releases.

Tasting notes Dailuaine 16 years old:

GS – Barley, sherry and nuts on the substan-tial nose, developing into maple syrup. Medium-bodied, rich and malty in the mouth, with more sherry and nuts, plus ripe oranges, fruitcake, spice and a little smoke. The finish is lengthy and slightly oily, with almonds, cedar and slightly smoky oak.

16 years old

Dalmore

[dal•moor]

Owner: **Region/district:**
Whyte & Mackay Ltd   Northern Highlands
(Emperador Inc)

Founded: **Status:**   **Capacity:**
1839   Active (vc)   4 000 000 litres

Address: Alness, Ross-shire IV17 0UT

Website: **Tel:**
thedalmore.com   01349 882362

The spirit from this distillery may start its life in bourbon casks, but to create the character of Dalmore single malt, ex-sherry casks are absolutely crucial. Equally important is to have a supplier of top-class sherry butts.

For more than a century, Whyte & Mackay have been working with one of Spain´s most well-known bodegas, Gonzalez Byass. The company was founded in 1835, just four years before Dalmore and is still family-run and in the hands of the fifth generation. With such a long business relationship, the Master Blender for Dalmore, Richard Paterson, has access to a continuous supply of the best sherry butts available. The vast majority of Dalmore new make is filled into ex-bourbon casks and then, after a number of years, they are placed into a variety of sherry casks. Dalmore single malt rarely gets a short finish, instead, it undergoes a second maturation of several years.

The distillery is equipped with a 9.9 ton stainless steel, semi-lauter mash tun, eight washbacks made of Oregon pine with a fermentation time of 50 hours and four pairs of stills. The spirit stills have water jackets, which allow cold water to circulate between the reflux bowl and the neck of the stills, thus increasing the reflux. The owners expect to do 23 mashes per week during 2016, producing 4 million litres.

The core range consists of **12, 15, 18, 25 year old** (limited to 3,000 bottles per year and the main part of the whiskies are considerably older than 25 years), **1263 King Alexander III** and **Cigar Malt**. In 2013 **Valour** was released for duty free and in summer 2016, a whole new range called Fortuna Meritas Collection was launched. Valour forms a part of this range with three new expressions being added; **Regalis** with a finish in Amoroso casks (oloroso sherry sweetened with PX grapes), **Luceo** with a final maturation in Apostoles casks (palo cortado sherry) and **Dominium** finished in Matusalem casks (oloroso sherry sweetened with PX grapes and at least 30 years old). Recent limited bottlings include new versions of the **21** and **30 year old** and, in autumn 2016, a **35 year old** and **Quintessence** with a finish in five different red wine casks.

History:

1839 Alexander Matheson founds the distillery.

1867 Three Mackenzie brothers run the distillery.

1891 Sir Kenneth Matheson sells the distillery for £14,500 to the Mackenzie brothers.

1917 The Royal Navy moves in to start manufacturing American mines.

1920 The Royal Navy moves out and leaves behind a distillery damaged by an explosion.

1922 The distillery is in production again.

1956 Floor malting replaced by Saladin box.

1960 Mackenzie Brothers (Dalmore) Ltd merges with Whyte & Mackay.

1966 Number of stills is increased to eight.

1982 The Saladin box is abandoned.

1990 American Brands buys Whyte & Mackay.

1996 Whyte & Mackay changes name to JBB (Greater Europe).

2001 Through management buy-out, JBB (Greater Europe) is bought from Fortune Brands and changes name to Kyndal Spirits.

2002 Kyndal Spirits changes name to Whyte & Mackay.

2007 United Spirits buys Whyte & Mackay. A 15 year old, and a 40 year old are released.

2008 1263 King Alexander III and Vintage 1974 are released.

2009 New releases include an 18 year old, a 58 year old and a Vintage 1951.

2010 The Dalmore Mackenzie 1992 Vintage is released.

2011 More expressions in the River Collection and 1995 Castle Leod are released.

2012 The visitor centre is upgraded and Constellaton Collection is launched.

2013 Valour is released for duty free.

2014 Emperador Inc buys Whyte & Mackay.

2016 Three new travel retail bottlings are released as well as a 35 year old and Quintessence.

Tasting notes Dalmore 12 years old:

GS – The nose offers sweet malt, orange marmalade, sherry and a hint of leather. Full-bodied, with a dry sherry taste though sweeter sherry develops in the mouth along with spice and citrus notes. Lengthy finish with more spices, ginger, Seville oranges and vanilla.

12 years old

Dalwhinnie

[dal•whin•nay]

Owner:	**Region/district:**
Diageo	Northern Highlands
Founded: **Status:**	**Capacity:**
1897 Active (vc)	2 200 000 litres
Address: Dalwhinnie, Inverness-shire PH19 1AB	
Website:	**Tel:**
malts.com	01540 672219 (vc)

When sulphury notes in a whisky are detected, they usually derive from bad sherry casks. Sulphur dioxide has been used for a long time by wine producers to prevent bacterial growth and this may affect the next liquid in the cask – namely whisky.

But sulphur will occur earlier in the production process as well, since grain naturally contains sulphur and during fermentation the impact on the spirit can be increased. Sulphury notes in a bottled whisky is scorned by most and that´s where the copper in the stills and condensers comes in to the picture. Copper effectively reduces the sulphury content. To complicate matters, however, there are distilleries (like Dalwhinnie) where sulphur is a sought after characteristic in the newmake. If you´re looking for a more robust and honeyed flavour, the sulphury start will effectively reduce the light green and grassy notes that you would otherwise end up with. Condensing the spirit with worm tubs, like at Dalwhinnie, Mortlach and Benrinnes, gives more sulphur because of the lesser copper contact in the worms. Longer maturation is also required to finally complete the elimination of sulphur.

Dalwhinnie distillery is equipped with a 7.3 ton full lauter mash tun and six wooden washbacks with the fermentation split into four short sessions at 60 hours and six long, fermenting over the weekend, at 110 hours. There is one pair of stills attached to worm tubs which was replaced with new ones in 2015. The 5-day production week for 2016 means 10 mashes per week which gives 1.4 million litres of alcohol in the year. Dalwhinnie is one of Diageo´s best selling single malts and comes in at sixth place with 1 million bottles sold in 2015. It is also the signature malt in one of the fastest increasing Scotch blends in the world right now – Buchanan´s – with its main markets in USA, Mexico and Venezuela.

The core range is made up of a **15 year old** and a **Distiller's Edition** with a finish in oloroso casks. A new addition, **Dalwhinnie Winter´s Gold**, was released in July 2015. Autumn 2015 saw the release of a limited **25 year old** and in August 2016, a **distillery exclusive** with no age statement was launched.

History:

1897 John Grant, George Sellar and Alexander Mackenzie commence building the facilities. The first name is Strathspey.

1898 The owner encounters financial troubles and John Somerville & Co and A P Blyth & Sons take over and change the name to Dalwhinnie.

1905 Cook & Bernheimer in New York, buys Dalwhinnie for £1,250 at an auction. The administration of Dalwhinnie is placed in the newly formed company James Munro & Sons.

1919 Macdonald Greenlees & Willliams Ltd headed by Sir James Calder buys Dalwhinnie.

1926 Macdonald Greenlees & Williams Ltd is bought by Distillers Company Ltd (DCL) which licences Dalwhinnie to James Buchanan & Co.

1930 Operations are transferred to Scottish Malt Distilleries (SMD).

1934 The distillery is closed after a fire in February.

1938 The distillery opens again.

1968 The maltings is decommissioned.

1987 Dalwhinnie 15 years becomes one of the selected six in United Distillers´ Classic Malts.

1991 A visitor centre is constructed.

1992 The distillery closes and goes through a major refurbishment costing £3.2 million.

1995 The distillery opens in March.

2002 A 36 year old is released.

2006 A 20 year old is released.

2010 A Manager´s Choice 1992 is released.

2012 A 25 year old is released.

2014 A triple matured bottling without age statement is released for The Friends of the Classic Malts.

2015 Dalwhinnie Winter´s Gold and a 25 year old are released.

2016 A distillery exclusive without age statement is released.

15 years old

Tasting notes Dalwhinnie 15 years old:

GS – The nose is fresh, with pine needles, heather and vanilla. Sweet and balanced on the fruity palate, with honey, malt and a very subtle note of peat. The medium length finish dries elegantly.

Deanston

[deen•stun]

Owner:
Burn Stewart Distillers
(Distell Group Ltd)

Region/district:
Southern Highlands

Founded: 1965
Status: Active (vc)
Capacity: 3 000 000 litres

Address: Deanston, Perthshire FK16 6AG

Website: deanstonmalt.com
Tel: 01786 843010

With its huge water turbine, Deanston is Scotland's only self-sufficient distillery when it comes to electricity. Therefore it seems only natural that they take the next step on the environmental path releasing their first organic whisky.

Deanston was built in the 1960s when an 18th century mill was transformed into a distillery. For many years it quietly lingered in the shadows of other distilleries and it wasn't until quite recently that consumers started to discover this whisky. Two reasons can be ascribed for this phenomenon. First, the master blender at the time, Ian MacMillan, changed the way the whisky was produced. He bottled it at a higher strength, didn't chill-filter it nor did he add colouring. At the same time an excellent visitor centre was opened in 2012.

The distillery is equipped with an 11 ton traditional open top, cast iron mash tun, eight stainless steel washbacks with an average fermentation time of 80 hours and two pairs of stills with ascending lyne arms. The distillery is doing 10 mashes per week and producing 2 million litres of alcohol. Having already started in 2000, a small part of organic spirit is being produced yearly.

The core range is a **12 year old**, an **18 year old** (released in 2015), as well as **Virgin Oak**. The latter is a non-age statement malt with a finish in virgin oak casks. Recent limited releases include an exclusive to the American market, an **18 year old** finished in cognac for more than 6 years, and a **20 year old** cask strength. There have already been talks about an **Organic Deanston** since at least 2012 and in spring 2016 it finally came to fruition. Certified as organic by the Organic Food Federation, it is a 15 year old and, although initially only available in Germany and through global travel retail, it will become a limited annual release. For those who travel to the distillery, there is a reward in the form of some exclusive bottlings – **Sherry Oak, Vintage 1974, 11 year old Marsala finish** and the new **Portwood Finish** which was released in July 2016.

History:

1965 A weavery from 1785 is transformed into Deanston Distillery by James Finlay & Co. and Brodie Hepburn Ltd Brodie Hepburn also runs Tullibardine Distillery.

1966 Production commences in October.

1971 The first single malt is named Old Bannockburn.

1972 Invergordon Distillers takes over.

1974 The first single malt bearing the name Deanston is produced.

1982 The distillery closes.

1990 Burn Stewart Distillers from Glasgow buys the distillery for £2.1 million.

1991 The distillery resumes production.

1999 C L Financial buys an 18% stake of Burn Stewart.

2002 C L Financial acquires the remaining stake.

2006 Deanston 30 years old is released.

2009 A new version of the 12 year old is released.

2010 Virgin Oak is released.

2012 A visitor centre is opened.

2013 Burn Stewart Distillers is bought by South African Distell Group for £160m

2014 An 18 year old cognac finish is released in the USA.

2015 An 18 year old is released.

2016 Organic Deanston is released.

18 years old

Tasting notes Deanston 12 years old:

GS – A fresh, fruity nose with malt and honey. The palate displays cloves, ginger, honey and malt, while the finish is long, quite dry and pleasantly herbal.

Dufftown

Together with Glen Ord and Glendullan, Dufftown make up the new mega single malt brand, The Singleton. Established ten years ago, the different versions were earmarked for different regions, but can now all be found globally.

The Singleton is positioned by Diageo as a "recruitment malt" intended to lead consumers into the single malt category, as opposed to their "discovery malts" (Talisker and Lagavulin) and "prestige malts" (Mortlach and the Special Releases). The owners are now working on the ambitious goal to make The Singleton the world´s number one malt whisky brand. Currently in fifth place, it sells 5.4 million bottles, compared to Glenfiddich´s 13.1 million.

Dufftown distillery is equipped with a 13 ton full lauter mash tun, 12 stainless steel washbacks and three pairs of stills. All stills furthermore have sub coolers. The style of Dufftown single malt is green and grassy which is achieved by a clear wort and long fermentation (75 hours minimum). Add to that, a slow distillation and the fact that the stills are filled with small volumes to allow as much copper contact as possible, you have what gives it its real character. Dufftown has been working 24/7 since 2007 and during 2016 they will be doing 6 million litres of alcohol.

The core range consists of **The Singleton of Dufftown 12, 15** and **18 year old**. In 2013 a new sub-range exclusive to duty free was launched. The first two releases were **Trinité** and **Liberté** and yet a third release, **Artisan**, was added in spring of 2014. New releases, however, didn´t stop there. March 2014 saw the launch of two new bottlings for domestic markets in Western Europe; **Tailfire** and **Sunray** and the two were followed in autumn 2014 by a new entry level bottling called **Spey Cascade**. Limited releases appear from time to time. The two latest, released in April 2016 were exclusive to Hong Kong – a **21 year old** matured in sherry casks and a **25 year old** from ex bourbon casks. In 2013, the first official cask strength bottling from the distillery was launched as part of the Special Releases, **The Singleton of Dufftown 28 year old**.

[duff•town]

Owner: Diageo	**Region/district:** Speyside
Founded: 1896	**Status:** Active	**Capacity:** 6 000 000 litres

Address: Dufftown, Keith, Banffshire AB55 4BR

Website: malts.com thesingleton.com	**Tel:** 01340 822100

History:

1895 Peter Mackenzie, Richard Stackpole, John Symon and Charles MacPherson build the distillery Dufftown-Glenlivet in an old mill.

1896 Production starts in November.

1897 The distillery is owned by P. Mackenzie & Co., who also owns Blair Athol in Pitlochry.

1933 P. Mackenzie & Co. is bought by Arthur Bell & Sons for £56,000.

1968 The floor maltings is discontinued and malt is bought from outside suppliers. The number of stills is increased from two to four.

1974 The number of stills is increased from four to six.

1979 The stills are increased by a further two to eight.

1985 Guinness buys Arthur Bell & Sons.

1997 Guinness and Grand Metropolitan merge to form Diageo.

2006 The Singleton of Dufftown 12 year old is launched as a special duty free bottling.

2008 The Singleton of Dufftown is made available also in the UK.

2010 A Manager´s Choice 1997 is released.

2013 A 28 year old cask strength and two expressions for duty free - Unité and Trinité - are released.

2014 Tailfire, Sunray and Spey Cascade are released.

Singleton of Dufftown 12 year

Tasting notes Dufftown 12 years old:

GS – The nose is sweet, almost violet-like, with underlying malt. Big and bold on the palate, this is an upfront yet very drinkable whisky. The finish is medium to long, warming, spicy, with slowly fading notes of sherry and fudge.

Edradour

[ed•ra•dow•er]

Owner:
Signatory Vintage
Scotch Whisky Co. Ltd

Region/district:
Southern Highland

Founded:
1825

Status:
Active (vc)

Capacity:
130 000 litres

Address: Pitlochry, Perthshire PH16 5JP

Website:
edradour.com

Tel:
01796 472095

After 15 years as an independent bottler, Andrew Symington in 2002 finally got what he was looking for – a distillery of his own which could complement the rest of the business.

After a series of attempts to buy distilleries like Scapa, Glenturret and Ardbeg, he was finally rewarded when Pernod Ricard sold him Edradour in 2002. Symington certainly had vision and foresight! Established producers are nowadays reluctant to sell whisky to independent bottlers, but if you produce your own whisky, you can always swap casks. At the same time Symington has managed to establish Edradour single malt as a brand of its own, admittedly small quantities, but with devoted followers nevertheless. Its success has been so stellar that a second distillery with two new stills is being planned for the near future, which could increase its capacity to 400,000 litres of alcohol. Edradour is a very busy place. The reason is not so much because of its huge production, but because of the many visitors who are attracted to one of the most picturesque distilleries in Scotland.

The distillery is equipped with an open, traditional cast iron mash tun with a mash size of 1.15 tonnes. The two washbacks are made of Oregon pine and two stills are connected to a more than 100 year old wormtub. In 2016 they will be doing 6 mashes per week and 130,000 litres of alcohol in the ensuing year, of which 26,000 litres will be heavily peated.

The core range consists of **10 year old**, **12 year old Caledonia Selection** (oloroso finish), **Cask Strength Sherry 14 year old**, **Cask Strength Bourbon 12 year old** and **Fairy Flag**, a 15 year old Oloroso finish. A series of wood finishes under the name **Straight From The Cask** (SFTC), are all bottled at cask strength. In addition to this, there is also a range of wood maturations, aged 8-12 years. Limited releases in 2016 include a **15 year old**, a **2006 Sauternes cask**, the 11th release of the bourbon matured **2003 Vintage** and a **22 year old Sauternes finish** from 1993. The first release of the heavily peated Ballechin was in 2006 and a number of limited bottlings followed until 2014 when the core **Ballechin 10 year old** was launched.

History:

1825 Probably the year when a distillery called Glenforres is founded by farmers in Perthshire.

1837 The first year Edradour is mentioned.

1841 The farmers form a proprietary company, John MacGlashan & Co.

1886 John McIntosh & Co. acquires Edradour.

1933 William Whiteley & Co. buys the distillery.

1982 Campbell Distilleries (Pernod Ricard) buys Edradour and builds a visitor centre.

1986 The first single malt is released.

2002 Edradour is bought by Andrew Symington from Signatory for £5.4 million. The product range is expanded with a 10 year old and a 13 year old cask strength.

2003 A 30 year old and a 10 year old are released.

2004 A number of wood finishes are launched as cask strength.

2006 The first bottling of peated Ballechin is released.

2007 A Madeira matured Ballechin is released.

2008 A Ballechin matured in Port pipes and a 10 year old Edradour with a Sauternes finish are released.

2009 Fourth edition of Ballechin (Oloroso) is released.

2010 Ballechin #5 Marsala is released.

2011 Ballechin #6 Bourbon and a 26 year old PX sherry finish are released.

2012 A 1993 Oloroso and a 1993 Sauternes finish as well as the 7th edition of Ballechin (Bordeaux) are released.

2013 Ballechin Sauternes is released.

2014 The first release of a 10 year old Ballechin.

2015 Fairy Flag is released.

12 years old

Tasting notes Edradour 10 years old:

GS – Cider apples, malt, almonds, vanilla and honey ar present on the nose, along with a hint of smoke and sherry. The palate is rich, creamy and malty, with a persistent nuttiness and quite a pronounced kick of slightly leathery sherry. Spices and sherry dominate the medium to long finish.

Fettercairn

[fett•er•cairn]

Owner: **Region/district:**
Whyte & Mackay (Emperador)   Eastern Highlands

Founded: **Status:**   **Capacity:**
1824   Active (vc)   3 200 000 litres

Address: Fettercairn, Laurencekirk, Kincardineshire
AB30 1YB

Website: **Tel:**
fettercairndistillery.co.uk   01561 340205

Among several prominent owners of Fettercairn over the years we find Joseph Hobbs – a Scot who had immigrated to Canada and later returned to his native country.

A highly innovative man both when it came to ideas on production, as well as sales and marketing, Hobbs was involved with several Scottish distilleries in the 1940s and 50s. He was also an active opponent against the Scotch Whisky Association which he thought resembled a cartel where the big companies did their utmost to set spanners in the works for smaller independent producers. He subsequently formed the Independent Scotch Whisky Association in 1951 with 40 member companies and its first priority was to be able to continue to export whisky younger than the stipulated three years. A spokesman for SWA claimed that "Whisky under three years old is a sick spirit. Sick in spirit and violent in the throat of man". Hobbs and his associates, on the other hand, claimed that "...after some years of selling 18-month old whisky to many countries, we have not had one complaint as to its quality". Eventually, Hobbs and his friends lost the battle. In order for it to be called Scotch, the whisky must at least be three years old and must have been matured only in Scotland.

Fettercairn distillery is equipped with a traditional cast iron mash tun with a copper canopy, eight wooden washbacks and two pairs of stills. When collecting the middle cut, cooling water is allowed to trickle along the outside of the spirit still neck. This is done in order to increase reflux and thereby producing a lighter and cleaner spirit. For 2016 the production will be 24 mashes per week, reaching 2,2 million litres of alcohol for the year.

The core range consists of **Fettercairn Fior** without age statement and three older whiskies – **24, 30** and **40 year old**. The greatest part of Fior comprises of whiskies aged 14 and 15 years with an addition of a 5 year old peated whisky. In 2011 another whisky without age statement was launched, **Fettercairn Fasque**, which contains slightly younger whiskies than Fior and only 5% is peated whisky.

History:

1824 Sir Alexander Ramsay founds the distillery.

1830 Sir John Gladstone buys the distillery.

1887 A fire erupts and the distillery is forced to close for repairs.

1890 Thomas Gladstone dies and his son John Robert takes over. The distillery reopens.

1912 The company is close to liquidation and John Gladstone buys out the other investors.

1926 The distillery is mothballed.

1939 The distillery is bought by Associated Scottish Distillers Ltd. Production restarts.

1960 The maltings discontinues.

1966 The stills are increased from two to four.

1971 The distillery is bought by Tomintoul-Glenlivet Distillery Co. Ltd.

1973 Tomintoul-Glenlivet Distillery Co. Ltd is bought by Whyte & Mackay Distillers Ltd.

1974 The mega group of companies Lonrho buys Whyte & Mackay.

1988 Lonrho sells to Brent Walker Group plc.

1989 A visitor centre opens.

1990 American Brands Inc. buys Whyte & Mackay for £160 million.

1996 Whyte & Mackay and Jim Beam Brands merge to become JBB Worldwide.

2001 Kyndal Spirits buys Whyte & Mackay from JBB Worldwide.

2002 The whisky changes name to Fettercairn 1824.

2003 Kyndal Spirits changes name to Whyte & Mackay.

2007 United Spirits buys Whyte & Mackay. A 23 year old single cask is released.

2009 24, 30 and 40 year olds are released.

2010 Fettercairn Fior is launched.

2012 Fettercairn Fasque is released.

Tasting notes Fettercairn Fior:

GS – A complex, weighty nose of toffee, sherry, ginger, orange and smoke. More orange and smoke on the palate, with a sherried nuttiness and hints of treacle toffee. Mild, spicy oak and a touch of liquorice in the lengthy finish.

Fior

Glenallachie

[glen•alla•key]

Owner: **Region/district:**
Chivas Brothers   Speyside
(Pernod Ricard)

Founded:	**Status:**	**Capacity:**
1967	Active	4 000 000 litres

Address: Aberlour, Banffshire AB38 9LR

Website: **Tel:**
-                              01542 783042

Glenallachie lies right in the middle of Speyside with the town of Aberlour being situated a few kilometres to the north and with the imposing Benrinnes mountain silhouetted in the south. The building at the distillery itself, however, is not as eye-catching.

Built in 1967, this is a working distillery with no pagoda roof and no visitor centre, and built in the typical, efficient style of the 1960s. It was founded by Charles Mackinlay Ltd, a well regarded whisky firm established in the 19th century, but taken over by Scottish & Newcastle Breweries in 1961. This was a golden era for Scotch whisky and Scottish & Newcastle decided to establish themselves within the lucrative spirits business, complementing its beer production. It was, however, with the current owners, Pernod Ricard, that the distillery was to be commissioned to be the supplier of malt whisky for the blend Clan Campbell. The brand, created in the 1930s, was introduced to the French market in 1984 and is currently one the most popular whiskies in the country. During the last five years though, sales have dropped and a re-launch of the brand was made recently to stop the decline. A total of 19 million bottles were sold in 2015.

The process structure of Glenallachie was designed by the famous whisky architect, William Delmé Evans, and it also became his last distillery project. With Glenallachie, he finally managed to design the gravity-fed distillery that he had been planning since the 1940s. The distillery is now equipped with a 9.4 ton semi-lauter mash tun, six washbacks made of mild steel, but lined with stainless steel, plus another two washbacks which have been brought in from Caperdonich which was demolished in 2011. There are also two pairs of unusually wide stills.

Until recently, the only official bottling from Glenallachie has been a **cask strength** from **2000**, which was released in 2014. This was an exclusive for Chivas´ visitor centres but has now been withdrawn.

History:

1967 The distillery is founded by Mackinlay, McPherson & Co., a subsidiary of Scottish & Newcastle Breweries Ltd. William Delmé Evans is architect.

1985 Scottish & Newcastle Breweries Ltd sells Charles Mackinlay Ltd to Invergordon Distillers which acquires both Glenallachie and Isle of Jura.

1987 The distillery is decommissioned.

1989 Campbell Distillers (Pernod Ricard) buys the distillery, increases the number of stills from two to four and takes up production again.

2005 The first official bottling for many years is a Cask Strength Edition from 1989.

2000 14 years old

Tasting notes Glenallachie 14 years old:

GS – The nose offers pineapple and banoffee pie, becoming spicier in time. The palate yields big orange spice notes, honey and caramel. Long, sweet and spicy in the finish.

Glenburgie

[glen•bur•gee]

Owner:	**Region/district:**
Chivas Brothers	Speyside
(Pernod Ricard)	

Founded:	**Status:**	**Capacity:**
1810	Active	4 200 000 litres

Address: Glenburgie, Forres, Morayshire IV36 2QY

Website:	**Tel:**
-	01343 850258

Glenburgie single malt, together with Miltonduff, form the backbone of the Ballantine´s blended Scotch, a whisky that is second only to Johnnie Walker on the Scotch sales top list.

But while Johnnie Walker in the early 2000s sold twice as many bottles as Ballantine, they now sell four times that amount. That´s why it must be gratifying for Chivas Brothers to see volumes of Ballantine´s increase in 2015 for the first time in five years to 75 million bottles. That´s one third of what Johnnie Walker sells.

For slightly more than two decades, 1958-1981, a couple of very special stills were operative at Glenburgie. Instead of the traditional swan neck, the so called Lomond stills had columns with a number of plates inside. The plates were adjustable and the thinking was to be able to produce different kinds of newmake from the same still. The idea however, was short-lived, but the whisky that the Lomond stills produced got its own name, Glencraig, named after the former product director of Ballantines, William Craig. With a bit of luck bottles of Glencraig can still be found from independent bottlers. Two of these were released in 2012 and 2013 by Gordon & MacPhail and Signatory.

Glenburgie distillery lies well hidden at the end of a side road to the A96 between Forres and Elgin. It was founded in 1810 as Kilnflat distillery, but the buildings that we see today are of a much later date, having been built in 2003 when the old distillery was demolished. Glenburgie is equipped with a 7.5 ton full lauter mash tun, 12 stainless steel washbacks with a fermentation time of 52 hours and three pairs of stills. The majority of the production is filled into bourbon casks and a part thereof is matured in four dunnage, two racked and two palletised warehouses.

The only current, official bottling is a **17 year old** cask strength, distilled in 1999 and bottled in 2016 in the new range The Distillery Reserve Collection which can be found at Chivas´ visitor centres.

History:

1810 William Paul founds Kilnflat Distillery. Official production starts in 1829.

1870 Kilnflat distillery closes.

1878 The distillery reopens under the name Glenburgie-Glenlivet, Charles Hay is licensee.

1884 Alexander Fraser & Co. takes over.

1925 Alexander Fraser & Co. files for bankruptcy and the receiver Donald Mustad assumes control of operations.

1927 James & George Stodart Ltd (owned by James Barclay and R A McKinlay since 1922) buys the distillery which by this time is inactive.

1930 Hiram Walker buys 60% of James & George Stodart Ltd.

1936 Hiram Walker buys Glenburgie Distillery in October. Production restarts.

1958 Lomond stills are installed producing a single malt, Glencraig. Floor malting ceases.

1981 The Lomond stills are replaced by conventional stills.

1987 Allied Lyons buys Hiram Walker.

2002 A 15 year old is released.

2004 A £4.3 million refurbishment and reconstruction takes place.

2005 Chivas Brothers (Pernod Ricard) becomes the new owner through the acquisition of Allied Domecq.

2006 The number of stills are increased from four to six in May.

17 year old cask strength

Tasting notes Glenburgie 20 years old:

GS – The nose is very floral, sweet and fruity. Peaches, apricots and nougat. Silky palate texture, with deep fruit notes that become more citric, with cream and hazelnuts. Nutty in the finish, drying slightly with mild oak.

Glencadam

[glen•ka•dam]

Owner: **Region/district:**
Angus Dundee Distillers   Eastern Highlands

Founded: **Status:**   **Capacity:**
1825   Active   1 300 000 litres

Address: Brechin, Angus DD9 7PA

Website: **Tel:**
glencadamdistillery.co.uk   01356 622217

Few single malts fit the description "underrated, overlooked and hidden gem" better than Glencadam. Neglected by previous owners, at least when it came to releasing official bottlings, the distillery suddenly resurrected and came out of the closet in 2005.

It was then that Angus Dundee launched the first official expression – a 15 year old. Ever since, new releases have cropped up regularly, but not with such frenzy as seen in 2016. No less than six new versions have seen the light of day this year. Until recently, all bottlings from Glencadam have been un chill-filtered and bottled at 46% or more, but with the new Origin 1825, they have made an exception. This new introduction to the range carries no age statement and is bottled at 40%.

The heavy rains in January 2016, forced the distillery to close temporarily because of flooding. With three feet of water in the still house, there was extensive damage to the electrical system. The last time the distillery had similar problems was in 2007.

Glencadam distillery is equipped with a traditional, 4.9 ton cast iron mash tun, six stainless steel washbacks with a fermentation time of 52 hours and one pair of stills. The distillery is currently working seven days a week, which enables 16 mashes per week and 1.3 million litres of alcohol per year. Glencadam is not only a busy distillery, but also hosts a huge filling and bottling plant with 16 large tanks for blending malt and grain whisky. Angus Dundee has a huge range of blended Scotch brands in its portfolio and is represented in more than 70 countries, not least of all China, where The Angus blend has recently been launched.

The core range from last year is made up of **10, 15** and **21 year old**. With the new releases, the range has now been expanded to eight bottlings. The new ones are **Origin 1825**, a combination of bourbon barrels and oloroso sherry butts, a **17 year old port finish**, a **19 year old oloroso finish** (replacing the 14 year old), an **18 year old** and a **25 year old**. Recent limited editions include a **33 year old single cask** from 1982.

History:

1825   George Cooper founds the distillery.

1827   David Scott takes over.

1837   The distillery is sold by David Scott.

1852   Alexander Miln Thompson becomes the owner.

1857   Glencadam Distillery Company is formed.

1891   Gilmour, Thompson & Co Ltd takes over.

1954   Hiram Walker takes over.

1959   Refurbishing of the distillery.

1987   Allied Lyons buys Hiram Walker Gooderham & Worts.

1994   Allied Lyons changes name to Allied Domecq.

2000   The distillery is mothballed.

2003   Allied Domecq sells the distillery to Angus Dundee Distillers.

2005   The new owner releases a 15 year old.

2008   A re-designed 15 year old and a new 10 year old are introduced.

2009   A 25 and a 30 year old are released in limited numbers.

2010   A 12 year old port finish, a 14 year old sherry finish, a 21 year old and a 32 year old are released.

2012   A 30 year old is released.

2015   A 25 year old is launched.

2016   Origin 1825, 17 year old port finish, 19 year old oloroso finish, an 18 year old and a 25 year old are released.

GLENCADAM

AGED **10** YEARS

The Rather Delicate
HIGHLAND SINGLE MALT
SCOTCH WHISKY

10 years old

Tasting notes Glencadam 10 years old:

GS – A light and delicate, floral nose, with tinned pears and fondant cream. Medium-bodied, smooth, with citrus fruits and gently-spiced oak on the palate. The finish is quite long and fruity, with a hint of barley.

GlenDronach

[glen•dro•nack]

Owner:	**Region/district:**
Benriach Distillery Co	Highlands
(Brown Forman)	

Founded:	**Status:**	**Capacity:**
1826	Active (vc)	1 400 000 litres

Address: Forgue, Aberdeenshire AB54 6DB

Website:	**Tel:**
glendronachdistillery.com	01466 730202

One of the biggest players in the world of spirits, and producers of the most sold American whiskey, Brown Forman, has been eyeing the Scotch whisky category for a long time.

In 2004, when Glenmorangie came up for grabs, the US company put in a bid. Perhaps they saw themselves as the obvious buyers. After all, at the time they distributed the brand in the US and had a 10% minority share. But their plans didn´t materialise – Moet Hennessy beat them to it and they thus sold their 10% of Glenmorangie shares. Twelve years later, they were more successful when they acquired BenRiach Distillery Company with three distilleries, including GlenDronach for £285m.

The distillery equipment at GlenDronach consists of a 3.7 ton cast iron mash tun with rakes, nine washbacks made of larch with a fermentation time of 60 to 90 hours and two pairs of stills. The plan is to produce 1.2 million litres of alcohol during 2016. The distillery has lately made small volumes of peated spirit, and for 2016 it will be 40,000 litres with a phenol specification of 38ppm.

The core range is **The Hielan 8 years, Original 12 years, Allardice 18 years, Parliament 21 years** and **Grandeur 25 years** where the 8th release was made in September 2016. The popular **15 year old Revival** is currently out of range, but should be back in circulation by 2018. However, a new addition to the core range appeared in November 2015 with the first (at least in modern times) **Peated GlenDronach**. Without age statement, the whisky has been matured in bourbon casks and then finished in a combination of oloroso and PX sherry casks. The **12 year old Sauternes finish** is the only remaining wood finish with a possibility of more being added in autumn 2016. The first **cask strength** expression was released in 2012 and batch number 6 was launched in August 2016. Batch 14 of the **single casks** was released in summer 2016, while the limited **20 year old GlenDronach Octaves** released in autumn 2015, represents the first GlenDronach that has been finished in the smaller (50 litres) octave casks. This was replaced in summer 2016 by **Octaves Classic** which has had a full maturation for around seven years in the smaller casks.

History:

1826 The distillery is founded by a consortium with James Allardes as one of the owners.

1837 Parts of the distillery is destroyed in a fire.

1852 Walter Scott (from Teaninich) takes over.

1887 Walter Scott dies and Glendronach is taken over by a consortium from Leith.

1920 Charles Grant buys Glendronach for £9,000.

1960 William Teacher & Sons buys the distillery.

1966 The number of stills is increased to four.

1976 Allied Breweries takes over William Teacher & Sons.

1996 The distillery is mothballed.

2002 Production is resumed on 14th May.

2005 The distillery closes to rebuild from coal to in-direct firing by steam. Reopens in September. Chivas Brothers (Pernod Ricard) becomes new owner through the acquisition of Allied Domecq.

2008 Pernod Ricard sells the distillery to the owners of BenRiach distillery.

2009 Relaunch of the whole range including 12, 15 and 18 year old.

2010 A 31 year old, a 1996 single cask and a total of 11 vintages and four wood finishes are released. A visitor centre is opened.

2011 The 21 year old Parliament and 11 vintages are released.

2012 A number of vintages are released.

2013 Recherché 44 years and a number of new vintages are released.

2014 Nine different single casks are released.

2015 The Hielan, 8 years old, is released.

2016 Brown Forman buys the distillery. Peated GlenDronach and Octaves Classic are released.

Tasting notes GlenDronach 12 years old:

GS – A sweet nose of Christmas cake fresh from the oven. Smooth on the palate, with sherry, soft oak, fruit, almonds and spices. The finish is comparatively dry and nutty, ending with bitter chocolate.

12 years old Original

Glendullan

[glen•dull•an]

Owner:	**Region/district:**
Diageo	Speyside
Founded: **Status:**	**Capacity:**
1897 Active	5 000 000 litres

Address: Dufftown, Keith, Banffshire AB55 4DJ

Website:	**Tel:**
www.malts.com	01340 822100

Glendullan is one of three Diageo distilleries working under the brand name The Singleton. Glen Ord and Dufftown are the other two.

During the last decade, The Singleton of Glendullan could only be found in the American market and sometimes in Duty Free. Recently though, the brand was rolled out to the rest of the world. The reason for this is that Diageo has decided to challenge the single malts category leader, Glenfiddich, with the aim of becoming the biggest single malt brand in the world. From the very beginning, more than ten years ago, it was decided that each of the three should operate in different geographical areas – Glendullan in America, Dufftown in Europe and Glen Ord in Asia – but all three will now be available worldwide.

Glendullan distillery is situated just one minute`s drive east of Glenfiddich near a river which, despite of the distillery´s name isn´t Dullan, but Fiddich. The confluence of the two rivers lies just a mile to the south of Glendullan. The equipment consists of a 12 ton full lauter stainless steel mash tun, 8 washbacks made of larch and two made of stainless steel with a fermentation time of 75 hours to promote a green/grassy character of the whisky, as well as three pairs of stills. In 2016 the distillery will be doing 21 mashes per week, producing 5 million litres of alcohol.

Until 2007, Glendullan single malt was just sold as a 12 year old in the Flora & Fauna range. During that same year it was re-launched, together with Dufftown and Glen Ord, under the name Singleton. The core range from Glendullan is **12, 15** and **18 year old**. In summer 2013 a new sub-range exclusive to duty free was launched, The Singleton Reserve Collection with **Liberty** and **Trinité**. These bottlings were replaced in autumn 2015 by **Classic** (which is matured in American oak), **Double Matured** (matured separately in American and European oak and then married together) and **Master´s Art** (with a finish in Muscat casks). In autumn 2014, a Glendullan single malt was, for the first time, launched as part of the Special Releases – a **38 year old** distilled in 1975.

History:

1896 William Williams & Sons, a blending company with Three Stars and Strahdon among its brands, founds the distillery.

1902 Glendullan is delivered to the Royal Court and becomes the favourite whisky of Edward VII.

1919 Macdonald Greenlees buys a share of the company and Macdonald Greenlees & Williams Distillers is formed.

1926 Distillers Company Limited (DCL) buys Glendullan.

1930 Glendullan is transferred to Scottish Malt Distillers (SMD).

1962 Major refurbishing and reconstruction.

1972 A brand new distillery is constructed next to the old one and both operate simultaneously during a few years.

1985 The oldest of the two distilleries is mothballed.

1995 The first launch of Glendullan in the Rare Malts series is a 22 year old from 1972.

2005 A 26 year old from 1978 is launched in the Rare Malts series.

2007 Singleton of Glendullan is launched in the USA.

2013 Singleton of Glendullan Liberty and Trinity are released for duty free.

2014 A 38 year old is released.

2015 Classic, Double Matured and Master´s Art are released.

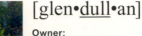

Tasting notes Singleton of Glendullan 12 years:

GS – The nose is spicy, with brittle toffee, vanilla, new leather and hazelnuts. Spicy and sweet on the smooth palate, with citrus fruits, more vanilla and fresh oak. Drying and pleasingly peppery in the finish.

12 years old

Glen Elgin

[glen el•gin]

Owner:
Diageo

Region/district:
Speyside

Founded: | **Status:** | **Capacity:**
1898 | Active | 2 700 000 litres

Address: Longmorn, Morayshire IV30 8SL

Website:
malts.com

Tel:
01343 862100

Glen Elgin was one of the last distilleries to be built in the 19th century and, at least since the 1930s, it has been one of the signature malts of the White Horse blend.

White Horse is one of the legendary blends and it takes its name from an equally legendary inn in Edinburgh. Situated in Canongate, The White Horse Inn was the starting place for the eight-day coach trip to London. It was built in 1623 by Lawrence Ord and soon afterwards it came into the possession of the Mackie family. There is written evidence that the inn was conveyed by John Mackie to his son, Alexander Mackie, in 1650. More than 200 years later, the White Horse name was taken into use for whisky which was blended by the Mackies with the name registered as a trademark in 1890. It was the dynamic Peter Mackie, owner of several distilleries at the time, including Lagavulin, who built up the brand to become one of the whisky world's most famous. Part of the glory has been lost along the way, but White Horse still belongs to the top 20 most sold brands with sales around 20 million bottles annually in key markets spread across the world: i. a. Japan, Greece, Brazil and South Africa.

The distillery is equipped with an 8.4 tonnes Steinecker full lauter mash tun from 2001, nine washbacks made of larch and six small stills. Three of the washbacks were installed as late as 2012 in the extended tun room, which meant that the production capacity had increased by 50%. Having moved recently from a 7 day operation to 5 days, the distillery is now working with a combination of short and long fermentations between 80 and 120 hours. The stills are connected to six wooden worm tubs where the spirit vapours are condensed. A new boiler was installed in December 2014, replacing the two, old existing ones. During 2016, they will be doing 12 mashes per week which translates to a production of 1.6 million litres.

The only official bottling is a **12 year old**, but older expressions (up to 32 years) have been released in limited numbers during the last decade.

History:

1898 The former manager of Glenfarclas, William Simpson and banker James Carle found Glen Elgin.

1900 Production starts in May but the distillery closes just five months later.

1901 The distillery is auctioned for £4,000 to the Glen Elgin-Glenlivet Distillery Co. and is mothballed.

1906 The wine producer J. J. Blanche & Co. buys the distillery for £7,000 and production resumes.

1929 J. J. Blanche dies and the distillery is put up for sale again.

1930 Scottish Malt Distillers (SMD) buys it and the license goes to White Horse Distillers.

1964 Expansion from two to six stills plus other refurbishing takes place.

1992 The distillery closes for refurbishing and installation of new stills.

1995 Production resumes in September.

2001 A 12 year old is launched in the Flora & Fauna series.

2002 The Flora & Fauna series malt is replaced by Hidden Malt 12 years.

2003 A 32 year old cask strength from 1971 is released.

2008 A 16 year old is launched as a Special Release.

2009 Glen Elgin 1998, a single cask in the new Manager´s Choice range is released.

12 years old

Tasting notes Glen Elgin 12 years old:

GS – A nose of rich, fruity sherry, figs and fragrant spice. Full-bodied, soft, malty and honeyed in the mouth. The finish is lengthy, slightly perfumed, with spicy oak.

Glenfarclas

[glen•fark•lass]

Owner:
J. & G. Grant

Region/district:
Speyside

Founded: **Status:**
1836   Active (vc)

Capacity:
3 500 000 litres

Address: Ballindalloch, Banffshire AB37 9BD

Website:
glenfarclas.co.uk

Tel:
01807 500257

Over the years there have been plenty of offers from other companies to buy Glenfarclas distillery, but none that has reached the public ear. Every offer has been politely turned down by the owners, the Grant family, since 150 years ago.

It is not strange that the distillery has been courted by potential buyers. Glenfarclas single malt has always had a solid reputation amongst blenders as being one of the Top Class whiskies and therefore a fair share of the production is sold to other companies for blends each year. The distillery is also known for its devotion to sherry casks, an expensive way to mature whisky nowadays as ex-sherry casks can be hard to come by. Glenfarclas way of solving this has been to build a 25 year long relationship with José y Miguel Martin bodega which supplies all their casks.

The distillery is equipped with a 16.5 ton semi-lauter mash tun and twelve stainless steel washbacks with an average fermentation time of 75 hours. There are three pairs of directly fired stills and the wash stills are equipped with rummagers. This is a copper chain rotating at the bottom of the still to prevent solids from sticking to the copper. There are 34 dunnage warehouses on-site with the capacity of holding 65,000 casks. In 2016, the distillery will produce 8 mashes a week for 38 weeks, resulting in 2.1 million litres of pure alcohol. Glenfarclas single malt has always been highly ranked among whisky aficionados and close to 800,000 bottles is sold annually.

The Glenfarclas core range consists of the **8, 10, 12, 15, 21** and **25 year old**, as well as the **105 Cask Strength**. There is also a **17 year old** destined for the USA, Japan and Sweden. Also in the core range, is the lightly sherried **Glenfarclas Heritage** without age statement. The soon to be re-launched **30** and **40 year olds** were previously part of the core range, but due to limited stock should now be carried over to limited bottlings. An **18 year old** exclusive to travel retail was launched in 2014.

The owners quite often make spectacular limited releases and the frequency and rarity of the expressions clearly show the impressive selection that they have available in their warehouses. In 2014, the first of six releases in a new range named The Generations Range (representing the six generations of the family) have appeared. It was a **1966 Fino** maturation which was followed in 2015 by the **1956 Sherry** cask. The third bottling, a **50 year old** matured in oloroso casks, appeared in spring 2016 and later in the year the final three expressions were launched; a **1981** matured in **port pipes**, a **1986 cask strength** and a **40 year old** from 1976. Few, if any other producer, have the opportunity to offer six such whiskies in just two years! Another limited release in 2015 was a bottling to celebrate the 150ᵗʰ anniversary of the Grants taking over Glenfarclas. It was named **£511.19s.0d Family Reserve**, being the amount paid for the distillery by John Grant on 8 June 1865. The owners also continue to release bottlings in their **Family Casks** series with vintages ranging from 1954 to 2001.

History:

1836 Robert Hay founds the distillery on the original site since 1797.

1865 Robert Hay passes away and John Grant and his son George buy the distillery. They lease it to John Smith at The Glenlivet Distillery.

1870 John Smith resigns in order to start Cragganmore and J. & G. Grant Ltd takes over.

1889 John Grant dies and George Grant takes over.

1890 George Grant dies and his widow Barbara takes over the license while sons John and George control operations.

1895 John and George Grant take over and form The Glenfarclas-Glenlivet Distillery Co. Ltd with the infamous Pattison, Elder & Co.

1898 Pattison becomes bankrupt. Glenfarclas encounters financial problems after a major overhaul of the distillery but survives by mortgaging and selling stored whisky to R. I. Cameron, a whisky broker from Elgin.

1914 John Grant leaves due to ill health and George continues alone.

1948 The Grant family celebrates the distillery's 100ᵗʰ anniversary, a century of active licensing. It is 9 years late, as the actual anniversary coincided with WW2.

1949 George Grant senior dies and sons George Scott and John Peter inherit the distillery.

1960 Stills are increased from two to four.

1968 Glenfarclas is first to launch a cask-strength single malt. It is later named Glenfarclas 105.

1972 Floor maltings is abandoned and malt is purchased centrally.

1973 A visitor centre is opened.

1976 Enlargement from four stills to six.

History continued:

2001 Glenfarclas launches its first Flower of Scotland gift tin which becomes a great success and increases sales by 30%.

2002 George S Grant dies and is succeeded as company chairman by his son John L S Grant

2003 Two new gift tins are released (10 years old and 105 cask strength).

2005 A 50 year old is released to commemorate the bi-centenary of John Grant´s birth.

2006 Ten new vintages are released.

2007 Family Casks, a series of single cask bottlings from 43 consecutive years, is released.

2008 New releases in the Family Cask range. Glenfarclas 105 40 years old is released.

2009 A third release in the Family Casks series.

2010 A 40 year old and new vintages from Family Casks are released.

2011 Chairman´s Reserve and 175th Anniversary are released.

2012 A 58 year old and a 43 year old are released.

2013 An 18 year old for duty free is released as well as a 25 year old quarter cask.

2014 A 60 year old and a 1966 single fino sherry cask are released.

2015 A 1956 Sherry Cask and Family Reserve are released.

2016 40 year old, 50 year old, 1981 Port and 1986 cask strength are released.

Tasting notes Glenfarclas 10 year old:

GS – Full and richly sherried on the nose, with nuts, fruit cake and a hint of citrus fruit. The palate is big, with ripe fruit, brittle toffee, some peat and oak. Medium length and gingery in the finish.

105 Cask Strength

50 years old

18 years old

Family Cask 1959

10 years old

Heritage

40 years old

Glenfiddich

[glen•fidd•ick]

Owner:
William Grant & Sons

Region/district:
Speyside

Founded: 1886
Status: Active (vc)
Capacity: 14 000 000 litres

Address: Dufftown, Keith, Banffshire AB55 4DH

Website:
glenfiddich.com

Tel:
01340 820373 (vc)

In 2014 Glenfiddich lost its spot as the world´s most sold single malt to Glenlivet, a position the brand had held at least since 1963. Just a year later, however, it seemed as if order was restored.

According to the latest figures from the IWSR, Glenfiddich has managed to beat its rival by 143,000 bottles during 2015, which isn't a lot considering that Glenfiddich had sold 13.1 million bottles during the year. It almost seems destined that the recovered top ranking has coincided with the start of a huge expansion of the distillery. A whole new distillery is being built on the grounds and, if everything goes according to plan, it will start producing by the end of 2018. The new unit will be equipped with one mash tun, 16 washbacks, 5 wash stills and 10 spirit stills. When the expansion is finished, the combined capacity of the two distilleries will be 20 million litres. On the other hand its closest competitors are not being idle either. Macallan will start production in its new distillery in 2017, which in theory will give it a total capacity (including the current distillery) of 26 million litres while Glenlivet, due to an expansion which has already commenced, may reach a total capacity of 30 million litres in a couple of years' time.

Glenfiddich distillery is equipped with two, stainless steel, full lauter mash tuns – both with a 10 ton mash. There are 24 Douglas fir washbacks and eight stainless steel washbacks which were installed late in 2012, all having a fermentation time of 68 hours. There are two still rooms with a total of 11 wash stills and 20 spirit stills. Three of them were added in autumn 2014 and, although it did not increase its capacity, had the desired effect of making the production smoother. The production for 2016 will be 68 mashes per week and 13.65 million litres of pure alcohol.

The core range consists of **12, 15, 18** and **21 year old**, **Rich Oak 14 year old** and **15 year old Distillery Edition**. Included in the core range, although in limited quantities, are **Malt Master´s Edition** and the **26 year old Glenfiddich Excellence**. Some older expressions have also been released over the years – which include **30, 40** and **50 year old** as well as the **38 year old Glenfiddich Ultimate**. In 2014, **Glenfiddich The Original** was released, created to replicate the flavour profile of the legendary Straight Malt from the early 1960s. The same year, **Glenfiddich Gallery** was introduced where Malt Master, Brian Kinsman, has selected 36 different casks from 1958 to 1996. In autumn 2015 an exclusive to the US market was released by way of a **14 year old** matured in bourbon casks. Two bottlings in the Experimental Series were released in September 2016; **IPA Experiment** with a finish in IPA beer casks and **Project XX** where the casks were selected by 20 brand ambassadors. Included in the duty free range are three Age of Disvovery bottlings; **Madeira cask, Bourbon cask** and **Red Wine cask finish** as well as the Cask Collection with **Select Cask, Reserve Cask, Vintage Cask** and, since 2016, **Finest Solera**. Another duty free exclusive is **Glenfiddich Rare Oak 25 years**, which was launched in 2014.

History:

1886 The distillery is founded by William Grant, 47 years old, who had learned the trade at Mortlach Distillery. The equipment is bought from Mrs. Cummings of Cardow Distillery. The construction totals £800.

1887 The first distilling takes place on Christmas Day.

1892 William Grant builds Balvenie.

1898 The blending company Pattisons, largest customer of Glenfiddich, files for bankruptcy and Grant decides to blend their own whisky. Standfast becomes one of their major brands.

1903 William Grant & Sons is formed.

1957 The famous, three-cornered bottle is introduced.

1958 The floor maltings is closed.

1963 Glennfiddich becomes the first whisky to be marketed as single malt in the UK and the rest of the world.

1964 A version of Standfast's three-cornered bottle is launched for Glenfiddich in green glass.

1969 Glenfiddich becomes the first distillery in Scotland to open a visitor centre.

1974 16 new stills are installed.

2001 1965 Vintage Reserve is launched in a limited edition of 480 bottles. Glenfiddich 1937 is bottled (61 bottles).

2002 Glenfiddich Gran Reserva 21 years old, finished in Cuban rum casks is launched. Caoran Reserve 12 years is released. Glenfiddich Rare Collection 1937 (61 bottles) is launched and becomes the oldest Scotch whisky on the market.

2003 1973 Vintage Reserve (440 bottles) is launched.

2004 1991 Vintage Reserve (13 years) and 1972 Vintage Reserve (519 bottles) are launched.

History continued:

2005 Circa £1.7 million is invested in a new visitor centre.

2006 1973 Vintage Reserve, 33 years (861 bottles) and 12 year old Toasted Oak are released.

2007 1976 Vintage Reserve, 31 years is released in September.

2008 1977 Vintage Reserve is released.

2009 A 50 year old and 1975 Vintage Reserve are released.

2010 Rich Oak, 1978 Vintage Reserve, the 6th edition of 40 year old and Snow Phoenix are released.

2011 1974 Vintage Reserve and a 19 year old Madeira finish are released.

2012 Cask of Dreams and Millenium Vintage are released.

2013 A 19 year old red wine finish and 1987 Anniversary Vintage are released. Cask Collection with three different expressions is released for duty free.

2014 The 26 year old Glenfiddich Excellence, Rare Oak 25 years and Glenfiddich The Original are released.

2015 A 14 year old for the US market is released.

2016 Finest Solera is released for travel retail. Two expression in the Experimental Series are launched; Project XX and IPA Experiment.

Tasting notes Glenfiddich 12 year old:

GS – Delicate, floral and slightly fruity on the nose. Well mannered in the mouth, malty, elegant and soft. Rich, fruit flavours dominate the palate, with a developing nuttiness and an elusive whiff of peat smoke in the fragrant finish.

Project XX

18 years old

IPA Experiment

12 years old

Reserve Cask

Select Cask

Rich Oak

The Original

Glen Garioch

[glen gee•ree]

Owner: Morrison Bowmore (Suntory)
Region/district: Eastern Highlands

Founded: 1797
Status: Active (vc)
Capacity: 1 370 000 litres

Address: Oldmeldrum, Inverurie, Aberdeenshire AB51 0ES

Website: glengarioch.com
Tel: 01651 873450

For many years, Glen Garioch was the easternmost whisky distillery in Scotland. In 2016 the title was passed on to Lone Wolf, a distillery which opened within the premises of the well-known brewery, BrewDog, in Ellon north of Aberdeen.

On the other hand, Glen Garioch can rejoice at being one of the three oldest distilleries in Scotland. The official opening year was 1797, but already in 1785, spirit from Glen Garioch was announced in the Aberdeen Journal. The Manson family who founded and owned the distillery for many decades, gained prominence in more areas than just with whisky production. John Manson junior married a cousin of the famous explorer, David Livingstone, and their son, Patrick Manson, was widely known as the father of tropical medicine. He had linked the connection between mosquitoes and several diseases and was often referred to as Mosquito Manson.

Glen Garioch single malt is typically unpeated, but smoky notes can easily be detected in expressions distilled before 1994 when their own floor maltings closed. Until then, the malt was peated with a specification of 8-10ppm.

The distillery is equipped with a 4 ton full lauter mash tun, eight stainless steel washbacks with a fermentation time of 48 hours and one pair of stills. There is also a third still, which has not been used for a long time. The spirit is tankered to Glasgow, filled into casks and returned to the distillery's four warehouses. During 2016 the production will be 7 mashes per week and around 450,000 litres in the year.

The core range is the **1797 Founder's Reserve** (without age statement) and a **12 year old**, both of them bottled at 48% and un chill-filtered. Recent limited releases include **Virgin Oak** – the first Glen Garioch fully matured in virgin American white oak – and a **15 year old Renaissance**. The latter was the first in a new range called Glen Garioch Renaissance Collection.

History:

1797 John Manson founds the distillery.

1798 Thomas Simpson becomes licensee.

1827 Ingram, Lamb & Co. bcome new owners.

1837 The distillery is bought by John Manson & Co.

1908 William Sanderson buys the distillery.

1933 Sanderson & Son merges with the gin maker Booth's Distilleries Ltd.

1937 Booth's Distilleries Ltd is acquired by Distillers Company Limited (DCL).

1968 Glen Garioch is decommissioned.

1970 It is sold to Stanley P. Morrison Ltd.

1973 Production starts again.

1978 Stills are increased from two to three.

1994 Suntory controls all of Morrison Bowmore Distillers Ltd.

1995 The distillery is mothballed in October.

1997 The distillery reopens in August.

2004 Glen Garioch 46 year old is released.

2005 15 year old Bordeaux Cask Finish is launched. A visitor centre opens in October.

2006 An 8 year old is released.

2009 Complete revamp of the range - 1979 Founders Reserve (unaged), 12 year old, Vintage 1978 and 1990 are released.

2010 1991 vintage is released.

2011 Vintage 1986 and 1994 are released.

2012 Vintage 1995 and 1997 are released.

2013 Virgin Oak, Vintage 1999 and 11 single casks are released.

2014 Glen Garioch Renaissance Collection 15 years is released.

Tasting notes Glen Garioch 12 years old:

GS – Luscious and sweet on the nose, peaches and pineapple, vanilla, malt and a hint of sherry. Full-bodied and nicely textured, with more fresh fruit on the palate, along with spice, brittle toffee and finally dry oak notes.

12 years old

The State of Scotch

six burning questions

Kevin Abrook,
Global Whisky Specialist
- Innovation, W Grant & Sons

1. The Millenials are often referred to as perhaps the most important consumer demographic today. Do you think Scotch whisky appeals to that category and what can the producers do to attract them and keep them interested?

This group is incredibly diverse; you cannot pigeonhole them. On the one hand there is a desire for authenticity and heritage; yet on the other, there is a desire for simplicity: "don't confuse me with detail, just let me enjoy it!" Quite often Millenials want both! They love innovation but also respect tradition and craftsmanship – this is where Scotch can appeal to Millenials. Remember the traditions of today were the innovations of yesterday. The history of Scotch is about great entrepreneurs who built a category. The key for brands is to have a good story, built on authenticity and heritage, to tell it well and to be genuine – people will see through anything false. Luckily Wm Grant & Sons is a family company with a rich history and appealing stories; built on a foundation of fantastic quality liquid. Everything hangs together, and has to for this audience.

However, whilst there is an obsession with Millenials, marketing people sometimes forget where the money is; the 55+; Baby Boomers and beyond. They've got bigger incomes; they've paid off their mortgages and their children have fled the nest in many cases. Their disposable income is at its peak. The 70-79 age group will be the fastest growing cohort through to 2030 as the global population ages; many of whom are very affluent, looking to enjoy the latter years of their lives and want to indulge themselves. This represents an opportunity for Scotch.

2. Several Scotch whisky producers have recently questioned the rules what can and can't be said on the label about the whisky. Should the legislation be changed, allowing more transparency?

I don't see it as a big issue. The point about blends is that there is no formula or recipe; it is about achieving a consistent style of flavour. Instead of focusing on the input, focus on the output: the taste. This is the defining characteristic of whisky; what separates the great and the good from the less good. Remember that c. 90% of all Scotch sold is blends. The detailed make-up of a whisky is important to single malt enthusiasts and whisky bloggers, but most people just want to know what a whisky tastes like. If they like it, fine; if not they'll look for something else – there's plenty of choice out there. What we don't want is miscommunication – you can have too much information. The 'geeks' will love it, but might it have the opposite effect to the wider whisky consumer? The detail becomes intimidating and daunting versus the whisky inside.

3. We see more and more Scotch whiskies being bottled without an age statement (NAS). Will that trend continue and, from a consumer point of view, is that all bad?

NAS is nothing new. For example we have been selling different expressions of Glenfiddich with and without age statements for decades. From an innovation perspective, NAS does allow us to experiment and to focus on flavour, which should be the overriding objective. A young whisky can add vibrancy to something older; similarly adding older whiskies gives layers and depth that you don't get with young whiskies; giving the consumer genuinely new flavours, which is a good thing.

4. Not a new discussion but one that does resurface from time to time. Does the quality of a whisky suffer from chill-filtration and colouring?

I don't think the quality of a whisky suffers, but the perception does. The majority of consumers don't even know about it, but if they were to see hazy whisky or variations in colour from one production to the next, they would have doubts about the quality of what's inside the bottle – people taste with their eyes. Likewise, perception is really important for whisky enthusiasts in the know who go out of their way to seek bottles that are 'original and unaltered'. Whilst blind taste tests have proved that people cannot tell the difference, logic has to be on their side: if you are filtering a whisky, you must be taking something out by definition. It's all about perception and that varies between blended drinkers and single malt drinkers. Happily we make both styles.

5. In the steps of flavoured vodka, flavoured whisky has become increasingly popular. Mostly bourbon and Irish whiskey but also Scotch. What are the benefits and downsides of this new trend?

A positive benefit of the flavoured whisky boom in the US is that it has not substituted volume from the mother brands which are growing. It has attracted new users to whiskey, particularly women, in the LDA – 25 year old age group. This generation has a sweet tooth, having grown up on Coke and 7-Up. These products have a sweeter taste profile, as indeed does American and Canadian whiskey.

The hope is that as these consumers become the next Millenials, their palates mature and they look for something with more authenticity and heritage, as today's Millennials do; then trade up to 'real' whisky. This is where Scotch can benefit by playing on the heritage and authentic stories that give it its appeal in the first place; something that consumers aspire to as they mature. Interestingly, there could be opportunities for The Girvan Patent Still single grain Scotch with its inherently sweeter taste profile.

6. Scotch whisky exports have declined in the last couple of years. Is the position of Scotch under threat and if so, what can be done to change the trend?

From a William Grant perspective, we take a long term view. Yes there has been a decline in exports recently due to a number of political and economic factors, but you cannot just chop and change production; when laying down stocks you have to think at least 12 years ahead. My feeling is that this is just a temporary trend. There is a move towards brown spirits with heritage and authenticity, particularly amongst Millennials as discussed above. There are also huge untapped opportunities. India is a massive market for example, with over 150 million 9 litre cases of 'Other whisky'. These drinkers aspire to Scotch, but cannot afford it yet. However, the Indian middle class is forecast to grow from around 50m today to 500m by 2030; just as the stocks we have laid down come of age.

Glenglassaugh

[glen•glass•ock]

Owner: | **Region/district:**
Glenglassaugh Distillery Co | Highlands
(BenRiach Distillery Co.) |

Founded: | **Status:** | **Capacity:**
1875 | Active (vc) | 1 100 000 litres

Address: Portsoy, Banffshire AB45 2SQ

Website: | **Tel:**
glenglassaugh.com | 01261 842367

The years between 1983 and 1986 were the darkest in recent Scotch whisky history. Consumer interest in the spirit was declining and the industry sat with a huge excess of whisky that was produced in the 1970s when the demand was high.

During those four years, no less than 17 distilleries stopped producing and all but one closed for good. For Glenglassaugh it didn't look good either, but after 22 years, the stills were fired once again in 2008. A group of private investors did an admirable job of putting the distillery on the map once more. After a few years it was obvious that they had underestimated the cost of resurrecting an old distillery and keeping it running. So when the distillery needed further investments, they decided to sell it to the owners of BenRiach and GlenDronach. Production, as well as new releases, has increased substantially over the last few years and from 2016, the distillery has American owners in that BenRiach Distillery Co was purchased by Brown-Forman.

The equipment of the distillery consists of a Porteus cast iron mash tun with rakes, four wooden washbacks and two stainless steel ones and one pair of stills. The production is 800,000 litres of pure alcohol, of which 40,000 litres is peated (30ppm). The main part (85%) is filled to be used as single malt while the rest is sold externally.

The core range is **Revival**, a 3 year old with a 6 month Oloroso finish, followed by **Evolution**, slightly older, matured in American oak and bottled at 50%. Then there is also **Torfa** which is peated (20ppm), matured in bourbon casks, bottled at 50% and without age statement. Limited releases include **30, 40** and **51 year old**, as well as various single casks where batch three was released in September. Two new limited releases also appeared in June 2016 – **Octaves Classic** and **Octaves Peated**. Both have been matured for around seven years in octaves (which are small casks holding approximately 60 litres) and are bottled at 48%.

History:

1873 The distillery is founded by James Moir.
1887 Alexander Morrison embarks on renovation work.
1892 Morrison sells the distillery to Robertson & Baxter. They in turn sell it on to Highland Distilleries Company for £15,000.
1908 The distillery closes.
1931 The distillery reopens.
1936 The distillery closes.
1957 Reconstruction takes place.
1960 The distillery reopens.
1986 Glenglassaugh is mothballed.
2005 A 22 year old is released.
2006 Three limited editions are released - 19 years old, 38 years old and 44 years old.
2008 The distillery is bought by the Scaent Group for £5m. Three bottlings are released - 21, 30 and 40 year old.
2009 New make spirit and 6 months old are released.
2010 A 26 year old replaces the 21 year old.
2011 A 35 year old and the first bottling from the new owners production, a 3 year old, are released.
2012 A visitor centre is inaugurated and Glenglassaugh Revival is released.
2013 BenRiach Distillery Co buys the distillery and Glenglassaugh Evolution and a 30 year old are released.
2014 The peated Torfa is released as well as eight different single casks and Massandra Connection (35 and 41 years old).
2015 The second batch of single casks is released.
2016 Octaves Classic and Octaves Peated are released.

Torfa

Tasting notes Glenglassaugh Evolution:

GS – Peaches and gingerbread on the nose, with brittle toffee, icing sugar, and vanilla. Luscious soft fruits dipped in caramel figure on the palate, with coconut and background stem ginger. The finish is medium in length, with spicy toffee.

Glengoyne

[glen•goyn]

Owner:
Ian Macleod Distillers

Region/district:
Southern Highlands

Founded: 1833

Status: Active (vc)

Capacity: 1 100 000 litres

Address: Dumgoyne by Killearn, Glasgow G63 9LB

Website: glengoyne.com

Tel: 01360 550254 (vc)

It seems as if the past two years of declining figures for the big companies haven´t affected the owners of Glengoyne at all. The past year has, in fact, meant a 23% increase in profits for Ian Macleod Distillers.

The optimism is high within the company and to be able to continue further expansion in some of their key markets (Africa, the Far East and the Americas), the company has secured a £60m bank loan in May 2016. Apart from Glengoyne and Tamdhu single malt, Ian Macleod also has several large blends of their own, like King Robert II for instance and also supply whisky to customers who want to have their own brands. One of its latest additions to the portfolio was Rocket Cat, a whisky infused with cinnamon and which was launched in Scandinavia in May 2016. This was the company´s first contribution to the growing range of flavoured whisky.

Glengoyne, with a magnificent location in the scenic region of the Trossarchs, is situated at the base of Dumgoyne Hill and right on the border between the Lowlands and the Highlands. Every year, around 60,000 visitors come to the distillery which offers no less than seven different tours and tastings.

The distillery is equipped with a 3.8 ton semi lauter mash tun. There are also six Oregon pine washbacks, as well as the rather unusual combination of one wash still and two spirit stills. Both short (56 hours) and long (110 hours) fermentations are practised. In 2016, the production will be split between 10 and 16 mashes per week which constitutes 920,000 litres of alcohol.

The core range of Glengoyne single malts consists of **10, 12, 15, 18, 21** and **25 year old**. The latter was launched in spring 2014 and is bottled at a higher strength (48%) than the rest (40-43%). There is also a **cask strength** (currently at 58.7%) without age statement. Recent limited releases include batch 4 of **The Teapot Dram**. The line-up for duty free is a **15 year old Distiller´s Gold** and a **First Fill 25 year old**. A distillery exclusive bottling is also available, currently a **15 year old single cask**.

History:

1833 The distillery is licensed under the name Burnfoot Distilleries by the Edmonstone family.

1876 Lang Brothers buys the distillery and changes the name to Glenguin.

1905 The name changes to Glengoyne.

1965 Robertson & Baxter takes over Lang Brothers and the distillery is refurbished. The stills are increased from two to three.

2001 Glengoyne Scottish Oak Finish (16 years old) is launched.

2003 Ian MacLeod Distillers Ltd buys the distillery plus the brand Langs from the Edrington Group for £7.2 million.

2005 A 19 year old, a 32 year old and a 37 year old cask strength are launched.

2006 Nine "choices" from Stillmen, Mashmen and Manager are released.

2007 A new version of the 21 year old, two Warehousemen´s Choice, Vintage 1972 and two single casks are released.

2008 A 16 year old Shiraz cask finish, three single casks and Heritage Gold are released.

2009 A 40 year old, two single casks and a new 12 year old are launched.

2010 Two single casks, 1987 and 1997, released.

2011 A 24 year old single cask is released.

2012 A 15 and an 18 year old are released as well as a Cask Strength with no age statement.

2013 A limited 35 year old is launched.

2014 A 25 year old is released.

15 years old

Tasting notes Glengoyne 15 years old:

GS – A nose of vanilla, ginger, toffee, vintage cars leather seats, and sweet fruit notes. The somewhat oily palate features quite lively spices, raisins, hazelnuts, and oak. The finish is medium in length and spicy to the end, with cocoa powder.

Glen Grant

[glen grant]

Owner: **Region/district:**
Campari Group Speyside

Founded:	**Status:**	**Capacity:**
1840	Active (vc)	6 200 000 litres

Address: Elgin Road, Rothes, Banffshire AB38 7BS

Website: **Tel:**
glengrant.com   01340 832118

One of the greatest personalities in the Scotch whisky industry retired as Distillery Manager of Glen Grant in spring 2016, but will remain Master Distiller with the role of overseeing the creation and launching of new Glen Grant expressions.

Dennis Malcolm was born at the Glen Grant malt plant in 1946 and began working at the distillery at the age of 15. During his career, Malcolm has been working at several distilleries in the Speyside area. In 1979 he was appointed manager at The Glenlivet and continued to be responsible for all Chivas Brothers' distilleries until 1999, when he went on to manage Balmenach distillery. Seven years later, he was persuaded by the new owners of Glen Grant, Campari, to come back to his "native" distillery. He was awarded an OBE (Order of the British Empire) in June 2016 for his contributions to the Scotch whisky industry, as well as for his 55 year long career. Dennis Malcolm was succeeded as distillery manager by Greig Stables.

The international breakthrough for Glen Grant single malt came in 1961 when the Italian, Armando Giovinetti, visited the distillery. He was so impressed by the product that he persuaded Douglas Mackessak, to appoint him as agent for Glen Grant in Italy. Glen Grant soon became the best selling malt whisky in Italy and still remains so today. Global sales have declined in the last couple of decades, but as much as 3.4 million bottles were nevertheless sold during 2015, which means that Glen Grant is currently in 8th place of the Top Ten single malts.

The distillery is equipped with a 12.3 ton semi-lauter mash tun, ten Oregon pine washbacks with a minimum fermentation time of 48 hours and four pairs of stills. The wash stills are peculiar in that they have vertical sides at the base of the neck and all eight stills are fitted with purifiers. This gives an increased reflux and creates a light and delicate whisky. A new, extremely efficient £5m bottling hall was inaugurated in 2013. It has a capacity of 12,000 bottles an hour and Glen Grant is the only one of the larger distillers bottling the entire production on site. In 2015 a second bottling line for the premium range was installed. During 2016, whisky will be produced for a total of two thirds of the year, while the same operators will be working in the bottling hall for the remainder of the year. In litres of alcohol, this translates to 2.5 million.

The Glen Grant core range consists of **Major's Reserve** with no age statement, a **5 year old** sold in Italy only and a **10 year old**. Two additions to the core range were made in June 2016 – a **12 year old** matured in both bourbon and sherry casks and an **18 year old** matured in bourbon casks. At the same time, the 16 year old was removed from the range. Summer 2016 also saw the introduction of a **12 year old non chill-filtered** expression bottled at 48% for the duty free market. Recent limited editions include a **50 year old** which was released in Hong Kong in 2014 and **Glen Grant Fiodh**, 43 years old and exclusive to Singapore.

History:

1840 The brothers James and John Grant, managers of Dandelaith Distillery, found the distillery.

1861 The distillery becomes the first to install electric lighting.

1864 John Grant dies.

1872 James Grant passes away and the distillery is inherited by his son, James junior (Major James Grant).

1897 James Grant decides to build another distillery across the road; it is named Glen Grant No. 2.

1902 Glen Grant No. 2 is mothballed.

1931 Major Grant dies and is succeeded by his grandson Major Douglas Mackessack.

1953 J. & J. Grant merges with George & J. G. Smith who runs Glenlivet distillery, forming The Glenlivet & Glen Grant Distillers Ltd.

1961 Armando Giovinetti and Douglas Mackessak found a friendship that eventually leads to Glen Grant becoming the most sold malt whisky in Italy.

1965 Glen Grant No. 2 is back in production, but renamed Caperdonich.

1972 The Glenlivet & Glen Grant Distillers merges with Hill Thompson & Co. and Longmorn-Glenlivet Ltd to form The Glenlivet Distillers. The drum maltings ceases.

History continued:

1973 Stills are increased from four to six.

1977 The Chivas & Glenlivet Group (Seagrams) buys Glen Grant Distillery. Stills are increased from six to ten.

2001 Pernod Ricard and Diageo buy Seagrams Spirits and Wine, with Pernod acquiring the Chivas Group.

2006 Campari buys Glen Grant for €115m.

2007 The entire range is re-packaged and re-launched and a 15 year old single cask is released. Reconstruction of the visitor centre.

2008 Two limited cask strengths - a 16 year old and a 27 year old - are released.

2009 Cellar Reserve 1992 is released.

2010 A 170th Anniversary bottling is released.

2011 A 25 year old is released.

2012 A 19 year old Distillery Edition is released.

2013 Five Decades is released and a bottling hall is built.

2014 A 50 year old and the Rothes Edition 10 years old is released.

2015 Glen Grant Fiodh is launched.

2016 A 12 year old and an 18 year old are launched and a 12 year old non chill-filtered is released for travel retail.

Tasting notes Glen Grant 12 year old:

GS – A blast of fresh fruit – oranges, pears and lemons – on the initial nose, before vanilla and fudge notes develop. The fruit carries over on to the palate, with honey, caramel and sweet spices. Medium in length, with cinnamon and soft oak in the finish.

12 years old   12 years old non chill-filtered   18 years old

10 years old   The Major´s Reserve

Glengyle

[glen•gajl]

Owner:
Mitchell´s Glengyle Ltd

Region/district:
Campbeltown

Founded: **Status:**
2004 Active

Capacity:
750 000 litres

Address: Glengyle Road, Campbeltown, Argyll PA28 6LR

Website:
kilkerran.com

Tel:
01586 551710

This is the year when the whisky from Glengyle will come of age. Admittedly, the first few bottles were already released in 2007 as three year olds, and more have followed every year since 2009 but, all along, the owners have had their minds set on this year´s launch.

Many producers are eager to release their first product, often at a young age and the reason, of course, is to create a positive cash flow. J & A Mitchell, owners of Glengyle, did the same, but mainly to afford the customers the opportunity to follow how the whisky has developed. Fittingly enough, the bottlings were called "Work in progress" so as to emphasise the fact that the final test is yet to come. Now, the end-product is finally ready, a 12 year old Kilkerran which was launched in August 2016. It is a vatting of bourbon- (70%) and sherry-matured (30%) whisky and this will now be the core expression going forward.

The distillery is equipped with a 4 ton semilauter mash tun, four washbacks made of larch with an average fermentation time of 96 hours and one pair of stills. Malt is obtained from the neighbouring Springbank and the same staff also runs operations. The capacity is 750,000 litres, but considerably smaller amounts have been produced over the years. The plan for 2016 is an increase from the previous year, but it shouldn´t involve more than 50,000 litres of alcohol. The production in 2016 will take place in November and December, except for a small run which will happen in August to coincide with the launch of the new 12 year old.

Although the bottlings so far haven´t revealed it, there is a lot of experimentation going on at Glengyle where different wood maturations, peated barley and even quadruple distillations are being used. The idea is to make limited releases from these experiments in the future. The core range now consists of the new **12 year old**, while the final Work in Progress was released in June 2015. As usual, there were two versions, bourbon and sherry, but what was different from previous releases was that they had been bottled at cask strength (54.1%)

History:

1872 The original Glengyle Distillery is built by William Mitchell.

1919 The distillery is bought by West Highland Malt Distilleries Ltd.

1925 The distillery is closed.

1929 The warehouses (but no stock) are purchased by the Craig Brothers and rebuilt into a petrol station and garage.

1941 The distillery is acquired by the Bloch Brothers.

1957 Campbell Henderson applies for planning permission with the intention of reopening the distillery.

2000 Hedley Wright, owner of Springbank Distillery and related to founder William Mitchell, acquires the distillery.

2004 The first distillation after reconstruction takes place in March.

2007 The first limited release - a 3 year old.

2009 Kilkerran "Work in progress" is released.

2010 "Work in progress 2" is released.

2011 "Work in progress 3" is released.

2012 "Work in progress 4" is released.

2013 "Work in progress 5" is released and this time in two versions - bourbon and sherry.

2014 "Work in progress 6" is released in two versions - bourbon and sherry.

2015 "Work in progress 7" is released in two versions - bourbon and sherry.

2016 Kilkerran 12 years old is released.

KILKERRAN

GLENGYLE DISTILLERY

CAMPBELTOWN

SINGLE MALT SCOTCH WHISKY

DISTILLED AT GLENGYLE DISTILLERY

PRODUCT OF SCOTLAND MATURED IN OAK

AGED 12 YEARS

12 years old

Tasting notes Kilkerran 12 year old:

GS – Initially, quite reticent on the nose, then peaty fruit notes develop. Oily and full on the palate, with peaches and more overt smoke, plus an earthy quality. Castor oil and liquorice sticks. Slick in the medium-length finish, with slightly drying oak and enduring liquorice.

The State of Scotch

six burning questions

Martin Markvardsen,
Senior Brand Ambassador,
Highland Park

1. The Millenials are often referred to as perhaps the most important consumer demographic today. Do you think Scotch whisky appeals to that category and what can the producers do to attract them and keep them interested?

It's a very important category of consumers. The industry is fully aware that they are the future. More things are happening on the web today than 10 years ago, such as Twitter tastings, competition etc. To keep them loyal to a single brand may take years as they will investigate differences between the distilleries and different countries. Story telling is a big part of selling whisky today. Every distillery has a story to tell, something for the consumers to associate with, and for them to remember the brand. I think today, it's a lot about involvement. Get people involved in what the distilleries are doing, make them feel part of something.

There is a no correct answer how to attract people as the approach is very different from market to market: having said that, I think to be innovative, and at the same time learn from the past, is something we all have to do. We need to have recruitment malts, but also malts that will keep people loyal.

2. Several Scotch whisky producers have recently questioned the rules what can and can´t be said on the label about the whisky. Should the legislation be changed, allowing more transparency?

Transparency is a good thing, but I don't think it has to be mandatory. For consumers it would be a way to see how the exact batch is put together and would give them an understanding how our whisky maker works. For some markets is would be a negative thing, especially for the brand owner. If the market is monopoly driven, like Finland, Norway, Sweden and Canada, then it would require that we apply for a new listing every time we change the batch. That of course can be solved in the future if the legislation will change.

3. We see more and more Scotch whiskies being bottled without an age statement (NAS). Will that trend continue and, from a consumer point of view, is that all bad?

I´m a big fan of NAS, and looking at the previous question, that's what I mean about having the freedom not always to be transparent. There´s a lot of fantastic NAS malts on the market, and we have to remember, it's NOT a new thing. For years, long before the talk of shortage of stocks in the Scottish warehouses, NAS was out there. I´m so sorry to say this, but today we hear people talking bad about NAS before they even tried it. That really annoys me. If the dram you have in your hand is good, drink it, enjoy it and then let's talk about it.

I honestly don't think that any distilleries today will compromise on the quality of the malts. The diversity in NAS is amazing, gives the whisky maker so many opportunities to create different flavors. What we often see at master classes, are people looking at each other, and agreeing that NAS is not so bad after all. Will the NAS disappear? No, I don't think so and I don't hope so. There might not be as many in the future, and we will see more age statement coming back, but NAS has always been there and will always be there.

4. Not a new discussion but one that does resurface from time to time. Does the quality of a whisky suffer from chill-filtration and colouring?

Well, in general I don't believe you can taste the E150 in whisky, and the test done with chill filtration and no chill filtration have shown the same. So why bother? If the whisky tastes good, isn't that what matters? No, is the simple answer, as we have different consumer groups today. The ones that just began the journey in to the whisky world, they don't have a huge knowledge yet. They go for the easy buy, not too complicated. They have no idea why their whisky goes cloudy, when or if they add water or ice to it. ……then we have the category that wants "the real deal". We need to look at both groups.

I'm a huge fan of not adding color into our malts. If the casks we use provide us with enough colour from the beginning, why adjust. There might be a slight difference in color from batch to batch, but that is what makes it fun to work with. Chill filtration, I still believe we have to do it when we bottle at 40% or 43% abv. Besides that, no reason to do it. The question will come up again and again, and we will see more companies, making more at 46% abv, no chill filtration and no colouring

5. In the steps of flavoured vodka, flavoured whisky has become increasingly popular. Mostly bourbon and Irish whiskey but also Scotch. What are the benefits and downsides of this new trend?

Let me just point out here; Scotch whisky is made from Grain, Yeast and Water. Flavoured mostly by the cask it's been matured in. Peat can be added in the process, when we dry the malt, to create smoke and peaty flavors. This is where the flavours should come from.

The benefits will of course be that we may attract new consumers and that we might get more impact in the on-trade business, but I think Scotch is powerful enough. As a liquor, with honey etc, I find it a great complement to our single malt, but it´s not whisky. Downsides here, will be that we will loose what we actually believe in. I think we can make a lot of "flavoured Scotch" be using cask finish, without adding artificial flavours to it.

6. Scotch whisky exports have declined in the last couple of years. Is the position of Scotch under threat and if so, what can be done to change the trend?

The sales of Scotch whisky have gone up and down the last century. Looking back to the first question about the Millenials, I think this covers it. We need to be better in diversity, stories, special editions, innovation, but never forget the basics and where Scotch whisky comes from. As long as the industry is true to the heritage and production, but still looks at innovation, I think sales will increase again. If I had the right and only answer how we can change the trend, I would probably have a different position in the company.

Glen Keith

[glen keeth]

Owner:
Chivas Brothers
(Pernod Ricard)

Region/district:
Speyside

Founded: 1957

Status: Active

Capacity: 6 000 000 litres

Address: Station Road, Keith, Banffshire AB55 3BU

Website: -

Tel: 01542 783042

For a while, Glen Keith was known as the spiritual home of Passport blended Scotch. The single malt from the distillery has been a substantial part of the popular brand for more than 50 years.

Created in 1965 by the master blender of Chivas Bros. at the time, Jimmy Laing, the blend has been one of the fastest growing during the last decade. In 2005, it was the 24th best selling Scotch and only ten years later it had climbed to place 11 with a sales increase of almost 200%! In 2015 it showed the biggest increase in volumes of all the Top 30 Scotch whiskies and this, in spite of the fact that the number one market for Passport, namely Brazil, is in a deep recession with severely reduced import of whisky as a consequence. Passport, however, is not relying just on one country and in 2015, 23 million bottles were sold to countries as far afield as Mexico, India and Eastern Europe.

Following 13 years of no production, Chivas Brothers started to reignite the work at the distillery in spring 2012. The old Saladin maltings were demolished and part of that area now holds a new building with a Briggs 8 ton full lauter mash tun and six stainless steel washbacks. In the old building there are nine new washbacks made of Oregon pine and six, old but refurbished stills. The stills have extremely long lyne arms and the desired character of the new make spirit is fruity. The distillery was re-opened in April 2013 and now has the capacity to do 6 million litres with the possibility of producing 40 mashes per week.

Glen Keith has sometimes functioned as an experimental workshop for whisky production including triple distillation, malt whisky from column stills and experiments on new strains of yeast. For a short period in the 1970s, there was also the production of two unusual single malts named Craigduff and Glenisla. They were never released by the owners but the independent bottler Signatory, has bottled them both.

The only current, official bottling is a **17 year old** cask strength bottled in 2016 in the new range The Distillery Reserve Collection which can be found at Chivas' visitor centres.

History:

1957 The Distillery is founded by Chivas Brothers (Seagrams).

1958 Production starts.

1970 The first gas-fuelled still in Scotland is installed, the number of stills increases from three to five.

1976 Own maltings (Saladin box) ceases.

1983 A sixth still is installed.

1994 The first official bottling, a 10 year old, is released as part of Seagram's Heritage Selection.

1999 The distillery is mothballed.

2001 Pernod Ricard takes over Chivas Brothers from Seagrams.

2012 The reconstruction and refurbishing of the distillery begins.

2013 Production starts again.

17 year old cask strength

Tasting notes Glen Keith 19 years old:

GS – Malt, cereal, figs and gingery banana on the nose. Smooth and viscous on the palate, white pepper, sweet sherry, fudge, and Madeira cake. Slighlty drying in the lengthy finish.

Glenkinchie

[glen•kin•chee]

Owner:
Diageo

Region/district:
Lowlands

Founded: **Status:** **Capacity:**
1837 Active (vc) 2 500 000 litres

Address: Pencaitland, Tranent,
East Lothian EH34 5ET

Website: **Tel:**
malts.com 01875 342004

One important reason for the huge interest that we see today in single malt whisky, was the introduction of the Classic Malts in 1988. Up until then, the selection of single malts was meagre, to say the least.

Diageo (or United Distillers as it was called at the time) decided to make some of their malts available in pubs and bars. Six of its distilleries were chosen, each one representing a certain region in Scotland and Glenkinchie was selected as an example of a Lowland whisky. But the most brilliant thing about it was the creation of the Classic Malts plinth, with room for all six bottles. This made it much easier for the bars to display the bottles and more visible to the consumers. One of the men behind the idea was James Espey who had been working for several whisky companies (including IDG and Chivas Bros.) with marketing and brand creation. Apart from the Classic Malts, Espey was involved in the development of Johnnie Walker Blue Label, Malibu and Bailey´s. In 2013 he received an OBE from the Queen for his work.

Glenkinchie is equipped with a full lauter mash tun (9 tonnes) and six wooden washbacks with a fermentation time of 60 hours. There is only one pair of stills but they, on the other hand, are very big – in fact, the wash still (30,963 litres) is the biggest in Scotland. Steeply descending lyne arms give very little reflux and condensation of the spirit vapours take place in a cast iron worm tub. In 2016, the distillery will be working a 5-day week with 10 mashes, producing around 2 million litres of alcohol. The proximity to Edinburgh is one reason why more than 40,000 visitors find their way to the distillery and its excellent visitor centre each year. Nowadays there´s even a shuttle bus that takes you straight from Edinburgh city centre to the distillery.

The core range consists of a **12 year old** and a **Distiller´s Edition** with a finish in amontillado sherry casks. There is also a new **distillery exclusive** without age statement. In October 2016, a **24 year old**, distilled in 1991 and bottled at 57.2% was launched as part of the Special Releases.

History:

1825 A distillery known as Milton is founded by John and George Rate.

1837 The Rate brothers are registered as licensees of a distillery named Glenkinchie.

1853 John Rate sells the distillery to a farmer by the name of Christie who converts it to a sawmill.

1881 The buildings are bought by a consortium from Edinburgh.

1890 Glenkinchie Distillery Company is founded. Reconstruction and refurbishment is on-going for the next few years.

1914 Glenkinchie forms Scottish Malt Distillers (SMD) with four other Lowland distilleries.

1939-
1945 Glenkinchie is one of few distilleries allowed to maintain production during the war.

1968 Floor maltings is decommissioned.

1969 The maltings is converted into a museum.

1988 Glenkinchie 10 years becomes one of selected six in the Classic Malt series.

1998 A Distiller's Edition with Amontillado finish is launched.

2007 A 12 year old and a 20 year old cask strength are released.

2010 A cask strength exclusive for the visitor centre, a 1992 single cask and a 20 year old are released.

2016 A 24 year old and a distillery exclusive without age statement are released.

Tasting notes Glenkinchie 12 years old:

GS – The nose is fresh and floral, with spices and citrus fruits, plus a hint of marshmallow. Notably elegant. Water releases cut grass and lemon notes. Medium-bodied, smooth, sweet and fruity, with malt, butter and cheesecake. The finish is comparatively long and drying, initially rather herbal.

12 years old

Glenlivet

[glen•liv•it]

Owner:
Chivas Brothers
(Pernod Ricard)

Region/district:
Speyside

Founded:
1824

Status:
Active (vc)

Capacity:
10 500 000 litres

Address: Ballindalloch, Banffshire AB37 9DB

Website:
theglenlivet.com

Tel:
01340 821720 (vc)

It was in 2014 that Glenlivet managed to break its main rival's, Glenfiddich, 50 year long domination. The brand's position as the world's most sold single malt, however, only lasted a year.

According to figures from the IWSR, Glenfiddich managed in 2015 to sell 143,000 bottles more which meant Glenlivet sold 12,973,000. Despite the setback, the owners can look back at an astonishing sales development for Glenlivet during the past five years with a phenomenal increase of 39% and the brand is still the number one single malt in the important USA market.

The distillery is equipped with a Briggs mash tun (13.5 ton capacity) and 16 wooden washbacks. There are seven pairs of stills, three of which are lined up in a beautiful stillhouse with a stunning view of Glen of the Livet. The plan for 2016 is to do 43 mashes per week which equates to 10.5 million litres of alcohol. A substantial expansion of the distillery is now underway. Construction began in 2015 and the size of the expansion is astounding. With no time frame announced, the plan is to construct two new distillery units towards the back of the existing warehouses. Each unit will consist of one mash tun, 16 washbacks and seven pairs of stills. When the entire expansion is ultimately completed, it would mean that Glenlivet's capacity would have tripled to well over 30 million litres!

The core range of Glenlivet is made up of **Founder's Reserve, 12 year old, 15 year old French Oak Reserve, 18 year old, 21 year old Archive** and **Glenlivet XXV**. A special range of un chill-filtered whiskies called Nadurra include **Nàdurra Oloroso Cask Strength** and **Nàdurra First Fill Selection Cask Strength** for domestic markets and both are also available in duty free, bottled at 48%. Two new expressions were released in autumn 2015 - the **Nàdurra Peated Whisky Cask Finish**, available at both cask strength and a 48% for duty free. The smoky notes come from a finish in casks that had previously held peated Scotch whisky.

The travel retail range also includes **Master Distiller's Reserve, Master Distiller's Reserve Solera Vatted**, as well as **Master Distiller's Reserve Small Batch**, all without age statement. In 2014 a **50 year old** became the inaugural bottling in a new range, The Winchester Collection with a second edition being released in September 2016. Alan Winchester, with 40 years in the industry, is Glenlivet's Master Distiller, as well as Distilling Manager for Chivas Brothers. In spring 2013, Winchester decided to challenge Glenlivet fans with a black bottle where only the alcohol strength was revealed. The idea with **The Glenlivet Alpha** (as it was named) was to get people to speculate what the content would be, based on their personal knowledge and experience. In July 2016, Winchester was in a playful mood again, when he launched **The Glenlivet Cipher** - once again in a black bottle and with the abv as the only information. This time the consumers were challenged to crack the code on the Glenlivet website by creating a flavour wheel with the help of videos and clues from Alan Winchester.

History:

1817 George Smith inherits the farm distillery Upper Drummin from his father Andrew Smith who has been distilling on the site since 1774.

1840 George Smith buys Delnabo farm near Tomintoul and leases Cairngorm Distillery.

1845 George Smith leases three other farms, one of which is situated on the river Livet and is called Minmore.

1846 William Smith develops tuberculosis and his brother John Gordon moves back home to assist his father.

1858 George Smith buys Minmore farm and obtains permission to build a distillery.

1859 Upper Drummin and Cairngorm close and all equipment is brought to Minmore which is renamed The Glenlivet Distillery.

1864 George Smith cooperates with the whisky agent Andrew P. Usher and exports the whisky with great success.

1871 George Smith dies and his son John Gordon takes over.

1880 John Gordon Smith applies for and is granted sole rights to the name The Glenlivet.

1890 A fire breaks out and some of the buildings are replaced.

1896 Another two stills are installed.

1901 John Gordon Smith dies.

1904 John Gordon's nephew George Smith Grant takes over.

1921 Captain Bill Smith Grant, son of George Smith Grant, takes over.

1953 George & J. G. Smith Ltd merges with J. & J. Grant of Glen Grant Distillery and forms the company Glenlivet & Glen Grant Distillers.

1966 Floor maltings closes.

1970 Glenlivet & Glen Grant Distillers Ltd merges with Longmorn-Glenlivet Distilleries Ltd and Hill Thomson & Co. Ltd to form The Glenlivet Distillers Ltd.

History continued:

1978 Seagrams buys The Glenlivet Distillers Ltd. A visitor centre opens.

1996 The visitor centre is expanded, and a multimedia facility installed.

2000 French Oak 12 years and American Oak 12 years are launched

2001 Pernod Ricard and Diageo buy Seagram Spirits & Wine. Pernod Ricard thereby gains control of the Chivas group.

2004 This year sees a lavish relaunch of Glenlivet. French Oak 15 years replaces the previous 12 year old.

2005 Two new duty-free versions are introduced – The Glenlivet 12 year old First Fill and Nadurra. The 1972 Cellar Collection (2,015 bottles) is launched.

2006 Nadurra 16 year old cask strength and 1969 Cellar Collection are released. Glenlivet sells more than 500,000 cases for the first time in one year.

2007 Glenlivet XXV is released.

2009 Four more stills are installed and Nadurra Triumph 1991 is released.

2010 Another two stills are commissioned and capacity increases to 10.5 million litres. Glenlivet Founder's Reserve is released.

2011 Glenlivet Master Distiller's Reserve is released for the duty free market.

2012 1980 Cellar Collection is released.

2013 The 18 year old Batch Reserve and Glenlivet Alpha are released.

2014 Nadurra Oloroso, Nadurra First Fill Selection, The Glenlivet Guardian's Chapter and a 50 year old are released.

2015 Founder's Reserve is released as well as two new expressions for duty free; Solera Vatted and Small Batch.

2016 The Glenlivet Cipher and the second edition of the 50 year old are launched.

Tasting notes Glenlivet 12 year old:

GS – A lovely, honeyed, floral, fragrant nose. Medium-bodied, smooth and malty on the palate, with vanilla sweetness. Not as sweet, however, as the nose might suggest. The finish is pleasantly lengthy and sophisticated.

Tasting notes Glenlivet Founder's Reserve:

GS – The nose is fresh and floral, with ripe pears, pineapple, tangerines, honey and vanilla. Medium-bodied, with ginger nuts, soft toffee and tropical fruit on the smooth palate. Soft spices and lingering fruitiness in the finish.

Master Distiller's Reserve Solera Vatted   Master Distiller's Reserve   The Glenlivet Cipher

21 years old Archive   Nàdurra Peated

Founder's Reserve   15 years old   12 years old

Glenlossie

[glen•loss•ay]

Owner:	**Region/district:**
Diageo	Speyside

Founded:	**Status:**	**Capacity:**
1876	Active	3 700 000 litres

Address: Birnie, Elgin, Morayshire IV30 8SS

Website:	**Tel:**
malts.com	01343 862000

Glenlossie was founded by a consortium of six men in 1876 and the list is a virtual "who-is-who" of the Scotch whisky industry of the late 19th century.

The best known was John Duff who had a background as manager of Glendronach. After ten years at Glenlossie he went abroad for a few years and, unsuccessfully, tried to build distilleries in South Africa and Kentucky. When he returned to Scotland he, together with two of his Glenlossie colleagues (George Thomson and Charles Shirres), founded Longmorn distillery and four years later BenRiach as well. Alexander Grigor Allan left Glenlossie to become part owner of both Talisker and Dailuaine while John Hopkins, a bottler and blender from Glasgow, took over Tobermory in 1890 and later founded Speyburn distillery.

Together with Glenkinchie and Linkwood, Glenlossie is one of the major contributors to the Haig Gold Label blend. During the early 1970s this famous brand was the first Scotch to sell one million cases (12 million bottles) in a year in the UK alone. The slogan that was used is still a classic; "Don´t be vague - ask for Haig". It has dipped in popularity since and parks at about 30th place on the top list with 4 million bottles being sold worldwide last year.

The distillery is equipped with one stainless steel full lauter mash tun (8 tonnes) and eight washbacks made of larch. There are also plans to install a further two stainless steel, exterior washbacks some time in the future. There are three pairs of stills with the spirit stills equipped with purifiers between the lyne arms and the condensers, thus increasing the reflux which, together with the 75-80 hour fermentation time, gives Glenlossie newmake its light and green/grassy character. A 5-day production is planned for 2016 with 12 mashes per week and 2 million litres for the year. Next to Glenlossie lies the much younger Mannochmore distillery and except for the two distilleries, a dark grains plant and a newly constructed bio-plant, the site also holds fourteen warehouses that can store 250,000 casks of maturing whisky.

The only official bottling of Glenlossie available today is a **10 year old**.

History:

1876 John Duff, former manager at Glendronach Distillery, founds the distillery. Alexander Grigor Allan (to become part-owner of Talisker Distillery), the whisky trader George Thomson and Charles Shirres (both will co-found Longmorn Distillery some 20 years later with John Duff) and H. Mackay are also involved in the company.

1895 The company Glenlossie-Glenlivet Distillery Co. is formed. Alexander Grigor Allan passes away.

1896 John Duff becomes more involved in Longmorn and Mackay takes over management of Glenlossie.

1919 Distillers Company Limited (DCL) takes over the company.

1929 A fire breaks out and causes considerable damage.

1930 DCL transfers operations to Scottish Malt Distillers (SMD).

1962 Stills are increased from four to six.

1971 Another distillery, Mannochmore, is constructed by SMD on the premises. A dark grains plant is installed.

1990 A 10 year old is launched in the Flora & Fauna series.

2010 A Manager´s Choice single cask from 1999 is released.

Tasting notes Glenlossie 10 years old:

GS – Cereal, silage and vanilla notes on the relatively light nose, with a voluptuous, sweet palate, offering plums, ginger and barley sugar, plus a hint of oak. The finish is medium in length, with grist and slightly peppery oak.

10 years old

The State of Scotch

six burning questions

Eddie Ludlow,
Whisky Evangelist,
The Whisky Lounge

1. The Millenials are often referred to as perhaps the most important consumer demographic today. Do you think Scotch whisky appeals to that category and what can the producers do to attract them and keep them interested?

Scotch whisky should and could appeal to this category of consumer but I think it needs to decide whether it is prepared to change – even slightly – with the times in order to do so. If we look at the real ale market and the proliferation of 'craft' beer in recent times, it is a far cry from the old days of the stereotypical warm, flat British pint of beer. Whether you like it or not, it is an exciting and vibrant marketplace now with exactly this type of consumer fully bought in paying very good money for it. Even the older, more established brewers have caught 'craft fever' and are doing the best to keep up.

Obviously it is slightly more difficult to get into making whisky as opposed to beer, and even if you do, you have to wait in reality 5-6 years before having anything half-way decent.

I think, therefore, the Scotch industry needs to look at itself and ask itself 'what do we want to look like' in the coming years.

2. Several Scotch whisky producers have recently questioned the rules what can and can´t be said on the label about the whisky. Should the legislation be changed, allowing more transparency?

I think, going back to the first question, that it is increasingly important that the SWA allows more transparency and therefore the ability to give consumers answers to the questions they might have on the bottle. Consumers are more and more informed and want to know what it is they are consuming. Surely this is a fundamental right and is of benefit to (nearly) all?

Absolutely look after the 'spirit' of Scotch and continue to defend it globally, but let John Glaser and other pioneers have fun, innovate and continue to help invigorate Scotch and bring us interesting and challenging products. In short I believe the current rules need to be assessed broadly and amended where needed to allow a bit more lee-way and not to the detriment of the rest of the industry.

3. We see more and more Scotch whiskies being bottled without an age statement (NAS). Will that trend continue and, from a consumer point of view, is that all bad?

I think the trend will continue until the current 'bubble' bursts, if indeed it does. Some of the best whiskies of old, that I continue to enjoy and recommend, such as Aberlour A'bunadh, Glenfarclas 105 and Ardbeg Uigeadail, are NAS. I have no problem with them at all if they are good whiskies, however there has been a trend, particularly in travel retail for nothing but NAS and not all of them are good. With the current stock situation for more mature casks apparently so desperate in Scotland I don't think this will end soon. I do think if distillers are more careful with the selection and vatting of NAS whiskies, there is no reason these cannot be of better quality

4. Not a new discussion but one that does resurface from time to time. Does the quality of a whisky suffer from chill-filtration and colouring?

I don't think this rule can be applied so generally. Some well-known and loved whiskies – single malt and blend alike – have undergone this process and it doesn't seem to affect their flavour or popularity. So many experts and distillers are divided by this subject and it is often difficult to discern what the right answer is. I think most of us, as whisky-lovers, would love to see all single malt, at least, non or unchill-filtered but it isn't going to happen. We are a small part of the whisky machine and the majority of whisky drinkers are not aware of these terms. Until they are and they demand the same we will not have a 'revolution'!

However, the good news is that even the larger distillers are recognising the benefits at least of keeping us geeks happy and are releasing more and more bottlings at 46% and unchill-filtered. So there is a choice out there, but I would never say dismiss a whisky purely on the basis of it not being unchill-filtered as you may well be missing out due to some miss-placed snobbery!

5. In the steps of flavoured vodka, flavoured whisky has become increasingly popular. Mostly bourbon and Irish whiskey but also Scotch. What are the benefits and downsides of this new trend?

The benefits are that it opens up the category to consumers who would otherwise be drinking something else. The idea being that the same consumer will 'graduate' to non-flavoured single malts or blends at some point in the future. I think the only downsides are the perception of those distillers producing these products by people who really don't see the point in them. I doubt I will be drinking them personally, as I think there is more than enough flavour already in most whiskies, but if it gets others into drinking and thinking whisky then I do not see the harm.

6. Scotch whisky exports have declined in the last couple of years. Is the position of Scotch under threat and if so, what can be done to change the trend?

I think if there was another country with aged stocks a-plenty of good whisky then the answer might be yes, it is under threat. However, there isn't. World whiskies that have garnered a lot of – well-deserved – attention, tend to be produced in much smaller quantities and are therefore a niche within a niche. Japan could possibly have challenged but their prices have risen beyond the point of being close to Scotch whiskies. Bourbon and particularly, so-called craft whiskies from the States are interesting and provide a shot in the arm to the market as a whole, but I don't think they present a threat to Scotch's position in the market.

However, it is vital that the Scotch market 'keeps up' with developments and doesn't stagnate. Education is also key. Stop bandying around stupid myths and hearsay regarding how aromas and flavours magically appear in the whisky. Be more open, transparent, innovative and be proud!

Glenmorangie

[glen•mor•run•jee]

Owner:
The Glenmorangie Co
(Moët Hennessy)

Region/district:
Northern Highlands

Founded:
1843

Status:
Active (vc)

Capacity:
6 000 000 litres

Address: Tain, Ross-shire IV19 1PZ

Website:
glenmorangie.com

Tel:
01862 892477 (vc)

Scotch single malt may have been bottled and sold overseas since the early 20th century, but not until the 1960s was it being promoted actively and the advantages of getting a head start are obvious.

Glenfiddich was first, followed by Glenlivet, Macallan and Glenmorangie and these four brands are still the Top 4 in sales more than 50 years later. In the beginning, promoting whisky was very much about lifestyle advertising and aimed mainly at reminding current consumers about the existence of the whisky, rather than attracting new ones. Glenmorangie went against the current trend when they in 1981 launched their highly successful "The 16 Men of Tain" campaign which would run for more than 25 years. The relevance here was to explain to the customer how much work went into the making of a bottle of Glenmorangie and, by featuring the people behind it, make them understand that it was a craft. Glenmorangie today, is the fourth most sold single malt in the world and has increased by 85% in the last seven years, not least in America. In 2015, 6.1 million bottles were sold.

The distillery is equipped with a full lauter mash tun with a charge of 10 tonnes, 12 stainless steel washbacks with a fermentation time of 52 hours and six pairs of stills. They are the tallest in Scotland and the still room is one of the most magnificent to be seen. Production for 2016 will be 32 mashes per week which equates to 6 million litres in the year.

The core range consists of **Original** (10 year old), **18** and **25 year old**. There are three 12 year old wood finishes: **Quinta Ruban** (port), **Nectar D'Or** (Sauternes) and **Lasanta** (sherry). Added to the core range is **Signet**, an unusual piece of work with 20% of the whisky having been made using chocolate malt. A series of bottlings, called Private Edition, started in 2009 with the release of the sherried **Sonnalta PX**. This has been followed up once a year with lightly peated **Finealta**, **Artein** extra matured in Sassicaia casks, **Ealanta** which was fully matured in virgin American oak, **Companta** which was a selection of whiskies matured for 14-18 years in a variety of casks and **Tùsail** which was made from floor malted Maris Otter. The 7th release appeared in February 2016 when **Milsean** was launched. Matured in ex-bourbon casks it was then finished in re-toasted ex-wine casks. In autumn 2015 **A Midwinter's Dram**, a vatting of ex-bourbon and ex-oloroso casks, was released as an exclusive to the UK market but will be made available in other countries during 2016. Glenmorangie has not been prioritising bottlings made for the travel retail market, but this changed in 2014 when **Dornoch**, extra matured in Amontillado sherry casks, was released. Soon after, a whole new duty free range (Glenmorangie's Legends) was presented. The first expression was **Duthac**, a vatting of whiskies matured in bourbon casks, PX sherry casks and charred, virgin oak casks. In spring 2016, two more bottlings in the range were released; **Tayne**, aged in amontillado sherry casks and **Tarlogan** with a maturation in both virgin oak and ex-bourbon casks.

History:

1843 William Mathesen applies for a license for a farm distillery called Morangie, which is rebuilt by them. Production took place here in 1738, and possibly since 1703.

1849 Production starts in November.

1880 Exports to foreign destinations such as Rome and San Francisco commence.

1887 The distillery is rebuilt and Glenmorangie Distillery Company Ltd is formed.

1918 40% of the distillery is sold to Macdonald & Muir Ltd and 60 % to the whisky dealer Durham. Macdonald & Muir takes over Durham's share by the late thirties.

1931 The distillery closes.

1936 Production restarts in November.

1980 Number of stills increases from two to four and own maltings ceases.

1990 The number of stills is doubled to eight.

1994 A visitor centre opens. September sees the launch of Glenmorangie Port Wood Finish which marks the start of a number of different wood finishes.

1995 Glenmorangie's Tain l'Hermitage (Rhone wine) is launched.

1996 Two different wood finishes are launched, Madeira and Sherry. Glenmorangie plc is formed.

1997 A museum opens.

2001 A limited edition of a cask strength port wood finish is released in July, Cote de Beaune Wood Finish is launched in September and Three Cask (ex-Bourbon, charred oak and ex-Rioja) is launched in October for Sainsbury's.

2002 A Sauternes finish, a 20 year Glenmorangie with two and a half years in Sauternes casks, is launched.

History continued:

2003 Burgundy Wood Finish is launched in July and a limited edition of cask strength Madeira-matured (i. e. not just finished) in August.

2004 Glenmorangie buys the Scotch Malt Whisky Society. The Macdonald family decides to sell Glenmorangie plc (including the distilleries Glenmorangie, Glen Moray and Ardbeg) to Moët Hennessy at £300 million. A new version of Glenmorangie Tain l´Hermitage (28 years) is released and Glenmorangie Artisan Cask is launched in November.

2005 A 30 year old is launched.

2007 The entire range gets a complete makeover with 15 and 30 year olds being discontinued and the rest given new names as well as new packaging.

2008 An expansion of production capacity is started. Astar and Signet are launched.

2009 The expansion is finished and Sonnalta PX is released for duty free.

2010 Glenmorangie Finealta is released.

2011 28 year old Glenmorangie Pride is released.

2012 Glenmorangie Artein is released.

2013 Glenmorangie Ealanta is released.

2014 Companta, Taghta and Dornoch are released.

2015 Túsail and Duthac are released.

2016 Milsean, Tayne and Tarlogan are released.

Tasting notes Glenmorangie Original 10 year old:
GS – The nose offers fresh fruits, butterscotch and toffee. Silky smooth in the mouth, mild spice, vanilla, and well-defined toffee. The fruity finish has a final flourish of ginger.

Tayne   Milsean   Tarlogan

Original 10 years old   Signet   Nectar D´Or

Glen Moray

[glen mur•ree]

Owner: La Martiniquaise (COFEPP)
Region/district: Speyside

Founded: 1897
Status: Active (vc)
Capacity: 5 700 000 litres

Address: Bruceland Road, Elgin, Morayshire IV30 1YE

Website: glenmoray.com
Tel: 01343 542577

Increased sales of Label 5 blended Scotch, where Glen Moray malt plays an important part, is one of the reasons for the expansion recently seen at Glen Moray distillery.

Label 5 is now the 9th best selling Scotch in the world with 31 million bottles. But this is not the only reason for the increased production. For Glen Moray single malt, the last few years have also led to increased sales. During the last year alone, volumes were up by 15% to 1.2 million bottles and it is now the fifth best selling single malt in the UK.

Since March 2016, the distillery is equipped with a new, highly efficient 11 ton full lauter mash tun with a 3 hour mash cycle compared to the previous one with a 7.5 hour cycle. There are 14 stainless steel washbacks placed outside with a fermentation time of 50-60 hours and nine stills. The three old wash stills were converted to spirit stills which make it a total of six and three new wash stills were constructed by Frilli in Italy. This means that the capacity has now gone from 3.3 million litres of alcohol to 5.7 million, but the owners have the option of reintroducing the old mash tun, adding a few more washbacks and two more wash stills which would increase the capacity to 8.9 million litres.

The distillery has been producing 7 days per week for many years and for 2016 that means 4.7 million litres, of which 250,000 litres will be heavily peated (50ppm) spirit. Peated production is fairly new to the distillery and did not start until 2009.

The Glen Moray single malt core range consists of **Classic, Classic Port** and **Classic Peated**. At the beginning of 2016, the range was expanded with **Classic Chardonnay Finish** and, in June, with a **Classic Sherry Finish**. All of them are without age statement. Furthermore, we can also find a **12 year old**, while the 10- and 16 year old will both be phased out, to be replaced by a **15-** and an **18 year old**. Recent limited releases include batch 3 of the **25 year old Port finish** and a collection of **1994 vintage** bottlings exclusively for the visitor centre.

History:

1897 West Brewery, dated 1828, is reconstructed as Glen Moray Distillery.

1910 The distillery closes.

1920 Financial troubles force the distillery to be put up for sale. Buyer is Macdonald & Muir.

1923 Production restarts.

1958 A reconstruction takes place and the floor maltings are replaced by a Saladin box.

1978 Own maltings are terminated.

1979 Number of stills is increased to four.

1996 Macdonald & Muir Ltd changes name to Glenmorangie plc.

1999 Three wood finishes are introduced - Chardonnay (no age) and Chenin Blanc (12 and 16 years respectively).

2004 Louis Vuitton Moët Hennessy buys Glenmorangie plc and a 1986 cask strength, a 20 and a 30 year old are released.

2005 The Fifth Chapter (Manager's Choice from Graham Coull) is released.

2006 Two vintages, 1963 and 1964, and a new Manager's Choice are released.

2007 New edition of Mountain Oak is released.

2008 The distillery is sold to La Martiniquaise.

2009 A 14 year old Port finish and an 8 year old matured in red wines casks are released.

2011 Two cask finishes and a 10 year old Chardonnay maturation are released.

2012 A 2003 Chenin Blanc is released.

2013 A 25 year old port finish is released.

2014 Glen Moray Classic Port Finish is released.

2015 Glen Moray Classic Peated is released.

2016 Classic Chardonnay Finish and Classic Sherry Finish are released as well as a 15 and an 18 year old.

Classic Peated

Tasting notes Glen Moray 12 years old:

GS – Mellow on the nose, with vanilla, pear drops and some oak. Smooth in the mouth, with spicy malt, vanilla and summer fruits. The finish is relatively short, with spicy fruit.

Glen Ord

[glen ord]

Owner:
Diageo

Region/district:
Northern Highlands

Founded: **Status:**
1838   Active (vc)

Capacity:
11 000 000 litres

Address: Muir of Ord, Ross-shire IV6 7UJ

Website:
malts.com

Tel:
01463 872004 (vc)

It only took ten years after the launch for The Singleton to become the world's fifth biggest single malt in terms of volume. Admittedly, the brand is made up of malts from three different distilleries, but the development is nonetheless impressive.

Of the three, Glen Ord is the biggest seller and, until recently, it could only be found in the Asian markets. Since autumn 2015, however, all three Singleton varieties (including Glendullan and Dufftown) can be found globally. The reason for this is Diageo's ambition to propel the Singleton brand to the world's number one single malt in the future.

Since 2011, Glen Ord distillery has been expanded rapidly in several stages and with the latest expansion in 2015, the distillery now has an impressive capacity of 11 million litres, making it the fifth biggest malt distillery in Scotland. The complete set of equipment now comprises of two stainless steel mashtuns, each with a 12.5 ton mash. There are 22 wooden washbacks with a fermentation time of 75 hours and no less than 14 stills. The expansion has been carried out in such a way that buildings being more than a century old (the old kiln and malt storage, as well as the Saladin maltings), have been elegantly utilized to house the new equipment. A major part of the site is occupied by the Glen Ord Maltings which was built in 1968. Equipped with 18 drums and with a capacity of 37,000 tonnes per year, it produces malt for several other Diageo distilleries. The excellent distillery visitor centre is well worth a visit and is to be found in the Visit Scotland top ten attractions.

The core range is the **Singleton of Glen Ord 12, 15** and **18 year old**. In 2013 a new sub-range, The Singleton Reserve Collection, exclusive to duty free, was launched. The first release was **Singleton of Glen Ord Signature**, followed by **Trinité**, **Liberté** and **Artisan**. Limited releases include a **32** and a **35 year old**, as well as a **cask strength**. The latest addition was **The Master's Casks 40 year old**, making it the oldest expression from the distillery so far. Only 999 bottles were released during the spring of 2015.

History:

1838 Thomas Mackenzie founds the distillery.

1855 Alexander MacLennan and Thomas McGregor buy the distillery.

1870 Alexander MacLennan dies and the distillery is taken over by his widow who marries the banker Alexander Mackenzie.

1877 Alexander Mackenzie leases the distillery.

1878 Alexander Mackenzie builds a new still house and barely manages to start production before a fire destroys it.

1896 Alexander Mackenzie dies and the distillery is sold to James Watson & Co. for £15,800.

1923 John Jabez Watson, James Watson's son, dies and the distillery is sold to John Dewar & Sons. The name changes from Glen Oran to Glen Ord.

1961 A Saladin box is installed.

1966 The two stills are increased to six.

1968 Drum maltings is built.

1983 Malting in the Saladin box ceases.

1988 A visitor centre is opened.

2002 A 12 year old is launched.

2003 A 28 year old cask strength is released.

2004 A 25 year old is launched.

2005 A 30 year old is launched as a Special Release from Diageo.

2006 A 12 year old Singleton of Glen Ord is launched.

2010 A Singleton of Glen Ord 15 year old is released in Taiwan.

2011 Two more washbacks are installed, increasing the capacity by 25%.

2012 Singleton of Glen Ord cask strength is released.

2013 Singleton of Glen Ord Signature, Trinité, Liberté and Artisan are launched.

2015 The Master's Casks 40 years old is released.

Tasting notes Glen Ord 12 years old:

GS – Honeyed malt and milk chocolate on the nose, with a hint of orange. These characteristics carry over onto the sweet, easy-drinking palate, along with a biscuity note. Subtly drying, with a medium-length, spicy finish.

12 years old

Glenrothes

[glen•roth•iss]

Owner: **Region/district:**
The Edrington Group   Speyside
(the brand is owned by Berry Bros)

Founded: **Status:**   **Capacity:**
1878   Active   5 600 000 litres

Address: Rothes, Morayshire AB38 7AA

Website: **Tel:**
theglenrothes.com   01340 872300

Glenrothes single malt has always been a favourite with the blenders. It became a part of Famous Grouse in 1896 and since the 1930s it has been vital for the character of Cutty Sark.

But it is the irony of fate that high quality sometimes puts a halt for a "quareer" of its own. It was simply too valuable for the blends to be launched as a single malt. It wasn't until 1994 that they decided to start bottling Glenrothes single malt. Thereafter, it didn't take long for the consumers to open their eyes to the dumpy bottle and the unusual concept of releasing vintages and, today, the brand sells around 800,000 bottles per year.

Glenrothes distillery is equipped with a 5.5 ton stainless steel full lauter mash tun. Twelve washbacks made of Oregon pine are in one room, whilst an adjacent modern tun room houses eight new stainless steel washbacks - all of them with a 58 hour fermentation time. The magnificent, cathedral-like still house has five pairs of stills performing a very slow distillation. In 2016, the distillery will be doing 44 mashes per week, producing just over 4 million litres of alcohol.

Even though Glenrothes started releasing bottlings ten years ago, without either vintage nor age statement, the vintages are admittedly the ones that have made the brand famous. Some of the more recent ones include the **1988, 1992, 1995** and **2001** vintages. Other core expressions include the **Select Reserve, Bourbon Cask Reserve** (formerly known as Alba Reserve), **Sherry Cask Reserve, Vintage Reserve** (made up of ten different vintages from 1989 to 2007) and, the latest edition, **Peated Cask Reserve.** The latter contains whisky from 1992 which has had additional maturation in casks that have formerly held Islay malt. The duty free range includes **Robur Reserve, Manse Reserve, Elder´s Reserve, Minister´s Reserve** and the exclusive **Oldest Reserve**, which is a vatting of vintages from 1971 to 1998. An addition to the range in 2016 was the **25 year old Ancestor´s Reserve.** Recent, limited releases include single casks from **1968, 1969** and **1970**.

History:

1878 James Stuart & Co. begins planning the new distillery with Robert Dick, William Grant and John Cruickshank as partners. Stuart has financial problems so Dick, Grant and Cruickshank terminate the partnership and continue the building.

1879 Production starts in December.

1884 The distillery changes name to Glenrothes-Glenlivet.

1887 William Grant & Co. joins forces with Islay Distillery Co. and forms Highland Distillers Company.

1897 A fire ravages the distillery.

1903 An explosion causes substantial damage.

1963 Expansion from four to six stills.

1980 Expansion from six to eight stills.

1989 Expansion from eight to ten stills.

1999 Edrington and William Grant & Sons buy Highland Distillers.

2002 Four single casks from 1966/1967 are launched.

2005 A 30 year old is launched together with Select Reserve and Vintage 1985.

2007 A 25 year old is released as a duty free item.

2008 1978 Vintage and Robur Reserve are launched.

2009 The Glenrothes John Ramsay, Alba Reserve and Three Decades are released.

2010 Berry Brothers takes over the brand.

2011 Editor´s Casks are released.

2013 2001 Vintage and the Manse Brae range are released.

2014 Sherry Cask Reserve and 1969 Extraordinary Cask are released.

2015 Glenrothes Vintage Single Malt is released.

2016 Peated Cask Reserve and Ancestor´s Reserve are released.

Select Reserve

Tasting notes Glenrothes Select Reserve:

GS – The nose offers ripe fruits, spice and toffee, with a whiff of Golden Syrup. Faint wood polish in the mouth, vanilla, spicy and slightly citric. Creamy and complex. Slightly nutty, with some orange, in the drying finish.

The State of Scotch

six burning questions

Euan Shand,
Owner and Chairman,
Duncan Taylor Scotch Whisky

1. The Millenials are often referred to as perhaps the most important consumer demographic today. Do you think Scotch whisky appeals to that category and what can the producers do to attract them and keep them interested?

I have never heard of this reference but since you have stated it, I have not found the Millenials to be the most important consumer demographic for the types of whiskies sold under my brands. I observe the Millenials in general as a group who look at whiskies as a product to mix with whatever fashionable mixer may be around. Our experience is of this group as well as others in International markets having a focus on mixology, the adulteration of fine whiskies. I´m fine with that if that is what they want to do. In the end of the day it´s consumer choice, they are buying it, do what they wish with it.

My only hope is that it may lead to them in the future to finding the beauty of Scotch in the purest form. Our modus operandi is to supply whiskies to all types of clients. We have never singled out a particular client group, whether that be Millenials or Octogenarians. We don't design for fashion, we produce for longevity. Millenials are very important to us but no more important than other age groups.

2. Several Scotch whisky producers have recently questioned the rules what can and can´t be said on the label about the whisky. Should the legislation be changed, allowing more transparency?

The legislation should be loose, to allow producers such as myself the opportunity to educate, to allow the consumer a chance to see the complexity of our brands, to understand the character of the finished product. There is nothing negative in letting people know exactly what they have in the glass. Tight legislation such as what is around today does nothing to further the interests of consumers, it protects brands that I suppose need to be protected in that they could be copied. Though copying the character of a brand in the whisky industry is not a huge hurdle, the taste profile can easily be done, so in the end of the day the legislation is rubbish. I´m all for transparency.

3. We see more and more Scotch whiskies being bottled without an age statement (NAS). Will that trend continue and, from a consumer point of view, is that all bad?

I have no concern about non age statement provided it does not obscure or dupe the consumer. As we all know a few years back a major drinks company substituted its single malt for a blended malt but retained the original design and packaging – that is misleading and downright dishonest. Also for example the inference of a product previously recognised as say a 12 year old having the same livery but now released containing an 8 year old, because the producer just didn't have enough stock, is immoral and wrong. In the end of the day it´s all down to taste and preference, let the consumer decide!

I can see the NAS trend continuing and no, I have no issue with it. As far as the consumer is concerned it should not prevent them from trying a brand. Age can be immaterial, its down to the quality and character of that brand and its perception by the consumer. I cant imagine anyone in the industry wants to sell an inferior whisky. If they do then it´s commercial suicide.

4. Not a new discussion but one that does resurface from time to time. Does the quality of a whisky suffer from chill-filtration and colouring?

Yes, it suffers! Whiskies that have gone through this process are substantially inferior to those that have not. I can name some major brands that to my taste are tainted by chemical colourings. Undrinkable. I fully understand that not everyone wants to drink a 46% plus whisky and that 40% is the industry norm, it does allow whiskies to go further by reducing with water and some people have the taste for blander whiskies so once again if consumers like it that way then all power to their elbows!

5. In the steps of flavoured vodka, flavoured whisky has become increasingly popular. Mostly bourbon and Irish whiskey but also Scotch. What are the benefits and downsides of this new trend?

Benefits being that it introduces whisky to the Millenials as discussed above, there can´t be any downsides as people have choice. They can do what they want – buy flavoured or non flavoured. If it introduces people to the huge and diverse character of Scotch Whisky then great. Over time I´m sure the flavoured stuff will become a little "wearing" and the consumers will move on as purists.

6. Scotch whisky exports have declined in the last couple of years. Is the position of Scotch under threat and if so, what can be done to change the trend?

No, it´s not under threat. Having been in this industry since 1973, I have seen threats come and go. It´s the nature of business, of trends, of fashions, of life. If we didn't have variation, life would be boring. The opinion over the past 20 years is that vodka would finish the Scotch Whisky industry. It hasn't. New, more marketed, brown spirits from Japan and the US have crept in and have found favour, but trends come and go. There is no great threat to Scotch Whisky, it is still one of the most consumed brown spirits in the world and will stay that way.

Of course it has peaks and troughs. Look at the price of a barrel of oil – I can´t see windpower knocking gasoline out over my lifetime, well not in the US anyway! The only threat to Scotch whisky is from the producers themselves, multinationals who have marketing teams chasing the next fashion. I watch our "esteemed" critics who are so easily influenced by fashion being drawn into "The Worlds Best Whisky" scenario, so much crap comes out of this, but that's life. Scotch Whisky will continue as it has done for hundreds of years. Yes, it will face hurdles but non more so than letting critics denounce the category for their own personal gain. Fashionistas will come and go. Investment bandwagons will come and go but Scotch whisky has been around for 100's of years and will stay that way. In my opinion there is no other spirit with the character and dimensions of Scotch Whisky.

Glen Scotia

[glen sko•sha]

Owner:
Loch Lomond Group
(majority owner Exponent)

Region/district:
Campbeltown

Founded: 1832
Status: Active (vc)
Capacity: 800 000 litres

Address: High Street, Campbeltown, Argyll PA28 6DS

Website: glenscotia.com
Tel: 01586 552288

From 1934, when Rieclachan closed, only two distilleries struggled on in what used to be called the whisky capital of the world, Campbeltown, on the southern point of the Kintyre peninsula, where no less than 33 distilleries were founded.

One such distillery, Springbank, achieved a cult status over time with a devoted crowd of fans. The other, Glen Scotia, was suffering from multiple changes in ownership and poor maintenance. This started to change a few years back and with new owners since 2014, it seems as if the distillery has a bright future. A substantial financial investment and an exciting new range of malts has put the distillery back on the map.

Glen Scotia is equipped with a traditional 2.8 ton cast iron mash tun, nine washbacks made of stainless steel and one pair of stills. The shortest fermentation time is 70 hours but can reach over 100 hours. For some years, the distillery had a very short middle cut (possibly the shortest in the industry), starting to collect the spirit at 71% and stopping at 68%. This has now changed and they come off spirit at 63%. The production in 2016 will be 10 mashes per week resulting in 500,000 litres of pure alcohol, of which 9% is a combination of lightly peated (17ppm) and heavily peated (54ppm) spirit.

Glen Scotia has been thoroughly upgraded and renovated during the last couple of years which includes a visitor centre which incorporates a tasting area and a shop. Warehousing capacity has also increased and the spirit produced is now stored on site.

Since spring 2015, the core range consists of three expressions; **Double Cask** (matured in bourbon casks and with a 3-4 months finish in PX sherry), **15 year old** (American oak and a short finish in oloroso casks) and the gently peated **Victoriana** which has been bottled at cask strength. A number of **single cask** bottlings available only at the distillery, have been released, the latest being on the Open Day of the distillery in May 2016.

History:

1832 The families of Stewart and Galbraith start Scotia Distillery.

1895 The distillery is sold to Duncan McCallum.

1919 Sold to West Highland Malt Distillers.

1924 West Highland Malt Distillers goes bankrupt and Duncan MacCallum buys back the distillery.

1928 The distillery closes.

1930 Duncan MacCallum commits suicide and the Bloch brothers take over.

1933 Production restarts.

1954 Hiram Walker takes over.

1955 A. Gillies & Co. becomes new owner.

1970 A. Gillies & Co. becomes part of Amalgated Distillers Products.

1979 Reconstruction takes place.

1984 The distillery closes.

1989 Amalgated Distillers Products is taken over by Gibson International and production restarts.

1994 Glen Catrine Bonded Warehouse Ltd takes over and the distillery is mothballed.

1999 The distillery re-starts under Loch Lomond Distillery supervision using labour from Springbank.

2000 Loch Lomond Distillers runs operations with its own staff from May onwards.

2005 A 12 year old is released.

2006 A peated version is released.

2012 A new range (10, 12, 16, 18 and 21 year old) is launched.

2014 A 10 year old and one without age statement are released - both heavily peated.

2015 A new range is released; Double Cask, 15 year old and Victoriana.

Tasting notes Glen Scotia Double Cask:

GS – The nose is sweet, with bramble and redcurrant aromas, plus caramel and vanilla. Smooth mouth-feel, with ginger, sherry and more vanilla. The finish is quite long, with spicy sherry and a final hint of brine.

Double Cask

Glen Spey

[glen spey]

Owner:	**Region/district:**
Diageo	Speyside
Founded: **Status:**	**Capacity:**
1878 Active	1 400 000 litres

Address: Rothes, Morayshire AB38 7AU

Website:	**Tel:**
malts.com	01340 831215

When W & A Gilbey bought Glen Spey in 1887, they became the first English company to buy a Scottish distillery. In the ensuing years they would acquire another two – Knockando and Strathmill.

For more than a century, W & A Gilbey was one of the most influential wine & spirits companies in the world. Today the name is surprisingly unknown, except for the gin which still carries the company's name. The two Gilbey brothers (later joined by a third) started as wine merchants in the mid 1800s and soon became involved in all aspects of the alcohol business. Apart from the three distilleries in Scotland, they also founded a distillery in Canada which made Black Velvet whisky and Smirnoff vodka. Subsequent to this, they took over a chateau in Bordeaux and they launched Spey Royal which still is one of Thailand's best-selling blended whiskies. When the company peaked, it had 22 distilleries in 18 countries. In 1962, the independence of the company was over when they merged with another company and a decade later it was absorbed by Grand Metropolitan and then Diageo.

The single malt from Glen Spey has its biggest importance in the blend J&B, where it is one of the signature malts. Ten years ago J&B was the second most sold Scotch after Johnnie Walker, but has since lost more than a third of its sales and now finds itself in fifth place with 43 million bottles being sold during 2015. The decline for J&B, which has its biggest market in southern Europe, was somewhat smaller during 2015 than the previous year and with the launch of a flavoured version in 2014 (J&B Urban Honey) Diageo is trying to create a new interest in the brand.

Glen Spey, hidden away in a side street in Rothes, is equipped with a semi-lauter mash tun, eight stainless steel washbacks and two pairs of stills, where the spirit stills are equipped with purifiers to obtain a lighter character of the spirit.

The core expression is the **12 year old** Flora & Fauna bottling. In 2010, two limited releases were made – a **1996 single cask** from new American Oak and a **21 year old** with maturation in ex-sherry American oak.

History:

1878 James Stuart & Co. founds the distillery which becomes known by the name Mill of Rothes.

1886 James Stuart buys Macallan.

1887 W. & A. Gilbey buys the distillery for £11,000 thus becoming the first English company to buy a Scottish malt distillery.

1920 A fire breaks out.

1962 W. & A. Gilbey combines forces with United Wine Traders and forms International Distillers & Vintners (IDV).

1970 The stills are increased from two to four.

1972 IDV is bought by Watney Mann which is then acquired by Grand Metropolitan.

1997 Guiness and Grand Metropolitan merge to form Diageo.

2001 A 12 year old is launched in the Flora & Fauna series.

2010 A 21 year old is released as part of the Special Releases and a 1996 Manager's Choice single cask is launched.

12 years old

Tasting notes Glen Spey 12 years old:

GS – Tropical fruits and malt on the comparatively delicate nose. Medium-bodied with fresh fruits and vanilla toffee on the palate, becoming steadily nuttier and drier in a gently oaky, mildly smoky finish.

Glentauchers

[glen•tock•ers]

Owner:
Chivas Brothers
(Pernod Ricard)

Region/district:
Speyside

Founded: 1897

Status: Active

Capacity: 4 200 000 litres

Address: Mulben, Keith, Banffshire AB55 6YL

Website: -

Tel: 01542 860272

James Buchanan, who founded Glentauchers in 1897, arrived in London thirteen years earlier to start his own business as a whisky blender. It was a booming market with fierce competition, but Buchanan differed from his competitors.

The ones he was up against were all sons and grandsons to men who had started in the trade many years earlier. There were reputable, family companies with names such as Walker, Dewar, Bell and Teacher. Buchanan, who had undertaken a five year apprenticeship with the whisky merchants, Charles Mackinlay & Co, couldn´t rely on tradition and reputation, but had to start with his own two hands. But he was not entirely alone. As a partner he had chosen W P Lowrie, a blending pioneer and one of the leaders of the trade. Lowrie, who was twenty years his senior, also owned several malt distilleries and so Buchanan couldn´t have chosen more wisely. With the assistance of Lowrie, his company soon became one of "The Big Three" with Dewar´s and Walker´s being the other two. The first blended whisky to rely on Glentauchers single malt was Buchanan´s own brand Black & White. As owners changed hands over the years, it became signature malt for Teacher´s and, today, it forms an integral part of Ballantine´s.

The distillery is equipped with a 12 ton stainless steel full lauter mash tun. There are six washbacks made of Oregon pine and three pairs of stills. The distillery is now doing 18 mashes per week and a total of 4 million litres per year. Most of the process at Glentaucher´s is done mechanically using traditional methods. The thought behind this is that new employees and trainees from Chivas Brothers will be able to work here for a while to learn the basic techniques of whisky production.

There are no official bottlings of Glentauchers, but Chivas Brothers have recently made an attempt to lift the whisky from obscurity. A range called Ballantine´s 17 year old Signature Distillery Editions was launched in order to highlight the four signature malts of the famous blend. The Glentaucher´s version was released in 2014 and is reserved for markets in Asia.

History:

1897 James Buchanan and W. P. Lowrie, a whisky merchant from Glasgow, found the distillery.

1898 Production starts.

1906 James Buchanan & Co. takes over the whole distillery and acquires an 80% share in W. P. Lowrie & Co.

1915 James Buchanan & Co. merges with Dewars.

1923 Mashing house and maltings are rebuilt.

1925 Buchanan-Dewars joins Distillers Company Limited (DCL).

1930 Glentauchers is transferred to Scottish Malt Distillers (SMD).

1965 The number of stills is increased from two to six.

1969 Floor maltings is decommissioned.

1985 DCL mothballs the distillery.

1989 United Distillers (formerly DCL) sells the distillery to Caledonian Malt Whisky Distillers, a subsidiary of Allied Distillers.

1992 Production recommences in August.

2000 A 15 year old Glentauchers is released.

2005 Chivas Brothers (Pernod Ricard) become the new owner through the acquisition of Allied Domecq.

Gordon & MacPhail
Glentauchers 1990

Tasting notes Glentauchers 1991 G&M:

GS – Fresh and floral aromas, with sweet fruits and peppery peaches. Medium to full-bodied in the mouth, with cereal and sweet spice. The finish is medium to long.

Glenturret

[glen•turr•et]

Owner:	**Region/district:**
The Edrington Group	Southern Highlands
Founded: **Status:**	**Capacity:**
1775 Active (vc)	340 000 litres

Address: The Hosh, Crieff, Perthshire PH7 4HA

Website:	**Tel:**
thefamousgrouse.com	01764 656565

If you want to be a bit dramatic, it took Glenturret 240 years to come out of the shadows as a single malt producer and a brand in its own right.

In 2015, the distillery celebrated its 240th anniversary as Scotland's oldest distillery (a statement which is sometimes debated). During all these years it was seldom known for its single malt. Instead, it was producing malt for blends and, more importantly, for the last 15 years has served as the spiritual home to The Famous Grouse. The Famous Grouse Experience is an excellent visitor centre with 70,000 visitors attending last year. Even though the big selling blend predominates here during a visit, Glenturret single malt has been allowed to take more space than ever before. Stuart Cassells, who in 2014 started as general manager at the visitor centre, plays a major part in this. He has identified Glenturret single malt as a hidden gem and has decided, together with the team at Edrington, to relaunch the brand.

Glenturret is equipped with a stainless steel, open mash tun, the only one left in Scotland where the mash is stirred by hand and where the draff at the end of the process must be removed manually. Furthermore, there are eight Douglas fir washbacks with a minimum fermentation time of 48 hours and one pair of stills with vertical condensers. From April 2016 to March 2017, the distillery will be producing 170,000 litres of alcohol. The main part of this, 120,000 litres, will be unpeated Glenturret, while the remaining part is made up of the heavily peated (80ppm in the barley) Ruadh Maor, which has been produced at the distillery since 2009 and is used mainly for blended whisky.

The **10 year old** is still available but, since November 2015, it has been joined by **Glenturret Sherry** (a combination of American and European oak seasoned with sherry), **Glenturret Triple Wood** (where ex bourbon casks complement the sherry casks) and **Glenturret Peated**. A number of limited releases have been made including **16, 18** and **26 year olds** and, in December 2015, the **32 year old James Fairlie** bottling - the oldest so far from the distillery – was released. The latest addition was the **16 year old Fly's 16 Masters** in summer 2016.

History:

1775 Whisky smugglers establish a small illicit farm distillery named Hosh Distillery.

1818 John Drummond is licensee until 1837.

1826 A distillery in the vicinity is named Glenturret, but is decommissioned before 1852.

1852 John McCallum is licensee until 1874.

1875 Hosh Distillery takes over the name Glenturret Distillery and is managed by Thomas Stewart.

1903 Mitchell Bros Ltd takes over.

1921 Production ceases and the buildings are used for whisky storage only.

1929 Mitchell Bros Ltd is liquidated, the distillery dismantled and the facilities are used as storage for agricultural needs.

1957 James Fairlie buys the distillery and re-equips it.

1959 Production restarts.

1981 Remy-Cointreau buys the distillery and invests in a visitor centre.

1990 Highland Distillers takes over.

1999 Edrington and William Grant & Sons buy Highland Distillers for £601 million. The purchasing company, 1887 Company, is a joint venture between Edrington (70%) and William Grant (30%).

2002 The Famous Grouse Experience, a visitor centre costing £2.5 million, is inaugurated.

2003 A 10 year old Glenturret replaces the 12 year old as the distillery's standard release.

2007 Three new single casks are released.

2013 An 18 year old bottled at cask strength is released as a distillery exclusive.

2014 A 1986 single cask is released.

2015 Sherry, Triple Wood and Peated are released.

2016 Fly's 16 Masters is released.

10 years old

Tasting notes Glenturret 10 years old:

GS – Nutty and slightly oily on the nose, with barley and citrus fruits. Sweet and honeyed on the full, fruity palate, with a balancing note of oak. Medium length in the sweet finish.

Highland Park

[hi•land park]

Owner:
The Edrington Group

Region/district:
Highlands (Orkney)

Founded: 1798
Status: Active (vc)
Capacity: 2 500 000 litres

Address: Holm Road, Kirkwall, Orkney KW15 1SU

Website:
highlandpark.co.uk

Tel:
01856 874619

There is evidence to suggest that Highland Park single malt was already exported to Norway, as well as to India in the late 1800s, but it wasn't until 1979 that the owners started promoting the whisky in a more structured manner.

The results were almost immediate and soon the brand had a large number of loyal followers. Ten years ago, the increasing sales figures came to an unexpected halt due to a shortage of stock. The reason for this was an irregular production towards the end of the 1990s. During the last five years, however, the supply has met the demand and sales have increased by 40% to 1.5 million bottles sold in 2015.

The distillery is equipped with a semi-lauter mash tun, twelve Oregon pine washbacks with a fermentation time between 50 and 80 hours, and two pairs of stills. The mash tun has a 12 tonnes capacity but is only filled to 50%. The plan for 2016 is to do 17 mashes per week for 45 weeks which translates to 2.2 million litres of alcohol. Highland Park is malting 30% of its malt themselves. There are five malting floors with a capacity of almost 36 tonnes of barley. The malt is dried for 18 hours using peat and the final 18 hours using coke. The phenol content is 30-40 ppm in its own malt and the malt which has been bought from Simpson's is unpeated. The two varieties are always mixed before mashing.

The core range of Highland Park consists of **12, 15, 18, 25, 30** and **40 year old**. In 2014, an addition to the core range without an age statement was released. **Dark Origins** is bottled at 46.8% and is made up of 80% first fill sherry casks, twice as many as for the standard 12 year old. However, from April 2017, both Dark Origins and the 15 year old will be gradually phased out and will be replaced by two new expressions. The Highland Park range for duty free, called the Warrior Series, mirrors the Viking heritage, which is of great importance to Orkney. **Svein, Einar** and **Harald** were released in spring 2013 and were followed by **Sigurd, Ragnvald** and **Thorfinn** in autumn of the same year. In 2016, two further additions to the range were made when the very limited **King Christian I** was launched and, later in spring, **Ingvar** was included as an exclusive to Taiwan.

Since 2009, there have been two ranges of limited bottlings celebrating Viking kings and Norse gods. The last and final release was **Odin** in 2015. However, starting in 2016, two new series have been introduced. One focuses on Norse mythology and the inaugurate launch was **Ice Edition** in March. This is a 17 year old, matured predominantly in ex-bourbon casks and bottled at 53.9%. The Ice Edition will be followed by the Fire Edition in 2017. The second range will be based on the distillery's five keystones (hand-turned malt, aromatic peat, cool maturation, sherry oak casks and harmonisation). The first release which was in August 2016 was **Hobbister**, bottled at 51.4%. It is named after Hobbister Moor where the distillery cuts the peat for the malting. This will be followed by another four bottlings in 2017.

History:

1798 David Robertson founds the distillery. The local smuggler and businessman Magnus Eunson previously operated an illicit whisky production on the site.

1816 John Robertson, an Excise Officer who arrested Magnus Eunson, takes over production.

1826 Highland Park obtains a license and the distillery is taken over by Robert Borwick.

1840 Robert's son George Borwick takes over but the distillery deteriorates.

1869 The younger brother James Borwick inherits Highland Park and attempts to sell it as he does not consider the distillation of spirits as compatible with his priesthood.

1895 James Grant (of Glenlivet Distillery) buys Highland Park.

1898 James Grant expands capacity from two to four stills.

1937 Highland Distilleries buys Highland Park.

1979 Highland Distilleries invests considerably in marketing Highland Park as single malt which increases sales markedly.

1986 A visitor centre, considered one of Scotland's finest, is opened.

1997 Two new Highland Park are launched, an 18 year old and a 25 year old.

1999 Highland Distillers are acquired by Edrington Group and William Grant & Sons.

2000 Visit Scotland awards Highland Park "Five Star Visitor Attraction".

2005 Highland Park 30 years old is released. A 16 year old for the Duty Free market and Ambassador's Cask 1984 are released.

History continued:

2006 The second edition of Ambassador´s Cask, a 10 year old from 1996, is released. New packaging is introduced.

2007 The Rebus 20, a 21 year old duty free exclusive, a 38 year old and a 39 year old are released.

2008 A 40 year old and the third and fourth editions of Ambassador´s Cask are released.

2009 Two vintages and Earl Magnus 15 year are released.

2010 A 50 year old, Saint Magnus 12 year old, Orcadian Vintage 1970 and four duty free vintages are released.

2011 Vintage 1978, Leif Eriksson and 18 year old Earl Haakon are released.

2012 Thor and a 21 year old are released.

2013 Loki and a new range for duty free, The Warriors, are released.

2014 Freya and Dark Origins are released.

2015 Odin is released.

2016 Hobbister, Ice Edition, Ingvar and King Christian I are released.

Tasting notes Highland Park 12 year old:

GS – The nose is fragrant and floral, with hints of heather and some spice. Smooth and honeyed on the palate, with citric fruits, malt and distinctive tones of wood smoke in the warm, lengthy, slightly peaty finish.

Tasting notes Highland Park Dark Origins:

GS – The nose offers bananas, milk chocolate-coated caramel and a hint of background soot. The palate is smooth, with dark chocolate, berries, spicy dry sherry and coal. The finish features black pepper, and is smoky, dry and lengthy.

Ingvar   Dark Origins   Hobbister

12 years old

18 years old

21 years old

Inchgower

[inch•gow•er]

Owner:
Diageo

Region/district:
Speyside

Founded:
1871

Status:
Active

Capacity:
3 200 000 litres

Address: Buckie, Banffshire AB56 5AB

Website:
malts.com

Tel:
01542 836700

Since Inchgower was in the possession of Arthur Bell & Sons for almost 50 years, it is no wonder that the single malt has for a long time formed an important part of Bell´s blended whisky.

And it is not playing second fiddle in the recipe either. It is there to add robust and spicy notes and if you look at the distillation process, it all makes sense. The wort from the mash tun is cloudy with part of the cereals left when it is pumped into the washbacks. A short fermentation time, around 50 hours, gives a nutty character to the newmake instead of a fruity one. The descending lyne arms on the stills allow very little room for reflux and a quick distillation gives little time for the copper to smooth out the robust, spicy character. Finally, they have an unusually wide spirit cut coming on spirit at 72% and they don´t stop collecting the spirit until 55%, which adds a hint of feinty notes as well.

Arthur Bell & Sons managed to keep their independence until 1984 when it was bought by Guinness and, later on, they became a part of the giant, Diageo. Bell´s blended Scotch is the second best selling blend in the UK and currently around tenth place in the world. Sales volumes have been stable during the last ten years and in 2015, 26 million bottles were sold.

After an extensive upgrade in 2012, the distillery is now equipped with an 8.6 ton stainless steel semilauter mash tun, six wooden washbacks and 2 pairs of stills with an unusual bend on the lyne arms. In 2016, the plan is to do 19 mashes per week and produce 3 million litres of alcohol in the year. Most of the production is matured elsewhere, but there are also five dunnage and four racked warehouses on site.

Inchgower is situated on the south side of Moray Firth and is difficult to miss as it is situated just at the A98 near the small fishing port of Buckie. If one is driving from Elgin towards Banff, it is even easier to spot the distillery as the name appears on the roof. Besides the official **Flora & Fauna 14 year old**, there have also been a few limited bottlings of Inchgower single malt. In 2010, for example, a **single sherry cask** distilled in **1993**, was released.

History:

1871 Alexander Wilson & Co. founds the distillery. Equipment from the disused Tochineal Distillery, also owned by Alexander Wilson, is installed.

1936 Alexander Wilson & Co. becomes bankrupt and Buckie Town Council buys the distillery and the family's home for £1,600.

1938 The distillery is sold on to Arthur Bell & Sons for £3,000.

1966 Capacity doubles to four stills.

1985 Guinness acquires Arthur Bell & Sons.

1987 United Distillers is formed by a merger between Arthur Bell & Sons and DCL.

1997 Inchgower 1974 (22 years) is released as a Rare Malt.

2004 Inchgower 1976 (27 years) is released as a Rare Malt.

2010 A single cask from 1993 is released.

14 years old

Tasting notes Inchgower 14 years old:

GS – Ripe pears and a hint of brine on the light nose. Grassy and gingery in the mouth, with some acidity. The finish is spicy, dry and relatively short.

Jura

[joo•rah]

Owner:	**Region/district:**
Whyte & Mackay	Highlands (Jura)
(Emperador Inc)	

Founded:	**Status:**	**Capacity:**
1810	Active (vc)	2 200 000 litres

Address: Craighouse, Isle of Jura PA60 7XT

Website:	**Tel:**
isleofjura.com	01496 820240

When Emperador bought Whyte & Mackay in 2014, the Philippine spirits company may have been the world´s largest producer of brandy by far, but is wasn´t truly a global company.

With the acquisition of Whyte & Mackay (including Jura and Dalmore) and a year later Bodegas Fundador in Spain, the company has grown considerably. With its products being sold in more than 100 countries, it is now one of the biggest drinks companies in the world. The growth will no doubt continue. Andrew Tan, the majority owner and chairman of Emperador and one of the richest men in the Philippines, has ambitious plans for his brands and will introduce Emperador brandy to the important North American market during the second half of 2016.

Jura distillery is equipped with one semi-lauter mash tun, six stainless steel washbacks with a fermentation time of 54 hours and two pairs of stills – the second tallest in Scotland. Working a 7-day week since 2011, they will be doing 28 mashes per week during 2016, which will include one month of peated production (at 50ppm) producing 2.3 million litres of alcohol in the year.

Sales volumes for Jura single malt have increased rapidly since 2010 and it is now the third most sold single malt in the UK after Glenfiddich and Glenmorangie. The increase may trigger the construction of a second distillery on site which could be operational within five years.

The core range consists of **Origin** (10 years), **Diurach´s Own** (16 years), **Superstition** (lightly peated), the peated **Prophecy** and **Jura Elixir**, a 12 year old matured in both American and European oak. **Turas-Mara**, a duty free exclusive with no age statement, was released in 2013. This year´s **Jura Tastival** bottling was a vatting of three whiskies aged for 14 to 19 years and all with a second maturation in different sherry casks. In September 2016, a limited **22 year old** with a pinot noir finish was released to mark the retirement of distillery manager Willie Cochrane who had been with the distillery for 39 years. The bottling was aptly named **"One For The Road"**.

History:

1810 Archibald Campbell founds a distillery named Small Isles Distillery.

1853 Richard Campbell leases the distillery to Norman Buchanan from Glasgow.

1867 Buchanan files for bankruptcy and J. & K. Orr takes over the distillery.

1876 Licence transferred to James Ferguson & Sons.

1901 Ferguson dismantles the distillery.

1960 Charles Mackinlay & Co. extends the distillery. Newly formed Scottish & Newcastle Breweries acquires Charles Mackinlay & Co.

1963 The first distilling takes place.

1985 Invergordon Distilleries acquires Charles Mackinlay & Co., Isle of Jura and Glenallachie from Scottish & Newcastle Breweries.

1993 Whyte & Mackay (Fortune Brands) buys Invergordon Distillers.

1996 Whyte & Mackay changes name to JBB (Greater Europe).

2001 The management buys out the company and changes the name to Kyndal.

2002 Isle of Jura Superstition is launched.

2003 Kyndal reverts back to its old name, Whyte & Mackay. Isle of Jura 1984 is launched.

2004 Two cask strengths (15 and 30 years old) are released in limited numbers.

2006 The 40 year old Jura is released.

2007 United Spirits buys Whyte & Mackay. The 18 year old Delmé-Evans and an 8 year old heavily peated expression are released.

2008 A series of four different vintages, called Elements, is released.

2009 The peated Prophecy and three new vintages called Paps of Jura are released.

2010 Boutique Barrels and a 21 year old Anniversary bottling are released.

2012 The 12 year old Jura Elixir is released.

2013 Camas an Staca, 1977 Juar and Turas-Mara are released.

2014 Whyte & Mackay is sold to Emperador Inc.

2016 The 22 year old "One For The Road" is released.

Tasting notes Jura 10 years old:

GS – Resin, oil and pine notes on the delicate nose. Light-bodied in the mouth, with malt and drying saltiness. The finish is malty, nutty, with more salt, plus just a wisp of smoke.

10 years old

Kilchoman

[kil•ho•man]

Owner:
Kilchoman Distillery Co.

Region/district:
Islay

Founded: **Status:** **Capacity:**
2005 Active (vc) 200 000 litres

Address: Rockside farm, Bruichladdich,
Islay PA49 7UT

Website: **Tel:**
kilchomandistillery.com 01496 850011

When Anthony Wills, the owner of Kilchoman, decided to hire a new general manager in 2010, he didn't have to search far. He managed to persuade John MacLellan at Bunnahabhain to take the job.

MacLellan started working at Bunnahabhain distillery in 1989 and eventually became the manager in 1997. He was instrumental in the re-launch of Bunnahabhain single malt and he was also the first to release a special bottling for the Islay Whisky Festival with all the other distilleries to follow later. At Kilchoman he launched two of the distillery's flagship expressions – 100% Islay and Machir Bay, and his vast experience had eased the introduction of Kilchoman to export markets. In March 2016, MacLellan sadly lost the battle to cancer, aged 60.

The distillery has its own floor maltings with a quarter of the barley requirements coming from fields that surround the distillery. At present, 20% of the malt requirement (peated to 20ppm) comes from own maltings, while the balance comes from Port Ellen (at 50ppm). A new malting floor and a new kiln will be installed by the end of 2016, enabling the owners to do 30% of the malting themselves. Other equipment include a stainless steel semi-lauter mash tun, six stainless steel washbacks (two of which were installed in January 2016) and one pair of stills. The distillery is currently doing 9 mashes per week which translates to almost 200,000 litres of alcohol.

The core range consists of **Machir Bay** and **Sanaig**. The latter was released in March 2016 and has been matured in a combination of ex-bourbon and ex-oloroso sherry casks. Limited, but regular releases are the sherry matured **Loch Gorm** and **100% Islay**, both with new editions in 2015. Recent, limited releases include a **Madeira cask** maturation released in 2015 and in 2016, a **Sauternes cask** matured and a new edition of the **Original Cask Strength**. The special Feis Ile 2016 bottling was an oloroso matured **2007 Vintage**. For the duty free market there is also **Coull Point**, which is around 5 years old, matured in bourbon casks and with a few weeks' finish in Oloroso sherry.

History:

2002 Plans are formed for a new distillery at Rockside Farm on western Islay.

2005 Production starts in June.

2006 A fire breaks out in the kiln causing a few weeks' production stop but malting has to cease for the rest of the year.

2007 The distillery is expanded with two new washbacks.

2009 The first single malt, a 3 year old, is released on 9th September followed by a second release.

2010 Three new releases and an introduction to the US market. John Maclellan from Bunnahabhain joins the team as General Manager.

2011 Kilchoman 100% Islay is released as well as a 4 year old and a 5 year old.

2012 Machir Bay, the first core expression, is released together with Kilchoman Sherry Cask Release and the second edition of 100% Islay.

2013 Loch Gorm and Vintage 2007 are released.

2014 A 3 year old port cask matured and the first duty free exclusive, Coull Point, are released.

2015 A Madeira cask maturation is released and the distillery celebrates its 10th anniversary.

2016 Sanaig and a Sauternes cask maturation are released.

Machir Bay

Tasting notes Kilchoman Machir Bay:

GS – A nose of sweet peat and vanilla, undercut by brine, kelp and black pepper. Filled ashtrays in time. A smooth mouth-feel, with lots of nicely-balanced citrus fruit, peat smoke and Germolene on the palate. The finish is relatively long and sweet, with building spice, chili and a final nuttiness.

Kininvie

[kin•in•vee]

Owner:
William Grant & Sons

Region/district:
Speyside

Founded: | **Status:** | **Capacity:**
1990 | Active | 4 800 000 litres

Address: Dufftown, Keith, Banffshire AB55 4DH

Website:
-

Tel:
01340 820373

When Kininvie was built in 1990 it was done with the thought in mind that the distillery should provide malt whisky for Grant´s blend. The malt from the neighbouring Glenfiddich and Balvenie was more needed for the company´s single malt bottlings.

It didn´t take long however, before Kininvie malt was used for a completely new brand as well. Monkey Shoulder, a blended malt, started selling in 2005 and Kininvie formed the backbone of the blend. It wasn´t a huge success from the very onset, but over the last five years, sales figures have increased by almost 400% to 1.6 million bottles being sold in 2015. When Drinks International asked 100 of the most influential bars in the world, Monkey Shoulder came in as the trendiest whisky and as the third most sold whisky after Johnnie Walker and Jameson.

Kininvie distillery consists of one still house with three wash stills and six spirit stills, neatly tucked away behind Balvenie. There is one stainless steel full lauter mash tun which is placed next to Balvenie´s in the Balvenie distillery and ten Douglas fir washbacks with a fermentation time of 65 hours can be found in two separate rooms next to the Balvenie washbacks. In 2016, the distillery will be doing 18 mashes per week and will produce approximately 2.6 million litres of pure alcohol.

The first time that Kininvie appeared as an official single malt bottling was in 2006, when a Hazelwood 15 year old was launched to celebrate the 105th birthday of Janet Sheed Roberts, the last, surviving grand-daughter of William Grant. In 2008 it was time to celebrate her 107th birthday with a Hazelwood 17 year old. It wasn't until autumn 2013 that Kininvie single malt was launched under its own name for the first time as a **23 year old**. The first batch was exclusive to Taiwan and was then followed by batch 2 for UK, USA and selected European markets. Batch 3 was offered globally. The end of 2015 saw the release of a **23 year old** core bottling. A **17 year old** is available in duty free and three **25 year old single casks** named First Drops, were launched in November 2015.

History:

1990 Kininvie distillery is inaugurated and the first distillation takes place on 25th June.

1994 Another three stills are installed.

2006 The first expression of a Kininvie single malt is released as a 15 year old under the name Hazelwood.

2008 In February a 17 year old Hazelwood Reserve is launched at Heathrow´s Terminal 5.

2013 A 23 year old Kininvie is launched in Taiwan.

2014 A 17 year old and batch 2 of the 23 year old are released.

2015 Batch 3 of the 23 year old is released and later in the year, the batches are replaced by a 23 year old signature bottling. Three 25 year old single casks are launched.

23 years old

Tasting notes Kininvie 17 years old:

GS – The nose offers tropical fruits, coconut and vanilla custard, with a hint of milk chocolate. Pineapple and mango on the palate, accompanied by linseed oil, ginger, and developing nuttiness. The finish dries slowly, with more linseed, plenty of spice, and soft oak.

Knockando

[nock•an•doo]

Owner:
Diageo.

Region/district:
Speyside

Founded: | **Status:** | **Capacity:**
1898 | Active | 1 400 000 litres

Address: Knockando, Morayshire AB38 7RT

Website: | **Tel:**
malts.com | 01340 882000

When distilleries change hands nowadays, the buyer is almost always from another spirits company, but it hasn´t always been the case.

For 25 years, until 1997, Knockando and several other distilleries were in the hands of Grand Metropolitan, a company founded in 1934. Originally a hotel business, the company expanded into such diverse fields as catering, bingo halls and breweries (and that was when Knockando came into the picture). It continued not only with tobacco companies and a variety of spirits brands (like Smirnoff for instance) but also with fast food companies like Burger King. In 1997, Grand Metropolitan merged with Guinness brewery to form Diageo .

For more than 60 years, Knockando single malt has been an important part of J&B blended Scotch. Just a decade ago, J&B was the second best selling Scotch in the world with 80 million bottles sold, but has now fallen to fifth place with 43 million bottles. Fortunately, Knockando also got off to an early start as a single malt as well. Introduced in 1976, it soon became very popular, not least in France and Spain. In 2015, 600,000 bottles were sold.

The distillery is equipped with a small (4.4 ton), semi-lauter mash tun, eight Douglas fir washbacks and two pairs of stills. Knockando has always worked a five-day week with 16 mashes per week, 8 short fermentations (50 hours) and 8 long (100 hours). In 2016 this will mean a production of 1.4 million litres of alcohol. The spirit is tankered away to Auchroisk and Glenlossie, and some of the casks are returned to the distillery for maturation in two dunnage and two racked warehouses. Knockando´s nutty character, a result of the cloudy worts coming from the mash tun, has given it its fame. However, in order to balance the taste, the distillers also wish to create the typical Speyside floral notes by using boiling balls on the spirit stills to increase reflux.

The core range consists of **12 year old, 15 year old Richly Matured, 18 year old Slow Matured** and the **21 year old Master Reserve**. In 2011 a **25 year old** matured in first fill European oak was released as part of the Special Releases.

History:

1898   John Thompson founds the distillery. The architect is Charles Doig.

1899   Production starts in May.

1900   The distillery closes in March and J. Thompson & Co. takes over administration.

1903   W. & A. Gilbey purchases the distillery for £3,500 and production restarts in October.

1962   W. & A. Gilbey merges with United Wine Traders (including Justerini & Brooks) and forms International Distillers & Vintners (IDV).

1968   Floor maltings is decommissioned.

1969   The number of stills is increased to four.

1972   IDV is acquired by Watney Mann who, in its turn, is taken over by Grand Metropolitan.

1978   Justerini & Brooks launches a 12 year old Knockando.

1997   Grand Metropolitan and Guinness merge and form Diageo; simultaneously IDV and United Distillers merge to United Distillers & Vintners.

2010   A Manager´s Choice 1996 is released.

2011   A 25 year old is released.

12 years old

Tasting notes Knockando 12 years old:

GS – Delicate and fragrant on the nose, with hints of malt, worn leather, and hay. Quite full in the mouth, smooth and honeyed, with gingery malt and a suggestion of white rum. Medium length in the finish, with cereal and more ginger.

Knockdhu

[nock•doo]

Owner:
Inver House Distillers
(Thai Beverages plc)

Region/district:
Highland

Founded: 1893   **Status:** Active (vc)   **Capacity:** 2 000 000 litres

Address: Knock, By Huntly, Aberdeenshire AB54 7LJ

Website: ancnoc.com

Tel: 01466 771223

With more than 50 years in the whisky business, the owners of Knockdhu, Inver House, is one of the dominant players in the industry today. But the company has had its fair share of ups and downs.

Founded in 1964 by an American, Harry Publicker, and based in Scotland, the company in its heyday employed over 1,000 people in Airdrie, North Lanarkshire. However, a serious decline for Scotch whisky in the late 70s and early 80s, combined with the death of Harry Publicker, had put an end to the glory days for the company. Intervention by way of a management buyout in 1988, Inver House managed to overcome the hard times and that same year, it bought its first distillery of five - Knockdhu. For many years, the distillery produced malt for the company´s blends but in 2003, a genuine investment was made in anCnoc single malt and, since then, the brand has gained more and more devoted followers. In 2015, 192,000 bottles were sold.

Knockdhu distillery is equipped with a 5 ton stainless steel lauter mash tun, eight washbacks made of Oregon pine with a fermentation time of 65 hours and one pair of stills with worm tubs, although the wash still is also equipped with a horizontal shell and tube condenser. For 2016 they plan to do 2 million litres of spirit of which 450,000 litres will be heavily peated (45ppm).

The core range consists of **12, 18** and **24 years old**, as well as a limited **Vintage 1975**. The 24 year old replaced the 22 year old in 2015. In addition to that there is the peated range with **Rascan**, **Peatlands** and, released end of September 2016, **Stack**. Previous expressions in the range (Rutter, Flaughter, Tushkar and Cutter) have now been sold out in most markets. The peated expressions are all between 8 and 12 years old. Every year a new vintage is released and in September 2014, it was a **2000** which was replaced by a **Vintage 2001** in March 2016. For the travel retail segment, two new expressions were released early in 2015 – **Black Hill Reserve** and the peated (13.5ppm) **Barrow**. Both have matured in bourbon casks and are bottled at 46%. In 2016, a collaboration with fashion designer, Patrick Grant, resulted in the limited **Blas**, matured in bourbon and sherry casks and bottled at 54%.

History:

1893 Distillers Company Limited (DCL) starts construction of the distillery.

1894 Production starts in October.

1930 Scottish Malt Distillers (SMD) takes over production.

1983 The distillery closes in March.

1988 Inver House buys the distillery from United Distillers.

1989 Production restarts on 6th February.

1990 First official bottling of Knockdhu.

1993 First official bottling of anCnoc.

2001 Pacific Spirits purchases Inver House Distillers at a price of $85 million.

2003 Reintroduction of anCnoc 12 years.

2004 A 14 year old from 1990 is launched.

2005 A 30 year old from 1975 and a 14 year old from 1991 are launched.

2006 International Beverage Holdings acquires Pacific Spirits UK.

2007 anCnoc 1993 is released.

2008 anCnoc 16 year old is released.

2011 A Vintage 1996 is released.

2012 A 35 year old is launched.

2013 A 22 year old and Vintage 1999 are released.

2014 A peated range with Rutter, Flaughter, Tushkar and Cutter is introduced.

2015 A 24 year old, Vintage 1975 and Peatlands are released as well as Black Hill Reserve and Barrow for duty free.

2016 Vintage 2001 and Blas are launchedas well as the peated Stack.

12 years old

Tasting notes anCnoc 12 years old:

GS – A pretty, sweet, floral nose, with barley notes. Medium bodied, with a whiff of delicate smoke, spices and boiled sweets on the palate. Drier in the mouth than the nose suggests. The finish is quite short and drying.

Lagavulin

[lah•gah•<u>voo</u>•lin]

Owner:
Diageo

Region/district:
Islay

Founded: **Status:**
1816   Active (vc)

Capacity:
2 450 000 litres

Address: Port Ellen, Islay, Argyll PA42 7DZ

Website:
malts.com

Tel:
01496 302749 (vc)

Last year two distilleries on Islay celebrated their bicentenaries, Laphroaig and Ardbeg, and in 2016 it was time for the third of the distilleries on the Kildalton coast, Lagavulin, to reach that milestone.

Twohundred years of legal distilling, that is. Already in 1742, whisky was produced on site through dozens of illegal stills, so called bothies. The founder of Lagavulin, John Johnston, hails from a family that has meant a lot to the production of whisky on the island and different members have also been involved in a number of distilleries. John managed Tallant distillery, among others, which closed in 1852, and he was also involved in Bowmore during a short period. His two sons, Alexander and Donald, founded Laphroaig and it remained in the family's ownership until 1954.

The sudden interest in smoky Islay whiskies that started in the early 1990s, can to a large extent be attributed to Lagavulin and the fact that it was marketed as one of the Classic Malts from 1988 onwards. For many years it was the most sold Islay single malt but has now been surpassed by Laphroaig, as well as Bowmore. One major reason was the lack of mature stock due to low production in the 1980s when they were working two-day shifts. The sales of Lagavulin have picked up in recent years though and with 1.9 million bottles sold in 2015, volumes are now close to that of Bowmore.

The distillery is equipped with a 4.4 ton stainless steel full lauter mash tun, ten washbacks made of larch with a 55 hour fermentation cycle and two pairs of stills. The spirit stills are actually larger than the wash stills and are filled almost to the brim. This diminishes the copper contact and that, together with a slow distillation, creates the rich and pungent character of Lagavulin single malt. Bourbon hogsheads are used, almost without exception, for maturation and all of the new production is stored on the mainland. The distillery is working 24/7 and the volume for 2016 will be around 2.45 million litres of alcohol.

The core range of Lagavulin is unusually limited and only consists of a **12 year old cask strength** (which actually forms part of the Special Releases but new bottlings appear every year), a **16 year old** and the **Distiller's Edition**, a Pedro Ximenez sherry finish. Two limited bottlings to celebrate the bicentenary were released in 2016. The first, in March, was an **8 year old** bottled at 48% and more bottles, also for the travel retail market, were released in the autumn. At the beginning of summer, a **25 year old** bottled at cask strength and matured in sherry casks was launched. It was released in honour of the 21 distillery managers that have overseen the distillery since its inception and their names can all be seen on the bottle. This was the first 25 year old from the distillery since 2002. Finally, the Islay Festival special release for 2016, bottled at 49.5%, is an **18 year old** vatting of whisky matured in refill American oak and ex bodega European oak.

History:

1816 John Johnston founds the distillery.

1825 John Johnston takes over the adjacent distillery Ardmore founded in 1817 by Archibald Campbell and closed in 1821.

1836 John Johnston dies and the two distilleries are merged and operated under the name Lagavulin. Alexander Graham, a wine and spirits dealer from Glasgow, buys the distillery.

1861 James Logan Mackie becomes a partner.

1867 The distillery is acquired by James Logan Mackie & Co. and refurbishment starts.

1878 Peter Mackie is employed.

1889 James Logan Mackie passes away and nephew Peter Mackie inherits the distillery.

1890 J. L. Mackie & Co. changes name to Mackie & Co. Peter Mackie launches White Horse onto the export market with Lagavulin included in the blend. White Horse blended is not available on the domestic market until 1901.

1908 Peter Mackie uses the old distillery buildings to build a new distillery, Malt Mill, on the site.

1924 Peter Mackie passes away and Mackie & Co. changes name to White Horse Distillers.

1927 White Horse Distillers becomes part of Distillers Company Limited (DCL).

1930 The distillery is administered under Scottish Malt Distillers (SMD).

1952 An explosive fire breaks out and causes considerable damage.

1962 Malt Mills distillery closes and today it houses Lagavulin's visitor centre.

1974 Floor maltings are decommisioned and malt is bought from Port Ellen instead.

History continued:

1988 Lagavulin 16 years becomes one of six Classic Malts.

1998 A Pedro Ximenez sherry finish is launched as a Distillers Edition.

2002 Two cask strengths (12 years and 25 years) are launched.

2006 A 30 year old is released.

2007 A 21 year old from 1985 and the sixth edition of the 12 year old are released.

2008 A new 12 year old is released.

2009 A new 12 year old appears as a Special Release.

2010 A new edition of the 12 year old, a single cask exclusive for the distillery and a Manager's Choice single cask are released.

2011 The 10th edition of the 12 year old cask strength is released.

2012 The 11th edition of the 12 year old cask strength and a 21 year old are released.

2013 A 37 year old and the 12th edition of the 12 year old cask strength are released.

2014 A triple matured for Friends of the Classic Malts and the 13th edition of the 12 year old cask strength are released.

2015 The 14th edition of the 12 year old cask strength is released.

2016 An 8 year old and a 25 year old are launched as well as the yearly 12 year old cask strength.

Tasting notes Lagavulin 16 year old:

GS – Peat, iodine, sherry and vanilla merge on the rich nose. The peat and iodine continue on to the expansive, spicy, sherried palate, with brine, prunes and raisins. Peat embers feature in the lengthy, spicy finish.

Distiller´s Edition   25 years old   8 years old

16 years old   12 years old cask strength

Laphroaig

[lah•<u>froyg</u>]

Owner: **Region/district:**
Beam Suntory   Islay

Founded: **Status:**   **Capacity:**
1815   Active (vc)   3 300 000 litres

Address: Port Ellen, Islay, Argyll PA42 7DU

Website: **Tel:**
laphroaig.com   01496 302418

One of the most difficult issues that a whisky producer has to deal with is managing the inventory of whiskies. You have to try and estimate the sales figures at least 10 years ahead in order to know how much you have to produce currently.

If you have a successful brand growing year by year, it makes it even more difficult. This has now become a problem for Laphroaig. It is, by far, the best selling Islay whisky and number seven of all single malts with close to 3.5 million bottles having been sold in 2015. The huge popularity of the brand has made it hard for the owners to offer some of the bottlings with an age statement simply because they don´t have enough stock of that particular age. That´s why the 18 year old was withdrawn last year and that´s also the reason why 75% of the upcoming new releases will be without age statement on the label.

Laphroaig is equipped with a 5.5 ton stainless steel full lauter mash tun and six stainless steel washbacks with a fermentation time of 55 hours. The distillery uses an unusual combination of three wash stills and four spirit stills, all fitted with ascending lyne arms. It is one of very few distilleries with its own maltings which produces 20% of its requirements. The barley is steeped in three waters for 51 hours and then spread out on two malting floors for 6 days. It is dried for 15 hours using peatsmoke and then for a further 19 hours with hot air. The own malt has a phenol specification of 40-60ppm, while the remaining malt from Port Ellen or the mainland lies between 35 and 45ppm. The distillery is running at full capacity which means 34 mashes per week and 3.3 million litres in the year. Around 70% of the production is reserved for single malts while the remaining 30% is used for blends. Laphroaig has one of the best visitor centres in the industry with tours at a variety of levels.

The core range consists of **Select** without age statement, **10 year old**, **10 year old cask strength**, **Quarter Cask**, **Triple Wood** and a **25 year old**. A new addition to the range, **Lore**, was launched in spring 2016. With no age statement, the whisky has been matured in a combination of first fill bourbon barrels, quarter casks and oloroso hogsheads. The travel retail range includes **Laphroaig PX**, matured in hogsheads and quarter casks with a finish in PX sherry casks and **Brodir port wood finish**. Two previous duty free bottlings, QA Cask and An Cuan Mor, have been discontinued and will be replaced by **Four Oak** and **The 1815 Edition** in 2017. Four Oak, bottled at 40%, is a vatting from four different casks – bourbon, quarter casks, virgin American oak and European oak hogsheads, while The 1815 Edition is a mix of first-fill, heavily charred bourbon barrels and new European oak hogsheads. Limited releases include three bottlings that were launched to celebrate the distillery´s bicentenary last year; **15 year old, 21 year old** and **32 year old**. The Feis Ile bottling for 2016 was a **Cairdeas**, matured in ex-bourbon hogsheads and finished in madeira casks. Finally, a limited **30 year old** was released later in 2016.

History:

1815   Brothers Alexander and Donald Johnston found Laphroaig.

1836   Donald buys out Alexander and takes over operations.

1837   James and Andrew Gairdner found Ardenistiel a stone's throw from Laphroaig.

1847   Donald Johnston is killed in an accident in the distillery when he falls into a kettle of boiling hot burnt ale. The Manager of neigh-bouring Lagavulin, Walter Graham, takes over.

1857   Operation is back in the hands of the Johnston family when Donald's son Dougald takes over.

1860   Ardenistiel Distillery merges with Laphroaig.

1877   Dougald, being without heirs, passes away and his sister Isabella, married to their cousin Alexander takes over.

1907   Alexander Johnston dies and the distillery is inherited by his two sisters Catherine Johnston and Mrs. William Hunter (Isabella Johnston).

1908   Ian Hunter arrives in Islay to assist his mother and aunt with the distillery.

1924   The two stills are increased to four.

1927   Catherine Johnston dies and Ian Hunter takes over.

1928   Isabella Johnston dies and Ian Hunter becomes sole owner.

1950   Ian Hunter forms D. Johnston & Company.

1954   Ian Hunter passes away and management of the distillery is taken over by Elisabeth "Bessie" Williamson, who was previously Ian Hunters PA and secretary. She becomes Director of the Board and Managing Director.

1967   Seager Evans & Company buys the distillery through Long John Distillery, having already acquired part of Laphroaig in 1962. The number of stills is increased from four to five.

History continued:

1972 Bessie Williamson retires. Another two stills are installed bringing the total to seven.

1975 Whitbread & Co. buys Seager Evans (now renamed Long John International) from Schenley International.

1989 The spirits division of Whitbread is sold to Allied Distillers.

1991 Allied Distillers launches Caledonian Malts. Laphroaig is one of the four malts included.

1994 HRH Prince Charles gives his Royal Warrant to Laphroaig. Friends of Laphroaig is founded.

1995 A 10 year old cask strength is launched.

2001 A 40 year old is released.

2004 Quarter Cask is launched.

2005 Fortune Brands becomes new owner.

2007 A vintage 1980 (27 years old) and a 25 year old are released.

2008 Cairdeas, Cairdeas 30 year old and Triple Wood are released.

2009 An 18 year old is released.

2010 A 20 year old for French Duty Free and Cairdeas Master Edition are launched.

2011 Laphroaig PX and Cairdeas - The Ileach Edition are released. Triple Wood is moved to the core range and replaced in duty free by Laphroaig PX.

2012 Brodir and Cairdeas Origin are launched.

2013 QA Cask, An Cuan Mor, 25 year old cask strength and Cairdeas Port Wood Edition are released.

2014 Laphroaig Select and a new version of Cairdeas are released.

2015 A 21 year old, a 32 year old sherry cask and a new Cairdeas are released and the 15 year old is re-launched.

2016 Lore, Cairdeas 2016 and a 30 year old are released.

Tasting notes Laphroaig Select:

GS – The nose offers chocolate and malt notes set against peat, citrus fruit and iodine. Citrus fruit is most apparent on the relatively light palate, along with ginger, cinnamon and dried fruits. The peat is muted. The finish offers bright spices, new oak and medicinal notes.

Tasting notes Laphroaig 10 year old:

GS – Old-fashioned sticking plaster, peat smoke and seaweed leap off the nose, followed by something a little sweeter and fruitier. Massive on the palate, with fish oil, salt and plankton, though the finish is quite tight and increasingly drying

Select

Quarter Cask

Lore

30 years old

QA Cask

10 years old

Cairdeas 2016

Four Oak

Linkwood

[link•wood]

Owner:	**Region/district:**
Diageo	Speyside
Founded: **Status:**	**Capacity:**
1821 Active	5 600 000 litres

Address: Elgin, Morayshire IV30 8RD

Website: **Tel:**
malts.com 01343 862000

When Alfred Barnard made his famous tour of 150 distilleries in Scotland, Ireland and England in 1886 he didn´t seem overly impressed with Linkwood. In his book about the journey, he only devoted one page to the distillery.

Two decades later, the interest in the distillery and its whisky had changed. One of the owners at the time, Innes Cameron, discovered the qualities that Linkwood single malt had as a blending component and today, blenders can only agree with him. The whisky makes an important contribution, not only to Diageo blends such as Johnnie Walker and White Horse, but is also included in whiskies from many other companies.

In 1962, a major refurbishment and expansion of the distillery took place. The old part of the distillery, which stopped producing in 1996, was equipped with worm tubs and had a slightly different character than the Linkwood of today. On two occasions during 2011-2013, the distillery has been expanded. The old distillery buildings facing Linkwood Road were demolished and an extension of the current still house, which houses two of the stills and the tunroom, was constructed. The only original buildings from 1872 left standing are No. 6 warehouse and the redundant, old kiln with the pagoda roof. The set up of equipment now is one 12.5 ton full lauter mash tun, 11 wooden washbacks and three pairs of stills. Like at Lagavulin, the spirit stills are larger than the wash stills but, unlike the distilling regime at the Islay distillery where the stills are filled almost to the brim, the Linkwood spirit stills are filled low. Here you want to make a clean, fresh newmake whereas the Lagavulin style, apart from being smoky, should be powerful and pungent. Production during 2016 will be a 5-day week translating to 3.6 million litres of alcohol.

The only official core bottling is a **12 year old** Flora & Fauna. In October 2016, a **37 year old** distilled in 1978 and bottled at 50.3%, was launched as part of the Special Releases.

History:

1821 Peter Brown founds the distillery.

1868 Peter Brown passes away and his son William inherits the distillery.

1872 William demolishes the distillery and builds a new one.

1897 Linkwood Glenlivet Distillery Company Ltd takes over operations.

1902 Innes Cameron, a whisky trader from Elgin, joins the Board and eventually becomes the major shareholder and Director.

1932 Innes Cameron dies and Scottish Malt Distillers takes over in 1933.

1962 Major refurbishment takes place.

1971 The two stills are increased by four. Technically, the four new stills belong to a new distillery referred to as Linkwood B.

1985 Linkwood A (the two original stills) closes.

1990 Linkwood A is in production again for a few months each year until 1996.

2002 A 26 year old from 1975 is launched as a Rare Malt.

2005 A 30 year old from 1974 is launched as a Rare Malt.

2008 Three different wood finishes (all 26 year old) are released.

2009 A Manager´s Choice 1996 is released.

2013 Expansion of the distillery including two more stills.

2016 A 37 year old is released.

12 years old

Tasting notes Linkwood 12 years old:

GS – Floral, grassy and fragrant on the nutty nose, while the slightly oily palate becomes increasingly sweet, ending up at marzipan and almonds. The relatively lengthy finish is quite dry and citric.

The State of Scotch

six burning questions

James Robertson,
International Sales Manager,
Terroir Distillers

1. The Millenials are often referred to as perhaps the most important consumer demographic today. Do you think Scotch whisky appeals to that category and what can the producers do to attract them and keep them interested?

I do think that Scotch Whisky appeals to them. In the past many of them saw Scotch as an old persons drink but now with the reinvigoration of the cocktail culture Scotch is right at the forefront of their minds especially with a focus on the classics. We have to be careful of over doing the stories, keep it simple and create/produce Scotch that appeals and is not over blown with marketing. One of the key messages for Scotch in this sector is that its all about referrals from customer to customer rather than relying on write ups from experts all the time. I have also noticed that more distilleries are focusing on the hand crafted aspect of whisky making, this certainly appeals to this sector and to others as well.

2. Several Scotch whisky producers have recently questioned the rules what can and can´t be said on the label about the whisky. Should the legislation be changed, allowing more transparency?

I cannot understand why the industry would not wish for transparency. If we are to attract new customers to the category they expect to know or want to know what is in the bottle that they are purchasing and drinking. By not doing this we are in danger of putting people off or in fact making them question the product and its authenticity. A good example of this is the wine trade where producers are more often than not explaining what grape variety is in the wine with the percentage used if it is a blend and why they have used the particular varieties. This immediately provides authenticity to the product and confidence in the brand. What have we got to hide, tell the consumer that would be my feeling.

3. We see more and more Scotch whiskies being bottled without an age statement (NAS). Will that trend continue and, from a consumer point of view, is that all bad?

I do not see the issue with NAS as long as the price reflects the quality. Many new customers for Scotch are used to drinking other non aged spirits. Of course I would say this as we have NAS at Tullibardine but that is mainly due to the closure of the distillery for about 10 years, but we have both NAS & aged whiskies in the range. I cannot see the trend disappearing, it is here to stay but it is essential that the consumer is informed about what the whiskies are in the NAS and how it was produced compared with the aged ones, look at what Compass Box do for example with their whiskies, no age, diverse & different. It goes back to transparency really and this is where NAS has become an issue with established whisky drinkers. It was not long ago that many in the industry were stating that age was all important and the older the whisky was the better it was going to be. It goes back to what I said before, its about the ratio of price and quality, if we do not get that right then the consumer is not going to be fooled into thinking that NAS is better than what was on offer before.

4. Not a new discussion but one that does resurface from time to time. Does the quality of a whisky suffer from chill-filtration and colouring?

This is a topic that certainly gets many people hot under the collar for sure. I personally would prefer to see non chill-filtration & no colouring as it means that the whisky is as close to what it was in the barrel. Its very similar to over filtration of wine as this does remove some of the core body and flavour and its the same with whisky. Why add colour when the cask can provide such a wonderful array of different hues. From experience many consumers are confused with the words chill-filtration and possibly do not understand the process anyway but I do think that more of them are now looking more into the way a whisky is made and becoming far more knowledgeable and thus wanting the whisky to be as natural as possible.

5. In the steps of flavoured vodka, flavoured whisky has become increasingly popular. Mostly bourbon and Irish whiskey but also Scotch. What are the benefits and downsides of this new trend?

Don't we already add flavour to whisky with the different casks that it is matured in! Maybe I am being a little old fashioned but I think that the different & subtle flavours that secondary casks that have had wine or even other spirits in them beforehand can provide the perfect door opener to a new generation of whisky drinker, especially those who know and drink wine. Of course to encourage more people to drink whisky we should certainly not ignore doing things differently. All of us in the industry are often asked the question how should I drink my whisky? In the end it is a personal choice to add water, ice or a mixer so therefore if the consumer likes the idea of a flavoured whisky then it certainly shouldn't be overlooked.

6. Scotch whisky exports have declined in the last couple of years. Is the position of Scotch under threat and if so, what can be done to change the trend?

I think that this has really happened due to political and economic upheavals. I truly believe that the huge growth of whisky being distilled around the world especially in the US & Canada only helps Scotch Whisky. It draws more consumers to drinking whiskey or whisky and inevitably sends them in the direction of Scotland. We should not stick our head in the sand though and thus we should continue to be innovative and creative with what we are producing. I think that what Compass Box have done over the past few years highlights this, they have made Scotch interesting to the new consumer and the existing one.

Loch Lomond

[lock low•mund]

Owner: **Region/district:**
Loch Lomond Group   Western Highlands
(majority owner Exponent Private Equity)

Founded: **Status:**   **Capacity:**
1965   Active   5 000 000 litres

Address: Lomond Estate, Alexandria G83 0TL

Website: **Tel:**
lochlomonddistillery.com   01389 752781

When Loch Lomond distillery (together with Glen Scotia and Glen Catrine bottling plant) was taken over by Exponent Private Equity, it proved to be a huge boost for the company.

The former owner, Sandy Bulloch, had done an excellent job when he built up his business to one of the biggest companies in the Scotch whisky industry, but with the new owners came a long awaited injection of money. The distilleries were both refurbished and expanded and the range of whiskies was completely overhauled. The company now has more than 200 people employed and its products are sold in over 80 countries. Their biggest seller is not a whisky, but Glen vodka, which is currently the second best selling spirit in the UK.

Loch Lomond distillery is equipped with one full lauter mash tun complemented by ten 25,000 litres and eleven 50,000 litres washbacks, all of which are made of stainless steel. The set-up of stills differs completely from any other distillery in Scotland. There are two, traditional, copper pot stills and six copper stills where the swan necks have been exchanged with rectifying columns. Furthermore, there is one Coffey still used for continuous distillation. And if this was not enough, an additional distillery with column stills producing grain whisky is housed in the same building. For the grain side of production there are twelve 100,000 litres and eight 200,000 litres washbacks. Its total capacity is 5 million litres of malt spirit and 18 million litres of grain.

The distillery used to produce a broad range of whiskies with two main brands – Loch Lomond and Inchmurrin. Further back in time, there were another 5-6 brands and several have contained peated whisky as well. With two new additions to the range in summer 2016 (the rest were launched in spring 2015), the range now consists of **Loch Lomond Original Single Malt** without age statement and the two new ones, **Loch Lomond 12** and **18 year old**, as well as two blends – the **Reserve** and the **Signature**. Furthermore, there are **Inchmurrin 12, 18** and a **Madeira Wood** without age statement, **Glengarry NAS** and **12 year old** and, finally, **Loch Lomond Single Grain**.

History:

1965   The distillery is built by Littlemill Distillery Company Ltd owned by Duncan Thomas and American Barton Brands.

1966   Production commences.

1971   Duncan Thomas is bought out.

1984   The distillery closes.

1985   Glen Catrine Bonded Warehouse Ltd buys Loch Lomond Distillery.

1987   The distillery resumes production.

1993   Grain spirits are also distilled.

1997   A fire destroys 300,000 litres of maturing whisky.

1999   Two more stills are installed.

2005   Inchmoan and Craiglodge as well as Inchmurrin 12 years are launched.

2006   Inchmurrin 4 years, Croftengea 1996 (9 years), Glen Douglas 2001 (4 years) and Inchfad 2002 (5 years) are launched.

2010   A peated Loch Lomond with no age statement is released as well as a Vintage 1966.

2012   New range for Inchmurrin released – 12, 15, 18 and 21 years.

2014   The distillery is sold to Exponent Private Equity. Organic versions of 12 year old single malt and single blend are released.

2015   Loch Lomond Original Single Malt is released together with a single grain and two blends, Reserve and Signature.

2016   A 12 year old and an 18 year old are launched.

Loch Lomond Original

Tasting notes Loch Lomond Original:

GS – Initially earthy on the nose, with malt and subtle oak. The palate is rounded, with allspice, orange, lime, toffee, and a little smokiness. Barley, citrus fruits and substantial spiciness in the finish.

Longmorn

[long•morn]

Owner:		**Region/district:**
Chivas Brothers		Speyside
(Pernod Ricard)		
Founded:	**Status:**	**Capacity:**
1894	Active	4 500 000 litres

Address: Longmorn, Morayshire IV30 8SJ

Website:	**Tel:**
-	01343 554139

The resemblance between the stills at Longmorn and those working at the Yoichi distillery in Japan may seem strange but it is no coincidence. It is all due to a young Japanese who came to Speyside in 1919.

Masataka Taketsuru had been sent off to Scotland by his boss, Shinjiro Torii, to gain knowledge about whisky production. Torii was the founder of what would later be named Suntory and he was anxious to expand his winemaking business also to produce whisky. Taketsuru arrived in Elgin in April 1919 and was welcomed at Longmorn distillery where he worked for five days. That practice, together with similar visits to other distilleries provided him with valuable information to be able to pilot the building of Yamazaki, the first designated Japanese whisky distillery, when once home in Japan. After a couple of years, Taketsuru was ready to build his own distillery, Yoichi on Hokkaido, and there he used a lot of what he had learnt during the five days as an apprentice at Longmorn.

In 2012, Longmorn distillery was completely revamped and expanded. A new 8.5 ton Briggs full lauter mash tun replaced the old, traditional tun and seven of the eight, old stainless steel washbacks were moved to the new tun room and an additional three were installed. There are currently four pairs of stills, all fitted with sub-coolers and the wash stills now have external heat exchangers. The production capacity has also increased by 30% to 4.5 million litres.

Longmorn single malt is often referred to as a hidden gem or the whisky blender's favourite, and to the owners, Chivas Brothers, the whisky has become an integral part of several of their blends, especially Chivas Regal 18 year old and Royal Salute. Sales of Longmorn single malt today are minuscule and only one widely available expression exists. In 2015, **The Distiller's Choice** (with no age statement) replaced the 16 year old as the only core bottling. Apart from that, a **16 year old cask strength** bottling (59.6%) in the new range, The Distillery Reserve Collection, can also be found at Chivas' visitor centres.

History:

1893 John Duff & Company, which founded Glenlossie already in 1876, starts construction. John Duff, George Thomson and Charles Shirres are involved in the company. The total cost amounts to £20,000.

1894 First production in December.

1897 John Duff buys out the other partners.

1898 John Duff builds another distillery next to Longmorn which is called Benriach (at times aka Longmorn no. 2). Duff declares bankruptcy and the shares are sold by the bank to James R. Grant.

1970 The distillery company is merged with The Glenlivet & Glen Grant Distilleries and Hill Thomson & Co. Ltd. Own floor maltings ceases.

1972 The number of stills is increased from four to six. Spirit stills are converted to steam firing.

1974 Another two stills are added.

1978 Seagrams takes over through The Chivas & Glenlivet Group.

1994 Wash stills are converted to steam firing.

2001 Pernod Ricard buys Seagram Spirits & Wine together with Diageo and Pernod Ricard takes over the Chivas group.

2004 A 17 year old cask strength is released.

2007 A 16 year old is released replacing the 15 year old.

2012 Production capacity is expanded.

2015 The Distiller's Choice is released.

The Distiller's Choice

Tasting notes Longmorn Distiller's Choice:

GS – Barley sugar, ginger, toffee and malt on the sweet nose. The palate reveals caramel and milk chocolate, with peppery Jaffa orange. Toffee, barley and a hint of spicy oak in the medium-length finish.

Macallan

[mack•al•un]

Owner:	**Region/district:**
Edrington Group	Speyside

Founded:	**Status:**	**Capacity:**
1824	Active (vc)	11.000 000 litres

Address: Easter Elchies, Craigellachie, Morayshire AB38 9RX

Website:	**Tel:**
themacallan.com	01340 871471

Macallan is the third most sold single malt in the world. With a sales increase during the past few years of over 25 % and with 9.5 million bottles being sold in 2015, the owners are now forced to review the production capacity.

A completely new distillery is being constructed and when it is ready to start production in autumn 2017, it will be Scotland's biggest malt distillery with a capacity of 15 million litres. The information regarding the number of stills in the new plant has varied. The latest information released by the owners is that there will be 24 stills. The new distillery will be shaped like five hills with meadow grass on the roof. The total cost of the project will be a staggering £100m! This includes a new cooperage and more warehouses as well. Until the distillery is ready, production currently takes place in two separate plants. The number one plant holds an 8.3 ton full lauter mash tun, 19 stainless steel washbacks, five wash stills and ten spirit stills. The number two plant comprises of a 6.7 ton semi-lauter mash tun, six wooden washbacks and three made of stainless steel, two wash stills and four spirit stills. The plan for 2016 is to do 73 mashes per week which means that they will end up with 11 million litres of alcohol. For the last couple of years, the distillery has been using the Concerto variety of barley, but 15% of the requirement is made up of Momentum which is a strain exclusive to Macallan.

The core range for Macallan consists of the 1824 Series – **Gold, Amber, Sienna** and **Ruby**. The whiskies are sold without age statement and have been matured in ex-sherry casks, but the origin of the oak and the age of the whisky will vary. Macallan's two previous ranges, **Sherry Oak (12, 18, 25** and **30 year old)** and **Fine Oak (10, 12, 15, 17, 18, 21, 25** and **30 year old)** will gradually be phased out, but will still be available for purchase in selected markets for a fairly long period of time. In spring 2016 a new core expression, the **12 year old Double Cask,** was released in Taiwan and in the USA. The plan is to launch it to other markets as well during 2016. It has been matured in a mix of sherry casks from both American and European oak. At the same time, the first in a new series of limited bottlings, **Edition No 1**, was launched and this was followed by **Edition No 2** in the autumn of 2016. In 2014, an extension of the range called 1824 Masters Series was launched. Four prestige expressions, all sherry matured and bottled in Lalique decanters, have been included – **Rare Cask, Reflexion, No.6** and **M**. The Macallan duty free range (called the 1824 Collection) holds five expressions; **Select Oak, Whisky Maker's Edition, Estate Reserve, Oscuro** and **Rare Cask Black**. The latter, released in autumn 2015, was made up of 100 sherry-seasoned casks but what is unusual is that it is lightly peated. Introduced in 2005, The Six Pillars Collection of ultra rare whiskies came to an end with the final release in summer 2016 - the 65 year old, **The Peerless Spirit**. Finally, **The Fine & Rare** range showcases vintages from 1926 to 1990.

History:

1824   The distillery is licensed to Alexander Reid under the name Elchies Distillery.

1847   Alexander Reid passes away and James Shearer Priest and James Davidson take over.

1868   James Stuart takes over the licence. He founds Glen Spey distillery a decade later.

1886   James Stuart buys the distillery.

1892   Stuart sells the distillery to Roderick Kemp from Elgin. Kemp expands the distillery and names it Macallan-Glenlivet.

1909   Roderick Kemp passes away and the Roderick Kemp Trust is established to secure the family's future ownership.

1965   The number of stills is increased from six to twelve.

1966   The trust is reformed as a private limited company.

1968   The company is introduced on the London Stock Exchange.

1974   The number of stills is increased to 18.

1975   Another three stills are added, now making the total 21.

1984   The first official 18 year old single malt is launched.

1986   Japanese Suntory buys 25% of Macallan-Glenlivet plc stocks.

1996   Highland Distilleries buys the remaining stocks. 1874 Replica is launched.

1999   Edrington and William Grant & Sons buys Highland Distilleries (where Edrington, Suntory and Remy-Cointreau already are shareholders) for £601 million. They form the 1887 Company which owns Highland Distilleries with 70% held by Edrington and 30% by William Grant & Sons (excepting the 25% share held by Suntory).

No.17
WASHBACK

History continued:

2000 The first single cask from Macallan (1981) is named Exceptional 1.

2001 A new visitor centre is opened.

2002 Elegancia replaces 12 year old in the duty-free range. 1841 Replica, Exceptional II and Exceptional III are also launched.

2003 1876 Replica and Exceptional IV, single cask from 1990 are released.

2004 Exceptional V, single cask from 1989 is released as well as Exceptional VI, single cask from 1990. The Fine Oak series is launched.

2005 New expressions are Macallan Woodland Estate, Winter Edition and the 50 year old.

2006 Fine Oak 17 years old and Vintage 1975 are launched.

2007 1851 Inspiration and Whisky Maker´s Selection are released as a part of the Travel Retail range. 12 year old Gran Reserva is launched in Taiwan and Japan.

2008 Estate Oak and 55 year old Lalique are released.

2009 Capacity increased by another six stills. The Macallan 1824 Collection and a 57 year old Lalique bottling is released.

2010 Oscuro is released for Duty Free.

2011 Macallan MMXI is released for duty free.

2012 Macallan Gold, the first in the new 1824 series, is launched.

2013 Amber, Sienna and Ruby are released.

2014 1824 Masters Series (with Rare Cask, Reflexion and No. 6) is released.

2015 Rare Cask Black is released.

2016 Edition No. 1 and 12 year old Double Cask are released.

Tasting notes Macallan Gold:

GS – The nose offers apricots and peaches, fudge and a hint of leather. Medium-bodied, with malt, walnuts and spices on the palate. Quite oaky in the medium-length finish.

Tasting notes Macallan Amber:

GS – Sweet sherry, malt, spicy fudge and a hint of cinnamon on the nose. Sherry and malt carry over from the nose to the palate, with ginger emerging in time. Christmas cake flavours and Jaffa orange in the relatively lengthy finish.

Tasting notes Macallan 12 year old sherry oak:

GS – The nose is luscious, with buttery sherry and Christmas cake characteristics. Rich and firm on the palate, with sherry, elegant oak and Jaffa oranges. The finish is long and malty, with slightly smoky spice.

Amber   Sienna   Ruby

15 years old   12 years old   12 years old
Fine Oak   Double Cask   Sherry Cask

Gold   Rare Cask Black   Reflexion   Rare Cask

Macduff

[mack•duff]

Owner:
John Dewar & Sons Ltd
(Bacardi)

Region/district:
Highlands

Founded: 1960
Status: Active
Capacity: 3 340 000 litres

Address: Banff, Aberdeenshire AB45 3JT

Website: lastgreatmalts.com
Tel: 01261 812612

The owners may have recently re-launched The Deveron single malt from Macduff, but there is no doubt that the distillery's most important task is to produce single malt for the successful William Lawson´s blended Scotch.

A somewhat incredible increase in sales during the last decade, led to the fact that the brand in 2012 had outdone its "sister brand" Dewar´s White Label in popularity. As a matter of fact, at the same time it had climbed from 14th place to become number six on the Top Twenty list of Scotch. Lawson´s has gained market shares in many countries around the world, but the development in Russia probably impresses the most. Introduced into the country in 2008, by 2014 it had become not only the biggest Scotch but also the number one imported spirit in Russia. The importance of Russia as a market was emphasised in spring 2016, when Bacardi signed a deal with the Russian company, Synergy, where the blend will be bottled at their plant outside Moscow. This is the first time in modern days that an international spirits brand has moved bottling operations to Russia.

The distillery is equipped with a stainless steel semi-lauter mash tun and nine washbacks made of stainless steel with a fermentation time between 49 and 55 hours. There is also a rather unusual set-up of five stills – two wash stills and three spirit stills. In order to fit the stills into the still room, the lyne arms on four of the stills are bent in a peculiar way and on one of the wash stills it is U-shaped. In 2016 the distillery will be doing 25 mashes per week, producing 2.8 million litres of alcohol.

Official bottlings from Macduff have always been made under the name Glen Deveron. When a completely new range of bottlings was launched in September 2015, the name had changed to The Deveron. The core range now consists of a **10 year old**, exclusive to France, as well as a **12** and **18 year old**. For duty free, a new range was launched in 2013 under the name The Royal Burgh Collection encompassing a **16**, a **20** and a **30 year old**.

History:

1960 The distillery is founded by Marty Dyke, George Crawford, James Stirrat and Brodie Hepburn (who is also involved in Tullibardine and Deanston). Macduff Distillers Ltd is the name of the company.

1964 The number of stills is increased from two to three.

1967 Stills now total four.

1972 William Lawson Distillers, part of General Beverage Corporation which is owned by Martini & Rossi, buys the distillery from Glendeveron Distilleries.

1990 A fifth still is installed.

1993 Bacardi buys Martini Rossi (including William Lawson) and eventually transfered Macduff to the subsidiary John Dewar & Sons.

2013 The Royal Burgh Collection (16, 20 and 30 years old) is launched for duty free.

2015 A new range is launched - 10, 12 and 18 years old.

12 years old

Tasting notes The Deveron 12 years old:

GS – Soft, sweet and fruity on the nose, with vanilla, ginger, and apple blossom. Medium-bodied, gently spicy, with butterscotch and Brazil nuts. Caramel contrasts with quite dry spicy oak in the finish.

Mannochmore

[man•och•moor]

Owner:	**Region/district:**
Diageo	Speyside
Founded: **Status:**	**Capacity:**
1971 Active	6 000 000 litres

Address: Elgin, Morayshire IV30 8SS

Website:	**Tel:**
malts.com	01343 862000

Mannochmore was built in 1971 by DCL, the predecessor of Diageo when interest in Scotch whisky was booming. At the same time another four distilleries opened in the Speyside area.

DCL was at this time regarded as the grand old man of the Scotch whisky industry. It had already been founded in 1877 and for a large part of the 20th century the company had dominated the market. By 1982 it owned 46 of the 119 malt distilleries and 5 of the 12 grain distilleries. In terms of ownership, it was even more dominant than what Diageo is today. But the large number of distilleries didn't tell the whole story. Since the 1960s, the company had steadily lost market shares. It was run in a traditional but inefficient way and there was an imminent threat from its competitors. As the whisky market started deflating towards the beginning of the 1980s, the company became a target for buyers and in 1986 DCL was acquired by the giant brewer, Guinness.

The Glenlossie/Mannochmore complex, south of Elgin, is a busy site with 14 warehouses holding 250,000 casks from many of Diageo's 28 distilleries. There is also a dark grains plant which converts pot ale into cattle feed, as well as a newly installed biomass burner which generates draff into steam which will power the entire site. And, of course, there are two distilleries with Glenlossie having been built almost a hundred years before its younger sister, Mannochmore. Five years ago, the two distilleries produced a combined total of 5 million litres – a figure which today, thanks largely to a powerful expansion and switching to 7-day weeks, has almost doubled to 9 million litres. Mannochmore has now outgrown its older sibling and accounts for two thirds of the capacity. Since summer 2013 the distillery is equipped with an 11 ton Briggs full lauter mash tun, eight wooden washbacks and another eight external made of stainless steel and four pairs of stills.

The only current official bottling of Mannochmore is a **12 year old** Flora & Fauna. In October 2016, a **25 year old** distilled in 1990 and bottled at 53.4%, was launched as part of this year's Special Releases.

History:

1971 Distillers Company Limited (DCL) founds the distillery on the site of their sister distillery Glenlossie. It is managed by John Haig & Co. Ltd.

1985 The distillery is mothballed.

1989 In production again.

1992 A Flora & Fauna series 12 years old becomes the first official bottling.

2009 An 18 year old is released.

2010 A Manager´s Choice 1998 is released.

2013 The number of stills is increased to four.

2016 A 25 year old cask strength is released.

12 years old

Tasting notes Mannochmore 12 years old:

GS – Perfumed and fresh on the light, citric nose, with a sweet, floral, fragrant palate, featuring vanilla, ginger and even a hint of mint. Medium length in the finish, with a note of lingering almonds.

Miltonduff

[mill•ton•duff]

Owner:
Chivas Brothers
(Pernod Ricard)

Region/district:
Speyside

Founded: **Status:**
1824   Active

Capacity:
5 800 000 litres

Address: Miltonduff, Elgin, Morayshire IV30 8TQ

Website: **Tel:**
-                    01343 547433

Miltonduff distillery is situated 7 kilometres south-west of Elgin, in peaceful rural surroundings called Pluscarden. Once called the Garden of Scotland, this is excellent land for growing barley.

This was one of the reasons for an abbey to be founded here by Alexander II in 1230. The influence of the abbey grew and a big part of the surroundings soon belonged to the monks of Pluscarden, including the site where Miltonduff now lies. The clear water from the Black Burn and the surplus of good barley created good conditions for building a brew house and producing beer and, who knows, perhaps even whisky. In any case, there is a legend which tells the story of a ceremony in the 15th century where the abbot, kneeling on a stone, blessed the water "and any product distilled there from". What is believed to be the stone, can now be seen imbedded in the water wheel pit at Miltonduff distillery. True or not, the Glen of Pluscarden has long been a haven for whisky production and, at one time, there were at least fifty illicit stills in the area.

Miltonduff distillery is equipped with an 8 tonne full lauter mash tun with a copper dome, 16 stainless steel washbacks with a fermentation time of 56 hours and six, large stills. The lyne arms are all sharply descending which allows for very little reflux. This makes for a rather robust and oily newmake in contrast to the lighter and more floral Glenburgie. Together, the two malts form the backbone of Ballantine's – the second biggest Scotch in the world after Johnnie Walker.

The most recent official bottling of Miltonduff is a **1997, 15 year old**, which was released in Chivas Brothers' cask strength series and is available only at Chivas' visitor centres. In 2013, a special Miltonduff version of the 17 year old Ballantine's was launched in its Signature Distillery Editions range. The idea is to highlight the four signature malts of the world's number 2 blended Scotch. The first two (Scapa and Glenburgie) were released in 2012 and the fourth and final one (Glentaucher's) came in 2014.

History:

1824 Andrew Peary and Robert Bain obtain a licence for Miltonduff Distillery. It has previously operated as an illicit farm distillery called Milton Distillery but changes name when the Duff family buys the site it is operating on.

1866 William Stuart buys the distillery.

1895 Thomas Yool & Co. becomes new part-owner.

1936 Thomas Yool & Co. sells the distillery to Hiram Walker Gooderham & Worts. The latter transfers administration to the newly acquired subsidiary George Ballantine & Son.

1964 A pair of Lomond stills is installed to produce the rare Mosstowie.

1974 Major reconstruction of the distillery.

1981 The Lomond stills are decommissioned and replaced by two ordinary pot stills, the number of stills now totalling six.

1986 Allied Lyons buys 51% of Hiram Walker.

1987 Allied Lyons acquires the rest of Hiram Walker.

1991 Allied Distillers follow United Distillers' example of Classic Malts and introduce Caledonian Malts in which Tormore, Glendro-nach and Laphroaig are included in addition to Miltonduff. Tormore is later replaced by Scapa.

2005 Chivas Brothers (Pernod Ricard) becomes the new owner through the acquisition of Allied Domecq.

1998 16 years old

Tasting notes Miltonduff 16 years old:

GS – Vanilla and pine on the nose, with soft toffee and a hint of cinnamon. Zesty orange, mixed nuts and cocoa on the palate. The finish is long, nutty and slighlty citric.

Mortlach

[mort•lack]

Owner: Diageo   **Region/district:** Speyside

Founded: 1823   **Status:** Active   **Capacity:** 3 800 000 litres

Address: Dufftown, Keith, Banffshire AB55 4AQ

Website: malts.com   **Tel:** 01340 822100

In his immortal bible, the Malt Whisky Companion, Michael Jackson devotes an entire chapter to what he calls regional characteristics in the flavour.

This approach has been forsaken more and more as heavily peated whiskies can be found in Speyside and big, bold whiskies can be produced in the Lowlands. One distillery which has not always conformed is Mortlach. Although it is situated in Dufftown, in the very heart of Speyside, it has never been known for a light and fruity character. Instead it's a meaty heavyweight which takes time to mature. Jackson himself calls it "a secret star" and the whisky has, notwithstanding, always had devoted followers.

The distillery was closed from May to October 2015 when major works were carried out. Four washbacks were replaced, a larger yeast tank was installed and some of the necks, shoulders and lye pipes on some of the stills were also replaced. After the re-opening, production was slowly jacked up to 16 mashes per week in early 2016, with the objective of producing 3.8 million litres of alcohol. A decision to expand the distillery and double the production has now been put on hold.

The distillery is equipped with a 12 tonnes full lauter mash tun, six washbacks made of larch and six stills in various sizes, all of them being attached to worm tubs for cooling the spirit vapours. There are three wash stills and three spirit stills where the No. 3 pair acts as a traditional double distillation. The low wines from wash stills No. 1 and 2 are directed to the remaining two spirit stills according to a certain distribution. In one of the spirit stills, called Wee Witchie, the charge is redistilled twice and, with all the various distillations taken into account, it could be said that Mortlach is distilled 2.8 times.

The core range consists of **Rare Old** with no age statement and matured mostly in first fill bourbon casks, but also in ex sherry casks, **Special Strength**, which is exclusive to duty free, similar to Rare Old but bottled at 49%. Then there is an **18 year old** matured in a combination of first fill sherry casks and re-fill American oak, as well as a **25 year old**, which is predominantly matured in re-fill American oak.

History:

1823 The distillery is founded by James Findlater.

1824 Donald Macintosh and Alexander Gordon become part-owners.

1831 The distillery is sold to John Robertson for £270.

1832 A. & T. Gregory buys Mortlach.

1837 James and John Grant of Aberlour become part-owners. No production takes place.

1842 The distillery is now owned by John Alexander Gordon and the Grant brothers.

1851 Mortlach is producing again after having been used as a church and a brewery for some years.

1853 George Cowie joins and becomes part-owner.

1867 John Alexander Gordon dies and Cowie becomes sole owner.

1895 George Cowie Jr. joins the company.

1897 The number of stills is increased from three to six.

1923 Alexander Cowie sells the distillery to John Walker & Sons.

1925 John Walker becomes part of Distillers Company Limited (DCL).

1964 Major refurbishment.

1968 Floor maltings ceases.

1996 Mortlach 1972 is released as a Rare Malt.

1998 Mortlach 1978 is released as a Rare Malt.

2004 Mortlach 1971, a 32 year old cask strength is released.

2014 Four new bottlings are released - Rare Old, Special Strength, 18 year old and 25 year old.

Tasting notes Mortlach Rare Old:

GS – Fresh and fruity on the nose, majoring in peaches and apricots. Parma violets, milk chocolate, and finally caramel. Fruit carries over from the nose to the nutty palate, with cinnamon spice. The finish is relatively long and spicy.

Rare Old

Oban

[oa•bun]

Owner:
Diageo

Region/district:
Western Highlands

Founded: 1794

Status: Active (vc)

Capacity: 870 000 litres

Address: Stafford Street, Oban, Argyll PA34 5NH

Website: malts.com

Tel: 01631 572004 (vc)

For a short period of time, the infamous Pattison brothers were involved in Oban distillery, owning a part of it in the last shivering years of the 19th century.

In 1898 the owner of Aultmore distillery, Alexander Edward, also acquired Oban and merged the two distilleries. Involved in the deal were Robert and Walter Pattison, whisky blenders in Leith. Shortly afterwards, the flotation of the Oban and Aultmore Distillery Co. gave Robert Pattison alone a profit of £40,000, which he spent on his lavish house. Both brothers led extravagant lives, but their fame in the whisky history was accentuated when their fraudulent business methods based on inflated stock figures, unsecured loans and embezzlement were revealed. Predictably, their company was forced into liquidation. A huge part of the industry were in business with the Pattisons and many followed in the crash that in 1899 marked the start of a 50 year long barren path for Scotch whisky.

Oban distillery is one of Scotland's oldest distilleries as well as one of the few remaining urban distilleries. The town of Oban was more or less just a fishing village when the distillery was built and it now features prominently right in the heart of the town. The equipment consists of a 7 ton traditional stainless steel mash tun with rakes, four washbacks made of European larch and one pair of stills. Attached to the stills is a rectangular, stainless steel, double worm tub to condensate the spirit vapours. One washback will fill the wash still twice. However, the character of Oban single malt is dependent on long fermentations (110 hours), hence they can only manage six mashes per week, giving it five long fermentations and one short one. The production for 2016 will be slightly more than 800,000 litres. The distillery also boasts one of the best visitor centres in the business with 35,000 visitors every year.

The core range consists of **Little Bay** (released in 2015) a **14 year old**, an **18 year old** exclusive for USA and a **Distiller's Edition** with a montilla fino sherry finish. In 2013 a **21 year old** was launched as part of the Special Releases and in autumn 2016, a distillery exclusive without age statement was released.

History:

1793 John and Hugh Stevenson found the distillery.

1820 Hugh Stevenson dies.

1821 Hugh Stevenson's son Thomas takes over.

1829 Bad investments force Thomas Stevenson into bankruptcy. His eldest son John takes over.

1830 John buys the distillery from his father's creditors for £1,500.

1866 Peter Cumstie buys the distillery.

1883 Cumstie sells Oban to James Walter Higgins who refurbishes and modernizes it.

1898 The Oban & Aultmore-Glenlivet Co. takes over with Alexander Edwards at the helm.

1923 The Oban Distillery Co. owned by Buchanan-Dewar takes over.

1925 Buchanan-Dewar becomes part of Distillers Company Limited (DCL).

1931 Production ceases.

1937 In production again.

1968 Floor maltings ceases and the distillery closes for reconstruction.

1972 Reopening of the distillery.

1979 Oban 12 years is on sale.

1988 United Distillers launches Classic Malts and Oban 14 year old is included.

1998 A Distillers' Edition is launched.

2002 The oldest Oban (32 years) so far is launched.

2004 A 1984 cask strength is released.

2009 Oban 2000, a single cask, is released.

2010 A no age distillery exclusive is released.

2013 A limited 21 year old is released.

2015 Oban Little Bay is released.

2016 A distillery exclusive without age statement is released.

14 year old

Tasting notes Oban 14 years old:

GS – Lightly smoky on the honeyed, floral nose. Toffee, cereal and a hint of peat. The palate offers initial cooked fruits, becoming spicier. Complex, bittersweet, oak and more gentle smoke. The finish is quite lengthy, with spicy oak, toffee and new leather.

Pulteney

[poolt•ni]

Owner:
Inver House Distillers
(Thai Beverages plc)

Region/district:
Northern Highlands

Founded: 1826 **Status:** Active (vc) **Capacity:** 1 800 000 litres

Address: Huddart St, Wick, Caithness KW1 5BA

Website: oldpulteney.com **Tel:** 01955 602371

Pulteney distillery is named after Sir William Pulteney who, at the beginning of the 1800s, decided to build an entirely new town with a fishing harbour situated next to Wick in the very north of Scotland.

Pulteney, as governor of the British Fisheries Society, gave the famous engineer, Thomas Telford, the assignment to build the city named Pulteneytown, to the south side of the river Wick. One of the reasons was to supply work to the many farmers who were evicted from their homes during the Highland Clearances. Over time, the town got the reputation of being the biggest herring port in Europe and, during its heydays, 800 boats could set sail from the harbour during a single day.

The distillery is equipped with a stainless steel semi-lauter mash tun clad with wood and with a copper canopy. There are six washbacks dating from the 1920s all made from Corten steel and are due to be replaced with stainless steel in 2016. Fermentation time is a mix of short cycles (of 50 hours) and long ones (of 110 hours). The wash still, equipped with a huge boil ball and a very thick lye pipe, is quaintly chopped off at the top. Both stills use stainless steel worm tubs for condensing the spirit. The plan for 2016 is to produce 1.6 million litres of alcohol.

The core range of Old Pulteney comprises of **12, 17, 21** and **35 year old**. To complement the bottlings with age statements, a new, un chillfiltered expression with no age statement was introduced in 2013 – **Old Pulteney Navigator**. During that same year, the owners started to release a series of whiskies, all destined for duty free and named after lighthouses that are scattered all around Wick. **Noss Head** is matured in ex-bourbon American oak, while **Duncansby Head** and **Dunnet Head** are a mix of ex-bourbon and ex-sherry. A limited **Vintage 1990**, which was released in 2013, was replaced by a **1989 Vintage** in 2015, together with the second release of the 35 year old. The French market is important to Pulteney and during autumn 2015, the third edition of **Flotilla** (this time a vintage 2005) was released exclusively to France.

History:

1826 James Henderson founds the distillery.

1920 The distillery is bought by James Watson.

1923 Buchanan-Dewar takes over.

1930 Production ceases.

1951 In production again after being acquired by the solicitor Robert Cumming.

1955 Cumming sells to James & George Stodart, a subsidiary to Hiram Walker & Sons.

1958 The distillery is rebuilt.

1959 The floor maltings close.

1961 Allied Breweries buys James & George Stodart Ltd.

1981 Allied Breweries changes name to Allied Lyons.

1995 Allied Domecq sells Pulteney to Inver House Distillers.

1997 Old Pulteney 12 years is launched.

2001 Pacific Spirits (Great Oriole Group) buys Inver House at a price of $85 million.

2004 A 17 year old is launched.

2005 A 21 year old is launched.

2006 International Beverage Holdings acquires Pacific Spirits UK.

2010 WK499 Isabella Fortuna is released.

2012 A 40 year old and WK217 Spectrum are released.

2013 Old Pulteney Navigator, The Lighthouse range (3 expressions) and Vintage 1990 are released.

2014 A 35 year old is released.

2015 Dunnet Head and Vintage 1989 are released.

Tasting notes Old Pulteney 12 years old:

GS – The nose presents pleasingly fresh malt and floral notes, with a touch of pine. The palate is comparatively sweet, with malt, spices, fresh fruit and a suggestion of salt. The finish is medium in length, drying and decidedly nutty.

12 years old

Royal Brackla

[royal brack•lah]

Owner:
John Dewar & Sons
(Bacardi)

Region/district:
Highlands

Founded: **Status:**   **Capacity:**
1812   Active   4 000 000 litres

Address: Cawdor, Nairn, Nairnshire IV12 5QY

Website: **Tel:**
lastgreatmalts.com   01667 402002

In 1998, Royal Brackla distillery became a small pawn in the game when one of the biggest deals ever in the drinks industry was concluded.

The year before, Grand Metropolitan and Guinness merged to form the giant, Diageo. Anti-trust authorities reacted vehemently and demanded that Diageo sell off all its interests in John Dewar & Sons so that they wouldn't have too much of a stranglehold on the Scotch whisky market. More than 20 companies vied for the bid, which, of course, pushed up the price. Bacardi-Martini was ultimately the victorious bidder with a staggering amount of £1,15bn. This enabled them to acquire the Dewar´s brand, including Bombay gin and four distilleries, among them being Royal Brackla.

Even with the new owners, bottlings of Royal Brackla single malt were scarce. There was only a 10 year old to be found and one of the reasons was that no stock was included in the deal with Diageo when the distillery changed ownership. But in 2014, Dewar´s decided to make a relaunch of their single malt range from all five distilleries and they called it The Last Great Malts.

Royal Brackla is equipped with a 12.5 tonnes full lauter mash tun from 1997. There are six wooden washbacks and another two made of stainless steel which have been placed outside. Finally, there are also two pairs of stills. In 2016, the distillery will be doing between 16 and 17 mashes per week which translates to 3.5 million litres of alcohol per year. In 2015 a biomass boiler (fired with wood-chips) replaced the old, heavy fuel oil boiler. Not only will this contribute to a 5,000 tonnes reduction of CO_2 emissions, but it will also be 50% more energy efficient.

The new core range introduced in 2015 and replacing the 10 year old, consists of a **12, 16** and **21 year old**. There are also plans for a possible release of a **30 year old** in the near future. Recent, limited releases include a **25 year old** and a **35 year old**. The latter, launched in April 2014 at Changi airport in Singapore, is the oldest official Royal Brackla ever.

History:

1812   The distillery is founded by Captain William Fraser.

1833   Brackla becomes the first of three distilleries allowed to use 'Royal' in the name.

1852   Robert Fraser & Co. takes over the distillery.

1897   The distillery is rebuilt and Royal Brackla Distillery Company Limited is founded.

1919   John Mitchell and James Leict from Aberdeen purchase Royal Brackla.

1926   John Bisset & Company Ltd takes over.

1943   Scottish Malt Distillers (SMD) buys John Bisset & Company Ltd and thereby acquires Royal Brackla.

1964   The distillery closes for a big refurbishment
-1966   and the number of stills is increased to four. The maltings closes.

1970   Two stills are increased to four.

1985   The distillery is mothballed.

1991   Production resumes.

1993   A 10 year old Royal Brackla is launched in United Distillers´ Flora & Fauna series.

1997   UDV spends more than £2 million on improvements and refurbishing.

1998   Bacardi–Martini buys Dewar´s from Diageo.

2004   A new 10 year old is launched.

2014   A 35 year old is released for Changi airport in Singapore.

2015   A new range is released; 12, 16 and 21 year old.

12 years old

Tasting notes Royal Brackla 12 years old:

GS – Warm spices, malt and peaches in cream on the nose. The palate is robust, with spice and mildly smoky soft fruit. Quite lengthy in the finish, with citrus fruit, mild spice and cocoa powder.

Royal Lochnagar

[royal loch•nah•gar]

Owner: Diageo	**Region/district:** Eastern Highlands
Founded:	**Status:**	**Capacity:**
1845	Active (vc)	500 000 litres

Address: Crathie, Ballater, Aberdeenshire AB35 5TB

Website: malts.com	**Tel:** 01339 742700

Royal Lochnagar may well be Diageo´s smallest distillery with small quantities of their single malt being bottled, but the distillery has an important role to play in South Korea.

In 2002, the country was the fourth biggest export market for Scotch whisky but since then, mainly due to a bad economic climate, the figures have dropped by more than 50%. In spite of that, the biggest blends still sell in the range of 5 to 10 million bottles per year and the biggest of them all is Windsor, launched in 1996, where Royal Lochnagar is the signature malt. In second place we find Pernod Ricard´s Imperial and in third place we have Scotch Blue from Lotte Chilsung. The latter used to be produced by Burnt Stewart and Angus Dundee Distillers.

The distillery is one of two operating distilleries which can boast with a Royal Warrant, the other being Royal Brackla. There was a third distillery, Glenury Royal, just south of Aberdeen, but it closed in 1983 and was later demolished. In December 2015, Royal Lochnagar suffered severe flooding with water levels in the distillery above 50 centimetres and production had to stop for seven weeks.

The distillery is equipped with a 5.4 ton open, traditional stainless steel mash tun. There are three wooden washbacks, with short fermentations of 70 hours and long ones of 110 hours. The two stills are quite small with a charge in the wash still of 6,100 litres and 4,000 litres in the spirit still and the spirit vapours are condensed in cast iron worm tubs. The whole production is filled on site with around 1,000 casks being stored in its only warehouse, while the rest is sent to Glenlossie. Four mashes per week during 2016 will result in 450,000 litres of pure alcohol.

The core range consists of the **12 year old** and **Selected Reserve**. The latter is a vatting of casks, usually around 18-20 years of age. The Distiller´s Edition was discontinued a couple of years ago but in August 2016, a new distillery exclusive without age statement was released. In autumn 2015 one of the oldest bottlings from the distillery was launched, a **36 year old single cask**.

History:

- 1823 James Robertson founds a distillery in Glen Feardan on the north bank of River Dee.
- 1826 The distillery is burnt down by competitors but Robertson decides to establish a new distillery near the mountain Lochnagar.
- 1841 This distillery is also burnt down.
- 1845 A new distillery is built by John Begg, this time on the south bank of River Dee. It is named New Lochnagar.
- 1848 Lochnagar obtains a Royal Warrant.
- 1882 John Begg passes away and his son Henry Farquharson Begg inherits the distillery.
- 1896 Henry Farquharson Begg dies.
- 1906 The children of Henry Begg rebuild the distillery.
- 1916 The distillery is sold to John Dewar & Sons.
- 1925 John Dewar & Sons becomes part of Distillers Company Limited (DCL).
- 1963 A major reconstruction takes place.
- 2004 A 30 year old cask strength from 1974 is launched in the Rare Malts series (6,000 bottles).
- 2008 A Distiller´s Edition with a Moscatel finish is released.
- 2010 A Manager´s Choice 1994 is released.
- 2013 A triple matured expression for Friends of the Classic Malts is released.
- 2016 A distillery exclusive without age statement is released.

WASHBACK No.3

12 years old

Tasting notes Royal Lochnagar 12 years old:

GS – Light toffee on the nose, along with some green notes of freshly-sawn timber. The palate offers a pleasing and quite complex blend of caramel, dry sherry and spice, followed by a hint of liquorice before the slightly scented finish develops.

Scapa

[ska•pa]

Owner:
Chivas Brothers
(Pernod Ricard)

Region/district:
Highlands (Orkney)

Founded: 1885
Status: Active
Capacity: 1 300 000 litres

Address: Scapa, St Ola, Kirkwall, Orkney KW15 1SE

Website:
scapamalt.com

Tel:
01856 876585

Scapa distillery overlooks Scapa Flow, a sheltered bay which was used by the Royal Navy as a naval base during both world wars. The links between the distillery and the navy, however, are not merely geographical.

During the First World War, the distillery was used by Admiral Jellicoe as his base and he also saved the distillery from a fire during his tenure. In May 1916, Jellicoe led his fleet against the Germans in the Battle of Jutland near the coast of Denmark. It was the largest naval battle of the war and to commemorate the centenary, a special single cask Scapa was launched in May of this year. The profits from the sales will be donated to Royal National Lifeboat Institution.

Scapa distillery has long lived in the shadows of Highland Park which is situated in Kirkwall, just a few kilometres away. In spring 2015, however, things started to change. A visitor centre was opened, a new expression was released and production increased. Ever since Pernod Ricard assumed ownership in 2005, the distillery has only been working 3-4 days per week. From 2015 the production has been increased to 7 days, which means 1 million litres of alcohol per year including a small part of peated production as well

The equipment consists of a 2.9 ton semi-lauter mash tun with a copper dome, eight washbacks (four made of Corten steel and four of stainless steel) and two stills. Due to the increased production, fermentation time is now down to 52 hours from the previous 160 hours. The wash still is only one of two surviving Lomond stills in the industry but on the Scapa Lomond still, the adjustable plates have been removed.

The 16 year old has been phased out and replaced by **Scapa Skiren**, which was introduced in 2015. Matured in first fill bourbon, it doesn´t carry an age statement. **Scapa Jutland**, a 16 year old single cask for sale at the distillery only, was released in May 2016. There are also two cask strength vintages, **1992** and **2003**, both part of the new range The Distillery Reserve Collection which can be found at Chivas´ visitor centres.

History:

1885 Macfarlane & Townsend founds the distillery with John Townsend at the helm.

1919 Scapa Distillery Company Ltd takes over.

1934 Scapa Distillery Company goes into voluntary liquidation and production ceases.

1936 Production resumes.

1936 Bloch Brothers Ltd (John and Sir Maurice) takes over.

1954 Hiram Walker & Sons takes over.

1959 A Lomond still is installed.

1978 The distillery is modernized.

1994 The distillery is mothballed.

1997 Production takes place a few months each year using staff from Highland Park.

2004 Extensive refurbishing takes place at a cost of £2.1 million. Scapa 14 years is launched.

2005 Production ceases in April and phase two of the refurbishment programme starts. Chivas Brothers becomes the new owner.

2006 Scapa 1992 (14 years) is launched.

2008 Scapa 16 years is launched.

2015 The distillery opens for visitors and Scapa Skiren is launched.

Tasting notes Scapa Skiren:

GS – Lime is apparent on the early nose, followed by musty peaches, almonds, cinnamon, and salt. More peaches on the palate, with tinned pear and honey. Tingling spices in the drying finish, which soon becomes slightly astringent.

Scapa Skiren

Speyburn

[spey•burn]

Owner:
Inver House Distillers
(Thai Beverages plc)

Region/district:
Speyside

Founded:
1897

Status:
Active

Capacity:
4 200 000 litres

Address: Rothes, Aberlour, Morayshire AB38 7AG

Website:
speyburn.com

Tel:
01340 831213

For many years there has been a rivalry between the two Inver House single malt brands, Speyburn and Pulteney, as to which will outsell the other. There is now no doubt that Speyburn definitely has the advantage.

Sales of Speyburn increased by 37% in 2014 and another 49% in 2015, which means a total of more than 1 million bottles! The biggest stronghold for the brand is, by far, the American market and this goes back many years. The strong position in the USA can probably be attributed to the fact that Inver House has had American owners for the first 24 years. Publicker Industries founded the company in 1964 and then sold it to Standard Brands in 1979. A management buyout in 1988, however, ended the American ownership. The relationships that were established during these years led to an agreement in 1993 with Barton Brands to distribute Speyburn single malt on the American market. The agreement with Barton expired in 2009 and since 2015, the US importer for all the Inver House brands has been 375 Park Avenue Spirits.

An impressive expansion of the distillery commenced during 2014 and was completed during the spring of 2015. The expansion had cost £4m and included a new, 6 ton stainless steel mash tun. Four of the six wooden washbacks were kept but they have also expanded with no less than 15 washbacks made of stainless steel. Finally, the existing wash still was converted to a spirit still of exactly the same shape as the other one, while a new and much larger wash still was installed. The two spirit stills are connected to a worm tub while the wash still is fitted with a shell and tube condenser. The fermentation time has also been lengthened from the original 48 hours to a minimum of 72 hours. The result of the expansion was a doubling of the capacity to 4.2 million litres.

The core range of Speyburn single malt is the **10 year old** and **Bradan Orach** without age statement. In September 2015, **Arranta Casks** was released as a limited USA exclusive. A second release was made in 2016.

History:

1897 Brothers John and Edward Hopkin and their cousin Edward Broughton found the distillery through John Hopkin & Co. They already own Tobermory. The architect is Charles Doig. Building the distillery costs £17,000 and the distillery is transferred to Speyburn-Glenlivet Distillery Company.

1916 Distillers Company Limited (DCL) acquires John Hopkin & Co. and the distillery.

1930 Production stops.

1934 Productions restarts.

1962 Speyburn is transferred to Scottish Malt Distillers (SMD).

1968 Drum maltings closes.

1991 Inver House Distillers buys Speyburn.

1992 A 10 year old is launched as a replacement for the 12 year old in the Flora & Fauna series.

2001 Pacific Spirits (Great Oriole Group) buys Inver House for $85 million.

2005 A 25 year old Solera is released.

2006 Inver House changes owner when International Beverage Holdings acquires Pacific Spirits UK.

2009 The un-aged Bradan Orach is introduced for the American market.

2012 Clan Speyburn is formed.

2014 The distillery is expanded.

2015 Arranta Casks is released.

10 years old

Tasting notes Speyburn 10 years old:

GS – Soft and elegant on the spicy, nutty nose. Smooth in the mouth, with vanilla, spice and more nuts. The finish is medium, spicy and drying.

Speyside

[spey•side]

Owner:
Speyside Distillers Co.

Region/district:
Speyside

Founded: 1976

Status: Active

Capacity: 600 000 litres

Address: Glen Tromie, Kingussie, Inverness-shire PH21 1NS

Website:
speysidedistillery.co.uk

Tel:
01540 661060

When Harvey´s of Edinburgh took over Speyside distillery in 2012, they had been buying whisky from the distillery for almost twenty years. The bulk of the whisky was sold as Spey whisky in Asia and this still remains as its main market.

The owner of the company, John Harvey McDonough, spent three years in Taiwan in the 1990s working for IDV. The network that he has established has made Taiwan the single most important market for Spey single malt. More than 1 million bottles are sold every year, making it the third biggest single malt in the country, but another 20 countries have also become aware of the whisky. In 2015, the company managed to hire the ex-footballer, Michael Owen, as the figure-head for the brand.

Speyside produces on a small-scale and is set in beautiful surroundings. The distillery is equipped with a 4 ton semi-lauter mash tun, four stainless steel washbacks with a fermentation time of 48 hours and one pair of stills. In 2016 they will be working a 6 day week with a total production of 600,000 litres of alcohol. There are also plans to build a second distillery in Rothiemurches near Aviemore.

The core range of Spey single malt is made up of **Tenné** (with a 6 months finish in tawny port), **12 year old** (6 months finish in new American oak), **18 year old** (sherry matured), **Chairman´s Choice** and **Royal Choice**. The latter two are multi-vintage marriages from both American and European oak. Destined for export markets is also **Black Burn** without age statement. Limited releases during 2016 include **"Byron´s Choice - The Marriage"** bourbon matured and finished in port casks and **Spey Cask 27** which comes from the very first distillation in December 1990 and bottled at cask strength (55.1%) and which is neither coloured nor chill-filtered. Finally, **Beinn Dubh** which replaced the famous black whisky, Cu Duhb, is now part of the core range with a no age statement core version, as well as several special editions, including a **20 year old**. The new owners also produce blended whisky for selected export markets such as Scotch Guard and Glen Hood.

History:

1956 George Christie buys a piece of land at Drumguish near Kingussie.

1957 George Christie starts a grain distillery near Alloa.

1962 George Christie (founder of Speyside Distillery Group in the fifties) commissions the drystone dyker Alex Fairlie to build a distillery in Drumguish.

1986 Scowis assumes ownership.

1987 The distillery is completed.

1990 The distillery is on stream in December.

1993 The first single malt, Drumguish, is launched.

1999 Speyside 8 years is launched.

2000 Speyside Distilleries is sold to a group of private investors including Ricky Christie, Ian Jerman and Sir James Ackroyd.

2001 Speyside 10 years is launched.

2012 Speyside Distillers is sold to Harvey´s of Edinburgh.

2014 A new range, Spey from Speyside Distillery, is launched (NAS, 12 and 18 year old).

2015 The range is revamped again. New expressions include Tenné, 12 years old and 18 years old.

2016 "Byron´s Choice - The Marriage" and Spey Cask 27 are released.

12 years old

Tasting notes Spey 12 years old:

GS – Malt and white pepper on the nose, with a mildly savoury background. The palate features vanilla, orange, hazelnuts and cloves. Black pepper and lively oak in the medium-length finish.

The State of Scotch

six burning questions

Sukhinder Singh,
Owner,
The Whisky Exchange

1. The Millenials are often referred to as perhaps the most important consumer demographic today. Do you think Scotch whisky appeals to that category and what can the producers do to attract them and keep them interested?

We see from customers at our shop that there are many new faces asking about whisky from a basic level and it is interesting that at our monthly whisky tastings, about 50% of the attendees are first timers and aged between 20-35 showing that the interest is definitely there. I have always said that whisky is a complicated subject and the only way to learn is by trying the product and through education. Most brands today have ambassadors and there are multiple shows and fairs in most countries of the world. As long as we all do our part in educating the consumer, all is good.

Once a person falls in love with whisky, they become a customer for life. The Millenial demographic has a long journey ahead and it is important to keep them interested. The market has changed greatly, there are now so many styles of whisky in terms of flavour and packaging. Whiskies are available from many different wood types and then there is the new wave of products with interesting and non-traditional names such as Monkey Shoulder, Haig Club, etc. In other words there is something for everyone and as long as the liquid is good, we are on to a winner.

2. Several Scotch whisky producers have recently questioned the rules what can and can´t be said on the label about the whisky. Should the legislation be changed, allowing more transparency?

There are, of course, positives and negatives to this. Whisky is already a complicated product, so too much information can be confusing. I feel other things are more important – anything that can help improve the quality of the final product such as increasing the minimum age you can bottle Scotch from 3 years old to, say, 5 years old. More honesty will have its challenges, a lot more education around the products would be required but in the long term I am sure the results will be positive so the answer is yes. Another important point to make is that transparency will be an option not a necessity so each can do as they please.

3. We see more and more Scotch whiskies being bottled without an age statement (NAS). Will that trend continue and, from a consumer point of view, is that all bad?

We all know that there are two arguments for no age statement whiskies. One being that it gives the blenders more flexibility to use a wide array of ages to make something which can be more interesting and complex. The other is that the success of whisky and the difficulty in long term forecasting has led to a shortage of aged stocks, this pressure on some brands has forced them to use younger stocks alongside aged stock to fill the gap. However adding an age statement with the lowest age might not necessarily command the prices they wish to achieve.

I agree that there are some amazing no-age products, such as Johnnie Walker Blue Label and Aberlour A'Bunadh. The problem is that some products which have been released as a no age are sadly not up to scratch in terms of liquid quality. They are overpackaged but underdeliver. Some no-age products, such as many of the Compass Box whiskies are focused on liquid quality with great packaging and have over time gained an amazing following of consumers. Products like these are what will bring new consumers to the category. Yes, many more no-age products will be released and some will shine, others will fail and be discontinued and hopefully will be forgotten in people's memory.

4. Not a new discussion but one that does resurface from time to time. Does the quality of a whisky suffer from chill-filtration and colouring?

There is no doubt that non-chill-filtration and no colouring can make a vast difference to the texture and taste of a whisky. Companies spend so much time and effort to create amazing spirit, they spend thousands of pounds on wood and then wait years for the liquid to mature. Non-chill-filtration is such a simple, inexpensive practice that it surprises me why more companies do not do it, especially for higher-strength whiskies of 46% and above. I can understand why companies that bottle at lower strengths do not do it, as cloudy whiskies are not very pleasing to the eye. I have personally experienced cases where customers have returned cloudy whiskies where they were low strength and non-chill-filtered

5. In the steps of flavoured vodka, flavoured whisky has become increasingly popular. Mostly bourbon and Irish whiskey but also Scotch. What are the benefits and downsides of this new trend?

I am not sure if this is following flavoured vodka, it is more like alcopops (sweet and fruity and horrible !!). I dislike products that are flavoured and sweetened and pretend to be something they are not; in most cases they are closer to being a liqueur. I believe these type of products are more of a phase and will not last the test of time and could actually be negative for the category. If these products are to exist, there needs to be a new classification or they need to be labelled as liqueurs so it is clear where these products sit. Jack Daniels Honey has probably been the most successful of these products, it is cleverly labelled with the brand name Jack Daniels making the consumer think it is a flavoured whiskey. I know it has sugar so cannot be called whiskey but I wonder if it actually has any whiskey in it?

6. Scotch whisky exports have declined in the last couple of years. Is the position of Scotch under threat and if so, what can be done to change the trend?

Whisky has had a very successful number of years of growth, but with most countries of the world now producing whisky, this growth had to slow down. Markets like India and China have not grown as expected but I am sure it is just a matter of time before they come back and sales boom again. For Scotch to remain at the pinnacle of the whisky category, it needs to keep quality the top priority – this is why we all fell in love with whisky in the first place.

Springbank

[spring•bank]

Owner:
Springbank Distillers
(J & A Mitchell)

Region/district:
Campbeltown

Founded: 1828

Status: Active (vc)

Capacity: 750 000 litres

Address: Well Close, Campbeltown, Argyll PA28 6ET

Website: springbankdistillers.com

Tel: 01586 551710

Springbank has always been a distillery which goes its own way. It´s been in the Mitchell family since 1837 and the chairman today is Hedley Wright, the great-great-grandson of one of the founders.

When all the other distilleries in Campbeltown have crumbled, and there have been more than 30, Springbank, together with Glen Scotia, were the only ones that survived. It was closed for a few years in the 1980s but the owner´s determination to stick to traditional production methods has not only carried the distillery through hardships, but has also turned the malt into a cult whisky. For Hedley Wright, the distillery is not there just to produce whisky, but also create jobs and security for the future for families living in Campbeltown. In 2014, Springbank became the first distillery in Scotland to become a Living Wage employer, which means that the 70 people who are employed there are paid more than the legally-enforced minimum wage.

The distillery is equipped with a 3.5 ton open cast iron mash tun, six washbacks made of Scandinavian larch with a fermentation time of up to 110 hours, one wash still and two spirit stills. The wash still is unique in Scotland, as it is fired by both an open oil-fire and internal steam coils. Ordinary condensers are used to cool the spirit vapours, except in the first of the two spirit stills, where a worm tub is used. Springbank is also the only distillery in Scotland that malts its entire need of barley using own floor maltings.

Springbank produces three distinctive single malts with different phenol contents in the malted barley. Springbank is distilled two and a half times (12-15ppm), Longrow is distilled twice (50-55 ppm) and Hazelburn is distilled three times and unpeated. When Springbank is produced, the malted barley is dried using 6 hours of peat smoke and 30 hours of hot air, while Longrow requires 48 hours of peat smoke only to achieve its character. In 2016 a total of 150,000 litres will be produced of which 10% is Longrow and 10% Hazelburn.

The core range is Springbank **10, 15** and **18 year old**, as well as **12 year old cask strength**. There are also limited but yearly releases of a **21 year old** and a **25 year old**. Longrow is represented by **Longrow** without age statement, the **18 year old** and the **Longrow Red**. The 2015 edition of the latter was a **New Zealand pinot noir** finish and it will be followed up in 2017 by a whisky that got its final character from **South African malbec** casks. Finally, there is Hazelburn where the core range consists of a **10 year old** and the new **Hazelburn Sherry Wood** bottled at cask strength which will be replacing the 12 year old in 2017.

Recent, limited editions have included the second release of **Springbank Green**, a 13 year old made of organic barley and matured in oloroso sherry casks. In February 2016 we saw the return of **Springbank Local Barley**. This time it is a 16 year old, the first in a series of five to be released during the coming years. October 2016 also saw the launch of a **9 year old Hazelburn** with a finish in **barolo casks**.

History:

1828 The Reid family, in-laws of the Mitchells (see below), founds the distillery.

1837 The Reid family encounters financial difficulties and John and William Mitchell buy the distillery.

1897 J. & A. Mitchell Co Ltd is founded.

1926 The depression forces the distillery to close.

1933 The distillery is back in production.

1960 Own maltings ceases.

1969 J. & A. Mitchell buys the independent bottler Cadenhead.

1979 The distillery closes.

1985 A 10 year old Longrow is launched.

1987 Limited production restarts.

1989 Production restarts.

1992 Springbank takes up its maltings again.

1997 First distillation of Hazelburn.

1998 Springbank 12 years is launched.

1999 Dha Mhile (7 years), the world's first organic single

2000 A 10 year old is launched.

2001 Springbank 1965 'Local barley' (36 years), 741 bottles, is launched.

2002 Number one in the series Wood Expressions is a 12 year old with five years on Demerara rum casks. Next is a Longrow sherry cask (13 years). A relaunch of the 15 year old replaces the 21 year old.

2004 Springbank 10 years 100 proof is launched as well as Springbank Wood Expression bourbon, Longrow 14 years old, Springbank 32 years old and Springbank 14 years Port Wood.

2005 Springbank 21 years, the first version of Hazelburn (8 years) and Longrow Tokaji Wood Expression are launched.

157

History continued:

2006 Longrow 10 years 100 proof, Springbank 25 years, Springbank 9 years Marsala finish, Springbank 11 years Madeira finish and a new Hazelburn 8 year old are released.

2007 Springbank Vintage 1997 and a 16 year old rum wood are released.

2008 The distillery closes temporarily. Three new releases of Longrow - CV, 18 year old and 7 year old Gaja Barolo.

2009 Springbank Madeira 11 year old, Springbank 18 year old, Springbank Vintage 2001 and Hazelburn 12 year old are released.

2010 Springbank 12 year old cask strength and a 12 year old claret expression together with new editions of the CV and 18 year old are released. Longrow 10 year old cask strength and Hazel burn CV are also new.

2011 Longrow 18 year old and Hazelburn 8 year old Sauternes wood expression are released.

2012 New releases include Springbank Rundlets & Kilderkins, Springbank 21 year old and Longrow Red.

2013 Longrow Rundlets & Kilderkins, a new edition of Longrow Red and Springbank 9 year old Gaja Barolo finish are released.

2014 Hazelburn Rundlets & Kilderkins, Hazelburn 10 year old and Springbank 25 years old are launched.

2015 New releases include Springbank Green 12 years old and a new edition of the Longrow Red.

2016 Springbank Local Barley and a 9 year old Hazelburn barolo finish are released.

Tasting notes Springbank 10 years old:

GS – Fresh and briny on the nose, with citrus fruit, oak and barley, plus a note of damp earth. Sweet on the palate, with developing brine, nuttiness and vanilla toffee. Long and spicy in the finish, coconut oil and drying peat.

Tasting notes Longrow NAS:

GS – Initially slightly gummy on the nose, but then brine and fat peat notes develop. Vanilla and malt also emerge. The smoky palate offers lively brine and is quite dry and spicy, with some vanilla and lots of ginger. The finish is peaty with persistent, oaky ginger.

Tasting notes Hazelburn 10 years old:

GS – Pear drops, soft toffee and malt on the mildly floral nose. Oiliness develops in time, along with a green, herbal note and ultimately brine. Full-bodied and supple on the smoky palate, with barley and ripe, peppery orchard fruits. Developing cocoa and ginger in the lengthy finish.

Springbank 15 years   Hazelburn 12 years   Springbank 21 years

Springbank Local Barley

Springbank 10 years old   Longrow

Strathisla

[strath•eye•la]

Owner:
Chivas Bros (Pernod Ricard)

Region/district:
Speyside

Founded: 1786
Status: Active (vc)
Capacity: 2 450 000 litres

Address: Seafield Avenue, Keith, Banffshire AB55 5BS

Website:
maltwhiskydistilleries.com

Tel:
01542 783044

In 2016, Strathisla in Keith celebrates its 230th anniversary as one of Scotland´s oldest distilleries. It is also one of the prettiest and most photographed distilleries in Scotland.

Every year, 15,000 visitors come here not only for the distillery, but also to learn more about one of the most iconic of blended whiskies – Chivas Regal. Strathisla is the spiritual home to the popular brand and is also the signature malt of the blend. Launched in 1909, Chivas Regal today is the third best selling blend in the world with a core range of 12, 18 and 25 year old versions. But regularly, new and limited expressions are also being launched. The Mizunara Edition in 2013 was finished in Japanese oak, while Chivas Regal Extra with no age statement and launched in 2014, had a larger proportion of oloroso sherry casks than the 12 year old. One year later came the pinnacle of the Chivas range – Chivas Regal The Icon. All the whiskies that are included are well over 25 years old and some of the twenty different malts come from distilleries that have long since been closed. In 2015, Chivas Regal sold a total of 53 million bottles and it is also the third best selling spirits brand in the duty free category after Johnnie Walker and Absolut Vodka.

The distillery is equipped with a 5 ton traditional mash tun with a raised copper canopy, seven washbacks made of Oregon pine and three of larch – all with a 54 hour fermentation cycle. There are two pairs of stills in a cramped, but very charming still room. The wash stills are of lantern type with descending lyne arms and the spirit stills have boiling balls and the lyne arms are slightly ascending. The spirit produced at Strathisla is piped to nearby Glen Keith distillery for filling or to be tankered away. A small amount is stored on site in two racked and one dunnage warehouse.

The core expression is the **12 year old** but there are also two cask strength bottlings in the new range The Distillery Reserve Collection which can be found at Chivas´ visitor centres; a **17 year old** and a **25 year old**.

History:

1786 Alexander Milne and George Taylor found the distillery under the name Milltown, but soon change it to Milton.

1823 MacDonald Ingram & Co. purchases the distillery.

1830 William Longmore acquires the distillery.

1870 The distillery name changes to Strathisla.

1880 William Longmore retires and hands operations to his son-in-law John Geddes-Brown. William Longmore & Co. is formed.

1890 The distillery changes name to Milton.

1940 Jay (George) Pomeroy acquires majority shares in William Longmore & Co. Pomeroy is jailed as a result of dubious business transactions and the distillery goes bankrupt in 1949.

1950 Chivas Brothers buys the run-down distillery at a compulsory auction for £71,000 and starts restoration.

1951 The name reverts to Strathisla.

1965 The number of stills is increased from two to four.

1970 A heavily peated whisky, Craigduff, is produced but production stops later.

2001 The Chivas Group is acquired by Pernod Ricard.

Tasting notes Strathisla 12 years old:

GS – Rich on the nose, with sherry, stewed fruits, spices and lots of malt. Full-bodied and almost syrupy on the palate. Toffee, honey, nuts, a whiff of peat and a suggestion of oak. The finish is medium in length, slightly smoky and a with a final flash of ginger.

12 years old

Strathmill

[strath•mill]

Owner:
Diageo

Region/district:
Speyside

Founded: **Status:** **Capacity:**
1891 Active 2 600 000 litres

Address: Keith, Banffshire AB55 5DQ

Website: **Tel:**
malts.com 01542 883000

Strathmill distillery is beautifully situated in a valley next to the river Isla in Keith, one of the major whisky towns of Speyside with two more distilleries – Strathisla and Glen Keith.

Two stately pagoda roofs, together with a couple of beautiful, traditional dunnage warehouses (with an additional two racked) creates the right distillery atmosphere. Once a corn mill, Strathmill was converted into a distillery in the late 1800s. The official foundation year is 1891 but some evidence suggests that the old mill had already served as a distillery from 1820 to 1831 under the name of Strathisla. The distillery that we today know by that name, was founded far earlier in 1786, but for nearly 90 years the distillery's name had varied between Milltown and Milton.

The equipment consists of a 9 ton stainless steel semi-lauter mash tun and six stainless steel washbacks with an 83 hour fermentation period. There are two pairs of stills and Strathmill is one of a select few distilleries still using purifiers on the spirit stills. This device is mounted between the lyne arm and the condenser and acts as a mini-condenser, allowing the lighter alcohols to travel towards the condenser and forcing the heavier alcohols to go back into the still for another distillation. The result is a lighter and fruitier spirit. The distillery had a short spell of 7-day production during 2015 but is now back to its normal 5-day week working 24 hours per day. That means 10 mashes per week and 1.8 million litres of alcohol in the year.

The whisky from Strathmill has always been an important component in J & B blended whisky. Until 2005, the brand was the second best-selling blend in the world after Johnnie Walker, but has since been surpassed by Ballantine's, Chivas Regal and Grant's. In 2015, 43 million bottles were sold with the largest markets being in France, Spain and the USA.

The only official bottling is the **12 year old Flora & Fauna**, but a limited **25 year old** was launched in 2014 as part of the Special Releases.

History:

1891 The distillery is founded in an old mill from 1823 and is named Glenisla-Glenlivet Distillery.

1892 The inauguration takes place in June.

1895 The gin company W. & A. Gilbey buys the distillery for £9,500 and names it Strathmill.

1962 W. & A. Gilbey merges with United Wine Traders (including Justerini & Brooks) and forms International Distillers & Vintners (IDV).

1968 The number of stills is increased from two to four and purifiers are added.

1972 IDV is bought by Watney Mann which later the same year is acquired by Grand Metropolitan.

1993 Strathmill becomes available as a single malt for the first time since 1909 as a result of a bottling (1980) from Oddbins.

1997 Guinness and Grand Metropolitan merge and form Diageo.

2001 The first official bottling is a 12 year old in the Flora & Fauna series.

2010 A Manager´s Choice single cask from 1996 is released.

2014 A 25 year old is released.

12 years old

Tasting notes Strathmill 12 years old:

GS – Quite reticent on the nose, with nuts, grass and a hint of ginger. Spicy vanilla and nuts dominate the palate. The finish is drying, with peppery oak.

Talisker

[tal•iss•kur]

Owner: **Region/district:**
Diageo   Highlands (Skye)

Founded: **Status:**   **Capacity:**
1830   Active (vc)   2 700 000 litres

Address: Carbost, Isle of Skye,
Inverness-shire IV47 8SR

Website: **Tel:**
malts.com   01478 614308 (vc)

The distillery's first 50 years were characterised by bankruptcies, fraud and owners going to prison. It wasn't until 1880 that Talisker was acquired by two men who were both influential and had a good reputation in the whisky industry.

Alexander Grigor Allan had founded Glenlossie a few years prior and the spirits merchant, Roderick Kemp, a few years later acquired Macallan. They decided to modernise Talisker which at that time only produced 180,000 litres annually, in comparison to the 2.7 million litres being produced today. The distillery gravitated towards a more stable future, but Talisker wasn´t known as single malt until it became one of six original Classic Malts in 1988. However, it is only during the last decade that the sales have accelerated in earnest with an increase of 235% to 2.4 million bottles sold in 2015. Behind the success story lays a very deliberate strategy from the owners. Smoky whisky may have become hugely popular but the medium peated Talisker also appeals to the consumers who find Islay whisky too overpowering. With a phenol specification of 18-20 ppm in the barley, which gives it a phenol content of 5-7 ppm in the new make, Talisker is not as heavily peated as some of its cousins on Islay.

The distillery is equipped with a stainless steel lauter mash tun with a capacity of 8 tonnes, eight washbacks made of Oregon pine and five stills (two wash stills and three spirit stills), all of which are connected to wooden wormtubs. The wash stills are equipped with a special type of purifiers, which use the colder outside air, and have a u-bend in the lyne arm. The purifiers and the peculiar bend of the lyne arms allow for more copper contact and increase the reflux during distillation. The fermentation time is quite long (65-75 hours) and the middle cut from the spirit still is collected between 76% and 65% which, together with the phenol specification, gives a medium peated spirit. Production in 2016 will be around 18 mashes per week which accounts for 2.7 million litres of alcohol.

An excellent and newly refurbished visitor centre is, despite the remote location on the Isle of Skye, one of the most popular in the industry and more than 65,000 people frequent it every year.

The range of Talisker single malts has been given plenty of attention in recent years. With its new expressions, Talisker's core range now consists of **Skye** and **Storm**, both without age statement, **10, 18, 25** and **30 year old, Distiller's Edition** with an Amoroso sherry finish, **Talisker 57° North** which is released in small batches, and **Port Ruighe**. The latter, which is pronounced Portree after the main town on Isle of Skye, has a finish in ruby port casks. There is also **Dark Storm**, the peatiest Talisker so far, which is exclusive to duty free. A second bottling for duty free, **Neist Point**, was launched in December 2015. Recent limited releases include a **27 year old** which was launched in the autumn of 2013 and a **distillery exclusive** without age statement in autumn 2016.

History:

1830 Hugh and Kenneth MacAskill, sons of the local doctor, found the distillery.

1848 The brothers transfer the lease to North of Scotland Bank and Jack Westland from the bank runs the operations.

1854 Kenneth MacAskill dies.

1857 North of Scotland Bank sells the distillery to Donald MacLennan for £500.

1863 MacLennan experiences difficulties in making operations viable and puts the distillery up for sale.

1865 MacLennan, still working at the distillery, nominates John Anderson as agent in Glasgow.

1867 Anderson & Co. from Glasgow takes over.

1879 John Anderson is imprisoned after having sold non-existing casks of whisky.

1880 New owners are now Alexander Grigor Allan and Roderick Kemp.

1892 Kemp sells his share and buys Macallan Distillery instead.

1894 The Talisker Distillery Ltd is founded.

1895 Allan dies and Thomas Mackenzie, who has been his partner, takes over.

1898 Talisker Distillery merges with Dailuaine-Glenlivet Distillers and Imperial Distillers to form Dailuaine-Talisker Distillers Company.

1916 Thomas Mackenzie dies and the distillery is taken over by a consortium consisting of, among others, John Walker, John Dewar, W. P. Lowrie and Distillers Company Limited (DCL).

1928 The distillery abandons triple distillation.

1960 On 22nd November the distillery catches fire and substantial damage occurs.

1962 The distillery reopens after the fire.

TALISKER

History continued:

1972 Own malting ceases.

1988 Classic Malts are introduced, Talisker 10 years included. A visitor centre is opened.

1998 A new stainless steel/copper mash tun and five new worm tubs are installed. Talisker is launched as a Distillers Edition with an amoroso sherry finish.

2004 Two new bottlings appear, an 18 year old and a 25 year old.

2005 To celebrate the 175th birthday of the distillery, Talisker 175th Anniversary is released. The third edition of the 25 year old cask strength is released.

2006 A 30 year old and the fourth edition of the 25 year old are released.

2007 The second edition of the 30 year old and the fifth edition of the 25 year old are released.

2008 Talisker 57° North, sixth edition of the 25 year old and third edition of the 30 year old are launched.

2009 New editions of the 25 and 30 year old are released.

2010 A 1994 Manager´s Choice single cask and a new edition of the 30 year old are released.

2011 Three limited releases - 25, 30 and 34 year old.

2012 A limited 35 year old is released.

2013 Four new expressions are released – Storm, Dark Storm, Port Ruighe and a 27 year old.

2014 A bottling for the Friends of the Classic Malts is released.

2015 Skye and Neist Point are released.

2016 A distillery exclusive without age statement is released.

Tasting notes Talisker 10 years old:

GS – Quite dense and smoky on the nose, with smoked fish, bladderwrack, sweet fruit and peat. Full-bodied and peaty in the mouthy; complex, with ginger, ozone, dark chocolate, black pepper and a kick of chilli in the long, smoky tail.

Tasting notes Talisker Storm:

GS – The nose offers brine, burning wood embers, vanilla, and honey. The palate is sweet and spicy, with cranberries and blackcurrants, while peat-smoke and black pepper are ever-present. The finish is spicy, with walnuts, and fruity peat.

Port Ruighe

Storm

Skye

Neist Point

Dark Storm

10 years old

18 years

Distiller´s Edition

Tamdhu

[tam•doo]

Owner:
Ian Macleod Distillers

Region/district:
Speyside

Founded: **Status:**
1896   Active

Capacity:
4 000 000 litres

Address: Knockando, Aberlour,
Morayshire AB38 7RP

Website:
tamdhu.com

Tel:
01340 872200

The late 19th century was the era of the blenders. The continuous still, invented in the 1820s had hugely streamlined the production of grain whisky and the Spirits Act of 1860 made it legal to blend grain and malt whisky in bond.

During the 1890s the big blending companies searched far and wide for more spirit for their increasingly popular brands. It was therefore not strange that several companies were interested when William Grant (not of Glenfiddich fame) came up with the idea of building a modern distillery in Knockando near the River Spey. The names of the investors in Tamdhu distillery reads like a list of the most influential whisky companies of the time; John Walker & Sons, John Dewar & Sons, Robertson & Baxter, William Sanderson and Bulloch Lade. Unfortunately for William Grant, his personal economic difficulties forced him to sell his share of the company and he was out of the picture after only two years.

The distillery is equipped with an 11.85 tonne semilauter mash tun, nine Oregon pine washbacks with a fermentation time of 59 hours and three pairs of stills. There are four dunnage warehouses, one racked and seven palletised with another two being built in 2016. The oldest cask in stock dates back to 1961. Production in 2016 has increased in comparison to the previous year and they are now doing 16 mashes per week which translates to 3.1 million litres for the entire year. Since last year, the production process at Tamdhu has become fully automated from mashing in right through to distillation. The distillery was closed in March 2016 when the heating system was changed from heavy oil to gas.

The owners, Ian Macleod, are committed to maturing Tamdhu single malt in sherry casks but the flavour is further enhanced by the fact that they are using both American and European oak. The core range consists of a **10 year old** matured in first and second fill sherry casks and the un chill-filtered **Tamdhu Batch Strength**, bottled at 58.8%. The owners plan to release a 50 year old in 2017.

History:

1896   The distillery is founded by Tamdhu Distillery Company, a consortium of whisky blenders with William Grant as the main promoter. Charles Doig is the architect.

1897   The first casks are filled in July.

1898   Highland Distillers Company, which has several of the 1896 consortium members in managerial positions, buys Tamdhu Distillery Company.

1911   The distillery closes.

1913   The distillery reopens.

1928   The distillery is mothballed.

1948   The distillery is in full production again in July.

1950   The floor maltings is replaced by Saladin boxes when the distillery is rebuilt.

1972   The number of stills is increased from two to four.

1975   Two stills augment the previous four.

1976   Tamdhu 8 years is launched as single malt.

2005   An 18 year old and a 25 year old are released.

2009   The distillery is motbalded.

2011   The Edrington Group sells the distillery to Ian Macleod Distillers.

2012   Production is resumed.

2013   The first official release from the new owners – a 10 year old.

2015   Tamdhu Batch Strength is released.

10 years old

Tasting notes Tamdhu 10 years old:

GS – Soft sherry notes, new leather, almonds, marzipan and a hint of peat on the nose. Very smooth and drinkable, with citrus fruit, gentle spice and more sweet sherry on the palate. Persistent spicy leather, with a sprinkling of black pepper in the finish.

Tamnavulin

TAMNAVULIN DISTILLERY

[tam•na•voo•lin]

Owner:	**Region/district:**
Whyte & Mackay (Emperador)	Speyside

Founded:	**Status:**	**Capacity:**
1966	Active	4 000 000 litres

Address: Tomnavoulin, Ballindalloch, Banffshire AB3 9JA

Website:	**Tel:**
-	01807 590285

The founder of Tamnavulin, Invergordon Distillers, was incorporated in 1959 and the company´s greatest asset was the huge grain distillery on Cromarty Firth which started production two years later.

One of the company's earliest members of staff, who became managing director in 1983, was Chris Greig. Being an influential businessman, he contributed considerably to the expansion of the Scotch whisky industry. He was one of the first to bottle and sell single grain with the intention of attracting new consumer groups, a trend which we now can see is growing stronger. In 1990 he also predicted that Russia and Eastern Europe would become important markets for Scotch whisky in the near future and the developments during the past five years have proved him right. For Invergordon´s account, he didn't just open Tamnavulin in 1966. He also acquired Bruichladdich, Jura, Tullibardine and Deanston. Greig died in 2012 at the age of 1977.

Tamnavulin distillery is equipped with a full lauter mash tun with a 10.7 ton capacity, nine washbacks made of stainless steel (five of which were installed in summer 2015) with a fermentation time of 48 hours and three pairs of stills. Two racked warehouses (10 casks high) on site have a capacity of 35,000 casks with the oldest ones dating back to 1967, but several of the casks are from other distilleries. During 2016, the owners will be doing 16 mashes per week which equates to around 3.5 million litres per year. From 2010 to 2013, part of the yearly production (around 5%) was heavily peated with a phenol specification in the barley of 55ppm.

Almost the entire production goes to blended whiskies as a result of a 12 year gap which occurred between 1995 and 2007 where there was no production, coupled with the fact that there was not that much stock of older whisky in the warehouse. Since a 12 year old Tamnavulin was discontinued several years ago, there has been no official bottling.

At least until autumn 2016 when, surprisingly, a **Tamnavulin Double Cask** with a sherry finish, was released as an exclsuive for the UK market to celebrate the distillery´s 50th anniversary.

History:

1966 Tamnavulin-Glenlivet Distillery Company, a subsidiary of Invergordon Distillers Ltd, founds Tamnavulin.

1993 Whyte & Mackay buys Invergordon Distillers.

1995 The distillery closes in May.

1996 Whyte & Mackay changes name to JBB (Greater Europe).

2000 Distillation takes place for six weeks.

2001 Company management buy out operations for £208 million and rename the company Kyndal.

2003 Kyndal changes name to Whyte & Mackay.

2007 United Spirits buys Whyte & Mackay. Tamnavulin is opened again in July after having been mothballed for 12 years.

2014 Whyte & Mackay is sold to Emperador Inc.

2016 Tamnavulin Double Cask is released.

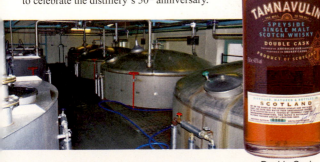

Double Cask

Tasting notes Tamnavulin 12 years old:

GS – Delicate and floral on the nose, with light malt and fruit gums. Light to medium bodied, fresh, malty and spicy on the palate, with a whiff of background smoke. The finish is medium in length, with lingering spice, smoke, and notes of caramel.

Teaninich

[tee•ni•nick]

Owner:
Diageo

Region/district:
Northern Highlands

Founded: 1817

Status: Active

Capacity: 9 800 000 litres

Address: Alness, Ross-shire IV17 0XB

Website:
malts.com

Tel:
01349 885001

The 1960s and 1970s was an amazing time for Scotch whisky. Business was booming and the optimism for the future was great. No less than sixteen new distilleries were built during these two decades.

Teaninich wasn´t one of them, as it had been around for more than 150 years. But it was, nevertheless, decided by the owners, DCL, that the distillery needed both a major upgrade and increased capacity. A completely new distillery with six stills was built next to the old with four stills and, all of a sudden, it had become one of the largest distilleries at the time with a capacity of six million litres. The two distilleries worked side by side for fifteen years until they both closed in 1985. The optimism had to give way to brutal honesty due to receding demand and increasing stock. But for the new distillery, the silence didn't last for very long. In 1991, Teaninich was producing again.

If one fast forwards to 2015, the distillery is once again one of the biggest in the industry. A huge expansion was conducted where the original setup with ten washbacks and six stills was doubled. Three of the existing wash stills were altered into spirit stills so that the old still house would house all six spirit stills, while a new house was built for the new wash stills. Teaninich has a very unusual mashing technique. It is one of only two Scottish distilleries (Inchdairnie being the other) using a mash filter instead of a mash tun. The malt is ground into fine flour without husks in an Asnong hammer mill. Once the grist has been mixed with water, the mash passes through a Meura 2001 mash filter where the wort is collected. Water is added to the filter for a second time and a second run of mash is obtained. The procedure is repeated three times until a washback is filled. A brand new filter with a 14 ton mash has been installed to cope with the larger volumes. Commissioning of the new equipment began in April 2015 and full production wasn´t reached until November. There were also plans to build a completely new distillery on the same grounds as Teaninich but these plans have now been postponed.

The only official core bottling is the **10 year old** in the Flora & Fauna series.

History:

1817 Captain Hugh Monro, owner of the estate Teaninich, founds the distillery.

1831 Captain Munro sells the estate to his younger brother John.

1850 John Munro, who spends most of his time in India, leases Teaninich to the infamous Robert Pattison from Leith.

1869 John McGilchrist Ross takes over the licence.

1895 Munro & Cameron takes over the licence.

1898 Munro & Cameron buys the distillery.

1904 Robert Innes Cameron becomes sole owner of Teaninich.

1932 Robert Innes Cameron dies.

1933 The estate of Robert Innes Cameron sells the distillery to Distillers Company Limited.

1970 A new distillation unit with six stills is commissioned and becomes known as the A side.

1975 A dark grains plant is built.

1984 The B side of the distillery is mothballed.

1985 The A side is also mothballed.

1991 The A side is in production again.

1992 United Distillers launches a 10 year old Teaninich in the Flora & Fauna series.

1999 The B side is decommissioned.

2000 A mash filter is installed.

2009 Teaninich 1996, a single cask in the new Manager´s Choice range is released.

2014 Another six stills and eight washbacks are installed and the capacity is doubled.

2015 The distillery is expanded with six new stills and the capacity is doubled.

10 years old

Tasting notes Teaninich 10 years old:

GS – The nose is initially fresh and grassy, quite light, with vanilla and hints of tinned pineapple. Mediumbodied, smooth, slightly oily, with cereal and spice in the mouth. Nutty and slowly drying in the finish, with pepper and a suggestion of cocoa powder notes.

Tobermory

[tow•bur•mo•ray]

Owner:
Burn Stewart Distillers
(Distell Group Ltd)

Region/district:
Highland (Mull)

Founded: 1798

Status: Active (vc)

Capacity: 1 000 000 litres

Address: Tobermory, Isle of Mull, Argyllsh. PA75 6NR

Website: tobermorydistillery.com

Tel: 01688 302647

Tobermory, the only distillery on the Isle of Mull, has always been a bit of an "under-the-radar" distillery with its single malts often difficult to find.

A recent revamp of the core range has not made it any easier. The only bottlings left are two expressions of the peated version Ledaig, while the 15 year old Tobermory has been discontinued and the 10 year old is now only available for purchase at the distillery. The latter, though, will return to global markets in a few years' time. The reason may be the success that the owner's have with the two blended whiskies where Tobermory single malt plays an important part; Black Bottle and Scottish Leader, the biggest selling blend in Taiwan and popular in South Africa as well. Scottish Leader was relaunched in 2014 and now contains a higher proportion of single malt than before, which may have put pressure on the stock situation. In 2016, Kirstie McCallum replaced Ian Macmillan as the company's lead blender for both the blends and the malts. Kirstie has been in the company for ten years, working both as a blender and brand ambassador, while Macmillan has left to become distillery manager for Bladnoch.

The distillery is equipped with a traditional 5 ton cast iron mash tun, four wooden washbacks with a fermentation time of 50 to 90 hours and two pairs of stills. Two of the stills were replaced in August 2014. The owner's plans are to do 8 mashes per week and 750,000 litres of alcohol in 2016 with a 50/50 split between Ledaig and Tobermory.

The core range from Tobermory distillery is the **10 and 18 year old Ledaig** with **10 year old Tobermory** now available only in the distillery shop together with a **Tobermory 20 year old** and **Ledaig 18 year old** – both bottled at cask strength and with a second maturation in PX casks. Recent limited bottlings include the **42 year old Ledaig Dùsgadh** (the oldest bottling ever of Ledaig), **Ledaig 1996** and a **42 year old Tobermory**. In summer 2016, a **cask strength version** of the latter was released for travel retail. Two exclusives for the German market were released in April 2016 – the bourbon matured **Tobermory 18 year old** and the **20 year old Tobermory** with a sherry finish.

History:

1798 John Sinclair founds the distillery.

1837 The distillery closes.

1878 The distillery reopens.

1890 John Hopkins & Company buys the distillery.

1916 Distillers Company Limited (DCL) takes over John Hopkins & Company.

1930 The distillery closes.

1972 A shipping company in Liverpool and the sherrymaker Domecq buy the buildings and embark on refurbishment. When work is completed it is named Ledaig Distillery Ltd.

1975 Ledaig Distillery Ltd files for bankruptcy and the distillery closes again.

1979 The estate agent Kirkleavington Property buys the distillery, forms a new company, Tobermory Distillers Ltd and starts production.

1982 No production. Some of the buildings are converted into flats and some are rented to a dairy company for cheese storage.

1989 Production resumes.

1993 Burn Stewart Distillers buys Tobermory for £600,000 and pays an additional £200,000 for the whisky supply.

2002 Trinidad-based venture capitalists CL Financial buys Burn Stewart Distillers for £50m.

2005 A 32 year old from 1972 is launched.

2007 A Ledaig 10 year old is released.

2008 A limited edition Tobermory 15 year old is released.

2013 Burn Stewart Distillers is sold to Distell Group Ltd. A 40 year old Ledaig is released.

2015 Ledaig 18 years and 42 years are released together with Tobermory 42 years.

Tasting notes Tobermory 10 years old:

GS – Fresh and nutty on the nose, with citrus fruit and brittle toffee. A whiff of peat. Medium-bodied, quite dry on the palate with delicate peat, malt and nuts. Medium finish with a hint of mint and a slight citric tang.

Tasting notes Ledaig 10 years old:

GS – The nose is profoundly peaty, sweet and full, with notes of butter and smoked fish. Bold, yet sweet on the palate, with iodine, soft peat and heather. Developing spices. The finish is medium to long, with pepper, ginger, liquorice and peat.

10 years old

Tomatin

[to•mat•in]

Owner: **Region/district:**
Tomatin Distillery Co   Highland
(Takara Shuzo Co., Kokubu & Co., Marubeni Corp.)

Founded: **Status:**   **Capacity:**
1897   Active (vc)   5 000 000 litres

Address: Tomatin, Inverness-shire IV13 7YT

Website: **Tel:**
tomatin.com   01463 248144 (vc)

Tomatin is probably one of the best examples of a distillery that has changed from the production of bulk whisky into one building a brand.

This becomes very apparent when one looks at the production figures which have gone from 12 million litres annually in the late 1970s to 2 million litres for 2016. For Tomatin there is obviously more money to be made from a range of aged quality single malts than selling tanks of young whisky to third parties. This transition slowly started a decade ago when the hard-to-find 10 year old was traded for a range of different varieties. Since then, the range has been expanded and a sub-range of peated expressions, Cù Bòcan, has also been introduced. During these ten years sales volumes have gone from 100,000 bottles to 460,000 bottles being sold in 2015, with USA as one of the most important markets.

The distillery is equipped with one 8 tonne stainless steel mash tun, 12 stainless steel washbacks with a fermentation time from 54 to 108 hours and six pairs of stills (only four of the spirit stills are still in use). The goal is to produce 2.5 million litres in 2015, of which 100,000 litres will be peated at 30-35ppm.

The entire core range was rebranded in 2016 with new bottles and labels. Today it consists of **Legacy** (without age statement), **12, 18** and **36 year old** (introduced in June 2015). Included are also **Cask Strength**, **14 year old port finish** and a **Vintage 1988**. Recent limited releases include a **1981 Vintage** and **Contrast** – a pack of two bottles (bourbon and sherry matured) with whiskies from six vintages. A new range of 40-year-old-plus whiskies was introduced in July 2016. The first expression in the Warehouse 6 Collection was a **44 year old single cask** matured in oloroso sherry casks.

The first official release of a peated Tomatin was Cù Bòcan in 2013 and it has now become a stand-alone brand. The range has been expanded and now includes a **1989 Vintage, Cù Bòcan Sherry, Cù Bòcan Virgin Oak** and **Cù Bòcan Bourbon**. In summer 2016, two new vintages were launched - **1988** and **2005**.

History:

1897 The distillery is founded by Tomatin Spey Distillery Company.

1906 Production ceases.

1909 Production resumes through Tomatin Distillers.

1956 Stills are increased from two to four.

1958 Another two stills are added.

1961 The six stills are increased to ten.

1974 The stills now total 23 and the maltings closes.

1985 The distillery company goes into liquidation.

1986 Takara Shuzo Co. and Okara & Co., buy Tomatin through Tomatin Distillery Co.

1998 Okara & Co is liquidated and Marubeni buys out part of their shareholding.

2004 Tomatin 12 years is launched.

2005 A 25 year old and a 1973 Vintage are released.

2006 An 18 year old and a 1962 Vintage are launched.

2008 A 30 and a 40 year old as well as several vintages from 1975 and 1995 are released.

2009 A 15 year old, a 21 year old and four single casks (1973, 1982, 1997 and 1999) are released.

2010 The first peated release - a 4 year old exclusive for Japan.

2011 A 30 year old and Tomatin Decades are released.

2013 Cù Bòcan, the first peated Tomatin, is released.

2014 14 year old port finish, 36 year old, Vintage 1988, Tomatin Cuatro, Cù Bòcan Sherry Cask and Cù Bòcan 1989 are released.

2015 Cask Strength and Cù Bòcan Virgin Oak are released.

2016 A 44 year old Tomatin and two Cù Bòcan vintages (1988 and 2005) are released.

12 years old

Tasting notes Tomatin 12 years old:

GS – Barley, spice, buttery oak and a floral note on the nose. Sweet and medium-bodied, with toffee apples, spice and herbs in the mouth. Medium-length in the finish, with sweet fruitiness.

Tomintoul

[tom•in•towel]

Owner:	**Region/district:**
Angus Dundee Distillers	Speyside

Founded:	**Status:**	**Capacity:**
1965	Active	3 300 000 litres

Address: Ballindalloch, Banffshire AB37 9AQ

Website:	**Tel:**
tomintouldistillery.co.uk	01807 590274

Being an independent bottler means that you're dependant on whisky producers in order to acquire stock. As mature whisky has become very scarce, the distillers have become more reluctant to sell whisky to the blenders.

A few of the bigger blenders have been proactive to prevent them from running out of whisky by either building or buying a distillery and one of the first was Angus Dundee. The company, founded in 1950 by Terry Hillman, is now run by his two children, Aaron and Tania. In 2000 they bought Tomintoul and in 2003 they acquired Glencadam. They also own a big bottling plant in Coatbridge near Glasgow. With a turnover of £55m last year they sell their own products in more than 70 countries, as well as providing bulk whisky for own-label products. Recently they have also jumped on the single grain whisky bandwagon and have released three versions of Strathcolm (no age, 8 and 12 years).

Tomintoul distillery is equipped with a 11.6 ton semi lauter mash tun, six stainless steel washbacks and two pairs of stills. There are currently 15 mashes per week, which means that capacity is used to its maximum, and a number of racked and palletised warehouses have a storage capacity of 120,000 casks. The malt used for mashing is unpeated, but every year around 360,000 litres of heavily peated spirit (55ppm) is produced. On the site there is also a blend centre with 14 large blending vats.

The core range consists of a **10, 14, 16 and 25 year old** as well as the new addition, **Tlàth** without age statement, which was released in August 2016. There are also two finishes; a **12 year old** with an extra maturation in **sherry** casks and the newly released **15 year old port finish**. The peaty side of Tomintoul is represented by **Peaty Tang** and, as a standalone range, **Old Ballantruan** and **Old Ballantruan 10 year old**. The recent years' limited releases include a **1976 Vintage** (the latest bottling from 2013) and a **Single Cask** (the most recent being from 1977) but the real treat came in February 2016 with the release of a **40 year old**. Only 500 bottles were filled.

History:

1965 The distillery is founded by Tomintoul Distillery Ltd, which is owned by Hay & MacLeod & Co. and W. & S. Strong & Co.

1973 Scottish & Universal Investment Trust, owned by the Fraser family, buys the distillery. It buys Whyte & Mackay the same year and transfers Tomintoul to that company.

1974 The two stills are increased to four and Tomintoul 12 years is launched.

1978 Lonrho buys Scottish & Universal Investment Trust.

1989 Lonrho sells Whyte & Mackay to Brent Walker.

1990 American Brands buys Whyte & Mackay.

1996 Whyte & Mackay changes name to JBB (Greater Europe).

2000 Angus Dundee plc buys Tomintoul.

2002 Tomintoul 10 year is launched.

2003 Tomintoul 16 years is launched.

2004 Tomintoul 27 years is launched.

2005 A young, peated version called Old Ballantruan is launched.

2008 1976 Vintage and Peaty Tang are released.

2009 A 14 year old and a 33 year old are released.

2010 A 12 year old Port wood finish is released.

2011 A 21 year old, a 10 year old Ballantruan and Vintage 1966 are released.

2012 Old Ballantruan 10 years old is released.

2013 A 31 year old single cask is released.

2015 Five Decades and a 40 year old are released.

2016 A 40 year old and Tlàth without age statement are launched.

10 years old

Tasting notes Tomintoul 10 years old:

GS – A light, fresh and fruity nose, with ripe peaches and pineapple cheesecake, delicate spice and background malt. Medium-bodied, fruity and fudgy on the palate. The finish offers wine gums, mild, gently spiced oak, malt and a suggestion of smoke.

Tormore

[tor•more]

Owner: Chivas Bros (Pernod Ricard) **Region/district:** Speyside

Founded: 1958 **Status:** Active **Capacity:** 4 400 000 litres

Address: Tormore, Advie, Grantown-on-Spey, Morayshire PH26 3LR

Website: tormoredistillery.com **Tel:** 01807 510244

Tormore is a distillery full of contradictions; a grandiose building sitting right next to the busy A95 right in the middle of Speyside and yet, almost completely unknown as a single malt brand.

When it was planned in the early 1950s, it was the decision by the owners (Schenley Industries) that it should become a model distillery and the famous architect, Sir Albert Richardson, was called in and no expenses were saved. The roof on the distillery building alone (made out of copper) cost £40,000 (in today's money £650,000). The distillery is strategically positioned within the boundaries of Cairngorm National Park, a part of Scotland with great natural values. Recently Chivas brothers have planted more than 15,000 pinewood trees on the Tormore site, in order to save endangered bird species such as the black grouse and capercaillie.

Tormore single malt is an important part of the legendary Long John blended Scotch which was established in 1909. The brand has seen better days but still managed to sell 4 million bottles last year. It was acquired by the American company, Schenley Industries, in 1956. Included in the purchase price was Glenugie distillery, which is situated in the far northeast and Strathclyde grain distillery which is found in Glasgow. A couple of years thereafter they built Kinclaith, a malt distillery which was found within the Strathclyde complex, but by then the plan to build Tormore was already in place.

Following an upgrade in 2012, Tormore is now equipped with a stainless steel full lauter mash tun, 11 stainless steel washbacks and four pairs of stills. Tormore single malt is known for its fruity and light character which is achieved by a clear wort, a slow distillation and by using purifiers on all the stills.

Nearly everything that is produced at Tormore is used for blended Scotch but, since spring 2014, there is a **14 year old** bottled at 43% and a **16 year old**, un chill-filtered and bottled at 48%. Both have been matured in American oak. The new versions were first introduced in France but later rolled out to other markets.

History:

1958 Schenley International, owners of Long John, founds the distillery.

1960 The distillery is ready for production.

1972 The number of stills is increased from four to eight.

1975 Schenley sells Long John and its distilleries (including Tormore) to Whitbread.

1989 Allied Lyons (to become Allied Domecq) buys the spirits division of Whitbread.

1991 Allied Distillers introduce Caledonian Malts where Miltonduff, Glendronach and Laphroaig are represented besides Tormore. Tormore is later replaced by Scapa.

2004 Tormore 12 year old is launched as an official bottling.

2005 Chivas Brothers (Pernod Ricard) becomes new owners through the acquisition of Allied Domecq.

2012 Production capacity is increased by 20%.

2014 The 12 year old is replaced by two new expressions - 14 and 16 year old.

14 years old

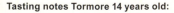

Tasting notes Tormore 14 years old:

GS – Vanilla, butterscotch, summer berries and light spice on the nose. Milk chocolate and tropical fruit on the smooth palate, with soft toffee. Lengthy in the finish, with a sprinkling of black pepper.

Tullibardine

[tully•bar•din]

Owner:
Picard Vins & Spiritueux

Region/district:
Highlands

Founded: 1949

Status: Active (vc)

Capacity: 3 000 000 litres

Address: Blackford, Perthshire PH4 1QG

Website:
tullibardine.com

Tel:
01764 682252

When a consortium bought the closed Tullibardine distillery from Whyte & Mackay in 2003, they had great plans which included building a retail village next to the distillery.

The location in Blackford, just off the busy A9 seemed like a perfect place and to quote one of the new directors, Douglas Ross, "This is not a traditional distillery purchase, but the development and creation of a unique visitor attraction". At first it was deemed a success and the distillery had an advantage with all the visitors to the shops, but after the property crash in 2009, things became tougher. The owners sold the distillery and the retail centre to a French company in 2011 and in 2014 the last shops were closed. As the interest for Tullibardine whisky had grown, the facilities were needed for other purposes In 2016 a bottling line, a vatting hall and more warehouses stood ready to be utilised as well as a cooperage.

This is also the spiritual home to the famous brand, Highland Queen. First launched in 1893 the brand had its heyday in the 1970s when it was popularly sold all over the world. In 2008, it was taken over by the Picard family. The range, with Tullibardine single malt as a key component, now consists of three blends and six single malts, the oldest being a 40 year old.

The equipment at Tullibardine consists of a 6 ton stainless steel semi-lauter mash tun, nine stainless steel washbacks with a minimum fermentation of 52 hours and two pairs of stills. In 2016 the owners expect to produce 2.5 million litres of alcohol.

The range of Tullibardine single malts was completely revamped in 2013 and now consists of **Sovereign**, a bourbon matured core expression without age statement, three wood finishes; **225 Sauternes finish**, **228 Burgundy finish** and **500 Sherry finish** and two older bottlings – a **20 year old** and a **25 year old**. A **60 year old** was released in 2015, as the first in a new range called Custodian Collection and it was followed up in September 2016 by yet another old expression – a **Vintage 1970**. At the same time a **2004 vintage** named **The Murray** was released – the first cask strength Tullibardine made this century.

History:

1949 The architect William Delmé-Evans founds the distillery.

1953 The distillery is sold to Brodie Hepburn.

1971 Invergordon Distillers buys Brodie Hepburn Ltd.

1973 The number of stills increases to four.

1993 Whyte & Mackay (owned by Fortune Brands) buys Invergordon Distillers.

1994 Tullibardine is mothballed.

1996 Whyte & Mackay changes name to JBB (Greater Europe).

2001 JBB (Greater Europe) is bought out from Fortune Brands by management and changes name to Kyndal (Whyte & Mackay from 2003).

2003 A consortium buys Tullibardine for £1.1 million. The distillery is in production again by December.

2005 Three wood finishes from 1993, Port, Moscatel and Marsala, are launched together with a 1986 John Black selection.

2006 Vintage 1966, Sherry Wood 1993 and a new John Black selection are launched.

2007 Five different wood finishes and a couple of single cask vintages are released.

2008 A Vintage 1968 40 year old is released.

2009 Aged Oak is released.

2011 Three vintages (1962, 1964 and 1976) and a wood finish are released. Picard buys the distillery.

2013 A completely new range is launched – Sovereign, 225 Sauternes, 228 Burgundy, 500 Sherry, 20 year old and 25 year old.

2015 A 60 year old Custodian Collection is released.

2016 A Vintage 1970 and The Murray from 2004 are released.

Tasting notes Tullibardine Sovereign:

GS – Floral on the nose, with new-mown hay, vanilla and fudge. Fruity on the palate, with milk chocolate, brazil nuts, marzipan, malt, and a hint of cinnamon. Cocoa, vanilla, a squeeze of lemon and more spice in the finish.

Sovereign

Topping out at Kingsbarns Distillery

New
distilleries

This section is reserved for distilleries
that were established in the last decade and the vast majority
of them have not yet released any whisky.
It is an interesting group of distilleries ranging from industrial giants
producing more than 10 million litres every year to craft distilleries aiming
at a yearly production of 20-30,000 litres.
Four distilleries have been added since last year and they all have
one thing in common – innovation. They are stretching the limits when
it comes to production technique whether it be mashing,
fermentation, distillation or maturation.

Wolfburn

[wolf•burn]

Owner:
Aurora Brewing Ltd.

Region/district:
Northern Highlands

Founded: | **Status:**
2013 | Active

Capacity:
135 000 litres

Address: Henderson Park, Thurso,
Caithness KW14 7XW

Website:
wolfburn.com

Tel:
01847 891051

This is now the most northerly distillery on the Scottish mainland (thereby displacing Pulteney in Wick). The distillery is situated in an industrial area on the outskirts of Thurso and actually doesn't resemble a distillery as we are used to seeing it.

There are four, large, newly constructed buildings of which one is the distillery, while the other three are warehouses and a bottling plant. The owners have chosen a site that is situated 350 metres from the ruins of the old Wolfburn Distillery which was founded in 1821 and subsequently closed down during the latter half of the 19th century. Construction work commenced in August 2012 and the first newmake came off the stills at the end of January 2013. From the very onset, before the equipment was ordered, the company hired Shane Fraser as the distillery manager. Shane had previously worked at Lochnagar and Oban and had for the last seven years been distillery manager at Glenfarclas. From the early design stages of the project, he was involved in determining the character of the future whisky.

The distillery is equipped with a 1.1 ton semi-lauter stainless steel mash tun with a copper canopy, four stainless steel washbacks with a fermentation time of 70-92 hours, holding 5,500 litres each, one wash still (5,500 litres) and one spirit still (3,600 litres). Each mash takes about 6 hours and the run in the spirit still is 10 minutes of foreshots, 2 hours of spirit cut and 2 hours on feints. Wolfburn uses a mix of casks: approximately one third of the spirit is laid down in ex-bourbon quarter casks, a further third is in ex-bourbon hogsheads as well as barrels, and the final third is laid down in ex-sherry butts. The owners expect to produce 132,000 litres of pure alcohol in 2016.

The main part of the malt is unpeated and the intention is to create a smooth whisky. However, since 2014, a lightly peated (10 ppm) spirit has also been produced. The inaugural bottling from the distillery appeared in early 2016 and had a smoky profile due to the fact that it had partly been matured in quarter casks from Islay. This limited release was followed by a more widely available bourbon matured whisky which in September 2016 was re-named Northland. At the same time a second bottling appeared, Aurora, a vatting of ex-bourbon and ex-oloroso casks.

Kingsbarns

[kings•barns]

Owner:
Wemyss family

Region/district:
Lowlands

Founded: | **Status:** | **Capacity:**
2014 | Active (vc) | 600 000 litres

Address: East Newhall Farm, Kingsbarns,
St Andrews KY16 8QE

Website:
kingsbarnsdistillery.com

Tel:
01333 451300

The plans for this distillery near St Andrews in Fife, were drafted in 2008 and came to fruition in 2014 when the distillery was opened.

The idea, initiated by Doug Clement, was to restore a dilapidated farmhouse from the late 18th century and turn it into a modern distillery. Initial advice came from Bill Lark, known as the godfather of modern whisky-making in Australia. Planning permission was received in March 2011 while the founder continued the battle for funding. The turning point came in September 2012 when the Scottish government awarded a grant of £670,000. This, in turn, led to the Wemyss family agreeing to inject £3m into the project and becoming the new owners. The family owns and operates the independent bottling company, Wemyss Malts, and adding a distillery of their own to the portfolio will, of course, facilitate the whisky business in the future.

Construction began in June 2013 and the distillery was officially opened on 30th November 2014 on St Andrew´s Day. Commissioning of the distillery began in January 2015 with the first casks being filled early in March. The distillery is equipped with a 1.5 ton stainless steel mash tun, four 7,500 litre stainless steel washbacks with

a fermentation time of 65-80 hours, one 7,500 litre wash still and one 4,500 litre spirit still. The lyne arms are long and distillation is slow to increase reflux. Local Fife malted barley is to produce a fruity, Lowland style spirit and predominantly, first fill bourbon barrels are used for maturation, together with some sherry butts. Around 140,000 litres of alcohol will be produced during 2016, although there is capacity for larger production in the future.

Peter Holroyd, with experience in the brewing business, became the distillery manager, while the founder of the project and the one who tirelessly fought to implement it, Doug Clement, is the visitor centre manager. There are currently two different types of tours for visitors to choose from. Since Kingsbarns is newly established, they cannot of course offer the visitors a taste of their own single malt, but the new make spirit is available, both for tasting on the tour and in the shop. On the other hand, sister company Wemyss Malts, as an independent bottler, offers an extensive range of whiskies from single malts to blends that can either be enjoyed at the distillery or bought in the shop.

Wemyss is a family-owned company based in Edinburgh, founded in 2005. The family also owns other companies in the field of wine and gin.

Ballindalloch

[bal•lin•da•lock]

Owner:	**Region/district:**
The Macpherson-Grant family	Speyside
Founded: **Status:**	**Capacity:**
2014 Active (vc)	100 000 litres

Address: Ballindalloch, Banffshire AB37 9AA

Website:	**Tel:**
ballindallochdistillery.com	01807 500 331

In the heart of Speyside, the owners of Ballindalloch Castle, the Macpherson-Grant family, decided in 2012 to turn a steading from 1820 into a whisky distillery.

Previous generations of the family had been involved in distilling from the 1860s and from 1923 to 1965, they owned part of Cragganmore distillery, not far away from the castle. The old farm building was meticulously renovated with attention given to every little detail and the result is an amazingly beautiful distillery which can be seen from the A95 between Aberlour and Grantown-on-Spey.

Ballindalloch distillery takes its water from the nearby Garline Springs and all the barley (currently Concerto) is grown on the Estate. All of the distillery equipment are gathered on the second floor which makes it easy for visitors to get a good view of the production. The equipment consists of an extraordinary 1 ton semi lauter, copper clad mash tun with a copper dome. There are four washbacks made of Oregon pine with two short (66 hours) fermentations per week and three long (114 hours). Finally there is a 5,000 litre lantern-shaped wash still and a 3,600 litre spirit still with a reflux ball. Both stills are connected to

two wooden worm tubs for cooling the spirit vapours. The distillery is run by three persons only and, with no automation or computers. Charlie Smith who has more than 40 years' experience within the industry, some of which was as manager at Talisker, was called in as distillery manager. He was retired at the end of 2015 when Colin Poppy succeeded him. The distillery came on stream in September 2014 and was officially opened 16th April 2015 by Prince Charles. The distillery is working 5 days a week, making 100,000 litres of alcohol. The idea is to produce a robust and bold whisky, enhanced not least by the use of worm tubs. Initially, they will fill the spirit into ex-bourbon and ex-sherry casks, but experiments with other types of casks are also in the pipeline. The one warehouse on site, filled up quickly and in May 2015 they started to move casks into a second warehouse close to Glenfarclas distillery. In April 2016, the 1,000th cask was filled since the opening.

The distillery is open for visitors by appointment and the stylish tasting rooms have been decorated with many objects from the family's castle. There is also the opportunity to take part in The Art of Whisky Making experience, which means spending a day with the crew and learning about whisky from mashing to warehousing.

Ardnamurchan

[ard•ne•mur•ken]

Owner:
Adelphi Distillery Ltd

Region/district:
Western Highlands

Founded:
2014

Status:
Active (vc)

Capacity:
500 000 litres

Address: Glenbeg, Ardnamurchan, Argyll PH36 4JG

Website:
adelphidistillery.com

Tel:
01972 500 285

The success for the independent bottler, Adelphi Distillery, has forced the owners to build their own distillery.

The chosen site is Glenbeg on the Ardnamurchan peninsula, just north of Isle of Mull, which makes it the most westerly distillery on mainland Scotland. It is a stunning location, on the shores of Loch Sunart, overlooking the Atlantic. Most of the buildings were completed by August 2013, the equipment started to arrive in the autumn and, finally on 11th July 2014, the distillery came on stream. The distillery was officially opened two weeks later by Princess Anne.

The distillery is equipped with a 2 tonne semi lauter mash tun made of stainless steel with a copper canopy, four oak washbacks and three made of stainless steel, a wash still (10,000 litres) and a spirit still (6,000 litres). The four wooden washbacks are very special because they were retrieved in France, where they had been used as cognac vats, were dismantled and then rebuilt at Ardnamurchan. Minimum fermentation time is 72 hours. The production started with 2 mashes per week and has now increased to five, which

means around 180,000 litres per year with the intention of moving to 300,000 litres sometime soon. Two different styles of whisky are produced; peated for six months of the year and unpeated for the rest. For the peated spirit, the barley has a phenol specification of 30-35ppm. Currently, there are close to 2000 casks of maturing spirit on site. The ultimate goal is to be self-sufficient with malted barley, but the plans for their own malting floors have now been postponed.

The owners have put in a lot of effort into creating a distillery whose environmental footprint is as small as possible. All the power and heat requirements for the distillery come from local renewables – the river that provides the distillery's cooling water has a hydro-electricity generator and the biomass boiler is fuelled by woodchip from the local forestry.

Adelphi Distillery is named after a distillery which closed in 1902. The company is owned by Keith Falconer and Donald Houston, with Alex Bruce as Managing Director. Their whiskies are always bottled at cask strength, uncoloured and un chillfiltered. Adelphi bottles around 50 casks a year.

Annandale

[ann•an•dail]

Owner:	**Region/district:**
Annandale Distillery Co.	Lowlands
Founded: **Status:**	**Capacity:**
2014 Active (vc)	500 000 litres

Address: Northfield, Annan, Dumfriesshire DG12 5LL

Website:	**Tel:**
annandaledistillery.co.uk	01461 207817

In 2010 Professor David Thomson and his wife, Teresa Church, obtained consent from the local council for the building of the new Annandale Distillery in Dumfries and Galloway in the south-west of Scotland.

The old one had been producing since 1836 and was owned by Johnnie Walker from 1895 until it closed down in 1918. From 1924 to 2007, the site was owned by the Robinson family, who were famous for their Provost brand of porridge oats. The old distillery was used as a drying plant for the oats. David Thomson began the restoration of the site in June 2011 with the two, old sandstone warehouses being restored to function as two-level dunnage warehouses. The distillery was in a poor condition and the mash house and the tun room was largely reconstructed while the other buildings were refurbished substantially. The total cost, including restoration, construction and new equipment amounted to £10.5m.

Entering the production area of the new distillery is like walking into a beautiful village church. First you run into the 2.5 ton semi-lauter mash tun with an elegant copper dome. Then, with three wooden washbacks (a fermentation time of 72-96 hours) on each side, you are guided up to the two spirit stills (4,000 litres). Once you have reached them, you find the wash still (12,000 litres) slightly hidden behind a wall. The capacity is 500,000 litres per annum but, to begin with, they will only work one shift, which means 6 mashes per week and 250,000 litres. The casks used for maturation are first fill and second fill bourbon barrels but sherry butts were also filled in November 2015 and then again in the summer 2016.

The first cask was filled on 15 November 2014 and both unpeated and peated (45ppm) whisky is distilled. The unpeated version will be called Man o´ Words inspired by the poet, Robert Burns, while the peated version will be named Man o´ Sword, named after King Robert the Bruce. In spring 2015, the distillery decided to put up the first 100 casks that were filled for sale. Prices vary, but cask number one has a price tag of £1m. The old maltings, with the kiln and original pagoda roof, have been turned into an excellent visitor centre and the owners hope to attract 50,000 visitors to the distillery in the future.

Inchdairnie

[inch•dairnie]

Owner:
John Fegus & Co. Ltd

Region/district:
Lowlands

Founded: **Status:**
2015   Active

Capacity:
2 000 000 litres

Address: Whitecraigs Rd, Glenrothes, Fife KY6 2RX

Website:
inchdairniedistillery.com

Tel:
01595 510010

The majority of new and planned distilleries in Scotland (except the ones built by the biggest companies) are quite small with a capacity of 50-500,000 litres.

A rare exception is Inchdairnie, which was officially opened in May 2016, a few miles west of Glenrothes in Fife. The distillery will be able to distil 2 million litres per year with a possibility of expanding to 4 million litres. The distillery is owned by John Fergus & Co. which was founded by Ian Palmer in 2011. Palmer has 40 years of experience in the Scotch whisky industry and his latest position was general manager for Glen Turner. He is a minority share holder, with CES Whisky holding the rest of the shares. CES, in turn, is owned by Copenhagen Fortuna which means that Inchdairnie is the first distillery in Scotland having Danish owners.

Inchdairnie is, in many ways, an unusual distillery. With an investment of £10m, it took only 18 months to build and the distillery is equipped with a Meura mash filter, instead of a traditional mash tun. There is only one distillery in Scotland, Teaninich, that already uses this technique.

Working with a mash filter also means a hammer mill must be used to create a finer grist compared to, for example, a Porteus mill. There are four washbacks with a fermentation time of 72 hours and one pair of traditional pot stills with double condensers and aftercoolers to increase the copper to spirit ratio. The two stills are complemented by a Lomond still with six plates to provide the opportunity for triple distillation and experimental distillation. Innovation, however, doesn't stop there. Normally, one uses spring barley to produce Scotch whisky. At Inchdairnie they will also be using winter barley, which is harder to handle in the mashing process due to the high protein content. On the other hand, using winter barley will enhance the flavour of the whisky. A unique yeast recipe combining beer-, wine- and distiller´s yeast is used and high gravity fermentation will create a fruitier character of the newmake.

Two main styles of whisky will be produced. Strathenry (80% of the production) will be used for blended whisky, not least by Macduff International (producers of Islay Mist and Lauder´s) while Inchdairnie will be matured to be sold as a single malt in the future. There are also plans to produce peated whisky (20ppm), starting at the end of 2016.

Daftmill

[daf•mil]

Owner:
Francis Cuthbert

Region/district:
Lowlands

Founded:
2005

Status:
Active

Capacity:
c 65 000 litres

Address: By Cupar, Fife KY15 5RF

Website:
daftmill.com

Tel:
01337 830303

Permission was granted in 2003 for a steading at Daftmill Farmhouse in Fife, just a few miles west of Cupar and dating back to 1655, to be converted into a distillery.

The first distillation was on 16th December 2005 and around 20,000 litres are distilled in a year. A little less was produced in 2013 when a new boiler was fitted. It is run as a typical farmhouse distillery. The barley is grown on the farm and they also supply other distilleries. Of the total 800 tonnes that Francis Cuthbert harvests in a year, around 100 tonnes are used for his own whisky. The malting is done without peat at Crisp´s in Alloa. The equipment consists of a one tonne semi-lauter mash tun with a copper dome, two stainless steel washbacks with a fermentation between 72 and 100 hours and one pair of stills with slightly ascending lyne arms. The equipment is designed to give a lot of copper contact, a lot of reflux. The wash still has a capacity of

3,000 litres and the spirit still 2,000 litres.

Francis Cuthbert´s aim is to do a light, Lowland style whisky similar to Rosebank. In order to achieve this they have very short foreshots (five minutes) and the spirit run starts at 78% to capture all of the fruity esters and already comes off at 73%. The spirit is filled mainly into ex-bourbon casks, always first fill, but there are also a few sherry butts in the two dunnage warehouses.

Taking care of the farm obviously prohibits Francis from producing whisky full time. His silent season is during spring and autumn when work in the fields take all of his time. Whisky distillation is therefore reserved for June-August and November-February. The whisky in the warehouse is now 10 years old and whisky enthusiasts have been asking for years when the first bottling is due. Francis however doesn´t seem to be in a hurry or as he himself puts it "patience is a virtue".

Abhainn Dearg

[aveen jar•rek]

Owner:
Mark Tayburn

Region/district:
Islands (Isle of Lewis)

Founded:
2008

Status:
Active

Capacity:
c 20 000 litres

Address: Carnish, Isle of Lewis,
Na h-Eileanan an Iar HS2 9EX

Website:
abhainndearg.co.uk

Tel:
01851 672429

In September 2008, spirit flowed from a newly constructed distillery in Uig on the island of Lewis in the Outer Hebrides.

This was the first distillery on the island since 1840 when Stornoway distillery was closed. The Gaelic name of the new distillery is Abhainn Dearg which means Red River, and the founder and owner is Mark "Marko" Tayburn who was born and raised on the island. Part of the distillery was converted from an old fish farm while some of the buildings are new. There are two 500 kg mash tuns made of stainless steel and two 7,500 litre washbacks made of Douglas fir with a fermentation time of 4 days. The wash still has a capacity of 2,112 litres and the spirit still 2,057 litres. Both have very long necks and steeply descending lye pipes leading out into two wooden worm tubs. Both bourbon and sherry casks are used for maturation. The plan was to use 100% barley grown on Lewis and in 2013

the first 6 tonnes of Golden Promise (15% of the total requirement) were harvested. In 2015, the owner reported that all the barley needed for the production, now came from the island.

The first release from the distillery was The Spirit of Lewis (matured for a short time in sherry casks) in 2010 and the first single malt was a limited release (2,011 bottles) of a 3 year old in October 2011, followed up by a cask strength version (58%) in 2012. The owners currently still offer Spirit of St Lewis and the 3 year old single malt and it seems the plan is to await the release of a 10 year old in 2018.

Ailsa Bay

[ail•sah bey]

Owner: William Grant & Sons

Region/district: Lowlands

Founded: 2007 **Status:** Active **Capacity:** 12 000 000 litres

Address: Girvan, Ayrshire KA26 9PT

Website: -

Tel: 01465 713091

Commisioned in September 2007, it only took nine months to build this distillery on the same site as Girvan Distillery near Ayr on Scotland's west coast.

Until recently, it was equipped with a 12,5 tonne full lauter mash tun, 12 washbacks made of stainless steel and eight stills. In August 2013 however, it was time for a major expansion when yet another mash tun, 12 more washbacks and eight more stills were commissioned, doubling the capacity to 12 million litres of alcohol.

Each washback will hold 50,000 litres and fermentation time is 60 hours for the heavier styles and 72 hours for the lighter "Balveniestyle". The stills are made according to the same standards as Balvenie's and two of the wash stills and two of the spirit stills have stainless steel condensers instead of copper. That way, they have the possibility

of making batches of a more sulphury spirit if desired. A unique feature is the octangular spirit safe which sits between the two rows of stills. Each side corresponds to one specific still. To increase efficiency and to get more alcohol, high gravity distillation is used. The wash stills are heated using external heat exchangers but they also have interior steam coils. The spirit stills are heated by steam coils. In 2016, the distillery will be producing 11.5 million litres of alcohol.

Five different types of spirit are produced. The most common is a light and rather sweet spirit. Then there is a heavy, sulphury style and three peated with the peatiest having a malt specification of 50ppm. The production is destined to become a part of Grant's blended Scotch which is currently the fourth most popular Scotch in the world with 53 million bottles sold in 2015. However, a peated single malt Ailsa Bay has also been released, in spring 2016, with more batches to follow.

Roseisle

[rose•eyel]

Owner: Diageo

Region/district: Highlands

Founded: 2009 **Status:** Active **Capacity:** 12 500 000 litres

Address: Roseisle, Morayshire IV30 5YP

Website: -

Tel: 01343 832100

Roseisle distillery is located on the same site as the already existing Roseisle maltings just west of Elgin. The distillery has won several awards for its ambition towards sustainable production.

The distillery is equipped with two stainless steel mash tuns with a 12.5 tonne charge each. There are 14 huge (115,500 litres) stainless steel washbacks and 14 stills with the wash stills being heated by external heat exchangers while the spirit stills are heated using steam coils. The spirit vapours are cooled through copper condensers but on three spirit stills and three wash stills there are also stainless steel condensers attached, that you can switch to for a more sulphury spirit. The plan for 2016 is to do 21 mashes per week and a total of 10,7 million litres of alcohol.

The total cost for the distillery was £40m and how to use the hot water in an efficient way was very much a focal

point from the beginning. For example, Roseisle is connected by means of two long pipes with Burghead maltings, 3 km north of the distillery. Hot water is pumped from Roseisle and then used in the seven kilns at Burghead and cold water is then pumped back to Roseisle. The pot ale from the distillation will be piped into anaerobic fermenters to be transformed into biogas and the dried solids will act as a biomass fuel source. The biomass burner on the site, producing steam for the distillery, covers 72% of the total requirement. Furthermore, green technology has reduced the emission of carbon dioxide to only 15% of an ordinary, same-sized distillery.

So far no substantial quantities of peated spirit has been distilled at Roseisle. Instead they are concentrating on producing a whisky with a light Speyside character. The fermentation time for this style is 90-100 hours and for a heavier style it is 50-60 hours.

Strathearn

[strath•earn]

Owner: Tony Reeman-Clark	**Region/district:** Southern Highlands
Founded: 2013 **Status:** Active	**Capacity:** c 30 000 litres
Address: Bachilton Farm Steading, Methven PH1 3QX	
Website: strathearndistillery.com	**Tel:** 01738 840 100

This is something as unique as Scotland´s first micro-distillery. Abhainn Dearg on the Isle of Lewis has the same capacity, but the stills at Strathearn are considerably smaller.

The brainchild of Tony Reeman-Clark, it is situated a couple of miles west of Methven near Perth. Gin production was started in August 2013 and the first whisky was filled into casks in October. The distillery uses the Maris Otter barley which was abandoned by other distillers years ago due to the low yield. Reeman-Clark prefers it though, because of the flavours that it contributes. All the equipment is fitted into one room and consists of a stainless steel mash tun, two stainless steel washbacks with a fermentation time of 4-5 days, one 1,000 litre wash still and a 500 litre spirit still. Both stills are of the Alambic type with vertical tube copper condensers. When they are producing gin, they simply detach the lyne arm and mount a copper

basket to the still to hold the botanicals. For maturation a variety of 50-100 litre casks are used; virgin French oak, virgin American oak and ex-sherry casks.

Reeman-Clark and his team have also been experimenting with other types of wood like chestnut, mullberry and cherry. According to the rules, spirit matured in anything other than oak, cannot be called Scotch whisky. This problem has been solved by labelling the content Uisge Beatha – the ancient name for Scotch. In an attempt to show how whisky would have been drunk a couple of hundred years ago, the company released this spirit, which had matured in 30-litre casks for only 28 days, in spring 2015. On the whisky side, both peated (35ppm) and un-peated whisky is produced and the first bottlings are expected to appear in December 2016. So far, apart from the Uisge Beatha and three types of new-make (un-peated, peated and triple distilled), four different gins have been released; Heather Rose, Citrus, Oaked Highland and Juniper.

Eden Mill

[eden mill]

Owner: Paul Miller	**Region/district:** Lowlands
Founded: 2014 **Status:** Active (vc)	**Capacity:** 80 000 litres
Address: St Andrews, Fife, KY16 0UU	
Website: edenmill.com	**Tel:** 01334 834038

In 2012, Paul Miller, the former Molson Coors sales director, with a background in the whisky industry (Diageo and Glenmorangie), opened up the successful Eden Brewery in Guardbridge 3 miles west of St Andrews.

The site was an old paper mill and only 50 metres away, there was a distillery called Seggie which was operative between 1810 and 1860 and owned by the Haig family. As an extension of the brewery, Paul decided to build a distillery called Eden Mill Distillery. The distillery, with a capacity of 80,000 litres per year, will mainly produce malt whisky, but gin is also on the map. The distillery is equipped with two wash stills and one spirit still of the alambic type. Made by Hoga in Portugal, all three stills are of the same size – 1,000 litres. Eden Mill is the first combined brewery and distillery in Scotland – a combination which

has proven so successful, especially in the USA. The brewery/distillery also has a visitor centre which already attracts 20,000 visitors a year.

Whisky production started in November 2014 and, waiting for the first whisky to be ready for release, Miller has already released several, young malt spirits – St Andrews Day, Hogmanay and Robert Burns Day, all of them being sold out by now. Different varieties of gin, on the other hand, have been launched continuously since the start, which include Hop, Love, Golf and Oak Gin. In 2016, the gin was launched in the USA and owners are also planning an introduction of the Chinese market. A new product category for the company has also been introduced – ready-to-drink gin cocktails. Of the whisky production, around 10,000 litres a year will be reserved for the distillery´s Private Cask Owners' Club, where customers can buy anything from octaves to hogsheads of whisky.

Dalmunach

[dal•moo•nack]

Owner:
Chivas Brothers

Region/district:
Speyside

Founded: | **Status:**
2015 | Active

Capacity:
10 000 000 litres

Address: Carron, Banffshire AB38 7QP

Website:
-

Tel:
-

One of the newest distilleries in Scotland, and one of the most beautiful, has been built on the site of the former Imperial distillery.

Imperial distillery was inaugurated in 1898 and was then owned by DCL (later to become Diageo) from 1916 until 2005, when Chivas Brothers took over. It was out of production for 60% of the time until 1998 when it was mothballed. The owners probably never planned to use it for distillation again as it was put up for sale in 2005 to become available as residential flats. Soon after, it was withdrawn from the market and, in 2012, a decision was taken to tear down the old distillery and build a new. Demolition of the old distillery began in 2013 and by the end of that year, nothing was left, except for the old warehouses.

Construction on the new Dalmunach distillery started in 2013 and it was commissioned in October 2014. The ex-

ceptional and stunning distillery is equipped with a 12 ton Briggs full lauter mash tun, 16 stainless steel washbacks with a fermentation time of 54 hours and 4 pairs of stills. The stills are positioned in a circle with a hexagonal spirit safe in the middle. The distillery, which cost £25m to build, has a capacity of 10 million litres and was officially opened in 2015 by Nicola Sturgeon, First Minister of Scotland.

Glasgow

[glas•go]

Owner:
Liam Hughes, Ian McDougall

Region/district:
Lowlands

Founded: | **Status:**
2015 | Active

Capacity:
200 000 litres

Address: 234 West George St, Glasgow G2 4QY

Website:
glasgowdistillery.com

Tel:
0141 4047191

There's been keen competition in the past year to see who builds what has been dubbed the first new distillery in Glasgow in more than one hundred years.

On the one hand there is Tim Morrison, the owner of AD Rattray, and his son, Andrew, who plan a distillery in the Ocean's Docks on the banks of the River Clyde. In the meanwhile, Liam Hughes and Ian McDougall from The Glasgow Distillery Company, backed up by Asian investors, have been working away on building another distillery at the Hillington Business Park and they finally beat the Morrison's to it. The first whisky was distilled in February 2015 and while awaiting that it will become at least three years old, they have already launched Makar Gin and different wood aged gins from own production. Whisky, however, is also being offered by the company. Prometheus, a sourced single malt where the distillery is not revealed, was

released in April 2015. It is a 26 year old, slightly peated sherry maturation from Speyside. The second release, a 27 year old, was released in February 2016 with a 28 year old already planned.

The distillery is equipped with a one ton mash tun, four wash backs (5,400 litres each), one 2,500 litre wash still, one 1,400 litre spirit still and one 450 litre gin still. In 2016, they will be producing 75,000 litres of pure alcohol, rising to 200,000 by the end of 2017. The first production of peated spirit (54ppm) also began in 2016 and was laid down in oloroso and amontillado sherry casks.

The fact that this would have been the first malt whisky distillery in Glasgow in more than 100 years, isn't entirely true. In 1958, Strathclyde grain distillery was founded and within that distillery, Kinclaith malt distillery was constructed which operated until 1975. Strathclyde is still a working distillery.

Harris

[har•ris]

Owner:	**Region/district:**
Isle of Harris Distillers Ltd.	Islands (Isle of Harris)

Founded:	**Status:**	**Capacity:**
2015	Active (vc)	230 000 litres

Address: Tarbert, Isle of Harris,
Na h-Eileanan an Iar HS3 3DJ

Website:	**Tel:**
harrisdistillery.com	01859 502212

Almost ten years ago, Anderson Bakewell had conjured up an idea that has now resulted in a distillery which has come to fruition on the Isle of Harris.

Bakewell, who has been connected to the island for more than 40 years, acquired the services of Simon Erlanger for the company´s benefit at an early stage. Erlanger, a former marketing director for Glenmorangie, is now MD of the new distillery, while Bakewell is chairman of the company. Construction started in 2014 and the distillery came into production in September 2015. The total cost for the whole project is £11.4m, but this sum probably also covers the cost for barley and casks until the first whisky is ready to be bottled. The distillery, located in Tarbert, is the second distillery after Abhainn Dearg on Lewis to be located in the Outer Hebrides.

The equipment consists of a 1.2 tonne semi lauter mash tun made of stainless steel but clad with American oak, 5 washbacks made of Oregon pine and with a fermentation time of 3-4 days, one 7,000 litre wash still and a 5,000 litre spirit still - both with descending lyne arms and made in Italy. During 2016, they will be doing 5 mashes per week producing 100,000 litres of pure alcohol. The style of the whisky, which will be called Hearach (the Gaelic word for a person living on Harris), will be medium peated with a phenol specification in the barley of 12-14ppm. The first spirit to be distilled in September 2015 was gin and this was followed by whisky in December. The gin has already been released and apart from traditional gin botanicals, local ingredients are also used such as sugar kelp.

With the new distillery, 20 new jobs have been created on the island, some of whom are working in the distillery visitor centre with an anticipated 40,000 guests in the first year.

Lone Wolf

[loan wolf]

Owner:	**Region/district:**
Brewdog plc.	Highlands

Founded:	**Status:**	**Capacity:**
2016	Active	450 000 litres

Address: Balmacassie Commercial Park, Ellon,
Aberdeenshire AB41 8BX

Website:	**Tel:**
brewdog.com	01358 724924

Founded in 2007 by James Watt and Martin Dickie, Brew Dog has grown to become the biggest independent brewery in the UK and is also the fastest-growing drinks producer in the country.

Today, the company has 540 employees producing 65 different beers and they have also managed to open 44 bars. A decision was made in 2014 to also open a distillery on the premises in Fellon, outside of Aberdeen. To manage the distillery, Steven Kearsley who has a background at several Diageo distilleries, was called in. Early on, Steven was determined that this should not be "just another" whisky distillery. To use his own words, it is multi-faceted and by that he means they will not limit themselves to just a few styles of spirits. Apart from malt whisky, there are also grain and rye, bourbon style whiskey, vodka, gin, rum and fruit brandies on offer.

The adjacent brew house will, of course, provide the distillery with the wash and for the distillation, the distillery has the following equipment; one 3,000 litre pot still with an 8 plate rectification column which will be used for stripping the wash for vodka, whisky and rum, another 3,000 litre still with a 60-plate column is used for the final distillation of vodka and whisky, a 600 litre pot still is dedicated to gin and brandy production, while a 50 litre pot still is used for research and experimentation. The last word is paramount to Steven. This will be an innovative distillery where, for example, cherry or apple wood may be used for drying the barley or other types of wood, other than just oak, may be used for maturation. Gin and vodka is already being produced (with a possible launch later in 2016) and distillation of whisky will probably commence by the end of the year.

Arbikie

[ar•bi•ki]

Owner:	Region/district:
The Stirling family	Eastern Highlands

Founded:	**Status:**	**Capacity:**
2015	Active	200 000 litres

Address: Inverkeilor, Arbroath, Angus DD11 4UZ

Website:	**Tel:**
arbikie.com	01241 830770

The Stirling family has been farming since the 17th century and the 2000-acre Arbikie Highland Estate in Angus has now been in their possession for four generations.

The three brothers (John, Iain and David) started their careers within other fields but have now returned to the family lands to open up a single-estate distillery. The definition of a single-estate distillery is that, not only does the whole chain of production take place on site, but all the ingredients are also grown on the farm. Ballindalloch is one example but Arbikie is the first to produce both brown and white spirits.

The first vodka from potatoes was distilled in October 2014 which was followed by gin in May 2015. Trials with malt whisky started in March 2015, has gone over to full production since October 2015.

The barley is grown in fields of their own and then sent to Boorts malt in Montrose, 7 miles away. The distillery, which is based in an old barn at the farm, is equipped with a stainless steel, semi-lauter mash tun with a 0.75 ton charge, four washbacks (two 4,400 litre and two 9,000 litre), one 4,000 litre wash still and one 2,400 litre spirit still. For the final stage of vodka and gin production, there is also a 40 plate rectification column. The whisky is mainly matured in ex bourbon barrels and ex sherry hogsheads.

The products released so far are Arbikie Vodka, Chilli Vodka made with chipotle chilli grown by Scotland's first chilli farm, Chillilicious and Arbikie Kirsty's Gin named after the master distiller, Kirsty Black. According to the owners, the style of their malt whisky will be unpeated Highland with a coastal influence. At the moment the Stirlings don´t intend to launch their first whisky any time soon. The plan is to release it at the age of 14 in 2030.

Dornoch

[dor•nock]

Owner:	Region/district:
Phil and Simon Thompson	Northern Highlands

Founded:	**Status:**	**Capacity:**
2016	Active	30 000 litres

Address: Castle Street, Dornoch, Sutherland, IV25 3 SD

Website:	**Tel:**
dornochdistillery.com	01862 810 216

Along with their parents, Phil and Simon Thompson have been running the Dornoch Castle Hotel in Sutherland for fifteen years.

The hotel is famous for its outstanding whisky bar and the two brothers are passionate about whisky and other spirits. So passionate in fact that they have decided to convert a 135-year old fire station into a distillery. The building is only 47 square metres and the brothers have struggled to fit all the equipment into the limited space. The distillery is equipped with a 300 kg stainless steel, semi-lauter mash tun, seven washbacks made of oak, a 1,000 litre wash still and a 600 litre spirit still. Both stills, made by Hoga in Portugal, have shell and tube condensers, but the brothers are no strangers when it comes to installing worm tubs in the future. The stills are directly fired using gas but they are also equipped with steam coils as an alternative heating method. There is also a 2,000 litre still with a column for

the production of gin and other spirits. The distillery will have a yearly capacity of 30,000 litres of pure alcohol of which approximately 15,000 litres are dedicated to whisky. The first distillation is scheduled for October 2016. As a way to make the financials add up initially, Phil and Simon have been using crowd funding.

Their interest in "old-style" whiskies produced in the 1960s and earlier, which is mirrored in the range that they offer in the bar, will also affect the production. All the barley will be floor malted and will originate from old heritage varieties, while brewer´s yeast will be used instead of distiller´s yeast. The plan is also to make the production organic. For maturation, they will be using different ex-sherry casks (fino, oloroso and PX), as well as casks that have previously held bourbon and rye. Initially, the whisky will be unpeated but the key word for this distillery is experimentation, so production in the future may involve peat.

Distilleries per owner

c = closed, d = demolished, mb = mothballed, dm = dismantled

Diageo
Auchroisk
Banff (d)
Benrinnes
Blair Athol
Brora (c)
Caol Ila
Cardhu
Clynelish
Coleburn (dm)
Convalmore (dm)
Cragganmore
Dailuaine
Dallas Dhu (c)
Dalwhinnie
Dufftown
Glen Albyn (d)
Glendullan
Glen Elgin
Glenesk (dm)
Glenkinchie
Glenlochy (d)
Glenlossie
Glen Mhor (d)
Glen Ord
Glen Spey
Glenury Royal (d)
Inchgower
Knockando
Lagavulin
Linkwood
Mannochmore
Millburn (dm)
Mortlach
North Port (d)
Oban
Pittyvaich (d)
Port Ellen (dm)
Rosebank (c)
Roseisle
Royal Lochnagar
St Magdalene (dm)
Strathmill
Talisker
Teaninich

Pernod Ricard
Aberlour
Allt-a-Bhainne
Braeval
Caperdonich (d)
Dalmunach
Glenallachie
Glenburgie
Glen Keith
Glenlivet
Glentauchers
Glenugie (dm)
Imperial (d)
Inverleven (d)
Kinclaith (d)
Lochside (d)
Longmorn
Miltonduff
Scapa
Strathisla

Tormore

Edrington Group
Glenrothes
Glenturret
Highland Park
Macallan

Inver House (Thai Beverage)
Balblair
Balmenach
Glen Flagler (d)
Knockdhu
Pulteney
Speyburn

John Dewar & Sons (Bacardi)
Aberfeldy
Aultmore
Craigellachie
Macduff
Royal Brackla

William Grant & Sons
Ailsa Bay
Balvenie
Glenfiddich
Kininvie
Ladyburn (dm)

Whyte & Mackay (Emperador)
Dalmore
Fettercairn
Jura
Tamnavulin

Morrison Bowmore (Beam Suntory)
Auchentoshan
Bowmore
Glen Garioch

Burn Stewart Distillers (Distell)
Bunnahabhain
Deanston
Tobermory

Benriach Dist. Co. (Brown Forman)
Benriach
Glendronach
Glenglassaugh

Loch Lomond Group
Glen Scotia
Littlemill (d)
Loch Lomond

Beam Suntory
Ardmore
Laphroaig

J & A Mitchell
Glengyle
Springbank

Glenmorangie Co. (LVMH)
Ardbeg
Glenmorangie

Angus Dundee Distillers
Glencadam
Tomintoul

Ian Macleod Distillers
Glengoyne
Tamdhu

Campari Group
Glen Grant

Isle of Arran Distillers
Arran

Signatory
Edradour

Tomatin Distillery Co.
Tomatin

J & G Grant
Glenfarclas

Rémy Cointreau
Bruichladdich

David Prior
Bladnoch (c)

Gordon & MacPhail
Benromach

La Martiniquaise
Glen Moray

Ben Nevis Distillery Ltd (Nikka)
Ben Nevis

Picard Vins & Spiritueux
Tullibardine

Harvey´s of Edinburgh
Speyside

Kilchoman Distillery Co.
Kilchoman

Cuthbert family
Daftmill

Mark Tayburn
Abhainn Dearg

Aurora Brewing Ltd
Wolfburn

Strathearn Distillery Ltd
Strathearn

Annandale Distillery Co.
Annandale

Adelphi Distillery Co.
Ardnamurchan

Wemyss
Kingsbarns

Mcpherson-Grant family
Ballindalloch

Paul Miller
Eden Mill

Isle of Harris Distillers
Harris

The Glasgow Distillery Company
Glasgow Distillery

John Fegus & Co. Ltd
Inchdairnie

Stirling family
Arbikie

Brewdog plc
Lone Wolf

Thompson family
Dornoch

Closed
distilleries

The distilleries on the following pages have all been closed and some of them even demolished. There are two of them where production may be resumed again; the new owners of the Coleburn site are using it for warehousing but have expressed an interest in starting distillation again, although with new equipment. At Dallas Dhu, on the other hand, the equipment is still intact and Historic Environment Scotland are in discussions with Diageo regarding a possible re-start of the distillery. New whiskies from some of the distilleries appear on a regular basis but for most of them chances are very slim of ever finding another bottling.

Banff

Owner:	Region:	Founded:	Status:
Diageo	Speyside	1824	Demolished

Banff's tragic history of numerous fires, explosions and bombings have contributed to its fame. The most spectacular incident was when a lone Junkers Ju-88 bombed one of the warehouses in 1941. Hundreds of casks exploded and several thousand litres of whisky were destroyed. The distillery was closed in 1983 and the buildings were destroyed in a fire in 1991. The distillery was owned for 80 years by the Simpson family but when their company filed for bankruptcy in 1932, it was sold to Scottish Malt Distillers which later would be a part of Diageo. When the distillery was at its largest it produced 1 million litres per year in three pairs of stills.

Bottlings:

There has only been one official Rare Malts bottling from 2004. A couple of independent bottlings from 1975 were released in 2012 and a 49 year old from Gordon & MacPhail (distilled in 1966) appeared in 2015.

Ben Wyvis

Owner:	Region:	Founded:	Status:
Whyte & Mackay	N Highlands	1965	Dismantled

The large grain distillery, Invergordon, today producing 36 million litres of grain whisky per year, was established in 1959 on the Cromarty Firth, east of Alness. Six years later a small malt distillery, Ben Wyvis, was built on the same site with the purpose of producing malt whisky for Invergordon Distiller´s blends. The distillery was equipped with one mash tun, six washbacks and one pair of stills. Funnily enough the stills are still in use today at Glengyle distillery. Production at Ben Wyvis stopped in 1976 and in 1977 the distillery was closed and dismantled.

Bottlings:

There have been only a few releases of Ben Wyvis. The first, a 27 year old, was released by Invergordon in 1999, followed by a 31 year old from Signatory in 2000 and finally a 37 year old from Kyndal (later Whyte & Mackay) in 2002. It is highly unlikely that there will be more Ben Wyvis single malt to bottle.

Brora

[bro•rah]

Owner:
Diageo

Founded:
1819

Status:
Closed

Region/district:
Northern Highlands

Capacity:
-

Although founded under the name Clynelish distillery in 1819, it is under the name Brora that the single malt has enjoyed its newfound fame during the past two decades.

The whisky has mostly appealed to peat freaks around the world but, for the first 140 years (and the final decade), it actually wasn't that peated. In 1967 DCL decided to build a new, modern distillery on the same site. This was given the name Clynelish and it was decided the old distillery, with a capacity of 1 million litres of alcohol, should be closed. Shortly after, the demand for peated whisky, especially for the blend Johnnie Walker, increased and the old site re-opened but now under the name Brora and the "recipe" for the whisky was changed to a heavily peated malt. This continued from 1969 to 1973 when production levels at Lagavulin and Talisker had increased to a sufficient level and after that the peatiness was reduced, even if single peated batches turned up until the late seventies. Brora closed permanently in 1983 but the buildings still stand next to the new Clynelish. The two stills, the feints receiver, the spirit receiver and the brass safe remain, while the warehouses are used for storage of spirit from Clynelish.

The first distillery was built in the time referred to as the Highland Clearances. Many land-owners wished to increase the yield of their lands and consequently went into large-scale sheep farming. Thousands of families were ruthlessly forced away and the most infamous of the large land-owners was the Marquis of Stafford who founded Clynelish (Brora) in 1819.

Since 1995 Diageo has regularly released different expressions of Brora in the Rare Malts series. The latest, which also became the last, appeared in 2003. In 2002 a new range was created, called Special Releases and bottlings of Brora have appeared ever since. In October 2016, it was time for the 15th release. This time it was a 38 year old distilled in 1977 and bottled at 48.6%. A total of 2,984 bottles were launched. This is the oldest Brora ever released as part of the Special Releases.

History:
- **1819** The Marquis of Stafford, 1st Duke of Sutherland, founds the distillery as Clynelish Distillery.
- **1827** The first licensed distiller, James Harper, files for bankruptcy and John Matheson takes over.
- **1828** James Harper is back as licensee.
- **1833** Andrew Ross takes over the license.
- **1846** George Lawson & Sons takes over.
- **1896** James Ainslie & Heilbron takes over and rebuilds the facilities.
- **1912** Distillers Company Limited (DCL) takes over together with James Risk.
- **1925** DCL buys out Risk.
- **1930** Scottish Malt Distillers takes over.
- **1931** The distillery is mothballed.
- **1938** Production restarts.
- **1960** The distillery becomes electrified (until now it has been using locally mined coal from Brora).
- **1967** A new distillery is built adjacent to the first one, it is also named Clynelish and both operate in parallel from August with the new distillery named Clynelish A and the old Clynelish B.
- **1969** Clynelish B is closed in April but reopened shortly after as Brora and starts using a heavily peated malt until 1973.
- **1975** A new mashtun is installed.
- **1983** Brora is closed in March.
- **1995** Brora 1972 (20 years) and Brora 1972 (22 years) are launched as Rare Malts.
- **2002** A 30 year old is the first bottling in the Special Releases.
- **2014** The 13th release of Brora – a 35 year old.
- **2015** The 14th release of Brora – a 37 year old.
- **2016** The 15th release of Brora – a 38 year old.

38 years old

Caperdonich

Owner:	Region:	Founded:	Status:
Chivas Bros.	Speyside	1897	Demolished

The distillery was founded by James Grant, owner of Glen Grant which was located in Rothes just a few hundred metres away. Five years after the opening, the distillery was shut down and was re-opened again in 1965 under the name Caperdonich. In 2002 it was mothballed yet again, never to be re-opened. Parts of the equipment were dismantled to be used in other distilleries within the company. In 2010 the distillery was sold to the manufacturer of copper pot stills, Forsyth's in Rothes, and the buildings were demolished. In the old days a pipe connected Caperdonich and Glen Grant for easy transport of spirit, ready to be filled.

Bottlings:

An official cask strength was released in 2005. Recent independent bottlings are a 21 year old distilled in 1994 from Douglas Laing and a 19 year old from 1995 from Berry Brothers.

Coleburn

Owner:	Region:	Founded:	Status:
Diageo	Speyside	1897	Dismantled

Like so many other distilleries, Coleburn was taken over by DCL (the predecessor of Diageo) in the 1930s. Although the single malt never became well known, Coleburn was used as an experimental workshop where new production techniques were tested. In 1985 the distillery was mothballed and never opened again. Two brothers, Dale and Mark Winchester, bought the buildings in 2004 with the intention of transforming the site into an entertainment centre - a plan that never materialised. Since 2014, the warehouses are used by Aceo Ltd, who bought independent bottler Murray McDavid in 2013, for storing their own whiskies as well as stock belonging to clients

Bottlings:

There has been one official Rare Malts bottling from 2000, and Independent bottlings are also rare. Two recent releases from Gordon & MacPhail are a 1972 bottled in 2013 and a 1981 bottled in 2015.

Convalmore

Owner:	Region:	Founded:	Status:
Diageo	Speyside	1894	Dismantled

This distillery is still intact and can be seen in Dufftown next to Balvenie distillery. The buildings were sold to William Grant's in 1990 and they now use it for storage. Diageo, however, still holds the rights to the brand. In the early 20th century, experimental distilling of malt whisky in continuous stills (the same method used for producing grain whisky) took place at Convalmore. The distillery closed in 1985. One of the more famous owners of this distillery was James Buchanan who used Convalmore single malt as a part of his famous blend Black & White. He later sold the distillery to DCL (later Diageo).

Bottlings:

A 28 year old was released by the owners in 2005. In autumn 2013, as part of the Special Releases, Diageo released a 36 year old distilled in 1977. The latest independent bottling was a 40 year old from 1975 released by Gordon & MacPhail in 2015.

Dallas Dhu

Owner:	Region:	Founded:	Status:
Diageo	Speyside	1898	Closed

Dallas Dhu distillery is located along the A96 between Elgin and Inverness and is still intact, equipment and all, but hasn't produced since 1983. Three years later, Diageo sold the distillery to Historic Scotland and it became a museum which is open all year round. In spring 2013 a feasibility study was commissioned by Historic Environment Scotland to look at the possibilities of re-starting production again. One of the founders of the distillery, Alexander Edwards, belonged to the more energetic men in the 19th century Scotch whisky business. Not only did he start Dallas Dhu but also established Aultmore, Benromach and Craigellachie and owned Benrinnes and Oban.

Bottlings:

There are two Rare Malts bottlings from Diageo, the latest in 1997. The latest from independents is a 1980 bottled in 2014 by Gordon & MacPhail.

Glen Albyn

Owner:	Region:	Founded:	Status:
Diageo	N Highlands	1844	Demolished

Glen Albyn was one of three Inverness distilleries surviving into the 1980s. Today, there is no whisky production left in the city. The first forty years were not very productive for Glen Albyn. Fire and bankruptcy prevented the success and in 1866 the buildings were transformed into a flour mill. In 1884 it was converted back to a distillery and continued producing whisky until 1983 when it was closed by the owners at the time, Diageo. Three years later the distillery was demolished.

Bottlings:

Glen Albyn has been released as a Rare Malt by the owners on one occasion. It is rarely seen from independents as well. In 2010, Signatory released a 29 year old and in 2012 a 1976 was bottled by Gordon & MacPhail.

Glenesk

Owner:	Region:	Founded:	Status:
Diageo	E Highlands	1897	Demolished

Few distilleries, if any, have operated under as many names as Glenesk; Highland Esk, North Esk, Montrose and Hillside. The distillery was one of four operating close to Montrose between Aberdeen and Dundee. Today only Glencadam remains. At one stage the distillery was re-built for grain production but reverted to malt distilling. In 1968 a large drum maltings was built adjacent to the distillery and the Glenesk maltings still operate today under the ownership of Boortmalt, the fifth largest producer of malt in the world. The distillery building was demolished in 1996.

Bottlings:

The single malt from Glen Esk has been bottled on three occasions as a Rare Malts, the latest in 1997. It is also very rare with the independent bottlers. Last time it appeared was in 2014 when Gordon & MacPhail released a 34 year old distilled in 1980.

Glen Flagler

Owner:	Region:	Founded:	Status:
InverHouse	Lowlands	1965	Demolished

In 1964 Inver House Distillers was bought by the American company, Publicker Industries, and that same year they decided to expand the production side as well. Moffat Paper Mills in Airdrie was bought and rebuilt into one grain distillery (Garnheath) and two malt distilleries (Glen Flagler and Killyloch). A maltings was also built which, at the time, became the biggest in Europe. The American interest in the Scotch whisky industry faded rapidly and Killyloch was closed in the early 1970s, while Glen Flagler continued to produce until 1985. A year later, Garnheath was closed only to be demolished in 1988.

Bottlings:

Glen Flagler was bottled as an 8 year old by the owners in the 1970s. The next releases came in the mid 1990s when Signatory launched a handful of bottlings distilled in the early 1970s. In 2003, Inver House released a Glen Flagler 1973. A peated version (15ppm) of Glen Flagler, produced until 1970, was called Islebrae.

Glenlochy

Owner:	Region:	Founded:	Status:
Diageo	W Highlands	1898	Demolished

Glenlochy was one of three distilleries in Fort William at the beginning of the 1900s. In 1908 Nevis merged with Ben Nevis distillery (which exists to this day) and in 1983 (a disastrous year for Scotch whisky industry when eight distilleries were closed), the time had come for Glenlochy to close for good. Today, all the buildings have been demolished, with the exception of the kiln with its pagoda roof and the malt barn which both have been turned into flats. For a period of time, the distillery was owned by an energetic and somewhat eccentric Canadian gentleman by the name of Joseph Hobbs who, after having sold the distillery to DCL, bought the second distillery in town, Ben Nevis.

Bottlings:

Glenlochy has occurred twice in the Rare Malts series. The most recent independent bottling is a 35 year old, distilled in 1980 and released by Signatory in 2015.

Glen Mhor

Owner:	Region:	Founded:	Status:
Diageo	N Highlands	1892	Demolished

Glen Mhor is one of the last three Inverness distilleries and probably the one with the best reputation when it comes to the whisky that it produced. When the manager of nearby Glen Albyn, John Birnie, was refused to buy shares in the distillery he was mana-ging, he decided to build his own and founded Glen Mhor. Almost thirty years later he also bought Glen Albyn and both distilleries were owned by the Birnie family until 1972 when they were sold to DCL. Glen Mhor was closed in 1983 and three years later the buildings were demolished. Today there is a supermarket on the site.

Bottlings:

Glen Mhor has appeared on two ocasions as Rare Malts. The most recent independent bottling is a 50 year old distilled in 1965 and with 8 years extra maturation in a first fill sherry butt. It was released in 2016 by Signatory.

Glenugie

Owner:	Region:	Founded:	Status:
Chivas Bros	E Highlands	1831	Demolished

Glenugie, positioned in Peterhead, was the most Eastern distillery in Scotland, producing whisky for six years before it was converted into a brewery. In 1875 whisky distillation started again, but production was very intermittent until 1937 when Seager Evans & Co took over. Eventually they expanded the distillery to four stills and the capacity was around 1 million litres per year. After several ownership changes Glenugie became part of the brewery giant, Whitbread, in 1975. The final blow came in 1983 when Glenugie, together with seven other distilleries, was closed never to open again.

Bottlings:

The first official bottling of Glenugie came as late as in 2010 when Chivas Bros (the current owners of the brand) released a 32 year old single sherry cask in a new range called Deoch an Doras. Recent independent bottlings include a 33 year old with 8 years Oloroso finish from Signatory, released in 2011.

Glenury Royal

Owner:	Region:	Founded:	Status:
Diageo	E Highlands	1825	Demolished

Glenury Royal did not have a lucky start. Already a few weeks after inception in 1825, a fire destroyed the whole kiln, the greater part of the grain lofts and the malting barn, as well as the stock of barley and malt. Just two weeks later, distillery worker James Clark, fell into the boiler and died after a few hours. The founder of Glenury was the eccentric Captain Robert Barclay Allardyce, the first to walk 1000 miles in 1000 hours in 1809 and also an excellent middle-distance runner and boxer. The distillery closed in 1983 and part of the building was demolished a decade later with the rest converted into flats.

Bottlings:

Bottled as a Rare Malt on three occasions. Even more spectacular were three Diageo bottlings released 2003-2007; two 36 year olds and a 50 year old. In early 2012 a 40 year old was released. There are few independent bottlings, the latest being a 38 year old released in 2012 by Gordon & MacPhail.

Imperial

Owner:	Region:	Founded:	Status:
Chivas Bros	Speyside	1897	Demolished

Rumours of the resurrection of this closed distillery have flourished from time to time during the last decade. Eight years ago, the owner commissioned an estate agent to sell the buildings and convert them into flats. Shortly after that, Chivas Bros withdrew it from the market. In 2012, the owners announced that a new distillery would be built on the site, ready to start producing in 2015. Demolition of the old distillery began and in spring 2015 the new Dalmunach distillery was commissioned. In over a century, Imperial distillery was out of production for 60% of the time, but when it produced it had a capacity of 1,6 million litres per year.

Bottlings:

The 15 year old official bottling is impossible to find these days but independents are more frequent. Signatory released a 20 year old in 2015 and in the same year, Gordon & MacPhail released a 19 year old from 1996.

Inverleven

Owner:	Region:	Founded:	Status:
Chivas Bros	Lowlands	1938	Demolished

Dumbarton was the largest grain distillery in Scotland when it was built in 1938. It was mothballed in 2002 and finally closed in 2003 when Allied Domecq moved all their grain production to Strathclyde. On the same site, Inverleven malt distillery was built, equipped with one pair of traditional pot stills. In 1956 a Lomond still was added and this still (with the aid of Inverleven's wash still), technically became a second distillery called Lomond. Inverleven was mothballed in 1991and finally closed. The Lomond still is now working again since 2010 at Bruichladdich.

Bottlings:

The first official bottling of Inverleven came in 2010 when Chivas Bros released a 36 year old in a range called Deoch an Doras. The latest independent was a 1986 released by Gordon & MacPhail in 2015. The same year, Wm Grant released Ghosted Reserve, a 26 year old vatting of Ladyburn and Inverleven.

Killyloch

Owner:	Region:	Founded:	Status:
InverHouse	Lowlands	1965	Demolished

When Publicker Industries launched the Inver House brand in the USA in the 1950s, it soon became a success and the company realised they had to invest in their own grain- and maltwhisky production. A paper mill in Airdrie was rebuilt into a grain distillery (Garnheath) and two malt distilleries (Glen Flagler and Killyloch). However, after the boom in the 1960s, the American interest in Scotch whisky faded and Killyloch (originally named Lillyloch after the water source) was closed in the early 1970s, while Glen Flagler continued to produce until 1985. Garnheath stopped production in 1986 and was demolished in 1988.

Bottlings:

While Glen Flagler was bottled regularly by the owners during the 1970s, Killyloch single malt seem to have been used solely for blends. Killyloch was released a couple of times in the mid 1990s by Signatory and then again in 2003 when Inver House bottled a Killyloch 1967 which is said to have been a vatting of the last six casks from the distillery.

Kinclaith

Owner:	Region:	Founded:	Status:
Chivas Bros	Lowlands	1957	Demolished

This was the last malt distillery to be built in Glasgow and was constructed on the grounds of Strathclyde grain distillery by Seager Evans (later Long John International). Strathclyde still exists today and produces 40 million litres of grain spirit per year. Kinclaith distillery was equipped with one pair of stills and produced malt whisky to become a part of the Long John blend. In 1975 it was dismantled to make room for an extension of the grain distillery. It was later demolished in 1982.

Bottlings:

There are no official bottlings of Kinclaith. The latest from independents came in 2009 when Signatory released a 40 year old distilled in 1969. In 2005, Duncan Taylor and Signatory both released 35 year old bottlings.

Ladyburn

Owner:	Region:	Founded:	Status:
W Grant & Sons	Lowlands	1966	Dismantled

In 1963 William Grant & Sons built their huge grain distillery in Girvan in Ayrshire. Three years later they also decided to build a malt distillery on the site which was given the name Ladyburn. The distillery was equipped with two pairs of stills and they also tested a new type of continuous mashing. The whole idea was to produce malt whisky to become a part of Grant's blended whisky. The distillery was closed in 1975 and finally dismantled during the 1980s. In 2008 a new malt distillery opened up at Girvan under the name Ailsa Bay.

Bottlings:

No less than three official bottlings (40, 41 and 42 years old) appeared in 2014/2015 while an independent 40 year old under the name Rare Ayrshire was released by Signatory in 2015. The same year, Wm Grant released Ghosted Reserve, a 26 year old vatting of Ladyburn and Inverleven.

Littlemill

Owner:	Region:	Founded:	Status:
Loch Lomond Co.	Lowlands	1772	Demolished

Until 1992 when production stopped, Littlemill was Scotland´s oldest working distillery and could trace its roots back to 1772, possibly even back to the 1750s! Triple distillation was practised at Littlemill until 1930 and after that some new equipment was installed, for example, stills with rectifying columns. The stills were also isolated with aluminium. The goal was to create whiskies that would mature faster. Two such experimental releases were Dunglas and Dumbuck. In 1996 the distillery was dismantled and part of the buildings demolished and in 2004 much of the remaining buildings were destroyed in a fire.

Bottlings:

Official bottlings still occur – in August 2015 a 25 year old was released. Several independent bottlings have been released lately, including a 24 year old Pearls of Scotland from 1991 and a 27 year old from 1988, released by Hunter Laing.

Lochside

Owner:	Region:	Founded:	Status:
Chivas Bros	E Highlands	1957	Demolished

Originally a brewery for two centuries, In the last 35 years of production Lochside was a whisky distillery. The Canadian, Joseph Hobbs, started distilling grain whisky and then added malt whisky production in the same way as he had done at Ben Nevis and Lochside. Most of the output was made for the blended whisky Sandy MacNab´s. In the early 1970s, the Spanish company DYC became the owner and the output was destined for Spanish blended whisky. In 1992 the distillery was mothballed and five years later all the equipment and stock were removed. All the distillery buildings were demolished in 2005.

Bottlings:

There are no recent official bottlings. In 2016, a 47 year old single malt was released by Cooper´s Choice and the same year saw a 52 year old single grain Lochside from Hunter Laing. Four years ago there was also an unusual single blend released by Adelphi Distillers.

Millburn

Owner:	Region:	Founded:	Status:
Diageo	N Highlands	1807	Dismantled

The distillery is the oldest of those Inverness distilleries that made it into modern times and it is also the only one where the buildings are still standing. It is now a hotel and restaurant owned by Premier Inn. With one pair of stills, the capacity was no more than 300,000 litres. The problem with Millburn distillery was that it could never be expanded due to its location, sandwiched in between the river, a hill and the surrounding streets. It was bought by the London-based gin producer Booth´s in the 1920s and shortly after that absorbed into the giant DCL. In 1985 it was closed and three years later all the equipment was removed.

Bottlings:

Three bottlings of Millburn have appeared as Rare Malts, the latest in 2005. Other bottlings are scarce. The most recent was a 33 year old distilled in 1974, released by Blackadder in 2007.

North Port

Owner:	Region:	Founded:	Status:
Diageo	E Highlands	1820	Demolished

The names North Port and Brechin are used interchangeably on the labels of this single malt. Brechin is the name of the city and North Port comes from a gate in the wall which surrounded the city. The distillery was run by members of the Guthrie family for more than a century until 1922 when DCL took over. Diageo then closed 21 of their 45 distilleries between 1983 and 1985 of which North Port was one. It was dismantled piece by piece and was finally demolished in 1994 to make room for a supermarket. The distillery had one pair of stills and produced 500,000 litres per year.

Bottlings:

North Port was released as a Rare Malt by Diageo twice and in 2005 also as part of the Special Releases (a 28 year old). Independent bottlings are very rare - the latest (distilled in 1977) was released by Cadenhead´s in 2016.

Port Ellen

Owner:
Diageo

Region/district:
Islay

Founded: **Status:**
1825   Dismantled

Capacity:
-

When Port Ellen closed in 1983 it was one of three Islay distilleries owned by Diageo (then DCL). The other two were Lagavulin and Caol Ila who had been operating uninterruptedly for many years.

Port Ellen, mothballed since 1930, had only been producing for 16 years since re-opening, which made it easy for the owners to single out which Islay distillery was to close when malt whisky demand decreased. It was also the smallest of the three, with an annual output of 1,7 million litres of alcohol.

The stills were shipped abroad early in the 1990s, possibly destined for India, and the distillery buildings were destroyed shortly afterwards. The whisky from Port Ellen is so popular, however, that rumours of distilling starting up again, do flourish from time to time.

Today, the site is associated with the huge drum maltings that was built in 1973. It supplies all Islay distilleries and a few others, with a large proportion of their malt. There are seven germination drums with a capacity of handling 51 tonnes of barley each. Three kilns are used to dry the barley and for every batch, an average of 6 tonnes of peat are required which means 2,000 tonnes per year. The peat was taken from Duich Moss until 1993 when conservationists managed to obtain national nature reserve status for the area in order to protect the thousands of Barnacle Geese that make a stop-over there during their migration. Nowadays the peat is taken from nearby Castlehill.

Besides a couple of versions in the Rare Malts series, Diageo began releasing one official bottling a year in 2001. The single malt soon became a target for collectors and whisky enthusiasts alike and prices have increased rapidly in the last years. In October 2016, it was time for the 16th bottling as part of the Special Releases. This year it was a 37 year old distilled in 1978 and bottled at 55.2%. A total of 2,940 bottles were launched and this is the oldest Port Ellen ever to appear in the Special Releases series.

History:

1825   Alexander Kerr Mackay assisted by Walter Campbell founds the distillery. Mackay runs into financial troubles after a few months and his three relatives John Morrison, Patrick Thomson and George Maclennan take over.

1833   John Ramsay, a cousin to John Morrison, comes from Glasgow to take over.

1836   Ramsay is granted a lease on the distillery from the Laird of Islay.

1892   Ramsay dies and the distillery is inherited by his widow, Lucy.

1906   Lucy Ramsay dies and her son Captain Iain Ramsay takes over.

1920   Iain Ramsay sells to Buchanan-Dewar who transfers the administration to the company Port Ellen Distillery Co. Ltd.

1925   Buchanan-Dewar joins Distillers Company Limited (DCL).

1930   The distillery is mothballed.

1967   In production again after reconstruction and doubling of the number of stills from two to four.

1973   A large drum maltings is installed.

1980   Queen Elisabeth visits the distillery and a commemorative special bottling is made.

1983   The distillery is mothballed.

1987   The distillery closes permanently but the maltings continue to deliver malt to all Islay distilleries.

2001   Port Ellen cask strength first edition is released.

2014   The 14th release of Port Ellen - a 35 year old from 1978.

2015   The 15th release of Port Ellen - a 32 year old from 1983.

2016   The 16th release of Port Ellen - a 37 year old from 1978.

37 years old

Parkmore

Owner:	Region:	Founded:	Status:
Edrington	Speyside	1894	Dismantled

The distillery, located in Dufftown close to Glenfiddich, was built during the great whisky boom in the late 1890s. In 1900, it was taken over by James Watson & Co. which, in turn, was bought by John Dewar & Sons. From 1925 to the last distillation in 1931, the distillery was owned by Distiller's Company Limited. The whisky from Parkmore never maintained a high quality, apparently because of problems with the water source. The water was taken from an area that is now used as a limestone quarry. The beautiful buildings remain today and are used by Edrington for warehousing.

Bottlings:

No bottles of Parkmore single malt have been offered for sale since 1995 when one was auctioned by Christie's. It is not unlikely though, that the odd bottle may be hiding in private collections.

Pittyvaich

Owner:	Region:	Founded:	Status:
Diageo	Speyside	1974	Demolished

The life span for this relatively modern distillery was short. It was built by Arthur Bell & Sons on the same ground as Dufftown distillery which also belonged to them and the four stills were exact replicas of the Dufftown stills. Bells was bought by Guinness in 1985 and the distillery was eventually absorbed into DCL (later Diageo). For a few years in the 1990s, Pittyvaich was also a back up plant for gin distillation (in the same way that Auchroisk is today) in connection with the production of Gordon's gin having moved from Essex till Cameronbridge. The distillery was mothballed in 1993 and has now been demolished.

Bottlings:

An official 12 year old Flora & Fauna can no longer be found but the latest official bottling was a 25 year old, released in 2015 as a part of the yearly Special Releases.

Rosebank

Owner:	Region:	Founded:	Status:
Diageo	Lowlands	1798	Dismantled

When Rosebank in Falkirk was mothballed in 1993, there were only two working malt distilleries left in the Lowlands – Glenkinchie and Auchentoshan. The whisky from the distillery has always had a great amount of supporters and there was a glimmer of hope that a new company would start up the distillery again. At the beginning of 2009 though, most of the equipment was stolen and furthermore, Diageo has indicated that they are not interested in selling the brand. The buildings are still intact and most of them have been turned into restaurants, offices and flats. The whisky from Rosebank was triple distilled.

Bottlings:

The official 12 year old Flora & Fauna is now almost impossible to find but in 2014 a 21 year old Special Release appeared. The latest independent bottling was a 1990, bottled and released by Gordon & MacPhail in 2015.

St Magdalene

Owner:	Region:	Founded:	Status:
Diageo	Lowlands	1795	Dismantled

At one time, the small town of Linlithgow in East Lothian had no less than five distilleries. St Magdalene was one of them and also the last to close in 1983. The distillery came into ownership of the giant DCL quite early (1912) and was at the time a large distillery with 14 washbacks, five stills and with the possibility of producing more than 1 million litres of alcohol. Ten years after the closure the distillery was carefully re-built into flats, making it possible to still see most of the old buildings, including the pagoda roofs.

Bottlings:

These include two official bottlings in the Rare Malts series. In 2008/2009 a handful of independent releases appeared, all of them distilled in 1982 and released by Ian MacLeod, Douglas Laing, Blackadder, Signatory and Berry Brothers. The latest was a 33 year old, distilled in 1982 and released by Gordon & MacPhail in 2015.

Brora Distillery in the 1930s

Single Malts
from Japan

There are slim pickings these days
on the Japanese single malt whisky shelves. Nikka now offers
just a pair of NAS releases as its entire single malt range.
Suntory's age-statement malts are available in theory,
but on such strict allocation that one might be forgiven for thinking
they have also been discontinued. For the malt aficionado, Suntory's range
is in reality a choice between the Yamazaki NAS or the Hakushu NAS.
The third biggest player, Kirin, discontinued the only single malt
in its portfolio back in the fall of 2015.

The refrain from all quarters is that "stocks are low and demand high". Another way to put it would be: "We need the stock for our workhorses – the blends." The domestic market for Japanese blended whiskies is estimated at around 10.68 million cases. Suntory's Kakubin is the undisputed market leader, selling 3.76 million cases in 2015 – a 14% increase from the year before. The second-best selling blend in Japan is 'Black Nikka', with 2.75 million cases sold in 2015.

To mark the 60th anniversary of the 'Black' brand, Nikka released a special edition 'Blender's Spirit' in the fall of 2016. The company is hoping that will push sales through the 3 million-case barrier. Together, Kakubin and Black Nikka account for 61% of the total domestic blended whisky market. It's difficult to make a dent in this for the other producers, but they're trying. Kirin's 'Fujisanroku Tarujuku 50°' (219,000 cases sold in 2015) is a case in point. They released a new version in March 2016. "The key concept for this expression," says chief blender Jota Tanaka, "was to deliver a blended whisky as close to the whisky straight out of the barrel as possible so that people could enjoy both a barrel tasting and the art of blending in one and the same dram." Bottled at 50% abv, the new version is unique among entry-level Japanese blended whiskies in being non-chill filtered.

Abroad, the selection is also leaning more and more towards blended whiskies. Suntory's Hibiki sold 138,000 cases in 2015, which is a whopping 44% hike from the year before. Beam Suntory even released a new blended whisky, Toki, limited (for the time being?) to the North American market. This was launched in the U.S. in June 2016, and in Canada the month after. It was promoted as the ideal base for a highball.

For the smaller players, this would seem like an opportunity to fill a void, but stocks are low across the board. Malt from iconic closed distilleries such as Karuizawa and Hanyu is all but gone. The active 'craft distilleries', Chichibu, Mars Shinshu and Eigashima, are busy distilling our future dream malts. They cannot afford to bottle their oldest stock – 8 years old for Chichibu and Eigashima, 5 years old for Mars Shinshu aside from a handful of pre-1991 casks – because they know the future lasts a long time. Blended whiskies are their bread and butter too, with most of them sourcing grain whisky from abroad.

Going with the grain

The big trio have all been spotlighting grain whisky to various degrees. Unusually it's been Kirin at the head of the pack, at least in terms of quality. Their premium, very limited and very expensive offerings in recent years have always been impressive, and in 2016 they were rewarded with a trophy at the World Whiskies Awards. For Kirin the grain releases have been about showing what they're capable of, and having a little fun.

For Suntory and Nikka it's much more an essential pivot to keep retail space. Nikka's Coffey Grain, once an occasional limited release, has become a fixture, alongside Suntory's most prominent new whisky release, The Chita. For most of its 44 years, the Chita grain facility has been quietly churning out whiskies, mainly from corn, for the company's blends. Now and again single grain bottlings appeared, most notably in distillery gift shops. But in 2015, with some fanfare, the company released The Chita as a permanent offering in packaging that made it clear this was designed as a sister to the single malts. The company pitched it as a new base for a highball.

The low supply of Japanese whisky has also led to some 'creative' (some may prefer the word 'questionable') responses. More than a few 'rice whiskies' launched in 2016. Most of them went straight to the docks. Given the loose definition of whisky in Japan, it is hard to know how exactly these 'whiskies' are produced. It's almost certain that in most parts of the world, these products wouldn't fall in the whisky category.

Provenance is another very loosely-regulated concept in Japan as far as whisky is concerned. Seeking to take advantage of the lack of 'domestic malts' in the marketplace, Matsui Shuzo, a liquor producer based in Tottori, launched a range under the name 'Kurayoshi' in labels that were so clearly based on Yamazaki that it's a wonder Suntory's lawyers haven't had a word. The Kurayoshi 18 year old

contains mostly, or even exclusively (the company isn't clear on this point), malt whisky imported from abroad. In the past, producers could get away with this, but times have changed. Matsui may be able to fool some people, but most whisky fans in Japan are appalled by what they perceive as a dishonest way of cashing in on the current craze.

Fortunately, there are plenty of honest responses to the thirst for Japanese whisky. There are five new faces in this year's Japan chapter. Some are expansions of existing liquor businesses. Others are brand new ventures. All of them are betting that people's interest in Japanese whisky won't be extinguished by a few years of paucity.

First out of the gate in 2016 was Kiuchi, a sake company turned beer brewing phenomenon with a have-a-crack-at-it attitude to everything. They started distilling in February 2016. Then came Sasanokawa, a company with a long track record in whisky production, though not until this year with anything that resembled a classic whisky distilling set-up. They began test distilling in gleaming new pot stills in the late spring. The people who make Mars whisky built a second distillery on the island of Kyushu and doubled fired up the stills at the tail end of the year. Gourmet trading company Kenten Jitsugyo have built perhaps the most traditional of the new distilleries on the opposite side of Hokkaido from Yoichi. At time of writing they had November 2016 pencilled in as their start date. Rounding out the list is a new operation in Shizuoka, a short hop from the Pacific coast. If the tax authorities play along, they'll be distilling malt early next year, and if nothing else, the provenance of some of their equipment will have whisky fans intrigued.

Most of them have noticed that they'll cross the 3-year whisky threshold around the time of the Tokyo Olympics.

Nicholas Coldicott is the former editor-in-chief of Eat magazine, former drink columnist for The Japan Times and former contributing editor at Whisky Magazine Japan. He currently works for Japan's national broadcaster, NHK, and writes a drink column for CNNgo.com.

Stefan Van Eycken grew up in Belgium and Scotland and moved to Japan in 2000. Editor of Nonjatta, he is also the man behind the 'Ghost series' bottlings and the charity event 'Spirits for Small Change'. He's on the Japanese panel of the WWA and is currently working on a book about the history of whisky making in Japan.

Akkeshi

Owner:
Kenten Jitsugyo

Location:
Hokkaido

Founded:
2015

Capacity:
100,000 l

Malt whisky range:
none yet

In 2016, quite a few new distilleries were added to the Japanese whisky map. Most were expansions of existing liquor operations. Akkeshi is one of two distilleries to be built from the ground up.

It's located in the town of the same name on the east coast of Hokkaido. It's quite a remote area with particularly harsh winters, but that didn't scare the people behind the project. It's close to the sea and surrounded by beautiful wetlands with an abundance of peat, so it ticked all the right boxes.

Construction began in October 2015 and continued through the harsh winter months. Most of the equipment was made by Forsyths in Scotland. The pot stills arrived in August 2016. The first distilling season was a very short one: November and December 2016. Unlike most distilleries, which close for maintenance during the hot summer months, Akkeshi will be closed during the winter. Temperatures can drop to -20°C which makes it challenging to run a distillery.

The plan for 2017 is to distill 7 days a week. The production target for the first full season is 100,000 litres. From 2018 onwards, the team is hoping to produce 300,000 litres of new-make a year. Initially, most of the barley used will be non-peated. From 2017, the peated production will be increased. Eventually, the Akkeshi distillery team is also hoping to use local barley and local peat. The stills at Akkeshi (5kl and 3.6kl) are pear-shaped, inspired by those at Lagavulin. The idea is to produce a rich, heavy spirit.

The initial plan is to fill into ex-bourbon wood, ex-sherry wood and mizunara. In due course, that will be expanded to include red wine casks (from France and Australia), rum barrels, Cognac casks, Sauternes casks as well as some less orthodox wood types. There is one small warehouse on site, but the Akkeshi team is keen to explore the effect of micro-climate on the maturation process, so in the future, the idea is to construct one warehouse up in the mountains and another one right by the sea.

Establishing Akkeshi as a quality single malt is the immediate goal, but the people behind the distillery have even bigger dreams: making blended whiskies entirely in-house. Most smaller distilleries in Japan source their grain whisky from abroad, but this company is keen to do everything itself. This would entail setting up another distillery to produce the grain – perhaps in another part of Hokkaido.

Asaka

Owner:
Sasanokawa Shuzo

Location:
Fukushima P.

Founded:
2015

Capacity:
40-50,000 l

Malt whisky range:
none yet

Asaka is a brand new distillery but operator Sasanokawa has been around for a while. The company was founded in 1765. They turned their hand to whisky making right after World War II.

A scarcity of rice was throwing a spanner in the works of their sake business, but there was a huge demand for whisky, particularly from the Allied occupation. Sasanokawa applied for a license to make whisky in 1945 and the year after that they got to work. Their focus was on the lowest grade of blended whisky, for which malt whisky as a component was not a legal necessity. Just like others in the field, they 'made' whisky by using surplus industrial alcohol from the war effort that was coloured, flavoured and mixed with other types of booze to look and taste like whisky.

As the economy recovered so did people's palates, so Sasanokawa – looking to up their game – started making whisky in makeshift stills (not made out of copper). Sales weren't always great but the structure of the company kept their whisky business afloat. Sake production took up about 200 days of the year, and whisky making kept the team busy the rest of the year. During the 1980s, Sasanokawa became one of the three big players of the 'ji whisky' boom (usually translated as 'craft whisky', but perhaps 'crafty whisky' is a better way of putting it), along with Hombo Shuzo and Toa Shuzo.

With demand for Japanese whisky at an all-time high, but supply rather low, Sasanokawa decided to set up a proper malt whisky distillery in 2015, the company's 250th anniversary. They looked into ordering pot stills from Forsyths in Scotland but quickly discovered there was a four-year lead time. Domestic maker Miyake Industries could get the job done in less than a year, so that proved to be an easy decision. By December 2015, the two small pot stills (1,000 litres and 2,000 liters) had been installed in a vacant warehouse, and by June 2016 the distillery was ready to start producing. Their plan is to distill year round, except for a silent period in the summer when it becomes unbearably hot in the area. Most of the production will be non-peated, with the weeks leading up to the summer break reserved for some peated runs. Maturation will be mainly in ex-bourbon casks.

Chichibu

Owner:
Venture Whisky

Location:
Saitama P.

Founded:
2008

Capacity:
80,000 l

Malt whisky range:
Occasional limited releases

Japan's new crop of distillery owners can only dream of having the start that Ichiro Akuto and his Chichi crew have enjoyed.

Demand so vastly outstrips supply that there is close to zero chance of finding a bottle on retail shelves, and anyone with the connections to get hold of a bottle can expect to pay an astonishing sum for something that isn't yet 10 years old. The reasons Chichibu shot straight to cult status is, of course, Akuto's single cask bottlings from his family's now-dismantled Hanyu distillery. Bottles of Ichiro's Malt with playing card labels are now serious collectors items. But that wouldn't have meant much if the new distillery wasn't any good.

Akuto says it's getting harder and harder to find the casks he wants, so he's buying mizunara from Hokkaido and making his own. His team has been studying with a local cooper to pick up techniques that would otherwise be lost, since the cooper has no sucessor, and they've opened an off-site cooperage. That's where they chop bourbon barrels into "chibidaru", his word for a quarter cask.

Around 10% of the barley they use is malted on-site, and that's a figure they hope will grow as they set their sights on being as local as possible. They've been using local peat, and devote the final two months before the summer break to distilling peated malt. The Chichibu process is more hands-on than in many distilleries. The mashman uses a wooden paddle to stir, and the stillman opens the spirit safe and samples the distillate to decide when to cut. The two stills are small with steep arms for a rich spirit. The distillate is aged, without temperature controls, in Chichibu's seesawing climate. Founder Ichiro Akuto says the fluctuations speed up the aging process. As other whisky makers are shedding their age statements, Akuto says his midterm focus is on releasing his first 10 year old. Expect that to arrive in 2020.

Tasting note The Peated 2015:
Very peat-forward, but the smoke is supported by honeydew melon with prosciutto, grilled apple pie, crema catalana and a myriad other treats. On the palate, you get all of that with citrus and spice.

Fuji Gotemba

Owner:
Kirin Holdings

Location:
Shizuoka P.

Founded:
1973

Capacity:
2,000,000 l

Malt whisky range:
Occasional limited releases

The bad news from Fuji Gotemba is that Kirin has axed the only single malt whisky in its line-up. The Fujisanroku 18 years old was sent into retirement in late 2015. For the time being, any bottles of Fuji Gotemba malt will be grab-em-while-you-can limited releases.

The good news, for the French at least, is that Kirin is about to export its whisky for the first time ever. The company will send some of its newly reformulated Fuji-sanroku 50 blend, bottled, as the name suggests, at 50% to Paris, which has long been Europe's capital of Japanese whisky. It's composed of malt and grain whiskies made at the distillery located in a forested area at the foot of Mount Fuji.

The other big news of the year for Fuji Gotemba was the 2016 World Whiskies Awards trophy for Best Single Grain. The winner was a 25 Years Old release composed of whiskies aged in Bourbon barrels. And like so many headline-grabbing Japanese releases, it's all gone now. But chief blender Jota Tanaka proved he has the stock and skill to show how good grain can be. Tanaka says Kirin is planning to issue Blender's Choice Single Malt and Single Grain releases every year. He also says everything he does, from selecting his malt or grain all the way through to mashing, fermentation, distillation and ageing, is designed to create clean and estery flavours.

Fuji Gotemba was originally a joint venture between Kirin, Seagram and Chivas, but Kirin took full control in in 2002. Much of the output goes into domestic blends at the cheaper end of the market, under names with international connotations, such as Boston Club, Ocean Lucky Gold and Robert Brown.

The distillery has an unusually diverse range of equipment, with two sets of pot stills, as well as kettles, a doubler and various columns. They distill grain in columns and kettles. And a Four Roses connection means the warehouses are dominated by bourbon barrels.

Hakushu

Owner: Beam Suntory
Location: Yamanashi P.
Founded: 1973
Capacity: 4,000,000 l

Malt whisky range:
NAS, 12, 18, 25 year old plus occasional limited releases

Miyagikyo

Owner: Nikka Whisky
Location: Miyagi P.
Founded: 1969
Capacity: 3,000,000 l

Malt whisky range:
NAS, Coffey malt, Coffey grain

The range of whiskies listed above is more than a little misleading. In reality, most of the time in Japan, you'll find NAS and nothing else.

What was once the biggest whisky distillery in the world is going through a quiet spell, at least from the outside. Inside, of course, they're distilling as much as they can to supply complexity to the blends and fill the casks that will, hopefully, make older Hakushu a fixture once more on shop shelves.

The Hakushu complex in Japan's Southern Alps offers an impressive visitor experience. The buildings are speckled around a forested area, along with a plant bottling Japan's top-selling mineral water – Minami Alps Tennensui – the same stuff that goes into Hakushu whisky.

Hakushu has 16 pot stills in a vast array of shapes and angles. There were once many more. Back in the 1980s, Hakushu had 36 stills turning out an estimated 30 million litres of spirit a year. If the enthusiasm for Japanese whisky continues at this pace, perhaps we'll see similar numbers again.

Suntory distills non-peated, lightly peated and heavily peated malt here. With the variety of stills and casks, the blenders have a lot of styles to play with. In years past, the company would show off the variety via limited releases. Those releases have dried up, and the company isn't saying whether we can expect any more soon, though the smart money says no.

There's also a grain facility on site with continuous stills. It produces only a tenth the output of Suntory's main grain distillery near Nagoya, but the focus here is experimentation. They produce small-run test batches of different kinds of grain – another sign that the people at Suntory are never ready to rest on their laurels.

Nikka was the first of Japan's whisky makers to open a second distillery. By the late 1960s, founder Taketsuru needed to boost production capacity.

Rather than expanding Yoichi, he decided to build a new facility that would produce something lighter, fruitier and more elegant. He reportedly spent three years searching for the right spot, until he found a secluded, humid location in Miyagi Prefecture on Japan's main island of Honshu. Nestled between mountains and encircled by rivers, it had the purity of air and water he was looking for.

The distillery was named after the nearby city of Sendai until 2001, when Asahi bought the company and renamed it Miyagikyo. It had four stills when it first opened, but expanded in 1979, 1989 and 1999. It now has eight pot stills and 22 steel washbacks. The stills are all large and have boil bulbs with upward lyne arms, and the malt that goes into them is unpeated or very lightly peated, to produce a light, fruity spirit. The site also houses two enormous Coffey stills imported from Scotland. They were originally housed in Nishinomiya, Hyogo Prefecture, but shipped to Sendai after an earthquake there.

Miyagikyo often sits in the shadow of its sister distillery, Yoichi, but Nikka's Coffey Grain and Coffey Malt have shone a brighter light on the fruitier sister facility, and if you make it to the distillery in person you can also pick up some NAS key malt bottles. The only bottle that comes out these days with the Chinese characters for Miyagikyo on the label is the entry level NAS releases. But this is also the malt that tempers the mighty Yoichi in the multi-award winning Taketsuru pure malts, which you can still find on sale on a good day.

Tasting note Hakushu NAS:

Green in all senses of the word. Cucumber and mint on the nose. On the palate, mossy twigs and citrus, with faint smoke emerging later on. The finish is long and woody.

Tasting note Miyagikyo NAS (2015 release):

Apples and pears on the nose with grassy and light floral elements; dried fruits, vanilla and anise on the palate, with a tiny bit of bitterness and some milk chocolate on the finish.

Nukada

Owner: Kiuchi Shuzo
Location: Ibaraki P.
Founded: 2016
Capacity: t. b. d.
Malt whisky range: none yet

Okayama

Owner: Miyashita Shuzo
Location: Okayama P.
Founded: 2011
Capacity: t. b. d.
Malt whisky range: none yet

The Kiuchi Brewery has been producing sake since 1823, but it's much better known for the beer it began making in 1996: Hitachino Nest.

More recently, the company has been making shochu distilled from sake lees, a dry-hopped, barrel-aged umeshu, and planted Chardonnay and Merlot vines to have a crack at wine. Whisky was a natural next step, especially since they had all the brewing equipment already in place. Production manager Toshiyuki Kiuchi is an avid malt collector who felt that the current offerings from his homeland didn't represent what Japanese whisky should be, so he's on a mission to redefine it.

He bought a hybrid system from China – a 1,000 litre pot still and column – and set it up, for now, on the second floor of a beer warehouse. There are plans to add a 5,000 litre pot still and give the whole operation a more formal home soon. The same brewhouse that tuns out the multi-award-winning beer is producing the wash. Essentially, they're distilling their pilsner, minus the hops and wheat. Most of the malt comes from Germany or Belgium, but the company is experimenting with local barley too. They've revived a strain that was all but wiped out after the war, though for now it's earmarked for the beer.

Kiuchi tapped a member of his brewing crew, 27 year old Isamu "Sam" Yoneda, to run the whisky making operation. Yoneda has the perfect heritage: he's half Scottish, half Japanese. It's a one-man operation. Yoneda comes from a beer background, but has been getting some invaluable distilling tips from Suntory's former chief blender Seiichi Koshimizu, who is reportedly eager to start some projects with the fledgling operation.

Koshimizu may well be drawn by the experimental mindset at Kiuchi. They've been playing with different yeasts, including a Weizen yeast that imparts a kind of non-peat smokiness. Yoneda says they want to create something that has the impact of peat, without using peat. He is filling a wide variety of casks, including cream sherry, Japanese wine, Koval bourbon, new American oak, Japanese oak, and Japanese oak barrels fitted with cherry wood heads. Yoneda says they are also thinking of trying casks that previously held their beers. And he is distilling hopped wort and mixtures of barley and wheat, though it's not clear whether the more experimental releases will make it to market. Early tastings suggest the malt aged in sherry wood is one to watch.

Miyashita Shuzo is a multitasking liquor producer based in Okayama. The company was founded in 1915 as a sake brewery. In 1983, they started making shochu and in 1994 they became one of the pioneers of Japanese craft beer.

They entered the whisky business after witnessing the highball boom. The brewing and distilling know-how was already there and much of the infrastructure to make whisky, too. All it took was a few extra steps.

In 2003, Miyashita started single-distilling some of their hoppy beer in a stainless steel shochu still. They filled this into American white oak and kept a close watch on it. Encouraged by the way this distilled beer was maturing, they started thinking about producing whisky. They acquired their license in 2011 and immediately got to work, using the equipment already in place. Mashing and fermentation was done in the equipment for beer making; distillation was carried out under low pressure in their shochu still by running it twice. Stainless steel and whisky are awkward bedfellows and the folks at Miyashita must have realized this. By July 2015, a brand new copper hybrid still had been installed on the premises by German maker Holstein.

Okayama is a traditional barley growing region and Miyashita is keen on using local barley. They source a local variety known as 'Sky Golden' from farmers in the region and send it to a malting company 750 kilometres away before it is trucked back to the distillery. This comes at a considerable expense. All in all, this makes using the local barley about 5 times as expensive as using imported barley. Since they can't get enough locally, half of their malted barley is imported from Germany. Still, no other distillery in Japan uses as much local barley as Okayama.

At the time of writing, distillation takes place once a week all year round. Atypically for a new distillery, most of the wood filled is ex-sherry and ex-brandy. They also have two 400 litre mizunara casks filled in January 2016 resting in the warehouse.

In 2016, some new-make was released in 200ml bottles. This showed a lot of promise. It's fair to assume, however, that it will be a while before a fully mature expression of Okayama is available.

Shinshu

Owner:	Location:	Founded:	Capacity:
Hombo Shuzo	Nagano P.	1985	40,000 l

Malt whisky range:
Komagatake (various limited edition releases)

Strikes and gutters – that's the Mars whisky history summed up in three words.

Parent company Hombo Shuzo got a license to distil whisky in 1949, but for the first decade simply blended sourced components with neutral spirits produced in-house. In 1960, founder Kiichiro Iwai set up a distillery in Yamanashi prefecture and began producing a heavy, smoky style of whisky. It didn't sell well, and after nine years he called it a day. In 1978, the Hombo Shuzo people were ready to give it another go, but they were using the old site for winemaking, so they started looking for a new one. In the meantime, they set up in Kagoshima, on the southern island of Kyushu, and made whisky in Iwai's style. In 1985, they moved north to Shinshu and changed to a lighter style. They were forced to mothball that plant in 1992 as people were switching to shochu. In 2011, with whisky booming again, they fired up the stills once more.

Production is limited to winter, after which the team switches to making beer, umeshu and other spirits, but lately they've been stretching their whisky season so 'winter' is now 6 months long. In November 2014, they replaced the old pot stills with new ones. They now produce four types of distillate (non-peated and peated at 3.5, 20 and 50ppm). They're exploring the influence of climate on the maturation process by sending some casks to the old site in Kagoshima, and some to the humid Yakushima island.

In 2015, Hombo launched 'Rindo', the first in the series 'Nature of Shinshu'. With this series, Hombo is seeking to bridge the decades by combining malt from the new regime with malt from the pre-1992 era. In 2016, they released their oldest single malt to date, a 30 year old. We won't be seeing many more releases like this in the future, though. Stock from the pre-1992 era is dwindling fast so the company is pushing their post-2011 production in the marketplace.

Tasting note Komagatake Sherry & American White Oak 2011:

Bears its youth on its sleeve. On the nose, white chocolate, rhubarb jam, apple compote with lots of lemon; on the palate, a slightly perplexing mix of stewed fruits, goya and grapefruit peel,

Shizuoka

Owner:	Location:	Founded:	Capacity:
Gaia Flow Distilling	Shizuoka P.	2015	t.b.d.

Malt whisky range:
none yeat

Shizuoka Distillery founder Taiko Nakamura was inspired by a visit to Islay in 2012. It was Kilchoman in particular that prompted him to set up a craft distillery in Japan.

To get a foot in the door of the liquor business, he reconfigured the renewable energy company he had set up earlier that year and started importing whisky, gin and other liquors. In May 2014, he put in an order for two pot stills with Forsyths in Scotland. At the time, he hadn't found a site. A month later, he picked the Tamakawa area of Shizuoka city. A year later, he bought the old Karuizawa distillery equipment at auction. Most of it wasn't going to be useful but a few key pieces of equipment will be put to good use. Of the four Karuizawa pot stills, the newest one – fixed and with a new heating system – will get a new life. The Porteus malt mill, the destoner and a hoops press machine will also be coming back to life in Shizuoka. Other pieces of equipment from Karuizawa that have outlived their usefulness will be put on display. Now all he needs is a licence. In Japan, where starting a distillery from scratch is a rare occurrence, it's unclear how long that will take.

The distillery is located in a beautiful valley beside a tributary of the Abe river. It's surrounded by small tea farms and forested mountains. The climate is mild all year round. Even in the winter, temperatures rarely drop below zero. The main distillery building is inspired by the Karuizawa distillery. Everything from milling to filling takes place under one roof, but in different rooms. Uniquely for Japan, the 'visitor experience' is integrated into the design of the distillery, with careful consideration given to the way the landscape outside is visible from various points in the distillery.

Most of the production will be non-peated, with a short period reserved for peated malt. Nakamura is planning to use local barley as soon as the distillery is ready. At the time of writing, there were four 7,000 litre wooden wash backs made from Oregon pine. The plan is to eventually have 12, most of them wooden. They will have 3 stills: the Karuizawa still will function as a wash still, with 2 new stills made by Forsyths, both with a boil ball. The new wash still will be direct heated; the old Karuizawa still and the new spirit still will be indirect heated. According to Nakamura, the idea is to produce a "light, delicate spirit". This will be a contrast with the type of spirit made by most of the younger Japanese craft distilleries – Chichibu, Tsunuki and Akkeshi – which is on the heavier side of the spectrum.

Tsunuki

Owner: Hombo Shuzo
Location: Kagoshima P.
Founded: 2016
Capacity: t. b. d.

Malt whisky range:
none yet

White Oak

Owner: Eigashima Shuzo
Location: Hyogo P.
Founded: 1984
Capacity: 47,000 l

Malt whisky range:
Akashi NAS and occasional, limited releases

In 2016, Hombo surprised the Japanese whisky community by announcing their plans to set up a second whisky distillery at their Tsunuki Kishogura site in Kagoshima. This is the Hombo family's home base so it's not just another location.

There is a lot of history involved. The company was born there in 1872 and the current president, Kazuto Hombo, was born next door and grew up there, so it's a bit like bringing the spirit home.

At Shinshu, they reached the limits of production in 2015. The decision to set up a second distillery wasn't just about increasing volume, though. The people at Hombo are interested in exploring terroir. They want a new malt whisky that is radically different, not by engineering the difference in one place, but by allowing the natural environmental conditions to play their part. At Shinshu, those conditions are the majestic mountains. At Tsunuki there is Sakurajima, the active volcano. At Shinshu, distillation takes place at high altitude; at Tsunuki, it is a stone's throw from the sea. Tsunuki is also the southernmost whisky distillery in Japan, and the only one on the island of Kyushu.

Construction of the Tsunuki distillery began in May 2016. Hombo asked domestic maker Miyake Industries to make the pot stills (5,800 litres and 3,300 litres). Their shape was inspired by a famous distillery on Islay (the wash-still is onion-shaped), and the idea is to produce a spirit that's on the heavier side of the spectrum.

Miyake has had a busy time recently, with brewers and distillers opting to pay a premium for a quick delivery rather than joining the Forsyths waiting list. The stills had to be trucked at night more than 1,000 kilometres from Miyake's factory in Gunma prefecture on Japan's main island of Honshu all the way to Kagoshima.

Hombo Shuzo is planning to set up a visitor centre on site. Aside from the new malt distillery, which should be ready by November 2016, people will also be able to see the old 7-story continuous still that was used there from 1956 until the mid-70s to make neutral spirits. The old stone sake brewery buildings on site are noteworthy, too. Fans of 007 may also be interested in visiting nearby Akime, where part of You Only Live Twice was shot in the summer of 1966.

Eigashima is a bit of an anomaly on the Japanese whisky scene. Even with demand at an all-time high, they keep taking it easy… just as they have for the past 100 years.

On paper, it's the oldest whisky distillery in Japan. They acquired a distilling license in 1919, four years before Yamazaki, but it took them four decades to get started. And it took them another four decades to release their first single malt. That was an 8 year old in 2007, and it wasn't until 2013 that they released their first single cask bottling. But whisky production was never a priority for Eigashima: they make their money with sake and shochu. When they entered the single malt market, whisky accounted for less than 1% of their total sales. They've expanded production to five months of the year, but we're still talking low single digits in sales percentage.

The current distillery was built in 1984. After a period of using malt with varying peat levels, they switched to Crisp Malting and now use lightly peated (5ppm). All production is matured on site, near the Akashi strait.

They used up their oldest casks for a 15 year old released in 2013, so the oldest stock left in the warehouses is approaching 9 years at the time of writing – and there's not very much of that. For a while, it rained young single cask bottlings (mostly 5 years old). But the recent dearth suggests they're listening to what the spirit has to say, rather than imposing a time-line of their own. That's to be applauded given the craze for any and all Japanese whisky. Since 2015, there haven't been any new releases. Hopefully this is a case of 'good things come to those who wait'.

Tasting note Akashi NAS:

The deep colours and surprisingly warm nose, tips you off that there's a sherry influence. There's a peach tea and autumn fruits when you sip, and a fairly short finish.

Yamazaki

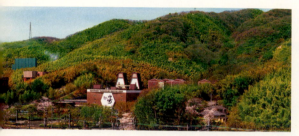

Owner:	Location:	Founded:	Capacity:
Beam Suntory	Osaka P.	1923	6,000,000 l

Malt whisky range:
NAS, 12, 18, 25 years old and occasional limited releases.

This is where it all began, nearly a century ago, in a lush, humid valley between Osaka and Kyoto. Yamazaki was the perfect location for Japan's first whisky distillery for several reasons.

The Suntory people will tell you about the quality of the local water, how tea ceremony pioneer Sen no Rikyu reportedly drew his water from this area, and how the bamboo forests surrounding the distillery are a sign of how pure the water is. It probably didn't hurt the business plan that the site is almost touching distance from Osaka, Kyoto and Kobe, and in easy reach of the capital.

Suntory founder Shinjiro Torii wanted to make a whisky suited to the Japanese palate, and ironically ended up making one that people around the world clamour for. The distillery underwent a billion-dollar expansion in 2013, with engineers installing 4 more pot stills, taking the total to 16.

It was the first expansion in 45 years. The stills are varied in size and shape, some with boil balls, some without, some direct fired, some using steam, some with steep arms, some with straight ones, to produce a miscellany of styles. This is also where most of Suntory's blending goes on, in a room with a snaking kaleidoscope of hundreds of whisky styles.

The number of official expressions in the Yamazaki single malt line-up didn't change last year, but the number of bottles making their way out sure seemed to. Only the NAS is easy to find these days. Still, the company found the stock to release 5,000 bottles of Yamazaki Sherry Cask 2016. It's a style that will now always be associated with Jim Murray, after he named it whisky of the year in his 2015 bible, and the 2016 release uses the same lot as its base. The connection between Yamazaki and sherry cask actually goes right back to the beginning of the distillery's history, when the very first whiskies were aged in barrels from Spain that the company had been using for its sweet wine.

Yamazaki is more accessible than most Japanese distilleries – just a 15-minute train ride from Kyoto. The tours, in English, are impressive, and the onsite museum got an overhaul in 2016.

Tasting note Yamazaki NAS:

Zesty nose, with some sawdust and strawberry. Lots of bourbon influences on the palate, with creamy vanilla, creme brulee, but also some spice. A relatively short, sharp finish. Superb for its price bracket.

Yoichi

Owner: Nikka Whisky   **Location:** Hokkaido   **Founded:** 1934   **Capacity:** 2,000,000 l

Malt whisky range:
NAS and occasional limited releases.

Masataka Taketsuru probably wasn't thinking about logistics when he picked Yoichi as the site of his dream distillery 80 years ago.

It's closer to Russia than it is to Tokyo and the Tsugaru Straits separated him from most of his customers. As anyone who's ever paid a visit can attest, it's miles from anywhere. Taketsuru was more interested in salty air and easy access to wood, coal, peat and water. He picked a spot just a kilometre from the Sea of Japan. That hewed closely to the kinds of distilleries he'd seen in Scotland, and Yoichi is still often described as Japan's most traditional distillery. But even Scotland's distilleries have given up on heating their still with a coal fire, as Yoichi still does.

Back in 1934 there was a single still that doubled as spirit and wash still. Nowadays there are 6 stills, coal-heated and featuring straight heads and downward lyne arms to produce a robust spirit. The varying angles of the lyne arms offer some diversity, as do the differing peat levels (0ppm,

4ppm and 35-50ppm). The on-site coopers work with new oak, sherry butts and bourbon barrels. Although the 'house style' is peaty and heavy, Yoichi is set up to create a wide range of distillates. Between various peating levels, yeast strains, mash bills, fermentation times, distillation methods and maturation types, it's said that Yoichi is capable of producing 3,000 different types of malt whisky.

The distillery released its first single malt, a 12 year old, in 1984, when Japan was in the grip of its first domestic whisky boom. It came out under the distillery's original name: Hokkaido. Asahi narrowed down the geography to the town of Yoichi when they bought Nikka Whisky Distilling in 2001.

In 2015, Nikka chopped its entire Yoichi range and introduced a NAS offering. The only way to get anything else with the distillery's name on it is to visit the gift shop, where you can find bottles of NAS key malts. And so the malts from Yoichi won't be winning any major awards these days, but the distillery manager did. Koichi Nishikawa was named manager of the year at the Icons of Whisky awards, just over a year after he took charge of the place.

Tasting note Yoichi NAS, (2015 release):

Barley sweetness, pencil shavings, over-ripe orchard fruits and soft smoke on the nose; oak and peat lead the dance on the palate with some candied orange peel thrown in; the finish is earthy and vegetal, with some tea on the side.

Dr. Graeme Macaloney, fermentation engineer and founder of the Victoria Caledonian Distillery in Victoria, Canada

Distilleries
around the globe

Including the subsections:
Europe
North America | Australia & New Zealand
Asia | Africa | South America

When I published the first Malt Whisky Year-book way back in 2005, this chapter contained a mere 33 distilleries producing malt whisky outside of Scotland and Japan. Twelve years later, the number stands at a staggering 287! If you were to include the ones that produce just about any kind of whisky, there would probably be close to 500 distilleries. Many of these are small and often distill other spirits as well. But there are also a handful who are dedicated to producing malt whisky alone and have the capacity to match many of the Scottish distilleries. These are naturally the ones that attract most attention. They have the possibility of producing volumes so large that they can, in fact, play a significant role in the whisky industry. But let us also be mindful of the smaller distilleries. Some of these have owners who are innovative and have fresh ideas that may well affect whisky production as we know it. Even if these smaller distilleries don´t manage to grow, their innovations probably won´t go unnoticed. Evidence of this is where established companies in the last couple of years have invested huge sums of money in these new and sometimes maverick whisky producers, just to be a part of something that may impact the whisky industry in the future.

Europe

Austria

Distillery: Whiskydistillery J. Haider, Roggenreith
Founded: 1995
Owner: Johann, Monika & Jasmin Haider
roggenhof.at

In the small village of Roggenreith in northern Austria, the Haider family has been distilling whisky since 1995 and three years later, the first Austrian whisky was released. In 2005, they opened up a Whisky Experience World with guided tours, a video show, whisky tasting and exhibitions. Roggenhof was the first whisky distillery in Austria and, over the years, production has steadily increased to 35,000 litres. The capacity currently stands at 100,000 litres per annum. The wash is allowed to ferment for 72 hours before it reaches either of the two 450 litre Christian Carl copper stills. The desired strength is reached in one single distillation, thanks to the attached column. The main part (70%) of the production are rye whiskies – Original Rye Whisky J.H., Pure Rye Malt J.H., Special Rye Malt J.H. and (since 2012) Special Rye Malt Peated J.H. The last three are made from 100% rye. A 10 year old Original Rye Selection was released recently. The current range of single malts made from barley is Single Malt J.H, Special Single Malt J.H. and Special Single Malt Peated J.H. In addition to that, some of these whiskies are also available as 9 year olds and bottled at a higher strength (46% instead of 41%). From time to time releases are also made in the Rare Selection range. Recent limited bottlings include Rare Selection Dark Rye Malt J.H., matured fot 6 years in eiswein barrels and a 3 year old Single Malt J.H. with a finish in Laphroaig casks.

Distillery: Reisetbauer, Kirchberg-Thening
Founded: 1994 (whisky since 1995)
Owner: Julia & Hans Reisetbauer
reisetbauer.at

This is a family-owned farm distillery near Linz in northern Austria specialising in brandies and fruit schnapps. Since 1995, a range of malt whiskies are also produced. The distillery is equipped with five 350 litre stills. All stills are heated, using hot water rather than steam, which, according to Hans Reisetbauer, allows for a more delicate and gentle distillation. The 70 hour-long fermentation takes place in stainless steel washbacks. Approximately 20,000 litres of pure alcohol destined for whisky making are produced annually, using local barley to make the unpeated malt. Casks are sourced locally from the best Austrian wine producers. The current range of whiskies have all been matured in casks that have previously contained Chardonnay and Trockenbeerenauslese and include a 7, a 12 and a 15 year old.

Other distilleries in Austria

Broger Privatbrennerei

Klaus, founded in 1976 (whisky since 2008)

www.broger.info

The production of whisky is supplementing the distillation and production of eau de vie from apples and pears. For their whisky, Broger buys peated malt in the UK and unpeated malt from Germany but also floor malted barley from Bohemia. The distillery is equipped with a 150 litre Christian Carl still. The total volume of whisky produced in a year is 2,500 litres. The current range of whiskies consists of five expressions; Triple Cask which is a blend of whiskies matured in bourbon, sherry and madeira casks, Medium Smoked which has been smoked using beech wood, Burn Out, a heavily peated whisky, Riebelmais, a corn whisky and the limited Distiller´s Edition which has been maturing in madeira casks and is bottled at cask strength (58,7%).

Destillerie Rogner

Rappottenstein, founded in 1997

www.destillerie-rogner.at

This distillery in Waldviertel in the northeast part of Austria has produced spirits from fruits and berries for more than a decade. Recently, Hermann Rogner has also added whisky to the range. Two of them are called Rogner Waldviertel Whisky 3/3 with the last figures referring to barley, wheat and rye being used for one of the

Jasmin Haider, the new CEO for Destilleri Haider since 2016 and Hans Reisetbauer, owner of Reisetbauer Distillery

expressions and three different kinds of malted barley for the other. There is also a whisky from 100% rye called Rye Whisky No. 13.

Destillerie Weutz
St. Nikolai im Sausal, founded in 2002

www.weutz.at

A family distillery with a history of producing schnapps and liqueur from fruits and berries. In 2004 Michael Weutz started cooperation with the brewer Michael Löscher and since then Weutz has added whisky to its produce based on the wash from the brewery. Since 2004, 14 different malt whiskies have been produced. Some of them are produced in the traditional Scottish style: Hot Stone, St. Nikolaus and the peated Black Peat. Others are more unorthodox, for example Green Panther, in which 5% pumpkin seeds are added to the mash, and Franziska based on elderflower. Annual production is currently at approximately 15,000 litres and for maturation casks made of French Limousin and Alliere oak are used.

Old Raven
Neustift, founded in 2004

www.oldraven.at

In 2004, a distillery was added to the Rabenbräu brewery by Andreas Schmidt. More than 250,000 litres of beer are produced yearly and the wash from the brewery is used for distillation of the 2,000 litres of single malt whisky. The triple distilled Old Raven comes in three expressions – Old Raven, Old Raven Smoky and the limited Old Raven R1 Smoky. The last one was filled into a PX sherry cask which had been used to mature Islay whisky.

Wolfram Ortner Destillerie
Bad Kleinkirchheim, founded in 1990

www.wob.at

Fruit brandies of all kinds make up the bulk of Wolfram Ortner´s produce, as well as cigars, coffee and other luxuries. For the last years he has also been producing malt whisky. New oak of different kinds (Limousin, Aliolier, Nevers, Vosges and American) is used for the maturation process. His first single malt, WOB DÖ MALT Vergin, began selling in 2001 and an additional product line, in which Ortner mixes his whisky with other distillates such as orange/moscatel, is called WOB Mariage.

Waldviertler Granit Destillerie
Waidhofen/Thaya, founded in 1995

www.granitdestillerie.at

The distillery has from 1995 established a comprehensive product portfolio of liquers and schnapps from all kinds of delectable berries and fruit. Whisky production started in 2006 and the owner, Günther Mayer, has not only released two different smoked single malts, but is also working with rye and dinkel.

Destillerie Hermann Pfanner
Lauterach, founded in 1854

www.pfanner-weine.com

Founded as an inn and brewery more than 150 years ago, the production soon turned to distillation of eau de vie and schnapps. In 2005, the current owner, Walter Pfanner, started whisky production and today 10,000 litres per year are filled into casks previously used for maturing sherry and sweet wines. The two core expressions are Pfanner Single Malt Classic and Single Malt Red Wood with a maturation in red wine casks. There are also two recent limited releases; a 4 year old single barrel matured in a PX sherry cask and the smoky Pfanner Whisky w-peated

Keckeis Destillerie
Rankweil, founded in 2003

www.destillerie-keckeis.at

Like so many other Austrian distilleries, it started with schnapps and eau de vie from fruit, in Keckeis´ case, mostly pears and apples. Whisky production started in 2008 and today one expression, Keckeis Single Malt is for sale as well as the new make Keckeis Baby Malt. Part of the barley has been smoked with beech and maturation takes place in small ex-sherry casks made of French Limousin oak.

Dachstein Destillerie
Radstadt, founded in 2007

www.mandlberggut.com

In 2007, Doris and Bernhard Warter added a distillery to their farm Mandlberggut. Apart from production of various spirits from berries, malt whisky is also produced. Maturation takes place in a mix of different casks – new Austrian oak, ex-sherry casks and red wine casks. Their only release so far is the five year old Rock-Whisky which is distilled 2,5 times.

Edelbrennerei Franz Kostenzer
Maurach/Achensee, founded in 1998

www.schnaps-achensee.at

The Kostenzer family is working on a huge range of different spirits, mainly from fruits and berries but whisky is also in the portfolio. Three expressions under the name Whisky Alpin have been released; a 6 year old single malt with a sherry cask finish, a 6 year old 100% single malt rye and a 3 year old single malt with smoky notes from beech wood.

Brennerei Ebner
Absam, founded in 1930

www.brennereiebner.at

A fourth generation brewer and distiller, Arno Pauli, began to make whisky at his combination of a guesthouse, brewery and distillery in 2005. The whisky production is just a small component of the business but, besides a single malt from barley, Pauli has also released whiskies made from maize, dinkel and wheat.

Belgium

Distillery:	Het Anker Distillery, Blasfeld
Founded:	1471 (whisky since 2003)
Owner:	Charles Leclef
	hetanker.be

Charles Leclef started out as a brewer and currently maintains this role at Brouwerij Het Anker. He also experimented with distillation of his own beer into whisky with some assistance from a nearby genever distiller. The first bottles under the name Gouden Carolus Singe Malt, appeared on the market in 2008. In 2010, he started a distillery of his own at the Leclef family estate, Molenberg, at Blaasfeld. The stills have been made by Forsyth´s in Scotland with a wash still capacity of 3,000 litres and a spirit still of 2,000 litres. The wash for the distillation is made at their own brewery in Mechelen and it is basically a Gouden Carolus Tripel beer without hops and spices and with a fermentation time of four to five days. Around 100,000 litres of alcohol are produced per year. The core expression is Gouden Carolus Single Malt where the whisky has matured for 30 months in ex-bourbon casks and the final six months in rejuvenated and re-charred casks made of European oak. In 2014 the limited Gold Fusion was released which is a vatting of the three year old Gouden Carolus and different 6 year old distillates made before their own distillery was built. End of 2014, a visitor centre was opened where you can buy a special version of their single malt called Pure Taste.

Distillery: The Owl Distillery, Grâce Hollogne
Founded: 1997
Owner: Etienne Bouillon, Christian Polis, Pierre Roberti

belgianwhisky.com

In October 2007, Belgium's first single malt, 'The Belgian Owl', was released. The next bottling came in 2008 but was exclusively reserved for private customers. The first commercial bottling was introduced in November 2008. A limited cask strength expression, 44 months old, was released in 2009 and more cask strength versions have followed. In the last couple of years, there have been several releases, 3 to 4 years old with most of them bottled at 46%, but also a couple of cask strength expressions. The distillery is equipped with a mash tun holding 2,1 tonnes per mash, four washbacks with a fermentation time of 60-100 hours and two stills from the 19th century (11,000 and 8,000 litres respectively) that had previously been used at the now demolished Caperdonich distillery in Rothes, Speyside. All the barley used for production comes from farms close to the distillery. The yearly production is around 50,000 litres of pure alcohol.

Czech Republic

Distillery: Gold Cock Distillery
Founded: 1877
Owner: Rudolf Jelinek a.s.

rjelinek.cz

The distilling of Gold Cock whisky started already in 1877. Today it is produced in three versions – a 3 year old blended whisky, a 12 year old single malt and the 22 year old Small Batch 1992 single malt. Production was stopped for a while but after the brand and distillery were acquired by R. Jelinek a.s., the leading Czech producer of plum brandy, the whisky began life anew. The malt whisky is double distilled in 500 litre traditional pot stills. The new owner has created a small whisky museum which is also home to

the club Friends of Gold Cock Whisky with private vaults, where any enthusiast can store his bottlings of Gold Cock.

Denmark

Distillery: Braunstein, Köge
Founded: 2005 (whisky since 2007)
Owner: Michael & Claus Braunstein

braunstein.dk

Denmark's first micro-distillery was built in an already existing brewery in Køge, just south of Copenhagen. The wash comes from the own brewery. A Holstein type of still, with four plates in the rectification column, is used for distillation and the spirit is distilled once. Peated malt is bought from Port Ellen, unpeated from Simpsons, but as much as 40% is from ecologically grown Danish barley. The lion's share of the whisky is stored in ex-bourbon (peated version) and first fill Oloroso casks (unpeated) from 190 up to 500 litres. The Braunstein brothers filled their first casks in 2007 and have since produced 50,000 litres annually. Their first release and the first release of a malt whisky produced in Denmark was in 2010 – a 3 year old single oloroso sherry cask called Edition No. 1 which was followed the same year by Library Collection 10:1, bottled at 46%. The most recent releases are Library Collection 15:2 (a peated version matured in bourbon and calvados casks) and Library Collection 16:1 (unpeated and matured in bourbon casks). For duty free, there is a special version called Danica.Braunstein which has also made an impact on the Chinese market where 5-6,000 bottles are sold yearly.

Distillery: Stauning Whisky, Stauning
Founded: 2006
Owner: Stauning Whisky A/S

stauningwhisky.dk

The first Danish purpose-built malt whisky distillery entered a more adolescent phase in 2009, after having experimented with two small pilot stills bought from Spain. More stills were installed in 2012 and they now have two wash stills and two spirit stills which yield a yearly production of 15,000 litres. The preconditions,

Prince Henrik of Denmark pays a visit to Stauning Distillery

however, were completely changed in December 2015 when it was announced that Diageo´s incubator fund project, Distill Ventures, would spend £10m to increase the capacity of Stauning. This means that by 2018, there will be no less than 26 stills which will increase the capacity to 800,000 litres of pure alcohol!

The aim has always been to be self-sustaining and Danish barley is bought and turned into malt on an own malting floor. The germinating barley usually has to be turned 6-8 times a day, but Stauning has constructed an automatic "grain turner" to do the job. Two core expressions are produced – Peated Reserve and Traditional Reserve – and the peat for the first one is acquired from one of few remaining peat bogs in Denmark. In 2012 the first edition of the two versions were released with slightly more than 700 bottles of each. The distillery has now established a core range including Traditional and Peated single malts as well as a Young Rye. Limited versions are also released; PX and oloroso finishes as well as the single malt finished in their own rye casks.

Other distilleries in Denmark

Fary Lochan Destilleri

Give, founded in 2009

www.farylochan.dk

This distillery, owned by Jens Erik Jørgensen, is situated in Jutland and the first cask was filled in December 2009. Jens Erik Jørgensen imports most of the malted barley from the UK, but he also malts some Danish barley by himself. A part of his own malted barley is dried using nettles instead of peat to create a special flavour. After mashing, it is fermented for five days in a 600 litre stainless steel washback. Distillation is performed in traditional copper pot stills – two smaller ones (300 and 200 litres) and a newly installed 1,200 litre still. The first whisky, lightly smoked, was released in 2013 and a number of bottlings have been released since then. A major expansion of the distillery, including a visitor centre, was made in 2015/2016 which increased both production as well as storage capacity.

Trolden Distillery

Kolding, founded in 2011

www.trolden.com

The distillery is a part of the Trolden Brewery which started in 2005. Michael Svendsen uses the wash from the brewery and ferments it for 4-5 days before a double distillation in a 325 litre alembic pot still. The spirit is filled in bourbon casks and production is quite small as brewing beer is the main task. The first release of the whisky (80 bottles), called Nimbus, came in November 2014 and was followed by Old No. 2. The third release is expected in December 2017.

Nordisk Brænderi/Thy Whisky

Fjerritslev, founded in 2009 (whisky since 2011)

www.nordiskbraenderi.dk, www.thy-whisky.dk

The production at this distillery, located in northern Jutland, is focused on gin, rum and aquavit. In 2011 however the owner, Anders Bilgram, and a local ecological farmer, Nicolaj Nicolajsen, decided to join forces and also produce a small amount of whisky from the barley grown in Nicolajsen´s fields. Within five years they have managed to fill 25 small casks of which three have been released under the name Thy Whisky, the first was in 2014 and the latest one in 2016.

Ørbæk Bryggeri/Nyborg Destilleri

Ørbæk, founded in 1997 (whisky since 2007)

www.oerbaek-bryggeri.nu

Niels Rømer and his son, Nicolai, have since 1997 run Ørbæk Brewery on the Danish island of Fyn. It is now one of many combinations of a micro-brewery and a micro-distillery where the wash from the brewery is used to produce whisky. In 2009 the first barrels of Isle of Fionia single malt were filled and the first release was made exactly three years later with further expressions the year after. The spirit production (a mix of whisky and rom) has been very small and intermittent over the years. In 2014, however, the owners bought an old railway workshop in Nyborg with the intention of converting it into a new and bigger distillery sometime during 2016.

Braenderiet Limfjorden

Sillerslev Havn, founded in 2013

www.braenderiet.dk

The latest distillery to come on stream in Denmark. The owner, Ole Mark, started production in June 2013 with a plan to do 1,000 to 1,500 litres the first year. Mashing and fermentation is carried out at a local brewery while distillation takes place in alambic type stills. Both peated and unpeated single malt as well as rye is produced. The first whisky will be released in 2016.

England

Distillery:	St. George´s Distillery, Roudham, Norfolk
Founded:	2006
Owner:	The English Whisky Co.
	englishwhisky.co.uk

St. George´s Distillery near Thetford in Norfolk was started by father and son, James and Andrew Nelstrop, and came on stream on12th December 2006. This made it the first English malt whisky distillery for over a hundred years. Customers, both in the UK and abroad, have had the opportunity to follow the development of the whisky via releases of new make, as well as 18 months old spirit, both peated and unpeated. These were called Chapters 1 to 4. Finally, in December 2009, it was time for the release of the first legal whisky called Chapter 5 – unpeated and without chill-filtering or colouring. This was a limited release but, soon afterwards, Chapter 6 was released in larger quantities. The next expression (Chapter 8) was a limited release of a lightly peated 3 year old, followed in June 2010 by Chapter 9 (with the same style but more readily available). Chapter 7, a 3 year old with 6 months finish in a rum cask, was launched in autumn 2010, together with Chapter 10, which has a sherry cask finish. The next bottling, Chapter 11, appeared in July 2011. This was the heaviest peated expression so far (50ppm) aged between 3 and 4 years matured in bourbon casks. October 2012 saw the release of the sherry cask matured Chapter 12. The next one, Chapter 13 is released twice a year – in spring for St. George´s Day and in autumn for Halloween. In late 2013, Chapter 14, basically an older version of Chapter 6, and Chapter 15, similar to Chapter 11 but twice the age, were released. In autumn 2014 Chapter 16, the first peated sherry maturation from the distillery, was launched and September 2015, it was time for Chapter 17, the first triple-distilled expression. Chapter 6 is at the moment the biggest seller followed by 9 and 11.

In summer 2013 a new series was introduced called The Black Range. The rationale behind the thinking was to have a more consistent product, predominantly for export and retail chains. Two expressions became available – Classic and Peated, both bourbon matured and bottled at 43%. In autumn 2016, they got a new look and were renamed Original and Smokey. In between the Chapter releases there are also very limited bottlings of the so called Founder´s Private Cellar. These are unique casks chosen by the founding chairman, James Nelstrop who died in September 2014. The last cask by his hand was released as The Final Signature in May 2015.

The distillery is equipped with a stainless steel semi-lauter mash tun with a copper top and three stainless steel washbacks with a fermentation time of 85 hours. There is one pair of stills, the wash still with a capacity of 2,800 litres and the spirit still of 1,800 litre capacity. First fill bourbon barrels are mainly used for maturation but the odd sherry, madeira and port casks have also been filled. Around 60% of production is unpeated and the rest is peated. The distillery capacity is 104,000 litres of pure alcohol and currently they are producing 50,000 litres per year. All the whiskies from the distillery are un chill-filtered and without colouring.

In late 2016, construction will commence on a new whisky shop and distillery bistro. The distilleries whisky shop stocks 300 whiskies from around the world as well as their own produce. Expect this to be open for spring 2017.

Other distilleries in England

The London Distillery Company

London, founded in 2012

www.londondistillery.com

The London Distillery Company is London´s first whisky distillery since Lea Valley closed its doors for the final time, more than a century ago. Founded in 2012 by whisky expert, Darren Rook, and former microbrewery owner, Nick Taylor, and, until recently, located in Battersea, the distillery started distilling gin at the beginning of February 2013. The owners have one still designated for gin called Christina and a second still, Matilda, is used exclusively for whisky production. The first release from the distillery in March 2013 was Dodd´s Gin. In December 2013 they finally got the licence to produce whisky and production started shortly thereafter. Both single malt and rye (100% as well as mixed with malted barley) are produced and the ratio between whisky and gin is 50:50. In September 2015, an unaged rye spirit was released under the name Spring-heeled Jack. Darren and his colleagues experiment with a huge variety of brewer´s yeast strains some of which originate from the early 1900s and also use rare barley varieties such as Plumage Archer and Maris Otter.

In December 2015, the distillery moved to a larger site in Bermondsey, close to Tower Bridge. In the near future, gin production will move to Battersea Power Station while whisky will continue to be produced in the new distillery. The plans is also to expand the capacity in early 2017 with yet another 2,100 litre still.

Lakes Distillery

Bassenthwaite Lake, founded in 2014

www.lakesdistillery.com

Headed by Paul Currie, who was the co-founder of Isle of Arran distillery, a consortium of private investors founded the distillery – the first whisky distillery in the Lake District for more than 100 years. It is housed in a converted Victorian farm near Bassenthwaite Lake. Production started in autumn 2014 and a visitor centre was opened a couple of months later. The distillery was officially opened by Princess Anne in July 2015. The £2,5m distillery is equipped with two stills for the whisky production, each with both copper and stainless steel condensers, and a third still for the distillation of gin. The capacity is 240,000 litres of pure alcohol and at the moment, they are producing 150,000 litres. To help create a cash flow, the company launched a British Isles blended whisky called The One in autumn 2013, where whisky had been sourced from a variety of producers around the UK. A sherry cask finish of The One has also been released. Well in advance of the first launch of a whisky having been produced at the distillery (possibly sometime in 2017), Currie has also released both a gin and a vodka.

Adnams Copper House Distillery

Southwold, founded in 2010

www.adnams.co.uk

Famous for their beer since 1872, the owners of Adnams Brewery in Suffolk installed a new brewhouse in their Sole Bay Brewery in 2008. Left with a redundant, old building, they decided to convert it into a distillery. Equipment was ordered from the famous German manufacturer, Carl GmbH; a 1,000 litre beer stripping still and an 850 litre copper pot still with a rectification column with 42 plates attached. Distillation began in December 2010 and, apart from whisky – gin, vodka and absinthe are also produced. Another two stills, tripling the capacity, were installed in early 2016. The first two whiskies from the distillery were released in December 2013 – Single Malt No. 1, a 3 year old matured in new French oak and Triple Grain No. 2 from malted barley, oats and wheat and matured in new American oak. Several whiskies have been added to the range since then, one of the latest being a Triple Malt, similar to the Triple Grain.

David Fitt, Chief Distiller for The English Whisky Company, and his latest creation, Original

The Cotswolds Distillery

Stourton, founded in 2014

www.cotswoldsdistillery.com

The distillery is the brainchild of Dan Szor, who acquired the Philip's Field Estate with two old stone buildings and started to convert them into a distillery. The main part of the equipment was in place towards the end of summer 2014 and production of both whisky and gin started in September. Three stills have been installed; one wash still (2,400 litres), one spirit still (1,600 litres) and a Holstein still (500 litres) for production of gin and other spirits. The rest of the equipment includes a 0.5 ton mash tun and eight stainless steel wash backs (four of which were installed in spring 2015). With the new fermenters installed, the distillery has a capacity of producing 300,000 bottles per year. The first product for sale was their Cotswolds Dry Gin in September 2014, while the first whisky, Organic Odyssey Single Malt, a vatting of whisky matured in ex-bourbon and red wine casks, will be released in 2017.

Chase Distillery

Rosemaund Farm, Hereford, founded in 2008

www.chasedistillery.co.uk

In 2002, William Chase founded Tyrrell's Crisps, a company which he later sold in 2008. During that same year, he started his new business, a distillery, on his farm in Hereford. Both businesses emanated from the same ingredient, namely potatoes. Chase's main product, and one which has already made success in more than 25 countries, is Chase Vodka which, unusually, is made of potatoes. Today more than 500,000 bottles are produced yearly and gins have also become part of the range. By the end of 2011, the first whisky was distilled and since then around 40 casks are filled every year. No release date has been set but Chase expects the first whisky will be launched as a 5 year old. The distillery is equipped with a copper still from Carl in Germany with a five plate column and an attached rectification column with another 42 plates. At 70 feet, the column is said to be the tallest of its kind in the world.

Finland ✛

Distillery:	Teerenpeli, Lahti
Founded:	2002
Owner:	Anssi Pyysing
	teerenpeli.com

The distillery, located in the company's restaurant in central Lahti, is equipped with one wash still (1,500 litres) and one spirit still (900 litres) and the average fermentation time in the washback is 70 hours. In 2010 a new mash tun was installed and later that month a new visitor centre was opened. A completely new distillery, with one 3,000 litre wash still and two 900 litre spirit stills, was opened in October 2015 in the same house as the brewery. The expansion means that the two units will quadruple the capacity to 160,000 litres per year. The old distillery will be used mainly for special runs such as organic or peated whiskies.

The first Teerenpeli Single Malt was sold as a 3 year old in 2005. Over the years more expressions have been made available, not only in Finland but also abroad. The core range now consists of a 10 year old matured in bourbon casks (released in 2015), Kaski wich is a 100% sherry maturation (launched in 2012) and Portti (to be released end of 2016) which is a 3 year old with another 1.5 years in port casks. Limited releases occur regularly. The four most recent are Rasi, a moscatel finish, Karhi (madeira finish), Aura which has been matured in the brewery's own porter casks and the smoky Suomi 100 (end of 2016) to celebrate the 100th anniversary of Finland's declaration of independence from Russia in 1917.

Other distilleries in Finland

Helsinki Distilling Company

Helsinki, founded in 2014

www.hdco.fi

The first privately-owned distillery in Helsinki for over a hundred years, was opened in 2014 by two Finns, Mikko Mykkänen and Kai Kilpinen, and one Irishman, Séamus Holohan. Production started in August with gin and the first whisky was distilled one month later. The distillery is equipped with one mash tun and three washbacks made of stainless steel and one 300 litre pot still with a 7 plate column. The current capacity is 12,000 litres per year but there are already plans to install a second still which would triple the output. The first gin, with lingonberry as one of the botanicals, was released in October 2014 and more gin as well as akvavit and applejack has followed since. On the whisky side, the focus is on rye, either with a mash bill of 75% rye and 25% barley or 100% rye, but also single malt made from barley. The owners have plans to also open an adjacent bar during 2016.

Valamo Distillery

Heinävesi, founded in 2014

www.valamodistillery.com

Over the centuries, there have been many examples of spirits (not least liqueurs) that have been produced in monasteries, but this is probably the first example of a monastery whisky. The Valamo Monastery in eastern Finland owns 51% of the distillery with the rest being divided among six private partners (Arttu Taponen, Samuli Taponen, Timo Kettunen, Arto Liimatta, Harri Turunen and Risto Toivanen). Experimental distillation started in 2011 in a small, 150 litre still. In 2015, production really began in earnest when the distillery was equipped with a 5,000 litre mash tun, four stainless steel washbacks and a 1,000 litre Carl still which is used for both the wash and the spirit distillation. Around 30,000 litres, both pea-ted and unpeated spirit, are produced yearly. Valamo monastery has been producing sacramental wine from berries for a long time and the empty wine casks, together with bourbon barrels, are used to mature the whisky. Apart from whisky, the distillery also produces spirits made from cloudberry and arctic bramble.

Portti - new in Teerenpeli's core range

France

Distillery:	Glann ar Mor, Pleubian, Bretagne
Founded:	1999
Owner:	Jean Donnay
	glannarmor.com

The owner of Glann ar Mor Distillery in Brittany, Jean Donnay, already started his first trials back in 1999. He then made some changes to the distillery and the process and regular production commenced in 2005. The distillery is very much about celebrating the traditional way of distilling malt whisky. The two small stills are directly fired and Donnay uses worm tubs for condensing the spirit. He practises a long fermentation in wooden washbacks and the distillation is very slow. For maturation, a variety of casks are used (first fill bourbon, ex-Sauternes casks, PX sherry etc.) and when the whisky is bottled, there is neither chill filtration nor caramel colouring. The full capacity is 50,000 bottles per year. Apart from France, the whisky is available in the UK, Sweden, Denmark, Germany, The Netherlands, Italy, Singapore, Taiwan, Canada and Japan.

There are two versions of the whisky from Glann ar Mor – the unpeated Glann ar Mor and the peated Kornog. Core expressions are usually bottled at 46% but every year a number of limited releases are made including single casks and cask strength bottlings. In 2015, Donnay also released his first rye whisky - Only Rye, made from 100% malted rye.

In summer 2015, the distillery was involved in a debate with the French INAO organization about the new rules regulating Geographical Indication (GI) for "Whisky Breton". Donnay felt that the regulations had been "tailor-made for industrial production" and this had put him, as an artisanal distiller, in an impossible situation. He announced that he would be closing the distillery but subsequently withdrew the decision a few weeks later after new talks were held with the INAO.

Jean Donnay has also embarked on a new project which entails building the ninth distillery on Islay. The initial plan was to open Gartbreck distillery some time in 2016 but so far construction has not started.

Distillery:	Distillerie Warenghem, Lannion, Bretagne
Founded:	1900 (whisky since 1994)
Owner:	Gilles Leizour
	distillerie-warenghem.com

Leon Warenghem founded the distillery at the beginning of the 20th century and in 1967 his grandson, Paul-Henri Warenghem, together with his associate, Yves Leizour, took over the reins. They moved the distillery to its current location on the outskirts of Lannion in Brittany. Today, the distillery is owned by the Leizour family and it was Gilles Leizour, taking over in 1983, who added whisky production to the repertoire. The first whisky, a blend called WB, was released in 1987 and in the ensuing year, the first single malt distilled in France, Armorik, was launched. The distillery is equipped with a 6,000 litres semi lautermash tun, four stainless steel washbacks and two, traditional copper pot stills (a 6,000 litres wash still and a 3,500 litres spirit still). Production has increased recently to 120,000 litres of pure alcohol per year and 30% thereof is grain spirit for their blends.

The single malt core range consists of Armorik Edition Originale and Armorik Sherry Finish. Both are around 4 years old, bottled at 40%, have matured in ex-bourbon casks plus a few months in sherry butts for the SherryFinish and are sold in supermarkets in France. Armorik Classic, a mix of 4 to 8 year old whiskies from bourbon and sherry casks and the 7 year old Armorik Double Maturation which has spent time in both new French oak and sherry wood are earmarked for export. Armorik Millesime is a limited bottling released occasionally while Maitre de Chai, a 6 year old with two years in a bourbon cask and four years in first fill oloroso, has been released a couple of times. The latest single malt bottling, launched in 2016, is the limited Armorik Dervenn which was matured in Breton oak casks. The first French rye ever was released in 2015. Named Roof Rye, the 8 year old whisky is a collaboration between the distillery and the famous bartender Guillaume Ferroni.

There are also three blended whiskies in the range; WB Whisky Breton which is 3-4 years old with 25% malt and 75% grain whisky, Galleg, same age but 50% malt whisky and Breizh, which is slightly older and 50% malt whisky. A total of 250,000 bottles were sold last year.

Warenghem Distillery with the new Dervenn Single Malt, un chill-filtered and with natural colour

Other distilleries in France

Distillerie Claeyssens de Wambrechies

Wambrechies, Hauts de France, founded in 1817 (whisky since 2000)

www.wambrechies.com

Claeyssens distillery is one of the oldest in France, tracing its history back to 1817 and located in a building classified as a historic monument in 1999. The distillery was originally famous for its genever, the traditional spirit consumed in the north of France, in Belgium and in Holland. In 2000, the distillery started to produce single malt whisky launching Wambrechies 3 year old in 2003, and an 8 year old version in 2009. In the spring of 2013, two 12 year old bottlings (the oldest French whiskies to date) were released: one aged in madeira casks and another in sherry casks, both bottled at 40%. Wambrechies whisky is also the heart of Bellevoye's triple malt whisky, launched by the independent bottler Sirech & Co at the end of 2015.

Domaine Mavela

Corsica, founded in 1991 (whisky since 2001)

www.domaine-mavela.com

Since 2001 whisky is produced in Corsica, the Mediterranean island off the Côte d'Azur. The creators of P&M are the brewer Dominique Sialleli, also responsible for the creation of Pietra beer in 1996, and Jean-Claude Venturini who set up the Mavela distillery in 1991. They got some help from the Alsacian Jean-Claude Meyer from the distillery of the same name. Distilled in a Holstein still and aged in ex-Corsican muscat casks, the P&M single malt was sold for the first time in 2004. Its unique taste of the Corsican maquis surprised many whisky amateurs before becoming a success. Two blends, P&M Whisky Corse and P&M Supérieur, were later released. In 2015 the line-up was modified to include a blend (P&M Vintage) and a single malt (P&M 7 years old).

Distillerie Meyer

Hohwarth, Grand Est, founded in 1958 (whisky since 2007)

www.distilleriemeyer.fr

The Meyer distillery was founded in 1958 by Fridolin Meyer, a fruit wholesaler who thought it would be an excellent way to make money from his unsold fruit. Together with his son Jean-Claude, who joined the company in 1975, Meyer soon became one of the most awarded distillers in France. At the beginning of the 2000's, Jean-Claude Meyer helped the Venturini family in Corsica to start producing whisky under the P&M brand, and this convinced him to produce his own whisky. With the help of his two sons, Arnaud and Lionel, they launched two no-age statement whiskies in 2007, just one year before the sudden death of Jean-Claude – one blend and one single malt. More than 500 casks are currently maturing in the new warehouse built in 2012. Meyer's, mainly sold in supermarkets in the Alsace area, is probably one of the best selling French whiskies right now. There are currently three different versions: Meyer's Pur Malt (a single malt), Meyer's Blend Supérieur and Oncle Meyer Blend Supérieur.

Distillerie des Menhirs

Plomelin, Bretagne, founded in 1986 (whisky since 1998)

www.distillerie.bzh

Ever since their great grand-mother bought a portable column still back in 1921 to "burn" cider, the Le Lay family has been distilling lambig (the traditional apple brandy of Brittany). In 1986, Guy and his wife Anne-Marie decide to settle down for good and the first lambig with the name Distillerie des Menhirs was released in 1989. Shortly after, Guy Le Lay came up with the idea of producing a 100% buckwheat whisky. Production started in 1998 and Eddu Silver was launched in 2002, followed by Eddu Gold in 2006, Eddu Silver Brocéliande in 2013 and Eddu Diamant in 2015. Nowadays, the Menhirs distillery is managed by Anne-Marie and Guy's sons:

Erwan, Kevin and Loïg. They were the ones who came up with the idea of producing the first French barley whisky distilled in a column still. Ed Gwenn (white cereal in English), aged for 4 years in ex-cognac barrels, was released for the first time in June 2016

Distillerie Gilbert Holl

Ribeauvillé, Grand Est, founded in 1979 (whisky since 2000)

www.gilbertholl.com

In 1979, Gilbert Holl began to distill occasionally in the back of his wine and spirits shop. He bought his first still in 1982 in order to produce eaux-de-vie with his own fruit: cherry plums, raspberries and cherries and in the beginning of 2000, he finally started distilling whisky in a very small still (150 litres). His first bottling, Lac'Holl, was put on sale in 2004 and was followed by Lac'Holl Junior in 2007 and Lac'Holl Vieil Or in 2009. Production of this light bodied whisky remains very limited.

Distillerie Hepp

Uberach, Grand Est, founded in 1972 (whisky since 2005)

www.distillerie-hepp.com

A family-owned distillery, Hepp started producing single malt whisky in 2005, on the initiative of the then owner's son, Yannick. Besides the regular expression, a no-age statement bottled at 42% under the brand Tharcis Hepp, two limited editions have been released, the first one aged in ex-plum cask, the second one under the name Johnny Hepp. As well as producing their own whisky, Hepp also supplies the independent bottler Denis Hanns with liquid for his Authentic Whisky Alsace.

Distillerie Rozelieures

Rozelieures, Grand Est, founded in 1860 (whisky since 2007)

www.whiskyrozelieures.com

Hubert Grallet had been distilling cherry plums for many years when his daughter married a barley farmer, Christophe Dupic: following a dare issued during a well-lubricated dinner, they decided to try their hand at whisky production, and launched the Glen Rozelieures brand in 2007. Four versions are currently available: the first two are aged in ex-fino sherry casks, the third is lightly peated and aged in Sauternes casks and the fourth is peated. In 2016, two single casks were released - ex-bourbon and ex-Vosne-Romanée (Burgundy red wine). Rozelieures is also bottled under the brand name Lughnasadh ("August" in Gaelic) for the Clair de Lorraine chain-store. The company also blends and bottles a blended malt, Whisky de France (30% Alsacian whisky, 70% Lorrain whisky).

Brûlerie du Revermont

Nevy sur Seille, Bourgogne-Franche Comté, founded in 1991 (whisky since 2003)

www.marielouisetissot-levin.com

For many years, the Tissot family were travelling distillers offering their services to the many wine producers in the Franche-Comté area. Relying upon a very unique distillation set-up, a Blavier still with three pots, designed and built in the early 1930's for the perfume industry, they have been producing single malt whisky since 2003. Whilst at the beginning all the whisky was distilled to order by Bruno Mangin, of the Rouget de Lisle Brewery, Pascal and Joseph Tissot launched their own whisky brand Prohibition in 2011. Aged in "feuillettes" (114 litres half-casks coopered specially for macvin and vin de paille french wines), the whisky is reduced to 41% or 42% and bottled uncoloured.

Rouget de Lisle

Bletterans, Bourgogne-Franche Comté, founded in 1994 (whisky since 2006),

www.brasserie-rouget-lisle.com

Rouget de Lisle is a micro-brewery created by Bruno Mangin and his wife. Having made a first unsuccessful attempt to distill in 1998, they tried again in 2006, commissioning the Brûlerie du Revermont to do it for them. This proved to be a good idea and the first Rouget De Lisle single malt whisky was released in 2009. In 2012, Bruno Mangin bought his own still, a Sofac Armagnac still with a capacity of 1,500 litres. Current bottlings are from the numerous casks he filled during his association with the Tissot family and which lie maturing in his own warehouse. The very first 100% Rouget de Lisle whisky won't be available until the end of 2017.

Distillerie Bertrand

Uberach, Grand Est, founded in 1874 (whisky since 2002)

www.distillerie-bertrand.com

The town of Uberach has only 1,000 inhabitants but two whisky distilleries, Uberach and Hepp. Distillerie Bertrand is an independent affiliate of Wolfberger, the large wine and eau-de-vie producer. The manager, Jean Metzger, gets the malt from a local brewer and then distils it in Holstein type stills. Two different types of whisky are produced. One is a single malt at 42,2%, non-chill filtered and with maturation in both new barrels and barrels which have previously contained the fortified wine Banyuls. The other is a single cask at 43,8% matured only in Banyuls barrels. The first bottles, aged 4 years, were released in 2006. Being a great wine connoisseur, Jean Metzger started to experiment with maturation and finishing whisky in a lot of other different ex-wine casks, including Arbois and Pupillin. This new range of whisky, Cask Jaune, is bottled in 50 cl beer type bottles. In September 2013, a very limited number of bottles of Uberach 10 year old were released for the Whisky Live Paris 10th anniversary. R8, launched in 2015 was aged in ex-Rasteau casks.

Distillerie de Northmaen

La Chapelle Saint-Ouen, Normandie, founded in 1997 (whisky since 2005)

www.northmaen.com

Northmaen is a craft brewery founded in 1997 by Dominique Camus and his wife. Every year since 2005, they have bottled and sold Thor Boyo, a 3 year old single malt, distilled in a small, mobile pot still. In 2009, a 5 year old cask strength (59%) version was launched and in 2013, the oldest version to date, an 8 year old bottled at 44% under the new brand name Sleipnir was released. For the first time a peated whisky, Fafnir, will be available from the end of 2015.

Distillerie Lehmann

Obernai, Grand Est, founded in 1850 (whisky since 2001)

www.distillerielehmann.com

The story of Lehmann distillery starts in 1850 when the family of the actual owner set up a still in Bischoffsheim. Yves Lehmann inherited the facility in 1982 but decided to move all the equipment to a new distillery in 1993. In 2001, he bought two Rump stills to produce single malt whisky which he ages exclusively in French white wine casks. The first regular bottling, aged for seven years in Bordeaux casks and bottled at 40%, was launched in 2008 under the brand Elsass Whisky. A second bottling, aged 8 years in Sauternes casks and bottled at 50%, followed soon after. The Côteaux-du-Layon casks have yet to be bottled.

Distillerie Brunet

Cognac, Nouvelle Aquitaine, founded in 1920 (whisky since 2006)

www.drinkbrenne.com

The Cognac area needs no introduction. With more than 5 000 stills in operation, the Poitou-Charentes region boasts the highest concentration of distillers in the world. But apart from cognac there is whisky produced here as well. The Brunet distillery, owned by Stéphane Brunet, started to distill whisky in 2006. His whisky, Tradition Malt, was launched in 2009 and has already found its way to the USA where it is sold under the brand Brenne, courtesy of Allison Patel. This young woman, whisky connoisseur and enthusiast, launched this as her own brand, surfing on the single malt wave and taking advantage of the fame of cognac. Each version, bottled at 40% comes from a single cask. In September 2015 a 10 year old version was released in small quantities in the USA.

Distillerie de Paris

Paris, Ile de France, founded in 2014

www.distilleriedeparis.com

The micro-distillation boom has come to Paris. Sébastien and Nicolas Julhès – two brothers in charge of one of Paris's best groceries – have set up a still in the heart of the French capital. The Distillerie de Paris is equipped with a 400 litre Holstein still configured to produce the equivalent of 50 litres of distillate at 65% per batch (double distillation). Distillation of gin and vodka started in January 2015, soon followed by brandy, rhum and grain spirit. The first single malt was distilled in June 2015.

Jean Metzger (left), owner of Distillerie Bertrand

Distillerie Ninkasi

Tarare, Auvergne-Rhône Alpes, founded in 1998 (whisky since 2015)

www.ninkasi.fr

The Ninkasi brewery in Lyon had plans to produce whisky already in 2009 but it wasn't until 2015 that they had the funds to make the plans a reality. The future whisky is distilled in a 2,500 litres still made by Prulho Chalvignac, using wash produced on site, and then aged in different types of cask. Production began in September 2015 and should reach cruising speed some time next year, producing around 10,000 litres of pure alcohol. In the long-term, Ninkasi is hoping to be able to use the on-site water source and to develop their own strain of yeasts.

Distillerie Kaerilis

Belle-Île, Bretagne, founded in 2011

www.kaeriliswhisky.com

Like many others, Fabien Mueller started his activity as an independent bottler. Since 2006, Kaerilis has released a range of whiskies distilled in Scotland with an additional maturation taking place on Belle-Île, a small island a few kilometres off the south coast of Brittany. Since 2011, the company also operates a small distillery located in the back of a shop in the main city of the island. The first bottles of An Toiseach Ar Bell'Isle are available since 2014. Fabien Mueller now dreams of growing his own barley and one day releasing a 100% Kaerilis whisky.

Brasserie Michard

Limoges, Nouvelle Aquitaine, founded in 1987 (whisky since 2011)

www.bieres-michard.com

The Limousin area is very well known for its forests of oak trees cherished by the cognac industry, but not really for its eaux-de-vie, nor for its whisky. However, that could change thanks to Michard, a brewery founded in 1987 by Jean Michard. On the initiative of his daughter, Julie, he bottled his first single malt in 2011. Using their own unique yeast, the first batch of their whisky is highly original and very fruity. Available in an 800 bottle limited edition, it has been followed by a second batch in late 2013. Unfortunately, due to problems with the French customs, Jean Michard has had to stop distilling for the time being. He is currently considering building a brand new distillery.

La Bercloise

Bercloux, Nouvelle Aquitaine, founded in 2000 (whisky since 2014)

www.bercloise.fr

After many trials of brewing whilst still a student, and a course in Ireland to hone his skills, Philippe Laclie opened his own brewery in 2000. The success encouraged him to increase production from 150 to 1,500 hectolitres in less than two years. In 2007 he decided to diversify by buying in some Scotch whisky and finishing it for a few months in Pineau des Charentes barrels. At the beginning of 2014, Philippe took the next step and invested around 100,000 euros by purchasing an 800 litre column still. After the first trial runs in June 2014, regular whisky production started in September. The first bottlings of Bercloux single malt spirit (3 and 9 months old) were released at the end of 2015 and in early 2016.

Domaine des Hautes-Glaces

Saint Jean d'Hérans, Auvergne-Rhône Alpes, founded in 2009
(whisky since 2013)

www.hautesglaces.com

At an altitude of 900 metres in the middle of the French Alps, Jérémy Bricka and Frédéric Revol have decided to produce whisky from the barley to the bottle! Apart from growing their own barley, all the parts of whisky production take place at the distillery – malting, brewing, distillation, maturation and bottling. Not only have they set out to create the first French single estate whisky, they are doing it organically. All of their cereal (mainly barley, but also rye) is harvested, malted, distilled and aged field by field and without any chemicals, in order to remain as faithful as possible to the expression of their unique terroir. Principium, the first whisky made at the distillery has been available since June 2014. The standard line-up includes two single malts, Les Moissons (100% malted barley) and Vulson (100% malted rye).

Dreumont

Neuville-en-Avesnois, Hauts de France, founded in 2005 (whisky since 2011)

www.ladreum.com

Passionate about beer, which he has been brewing for the past twenty years, Jérôme Dreumont founded his distillery in 2005. In 2011 he built his own 300 litre still and ran it for the first time in November the same year. Since then, he has been filling only one cask of double-distilled spirit per year, but intends to increase production soon. His first whisky, distilled from a mix of peated and non-peated barley, was released in March 2015 and was followed one year later by a second edition.

Distillerie du Castor

Troisfontaines, Grand Est, founded in 1985 (whisky since 2011)

www.distillerie-du-castor.com

Founded by Patrick Bertin, the distillery produces both fruit and pomace brandies. It is equipped with two small stills which have been used since 2011 by Patrick's son to distill single malt whisky. The malt is bought from Malteurop in Metz and brewed by a local brewery. The first distillation is carried out in the two stills whereas the low wines, mixed together, are re-distilled in the Carl still only. The distillate is aged in ex-white wine casks and then finished in ex-sherry casks. A first bottling of 1,100 bottles (bottled at 42%) was put on sale in June 2015 under the name St Patrick.

La Roche Aux Fées

Sainte-Colombe, Bretagne, founded in 1996 (whisky since 2010)

Gonny Keizer installed a micro-brewery in the Roche aux Fées county, next to the town of Sainte-Colombe en Ille-et-Vilaine in 1996. She is the first female master-brewer in France. In 2010, Gonny and her husband Henry bought themselves a portable automatic batch still made in 1950 in Nantes by Coyac. With a capacity of 400 litres, the still is wood-heated and is equipped with a worm-tub condenser. The first spirit was put into cask in 2010. In 2014 a distillery was built to shelter the still in a permanent manner. The first Roc'Elf bottling, distilled from three malted cereals (barley, wheat, oat), was released in January 2016.

Distillerie Castan

Villeneuve Sur Vère, Occitanie, founded in 1946 (whisky since 2010)

www.distillerie-castan.com

The Castan distilling story can be traced back to 1941 when Gilbert Castan bought a portable still. His son, Jacques, will go down in history as the last itinerant distiller in the county as his son Sébastien Castan, the third generation, in 2010 decided to permanently house the still in a distillery. The same year, he distilled his first whisky and aged the spirit in ex-Gaillac wine casks. Two bottlings of Vilanova Berbie were launched in 2013, with Vilanova Gost following in early 2014. These were the first in a series of two annual bottlings, some of them peated. The first smoky whisky, Vilanova Terrocita, was released towards the end of 2015.

Domaine de Bourjac

Broquiès, Occitanie, founded in 1994 (whisky since 2010)

www.domainedebourjac.com

Founded in 1994 by Olivier Toulouse and his wife, Domaine de Bourjac produces local wines from indigenous grape varieties. In 2010, Olivier, with the help of a local fruit eau-de-vie distiller, decided to produce malt whisky from local barley. The distillate was aged in ex-wine barrels and the first bottles of DDB were released in 2012. The same year, Olivier bought an old Charentais type still which he refurbished in order to put it to its original use: direct distillation with smoke recuperation through a tube wrapped around the kettle to help the heat repartition. Domaine de Bourjac produces about 400 bottles of certified organic whisky per year.

Alp Spirits

Pontcharra, Auvergne-Rhône Alpes, founded in 2002 (whisky since 2012)

www.mandrin.eu

Vincent Gachet, an IT professional, decided to become a brewer in 2002 opening the Brasserie Artisanale du Dauphiné in the suburbs of Grenoble, at Saint-Martin d'Hères. The first beers were released the same year under the Mandrin brand. In 2005, he joined forces with Gilles Gaudet, an ambulant brewer equipped with a four-kettle still. In 2012 they decided to produce whisky as well and every winter since then, Vincent Gachet goes to Pontcharra, where the ambulant still settles for the season, and distils his own brews. The first 400 bottles of Mandrin single malt were released end of 2015.

Ouche Nanon

Ourouer Les Bourdelins, Centre-Val de Loire, founded in 1996 (whisky since 2015)

www.ouche-nanon.fr

Behind the beautiful name (Nanon's orchard), hides a micro-brewery producing artisanal beer since 2010. In 2015, Thomas Mousseau acquired a Guillaume still from the 1930s, removed the little column and made it into a pot still, heated by a wood fire. A first single malt spirit (3 months old) was offered to crowdfunding contributors allowing him to set up his own distillery.

Germany

Distillery:	Whisky-Destillerie Blaue Maus, Eggolsheim-Neuses
Founded:	1980
Owner:	Robert Fleischmann
	fleischman-whisky.de

This is the oldest single malt whisky distillery in Germany and it celebrated its 30th anniversary in 2013. This was also a celebration of the first German single malt whisky which was distilled in 1983. It took, however, 15 years before the first whisky, Glen Mouse 1986, appeared. Fleischmann uses unpeated malt and the whisky matures for approximately eight years in casks of fresh German Oak. A completely new distillery became operational in April 2013. All whisky from Blaue Maus are single cask and there are currently around ten single malts in the range, for example Blaue Maus, Spinnaker, Krottentaler, Schwarzer Pirat, Grüner Hund, Mary Read, Austrasier and Old Fahr. Some of them are released at cask strength while others are reduced to 40%. To celebrate the 30th anniversary, some limited releases were made in June 2013 – for example, Blaue Maus and Spinnaker, both in 20 and 25 year old versions.

An unusual experiment was made in 2016 when the owners transported about a dozen of casks to the island of Sylt in the North Sea. The casks were lowered into the sea to continue the maturation process. Because of the tide, every six hours the casks were exposed to the air. None of the casks have been bottled so far.

Distillery:	Slyrs Destillerie, Schliersee
Founded:	1928 (whisky since 1999)
Owner:	Stetter family
	slyrs.de

Lantenhammer Destillerie in Schliersee, Bavaria was founded in 1928 and was producing mainly brandy until 1999 when whisky took preference, and in 2003 Slyrs Destillerie was founded. The malt, smoked with beech, comes from locally grown grain and the spirit is distilled in 1,500 litre stills. Maturation takes place in charred 225-litre casks of new American White Oak from Missouri. Investments in three new fermentation tanks (washbacks) and a malt silo during 2009/2010 increased the capacity and they are currently producing 150,000 bottles per year.

Slyrs Destilleri and one of their latest releases - Slyrs 51

The non chill-filtered whisky is called Slyrs after the original name of the surrounding area, Schliers. Around 40,000 bottles are sold annually. The core expressions are a 3 year old bottled at 43% and a cask strength version. In 2013, three limited versions were released – a PX sherry cask finish, an Oloroso finish and a Port finish. New editions of all three have since been released. In May 2015, 1,000 bottles of the distillery's first 12 year old whisky were released. A second edition was released in May 2016 and sold out in three hours! Another expression was launched in October 2015, Slyrs 51, which was bottled at 51%.

Distillery:	Hammerschmiede, Zorge
Founded:	1984 (whisky since 2002)
Owner:	Alexander Buchholz
	hammerschmiede.de

In keeping with many other small whisky producers on mainland Europe, Hammerschmiede's main products are spirits from fruit, berries and herbs and whisky distilling was only embarked on in 2002. In 2014, Alexander Buchholz, started the construction of a new still house with additional stills making it a total of five. The first bottles were released in 2006 under the name Glan Iarran. Today, all whisky produced has changed name to Glen Els. The core range consists of four expressions; Glen Els Journey with a blend of different maturations, Ember, which is woodsmoked, Unique Distillery Edition which is always from a sherry cask and Wayfare, bottled at cask strength. These whiskies are complemented by the Woodsmoked Malts, a range of single cask bottlings where the whisky is always smoked but has matured in a variety of casks, Four Seasons with six non-woodsmoked maturations (ruby port, madeira, bordeaux, marsala and sherry) and Elements, where the flavour of the whiskies reflect the four elements (air, water, fire, earth). Finally, there is the Alrik by Glen Els which, according to the owner, is the ultimate woodsmoked malt, usually matured in a PX sherry cask with an additional finish.

Other distilleries in Germany

Spreewälder Feinbrand- & Likörfabrik
Schlepzig, founded in 2004 (whisky production)
www.spreewaldbrennerei.de

The product range consists of different kinds of beers, eau-de-vie and rum, and since 2004 malt whisky is also included. The distillery is equipped with three stills with fractionating column and is fired by using gas. The annual production of whisky and rum is 15,000 litres per year. French Oak casks, that have previously contained wine made of Sylvaner and Riesling grapes, are used for maturation, as well as new Spessart oak casks. Torsten Römer released his first whisky; Sloupisti, as a 3 year old in 2007. Recent bottlings have been older (up to a 10 year old) and there is also a cask strength version.

Obsthof am Berg
Kriftel, founded in 1983 (whisky since 2009)
www.obsthof-am-berg.de, www.gilors.de

Holger and Ralf Heinrich are the third generation running this distillery and their focal point is to produce spirits from fruits and berries. In 2009 the two brothers started whisky production and the first release of their 3 year old single malt Gilors was in 2012. The whisky is non chillfiltered and the majority of the production is unpeated. For maturation they use 100-250 litre ex-sherry and ex-port casks with a yearly production of 1,200 litres. The two core expressions, Gilors fino sherry matured and Gilors port matured, are both 3 years old. Recent limited editions include the 4 year old Gilors Islay cask finish (1 year in new oak and 3 years in an Islay cask), Gilors Oloroso finish and, in spring 2016, Gilors Peated (made from peated malt and matured for three years in bourbon casks).

Bayerwald-Bärwurzerei und Spezialitäten-Brennerei Liebl
Kötzting, founded in 1970 (whisky since 2006)
www.coillmor.com

In 1970 Gerhard Liebl started spirit distillation from fruits and berries and in 2006 his son, Gerhard Liebl Jr., built a brand new whisky distillery. Maturation takes place in first or second fill ex-bourbon barrels, except for whisky which is destined to be bottled as single casks. Sherry, Port, Bordeaux and Cognac casks are used here. About 20,000 litres of whisky are produced annually and in 2009 the first 1,500 bottles bearing the name Coillmór were released. The current range is American oak (4 years), Port single cask (8 years), Albanach Peat (5 years), Bordeaux single cask (6 years), Bourbon peated (6 years), Oloroso sherry (5 years) and PX Sherry (6 years).

Brennerei Höhler
Aarbergen, founded in 1895 (whisky since 2001)
www.brennerei-hoehler.de

The main produce from this distillery in Hessen consists of different distillates from fruit and berries. The first whisky, a bourbon variety, was distilled in 2001 and released in 2004. Since then, Karl-Holger Höhler has experimented with different types of grain (rye, barley, spelt and oat). A couple of the more recent releases of his Whesskey (so called since it is from the province Hessen) are a Cara-Aroma Single Malt and single malts made from smoked (and not peated) barley.

Stickum Brennerei (Uerige)
Düsseldorf, founded in 2007
www.stickum.de

Uerige Brewery, founded in 1862, was completed with a distillery in 2007. The wash comes from their own brewery and the distillation takes place in a 250 litre column still. For the maturation they not only use new oak but also bourbon, sherry and port casks. The distillery produces around 700 bottles of their whisky BAAS per year and the first bottling (a 3 year old) was released in December 2010. In 2014 the owners released their first 5 year old whiskies – one matured in a sherry cask and the other in new oak.

Preussische Whiskydestillerie
Mark Landin, founded in 2009
www.preussischerwhisky.de

Cornelia Bohn purchased a closed-down distillery in 2009 in the Uckermark region, one hour's drive from Berlin. The distillery had been operational for 100 years up until WWII, when Russian soldiers took it apart and the last stills disappeared in the 1950s. Bohn installed a 550 litre copper still with a 4-plate rectification column attached. The spirit is distilled very slowly five to six times and is then matured in casks made of new, heavily toasted American white oak, German fine oak or German Spessart oak. Since 2013 only organic barley is used for the distillation. The first whisky was launched as a 3 year old in December 2012 and in 2014, three releases were made (March, June and September). From March 2015, all the whiskies from the distillery will be at least 5 years old. The whisky is always un chill-filtered without colouring and bottled at cask strength.

Kleinbrennerei Fitzke
Herbolzheim-Broggingen, founded in 1874 (whisky since 2004)
www.kleinbrennerei-fitzke.de

The main commerce for the distillery is the production of eau de viex and vodka, but they also distill whisky from different grains. Mashing, fermentation and distillation all take place at the distillery and for maturation they use 30 litre oak casks. For the first six months they use virgin oak and, thereafter, the spirit is filled into used barrels for another two and a half years. The first release of the Derrina single malt was in 2007 and new batches have been launched ever since. The different varieties of Derrina are either made from malted grains (barley, rye, wheat, oats etc.) or unmalted (barley, oats, buckwheat, rice, triticale, sorghum or maize).

Rieger & Hofmeister

Fellbach, founded in 1994 (whisky since 2006)

www.rieger-hofmeister.de

Marcus Hofmeister´s stepfather, Albrecht Rieger, started the distillery and when Marcus entered the business in 2006 he expanded it to also include whisky production. The first release of this Schwäbischer Whisky was in 2009 and currently there are two expressions in the range – a Single Malt matured in Pinot Noir casks and a Malt & Grain (50% wheat, 40% barley and 10% smoked barley) from Chardonnay casks. By the end of 2012 a malted rye was distilled and at the beginning of 2013 a lightly peated malt from barley.

Kinzigbrennerei

Biberach, founded in 1937 (whisky since 2004)

www.biberacher-whisky.de

Martin Brosamer is the third generation in the family and he is also the one who expanded the production in 2004 to include whisky. The total production of whisky is 2,000 litres annually. In the beginning, Martin filled small casks (50 litres) made of new oak but has progressively moved to larger casks. The first release in 2008 was Badische Whisky, a blend made from wheat and barley. Two years later came the 4 year old Biberacher Whisky, the first single malt and in 2012, the range was expanded with Schwarzwälder Rye Whisky and the smoky single malt Kinzigtäler Whisky.

Destillerie Kammer-Kirsch

Karlsruhe, founded in1961 (whisky since 2006)

www.kammer-kirsch.de

Like so many distilleries, production of spirits from various fruits and berries is the main focus for Kammer-Kirsch and they are especially known for their Kirschwasser from cherries. In 2006 they started a cooperation with the brewery, Landesbrauerei Rothaus, where the brewery delivers a fermented wash to the distillery and they continue distilling a whisky called Rothaus Black Forest Single Malt Whisky which matured in bourbon casks. The whisky was launched for the first time in 2009 and, every year in March, a new batch is released. Around 6,000 bottles are produced every year.

Alt Enderle Brennerei

Rosenberg/Sindolsheim, founded in 1988 (whisky since 2000)

www.alt-enderle-brennerei.de

While concentrating on the production of schnapps, gin, rum and absinthe, Joachim Alt and Michael Enderle produced their first malt whisky in 2000. They have two core expressions for sale – an 8 year old Neccarus and a recently released 12 year old. The latest limited release was the 7 year old, smoky Terrador. The whisky is matured in a combination of bourbon and sherry casks. In 2013 Neccarus was awarded as the best German whisky.

Brennerei Ziegler

Freudenberg, founded in 1865

www.brennerei-ziegler.de

Like so many other distilleries in Germany, Ziegler has distillation of spirits from fruits and berries as their main business, but has also added a small whisky production. One characteristic that distinguishes itself from most other distilleries is that the maturation takes place not only in oak casks, but also in casks made of chestnut! Their current bottling is a 5 year old called Aureum 1865 Single Malt and there is also a cask strength version.

AV Brennerei

Wincheringen, founded in 1824 (whisky since 2006)

www.avadisdistillery.de

For generations, the Vallendar family have been making schnapps and edelbrände on a farm in an area where France, Luxembourg and Germany's borders meet. Since 2006 the brothers Andreas and Carlo Vallendar, also produce malt whisky. Around 2,000 bottles per annum are available for purchase and the oak casks from France have previously been used for maturing white Mosel wine. Threeland Whisky is a 3 year old and the range also consists of two finishes – Oloroso and Port.

Birkenhof-Brennerei

Nistertal, founded in 1848 (whisky since 2002)

www.birkenhof-brennerei.de

The traditional production of edelbrände made from a delightful variety of fruits and berries was complemented with whisky production in 2002. The first release was a 5 year old rye whisky under the name Fading Hill in 2008. This was followed a year later by a single malt. The most recent bottlings are from 2016 with a single malt and single rye 6 years old.

Brennerei Faber

Ferschweiler, founded in 1949

www.faber-eifelbrand.de

Established as a producer of eau-de vie from fruits and berries, Ludwig Faber – the third generation of the owners – has included whisky production during the last few years. The only whisky so far is a single malt that has matured for 6 years in barrels made of American white oak.

Steinhauser Destillerie

Kressbronn, founded in 1828 (whisky since 2008)

www.weinkellerei-steinhauser.de

The distillery is situated in the very south of Germany, near Lake Constance, close to Austria. The main products are spirits which are derived from fruits, but whisky also has its own niche. The first release was the single malt Brigantia which was released in November 2011. It was triple distilled and only 111 bottles were released. More releases have fololwed since. The ultimate goal is to release a 12 year old in 2020 under the name of Constantia.

Weingut Simons

Alzenau-Michelbach, founded in 1879 (whisky since 1998)

www.feinbrenner.eu

The owner, Severin Simon, produces wine from his own vineyards, spirits from fruit as well as gin, vodka, rum and whisky. Until recently all the whisky was produced in a 150 litre still but a new still from Arnold Holstein was installed in June 2013, raising the whisky production from 300 litres per year to 3-5,000 litres. A pure pot still whisky has since been released and the first whisky from 100% malted barley was distilled in January 2013. In March 2016, the first whisky from the new still was released – a 100% rye.

Nordpfälzer Edelobst & Whiskydestille

Winnweiler, founded in 2008

www.nordpfalz-brennerei.de

This distillery owned by Bernhard Höning is based on the production of spirits from fruits but also distilling whisky. The first release was in 2011, a 3 year old single malt by the name Taranis with a full maturation in a Sauternes cask and in October 2013 a 4 year old from ex-bourbon casks with an Amarone finish was launched. Regular releases have occured since. In September 2013 a second distillery including a tasting room was opened and Höning is now producing 12 barrels of whisky per year.

Destillerie Drexler

Arrach, whisky since 2007

www.drexlers-whisky.de

The main business for Reinhard Drexler is the production of spirits from herbs, fruits and berries. In between he also finds the time to produce malt whisky and from August 2013 also rye whisky. The first release was Bayerwoid in 2011 which was followed up by the 3 year old No. 1 Single Cask Malt Whisky and a 100% malted rye whisky. The whisky matures in fresh American oak and casks that have previously been used for sherry, bourbon and cognac.

Destillerie & Brennerei Heinrich Habbel

Sprockhövel, founded in 1878 (whisky since 1977)

www.habbel.com

Already in 1977, Michael Habbel produced his first whisky from 85% rye and 15% malted barley. After a 10 year maturation in bourbon casks, the whisky was transferred into stainless steel tanks and wasn´t released until a few years ago as Habbel´s Uralter Whisky. Meanwhile, the distillery has produced different eau de vie, schnapps, vodka and gin. In spring of 2014 a designated whisky distillery called Hillock Park Distillery was opened on the premises and the plan is to produce 50 casks per year. A sample of the product has already been released in the shape of a newmake – Hillock White Dog (78% rye and 22% malted barley).

Märkische Spezialitäten Brennerei

Hagen, whisky since 2010

www.msb-hagen.de

Under the brand name Bonum Bono, Klaus Wurm and Christian Vormann produce spirits and liqueurs from various fruits. In autumn 2010 they added whisky to the range. Around 20 casks are produced yearly. The spirit is distilled four times, matured in ex-bourbon barrels in the distillery warehouse for 12 months and then brought to a cave, with low temperature and high humidity, 20 kilometres from the distillery for further maturation. The first releases were new make and aged spirit with the first 3 year old whisky, Tronje van Hagen, being released in 2013. More bottles followed in 2014. The whisky has now been renamed DeCavo ("from the cave", in allusion to where the maturation takes place).

Dürr Edelbranntweine

Neubulach, founded in 2002

www.blackforest-whiskey.com

Third generation distillers, Nicolas and Sebastian Dürr, began producing whisky in 2002. It wasn't until 2012 when their first single malt (limited to 200 bottles) reached the market. Doinich Daal Batch 1 was a 4 year old matured in a combination of bourbon and cognac casks. Batch two (Malachit and Azurit editions) was released in November 2014.

Brennerei Feller

Dietenheim-Regglisweiler, founded in 1903
(whisky since 2008)

www.brennerei-feller.de

Roland Feller, the owner of this old schnapps distillery, took up whisky production in 2008 and four years later he released his first single malt, the 3 year old Valerie (recent releases are 4 years old) matured in bourbon casks. It was later followed by Augustus and Augustus Corado, both single wheat whiskies with a port finish.

Tecker Whisky-Destillerie

Owen, founded in 1979 (whisky since 1989)

www.tecker.eu

Founded by one of the German whisky pioneers, Christian Gruel, the distillery is run by his grandchild Immanuel Gruel, since five

years back. Apart from a variety of eau de vie and other spirits, approximately 1,500 litres of whisky is produced annually. The core expression is the 5 year old Tecker Single Malt matured in sherry casks and a 5 year old Tecker Single Grain. Limited releases have included a cask strength 10 year old single malt and a cask strength 14 year old single grain.

Marder Edelbrände

Albbruck-Unteralpfen, founded in 1953 (whisky since 2009)

www.marder-edelbraende.de

Apart from a vast number of distillates from different fruits, Stefan Marder also produces whisky since 2009. The first release came in 2013 - the 3 year old Marder Single Malt matured in a combination of new American oak and sherry casks. One thousand bottles were released and the latest edition, matured in port pipes, was launched in July 2015.

Edelbrände Senft

Salem-Rickenbach, founded in 1988 (whisky since 2009)

www.edelbraende-senft.de

When Herbert Senft started whisky production, he experimented with a variety of different grains but, in future, he will be concentrating on whisky from 100% malted barley. The first 2,000 bottles of 3.5 year old Senft Bodensee Whisky were released in 2012 and they were later followed by a cask strength version (55%).

Sperbers Destillerie

Rentweinsdorf, founded in 1923 (whisky since 2002)

www.salmsdorf.de

Apart from distilling eau de vie and liqueurs from fruits, Helmut Sperber has also been producing whisky since 2002. At the moment, four different expressions have been released, all of them 7 years old – single malt matured in bourbon casks, single malt matured in a mix of sherry and bourbons casks, a sherrymatured single malt bottled at cask strength, as well as,a single grain whisky from a mix of bourbon, sherry and Spessart oak casks.

Schwarzwaldbrennerei Walter Seger

Calw-Holzbronn, founded in 1952 (whisky since 1990)

www.krabba-nescht.de

Incorporated with a restaurant, this distillery which, apart from producing eau de vie from berries and fruit, also produces whisky. The first single malt was launched in 2009 and at the moment, Walter Seger has two expressions in the range; the 4 year old Black-Wood single malt matured in amontillado sherry casks and an 8 year old wheat whisky.

Landgasthof Gemmer

Rettert, founded in 1908 (whisky since 2008)

www.landgasthof-gemmer.de

The current owner, Klaus Gemmer, is the fourth generation running this distillery, and he was also the one who introduced whisky production in 2008. Their only single malt is the 3 year old Georg IV which has matured for two years in toasted Spessart oak casks and finished for one year in casks that have contained Banyuls wine. Around 800 litres are produced per year.

Hausbrauerei Altstadthof

Nürnberg, founded in 1984

www.hausbrauerei-altstadthof.de

The brewery component of this establishment was founded in 1984 and later Reinhard Engel also added a distillery. He produced the first German organic single malt and the current range consists of the 4 year old Ayrer´s Red bottled at 43% and 58%, both matured in new American oak, Ayrer´s PX, bottled at 56% and finished in

PX sherry casks, Ayrer´s Bourbon, bottled at 51% and matured in bourbon barrels and Ayrer´s Master Cut, bottled at an exceptional 74.2%. There is also Ayrer´s White which is an 8 week old whisky spirit.

Destillerie Mösslein

Zeilitzheim, founded in 1984 (whisky since 1999)

www.frankenwhisky.de

Originally a winery but also producing a wide range of eau de vie from fruits, whisky production was brought on board in 1999. The first whisky was released in 2003 and, at the moment, the owner, Reiner Mösslein, can offer two types of whisky – a single malt and a grain whisky, both 5 years old.

Brennerei Josef Druffel

Oelde-Stromberg, founded in 1792 (whisky since 2010)

www.brennerei-druffel.de

Jochen Druffel is the seventh generation to run this old family distillery. A variety of different spirits are distilled with schnapps and liqueur made from plums as a speciality. The first single malt, Prum, was released in 2013 and had matured in a mix of different casks (bourbon, sherry, red wine and new Spessart oak) and was finished in small casks made of plum tree! In 2015, a 5 year old version was released.

Brauhaus am Lohberg

Wismar, whisky since 2010

www.brauhaus-wismar.de

This unique combination of a guesthouse, brewery and distillery is situated at the centre of Wismar in a building from the 15th century. Here Herbert Wenzel has been producing whisky since 2010. The first release of Baltach single malt was in December 2013. It was a 3 year old with a finish in sherry casks. The latest edition of Baltach was released in July 2016.

Wild Brennerei

Gengenbach, founded in 1855 (whisky since 2002)

www.wild-brennerei.de

The distillation of whisky constitutes only a small part of the production but Franz Wild has released two 5 year old whiskies – Wild Whisky Single Malt which has matured for three years in American white oak and another two in either sherry or port casks and Wild Whisky Grain, made from unmalted barley and with a similar maturation.

Brennerei Volker Theurer

Tübingen, founded in 1995

www.schwaebischer-whisky.de

Located in a guesthouse, this distillery which is run by Volker Theurer has been producing whisky since 1995. The first release was a 7 year old in 2003 and since then he has released Sankt Johann, an 8 year old single malt and the 9 year old Tammer which has been double matured in bourbon and sherry casks. Theurer is also selling a blended whisky called Original Ammertal Whisky.

Iceland

Distillery:	Eimverk Distillery, Reykjavik
Founded:	2012
Owner:	Thorelsson family
	flokiwhisky.is

The country´s first whisky distillery emanated from an idea in 2008 when the three Thorkelsson brothers discussed the possibility of producing whisky in Iceland. In 2011 a company was formed, the first distillation was made in the ensuing year and full scale production started in August 2013. Only organic barley grown in Iceland is used for the production and everything is malted on site. The barley variety is low in sugars and it takes 50% more barley than usual to produce a bottle of whisky. The distillery is equipped with an Arnold Holstein still and the annual capacity has recently been increased to 75,000 litres with a goal to reach 100,000 litres end of 2015. Fifty percent of the capacity is reserved for gin and aquavite and the rest for whisky. The first, limited whisky release is expected to be in 2017. Currently, the distillery is offering Flóki young malt, a spirit which has matured for one year in fresh oak. The owners also have Vor Gin and Vití Aquavit for sale. In summer 2014 the first smoky spirit was distilled, using both peat and sheep dung to dry the barley.

Republic of Ireland

Distillery:	Midleton Distillery, Midleton, Co. Cork
Founded:	1975
Owner:	Irish Distillers (Pernod Ricard)
	irishdistillers.ie

Midleton is by far the biggest distillery in Ireland and the home of Jameson´s Irish Whiskey. The distillery that we see today is barely 40 years old, but Jameson´s as a brand dates back much further. John Jameson, the founder, moved from Scotland to Ireland in 1777 and became part-owner in a distillery called Bow Street Distillery in Dublin. Some years later he became the sole owner and renamed the company John Jameson & Son.

In 1966, John Jameson & Son with their distillery in Bow Street, merged with John Power & Son, as well as Cork Distillery Company to form Irish Distillers Group. It was decided that the production of the three companies should move to Midleton Distillery in Cork. The result was that the Bow Street Distilllery was closed in 1971. Four years later an ultra modern distillery was built next to the old Midleton distillery and this is what we can see today, while the old distillery has been refurbished asa visitor attraction. The production at Midleton comprises of two sections – grain whiskey and single pot still whiskey. The grain whiskey is needed for the blends, where Jameson´s is the biggest seller. Single pot still whiskey, on the other hand, is unique to Ireland. This part of the production is also used for the blends but is being bottled more and more on its own.

Midleton distillery is equipped with mash tuns both for the barley side and the grain side. Until recently, there were 14 washbacks for grain and 10 for barley, four, large copper pot stills and 5 column stills. The hugely increased demand for Irish whiskey, and for Jameson's in particular, has now forced the owners to greatly expand their capacitiy. The expansion, which was completed in autumn 2013, included a completely new brew house and 24 washbacks, a new still house with three more pot stills (80,000 litres each) and six, new, larger columns replacing the existing ones. A new maturation facility with 40 warehouses has also been built in Dungourney, not far from Midleton. The investment for the whole expansion was €200m and the capacity of the distillery is now 64 million litres of pure alcohol. The sales increase over the past few years has also forced the owners to invest €17m to increase the bottling plant in Clondalkin. By 2017 they will be able to bottle 120 million bottles per year.

Of all the brands produced at Midleton, Jameson´s blended Irish whiskey is by far the biggest. In 2014 the brand sold 56 million bottles of which more than 40% was sold to the USA. Apart from the core expression with no age statement, there are 12 and 18 year olds, Black Barrel, Gold Reserve and a Vintage. In autumn 2015 a new range, Deconstructed, was released for travel retail with three bottlings - Bold, Lively and Round. Other blended whiskey brands include Paddy, Powers and the exclusive Midleton Very Rare. In recent years, Midleton has invested increasingly in their second category of whiskies, single pot still, and that range now includes Redbreast (12, 12 cask strength, 15, 21 year old, the sherrymatured Mano a Lámh and a new single cask), Green Spot (no age and the 12 year old Leoville Barton bordeaux finish), Yellow Spot 12 years old, Powers (John´s Lane, Signature and Three Swallow) and Barry Crocket Legacy. In spring of 2015, the unique single pot still Midleton Dair Ghaelach was launched. It is the first ever Irish whiskey to be finished in virgin Irish oak. It has been matured for between 15 and 22 years in bourbon casks before the finish in Irish oak. Ten different version reflecting ten different trees were released.

In autumn 2015, a new micro distillery adjacent to the existing distillery, was opened. With a production capacity of 400 casks per year, it will be used for experiments and innovation.

Distillery:	Tullamore Dew Distillery, Clonminch, Co. Offaly
Founded:	2014
Owner:	Wm Grant & Sons
	tullamoredew.com

Until 1954, Tullamore D.E.W. was distilled at Daly´s Distillery in Tullamore. When it closed, production was temporarily moved to Power´s Distillery in Dublin, and was later moved to Midleton Distillery and Bushmill´s Distillery. William Grant & Sons acquired Tullamore D.E.W. in 2010 and in March 2012, they announced that they were in the final stages of negotiations to acquire a site at Clonminch, situated on the outskirts of Tullamore. Construction of a new distillery began in May 2013 and in autumn 2014, the distillery was ready to start production. The construction will be executed in three phases where the first was a pot still distillery with the possibility to distil 1,8 million litres per year. In early 2016, it was increased to 3,6 million litres by the addition of more stills and washbacks. Finally, in May 2016, the company was seeking planning permission for a further development including a grain distillery with a capacity of doing 8 million litres of grain spirit.

Tullamore D.E.W. is the second biggest selling Irish whiskey in the world after Jameson with 10 million bottles sold in 2015. The core range consists of Original (without age statement), 12 year old Special Reserve and 10, 14 and 18 year old Single Malts. Recent limited releases include Trilogy (a triple blend whiskey matured in three types of wood) and Phoenix. As an exclusive to duty free, the Tullamore D.E.W Cider Cask Finish was launched in summer 2015. The whiskey had been finished for three months in casks that had previously been used to produce apple cider.

Distillery:	Cooley Distillery, Cooley, Co. Louth
Founded:	1987
Owner:	Beam Suntory
	kilbeggandistillingcompany.com

In 1987, the entrepreneur John Teeling bought the disused Ceimici Teo distillery and renamed it Cooley distillery. Two years later he installed two pot stills and in 1992 he released the first single malt from the distillery, called Locke´s Single Malt. Due to financial difficulties, the distillery was forced to close down but was re-opened in 1995. A number of brands were launched over the years and Teeling got several offers from companies wanting to buy Cooley. Finally, in December 2011 it was announced that Beam Inc. had acquired the distillery for $95m. The most important part of the takeover for Beam's was the Kilbeggan blended whiskey brand that had already reached some level of success on the American market. In spring 2014, Suntory took over Beam in a $16bn deal and the new company was renamed Beam Suntory.

Cooley distillery is equipped with one mash tun, four malt and six grain washbacks all made of stainless steel, two copper pot stills and two column stills. There is a production capacity of 650,000 litres of malt spirit and 2,6 million litres of grain spirit.

The Cooley range of whiskies consists of several brands. Connemara single malts, which are all more or less peated, consist of a no age, a 12 year old and a 22 year old. The other brand is Tyrconnel bottled without age statement. Other Tyrconnel expressions which have now been discontinued included a 15 year old single cask and several wood finishes. The distillery also produces the single grain Greenore where there currently are three expressions – 6 year old (created for the Swedish market), 8 year old and 18 year old. In spring 2015, the owners re-branded Greenore and it now goes under the name Kilbeggan single grain.

Midleton´s new still house

Distillery: Teeling Distillery
Founded: 2015
Owner: Teeling Whiskey Co.
teelingwhiskey.com

After the Teeling family had sold Cooley and Kilbeggan distilleries to Beam in 2011, the family started a new company, Teeling Whiskey. A wide range of whiskeys have been released since then, all made from stock made at Cooley which the family kept while selling the distilleries. However, all the while, they have planned for a new distillery of their own. John Teeling, the father of the family, has been working on his own project, turning Great Northern Brewery in Dundalk into a distillery. His sons, Jack and Stephen, beat him to it though, when they opened their own distillery in Newmarket, Dublin in June 2015 (it was actually commissioned already in March). This was the first new distillery in Dublin in 125 years.

The distillery is equipped with two wooden washbacks, four made of stainless steel and three stills made in Sienna, Italy; wash still (15,000 litres), intermediate still (10,000 litres) and spirit still (9,000 litres) and the capacity is 500,000 litres of alcohol. Both pot still and malt whisky will be produced and the total investment is 10 million euros. With the distillery in Dublin, the Teeling family are coming back to their roots. The family´s involvement in the whiskey industry started in 1782 when Walter Teeling owned a distillery on Marrowbone Lane in Dublin. One year after the opening, an amazing 60,000 people had been welcomed to the distillery! When the distillery opened, Revival, a bottling from old stock made at Cooley was released. In June 2016, it was time for Revival II – a 13 year old with 12 months finish in calvados casks.

Distillery: Walsh Whiskey Distillery, Carlow, Co. Carlow
Founded: 2016
Owner: Bernard Walsh, Illva Saronno
walshwhiskey.com

Bernard Walsh, CEO and owner of The Irishman Brands with whiskies like The Irishman and Writer´s Tears (both produced at Midleton), announced in autumn 2013 that he planned to build a distillery at Royal Oak, Carlow. It was later revealed that his company and thus the project in general, were backed up by the major Italian drinks company, Illva Saronno. Construction began in

late 2014 and the distillery was commissioned in March 2016. It is one of the largest whiskey distilleries in Ireland with a capacity of 2.5 million litres of alcohol. All types of whiskey will be produced including grain- malt- and pot still whiskey. The equipment consists of a 3 ton semi-lauter mash tun, six washbacks, a 15,000 litre wash still, a 7,500 litre intermediate still and a 10,000 litre spirit still. There is also a column still for grain whiskey production. Apart from producing whiskey for its own brands, the distillery has allocated 15% of the output for a small number of international partners and the first deal was concluded in May with the Finnish company, Altia, for a supply of both malt and grain whiskey for its brands.

Distillery: Great Northern Distillery, Dundalk, Co. Louth
Founded: 2015
Owner: The Irish Whiskey Co.
gndireland.com

The Irish Whiskey Company (IWC), which has the Teeling family as the majority owners, signed an agreement with Diageo in August 2013, thus taking over the Great Northern Brewery in Dundalk. Diageo was about to move the brewing operation to Dublin and the IWC started restructuring the site into Great Northern Distillery at a cost of €35m. When it became operational in August 2015, it became the second biggest distillery in Ireland after Midleton, with the capacity to produce 3.6 million litres of pot still whiskey and 8 million litres of grain spirit. The distillery is equipped with three columns for the grain spirit production and three pot stills for producing malt and single pot still whiskey. The distillery has been producing malt whiskey since September 2015 and the main part of the business will be to supply whiskey to private label brands, rather than under its own name. Great Northern Distillery is owned by the Teeling family and two former directors of Cooley Distillery, Jim Finn and David Hynes.

Distillery: Waterford Distillery, Waterford, Co. Waterford
Founded: 2015
Owner: Mark Reynier
waterforddistillery.ie

The former co-owner of Bruichladdich distillery on Islay, Mark Reynier, has always been a man of action. When he, more or less

Teeling Distillery in Newmarket, Dublin attracted 60,000 visitors in the first year

against his will, was forced to sell the Islay distillery in 2012, he soon started to consider building a new distillery and this time in Ireland. In 2014 he bought the Diageo-owned Waterford Brewery in south east Ireland and only 16 months later, in December 2015, the first spirit was distilled. The distillery is equipped with two pot stills and one column still and, even though grain spirit will be produced, malt whiskey will become the number one priority. The two pot stills have an interesting story. Built in 1972, they were used for 19 years at Inverleven distillery in Scotland until 1991 when the distillery closed. Later on, they were bought by Bruichladdich to be used in the planned Port Charlotte distillery. When that did not come to fruition, Reynier bought the pair of pot stills and shipped them to Waterford. In keeping with the business at Bruichladdich, local barley will be the main focus and Reynier will be sourcing the barley from 46 different Irish farms. The distillery has a capacity of 1 million litres but the owners have plans to go up to 3 million litres in the future. No other spirits will be distilled in order to create cash flow and Reynier`s expectation is that the first whiskey will be bottled in four to five years´ time.

Other distilleries in Ireland

Kilbeggan Distillery

Kilbeggan, Co. Westmeath, founded in 1757

www.kilbegganwhiskey.com

It was the owners of Cooley distillery with John Teeling at the forefront, who decided in 2007 to bring this distillery back to life and it is now the oldest producing whiskey distillery in the world. In 2011, Cooley Distillery was taken over by Beam Inc. and in spring 2014, Suntory bought Beam, which means that the current owners are the newly formed Beam Suntory. The distillery is equipped with a wooden mash tun, four Oregon pine washbacks and two stills with one of them being 180 years old. The production at the distillery spans over a wide range of techniques and whiskey varieties including malt whiskey, pure pot still whiskey (malted and unmalted barley mixed), rye whiskey from pot stills and triple distillation. The first single malt whiskey release (the 3 year old Kilbeggan Distillery Reserve) from the new production came in June 2010 and limited batches have been released thereafter. The core blended expression of Kilbeggan is a no age statement bottling but limited releases of aged Kilbeggan blend (15, 18 and 21 year

old) have occurred. To confuse matters, since spring 2015 there is also a Kilbeggan single grain, produced at Cooley, which used to be called Greenore.

West Cork Distillers

Skibbereen, Co. Cork, founded in 2004

www.westcorkdistillers.com

Started by John O´Connell, Denis McCarthy and Ger McCarthy in 2003 in Union Hall in West Cork, the distillery moved in 2013 to the present site. The distillery is equipped with four stills with the two wash stills coming from Sweden and the two spirit stills having been manufactured in Germany. The distillery is producing both malt whiskey and grain whiskey (from barley and wheat) and some of the malting is done on site. Apart from a range of vodka, gin and liqueurs, a 10 year old single malt and a blended whiskey are sold under the name West Cork. The Pogues Irish Whiskey, developed together with Barry Walsh and Springbank´s former production manager Frank McHardy and launched in collaboration with the Irish band The Pogues, was released in 2015.

Connacht Whiskey Company

Ballina, Co. Mayo, founded in 2016

connachtwhiskey.com

The distillery, which nestles on the banks of the River Moy in northwest Ireland, was founded by three Americans - Robert Cassell, Tom Jensen and PJ Stapleton - and one Irishman, David Stapleton. It is equipped with three pot stills which were made in Canada (comprising of 2500, 1800 and 1500 litres respectively) and the first distillation of whiskey was made in April 2016. Apart from malt whiskey and single pot still whiskey, the owners are also producing vodka, gin and poitin - all of which have already been released. It has the capacity to produce 300,000 litres of pure alcohol per year but for the first year, the plan is to do only 70,000 litres. Local barley is used and Robert Cassell, who is the Master Distiller, has decided to use a combination of several malts to create a special flavour. A visitor centre with different tours and tutored tastings opened in summer 2016. A sourced, single malt has also been released – namely the 10 year old Spade & Bushel.

Bernard Walsh - founder and co-owner of Walsh Whiskey Distillery

The Dingle Whiskey Distillery

Milltown, Dingle, Co. Kerry, founded in 2012

www.dingledistillery.ie

Permission to build a distillery in Dingle, County Kerry, was applied for in 2008 and was granted in 2009. The people whose brainchild it was, Oliver Hughes, founder of the Porterhouse group of pubs and Jerry O´Sullivan, managing director of Southbound Properties, planned to convert an old creamery into a distillery. In 2010, the former business partners went their separate ways and Oliver Hughes found a new location, the old Fitzgerald sawmills and set about transforming the site into a distillery. Three pot stills and a combined gin/vodka still were installed in June 2012 and the first production of gin and vodka was in October. Whisky distillation began in December and the plan is to produce 100,000 bottles per year. The first products that were launched were Dingle Original Gin and DD Vodka. The first whiskey, the limited Dingle Cask No. 2, was released in December 2015 and a general release is expected in autumn 2016. In July 2016, co-founder Oliver Hughes died unexpectadly at the age of 57.

The Shed Distillery

Drumshanbo, Co. Leitrim, founded in 2015

www.thesheddistillery.com

One of the newest distilleries in Ireland, The Shed Distillery was founded by entrepreneur Pat Rigney who is a veteran in the drinks business, having worked with brands like Bailey´s, Gilbey´s and Grant´s. The distillery cost €2m to build and is equipped with three Holstein stills with columns attached. The focus for the owners will be single pot still whiskey but the product range also includes potato vodka, gin and liqueurs. The first whiskey distillation was in January 2015.

Boann Distillery

Drogheda, Co. Meath, founded in 2016

boanndistillery.ie

One of the latest distilleries in Ireland to come on stream and being of a considerable size, Boann Distillery is owned by the Cooney family. Under forty years, Pat Cooney built the Gleeson Group up from a small independent bottler to a leading supplier and distributor in the drinks business. In 2012, he sold most of

the company to C&C Group and, together with his wife and five children, he started planning a distillery of their own. Assisted by the well-known whisky consultant, John McDougall, the distillery has taken shape and production will start in autumn 2016 Three copper pot stills (10,000, 7,500 and 5,000 litres respectively) were ordered from Italy and they have been supplemented by a 500-litre Bennett gin still. On top of that, the distillery is equipped with a state of the art brewing equipment and will also produce craft beers. There is also a visitor centre with bar and restaurant.

Glendalough Distillery

Newtown Mount Kennedy, Co. Wicklow, founded in 2012

glendaloughdistillery.com

The distillery was founded by five friends from Wicklow and Dublin in 2012. For the first three years, they acted as independent bottlers, sourcing their whisky mainly from Cooley distillery. A range of Glendalough whiskey was soon created with two single malts (7 and 13 years old) and a Double Barrel blend made from 90% corn and 10% malted barley and with a 3.5 year maturation in ex bourbon barrels and six months finish in oloroso casks. In 2015 Holstein stills were installed and gin production began, which was followed by whiskey in the ensuing autumn

Italy

Distillery:	Puni Destillerie, Glurns, South Tyrol
Founded:	2012
Owner:	Ebensperger family
	puni.com

The lack of a whisky distillery in Italy was rectified in February 2012 when the first spirit was distilled at Puni distillery, situated in South Tyrol in the north of Italy. It is owned and run by the Ebensperger family with Albrecht, the father, and one of his sons, Jonas, as the dominant figures. There are at least two things that distinguish this project from most others. One characteristic is the design of the distillery – a 13-metre tall cube made of red brick. The other is the raw material that they are using. They are making malt whisky but malted barley is only one of three cereals in the recipe. The other two are malted rye and malted wheat. The family calls

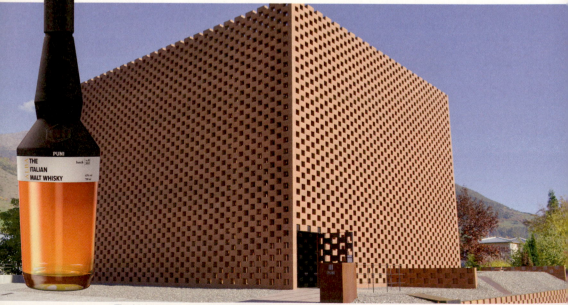

The highly original Puni Distillery in South Tyrol and their latest bottling - Puni Nero

it Triple Malt and it is their intention to use this combination of cereals for their main line of whiskies. In 2016, however, they also started distilling 100% malted barley and anticipate to release their first whisky from that production in 2019.

The distillery is equipped with five washbacks made of local larch and the fermentation time is 84 hours. There is one wash still (3,000 litres) and one spirit still (2,000 litres) and the capacity is 80,000 litres of alcohol per year. For maturation, mainly ex-Bourbon barrels and ex-Marsala casks are being used. Some of the casks are maturing in old bunkers from the Second World War.

In October 2015, it was time for the first release of, not one but two, Italian single malt whisky – both with natural colour and un chill-filtered. Puni Nova was matured in American white oak for three years while Puni Alba had been matured for three years in Marsala casks and then finished in Islay casks. The next release, in October 2016, was Puni Nero which had been matured in Pinot Nero casks from nearby wineries. A total of 3,000 bottles at 43% were released.

Liechtenstein

Distillery:	Brennerei Telser, Triesen
Founded:	1880 (whisky since 2006)
Owner:	Telser family
	brennerei-telser.com

The first distillery in Liechtenstein to produce whisky is not a new distillery. It has existed since 1880 and is now run by the fourth generation of the family. Traditions are strong and Telser is probably the only distillery in Europe still using a wood fire to heat the small stills (150 and 120 litres). Telser produces mainly spirits from fruits and berries, including grappa and vodka. For whisky, the distillery uses a mixture of three different malts (some peated) which are fermented and distilled separately. After an extremely long fermentation (lasting 10 days), the spirit is triple distilled and the three different spirits are blended and filled into pinot noir barriques and left to mature for a minimum of three years. The first bottling of Telsington was distilled in 2006 and released in 2009. In 2014, the name was changed from Telsington to Liechtenstein Whisky and edition VII, a 5 year old, matured in a pinot noir cask was released. This was followed in autumn 2015 by VIII and in spring 2016 by IX which had been matured in a pinot noir cask.

The Netherlands

Distillery:	Zuidam Distillers, Baarle Nassau
Founded:	1974 (whisky since 1998)
Owner:	Zuidam family
	zuidam.eu

Zuidam Distillers was started in 1974 as a traditional, family distillery producing liqueurs, genever, gin and vodka. The first release of a whisky, which goes by the name Millstone, was from the 2002 production and it was bottled in 2007 as a 5 year old. The current range is a 5 year old which comes in both peated and unpeated versions, American oak 10 years, French oak 10 years, Sherry oak 12 years and PX Cask 1999, a 14 year old bottled at 46%. Apart from single malts there is also a Millstone 100% Rye which is bottled at 50%. Recent limited releases include a 6 year old, triple distilled three grain whisky (equal parts of corn, rye and malted barley) and a 3 year old, triple distilled five grain whisky (wheat, corn, rye, spelt and malted barley).

The distillery has been expanded at an impressive pace during the last years and the equipment now consists of one mash tun for malt whisky, one for rye and genever and 10 washbacks (three of them installed in 2015). Furthermore, there are a total of five stills with

volumes ranging from 850 litres up to 5,000 litres. The total capacity is 280,000 litres of pure alcohol per year. But the expansion doesn´t stop at that. Patrick van Zuidam has plans to build a second distillery at a farm where they will be growing their own barley and rye as well. The distillery will be equipped with four pot stills (5,000 litres each) with the possibility of adding another six. In summer 2016, the company was still waiting for the final permits.

Other distilleries in The Netherlands

Us Heit Distillery

Bolsward, founded in 2002

www.usheit.com

This is one of many examples where a beer brewery also contains a whisky distillery. Frysk Hynder was the first Dutch whisky and made its debut in 2005 at 3 years of age. The barley is grown in surrounding Friesland and malted at the distillery. Some 10,000 bottles are produced annually and the whisky (3 to 5 years old) is matured in various casks – sherry, bourbon, red wine, port and cognac. A cask strength version has also been released.

Kalkwijck Distillers

Vroomshoop, founded in 2009

www.kalkwijckdistillers.nl

Lisanne Benus and her father Bert opened their distillery in 2009. Kalkwijck is located in Vroomshoop, in the rural eastern part of the Netherlands. Lisanne is one of the youngest whisky producers in the world and was trained by, amongst others, Patrick van Zuidam, the maker of Millstone whisky. The distillery is equipped with a 300 litre pot still still with a column attached. The main part of the production is jenever, korenwijn and liqueurs but whisky has been distilled since 2010. In spring 2015, the first single malt was released. Eastmoor is 3 years old, made from barley grown on the estate and bottled at 40%. The first release was only 200 bottles but a second edition was launched already in May.

Turv Exloo Distillery

Exloo, founded in 2016

www.turv.nl

This new distillery, founded and owned by Matthieu and Helmy Smakman, is equipped with eight 2,650 litre stainless steel washbacks and one 1,500 copper pot still with tho columns attached for further refinement of some of the products. The spirit safe is equipped with a new and unique technology which helps separate different alcohols on a molecular basis, thereby making it easier to collect those that contribute to the desired character of the spirit. The capacity of the distillery is 780,000 litres of alcohol and apart from malt- and grain whisky, a number of other spirits are produced including jenever, rum and gin. The main part of the whisky is matured in new American oak.

Stokerij Sculte

Ootmarsum, founded in 2004 (whisky since 2011)

www.stokerijsculte.nl

Gerard Velthuis started the distillery in 2004, focusing on spirits made from fruit. From 2011, malt whisky is also on the agenda. The distillery is equipped with a 500 litre stainless steel mashtun, 4 stainless steel washbacks with a fermentation time of 4-5 days and two Austrian made stills (250 and 110 litres respectively). The first Sculte Twentse Whisky was released in October 2014 and this was followed by a 4 year old in May 2016. Om both occasions 500 bottles were released. Velthuis is now working on new recipes, including a heavily peated, with the aim to start releasing them in 2019/2020. The whisky matures in casks, 55 litres up to 220 litres, made of Dutch oak

Northern Ireland

Distillery: Bushmill´s Distillery, Bushmills, Co. Antrim
Founded: 1784
Owner: Casa Cuervo

bushmills.com

Diageo, the owners of Bushmill´s since 2005, took the market by surprise when they announced in November 2014 that they were selling the distillery. This was Diageo´s only part of the vibrant, increasing Irish whiskey segment and commentators struggled to see the reason for the sale. The buyer was the tequila maker Casa Cuervo, producer of the well-known José Cuervo. Diageo already owned 50% of the company´s other, upscale tequila brand, Don Julio and with the deal, they got the remaining 50% as well as $408m.

Bushmills is the second biggest of the Irish distilleries after Midleton, with a capacity to produce 4,5 million litres of alcohol a year. In 1972 the distillery became a part of Irish Distillers Group which thereby gained control over the entire whiskey production in Ireland. Irish Distillers were later (1988) purchased by Pernod Ricard who, in turn, resold Bushmill´s to Diageo in 2005 at a price tag of €295.5 million. Since the take-over, Diageo invested heavily into the distillery and it now has ten stills with a production running seven days a week, which means 4,5 million litres a year. In December 2015, the new owners announced that they had applied for a planning permission to build a £30 million addition to the current distillery which would effectively double the production capacity. Included in the application were also plans to build a new visitor´s centre. Two kinds of malt are used at Bushmills, one unpeated and one slightly peated. The distillery uses triple distillation, which is the traditional Irish method.

Bushmill`s core range of single malts consists of a 10 year old, a 16 year old Triple Wood with a finish in Port pipes for 6-9 months and a 21 year old finished in Madeira casks for two years. There is also a 12 year old Distillery Reserve which is sold exclusively at the distillery and the 1608 Anniversary Edition. Black Bush and Bushmill´s Original are the two main blended whiskeys in the range. In spring 2016, Bushmill´s launched their first whiskey exclusive for duty free. The Steamship Collection will consist of three special cask matured whiskies plus a number of limited relea-

ses. The first part of the series was a no age-statement Sherry Cask Reserve. With close to 10 million bottles sold in 2015, Bushmill´s is the third most sold Irish whiskey after Jameson and Tullamore D.E.W.

Other distilleries in Northern Ireland

Echlinville Distillery

Kircubbin, Co. Down, founded in 2013

www.echlinville.com

Shane Braniff, who launched the Feckin Irish Whiskey brand in 2005, has had plans for a distillery of his own for some time now. Feckin Irish Whiskey, which has become popular in USA, has so far been produced at Cooley Distillery but when Beam Inc. bought the distillery in 2012, the new owners decided not to supply whiskey to independent bottlers. Shane had already started the building of the new distillery located near Kircubbin on the Ards Peninsula and some of the equipment was already in place when they were granted a license by Customs and Excise in May 2013. Only a few weeks later, the first spirit was distilled. A new stillhouse with more stills was opened up in autumn 2015 as well as a visitor´s centre in April 2016. Apart from Feckin Irish Whiskey, Braniff has also recently revived the old Dunville´s brand of blended whiskey and released a 10 year old single malt with a finish in PX sherry casks as a part of the same range. Apart from single pot still and single malt whiskey, Echlinville also produces vodka and gin.

Rademon Estate Distillery

Downpatrick, Co. Down, founded in 2012

shortcrossgin.com

Fiona and David Boyd-Armstrong opened their distillery on the Rademon estate in 2012, which was owned by Frank Boyd, the father of Fiona. Since its inception, their main product has been Short Cross gin which quickly became a success story. In summer 2015 the production was expanded into whiskey and during the first year, around 100 barrels were filled. The couple are now planning to put in more stills to cope with the increased production of Irish malt whiskey.

Bushmill´s Distillery

Norway

Distillery: Det Norske Brenneri, Grimstad
Founded: 1952 (whisky since 2009)
Owner: Norske Brenneri AS
detnorskebrenneri.no

The company was founded in 1952 by Karl Gustav Puntervold and for more than 50 years it mainly produced wine from apples and other fruits. The company was taken over by Karl Gustav's son, Ole, in 1977. In July 2005 the state monopoly in terms of production of spirits in Norway was abolished and Ole decided to take advantage of that. He started to produce aquavit, among other products, and the first products were launched during autumn 2005. Whisky production started in 2009 and two Holstein stills are used for the distillation with a current yearly production of around 2,500 litres of alcohol. In November 2012 the first single malt produced in Norway was released (1,750 bottles). It was a single ex-sherry butt called Audny and in spring 2013 another 1,750 bottles were released. The third release of Audny appeared in May 2015 and in autumn the same year, Eiktyrne, a 3,5 year old, oloroso matured was released. In January 2014, K.G. Puntervold and Det Norske Brenneri (known as Agder Brenneri at the time) were sold to the companies' biggest customer – Norske Brenneri AS.

Other distilleries in Noway

Myken Distillery
Myken, founded in 2014
www.mykendestilleri.no

The latest whisky distillery to open in Norway, was built in the most unlikely place one can imagine. Myken is a group of islands in the Atlantic ocean, 32 kilometres from mainland Norway and 25 kilometres north of the Arctic Circle. The largest island has 9 people living the year round and this is where Myken distillery was opened in 2014. The distillery produced the first spirit in December 2014. The distillery is equipped with one wash still (1,000 litres), one spirit still (700 litres) and one gin still (300 litres) – all alambic style, made in Spain and direct fired using propane gas burners. The fermentation time is 60-140 hours and the capacity is 20,000 litres

per year. During 2016, the owners expect to do 7,000 litres. There are already plans to expand the distillery with two more stills.

The main part of the production is from unpeated malt but the first peated distillation (35ppm) was made in summer 2016. The production water is desalinated sea water, supplied by a municipal facility and the distillery is blessed with cold Arctic water the year round for the cooling. The only spirit released so far is Myken Arctic Gin and the plan is to release the first whisky in autumn 2018. The distillery was in 2016 expanded with a small visitor centre.

Arcus
Gjelleråsen, founded in 1996 (whisky since 2009)
www.arcus.no

Arcus is the biggest supplier and producer of wine and spirits in Norway with subsidiaries in Denmark, Finland and Sweden. They are also the largest aquavit producer in the world and are involved in cognac production in France. The first whisky produced by the distillery was released in 2013. Under the name Gjoleid, two whiskies made from malted barley and malted wheat were released – one matured in ex-bourbon American oak and the other in ex-oloroso American oak. Both whiskies are 3,5 years old.

Spain

Distillery: Distilerio Molino del Arco, Segovia
Founded: 1959
Owner: Distilerias y Crianza del Whisky (DYC)
dyc.es

Spain's first whisky distillery is not a small artisan distillery like so many others on these pages. Established by Nicomedes Garcia Lopez in 1959 (with whisky distilling commencing three years later), this is a distillery with capacity for producing eight million litres of grain whisky and two million litres of malt whisky per year. In addition to that, vodka and rum are produced and there are in-house maltings which safeguard malted barley for the production. The distillery is equipped with six copper pot stills and there are 250,000 casks maturing on site. The blending and bottling plant has been relocated to the Anis Castellana plant at Valverde del Majano.

The big seller when it comes to whiskies is a blend simply called DYC which is around 4 years old. It is supplemented by an 8 year old blend and, since 2007, also by DYC Pure Malt, i. e. a vatted malt consisting of malt from the distillery and from selected Scottish distilleries. A brand new expression was also launched in 2009 to commemorate the distillery's 50th anniversary – a 10 year old single malt, the first from the distillery. A recent extension of the range is DYC Red One which is a cherry infused whisky-based spirit which is bottled at 30%.

Other distilleries in Spain

Destilerias Liber
Padul, Granada, founded in 2001
www.destileriasliber.com

This distillery is quite a bit younger than its competitor in Segovia, DYC. Destilerias Liber was founded in 2001 but did not start production until late 2002. Like so many other, newly established distilleries, they started distilling rum, marc and vodka – spirits that do not require maturation and can also instantaneously generate cash to the company. For the whisky production, the spirit is double distilled after a fermentation of 48-72 hours. Maturation takes place in sherry casks. The only available whisky on the market is a 5 year old single malt called Embrujo de Granada.

The stills at Myken Distillery in Norway

Sweden

Distillery: Box Destilleri, Bjärtrå
Founded: 2010
Owner: Box Destilleri AB
boxwhisky.se

This northern distillery, set in buildings from the 19th century that had previously been used both as a box factory (hence the distillery name), as well as a power plant, is equipped with a four-roller Boby mill, a semilauter mash tun with a capacity of 1,5 tonnes and three stainless steel washbacks which can hold 8,000 litres each. The wash still (3,800 litres) and the spirit still (2,500 litres) were both made by Forsyth´s in Scotland. The first distillation was made in November 2010 and the distillery is currently producing 100,000 litres of pure alcohol per year.

Box Destilleri is making two types of whisky – fruity/unpeated and peated. As regards the former, the malted barley comes from Sweden, whereas the peated malt is imported from Belgium where it has been dried using peat from Islay. The distillery manager, Roger Melander, wants to create a new make which is as clean as possible by using a very slow distillation process with lots of copper contact in the still. The flavour of the spirit is also impacted by the effective condensation using what might be the coldest cooling water in the whisky world, namely 2-6ºC, which is obtained from a nearby river. A fermentation time of 72-96 hours also affects the character. A majority of the casks (80%), from 500 litres down to 40 litres, are first fill bourbon but Oloroso casks, virgin oak and casks made from Hungarian oak have also been filled. An interesting experiment was also started in 2016 when 100 small casks made of Japanese oak (Quercus mongolica) were filled with new make.

The first whisky, The Pioneer, was released on 5th June 2014 and all 5,000 bottles were sold out in less than 7 hours! Between 3 and 4 years old, it was a vatting of unpeated and lightly peated whisky, predominantly from bourbon casks but also a small amount of ex-sherry. The whisky was the first in a range of four called Early Days Collection with Challenger, Explorer and Messenger to follow. The next range, 2nd Step Collection was launched in 2016 where a lightly peated whisky, predominantly from oloroso casks was the latest release (September 2016). Two months later, the distillery launched its first core release, Dàlvve (the sami word for winter), bottled at 46%. But the buck didn´t stop there! The company has now decided to let the rest of the world know about its whisky and during autumn, a PX finish was released in Asia while a whisky, matured in American oak and with a finish in virgin oak, was released globally.

In June 2014 a new visitor centre was opened and warehouse capacity has also recently been expanded.

Distillery: Mackmyra Svensk Whisky, Valbo
Founded: 1999
Owner: Mackmyra Svensk Whisky AB
mackmyra.se

Mackmyra´s first distillery was built in 1999 and, ten years later, the company revealed plans to build a brand new facility in Gävle, a few miles from the present distillery. In 2012, the distillery was ready and the first distillation took place in spring of that year. The total investment, which included a whisky village to be built within a ten year period, was expected to amount to approximately £50 million. The construction of the new distillery is quite extraordinary and with its 37 metre structure, it is perhaps one of the tallest distilleries in the world. Since April 2013, all the distillation takes place at the new gravitation distillery, while the old distillery will be used for special runs and marketing activities.

The company seems to have overcome the financial problems that they have suffered in early 2014 even if production volumes are still relatively small compared to previous years (the equivalent of 60,000 bottles were distilled in 2015 compared to 750,000 in 2013). In 2015, 214,000 bottles were sold which represents an increase of 19% from the previous year. Apart from Sweden and other Nordic countries, Mackmyra is exported to Germany, France, Belgium and the UK.

Mackmyra whisky is based on two basic recipes, one which produces a fruity and elegant whisky, while the other is smokier. The smoke does not stem from peat, but from the juniper wood and

Set in beautiful surroundings, Box Distillery is now taking a second step leading them to markets around the world

bog moss being used. The first release was in 2006 and the distillery now has four core expressions; Svensk Ek, Brukswhisky, the peated Svensk Rök and, new since 2015, MACK by Mackmyra which competes in the lower price segment. A range of limited editions called Moment was introduced in December 2010 and consists of exceptional casks selected by the Master Blender, Angela D`Orazio. Two of the latest editions are Jakt and XVI. The name of the latter derives from a visit to the distillery by the Swedish king, Carl XVI Gustaf in March 2009. At that time the now launched whisky was being distilled and filled into casks. Seasonal expressions are also released regularly with Blomstertid being one of the latest. The whisky had received a finish in casks that previously held cherry wine.

Other distilleries in Sweden

Smögen Whisky
Hunnebostrand, founded in 2010

www.smogenwhisky.se

In August 2010, Smögen Whisky on the west coast of Sweden, produced its first spirit and thus became the country´s third whisky distillery, following Mackmyra and Spirit of Hven. Pär Caldenby – a lawyer, whisky enthusiast and the author of Enjoying Malt Whisky is behind it all. The distillery is equipped with three washbacks (1,600 litres each), a wash still (900 litres) and a spirit still (600 litres). The distillery has the capacity to produce 35,000 litres of alcohol a year. Pär practices a slow distillation with unusually long foreshots (45 minutes) in order not to get a newmake with too many fruity esters. Heavily peated malt is imported from Scotland and the vision is to produce an Islay-type of whisky. The first release (1,600 bottles) from the distillery was the 3 year old Primör in March 2014. It was a vatting of eight casks made of new, European oak and one cask that had previously held Bordeaux wine and it was bottled at 63,7%. Releases during 2016 include French Quarter, a 4 year old matured in heavily toasted, new French oak, Single Cask No. 3 which is a 5 year old from a first fill Bordeaux barrique and Wee Swede where the 4 year old whisky from one bourbon barrel was filled into small, 30 litre casks made from

Swedish oak and after two months filled back into the barrel for marrying. Pär Caldenby has also released his own gin, Strane, in three versions – Merchant Strength (47.4%), Navy Strength (57.1%) and Uncut Strength (75.3).

Spirit of Hven
Hven, founded in 2007

www.hven.com

The second Swedish distillery to come on stream, after Mackmyra, was Spirit of Hven, a distillery situated on the island of Hven right between Sweden and Denmark. The first distillation took place in May 2008. Henric Molin, founder and owner, is a trained chemist and very concerned about choosing the right oak for his casks. The oak is left to air dry for three to five years before the casks are loaned to, especially, wine producers in both the USA and Europe. The distillery is equipped with a 0,5 ton mash tun, six washbacks made of stainless steel and one pair of stills – wash still 2,000 litres and spirit still 1,500 litres. Part of the barley is malted on site and for part of it he uses Swedish peat, sometimes mixed with seaweed and sea-grass, for drying. Around 15,000 litres of whisky is distilled per year and other products include rum made from sugar beet, vodka, gin, aquavit and calvados. The distillery was expanded in summer 2013 with a new warehouse, an upgraded bottling line and an advanced spirits laboratory.

The first whisky to hit the market, was the lightly peated Urania which was released in 2012. The second launch, in early 2013, was the start of a new series of limited releases called The Seven Stars. The first expression was the 5 year old, lightly peated Dubhe, which was followed by Merak, Phecda and, in 2016, Megrez. In June 2014 the limited cask strength single cask Sankt Ibb was released and later that year saw the launch of Sankt Claus, also bottled at cask strength and matured in ex-merlot casks. All the above have been limited releases but in autumn 2015 it was time for the distillery´s first readily available bottling - Tycho´s Star, named in honour of the famous astronomer Tycho Brahe, who lived and worked on the island in the 16th century.

Pär Caldenby (left), the owner of Smögen Distillery

Henric Molin, the owner of Spirit of Hven

Norrtelje Brenneri

Norrtälje, founded in 2002 (whisky since 2009)

www.norrteljebrenneri.se

This distillery, situated 70 kilometres north of Stockholm, was founded on a farm which has belonged to the owner's family for five generations. The production consists mainly of spirits from ecologically grown fruits and berries. Since 2009, a single malt whisky from ecologically grown barley is also produced. The whisky is double distilled in copper pot stills (400 and 150 litres respectively) from Christian Carl in Germany. Most of the production is matured in 250 litre Oloroso casks with a finish of 3-6 months in French oak casks which have previously held the distillery's own apple spirit. The first bottling was released in summer 2015 and several limited editions have followed.

Gammelstilla Whisky

Torsåker, founded in 2005

www.gammelstilla.se

Less than 30 kilometres from the better known Mackmyra lies another distillery since 2011 – Gammelstilla. The company was already founded in 2005 by three friends but today there are more than 200 shareholders. Unlike most of the other Swedish whisky distilleries, they chose to design and build their pot stills themselves. The wash still has a capacity of 600 litres and the spirit still 300 litres and the annual capacity is 20,000 litres per year. The first distillation took place in April 2012 with a plan to launch the first bottlings in 2016.

Gotland Whisky

Romakloster, founded in 2011

www.gotlandwhisky.se

This distillery, on the island of Gotland in the Baltic Sea, is situated in a decommissioned sugar works south of Visby. It is equipped with a wash still (1,600 litres) and a spirit still (900 litres) – both made by Forsyth's in Scotland. The local barley is ecologically grown and malted on site. The floor malting is made easier through the use of a malting robot of their own construction which turns the barley. The whisky is matured in a warehouse situated four metres underground. Both unpeated and peated whisky is produced and the capacity is 60,000 litres per year. The distillery came on stream in May 2012 and the first whisky, Isle of Lime, is planned to be released in autumn 2016.

Nordmarkens Destilleri

Holmedal, founded in 2016

www.nordmarkensdestilleri.se

The first spirit from the owners was distilled in 2015 when they were offered to use a competitor's distillery. Currently a distillery of their own is under construction and will probably be ready towards the end of 2016. Two stills (with a capacity of 900 and 600 litres each) were purchased from the closed Grythyttan distillery in December 2015 and included in the deal, was some matured single malt (4-5 years old). This was released in 2016 under the name Initium. The planned distillation capacity is 22,000 litres per year.

Switzerland

Distillery:	Whisky Castle, Elfingen, Aargau
Founded:	2002
Owner:	Ruedi Käser
	whisky-castle.com

The first whisky from this distillery in Elfingen, founded by Ruedi Käser, reached the market in 2004. It was a single malt under the name Castle Hill. Since then the range of malt whiskies has been expanded and today include Castle Hill Doublewood (3 years old matured both in casks made of chestnut and oak), Whisky Smoke Barley (at least 3 years old matured in new oak), Fullmoon (matured in casks from Hungary), Terroir (4 years old made from Swiss barley and matured in Swiss oak), Cask Strength (5 years old and bottled at 58%) and Edition Käser (71% matured in new oak casks from Bordeaux). Recent additions include Castle One (matured in Bordeaux casks) and Family Reserve (an 8 year old with a port finish). In 2010, new, open top fermenters were installed to add fresher and fruitier notes to the newmake. The owners have also cut down on the number of casks made from new oak and have added a variety of other casks to influence the spirit. The yearly production is between 8,000 and 10,000 litres and on the premises one can have a complete visitor's experience, which includes a restaurant as well as a shop.

Distillery:	Brauerei Locher, Appenzell
Founded:	1886 (whisky since 1999)
Owner:	Locher family
	saentismalt.com

This old, family-owned brewery started to produce whisky on a small scale in 1999 but from 2005, larger volumes have been produced. The equipment consists of a Steinecker mash tun, stainless steel wash backs and Holstein stills. Brauerei Locher is unique in using old (70 to 100 years) beer casks for the maturation. The core range consists of three expressions; Himmelberg, bottled at 43%, Dreifaltigkeit which is slightly peated having matured in toasted casks and bottled at 52% and, finally, Sigel which has matured in very small casks and is bottled at 40%. A range of limited bottlings under the name Alpstein is also available. After a few years in a beer cask, these whiskies have received a further maturation in casks that previously held other spirits or wine. The most recent, Edition XI, was released in 2016 and had matured in beer casks for two years and then another five years in sherry casks. Yet another limited range, Snow White, was introduced in 2013 and for the latest release (winter 2015) a 5 year old with one year's finish in casks that had previously held plum spirit, was chosen.

Other distilleries in Switzerland

Langatun Distillery

Langenthal, Bern, founded in 2007

www.langatun.ch

The distillery was built in 2005 and under the same roof as the brewery Brau AG Langenthal (which was already established in 2001). The reason for this co-habitation was to access a wash for distillation and thereby avoiding investments in mashing equipment. The casks used for maturation are all 225 litres and Swiss oak (Chardonnay), French oak (Chardonnay and red wine) and ex sherry casks are used. There are two 5 year old core expressions – Old Deer and the peated Old Bear, with being avaailable at 40% and 62% respectively. Among the latest releases are a single cask rye, Old Eagle, and a single cask "bourbon", Old Mustang.

Bauernhofbrennerei Lüthy

Muhen, Aargau, founded in 1997 (whisky since 2005)

www.swiss-single-malt.ch

This farm distillery started in 1997 by producing distillates from fruit, as well as grappa, absinthe and schnapps. The range was expanded to include whisky in 2005 which was distilled in a mobile pot still distillery. Lüthy's ambition is to only use grain from Switzerland in his production. Since it was impossible to obtain peated malt from Swiss barley, he decided to build his own floor maltings in 2009. The first single malt expression to be launched in 2008, was Insel-Whisky, matured in a Chardonnay cask and several releases hav since followed. Starting in 2010, the yearly bottling was given the name Herr Lüthy and the 10th release from these was in 2015, a Swiss Strohwein maturation (a wine similar to Amarone).

Brennerei Stadelmann

Altbüron, Luzern, founded in 1932 (whisky since 2003)

www.schnapsbrennen.ch

The distillery, founded by Hans Stadelmann in 2001, is equipped with three Holstein-type stills (150-250 litres) and the first whisky was distilled for a local whisky club in 2003. In 2006 it was bottled under the name Dorfbachwasser and finally, in 2010, the first official bottling from the distillery in the shape of a 3 year old single malt whisky was released. In autumn 2014, the sixth release was made, matured in a Bordeaux cask. The first whisky from smoked barley was distilled in 2012.

Etter Distillerie

Zug, founded in 1870 (whisky since 2007)

www.etter-distillerie.ch

This distillery was started in 1870 by Paul Etter and today it is the third and fourth generations who are running it. Their main produce is eau de vie from various fruits and berries. A sidetrack to the business was entered in 2007 when they decided to distil their first malt whisky. The malted barley was bought from a brewery, distilled at Etter, filled into wine casks and left to mature in moist caves for a minimum of three years. The first release was made in 2010 under the name Johnett Single Malt Whisky and this is currently sold as a 6 year old. In 2015, the limited Johnett Trinidad rum finish was released.

Spezialitätenbrennerei Zürcher

Port, Bern, founded in 1954 (whisky from 2000)

www.lakeland-whisky.ch

The first in the Zürcher family to distil whisky was Heinz Zürcher in 2000, who released the first 1,000 bottles of Lakeland single malt in 2003. Daniel and Ursula Zürcher took over in 2004. They continued their uncle's work with whisky and launched a second release in 2006. The main focus of the distillery is specialising in various distillates of fruit, absinth and liqueur but a Lakeland single malt is also in the range. The oldest version so far, appeared in August 2014. It was an 8 year old matured in an oloroso cask.

Whisky Brennerei Hollen

Lauwil, Baselland, founded in 1999

www.swiss-whisky.ch, www.single-malt.ch

The first Swiss whisky was distilled at Hollen in July 1999. The whisky from Brennerei Hollen is stored on French oak casks, which have been used for white wine (Chardonnay) or red wine (Pinot Noir). In the beginning most bottlings were 4-5 years old but in 2009 the first 10 year old was released and there has also been a 12 year old double wood, the oldest expression from the distillery so far.

Brennerei Hagen

Hüttwilen, Thurgau, founded in 1999

www.distillerie-hagen.ch

A triple distilled malt whisky is produced by Ueli Hagen in the small village of Hüttwilen in the northernmost part of Switzerland. The spirit is matured in bourbon barrels and the first produce was sold in 2002 as a 3 year old. Ueli Hagen produces mainly schnapps and absinth and distills around 300 bottles of malt whisky a year.

Wales

Distillery:	Penderyn Distillery, Penderyn
Founded:	2000
Owner:	Welsh Whisky Company Ltd.
	welsh-whisky.co.uk

In 1998 four private individuals started The Welsh Whisky Company and two years later, the first Welsh distillery in more than a hundred years started distilling. A new type of still, developed by David Faraday for Penderyn Distillery, differs from the Scottish and Irish procedures in that the whole process from wash to new make takes place in one single still. But that is not the sole difference. Every distillery in Scotland is required by law, to do the mashing and fermenting on site. At Penderyn, though, the wash (until summer 2014) was bought from a regional beer brewer and transported to the distillery on a weekly basis. Even though the distillery has been working 24 hours a day to keep up with the increasing demand, it became obvious in 2012 that they had to do something to increase its capacity.

In September 2013, a second still (almost a replica of the first still) was commissioned and in June 2014, two traditional pot stills, as well as their own mashing equipment was installed. The expansion, worth £1m, increased the production from 90,000 litres to 300,000 litres of alcohol per annum and will also allow the company to experiment with new styles and expressions of single malts.

The first single malt was launched in 2004. The core range consists of Penderyn Madeira Finish (46%), Penderyn Peated (46%), Penderyn Legend (madeira finish bottled at 41% and formerly known as Penderyn 41), Penderyn Myth (full bourbon maturation and bottled at 41%) and Penderyn Celt (a peated finish launched in August 2015 and bottled at 41%). Over the years, the company has released several single casks based on a port finish but recently a regular Port Finish bottled at 46% was launched.

A new range of whiskies called Icons of Wales was introduced in 2012 and the fourth edition, That Try, was released in June 2015. The bottling is celebrating the famous rugby match between Barbarians and All Blacks in 1973. The main markets for Penderyn are UK, France and Germany and the brand sells around 200,000 bottles per year. A visitor centre opened in 2008 and attracted 35,000 visitors last year.

The new Port Finish from Penderyn

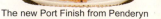

North America

USA

Distillery: Westland Distillery, Seattle, Washington
Founded: 2011
Owner: Lamb family
westlanddistillery.com

Unlike most of the new craft distilleries in the USA producing whiskey, Westland Distillery did not distil other spirits to finance the early stages of production. Until November 2012, Westland was a medium sized craft distillery where they brought in the wash from a nearby brewery and had the capacity of doing 60,000 litres of whiskey per year. During the summer of 2013 the owners, the Lamb family, moved to another location which is equipped with a 6,000 litre brewhouse, five 10,000 litre fermenters and two Vendome stills (7,560 and 5,670 litres respectively). The capacity is now 260,000 litres per year and currently they are making 160,000 litres. The malt for the production is sourced both locally, as well as from England, and the casks are predominantly heavy char, new American oak. Trials are also being conducted with ex-bourbon, ex-sherry and ex-port casks.

The first 5,500 bottles of their core expression, Westland American Single Malt Whiskey, were released in autumn 2013 followed by a limited one-off release called Deacon Seat. Both were mashed with a 5-malt grain bill and matured in heavily charred American oak. Since then, the owners have released a core range which now consists of American Single Malt Whiskey (October 2013), Peated Malt (October 2014) and Sherry Wood (December 2014). In addition to this, the distillery also releases different single cask bottlings. The latest addition is a range called Native Oak where unorthodox oak types are being used for maturation. The first, in summer 2016, was Westland Garryana where 20% of the whiskey had matured in Garry oak while the rest had been filled into American white oak. Quercus garryana is a type of oak native to the Pacific Northwest and very rarely used for whiskey maturation . In 2014, Westland partnered with Anchor Distilling Company to distribute their whiskey nationally. It is now available in all 50 states and it has also been launched in export markets such as Japan, France, the UK, Australia and Canada. In 2016 Westland was awarded World Craft Producer of the Year in the World Whiskies Awards.

Distillery: Stranahans Whiskey Distillery, Denver, Colorado
Founded: 2003
Owner: Proximo Spirits
stranahans.com

Stranahans, founded by Jess Graber and George Stranahan, was bought by New York based Proximo Spirits (makers of Hangar 1 Vodka and Kraken Rum among others) in 2010. A surprising decision was soon made to withdraw Stranahans Colorado Whiskey from all other markets, but Colorado. The owners claimed that they wanted to build up a significant stock before delivering nationally again. Apparently the stock has grown as the whiskey has now been sold acros the USA for more than a year.

Stranahans Colorado Whiskey is always made in batches aged from two to five years and since 2004, close to 200 batches have been released. Except for the core expression, a special version with different finishes is launched twice a year under the name Snowflake. In the 18th edition (Mount Evans) from November 2015, both madeira and port casks were involved and the 19th edition was released in June 2016. Since spring 2015, there is also another limited version of Stranahans called Diamond Peak which is a vatting of casks that are around 4 years old. In spring 2014, a bourbon by the name Tincup American Whiskey was released by Proximo Spirit,s with a lot of references made to Stranahans. It turned out that the whiskey had been distilled in Indiana and shipped to Stranahans where it was cut with local water and bottled.

Distillery: Balcones Distillery, Waco, Texas
Founded: 2008
Owner: Balcones Distilling Co.
balconesdistilling.com

The distillery was founded by Chip Tate but since end of 2014, he is no longer with the company. His exit was the result of a bitter feud between Tate and the company board, a feud which also included court hearings and restraining orders. A settlement was later made between the parties.

All of Balcones´ whisky is mashed, fermented and distilled on site and they were the first to use Hopi blue corn for distillation. Four

Westland´s Master Distiller, Matt Hoffman

different expressions of blue corn whiskey have been released so far – Baby Blue, bottled at 46%, True Blue which is a cask strength version, Brimstone Smoked Whiskey, a smoky version and True Blue 100, a 100 proof bottling of True Blue. The biggest seller, however, is the Texas Single Malt Whisky. Like the other whiskies it is un chill-filtered and without colouring. The most recent releases include batch 3 of Texas Rum and batch 2 of Texas Blue Corn Bourbon. A version of the Texas Single Malt finished in their rum casks has also been announced.

The demand for Balcones whiskies has grown rapidly and in January 2014, another four, small stills were installed. The big step though, was a completely new distillery which was built 5 blocks from the current site. Distillation started in February 2016 and the official opening was in April. The new distillery is equipped with one pair of stills and five fermenters with another set of stills going in during 2017. The plan for the old site is to use it as a pilot system for new products.

Distillery:	Clear Creek Distillery, Portland, Oregon
Founded:	1985
Owner:	Hood River Distillers
	clearcreekdistillery.com

Steve McCarthy was one of the first to produce malt whiskey in the USA and, like many other, smaller distilleries, they started by distilling eau-de-vie from fruit, especially pears, and then expanded the product line into whiskey. They began making whiskey in 1996 and the first bottles were on the market three years later. There is only one expression at the moment, McCarthy´s Oregon Single Malt 3 years old. The whiskey is reminiscent of an Islay and, in fact, the malt is purchased directly from Islay with a phenol specification of 30-40 ppm. It is only bottled twice a year and the next release is scheduled for October 2016. Maturation takes place in ex-sherry butts with a finish in new Oregon White Oak hogsheads. In early 2014, it was announced that Hood River Distillers was to take over the distillery with Steve McCarthy continuing as a consultant. Hood River Distillers, also based in Oregon, began in 1934 as a distillery but, since the 1960s, they have acted as a bottler and importer of spirits from other producers. One of their biggest sellers is the Canadian blended whisky Pendleton.

Distillery:	Charbay Winery & Distillery, St. Helena, California
Founded:	1983
Owner:	Miles and Marko Karakasevic
	charbay.com

Charbay was founded by Miles Karakasevic – a legend in American craft distilling – and the distillery is now run by his son Marko, the 13th generation in a winemaking and distilling family. With a wide range of products such as wine, vodka, grappa, pastis, rum and port, the owners decided in 1999 to also enter in to whiskey making. That year they took 20,000 gallons of Pilsner and double distilled it in their Charentais pot still. From this distillation, a 4 year old called Double-Barrel Release One (comprising of two barrels) was launched in 2002. There were 840 bottles at cask strength and non-chill filtered. The whiskey was quite unique since a ready beer, hops and all, rather than wash from a brewery was used. It took six years before Release II appeared in 2008 and in 2013 it was time for Release III. At 14 years old, it had spent the first six years in charred, new American oak. The remaining eight years it was allowed to mature in stainless steel tanks. This was followed by Release IV in autumn 2015 when 223 bottles of a 16 year old were launched. Other recent releases include Charbay R5 Whiskey matured in French oak for 21 months and S Whiskey Lot 211A which Marko created by distilling 6,000 gallons of Big Bear stout into 590 gallons of whiskey. It was then matured for 29 months in used French oak.

Distillery:	Edgefield Distillery, Troutdale, Oregon
Founded:	1998
Owner:	Mike and Brian McMenamin
	mcmenamins.com

Mike and Brian McMenamin started their first pub in Portland, Oregon in 1983. It has now expanded to a chain of more than 60 pubs and hotels in Oregon and Washington. More than 20 of the pubs have adjoining microbreweries and the chain's first distillery opened in 1998 at their huge Edgefield property in Troutdale with the first whiskey, Hogshead Whiskey, being bottled in 2002. Hogshead is still their number one seller. Another part of the

Cask selecting at Balcones Distillery

range is the Devil´s Bit, a limited bottling released every year on St. Patrick´s Day. For 2016 it was a four year old that had been matured in Edgefield Black Widow beer barrels. A second distillery was opened in 2011 at the company´s Cornelius Pass Roadhouse location in Hillsboro.

Distillery: High West Distillery, Park City, Utah
Founded: 2007
Owner: David Perkins
highwest.com

David Perkins has made a name for himself mainly because of the releases of several rye whiskies. None of these have been distilled at High West distillery. Perkins has instead, bought casks of mature whiskies and blended them himself. The first (released in 2008) was Rendezvous Rye, a mix of two whiskies (16 and 6 years old). Today this is part of the core range together with Double Rye (a blend of 2 and 16 year old whiskies), American Prairie Bourbon and the unusual Campfire. This is a blend of straight bourbon, straight rye and peated blended malt Scotch whisky. Limited releases include Yippe Ki-Yay Whiskey, a rye that has been aged in used vermouth and syrah barrels and A Midwinter Night´s Dram, a rye finished in port casks. In autumn 2015, they opened another distillery at Blue Sky Ranch in Wanship, Utah. It started off with two 6,000 litre pot still with the capacity of doing 700,000 litres of pure alcohol per year. The plan, however, is to eventually have 18 washbacks and four pot stills (with rectification columns attached) with the possibility of producing 1,4 million litres! Around 300,000 visitors come every year to the two sites in Park City and Wanship.

Distillery: Prichard´s Distillery, Kelso, Tennessee
Founded: 1999
Owner: Phil Prichard
prichardsdistillery.com

When Phil Prichard started his business in 1999, it became the first legal distillery for 50 years in Tennessee. Today, it is the third largest in the state after giants Jack Daniel's and George Dickel. In 2012 the capacity was tripled with the installation of a new 1,500 gallon mash cooker and three additional fermenters. The plan is to increase the capacity even further by adding a 1,500 gallon wash still and turning the old 550 gallon wash still into a spirit still. In spring 2014, a second distillery equipped with a new 400-gallon alembic copper still was opened at Fontanel in Nashville.

Prichard produces around 20,000 cases per year with different kinds of rum as the main track. The first single malt was launched in 2010 and later releases usually have been vattings from barrels of different age (some up to 10 years old). The whiskey range also includes rye, two bourbons and a Tennessee whiskey.

Distillery: RoughStock Distillery, Bozeman, Montana
Founded: 2008
Owner: Kari and Bryan Schultz
montanawhiskey.com

RoughStock buys its 100% Montana grown and malted barley and then mill and mash it themselves. The mash is not drained off into a wash, but brought directly from the mash tun into two 1,000 gallon open top wooden fermenters for a 72 hour fermentation before distillation in two Vendome copper pot stills (500 and 250 gallons). Maturation is on a mix of quarter casks and 225 litre barrels made from new American oak.

In 2009, the first bottles of RoughStock Montana Pure Malt Whiskey were released. Since then a single barrel bottled at cask strength has been added (Black Label Montana Whiskey) and apart from whiskey made from 100% malted barley, the product range also includes Spring Wheat Whiskey, Straight Rye Whiskey and Montana Bourbon Whiskey.

Distillery: Town Branch Distillery, Lexington, Kentucky
Founded: 1999
Owner: Alltech Lexington Brewing & Distilling Co.
lyonsspirits.com

Most of the producers of malt whiskey in the USA have a background in brewing, winemaking or distilling other spirits. This also applies to Lexington Brewing & Distilling Company, as whiskey production is derived from their production of Kentucky Ale. Dr Pearse Lyons' background is interesting – being the owner, the founder and a native of Ireland, he used to work for Irish Distillers in the 1970s. In 1980 he changed direction and founded Alltech Inc, a biotechnology company specializing in animal nutrition and feed supplements.

Alltech purchased Lexington Brewing Company in 1999, with the intent to produce an ale that would resemble both an Irish red ale and an English ale. In 2008, two traditional copper pot stills from Scotland were installed with the aim to produce Kentucky´s first malt whiskey. The first single malt whiskey was released in 2010 under the name Pearse Lyons Reserve and in 2011 it was time for a release of their Town Branch bourbon. It then took until 2014 before their third whiskey was released, the 4 year old Town Branch Rye. In 2012 the stills were relocated from the brewery to a new stand alone distillery building right across the street with a capacity of 450,000 litres of pure alcohol per year. In April 2015, Alltech started construction of a new brewery and distillery in Pikeville. The new unit will cost $13m to build and the plan is to start production in early 2017.

Distillery: St. George Distillery, Alameda, California
Founded: 1982
Owner: Jörg Rupf/Lance Winters
stgeorgespirits.com

The distillery is situated in a hangar at Alameda Point, the old naval air station at San Fransisco Bay. It was founded by Jörg Rupf, who came to California in 1979 and who was to become one of the forerunners when it came to craft distilling in America. In 1996, Lance Winters joined him and today he is Distiller, as well as co-owner. In 2005, the two were joined by Dave Smith who now has the sole responsibility for the whisky production.

The main produce is based on eau-de-vie which is produced from locally grown fruit, and vodka under the brand name Hangar One. Whiskey production was picked up in 1996 and the first single malt appeared on the market in 1999. St. George Single Malt used to be sold as a three year old but, nowadays, comes to the market as a blend of whiskeys aged from 4 to 16 years. The latest release was Lot 16 (October 2016) and every lot is around 3-4,000 bottles. A new addition to the range was released in April 2016. Baller is what Lance Winters describes as "a California take on the Japanese spin on Scotch whisky." Aged 3-4 years, this malt whiskey has been filtered through maple charcoal and then finished in casks that held house-made umeshu (a Japanese style of plum liqueur). Currently only available in California, Baller soon became a success especially to be used in a highball (hence the name).

Distillery: Tuthilltown Spirits, Gardiner, New York
Founded: 2003
Owner: Ralph Erenzo and Brian Lee
tuthilltown.com

Just 80 miles north of New York City, Ralph Erenzo and Brian Lee produce bourbon, single malt whiskey, rye whiskey, rum, vodka and gin. The first products came onto the shelves in 2006 in New York and the whiskey range now consists of Hudson Baby Bourbon, a 2-4 year old bourbon made from 100% New York corn and the company´s biggest seller by far, Four Grain Bourbon (corn, rye, wheat and malted barley), Single Malt Whiskey (aged in small, new, charred American oak casks), Manhattan Rye and New York Corn Whiskey. The spirits range also include Half Moon Orchard

Gin (made from wheat and apples), Indigenous Vodka, Roggen´s Rum and Tuthilltown Cassis. Hudson whiskey currently sells in all 50 states, in Europe, Australia and Hong Kong. A cooperative venture was announced between Tuthilltown and William Grant & Sons in 2010, in which W Grant acquired the Hudson Whiskey brand line in order to market and distribute it around the world. Tuthilltown Spirits remains an independent company that will continue to produce the different spirits. In 2014, the distillery site was expanded with a new packaging building and, not least, a whole new R&D building where the antique charentais brandy still will be used for new experiments.

Distillery:	Corsair Artisan, Bowling Green, Kentucky and Nashville, Tennessee
Founded:	2008
Owner:	Darek Bell, Andrew Webber and Amy Lee Bell
	corsairartisan.com

The two founders of Corsair Artisan, Darek Bell and Andrew Webber, were based in Nashville when they came up with the idea in 2008 to start up a distillery. At that time Tennessee law didn´t allow this, so the first distillery was opened across the border in Bowling Green, Kentucky. Two years later, the legislation in Tennessee had changed and a second distillery and brewery were opened up in Nashville. Apart from producing around 20 different types of beer, the brewery is also where the wash for all the whisky production takes place. In Nashville, they also have a 240 gallon antique copper pot still. For those spirits in the range that require a second distillation, the low wines are taken to Bowling Green and the custom made 50 gallon still from Vendome Copper. In spring 2015, the company established a malting facility in Nashville where they can floor malt their own grain and eventually there will also be a drum malting station.

Corsair Artisan has a wide range of spirits – gin, vodka, absinthe, rum and whiskey. The number of different whiskies released is growing constantly and Corsair Artisan is most likely the distillery in the USA which experiments the most with different types of grain. The big sellers are Triple Smoke Single Malt Whiskey (made from three different types of smoked malt with an addition of chocolate malt) and Ryemaggedon (made from malted rye and chocolate rye). The first whiskey made with hickory smoked malt from the Malthouse in Nashville, was Wildfire, released in autumn 2015. Recently, they also joined Few Spirits, Journeyman Distillery and Mississippi River Distilling Company in a venture where whiskey from all four distilleries were blended together.

Distillery:	Virginia Distillery, Lovingston, Virginia
Founded:	2008 (production started 2015)
Owner:	Virginia Distillery Company
	vadistillery.com

The whole idea for this distillery was conceived by Chris Allwood in 2007, but he left the company in 2010 and several changes in ownership have occurred since then, the last one being in spring 2016. Even though the copper pot stills arrived from Turkey in 2008 (having been bought second hand from the Turkish government), the company was struggling with the financing and the first distillation didn´t take place until November 2015. The distillery has the capacity of making 1.1 million litres of alcohol and is equipped with a 3.75 ton mash tun, 8 washbacks, a 10,000 litre wash still and a 7,000 litre spirit still.

Other distilleries in USA

Dry Fly Distilling
Spokane, Washington, founded in 2007
www.dryflydistilling.com

Dry Fly Distilling was the first grain distillery to open in Washington since Prohibition. The first batch of malt whisky was distilled in 2008 but the first bottling will probably not be released until early 2018. However, several other types of whisky have been released recently – Bourbon 101, Straight Cask Strength Wheat Whiskey, Port Finish Wheat Whiskey, Peated Wheat Whiskey and Straight Triticale Whiskey (triticale is a hybrid of wheat and rye). A new limited bottling, released in November 2015, is the triple distilled O´Danaghers which is a mix of barley, wheat and oats.

Triple Eight Distillery
Nantucket, Massachusetts, founded in 2000
www.ciscobrewers.com

In 1995 Cisco Brewers was established and five years later it was expanded with Triple Eight Distillery. The Nantucket facility consists of a brewery, winery and distillery. Apart from whiskey, Triple Eight also produces vodka, rum and gin. Whiskey production was moved to a new distillery in May 2007. The first 888 bottles of single malt whiskey were released on 8th August 2008 as an 8 year old. To keep in line with its theme, the price of these first bottles was also $888. More releases of Notch (as in "not Scotch") have followed, the latest being a 12 year old in spring 2015.

Cedar Ridge Distillery
Swisher, Iowa, founded in 2003
www.crwine.com

Jeff Quint and his wife, Laurie started Cedar Ridge Vineyards in 2003 and expanded the business soon afterwards to also include a distillery. After a while they moved to the present location in Swisher, between Cedar Rapids and Iowa City. The first whiskey, a bourbon, was released in 2010. Malt whiskey production started in 2005 and in 2013 the time had come for the launch of the first single malt. Four 15 gallon ex-bourbon barrels were bottled after having a finish in different secondary casks (port, rum, sherry and bourbon). More releases of the single malt have been made since then. A range of limited releases called Silver Label Single Malts has also been introduced including one made with chocolate malt, another finished for two years in a Sauternes cask while a third had been maturing in toasted cherry wood. A major expansion of the distillery was made in autumn 2014 when a grain silo, a malt mill, a new 20 barrel lauter mash tun, more washbacks and a 650 litre wash still were added.

Nashoba Valley Winery
Bolton, Massachusetts, founded in 1978
(whiskey since 2003)
www.nashobawinery.com

Nashoba Valley Winery is mainly about wines but over the last decade, the facilities have been expanded with a brewery and a distillery. The owner, Richard Pelletier, produces a wide range of spirits including vodka, brandy and grappa. Since 2003 malt whiskey is also being distilled. The malt is imported and the wash is produced at his own brewery. In autumn 2009, Stimulus, the first single malt was released. The second release of a 5 year old came in 2010 and it is Richard´s intention to release a 5 year old once a year. The first 10 year old single malt was released in autumn 2015 together with a 5 year old rye whiskey.

Woodstone Creek Distillery
Cincinnati, Ohio, founded in 1999
www.woodstonecreek.com

Don and Linda Outterson opened a farm winery in Lebanon, Ohio in 1999 and relocated to Evanston i Cincinnati in 2003 where a distillery was added to the business. In autumn 2014 they were forced to move again and the distillery/winery is now located a bit farther north in St. Bernard. If everything goes according to plans, the owners will have a brewery on site in the future as well. The first whiskey, a five grain bourbon, was released in 2008. In 2010, the Outtersons released a peated 10 year old single malt from malted barley and in 2012 this was followed up by a 12 year old unpeated single malt whiskey, Ridge Runner (a five-grain bourbon white dog) and a blended whiskey. A 13 year old single malt matured in a sherry cask has also been recently released.

Ballast Point Brewing & Distilling

San Diego, California, founded in 1996 (whiskey since 2008)

www.ballastpoint.com

Jack White and Yuseff Cherney founded Ballast Point Brewing Company in 1996. It soon became one of the most influential craft beer brewers in USA, with four production sites in the San Diego area and selling around 3 million cases per year. In December 2015, the company was bought by Constellation Brands (maker of Robert Mondavi wines and Svedka vodka) for the staggering sum of $1bn! The distilling side of Ballast Point started in 2008, and the first product to appear on the market was Old Grove gin in 2009. Vodka and rum have been released thereafter. Two whiskeys are produced; a single malt Devil's Share Whiskey and Devil's Share Bourbon, both of them matured for a minimum of three years. They were released for the first time in 2013 with batch 2 of the single malt and batch 3 of the bourbon released in spring 2015.

House Spirits Distillery

Portland, Oregon, founded in 2004

www.housespirits.com

In September 2015, Christian Krogstad and Matt Mount moved their distillery a few blocks to bigger premises. The main products for House Spirits used to be Aviation Gin and Krogstad Aquavit but with their new equipment they drastically increased whiskey capacity from 150 barrels per year to 4,000 barrels! The first three whiskies were released locally in 2009 and this was followed up by more bottlings in 2010 and 2011. In November 2012 it was time for the first, widely available single malt under the name of Westward Whiskey. It was a 2 year old, double pot distilled and matured in 2-char, new American oak. Recent releases have been 3 years old and now each release is a single barrel.

New Holland Brewing Co.

Holland, Michigan, founded in 1996 (whiskey since 2005)

www.newhollandbrew.com

This company started as a beer brewery, but after a decade, it opened up a micro-distillery as well; and the wash used for the beer is now also used for distilling whiskey. Until 2011, the spirit was double distilled in a 225 litre, self-constructed pot still. At that time, the capacity increased tenfold, mainly as a result of the installation of a restored 3,000-litre still built in 1932. The first cases of New Holland Artisan Spirits were released in 2008 and among them were Zeppelin Bend, a 3 year old (minimum) straight-malt whiskey which is now their flagship brand. This was followed by the single malt Double Down Barley, Walley Rye, Beer Barrel Bourbon Malt House Whiskey and Pitchfork Wheat Whiskey. Most recent bottlings include the 18 months old Cask & Smoke Whiskey, a single malt which was released in January 2016.

DownSlope Distilling

Centennial, Colorado, founded in 2008

www.downslopedistilling.com

The three founders were brought together by their interest and passion for craft-brewing when they started the distillery in 2008 and in 2009 they finally got their licence to start distilling. The distillery is equipped with two stills – one copper pot still made by Copper Moonshine Stills in Arkansas and a vodka still of an in-house design. The first whiskey, Double-Diamond Whiskey, was released in 2010. It was made from 65% malted barley and 35% rye and is still the core whiskey in the range. It was followed by a number of varieties of bourbon, rye and single malt. The most recent products include a 4 year old Double Diamond Whiskey finished in a cognac cask. All the malt whiskies are made from floor malted Maris Otter barley.

Do Good Distillery

Modesto, California, founded in 2013

dogooddistillery.com

Founded in 2013 by six friends and family members, and headed by Jim Harrelson, the goal is to make whiskey and, in particular, single malt. First production was in early autumn 2014 and from autumn 2015 a number of different releases have been made; Beechwood Smoked, Peat Smoked, Cherrywood Smoked - all of them single malts - and The Nighthawk bourbon. Most of the malt they are using is imported from Europe. Due to a recent expansion of the distillery (including two more stills) the owners can now produce the equivalent of 200,000 bottles per year.

Copper Fox Distillery

Sperryville, Virginia, founded in 2000

www.copperfox.biz

Copper Fox Distillery was founded in 2000 by Rick Wasmund. In 2005 they moved to another site where they built a new distillery and began distilling in 2006. Rick Wasmund has become one of the most unorthodox producers of single malt. He does his own floor malting of barley (also supplying several breweries) and it is dried using smoke from selected fruitwood. After mashing, fermentation and distillation, the spirit is filled into oak barrels, together with plenty of hand chipped and toasted chips of apple and cherry trees, as well as oak wood. Adding to the flavour, Wasmund also believes that this procedure drastically speeds up the time necessary for maturation. The first bottles of Wasmund's Single Malt (also known as Red Top) were just four months old but the current batches are more aged 12-16 months. There is also an older version, Blue Top, which has matured for up to 42 months. Other expressions in the distillery range include Copper Fox Rye Whiskey with a mash bill of 2/3 Virginia rye and 1/3 malted barley and two unaged spirits – Rye Spirit and Single Malt Spirit. In summer 2016, Rick Wasmund opened up a second distillery in Williamsburg..

Bull Run Distillery

Portland, Oregon, founded in 2011

www.bullrundistillery.com

Founded by former brewer, Lee Medoff, the distillery made its first distillation in autumn of 2011. The distillery is equipped with two pot stills (800 gallons each) and the main focus is on 100% Oregon single malt whiskey. Waiting for their own whiskey to mature, the company has been selling bourbon under the label Temperance Trader sourced from other producers, but blended and sometimes matured for an additional period at Bull Run. The first release of a single malt under the name Bull Run is expected during 2016.

Rogue Ales & Spirits

Newport, Oregon, founded in 2009

www.rogue.com

The company started in 1988 as a combined pub and brewery. Over the years the business gradually expanded and now consists of one brewery, two combined brewery/pubs, two distillery pubs (Portland and Newport) and five pubs scattered over Oregon, Washington and California. The main business is still producing Rogue Ales, but apart from whiskey, rum and gin are also distilled.

The first malt whiskey, Dead Guy Whiskey, was launched in 2009 and is based on five different types of barley. It is distilled twice in a 150 gallon Vendom copper pot still and the spirit is matured for one month in charred barrels made of American Oak. In April 2016, it was time for the first straight malt whiskey - Oregon Single Malt Whiskey, aged for at least two years. It is made from barley grown and floor malted on Rogue's own farm in Tygh Valley.

FEW Spirits

Evanston, Illinois, founded in 2010

fewspirits.com

Former attorney (and founder of a rock and roll band) Paul Hletko started this distillery in Evanston, a suburb in Chicago in 2010. It is equipped with three stills; a Vendome column still and two Kothe hybrid stills. Bourbon and rye have been on the market for a couple of years and the first single malt, with some of the malt being smoked with cherry wood, was released in early 2015. Apart from this, three distinctive types of gin are produced, which is unique because they have an unaged bourbon as a base instead of the usual neutral spirit.

Sons of Liberty Spirits Co.

South Kingstown, Rhode Island, founded in 2010

www.solspirits.com

Michael Reppucci started the distillery with the help of David Pickerell who was Master Distiller for Maker´s Mark for 13 years. This distillery is equipped with a stainless steel mash tun, stainless steel, open top fermenters and one 950 litre combined pot and column still from Vendome. Sons of Liberty is first and foremost a whiskey distillery, but the first product launched was Loyal 9 Vodka. In 2011 the double distilled Uprising American Whiskey was launched, made from a stout beer and it was followed in early 2014 by Battle Cry made from a Belgian style ale. Both Uprising and Battle Cry have also been released as sherry finishes.

Cut Spike Distillery (formerly Solas Distillery)

La Vista, Nebraska, founded in 2009

www.cutspikedistillery.com

Originally opened as Solas distillery in 2009, Brian McGee and Jason Payne later renamed it Cut Spike distillery. The first product to hit the market in 2009 was Joss Vodka while the Cuban-style Chava Rum was released in 2011. In 2010 single malt whiskey was distilled and the first 140 bottles in a batch of 2,000 were launched in August 2013. Every month 140 bottles were released until November 2014 when the second batch was launched. Batch 5 was released in summer 2016. Cut Spike Single Malt Whiskey is two years old and bottled at 43%. Apart from whiskey, the range from the distillery now consists of vodka and rum.

Green Mountain Distillers

Morristown, Vermont, founded in 2001

www.greendistillers.com

Green Mountain Distillers, a certified organic distillery, was started by Tim Danahy and Howie Faircloth. The first product to hit the shelves was Sunshine Vodka in 2004, followed in 2009 with two new versions – Organic Lemon and Organic Orange. However, a 100% organic malt whiskey has always been uppermost in their minds. The first batches were already distilled in September 2004, but unlike many other distillers in the USA, Tim and Howie decided to let it mature for quite a number of years and, at the moment, there has been no release. In summer 2015, the distillery moved to a new location in Morristown, Vermont.

Blue Ridge Distilling Co.

Bostic, North Carolina, founded in 2010

www.blueridgedistilling.com

After a career in commercial diving and salvage, Tim Ferris opted for a change. He took the crew from his company, Defiant Marine, and opened up a distillery in 2010. The equipment consists of a lauter mash tun, stainless steel fermenters and a modified Kothe still. For maturation they use 24 months air dried, toasted American oak. At least for the time being, their minds are totally set on single malt whisky and they produce around 20,000 cases per year. The first distillation was in June 2012 and already in December the first bottles of Defiant Single Malt Whisky were released.

Journeyman Distillery

Three Oaks, Michigan, founded in 2010

www.journeymandistillery.com

Before opening his own distillery, Bill Welter rented still time at Koval Distillery in Ravenswood to make sure he had an aged rye whiskey (Ravenswood Rye) available when his own distillery

Paul Hletko, founder and owner of FEW Spirits

was opened. The range of whiskies distilled at his own premises now include Last Feather Rye (a name change was made due to a trademark dispute) which is their biggest seller, Featherbone bourbon, Silver Cross Whiskey (equal parts of rye, wheat, corn and barley), W.R. Whiskey (un-aged rye), Kissing Cousins (bourbon finished in a Cabernet Sauvignon barrel) and Federalist 12 Rye. The first, limited release of Three Oaks Single Malt Whiskey was in October 2013 and was followed by another batch in July 2015. A major expansion of the distillery was made in 2015, including a new 5,500 litre still, five times the size of the previous.

Santa Fe Spirits

Santa Fe, New Mexico, founded in 2010

www.santafespirits.com

Colin Keegan, the owner of Santa Fe Spirits, is collaborating with Santa Fe Brewing Company which supplies the un-hopped beer that is fermented and distilled in a 1,000 litre copper still from Christian Carl in Germany. The whiskey gets a hint of smokiness from mesquite. The first product, Silver Coyote released in spring 2011, was an unaged malt whiskey. The first release of an aged (2 years) single malt whiskey, Colkegan, was in October 2013. By spring 2016 seven batches had been released. A new mash tun was installed in April 2016, increasing the production substantially.

Copperworks Distilling Company

Seattle, Washington, founded in 2013

www.copperworksdistilling.com

The founders of the distillery, Jason Parker and Micah Nutt, both come from a brewing background and that is also where their whiskey comes from. They obtain their wash from a local brewery and then ferment it on site. The distillery is equipped with two, large copper pot stills for the whiskey production, one smaller pot still for the gin and one column still. The whiskey is matured in 53-gallon charred, American oak barrels. The first distillation was in January 2014 and the first batch of the single malt was released in September 2016. Other spirits include vodka and gin, both based on malted barley.

Wood´s High Mountain Distillery

Salida, Colorado, founded in 2011

www.woodsdistillery.com

Even though the brothers PT and Lee Wood have released two different gins since they started production in 2012, it seems that whiskey will be their main product. After a very long fermentation (9 days) the spirit is double-distilled in a 350 gallon stripping still and a 50 gallon pot-column hybrid still and then filled into small casks (25-30 gallons). Their first expression, Tenderfoot Whiskey released in June 2013, is something as rare as a triple malt. The mash bill is 77% malted barley (a mix of chocolate malt and cherrywood smoked malt), 13% malted rye and 10% malted wheat. The next releases were Alpine Rye Whiskey, with a mash bill of 70% malted rye and 30% malted barley and a 16 months old whiskey made from local Oilman Imperial Stout.

Door County Distillery

Sturgeon Bay, Wisconsin, founded in 2011

www.doorcountydistillery.com

The Door Peninsula Winery was founded in 1974 and ten years later the current owners, the Pollman family, took over. It is a large facility including a shop and tasting rooms and attracts thousands of visitors every year. In 2011, the family decided to add a distillery to the site. The wash is brought in from a local brewery and distilled in a copper pot/column hybrid still. Gin, vodka and brandy are the main products but they also make roughly 100 gallons of single malt whiskey per year. The first Door County Single Malt was released as a one year old in 2013.

Immortal Spirits

Medford, Oregon, founded in 2008

www.immortalspirits.com

In the beginning, this distillery could be seen mainly as a labour of love by two home brewers, Jesse Gallagher and Enrico Carini, but they had their minds set on something bigger. The two stills (a 1,200 gallon pot still and an 88 gallon still for limited release runs)

Micah Nutt and Jason Parker - owners of Copperworks Distilling with their first single malt release

were designed and fabricated by themselves, and the wash used to come from a local brewery. After some time, a 2,000 gallon mash tun and three 2,000 gallon fermenters were installed, so not only is all of the production handled at the distillery, but the volumes have increased substantially as well. A young single malt, Early Whiskey was released in spring 2015 and this was followed by a limited four year old Single Barrel, released when they opened their new tasting room in November 2015. A year ago, Immortal Spirits was also one of the first distilleries in the USA, to start using Oregon oak for all of their single malts. Oregon oak (*Quercus garryana*) has deeper tannins than American white oak (*Quercus alba*) and resembles European oak.

Deerhammer Distilling Company
Buena Vista, Colorado, founded in 2010
www.deerhammer.com

The location of the distillery at an altitude of 2,500 metres with drastic temperature fluctuations and virtually no humidity, have a huge impact on the maturation of the spirit. Owners Lenny and Amy Eckstein found that their first whiskey, based on five varieties of malted barley, was ready to be released after only 9 months´ maturation in December 2012. The next bottling of the Down Time single malt was in June 2013 and, so far, they have released around 30 batches. Recent bottlings have been matured between 2 and 3 years. The distillery was upgraded in 2013 with more fermenters, a bigger mash tun and an additional 600 gallon pot still.

Hillrock Estate Distillery
Ancram, New York, founded in 2011
www.hillrockdistillery.com

What makes this distillery unusual, at least in the USA, is that they are not just malting their own barley – they are floor malting it. This a technique that has been abandoned even in Scotland, except for a handful of distilleries. Jeff Baker founded the distillery in 2011 and equipped it with a 250 gallon Vendome pot still and five fermentation tanks. The first spirit was distilled in November 2011. The first release from the distillery was in 2012, the Solera Aged Bourbon and in 2013 it was time for the first Single Malt whiskey. This was followed by the Double Cask Rye. New releases in 2014 were two versions of a Peated Single Malt (8-hour and 14-hour peat smoke) and in 2015 a 20-hour Peated Single Malt and two versions of Double Cask Rye (portfinished and madeirafinished) were launched. The distillery is now producing 1,000 cases a year but the owners are looking to increase that to 5,000.

Painted Stave Distilling
Smyrna, Delaware, founded in 2013
paintedstave.com

Like for so many other new distilleries, production for Painted Stave started with vodka and gin. Whiskey production started in 2014, first with bourbon and rye, then followed by whiskey from malted barley. Most of the whiskey production is centered on bourbon and rye but the owners, Ron Gomes and Mike Rasmussen, released a malt whisky made from peated malt, regular malt and corn in September 2015. They hope to have more malt whiskies in the core range in a year or two.

Long Island Spirits
Baiting Hollow, New York, founded in 2007
www.lispirits.com

Long Island Spirits is the first distillery on the island since the 1800s. The starting point for The Pine Barrens Whisky, the first single malt from the distillery, is a finished ale with hops and all. The beer is distilled twice in a potstill and matures for one year in a 10 gallon, new, American, white oak barrel. The whisky was first released in April 2012 The range also includes Rough Rider straight bourbon, Happy Warrior cask strength bourbon and a cask strength rye called Rough Rider Big Stick. The big seller for the owner,

Richard Stabile, is not a whisky, however, but LiV Vodka, made 100% from potatoes and selling 70,000 bottles per year.

Van Brunt Stillhouse
Brooklyn, New York, founded in 2012
www.vanbruntstillhouse.com

To the Whisky Trail in Scotland and the Kentucky Bourbon Trail, you can now add The Brooklyn Spirits Trail in New York, where no less than 11 distillers have teamed up to showcase their different spirits. One of them is Van Brunt Stillhouse, owned by Daric Schlesselman and located near the Red Hook waterfront. They made their first release of Van Brunts American Whiskey in December 2012, a mix of malted barley, wheat and a hint of corn and rye. This was followed by a malt whiskey from 100% malted barley, a wheated bourbon and a rye.

Civilized Spirits
Traverse City, Michigan, founded in 2009
www.civilizedspirits.com

Jon Carlson and Greg Lobdell developed a passion for craft beer and artisan spirits whilst they were attending the University of Michigan. Years later they founded Northern United Brewing Company which is the parent company of Civilized Spirits. The spirits are produced at a distillery on Old Mission Peninsula, just outside Traverse City in a 1,000 litre pot still with a 24-plate column attached. The whiskey side of the business includes Civilized Single Malt (at least 3 years old), Civilized Whiskey (made from locally grown rye), Civilized White Dog Whiskey (an unoaked wheat whiskey) and Civilized Bourbon.

Square One Brewery & Distillery
St. Louis, Missouri, founded in 2006
www.squareonebrewery.com

Steve Neukomm has been working with micro-breweries since 1999. In 2006 he opened a combined brewery and restaurant in St. Louis and two years later he was granted Missouri´s first micro-distilling licence. Apart from rum, gin, vodka and absinthe, Steve also produces J.J. Neukomm Whiskey, a malt whiskey made from toasted malt and cherry wood smoked malt.

Great Lakes Distillery
Milwaukee, Wisconsin, founded in 2004
www.greatlakesdistillery.com

The first distillery to open in Wisconsin since Prohibition, released its first product, Rehorst Vodka, in 2006. The distillery is focused on the production of absinthe, vodka, gin, brandy and rum, but there has also been the occasional distillation of whiskey. The only whiskey in the range at the moment is an American blended whiskey called Kinnickinnic. It is a mix of sourced bourbon, blended with malt and rye whiskey which is produced in the distillery. A one-off bottling was a Kinnickinnic with a second maturation in cabernet franc wine casks. Originally, the equipment consisted of a 250 litre Holstein still, three fermenters and a 1,000 litre cooker, but a second still installed in March 2015 has increased the capacity.

Hamilton Distillers
Tucson, Arizona, founded in 2011
www.hamiltondistillers.com

Since 1986 Stephen Paul has been working as a manufacturer of furniture made from local mesquite wood. Scraps from the shop were often brought home to fire the barbecue and he and his wife, being avid Scotch whisky drinkers, came up with the idea of drying barley over mesquite, instead of peat. They started their small distillery using a 40 gallon copper alembic still, but since 2014, a 500 gallon still is in place. In spring 2015, new malting equipment was installed which made it possible to malt the barley in 5,000 lbs batches, instead of the previous 70 lbs batches! Everything is done on site - from malting to maturation. The first, limited releases were made in 2013 and they now have three expressions of Whiskey del Bac in the range – aged Mesquite smoked (Dorado), aged unsmoked (Classic) and unaged Mesquite smoked (Clear).

Cornelius Pass Roadhouse Distillery

Hillsboro, Oregon, founded in 2011

www.mcmenamins.com

The distillery is owned by the McMenamin brothers who also have a chain of more than 60 pubs and hotels, as well as the Edgefield Distillery in Troutdale. The Hillsboro distillery is equipped with a 19th century Charentais alambic still. The first release was an un-aged whiskey called The White Owl (72% malted wheat and 28% malted barley) in 2012 and it was followed by a gin in 2013. In September 2014, an aged version (3 years) of the White Owl was released under the name Billy Whiskey. In addition to whiskey, the owners also produce and sell rum, gin and brandy.

Great Wagon Road Distilling Co.

Charlotte, North Carolina, founded in 2014

gwrdistilling.com

For Ollie Mulligan, a native of Ireland, everything started with a 15 litre still and him taking classes under some of the country´s master distillers. Over time, he invested in bigger stills and in February he installed a 3,000 litres Kothe still in his new 15,000 sq foot facility. The mash comes from a neighbouring brewery and the fermentation is made in-house in four tanks. The first batch of his Rua Single Malt was launched at Christmas 2015 and at least four or five batches have since followed, including vodka and Drumlish poteen.

Maine Craft Distilling

Portland, Maine, founded in 2013

www.mainecraftdistilling.com

This distillery started production in January 2013 and the founder, Luke Davidson, built most of the equipment himself. Currently they are offering vodka, gin, rum and Chesuncook, which is a botanical spirit using barley and carrot distillates! Since March 2014 there is also a single malt whiskey for sale – Fifty Stone. This is now released in limited batches. Luke Davidson is floor malting all the barley himself and due to a combustion of the kiln in November they had to postpone the whisky production until April 2014.

3 Howls Distillery

Seattle, Washington, founded in 2013

www.3howls.com

Inspired by whisky production in Scotland, Will Maschmeier and Craig Phalen started distillation in 2013. The Scottish connection is reflected in that all the malted barley is imported from Scotland including a small amount of peated malt. For the distillation they use a 300 gallon hybrid still with a stainless steel belly and a copper column. Their first whiskies were released at the end of 2013, a single malt and a hopped rye and these were followed in 2014 by a rye whiskey and a bourbon.

Montgomery Distillery

Missoula, Montana, founded in 2012

www.montgomerydistillery.com

In 2012, Ryan and Jenny Montgomery renovated the 19th century Pipestone Mountaineering building in Missoula and opened up a distillery. The barley and the rye is milled to a fine flour on site, using a hammer mill and the wash is then fermented on the grain. Distillation takes place in a 450 litre Christian Carl pot still with a 21 plate column attached. At the moment, they have around 65 barrels of single malt and 80 of rye maturing. The first whiskey was Early Release rye in summer 2015 which was followed by the 2 year old straight rye Sudden Wisdom. The first single malt may be released in late 2016.

Ranger Creek Brewing & Distilling

San Antonio, Texas, founded in 2010

www.drinkrangercreek.com

The owners of Ranger Creek (TJ Miller, Mark McDavid and Dennis Rylander) focus on beer brewing and whiskey production. They have their own brewhouse where they mash and ferment all their beers, as well as the beer going for distillation. The still is a 1,200 litre, 6-plate column still from Holstein. The first release was Ranger Creek .36 Texas Bourbon in 2011. Their first single malt, Rimfire, was launched early in 2013. Other expressions include Ranger Creek .44 Rye and the white dog, Ranger Creek .36 White.

Two James Spirits

Detroit, Michigan, founded in 2013

www.twojames.com

David Landrum and Peter Bailey named their distillery after their respective fathers, both named James. Equipped with a 500 gallon

The crew from Great Wagon Road Distilling with the owner, Ollie Mulligan, second from the left

pot still with a rectification column attached, the distillery started production in September 2013. Vodka, gin, bourbon and rye have already been released and they expect to launch their first single malt some time in 2016 as a 3 year old. Aged in ex-sherry casks the whiskey has been made from peated Scottish barley.

Brickway Brewery & Distillery (former Borgata)

Omaha, Nebraska, founded in 2013

www.drinkbrickway.com

Zac Triemert, who owns the distillery, together with Holly Mulkins, was involved in founding Solas distillery (later re-named Cut Spike distillery) in 2009, and left a couple of years ago to start Borgata. All the wash for the distillation comes from their own brewery and distillation takes place in a 550 gallon Canadain wash still, while the 400 gallon spirit still comes from Forsyth´s in Scotland. The owners are focused on single malt whiskey but they will also produce smaller amounts of bourbon and rye. Their first whisky, Borgata American Single Malt White Whisky, was released in May 2014. End of 2014 the distillery´s name was changed to Brickway following a dispute with Borgata Casino and the whiskey now goes under the name Brickway Single Malt whisky and is typically around one year old. Thirteen batches had been released by July 2016. One month later, their first two year old called Brickway Double Barrel Whisky was launched.

Seven Stills Distillery

San Francisco, California, founded in 2013

www.sevenstillsofsf.com

Although already founded in 2013 by Tim Obert and Clint Potter, the first whiskies to be released from the Seven Stills distillery were all produced at Stillwater distillery in Petaluma. Not until March 2016, had the two owners managed to find the perfect spot for their own distillery – Bayview, an area in the San Francisco environs. Equipped with a 300 gallon copper pot still from Artisan Still Design, as well as brewing equipment, a range of unorthodox whiskies are now being produced in the new location. Their whiskies are made from different beers including oatmeal stout, peanut butter milk stout, sour dough sour and coffee porter. The first vodka from the new production has already been released and the first whiskey is scheduled to be released in August 2016.

Tualatin Valley Distilling

Hillsboro, Oregon, founded in 2013

www.tvdistilling.com

Originally started as Willamette Valley Distilling, the founders (Jason O´Donnell and Corey Bowers) eventually changed the name to Tualatin Valley. The distillery is equipped with a 26 gallon, 4-plate column still for the brandies and a 100 litre pot still for whiskey. Maturation takes place in small (5 gallons) charred American oak barrels but experiments have also been made with Hungarian oak. The owners concentrate on whiskey production and the first distillation was in December 2013. The current range consists of two brands; Oregon Single Malt Whiskey and 50/50 American Whiskey (50% rye and 50% malted barley). The owners have also recently introduced a range of limited expressions of the single malt using different types of wood for smoking the barley. An expansion of the production capacity announced last year is currently on hold.

Vikre Distillery

Duluth, Minnesota, founded in 2012

www.vikredistillery.com

Joel and Emily Vikre fired up the still for their first distillation in November 2013. Gin and aquavit have already found their way to shops and bars in Minnesota and they also have three different kinds of whiskey maturing on site – Iron Range American Single Malt, Gunflint Bourbon and Temperance River Rye. The first releases of these are still a few years away, but in November 2015,

a young bourbon was launched. Sugarbush has been matured in port barrels first, and then finished in bourbon barrels that have been seasoned with maple syrup. The distillery was expanded in April 2016 with six new fermentation tanks.

Rennaisance Artisan Distillers

Akron, Ohio, founded in 2013

renartisan.com

The distillery is an outgrowth of a homebrew supply shop run by brothers John and Jim Pastor. So far they have, apart from whiskey, produced gin, brandy, grappa and limoncello. The first whiskey release, The King´s Cut single malt, was made from a grain bill including special malts such as toasted and caramel malts. It was launched in October 2014 and new batches appear every 6 months. Early 2016, a larger lauter mash tun was installed which increased production significantly.

Coppercraft Distillery

Holland, Michigan, founded in 2012

coppercraftdistillery.com

Located in Holland, close to Lake Michigan, this distillery is owned and operated by Walter Catton. He uses a stainless steel mash tun, six washbacks and two stills - one stripping still with stainless steel pot and copper column and a fractioning still with both pot and column made from copper. The first three whiskies - corn, wheat and malted rye - were released in summer 2014. Walter expects to release his first single malt sometime in 2016.

John Emerald Distilling Company

Opelika, Alabama, founded in 2014

www.johnemeralddistilling.com

In October 2013, John and Jimmy Sharp (father and son) obtained the final approval to build a distillery and already in July 2014 the production started. The first distillations were made in a small, 26 gallon pilot still, but a larger pot/column hybrid still with four plates was soon installed. The mashing is done in a lauter tun and the wash is fermented on the grain in stainless steel tanks. The main product will be an Alabama Single Malt which gets its character from barley smoked with a blend of southern pecan and peach wood. The first release of the single malt was made in March 2015. Around 6,000 litres of whiskey will be produced during the first year. Other products include rum and gin.

11 Wells Distillery

St. Paul, Minnesota, founded in 2013

11wells.com

Located in the middle of St. Paul, close to the Flat Earth Brewing Company, this new distillery is run by Bob McManus and Lee Egbert. The distillery is equipped with a 650 gallon mash tun, stainless steel open-top fermentation tanks and two stills - a 250 gallon stripping still designed by themselves and a 100 gallon Kothe hybrid pot/column still. Whiskey is the main product and the first two releases, aged bourbon and rye, were released in November 2014. A wheat whiskey was released in 2015, but the owners have still to release a whiskey made entirely from malted barley. The labels on the bottles have a serial number which for instance shows oak origin, char level, yeast type, mash bill and mash type.

Blaum Bros. Distilling

Galena, Illinois, founded in 2012

blaumbros.com

Heavily influenced by Scotch whisky, the two brothers Matthew and Mike Blaum opened their distillery in 2012 and began distilling in early 2013. The equipment consists of a 2,000 litre mash tun, five 2,000 litre wash backs and a 2,000 litre Kothe hybrid still. The whiskey is matured in American oak, oloroso sherry butts, madeira casks, port barrels and rum barrels. Apart from gin and vodka, the first two releases were the sourced Knotter Bourbon and Knotter Rye. The first whiskey from their own production was a rye in 2015. It will probably be another three years before their first single malt is released.

Sugar House Distillery

Salt Lake City, Utah, founded in 2014

sugarhousedistillery.net

James Fowler's background as a dedicated home brewer for more than 20 years, led him to the decision to build a distillery. Assisted by Eric Robinson, an experienced distiller formerly based at High West distillery, he started production in 2014. The first release was a vodka, followed later that year by a single malt whisky. More releases of the single malt were made in November 2015 and bourbon and rum have also been added to the range. The malt whisky is unpeated and non chill-filtered and has been maturing in 10-15 gallon barrels made of charred, new American oak.

Venus Spirits

Santa Cruz, California, founded in 2014

venusspirits.com

After having worked in the brewing business and organic food industry, Sean Venus decided to build his own distillery. Production, which started in May 2014, is focused on whiskey, but he has also released gin and spirits from blue agave. The first single malt was Wayward Whiskey, made from crystal malt and released in January 2015. This was followed up by a rye and later a bourbon. The distillation takes place in a hand pounded alembic still from Spain.

Oak N´ Harbor Distillery

Oak Harbor, Ohio, founded in 2014

oaknharbordistillery.com

Together with his wife Andrea, Joe Helle began distilling in December 2014 and only a week later his first single malt was on the shelves. Aptly named Six Days Seven Nights, it had been maturing for a week in small barrels made from Minnesota white oak. Since then, both a bourbon and a corn whiskey have been released. Other products include gin, apple brandy, rum and vodka. Oak N´Harbor is probably the only distillery in the USA run by a mayor! Joe Helle was elected end of 2015.

Bent Brewstillery

Roseville, Minnesota, founded in 2014

bentbrewstillery.com

After years of research and education in the arts of distilling and brewing, Bartley Blume decided to build a combined brewery and distillery. Production started in 2014 and apart from a range of beers, Blume is also producing gin and whiskey with plans for many other varieties. No whiskies have been released so far, but one called Kursed Single Malt is currently aging in a combination of charred oak and charred apple wood and yet another was distilled from an India Pale Ale.

Orange County Distillery

Goshen, New York, founded in 2013

orangecountydistillery.com

This is a true farm distillery where the owners, Bryan Ensall and John Glebocki, grow every ingredient on the farm, including sugar beet, corn, rye, barley and even the botanicals needed for their gin. They malt their own barley and even use their own peat when needed. Production started in April 2014 and the first products, gin and vodka, were selling in October of the same year. Since then, they have also launched a wide range of whiskies, including corn, bourbon, rye and peated single malt. The first aged single malt (at around 7 months) was launched in summer 2015 and batch # 3

was released in April 2016, together with a honey-flavoured corn whiskey.

Key West Distilling

Key West, Florida, founded in 2013

kwdistilling.com

The main track for Jeffrey Louchheim is to produce rum but he is also distilling whiskey. The mash is brought in from Bone Island Brewing, fermented, distilled and filled into new barrels or used rum barrels. The first release of Whiskey Tango Foxtrot was in July 2015 with more batches following in spring and summer 2016.

Thumb Butte Distillery

Prescott, Arizona, founded in 2013

thumbbuttedistillery.com

A variety of gin, dark rum and vodka, as well as whiskey are produced by the owners, Dana Murdock, James Bacigalupi and Scott Holderness. Rodeo Rye, Bloody Basin Bourbon and Central Highlands Single Malt have all now been released. Maris Otter barley is being used for the malt whiskies.

Seattle Distilling

Vashon, Washington, founded in 2013

seattledistilling.com

Paco Joyce and Tami Brockway Joyce produce gin, vodka, coffee liqueur, as well as a malt whiskey. The latter, named Idle Hour was first launched in 2013 with batch 7 being released in February 2016. The style is Irish with both malted and unmalted barley being used in the mashbill. A small amount of honey is also added during fermentation. The owners' source used wine casks from a local winery and then re-cooper and char them on site.

Hewn Spirits

Pipersville, Pennsylvania, founded in 2013

hewnspirits.com

Using a 130 gallon copper still, Sean Tracy is producing a variety of spirits including rum, gin and vodka. On the whiskey side there is Dark Hollow Bourbon, Red Barn Rye and the Reclamation American Single Malt Whiskey which was released for the first time in summer 2014. After maturing the malt whiskey in barrels for 1-4 months, Tracy does a second maturation in stainless steel vats where he also puts in charred staves of either chestnut or hickory wood. The second maturation lasts for two weeks.

Damnation Alley Distillery

Belmont, Massachusetts, founded in 2013

damnationalleydistillery.com

A small distillery but with a wide range of whiskies. Founded in 2013 by Alison DeWolfe, Jeremy Gotsch, Jessica Gotsch, Alex Thurston and Emma Thurston, the distillery produces vodka but mainly whiskey. Maturation takes place for 4-6 months in 5 gallon barrels. Among the varieties that can be mentioned are single malt, hopped single malt, smoked single malt (smoked with fruit wood), bourbon, rye and a house whiskey from barley, corn, rye and wheat. In June 2016, the first 2 year old whiskey from the distillery was released.

Wright & Brown Distilling Co.

Oakland, California, founded in 2015

wbdistilling.com

Founded by Earl Brown and Daniel Wright, this distillery is focused on barrel aged spirits, i. e. whiskey, rum and brandy. The first whiskey was distilled in 2015 and the first product, a rye whiskey, was released during the summer of 2016 with the first single malt due for release in spring 2017. The equipment is made up of a 500 gallon mash tun, 500 gallon stainless steel fermenters and a 250 gallon copper pot still from Vendome.

Stark Spirits

Pasadena, California, founded in 2013

starkspirits.com

Greg Stark and Karen Robinson-Stark, co-founders of the distillery, obviously share the interest for distilled spirits but, while Karen is focused on gin, Greg tends to concentrate on whiskey and rum. The first single malt whiskey was distilled in July 2015 and the first release was a barrel of peated single malt in February 2016 for one customer. The first official distillery release of single malt is scheduled for September 2016 with more to follow towards the end of the year. They have two stills with one reserved for all the peated production. Peated malt is bought from Baird´s in Scotland.

Cotherman Distilling

Dunedin, Florida, founded in 2015

cothermandistilling.com

All the whiskies made by Michael Cotherman and his wife, Tara Cupp, are from 100% malted barley. The mash is brought in from local breweries, fermented at the distillery and then distilled in a pot still and a 3-plate bubble-cap still. The first release which was towards the end of July 2016 was a single barrel. Apart from whiskey – gin and vodka are also produced.

Quincy Street Distillery

Riverside, Illinois, founded in 2011

quincystreetdistillery.com

Derrick Mancini has built up an impressive range of spirits during the last couple of years which ranges from gin, vodka and absinth to bourbon, corn whiskey and poteen. So far, single malt whiskey made from barley only forms a small part. The only single malt released so far is a 2 year old Golden Prairie which was in December 2015 and the next one isn´t due until the beginning of 2018.

Boston Harbor Distillery

Boston, Massachusetts, founded in 2015

bostonharbordistillery.com

This distillery was founded by a highly experienced "veteran" in the drinks business. In 1984, Rhona Kallman co-founded Boston Beer Company, which today is famous worldwide for its Samuel Adams beer and, since then, Kallman has made a huge contribution to the production of craft beer world-wide. The distillery started production in summer 2015 and while it concentrates mainly on whiskey, it is also making a variety of spirits based on different Samuel Adams´ beers. At the time of writing, the first bottling of their flagship brand, Putnam New England Malt Whiskey, had not appeared, but a launch was expected in early autumn of 2016. Apart from the distillery with its 150-gallon Vendome copper pot still, the facility consists of a shop, tasting room and an event space.

Liquid Riot Bottling Co.

Portland, Maine, founded in 2013

liquidriot.com

When Liquid Riot opened its doors, it was Maine´s first brewery/distillery/resto-bar. At the waterfront in the Old Port, Eric Michaud produces an extensive range of beers and spirits which include bourbon, rye, oat, single malt, rum, vodka and agave spirit. The Old Port single malt made from 80% cherry wood smoked malt was first released as a 16 month old late in 2014, with a second release one year later. Distillation is made in a German hybrid still with a 5 plate rectification column and the single malt is matured in ex-bourbon barrels.

Old Line Spirits

Baltimore, Maryland, founded in 2014

oldlinespirits.com

When the two former Naval Flight Officers, Mark McLaughlin and Arch Watkins, decided to start producing whiskey, they happened to meet Bob Stilnovich at an American Distilling Institute conference. Bob was looking to sell his Golden Distillery in the Pacific Northwest and Mark and Arch seized the opportunity. They did an apprenticeship alongside Bob for a few months and then sent

In the warehouse at Boston Harbor Distillery

all the equipment to Baltimore and the maturing stock to Kentucky. During the summer of 2016, distilling started at their new location in Baltimore and a couple of months prior, the first Old Line single malt, two to three years old and obviously from the Golden Distillery production, was released. A peated version is planned for a 2017 release.

Cannon Beach Distillery

Cannon Beach, Oregon, founded in 2012

cannonbeachdistillery.com

Having been introduced to home brewing during his college days, Mike Selberg later decided to enter into distilling as well. His philosophy about whisky making is never to make the same spirit twice. So far he´s managed to make 16 different whiskeys with six of them having been released, while the others are still maturing. Included in the releases are Embrued, a 2 year old made from malt smoked by using both applewood and cherrywood, New Branch with the starting point from a stout beer recipe and Strata 1 (the latest release) was made from 100% heavily peated malt from Baird´s. The next release (Strata 2) is due to be released in December. Distillation takes place in a 380 litre Vendome still with a 6-plate column. Mike is also producing rum, gin and agave spirit.

Witherspoon Distillery

Lewisville, Texas, founded in 2011

witherspoondistillery.com

Two former US Marines, Quentin Witherspoon and Ryan DeHart, own and run the distillery together with Natasha DeHart. The main products are bourbon, rum and Bonfire (a cinnamon-infused rum), but they also make small runs of Witherspoon Single Malt which is generally aged between 1 and 2 years. The whiskey is distilled in two 1,110 litre stills and the single malt is matured in new American oak and finished in rum casks.

River Sands Distillery

Kennewick, Washington, founded in 2011

riversandsdistillery.com

The company has been around since 1968 but the distillery only started in 2011. The principal owners are Paul and Deana Schiro and Russell and Ida Horn. Different types of gin and vodka are produced, as well as two single malts – Kennewick and R J Callaghan. They are aged for 1,5 years in charred American oak and then finished for 6 months in Hungarian oak. During the summer of 2016 a 100% malted rye was released as well.

Sound Spirits

Seattle, Washington, founded in 2010 (whiskey since 2012)

drinksoundspirits.com

When it opened, it was Seattle´s first craft distillery since prohibition. A number of different spirits are produced by the owner, Steven Stone, namely gin, vodka, aquavit, liqueurs and single malt whiskey. The first release of the 3 year old Madame Damnable single malt was in 2015 and another two releases have since followed.

Alley 6 Craft Distillery

Healdsburg, California, founded in 2014

alley6.com

A small craft distillery in Sonoma county where everything from milling and mashing to distilling, barrelling and bottling is done by Jason and Krystle Jorgensen. The main product is rye whiskey and the first bottles were released in summer 2015. Single malt production is on a smaller scale with the first bottles having been released towards the end of May 2016. The Jorgensen´s are

experimenting with a range of different barley varieties, mainly from Germany and Belgium and the spirit is distilled in a 500 litre alembic copper still..

Gray Skies Distillery

Grand Rapids, Michigan, founded in 2014

grayskiesdistillery.com

In 2014, Brandon Voorhees and Steve Vander Pol bought an industrial building for their grain-to-glass distillery but, due to extensive refurbishing, it took more than a year before the first spirit was distilled. The equipment is made up of a 1,800 litre mash kettle, four fermenters and a 2,500 litre pot still with an attached column. Vodka and gin have already been released while rye, bourbon and single malt whiskeys are still in the barrels. A young, single malt may be released late in 2016.

San Diego Distillery

San Diego, California, founded in 2015

sddistillery.com

Unlike many of the other new craft distilleries, Trent and Maria Tilton have decided to focus almost entirely on whiskey. For Trent, the inspiration came from tasting Lagavulin 16 year old for the first time in 2012. In March 2016 the first six whiskies were released; a bourbon, a rye and an Islay peated single malt – all three bottled at 90 proof and at cask strength. The next whiskey to appear will be the 7 Malt Whiskey, where malted rye and wheat are also included in the mash bill. Trent and Maria´s distillery model is based on small one-off batches that will be available in their tasting room only.

Dallas Distilleries Inc.

Garland, Texas, founded in 2008

dallasdistilleries.com

The distillery which is run and owned by Herman Beckley and Marshall Louis, is primarily focused on whiskey alone. The first products in their Herman Marshall range were launched in 2013. It was a bourbon and a rye and was later followed by a single malt. The latest addition which was released in November 2015, was Temptress Single Malt - a collaboration with Lakewood Brewing Company where the whiskey has been flavoured with a milk stout. An unusual feature at the distillery is the open top fermenters which are made from cypress wood.

Hard Times Distillery

Monroe, Oregon, founded in 2009

dallasdistilleries.com

James Stegall and Dudley Clark started off with just the one product, Sweet Baby Vodka, which was made from molasses. This was followed by a wasabi-flavoured vodka, moonshine from oats and barley and Appleshine made from apple juice. Eventually the two owners branched into the production of whiskey and the latest release is Eleventh Hour Whiskey, a single malt which is distilled twice in pot stills.

Spirit Hound Distillers

Lyons, Colorado, founded in 2012

spirithounds.com

Craig Engelhorn and his four partners got off to a tough start when they opened up their distillery in 2012. Eight months after they had started production, the whole town of Lyons was devastated by flooding, which filled the distillery building with half a metre of flood water and mud. The distillery was shut down and between the first six barrels of whiskey and barrel #7 , there was an 8 month gap. Rum, vodka and sambucca are on the production list, but their signature spirits are inherently gin and malt whiskey. The barley for the whiskey is grown, malted and peat-smoked in Alamosa by Colorado Malting and the whiskey released so far is straight, i.e. at least two years old. The first bottles (five single barrels) hit the shelves in summer 2015 with another release of 12 single barrels in spring 2016. All their whiskeys are matured in full-size American oak barrels with a #3 char.

Arizona Distilling Company

Tempe Arizona, founded in 2012

azdistilling.com

When Jason Grossmiller and his partners released their first whiskey, it was a bourbon sourced from Indiana. The ensuing releases, which started with Desert Durum made from wheat, have all been produced in their distillery. Humphrey's – a single malt – was first released in late 2014 and more bottles became available in summer 2015. Other products include gin, vodka and rye whiskey.

Canada 🇨🇦

Distillery:	Glenora Distillery, Glenville, Nova Scotia
Founded:	1990
Owner:	Lauchie MacLean
	glenoradistillery.com

Situated in Nova Scotia, Glenora was the first malt whisky distillery in Canada. The first launch of in-house produce came in 2000 but a whisky called Kenloch had been sold before that. This was a 5 year old vatting of some of Glenora's own malt whisky and whisky from Bowmore Distillery on Islay. The first expression, a 10 year old, came in September 2000 and was named Glen Breton and this is still the core expression under the name Glen Breton Rare. Glen Breton Ice (10 years old), the world's first single malt aged in an ice wine barrel, was launched in 2006 and since then several expressions have been launched, among them single casks and sometimes under the name Glenora. To celebrate the distillery's 25th anniversary, a limited (130 bottles) 25 year old single cask was released in summer 2015. This was complemented later in the year by yet another limited release, Jardine Specials, in honour of the founder and original owner of Glenora Distillery - Bruce Jardine.

Distillery:	Shelter Point Distillery, Vancouver Island, British Columbia
Founded:	2009
Owner:	Patrick Evans
	shelterpointdistillery.com

In 2005, Patrick Evans and his family decided to switch from the dairy side of farming to growing crops and they bought the Shelter Point Farm just north of Comox on Vancouver Island. Eventually the idea to transform the farm into a distillery was raised and with the help of some Scottish investors headed by Andrew Currie, who co-founded Arran Distillery in the early 1990s, the construction work began. The buildings were completed in 2009 and in May 2010 all the equipment was in place. This includes a one tonne mash tun, five washbacks made of stainless steel (5,000 litres each) and one pair of stills (a 5,000 litre wash still and a 4,000 litre spirit still). Evans already has plans for a major expansion of the distillery in 2017 and two 26,000 litre copper pot stills have already been acquired from the closed Hiram Walker distillery in Kelowna. To assist with the start up, Patrick Evans asked Mike Nicolson to join him and his operating manager, Jim Marinus. Mike is an experienced distiller having worked for many years at distilleries in Scotland. Distillation started in spring 2011 and the barley used for the distillation is grown on the farm. In May 2016, 7,000 bottles of the first single malt, 5 years old, were released. The plan for 2017, is to release another 17,000 bottles and the following year, increase to almost 30,000.

Distillery:	Victoria Caledonian Distillery, Victoria, British Columbia
Founded:	2016
Owner:	Graeme Macaloney et al
	victoriacaledonian.com

Scotsman and founder of the Victoria Caledonian Distillery, Graeme Macaloney, first worked as a student in the Black & White whisky factory. This had inspired him to study fermentation at Strathclyde University, followed by biochemical engineering at University College London, and then finally an industrial PhD in fermentation at Strathclyde. After working in a an ex-Distillers Company Limited (DCL) fermentation facility he re-mortgaged his house, raised $2.4m from Agriculture Canada, and several $million from over 250 Canadian whisky enthusiasts to finance and build the

The Victoria Caledonian Distillery team (left to right): Dr. Graeme Macaloney - founder & fermentation engineer, Dr. Jim Swan - maturation guru and Mike Nicolson – Master Distiller.

joint-second largest single malt distillery in Canada. As a helping hand Macaloney had Mike Nicolson, who previously worked at no less than 18 distilleries in Scotland. In addition, he had also acquired the services of Jim Swan, one of the foremost whisky consultants in the world and an expert in whisky maturation.

The distillery is equipped with a 1 ton semilauter mash tun, 7 stainless steel washbacks, a 5,500 litre wash still and a 3,600 litre spirit still from Forsyth. There is also a craft beer brewery on site. Distilling started in July 2016 and Macaloney is also planning for triple distilled pot still whiskey, as well as peated single malt once he has commissioned the planned traditional floor malting. A visitor centre has also been opened which offers tours on several levels of the distillery and the brewery, as well as tutored tastings. There is also the opportunity for whisky enthusiasts to buy 30-litre casks and to design their own whisky from a selection of five different new make options and ten different cask options.

Distillery:	Still Waters Distillery, Concord, Ontario
Founded:	2009
Owner:	Barry Bernstein and Barry Stein
	stillwatersdistillery.com

In 2009, Barry Bernstein and Barry Stein opened Still Waters distillery in Concord, on the northern outskirts of Toronto. The distillery is equipped with a 3,000 litre mash tun, two 3,000 litre washbacks and a Christian Carl 450 litre pot still. The still also has rectification columns for brandy and vodka production. The plan is to expand production sometime in 2016 which will increase the capacity by 2 to 3 times. The focus is on whisky but they also produce vodka, brandy and gin. Their first release was a triple distilled, single malt vodka and they have also released a Canadian whisky with distillate sourced from other producers. Their first single malt, named Stalk & Barrel Single Malt, was released in April 2013 and around 40 batches have followed since. In late 2014 it was time for their first rye whisky release, made from locally sourced 100% Ontario rye. In the future, rye will comprise about half of the total releases.

New releases from Pemberton and Shelter Point

Other distilleries in Canada

Victoria Spirits

Sidney, British Columbia, founded in 2008

www.victoriaspirits.com

This family-run distillery recently moved from Victoria on Vancouver Island to Sidney, 20 km to the north. Their best-selling product is Victoria Gin, which currently sells 10,000 bottles a year. Whisky production started in 2009 but has been very intermittent. The first and only single malt, Craigdarroch, was launched in early 2015. Only 250 bottles were released and more whisky can´t be expected for at least a couple of years.

Pemberton Distillery

Pemberton, British Columbia, founded in 2009

www.pembertondistillery.ca

Tyler Schramm started distilling in 2009, with vodka produced from potatoes as the first product. He used a copper pot still from Arnold Holstein and the first Schramm Vodka, was launched later that year. During the ensuing year, Tyler started his first trials, distilling a single malt whisky using organic malted barley from the Okanagan Valley. His aim is to produce 6-10 200 litre casks of whisky per year. The first release was in October 2013 when a limited 3 year old unpeated version was launched. Since autumn 2015, the owners have a regular expression called Pemberton Valley Organic Single Malt Whisky.

Okanagan Spirits

Vernon and Kelowna, British Columbia, founded in 2004

www.okanaganspirits.com

The first distillery named Okanagan was started in 1970 by Hiram Walker to which malt whisky production was added in 1981, but it closed in 1995. The main part of the production was shipped to Japan to be used by Suntory for their whisky blending. In 2004, forestry engineer, Frank Deiter, decided to make a career change and established Okanagan Spirits. A distillery was opened in Vernon and, later on, a second one was built in Kelowna. A variety of spirits made from fruits and berries as well as gin, vodka, absinthe and whisky ar being produced. Their core whisky is a blend of two 5 year old whiskies made from rye and corn with a small percentage of malted barley. Since 2013, there is also a 6 year old single malt in the range - The Laird of Fintry.

Yukon Spirits

Whitehorse, Yukon, founded in 2009

www.twobrewerswhisky.com

In 1997 Bob Baxter and Alan Hansen founded Yukon Brewing which more than 10 years later was expanded with also a small distillery. All of the whisky produced is made from malted grains but not only barley but also wheat and rye. The goal is to release small batches where they use a variety of malted and roasted grains and different fermentation techniques. The first 850 bottles of the 7 year old Two Brewer´s Yukon Single Malt Whisky were released in February 2016 and the portfolio is now based on four styles; Classic, Peated, Special Finishes and Innovative.

L B Distillers

Saskatoon, Saskatchewan, founded in 2012

www.lbdistillers.ca

The abbreviation for LB in the distillery name stands for Lucky Bastards and the luckiest bastard amongst the owners is Michael Goldney, who earned his nickname after winning the lottery in 2006. Joined by Cary Bowman and Lacey Crocker, he opened up the distillery in 2012. The first single malt whisky was released in summer 2016 but before that, the owners have released a fair amount of other spirits – vodka, gin and a variety of liqueurs.

Australia & New Zealand

Australia

Distillery: Lark Distillery, Hobart, Tasmania
Founded: 1992
Owner: Lark Distillery Pty Ltd.
larkdistillery.com.au

In 1992, Bill Lark was the first person for 153 years to take out a distillation licence in Tasmania. Since then he has not just established himself as a producer of malt whiskies of high quality, but has also helped to off-set several new distilleries. The success of the distillery forced Bill and his wife Lyn to start thinking of how to generate future growth and in 2013 they took on board a group of Hobart based investors as majority owners of the company. The Larks are still significant shareholders and Bill will now devote his time to being a global brand ambassador for Lark Distillery. In January 2014, they acquired Old Hobart Distillery and the Overeem brand.

Lark Distillery is situated on a farm at Mt Pleasant, 15 minutes' drive from Hobart. The whisky is double-distilled in a 1,800 litre wash still and a 600 litre spirit still and then matured in 100 litre "quarter casks". In 2015, more staff was hired and production was doubled compared to 2014. There are also plans to add another pair of stills to increase production even further. The old distillery site down in Hobart at the waterfront is now a cellar door and a showcase for Lark whisky.

The core product in the whisky range is the Classic Cask Single Malt Whisky at 43%, previously released as single casks but now a marriage of several casks. There is also the Distillers Selection at 46% and a Cask Strength at 58%, both of which are also single cask. Future plans include releases of special bottlings, for example, whisky matured in rum casks or finished in the distillery's own apple brandy casks..

Distillery: Bakery Hill Distillery, North Balwyn, Victoria
Founded: 1998
Owner: David Baker
bakeryhilldistillery.com.au

Since 2008, when Bakery Hill Distillery completed the installation of a 2,000 litre brewery, David Baker has had total control of all the processes from milling the grain to bottling the matured spirit. The first spirit at Bakery Hill Distillery was produced in 2000 and the first single malt was launched in autumn 2003. Three different versions are available – Classic and Peated (both matured in ex-bourbon casks) and Double Wood (ex-bourbon and a finish in French Oak). As Classic and Peated are also available as cask strength bottlings, they can be considered two more varieties. Most of the spirit is matured in ex-bourbon American oak from Jack Daniels and the 225 litre hogsheads are rebuilt into 100 litre barrels. Recently David started doing trials with three new wood finishes but an eventual release is still a couple of years away.

Distillery: Old Hobart Distillery, Blackmans Bay, Tasmania
Founded: 2005
Owner: Lark Distillery Pty Ltd.
overeemwhisky.com

Even though Casey Overeem did not start his distillery until 2007, he had spent several years experimenting with different types of distillation which were inspired by travels to Norway and Scotland. The distillery (previously known as Overeem Distillery) came on stream in 2007. The mashing is done at Lark distillery where Overeem also has his own washbacks and the wash is made to his specific requirement, among others, with his own yeast. In every mash, a mix of 50% unpeated barley and 50% slightly peated is used. The wash is then transported to Old Hobart Distillery where the distillation takes place in two stills (wash still of 1,800 litres and spirit still of 600 litres).

The range consists of Overeem Port Cask Matured and Overeem Sherry Cask Matured, both varieties available at 43% and 60%. In December 2013, Overeem Bourbon Cask Matured at 43% was released, followed by a 60% version in June 2014.

In January 2014, Old Hobart distillery was acquired by Lark Distillery Pty Ltd. The latter was formed during the summer of 2013 when a group of investors took a majority position in Lark distillery. Casey Overeem has now retired and his daugther, Jane, is the marketing manager for Lark and Overeem, as well as being the brand ambassador for Overeem.

Distillery: Tasmania Distillery, Cambridge, Tasmania
Founded: 1994
Owner: Patrick Maguire
tasmaniadistillery.com

Founded in 1994, it wasn't until the current owner, Patrick Maguire, took over that the distillery became a subject of interest. The distillery obtains wash from Cascade Brewery in Hobart and the spirit is then double distilled, although there is only one still at the distillery. In September 2014 the distillery moved to a new building about four times the size of the current facility. Production was also escalated and they are now distilling 7 days a week which means filling around 420 casks per year - 140 port pipes and 280 bourbon barrels.

The range comprises of Sullivan's Cove Single Cask, bottled at 47,5% and matured in either bourbon casks or French oak port casks and Sullivan's Cove Double Cask (40%) which is a marriage of port and bourbon casks. The age has increased over the years and currently they are bottling 12 to 15 year old whisky vintages. The distillery has won several awards for its whiskies during the last few years and to acknowledge that achievement, a very limited (only 2 bottles) release was made in August 2015. The Sullivan's Cove Manifesto is a vatting of whiskies that has been awarded World's Best Single Malt Whisky, as well as Best Australian Single Malt. Filled into 6 kg crystal decanters, the whiskies were sold on the same day that they were released and at a staggering price of $10,000 each. Version 2 of Manifesto is expected sometime in 2016.

Distillery: Hellyers Road Distillery, Burnie, Tasmania
Founded: 1999
Owner: Betta Milk Co-op
hellyersroaddistillery.com.au

Hellyer's Road Distillery is the largest single malt whisky distillery in Australia with a capacity of doing 100,000 litres of pure alcohol per year. The distillery is equipped with a 6.5 ton mash tun and the wash is fermented for 65 hours. There is only one pair of stills but they compensate for numbers by size. The wash still has a capacity of 40,000 litres and the spirit still 20,000 litres. The foreshots take around 4-5 hours and the middle cut will last for 24 hours, which is six to seven times longer compared to what is common practice in Scotland. Another interesting fact is that the pots on both stills are made of stainless steel while heads, necks and lyne arms are made of copper. Maturation takes place in ex-bourbon casks but they also use Tasmanian red wine barrels for part of it. .

The first whisky was released in 2006 and there are now seven varieties of Hellyers Road Single Malt Whisky in the core range: Original (with no age statement) and a peated bottled at cask strength are only available to visitors at the distillery. Original 10 year old, Original 12 year old, Port Cask 10 year old, a Pinot Noir finish and Slightly Peated are more readily available. There is also a Hellyer's Road Roaring 40´s reserved for export. End of 2014, the Henry´s Legacy Range was introduced. This is a new series of cask strength, single cask bottlings with The Gorge as the first release. The second, Saint Valentine´s Peak, appeared in July 2015.

Distillery:	Great Southern Distilling Company, Albany, Western Australia
Founded:	2004
Owner:	Great Southern Distilling Company Pty Ltd./ Cameron Syme
	limeburners.com.au

The distillery was built in Albany on the south-western tip of Australia in 2004 with whisky production commencing in late 2005. Throughout the initial years, production of whisky, brandy, vodka and gin took place in a set of sheds on the outskirts of Albany. A move was made in 2007 to a new, custom-built distillery with a visitor centre at Princess Royal Harbour. For the distillation, one wash still (1,800 litres) and one spirit still (580 litres) are used and a 600 litre copper pot antique gin still has also been installed. The goal for the production in 2016 is 25,000 litres.

The first expression of the whisky, called Limeburners, was released in 2008 and this is still the core bottling. Included in the range are also American Oak, Port Cask and Sherry Cask, all bottled at 43% as well as Peated which is bottled at 48%. A limited, heavily peated whisky, Darkest Winter bottled at 65.1%, was released in August 2016. A new addition to the range was released in 2012 – Tiger Snake, an Australian sour mash whisky based on corn, malted barley and rye. In December 2015, the company opened a second distillery combined with a cellar door and restaurang in Margaret River.

Distillery:	Nant Distillery, Bothwell, Tasmania
Founded:	2007
Owner:	Keith Batt
	nant.com.au

Nant distillery, in the Central Highlands of Tasmania, started when Queensland businessman, Keith Batt, bought the property in 2004. He refurbised the Historic Sandstone Water Mill on the estate and converted it into a whisky distillery. The first distillation took place in 2008. The distillery is equipped with a 1,800 litre wash still, a 600 litre spirit still and wooden washbacks for the fermentation.

Quarter casks of 100 litres, which previously held port, sherry and bourbon, are used for maturation. The first bottlings were released in 2010 and since 2012 the range consists of Nant Single Malt Whisky matured in either bourbon, sherry, port or pinot noir casks, bottled at 43%. There are also cask strength versions (63%) of all four. The latest additions to the range are Old Mill Reserve, matured in a combination of bourbon and sherry casks and bottled at 63% and White Oak which had been matured in virgin American oak and bottled at 43%.

In December 2015, Keith Batt filed for bankruptcy with debts of $16.2 million. This probably does not affect the work at the distillery as his shares in Nant Distilling are owned by a company under the direction of a family trust, of which Batt is not a beneficiary.

Other distilleries in Australia

New World Whisky Distillery

Essendon Fields, Melbourne, Victoria, founded in 2008

www.newworldwhisky.com.au

The distillery, founded by David Vitale, was until recently fitted into an old Qantas maintenance hangar at Essendon Fields, Melbourne´s original airport. The stills (an 1,800 litre wash still and a 600 litre spirit still) were bought from Joadja Creek Distillery in Mittagong and currently the yearly production is around 20,000 cases. At the end of October 2016, the distillery moved to a new and bigger site in Port Melbourne. The first whisky was released under the name Starward in 2013 and since then the range has been expanded. A range of limited releases called New World Projects has also been launched with a double maturation (re-fill and first fill port) as the latest addition.

In December 2015, the distillery was given a major boost when Diageo´s incubator fund project, Distill Ventures, announced that they would invest in the Australian company. The sum was not disclosed but it was said it would be used to boost production and help the company expand into new markets.

Archie Rose Distillery

William McHenry and Sons Distillery

Port Arthur, Tasmania, founded in 2011

www.mchenrydistillery.com.au

William McHenry was working as an employee at a biotech company in Sydney in 2006 when he first started considering a distillery of his own. In 2011 the decision was taken and he moved to Tasmania with his family. The copper still was delivered in October of that year and in January 2012 he started distilling. The distillery is equipped with a 500 litre copper pot still with a surrounding water jacket to get a lighter spirit. In 2013 he built a new 200 m² bond store to be able to increase production. To facilitate the cash flow, he produces a range of gin including Dry Gin, Sloe Gin, Navy Strength Gin and a Barrel Aged Gin. The first whisky release, 100 bottles made from Tasmanian Gairdner barley, aged in American oak casks from Maker's Mark for four years and finished in Australian ex-apera (sherry) barrels, was released in May 2016.

Archie Rose Distilling Company

Rosebery, New South Wales, founded in 2014

www.archierose.com.au

For many years brewing and spirit production was only a hobby for Will Edwards, but after a visit to craft distilleries in Brooklyn, New York, he decided to go ahead and build Sydney's first independent distillery. Archie Rose is situated just 5 km from the city centre and the first distillation was conducted in December 2014. Apart from producing single malt and rye whisky (both of which are currently maturing), Will has also produced and released gin and vodka. The first mash tun was completely manual, including stirring the mash by hand, but is has now been exchanged for a stainless steel lauter tun. Three copper pot stills (two for whisky and one for gin/vodka production) are all made in Tasmania. The single malt is both peated and unpeated and matures mainly in Australian ex-port and ex-sherry casks. Will has also introduced Tailored Spirits which allows customers to create their own gin, vodka or whisky based on their own preferences. The choices when it comes to whisky, include the size of the cask, as well as the wood type and the level of peating. The excellent distillery bar was named Sydney's Best New bar in 2015.

Launceston Distillery

Western Junction (near Launceston), Tasmania, founded in 2013

www.launcestondistillery.com.au

The distillery was founded in 2013 by five friends and the first distillation was in October 2015. The distillery is located in a hangar at Launceston Airport and initially, the owners will be distilling 100-200 litres per week with production planned to increase in the future. The equipment consists of a 1,100 litre stainless steel mash tun, stainless steel washbacks with a fermentation time of one week, a 1,600 litre wash still and a 700 litre spirit still - both with reflux balls. The newmake is filled into barrels which have previously held bourbon, sherry and port. The goal is to have the first whisky ready for release in early 2018.

Black Gate Distillery

Mendooran, New South Wales, founded in 2012

www.blackgatedistillery.com

This boutique distillery was opened by Brian and Genise Hollingworth in January 2012. Both mashing and fermentation are done at the distillery and since autumn 2013 they have also started peatsmoking the barley on site. The first products were vodkas and liqueurs with rum following. The first release of a single malt came in the beginning of 2015 when a sherrymatured expression was launched. One of the latest, in spring 2016, was a cask strength version of the previous but this time also lightly peated.

Redlands Estate Distillery

Kempton, Tasmania, founded in 2013

www.redlandsestate.com.au

Redlands Estate in Derwent Valley dates back to the early 1800s and was run mainly as a hop and grain farm. A few years ago, Peter and Elizabeth Hope bought the rundown property, restored it into

Launceston Distillery

a working farm including a distillery. In spring 2016, the distillery re-located to Dysart House, an old coaching inn in Kempton, which was built in 1842. The first spirit was double distilled in March 2013 in a 900 litre copper pot still and in 2016, yet another and bigger still (2,000 litre) was installed. The barley used is grown on the estate and it is also floor malted on site. The first whisky, which had been matured in a 20 litre pinot noir cask, was released in September 2015 and this was followed by several more releases.

Timboon Railway Shed Distillery

Timboon, Victoria, founded in 2007

www.timboondistillery.com.au

The small town of Timboon lies 200 kilometres southwest of Melbourne. Here, Tim Marwood established his combination of a distillery and a restaurant in 2007 in a renovated railway goods shed. Using a pilsner malted barley, Marwood obtains the wash (1,000 litres) from the local Red Duck microbrewery. The wash is then distilled twice in a 600 litre pot still. For maturation, resized (20 litres) and retoasted ex-port, tokay and bourbon barrels are used. The first release of a whisky, matured in port barrels, was made in 2010 and the latest expression, released in May 2016, was Tom´s Cut, bottled at 58%. Around 4,000 litres are produced yearly and Tim has plans to create a second range of peatsmoked whiskies.

Castle Glen Distillery

The Summit, Queensland, founded in 2009

www.castleglenaustralia.com.au

Established as a vineyard in 1990 by the current owner Cedric Millar, Castle Glen moved on to open up also a brewery and a distillery in 2009. Apart from wine and beer, a wide range of spirits are produced including rum, vodka, gin, absinthe and various eau de vies. Castle Glen is also the only whiskey (they use this spelling) distillery in Queensland. Malted barley is imported from Switzerland and the first whiskey, Castle Glen Limited Edition, was released as a 2 year old in early 2012.

Joadja Distillery

Joadja, New South Wales, founded in 2014

www.joadjadistillery.com.au

This distillery was originally founded by Mark Longobardi seven years ago but never went in to production. The stills were sold to

New World Whisky Distillery and the National Heritage Listed property (with no production equipment left) was bought by Valero Jimenez in March 2011. He applied for an Excise Licence and consulted with Bill Lark on how to start up the production. The first distillation was in December 2014 when the distillery was equipped with just the one still (800 litres), used for both the wash and the spirit run. In December 2015, a 2,400 litre wash still was installed together with another four washbacks. The owners plan to grow 30 acres of their own barley on the estate and also to malt it on site, using peat to dry it. The first whisky will probably be released in April 2017.

Mackey´s/Shene Distillery

Pontville, Tasmania, founded in 2015

www.mackeysdistillery.com.au, www.shene.com.au

Shene Distillery is scheduled to open end of December 2015 but distillation actually began already in 2007 in a different location. That was the year when Damian Mackey built a minute distillery in a shed on his property in New Town outside Hobart. Over the years, Mackey has patiently been experimenting and learning the trade and in spring 2016 the opportunity came for him to move his production to the Shene Estate at Pontville, 30 minutes north of Hobart. The estate, dating back to 1819, has been restored and is now owned by David and Anne Kemke. Prior to that, in September 2015, Mackey released his first single malt - a triple distilled, Irish-style malt whisky matured for 6 years in a port cask and more releases have followed. The first bottles from Mackey´s production at the Shene Distillery won´t be available until mid 2018.

Tin Shed Distilling Co.

Welland (Adelaide), South Australia, founded in 2013

www.iniquity.com.au

The first distillery founded by Ian Schmidt and Vic Orlow in 2004 was Southern Coast Distillers. They made their first whisky release in 2010, but two years later the operation folded due to a disagreement with a third partner. Ian and Vic, however, kept going and started a new business, Tin Shed Distilling Company. Initially they used equipment from the first distillery, but in 2014 this was supplemented by a 2,200 litre wash still and a new mash tun. The spirit is matured in 100 litre ex Australian fortified wine casks and the first single malt, under the name, Iniquity, was released as a 2 year old in autumn 2015. More releases have then followed.

Cardrona - the newest distillery in New Zealand

distillery experiences an Angel´s Share of 10-11%, mainly due to extreme variations in temperature and humidity in the Adelaide area, or as Ian Schmidt says; "It is mostly as hot as Hades and as dry as a dead dingo´s donger."

Mt Uncle Distillery

Walkamin, North Queensland, founded in 2001

www.mtuncle.com

When Mark Watkins founded the distillery in 2001, he started out by producing gin, rum and vodka - all of which soon became established brands on the market. After a few years, Watkins decided to add whisky production as well. Their first single malt, The Big Black Cock, first released in April 2014, is produced using local Queensland barley and has been matured for five years in a combination of French and American oak.

Loch Distillery

Loch, Victoria, founded in 2014

www.lochbrewery.com.au

Situated in an old bank building, this combined brewery and distillery has been producing since summer 2014. The owner, Craig Johnson, learnt about distilling from Bill Lark (like so many others have) before ordering his stills from Portugal. Gin has already been released while whisky production didn´t start until March 2015. The wash used for the whisky production comes from their own brewery. In June 2016, the distillery was expanded with a new, 400 litre alembic still.

Fanny´s Bay Distillery

Weymouth, Tasmania, founded in 2015

One of the newest additions to the Tasmanian whisky scene, the distillery was built by Mathew and Julie Cooper in 2014. Most of the equipment was actually constructed by Mathew himself and the distillery is equipped with a 400 litre copper pot still, a 600 litre mash tun and a 300 litre washback with a 7-8 day fermentation. The whisky starts in 20 litre port barrels and is then finished in small bourbon casks.

Applewood Distillery

Gumeracha, South Australia, founded in 2015

www.applewooddistillery.com.au

In their early twenties, Laura and Brendan Carter started Unico Zelo wines and, a few years later, expanded the business to also include perfumes. In 2015, a further expansion led to the Carter´s opening a distillery in the Adelaide Hills. To start with, gin, eau de vie and liqueurs were on the menu, but in summer 2015, whisky production was added. In March 2016, a 3 months old single malt spirit that had matured in ex-tawny casks was released.

New Zealand

Distillery:	New Zealand Malt Whisky Co., Oamary, South Island
Founded:	2000
Owner:	Extra Eight
	thenzwhisky.com, milfordwhisky.co.nz

In 2001, Warren Preston bought the entire stock of single malt and blended whisky from the decommissioned Wilsons Willowbank Distillery in Dunedin. The supplies that he acquired consisted of 400 casks of single malt whisky including production dating back to 1987. Before he bought it, the whisky was sold under the name Lammerlaw, but Preston renamed it Milford. Preston also had plans to build a distillery in Oamaru. In 2010, however, his company was evicted from its premises and later it was placed in receivership

but rescue came in the form of a syndicate of investors led by Tasmanian-based businessman Greg Ramsay. Their capital injection revived the company and plans to build a distillery still exist. Since early 2015, the company has been distilling trial batches of whisky at Workshops Whisky, a division of Kenny Beverages in Christchurch, a small distillery owned by Doug and Anthony Lawry.

The Milford range (10, 15, 18 and 20 years old) was released already when Warren Preston was the owner. With the new ownership, the range of expressions from the old stock has increased rapidly with South Island Single Malt (up to 25 years old), Dunedin Doublewood blend 16 years old, single casks from 1988 to 1993, Diggers & Ditch (a blended malt with whiskies from both New Zealand and Tasmania) and 1987. Touch.Pause.Enjoy. 27 years old, the oldest expression from the distillery so far. Among the most recent bottlings is Oamaruvian 16 year old, a blend including grain whisky that has been matured for six years in bourbon barrels and then another ten years in New Zealand red wine barrels.

Distillery:	Thomson Whisky Distillery, Auckland, North Island
Founded:	2014
Owner:	Thomson Whisky New Zealand Ltd.
	thomsonwhisky.com

The company started out as an independent bottler, sourcing their whiskies from the closed Willowbank Distillery in Dunedin, New Zealand. Two of the whiskies available are an 18 year old and a 21 year old single cask while the third, named Two Tone, is a vatting of whisky matured in American white oak and in European oak casks that had held New Zealand red wine. In April 2014, Rachel and Mathew Thomson opened up a small distillery (basically just a copper pot still) based at Hallertau Brewery in North West Auckland. The wash for the distillation comes from the brewery. In summer 2014, trials were made producing a whisky where the malt had been kilned using New Zealand Manuka wood. "Work-in-progress" bottles of the Manuka spirit were released in 2015 but the first whisky isn´t expected until 2017 or 2018.

Distillery:	Cardrona Distillery, Cardrona (near Wanaka), South Island
Founded:	2015
Owner:	Desiree and Ash Whitaker
	cardronadistillery.com

The mastermind behind the distillery, Desiree Whitaker, sold her dairy farm in South Canterbury to pursue her dream of building a distillery. She found a site in Cardrona Valley and met her husband, Ash, at the same time. Building on the distillery started in January 2015 and in October the first distillation was made. The distillery is equipped with 1.4 ton mash tun, six metal washbacks, one 2,000 litre wash still and a 1,300 litre spirit still. For production of single malt vodka there is also a Jacob Carl column still from Germany and for gin, a New Zealand built vapour infusion still. The two pot stills were made by the famous copper smiths in Scotland, Forsyth's Ltd and the owner and manager of the company, Richard Forsyth, even attended the distillery opening. One of the reasons for that could have been the fact that Richard Forsyth´s niece, Jennie Whitlock is the Cardrona distillery manager! The production capacity is one barrel per day and the whisky will be matured in sherry casks from Gonzales Byass and bourbon barrels from Breckinridge distillery in Colorado. The owners plan to release the first bottles in 2025 as a 10 year old.

Asia

India

Distillery: Amrut Distilleries Ltd., Bangalore
Founded: 1948
Owner: Jagdale Group

amrutwhisky.co.uk

The family-owned distillery, based in Bangalore, south India, started to distil malt whisky in the mid-eighties. The equivalent of 50 million bottles of spirits (including rum, gin and vodka) is manufactured a year, of which 1,4 million bottles is whisky. Most of the whisky goes to blended brands, but Amrut single malt was introduced in 2004. It was first introduced in Scotland, but can now be found in more than 20 countries and has recently been introduced to the American market. Funnily enough, it took until 2010 before it was launched in India.

The distillery, with a capacity of doing 200,000 litres of pure alcohol per year, is equipped with six washbacks with a fermentation time of 140 hours and two stills, each with a capacity of 5,000 litres. The barley is sourced from the north of India, malted in Jaipur and Delhi and finally distilled in Bangalore before the whisky is bottled without chill-filtering or colouring. The owners have plans to build yet another distillery adjacent to the present.

The Amrut core range consists of unpeated and peated versions bottled at 46%, a cask strength and a peated cask strength and, finally, Fusion which is based on 25% peated malt from Scotland and 75% unpeated Indian malt. Special releases over the years include Two Continents, where maturing casks have been brought from India to Scotland for their final period of maturation: Intermediate Sherry Matured where the new spirit has matured in ex-bourbon or virgin oak, then re-racked to sherry butts and with a third maturation in ex-bourbon casks: Kadhambam which is a peated Amrut which has matured in ex Oloroso butts, ex Bangalore Blue Brandy casks and then finally in ex rum casks; Amrut Herald with four years bourbon maturation in India and a final 18 months on the German island of Helgoland and, finally, Portonova with a maturation in bourbon casks, then 9 months in port pipes and

back to bourbon casks for the last 8 months. Both Portonova and Intermediate Sherry are annual limited editions, whereas new expressions of Kadhambam, Herald and Two Continents are released on a more irregular basis.

A big surprise for 2013 was the release of Amrut Greedy Angels, an 8 year old and the oldest Amrut so far. That was an astonishing achievement in a country where the hot and humid climate causes major evaporation during maturation. In 2015 it was time for an even older expression when the 10 year old Greedy Angel´s - Chairman´s Reserve was launched. Then, finally in 2016, the Amrut people managed to improve even further upon their previous attempts when 100 bottles of a 12 year old, the oldest whisky from India so far, were released. Recent, limited releases include the highly innovative Spectrum, where the whisky had matured in casks made of five different types of wood; new American oak, new French oak, new Spanish oak, ex PX casks and ex Oloroso casks. This was followed up in autumn 2016 with Amrut Double Cask, a vatting of a PX sherry cask and an ex-bourbon cask, as well as Amrut Rye Single Malt - the first rye whisky from the company. This was also the first 100% malted rye from Asia and actually one of only a few in the world!

Distillery: John Distilleries Jdl, Goa
Founded: 1992
Owner: Paul P John

pauljohnwhisky.com

Paul P John, who today is the chairman of the company, started in 1992 by making a variety of spirits including Indian whisky made from molasses. Their biggest seller today is Original Choice, a blend of extra neutral alcohol distilled from molasses and malt whisky from their own facilities. The brand, which was introduced in 1995/96 has since made an incredible journey. It is now the world´s 8th most sold whisky with sales of 128 million bottles in 2015.

John Distilleries owns three distilleries and produces its brands from 18 locations in India with its head office in Bangalore. The basis for their blended whiskies is distilled in column stills with a

The latest achievement from Amrut – Greedy Angels 12 year old, the oldest Indian whisky ever released

capacity of 500 million litres of extra neutral alcohol per year. In 2007 they set up their single malt distillery which is equipped with one pair of traditional copper pot stills with another set of stills being installed in early 2017. This will increase the malt whisky capacity to 1.5 million litres per year. The company released their first single malt in autumn 2012 and this was followed by several single casks bottled at cask strength. In May 2013 it was time for two more widely available core expressions, both made from Indian malted barley. Brilliance is unpeated and bourbon-matured while Edited, also matured in bourbon casks, has a small portion of peated barley in the recipe. The peat was brought in from Scotland but the malting process took place in India. At the beginning of 2014, two cask strength bottlings were released; Select Cask Classic (55,2%) and the quite heavily peated Select Cask Peated (55,5%). These are limited versions but will be released continuously. In 2015, finally, the third core expression was released. It was a 100% peated bottling called Bold, bottled at 46%. Recent limited releases from 2016, include three 7 year old single malts; Mars Orbiter, a peated whisky matured in American oak, Oloroso, unpeated and matured in oloroso butts and Kanya, unpeated from American oak. Currently the single malts are available in ten countries in Europe (including the UK, Germany and Scandinavia) as well as in Australia, Singapore, Taiwan and Malaysia.

Other distilleries in India

McDowell´s Distillery

Ponda, Goa, founded in 1988 (malt whisky)

unitedspirits.in

In 1826 the Scotsman, Angus McDowell, established himself as an importer of wines, spirits and cigars in Madras (Chennai) and the firm was incorporated in 1898. In the same town another Scotsman, Thomas Leishman, founded United Breweries in 1915. Both companies were bought by Vital Mallya around 1950 and eventually, under the leadership of Vijay Mallya, became the second largest producer of alcohol in the world after Diageo. Since 2014, after a business settlement involving several steps, Diageo controls

the majority of the shares in United Spirits.

United Spirits has more than 140 brands in their portfolio including Scotch whisky, Indian whisky, vodka, rum, brandy and wine. The absolute majority of United Spirits´ whiskies are Indian whisky, made of molasses while single malt sales are negligible. McDowell´s Single Malt is made at the distillery in Ponda (Goa) and sells 20,000 cases each year. It has matured for 3-4 years in ex-bourbon casks.

Rampur Distillery

Rampur Uttar Pradesh, founded in 1943

www.rampursinglemalt.com

This huge distillery is situated west of Delhi and around 100 kilometres from the Nepalese border. It was purchased in 1972 by G. N. Khaitan and is today owned by Radico Khaitan, the fourth biggest Indian liquor company. The distillery has a capacity of producing 75 million litres of whisky based on molasses, 30 million litres of grain whisky and 460,000 litres of malt whisky per year. The first whisky brand from Radico was 8PM, launched in 1999 and today sells around 50 million bottles yearly. The first single malt release, un-chill filtered and without age statement, appeared in May 2016.

Israel

Distillery:	The Milk & Honey Distillery, Jaffa
Founded:	2013
Owner:	Gal Kalkshtein et al.
	mh-distillery.com

This is the first whisky distillery that has been undertaken in Israel and the team behind the project comprises of Gal Kalkshtein, Simon Fried, Amit Dror and Nir Gilat. In addition to this, they are ably assisted by the well-known whisky consultant, Jim Swan. The distillery is equipped with a 1 ton stainless steel mash tun, two stainless steel washbacks and two copper stills (with a capacity of 9,000 and 3,500 litres each). The total capacity is 200,000 litres of pure alcohol. The first distillation was in March 2015 when the wash was brought in from a local brewery. In February 2016, the first in-house whisky production took place. Products released so far include Levantine gin, new make spirit and a couple of malt spirits of around 6-12 months old. The whisky is not matured on site near Tel Aviv. Instead, the owners experiment with maturation in a wide variety of climates, from dry deserts to hot and humid coastal areas.

Pakistan

Distillery:	Murree Brewery Ltd., Rawalpindi
Founded:	1860
Owner:	Bhandara family
	murreebrewery.com

Murree Brewery in Rawalpindi started as a beer brewery supplying the British Army. The assortment was completed with whisky, gin, rum, vodka and brandy. The core range of single malt holds two expressions – Murree´s Classic 8 years old and Murree´s Millenium Reserve 12 years old. In 2005 an 18 year old single malt was launched and the following year their oldest expression so far, a 21 year old, reached the market. There is also a Murree´s Islay Reserve, Vintage Gold, which is a blend of Scotch whisky and Murree single malt and a number of local, blended whiskies such as Vat No. 1, Lion and Dew of Himalaya. The brewery makes its own malt (using both floor maltings and Saladin box) and produces 2,6 million litres of beer every year and approximately 440,000 litres of whisky.

Brilliance – one of the big-sellers from Paul John

Taiwan

Distillery: Yuan Shan Distillery, Yanshan, Yilan County
Founded: 2005
Owner: King Car Food Industrial Co.

kavalanwhisky.com

In a short period of time, the Taiwanese single malt, Kavalan, has swept across the world like few other brands from outside the traditional group of whisky producing countries have ever done before. The merits for the rapid escalation of the establishment mainly lie with Master Blender, Ian Chang, and the well-known whisky consultant, Dr. Jim Swan, who have worked together since its inception in 2005. Yuan Shan distillery lies in the north-eastern part of the country, in Yilan County, just one hour's drive from Taipei.

The distillery is equipped with a 4 ton semi-lauter stainless steel mash tun with copper top and 16 closed stainless steel washbacks with a 60-72 hour fermentation time. There are five pairs of lantern-shaped copper stills with descending lye pipes. The capacity of the wash stills is 12,000 litres and of the spirit stills 7,000 litres. After 10-15 minutes of foreshots, the heart of the spirit run takes 2-3 hours. The cut points for the spirit run are 65%-55% to accommodate a complex and rich flavour profile. The spirit vapours are cooled using tube condensers, but because of the hot climate, subcoolers are also used. Some of the equipment was installed as late as in September 2015 which increased the capacity from 1.5 million to 4.5 million litres of alcohol. But that's not where the buck stops- rapid success for the brand has prompted the owners to increase the production even more. By the end of 2016, there will be a total of four mash tuns, 40 washbacks and 10 pairs of stills which will bring its capacity to 9 million litres per year! This means that Kavalan could, by then, be one of the ten largest malt whisky distilleries in the world!

On site, there are two five-story high warehouses and the casks are tied together (four and four) due to the earthquake risk. The climate in this part of Taiwan is hot and humid and on the top floors of the warehouses the temperature can easily reach 42°C. Hence the angel's share is quite dramatic – no less than 10-12% is lost every year. On the other hand, the heat speeds up the extraction of flavour from the casks which also makes the whisky mature quicker.

Predominantly, American white oak is used, since the owners have found that it is the type of wood that works the best for maturation in a subtropical climate.

The brand name for the whisky produced at Yuan Shan distillery is Kavalan. The name derives from the earliest tribe that inhabited Yilan, the county where the distillery is situated. Since the first bottling was released in 2008, the range has been expanded and now holds more than ten different expressions. The best seller globally is Classic Kavalan, bottled at either 40% or 43%. In 2011, an "upgraded" version of the Classic was launched in the shape of King Car Conductor – a mix of eight different types of casks, un chill-filtered and bottled at 46%. A port finished version called Concertmaster (currently the best selling Kavalan in the USA) was released in 2009 and, later that year, two different single cask bottlings were launched under the name Solist – one ex-bourbon and one ex-Oloroso sherry. It was the launch of these two expressions that made the rest of the world aware of Taiwanese whisky.

More expressions in the Solist series have been added and the range now consists of (apart from Bourbon and Sherry) Fino, Vinho Barrique (using Portuguese wine barriques), Manzanilla, Amontillado, PX, Moscatel and Port. All of these are bottled at cask strength but in 2012 two versions bottled at 46% were also introduced - Bourbon Oak and Sherry Oak. Other releases include Podium which is a vatting of whiskies from new American oak and a selection of re-fill casks and Distillery Reserve Peaty Cask. The latter, exclusively available at the distillery visitor centre, obtains its smoky flavour from maturation in ex-Islay casks. The distillery has produced whisky from peated barley as well, but this is still maturing. Whisky is, of course, the main product for Kavalan but, recently, production of gin has also started with the first release expected by the end of 2016.

Kavalan is being exported to more than 40 countries including the USA, the UK, France, Belgium, Italy, The Netherlands, Russia, Israel and Hong Kong. Apart from Taiwan, Europe and the US are the most important markets. Their ambition to establish themselves on the American market was evidenced by the message on eleven of the electronic billboards on Times square during autumn 2016. There is an impressive visitor centre on site and it was awarded Whisky Visitor Attraction of the Year in 2011 by the Whisky Magazine. No less than one million visitors come here annually. The owning company, King Car Group, with 2,000 employees, was already founded in 1956 and runs businesses in several fields; biotechnology and aquaculture, among others. It is also famous for its ready-to-drink coffee, Mr. Brown.

Yuan Shan Distillery, home of Kavalan Single Malt, is celebrating it's 10th anniversary in 2016

Other distilleries in Taiwan

Nantou Distillery

Nantou City, Nantou County, founded in 1978
(whisky since 2008)

en.ttl.com.tw

Nantou distillery is a part of the state-owned manufacturer and distributor of cigarettes and alcohol in Taiwan – Taiwan Tobacco and Liquor Corporation (TTL). Established as a government agency in the early 1900s, it was renamed Taiwan Tobacco and Wine Monopoly Bureau in 1947. Between 1947 and 1968 the Bureau exercised a monopoly over all alcohol, tobacco, and camphor products sold in Taiwan. It retained tobacco and alcohol monopolies until Taiwan's entry into the WTO in 2002.

There are seven distilleries and two breweries within the TTL group, but Nantou is the only with malt whisky production. The distillery is equipped with a full lauter Huppmann mash tun with a charge of 2.5 tonnes and eight washbacks made of stainless steel. The fermentation time is 60-72 hours and in order to regulate the fermentation, the washbacks are equipped with water-cooling jackets. There are two wash stills (9,000 and 5,000 litres) and two spirit stills (5,000 and 2,000 litres). All are equipped with shell and tube condensers, as well as aftercoolers. Malted barley is imported from Scotland and ex-sherry and ex-bourbon casks are used for maturation. Nantou Distillery also produces a variety of fruit wines and the casks that have stored lychee wine and plum wine are then used to give some whiskies an extra finish.

Due to extreme temperatures during summer, distillation only takes place from October to April. The hot and humid climate also increases the angle's share which is around 6-7%. Until recently, the spirit from Nantou has been unpeated, but in 2014, trials with peated malt brought in from Scotland were made.

The main product from the distillery is a blended whisky which comprises of malt whisky from Nantou, grain whisky from Taichung distillery and imported blended Scotch. In October 2013, two cask strength single malt whiskies were launched – one from bourbon casks and the other from sherry casks. The next expressions were Omar single malt, where several versions have been released, matured in either sherry or bourbon casks. A very special variety of Omar (only 700 bottles) had been finished in a lychee liqueur barrel.

Africa

South Africa

Distillery: James Sedgwick Distillery, Wellington, Western Cape

Founded: 1886 (whisky since 1990)

Owner: Distell Group Ltd.

threeshipswhisky.co.za

Distell Group Ltd. was formed in 2000 by a merger between Stellenbosch Farmers' Winery and Distillers Corporation, although the James Sedgwick Distillery was already established in 1886. The company produces a huge range of wines and spirits including the popular cream liqueur, Amarula Cream. James Sedgwick Distillery has been the home to South African whisky since 1990. The distillery has undergone a major expansion in the last years and is now equipped with one still with two columns for production of grain whisky, two pot stills for malt whisky and one still with six columns designated for neutral spirit. There are also two mash tuns and 23 washbacks. Grain whisky is distilled for nine months of the year, malt whisky for two months (always during the winter months July/August) and one month is devoted to maintenance. Three new warehouses have been built and a total of seven warehouses now hold 180,000 casks.

In Distell's whisky portfolio, it is the Three Ships brand, introduced in 1977, that makes up for most of the sales. The range consists of Select and 5 year old Premium Select, both of which are a blend of South African and Scotch whiskies. Furthermore, there is Bourbon Cask Finish, the first 100% South African blended whisky and the 10 year old single malt. The latter was launched for the first time in 2003 and the release in 2016 was the fifth and the first to carry a vintage. Apart from the Three Ships range, Distell also produces two 3 year old blended whiskies, Harrier and Knight, as well as South Africa's first single grain whisky, Bain's Cape Mountain.

In 2013 the Distell Group acquired the Scottish whisky group, Burn Stewart Distillers, including Bunnahabhain, Tobermory and Deanston distilleries as well as the blended whisky, Scottish Leader. The man who tirelessly worked to bring the Three Ships single malt to the market, was Andy Watts. After 25 years as the distillery manager, he has now taken on a new role in the company where he will be responsible for overseeing Distell's entire whisky portfolio, including the Scotch brands.

Omar Single Malt from Nantou Distillery

Two versions of the Three Ships Single Malt

South America

Argentina

Distillery:	La Alazana Distillery, Golondrinas, Patagonia
Founded:	2011
Owner:	Nestor Serenelli
	laalazanawhisky.com

The first whisky distillery in Argentina concentrating solely on malt whisky production was founded in 2011 and the distillation started in December of that year. Located in the Patagonian Andes to the South of Argentina, it was Pablo Tognetti, an old time home brewer, and his son-in-law, Nestor Serenelli who started it but end of 2014, Pablo Tognetti withdrew from the company. Today it´s Nestor and his wife Lila who own and run the distillery. They are both big fans of Scotch whisky and before they built the distillery, they toured Scotland to visit distilleries and to get inspiration. Even though the Serenelli´s are producing their whisky according to Scottish tradition, they are also firm believers in the "terroir" concept where local barley and water and, not least, climate will affect the flavour of the whisky. The distillery is equipped with a lauter mash tun, four stainless steel 1,100 litre washbacks with a fermentation time of 4 to 6 days and two stills – one 500 litres and another, recently installed, 1,300 litres. The second still made it possible to double the production to 8,000 litres a year.

The owners are aiming for a light and fruity whisky but they have also filled several barrels with peated whisky. Maturation is mostly in ex-bourbon casks but fresh PX sherry casks and toasted Malbec casks are also used. A visitor centre has recently been built and a grand, official opening of the distillery was held in November 2014. The first, limited release was made in December 2013. The latest bottling appeared in September 2016, a "classic" La Alazana (70% ex bourbon and 30% ex sherry). Occasional limited bottlings will continue to be released but the owners are planning for a core expression that is at least 8-10 years old.

Other distilleries in Argentina

Distillery Emilio Mignone & Cia

Luján, Buenos Aires province, founded in 2015

www.emiliomignoneycia.com.ar, www.emyc.com.ar

The distillery, founded and owned by the brothers Santiago and Carlos Mignone, became the second whisky distillery in Argentina. Inspired and mentored by Nestor and Lila Serenelli of La Alazana, the two brothers made their first distillation in November 2015. A number of tests followed and the first barrel was filled in July 2016. The distillery is equipped with a 200 litre open mash tun, a 250 litre washback with a 96 hour fermentation cycle and two stills, directly fired by natural gas. The plan for 2017 is to produce 1,000 litres and the first bottling will be released in 2019. A second and larger distillery may be built in the near future in Lago Puelo, Patagonia, where the Mignone family owns a farm.

Madoc Distillery

Dina Huapi, Rio Negro, founded in 2015

www.madocwhisky.com

In 2015 construction began on another whisky distillery in Patagonia. The founder, Pablo Tognetti, is no newcomer to whisky production as he was one of the founders of the Patagonian distillery, La Alazana. In 2015, he left the company and brought with him some of the equipment, as well as part of the maturing stock to build a new distillery in Dina Huapi, which is situated on the outskirts of the lake-side Andean ski resort, Bariloche. The existing equipment with a lauter mash tun, a washback and a copper pot still was complemented by a wash still and the first distillation took place in September 2016.

Nestor Serenelli, owner of La Alazana Distillery

The first casks maturing at Distilley Emilio Mignone

Brazil

Distillery: Union Distillery, Veranópolis
Founded: 1972
Owner: Union Distillery Maltwhisky Do Brasil Ltda
maltwhisky.com.br

The company was founded in 1948 as Union of Industries Ltd to produce wine. In 1972 they started to produce malt whisky and two years later the name of the company was changed to Union Distillery Maltwhisky do Brasil. In 1986 a co-operation with Morrison Bowmore Distillers was established in order to develop the technology at the Brazilian distillery. Most of the production is sold as bulk whisky to be part of different blends, but the company also has its own single malt called Union Club Whisky.

Distillery: Muraro Bebidas, Flores da Cunha
Founded: 1953
Owner: Muraro & Cia
muraro.com.br

This is a company with a wide range of products including wine, vodka, rum and cachaca and the total capacity is 10 million litres. Until recently, the blend Green Valley was the only whisky in the range. In November 2014, however, a new brand was introduced. It has the rather misleading name Blend Seven but it appears to be a malt whisky. The main market for the new whisky is The Carribean.

Pablo Tognetti, founder of Madoc Distillery

The Year
that was

Including the subsections:
The big players | The big brands | Changes in ownership
New distilleries | Bottling grapevine

To start off with, let´s just briefly get the feel of the temperature of the global spirits market. It is growing year by year, but what's alarming is that the pace is steadily declining. According to Euromonitor International, in 2015 a total of 29 billion bottles of spirits were sold in the world at a total value of £327 billion. The global spirits market grew by 11% from 2008 to 2013 and in 2014 volumes grew by a further 1.7%. But the global data agency also states that the growth in the last five years was down to 5.6% and for 2015 only 0.8%. Asia, North America, Africa and the Middle East are the regions that account for the growth, while Europe and Latin America are minimising the figures.

If we narrow it down to Scotch whisky, the producers had quite an eye-opener when the figures from 2014 were reported. For the first time in 10 years the values of the export had declined and by as much as almost 7%! One year later, the state of the industry could best be described as "not being out of the woods, but you could at least see the sky". Both values and volumes have declined this past year, but not as sharply as in 2014. Values were down by 2.4% and volumes by 2.8%. The main reason for the decline over the last two years has mainly been because of global economic and political instability. When the economy goes down, customers always tend to change their purchasing behaviour, by cutting down on luxury goods or migrating to cheaper local spirits. The latter behaviour is often noticed in parts of South- East Asia and Latin America. One significant detail worth noting during 2015 is that the sharpest decline in exported volumes applies to the countries whose economies are driven by oil and other commodities. The economic melt-down in Russia (also impacted by the Ukraine conflict), Brazil and Venezuela has obviously affected the import of whisky.

An obvious trend is that the Top 5 market´s share of the global exports has increased steadily over the last five years from 39% to 42%. If one looks at the Top 20 markets it becomes more apparent with an increase from 74% to 78%. This could indicate either that the established and sometimes assumed, mature markets haven´t been saturated yet and that there is still more growth to be had. It could also imply that some of the emerging markets have yet to establish a pattern of consumption that includes Scotch whisky. Especially in countries that are culturally inclined to drink white spirits, such a change could take longer than one would perhaps expect.

The decrease in volumes for blended Scotch was 1.7% and for value 3%. The latter figure can be compared to a disastrous decrease of 15% during the previous year. Single malt Scotch also lost volumes during 2015 (-1.8%) but, could on the other hand, compensate with a small increase in values (+0.4%) in comparison to a 12% increase in 2014. The continued interest in single malts is long-standing and since 2006, the single malt´s share of total Scotch whisky exports (that also includes bulk whisky) has gone from 7% to 9% and values have grown dramatically from 16% to 24%.

SINGLE MALT - EXPORT
Value: +0.4% to £916m
Volume: -1.8% to 103m bottles

BLENDED SCOTCH - EXPORT
Value: -3.0% to £2,7bn
Volume: -1.7% to 798m bottles

TOTAL SCOTCH - EXPORT
Value: -2.4% to £3,88bn
Volume: -2.8% to 1.16bn bottles

NB. Grain whisky, blended malt and bulk export are not included, except in the Total.

Looking at the detailed figures for each of the nine regions, six of them have shown both decreasing volumes and values, while the remaining three (North America, Australasia and Non EU Europe) accounted for an increase in both volumes and values.

The European Union

The producers may have been wooing the emerging markets for quite some time now but are, at the same time,

well aware of the importance that the European Union (excluding the UK) has for the sales of Scotch whisky. In terms of volume, 37% of the exports land in this region, while the value is marginally less (at 31%). If we focus just on single malts, the predominance is even clearer; in that 42% of the volumes and 40% of the values end up in the EU. The figures clearly indicate a market where consumers trade up for more expensive whiskies. However, during 2015 the volumes decreased by 2.6% while values were down by 3.6%.

EU — Top 3

France	volumes	-4%	values	-2%
Spain	volumes	-1%	values	-9%
Germany	volumes	-6%	values	+3%

For many years now, France has, in terms of volume, been the biggest importer of Scotch whisky in the world. Together with the USA, the two countries account for one in four bottles of Scotch exported and one third of the value. In spite of a strained economic climate during an extended time, Spain still remains at second place within the EU, although it still lags far behind France. Germany has over a period of time secured third place. What one should remember regarding Germany is that less than half the volumes imported are sold domestically. The rest is re-directed to other countries, not least Turkey and Belarus. Following the Top Three, two countries showed huge increases during 2015. The increase for Netherlands (values up by 29% and volumes by 15%) is remarkable, as is the development in Poland (values +19% and volumes +34%). As for the latter, the figures should be seen in the light of the equally big decrease of the previous year. These were due to a 15% tax rise that came into effect in January 2014. The overall trend in the country is that whisky increases

in popularity at the expense of vodka. Another interesting EU market in Eastern Europe is Bulgaria which admittedly declined in 2014, but bounced back the ensuing year with double digit increases. A group of countries which has been reliable markets is the Nordics. The interest, especially in single malts, has been growing steadily but during the last three years, volumes have fallen, as has been the case in 2015.

North America

The second biggest region in terms of value continues to be North America, which in 2013 eclipsed Asia into third place and during 2015 the gap has become even bigger. The figures meant a real boost compared to the previous year. Volumes were up 8% and values increased by 3%.

North America — Top 3

USA	volumes	-2%	values	+-0%
Mexico	volumes	+33%	values	+17%
Canada	volumes	+11%	values	+15%

USA is the biggest importer of Scotch in the world in terms of value, but in 2015 they didn't add to the growth for North America. The domestic varieties (bourbon and rye) continued to gain market shares, just like the previous year. The Scotch category that is suffering the most are the blends. The value of single malt Scotch in the US, on the other hand, had increased by 13%. But in the absence of success in the USA, Mexico and Canada stood up as saviours in the region. Since 2006, volumes of scotch imported to Mexico have gone up every year, but the 33% increase for last year was unprecedented and the country is now the fifth biggest market in the world!

Asia

Asia is still the third biggest region for scotch whisky (and the second biggest in terms of volumes) but the momentum it had until 2012, has been lost. Since that year, the value has fallen by 15%. Values for 2015 were down 3.5%, a smaller decline compared to 2014, while volumes decreased by 5%. More than 40% of the Scotch exports to the region are shipped in bulk to be bottled overseas or used in other beverages.

Asia — Top 3

Singapore	volumes	-8%	values	+5%
Taiwan	volumes	-9%	values	-10%
South Korea	volumes	-23%	values	-15%

Singapore is the number one market but, as has always been the case, the vast majority of the whisky is re-exported to other markets in the region, not least to ASEAN countries and China.

Taiwan, in second place, continues to be a strong market, especially for single malt. The single malt share of the total Scotch imports in 2015 was 37% in comparison to the USA (18%) and France (10%). However, both volumes and values were down in 2015, probably due to the current recession in the country. By spring 2016, the Taiwanese economy had contracted for the third quarter in a row.

South Korea was one of the first emerging markets to embrace Scotch but, for the seventh year in a row, sales have now decreased due to a difficult economic climate. Consumers are looking for cheaper spirit with lower alcohol. The biggest spirits category in the country is the domestic soju and, with the highly successful introduction in 2015 of a new sub-category, Fruit Soju, whisky is under even more pressure. Producers of Scotch are now trying to cover their losses by entering into the flavoured segment with whisky-based liqueurs, such as W Ice by Windsor from Diageo and Eclat by Imperial from Pernod Ricard.

In India, scotch whisky volumes were up by 30% and values increased by 20% in 2014 and, even though volumes remained unchanged in 2015 and values dropped by 4%, the country is still considered to be one of the most important markets for the future. Scotch whisky only accounts for about 1% of the Indian spirits market, so the prospects for growth are considerable. The obstacle so far has been the high import tariffs (150%), but there are ongoing negotiations to try and reduce them.

Central and South America

If one wants to trade in the fourth biggest region, then one requires nerves of steel. A majority of the markets are very volatile and large increases in sales one year can easily shift to a major decline the next. Exports to Central and South America is mainly about blended Scotch and, in 2015, only 670,000 bottles of single malt were shipped to the entire region to be compared to the equivalent of 118 million bottles of bulk and blended whisky. In 2015, volumes were down by 10.5% and values decreased by 8%.

Central & South America — Top 3

Brazil	volumes	-20%	values	-30%
Panama	volumes	-36%	values	-23%
Dom. Republic	volumes	+26%	values	+14%

The major disappointment during 2015 was undoubtedly Brazil. The previous year it was the fifth biggest market for Scotch in terms of volumes but, with a 20% decrease, it has in one year fallen to eighth place. The market is still hugely important and reportedly, North-eastern Brazil has the highest per capita consumption of Scotch whisky in the world!

One of the secrets behinds the whisky interest in Japan is the popular highball trend

The poor results of 2015 are mainly due to the recession, the deepest in the country in recent history and one which may continue during 2016, due to the political turmoil. In second place was Panama which also suffered severe decreases in 2015 and, even though the Dominican Republic, as well as Peru which is further down the list, was heading in the other direction, it was not enough to compensate for Brazil's decline. Venezuela, which as late as in 2012 was the biggest market for Scotch in the region, has completely fallen apart, mainly because of political and economic difficulties. The total value of exports to the country in 2012 was £102m and by the end of the book year 2015, the figure had plummeted by over 90% to £10m!

Africa

Africa, excluding South Africa, is still an undeveloped market for Scotch, but most of the big producers have begun to position themselves in order to be prepared when the consumer interest starts to escalate. In 2015, volumes were down by 11%, while values decreased by 12%.

Africa — Top 3

South Africa	volumes	-5%	values	-10%
Angola	volumes	-26%	values	-37%
Morocco	volumes	-10%	values	+2%

The biggest market on the continent, by far, is South Africa but, after having shown an increase over a long period of time, the market has disappointed the producers of Scotch two consecutive years. However, the decline has not been as significant as has been the case during 2014. Angola, still in second place despite a severe downturn in 2015, has experienced an upward spiral during the last few years and, part of the increase can be attributed to a huge amount of foreign nationals working in the country's expanding oil industry. What is worth noting regarding Africa, as indeed in many other regions, is that single malt goes against the current with an increase in value by 7% during 2015.

Middle East

Middle East was the only region where both volumes and value had increased in 2014 but, for 2015, this had changed to negative figures (volumes -5% and values -1%). On the positive side – the value of single malts has increased by no less than 29%.

Middle East - Top 3

UAE*	volumes	+-0%	values	+5%
Lebanon	volumes	-26%	values	-26%
Israel	volumes	+17%	values	+32%

* United Arab Emirates

With more than 50% of the volumes, the biggest market in the region is still the United Arab Emirates and, if we look at values, their dominance is even bigger, more than 60%. They are now the seventh biggest market for Scotch. However, most of the whisky is for religious reasons not consumed within the country. Instead, UAE acts as a distribution hub for parts of Africa, Asia and India. After being at the same levels for many years, the break-through for Israel as a whisky drinking nation finally came in 2009 and sales have continued to increase. Since 2012, values of Scotch exported to the country have soared by 150%!

European non EU-members

Export to European non EU-members have increased in recent years, perhaps not so much in terms of volume, but certainly in terms of value with an increase of 18% in three years. Figures for 2015 show volumes increasing by 9% and value by 8%.

Europe (non-EU) — Top 3

Turkey	volumes	+25%	values	+24%
Switzerland	volumes	-18%	values	-13%
Norway	volumes	+2%	values	-9%

The region is dominated by Turkey and Switzerland and The Top 3 markets represent 95% of the sales to the region.

Australasia

Australasia is the second smallest region, importing the equivalent of 33 million bottles of Scotch. Values increased by 5% in 2014 and volumes by 8.5%.

Australasia — Top 3

Australia	volumes	+12%	values	+7%
New Zealand	volumes	-21%	values	-12%
N. Caledonia	volumes	-15%	values	-7%

Australia is dominating with more than 90% of the value, placing the country in 11th place on the global list.

Eastern Europe

The name of this region is a bit misleading in that important Scotch importers such as Poland, Bulgaria and the Baltic states belong to Eastern Europe in a geographical sense, but at the same time they are EU members and their figures are included in that region. This means that when Eastern Europe is considered an important, emerging market by the Scotch industry – they often refer to EU countries such as the ones mentioned above, but also include non EU members in the east such as Russia, Ukraine and Georgia. Increasing export to this region came to a halt with the sharp decline in 2014 which continued in 2015. Volumes were down by 28% and values even more, by minus 34%.

Eastern Europe — Top 3

Georgia	volumes	-18%	values	-21%
Ukraine	volumes	-5%	values	-39%
Serbia	volumes	+3%	values	-4%

Buchanan´s blended Scotch is one of Diageo´s fastest growing whisky brands at the moment

The reason for this dramatic change is, of course, the crisis in Ukraine, which has resulted in trade sanctions imposed by the EU and the USA on Russia. If one just looks at the figures, direct export to the country has practically been obliterated over the last two years. However, whisky still indirectly finds its way to Russia through various hubs and the interest in Scotch from the Russian consumers is far from gone.

The neighbouring countries, Georgia and Ukraine, have also been affected, but not to the same extent. Still, the declining trend of 2014 has continued in 2015.

The big players

Diageo

When first looking at the results for Diageo for the fiscal year ending 30th June 2016, the figures are not that impressive. Net sales were down by 3% to £10.5bn while operating profits only increased by 1.6% to £2.8bn. However, one needs to critically examine what has really happened during the past year in order to get a proper picture. Diageo has been involved in several deals with competitors in order to focus on what is now to become its core business, i. e. spirits and beer. All of its wine business has been sold off to other companies and this will, of course, affect both sales and profits in the short run. So, if we eliminate the effects of these sales and look at organic results, it means that net sales have actually increased by 2.8%, while operating profits have climbed by 3.5%. With the sell-off of non-core assets (including Gleneagles hotel), Diageo has released £1 billion during the year, a sum that comes in handy when it needs to bring down the debts that emerged from the take-over of United Spirits two years ago – a deal that in the end had cost the company a staggering £1.12 billion!

If we look at the different regions, organic sales were up by 1-4% in all five regions, with Europe and North America

being particularly strong. The weakest regions were Latin America, mainly because of the decline in Brazil, and Asia-Pacific where sales in China and Korea were weak.

Scotch represents 24% of Diageo net sales and within that category, volumes of Johnnie Walker had increased by 5% to 226 million bottles while J&B had lost 3% to 43 million bottles. Of the single malts, its top three sellers showed strong performances; The Singleton was up by 19% to 5.8 million bottles, Talisker had improved by 7% to 2.4 million and Cardhu had increased by 1.5% to 2.3 million bottles.

Two years ago, Diageo sold off Bushmill´s Irish whiskey, a deal which raised many eyebrows. Numerous competitors are doing all they can to buy into the growing category of Irish whiskey, but Diageo has left it completely. A year later, Diageo´s CEO, Ivan Menezes, said that he was still pleased with the Bushmill´s deal, while reiterating that one could very well imagine a purchase within American whiskey if opportunity presented itself. The only major bourbon in the Diageo portfolio, Bulleit, is still relatively small (with 10 million bottles) compared to the category leader, Jim Beam (with 90 million).

Pernod Ricard

Pernod Ricard´s CEO, Alexandre Ricard, described fiscal 2016 (July 2015 to June 2016) as "solid and encouraging". If one considers the jump in net profits - up by 43% - you may well wonder why he was so modest. However, the increase is based on the previous year when the company took a €404m impairment charge for the Absolut vodka brand. If we, instead, look at the net profits, stripping out one-offs, they were down by 2% and operating profits had increased by a mere 2% to €2.28bn, while net sales for the 12 months had increased by 1% to €8.68bn. The forecast for next year´s profit is a low single-digit improvement.

The company has divided the world into three markets; Americas, where sales were up 4% mainly thanks to a solid

Sales of Pernod Ricard´s Passport Scotch have increased by 60% in the last four years

performance in the USA, Europe with sales up 1% mainly driven by growth in Spain and Asia-Rest of the World where sales had increased by 1%. This was largely due to the double-digit growth in India and Africa/Middle-East which had helped to offset difficulties in China and South Korea.

The biggest brand in the portfolio in terms of volumes is still Absolut vodka with 131 million bottles sold in the year. Those are more or less the same figures as five years ago given that vodka has proven to be a difficult category for many producers. The whisky side of the business is a mixed bag. While Ballantine´s increased by 5% to 75 million bottles, Chivas Regal had gone in the other direction and lost 5% to 53 million bottles. Jameson Irish whiskey is still the golden egg with a solid increase of 16% to 68 million bottles, while Glenlivet, finally, is steady around the 12 million bottle mark.

While Diageo has been busy cleaning up its portfolio by getting rid of its interest in the wine business, Pernod Ricard has had a quieter year with "business as usual" as its motto. In the struggle between the two leading drinks companies, the battle ground for the next year seems to be in the important USA market, where Diageo, for a long time, has been dominant, but Pernod Ricard now seems to be building up its forces. In India, on the other hand, the converse seems to be in place but with Diageo´s acquisition of United Spirits, the battle could be equally interesting.

Edrington

The results for Edrington for the fiscal year ending March 2016 reflected a tough and unstable market. Revenues totalling £574.6m were more or less the same as the previous year but pre-tax profits dropped dramatically by 13% to £146.4m. According to the company, there were several reasons for this; Macallan single malt faced strong competition in Taiwan. The Famous Grouse blend, while

still the category leader in the UK, was hard-pressed by a price war on the domestic market. The third reason was the strength of the pound against other currencies which also had a significant impact on sales.

The flagship brand for the company is Macallan which during the last three years have had sales of about 9.5 million bottles. Even if Taiwan was disappointing last year, the brand performed well in China, Russia and, in particular, the US where it is the number one Scotch single malt by value. The other high profile single malt, Highland Park, has shown strength over the past years and from 2014 to 2015 the volumes had increased by 7% to 1.5 million bottles.

On the blended side, Famous Grouse hasn´t experienced any major growth since 2007 but managed to sell 35 million bottles in 2015. Cutty Sark is still struggling to get back to the volumes of ten years ago. An intense marketing campaign over the last few years has not been able to fulfill that goal, but has more likely saved the brand from yet greater declines. But there is light at the end of the tunnel as last year the brand grew significantly ahead of its category in important markets such as Spain, Portugal and the USA.

The major area of concern for the company during the past year has been that of Brugal, the rum that Edrington acquired in 2008 and where large write-offs were made in the books between 2012 and 2014 due to the weak performance of the brand. In 2015, however, Brugal returned to profit in its core markets, the Dominican Republic and Spain.

A spokesperson for the company cautioned that "uncertain political, economic and trading conditions are likely to endure through 2016/2017." The Edrington Group is owned by a charitable trust, The Robertson Trust, established in 1961, which donated more than £18m to charitable organisations in Scotland during 2015/2016.

Gruppo Campari

It was a happy Campari CEO who announced the results for 2015 in March 2016. After three lean years, Bob Kunze-Concewitz, could report a 6.2% increase in sales to €1657m, while net profits had leapt by 36% to €175.4m. One-offs taken into consideration, the increase in profit was still an impressive 20%. The two biggest regions for Campari which account for 74% of the total sales are the Americas and the Southern Europe/Middle East/Africa region. The USA, in particular, has become increasingly important over the last few years.

The biggest brands in the group are called Global Priorities and include Campari, Aperol, Skyy and Wild Turkey, while their only Scotch single malt, Glen Grant, is labelled as a Regional Priorities brand. Volumes of Glen Grant have increased by 7% in the last two years and 3.4 million bottles were sold in 2015. Glen Grant is still the biggest single malt in Italy but volumes have steadily decreased during the last 10-15 years. This decline has, on the other hand, been compensated through growing volumes in the USA, France, Germany, Sweden, Australia and Mexico. The whole ranged was re-launched in summer 2016 and includes two new expressions (12 and 18 year old).

The Campari group, where the Garavoglia family owns 51% of the shares, has broadened its business base over the past few years through a series of successful acquisitions. It first started with SKYY vodka in 2001, and then continued with Glen Grant in 2006 which was followed by Wild Turkey bourbon in 2009. This trend has continued with Appleton rum in 2012, as well as the Canadian whisky distiller, Forty Creek, and Fratelli Averna in 2014. In just more than a decade, Campari has invested close onto €1.5bn in acquiring other companies.

Ian Macleod Distillers

The family-owned bottler and owner of Glengoyne and Tamdhu distilleries, is the tenth largest whisky firm in Scotland and was established in 1933. While some of the other distilleries have had their ups and downs over the last few years, Ian Macleod Distillers seems to have been unaffected through these turbulent times for the industry. In the last financial report, ending September 2015, the company showed an increase in pre-tax profits of £8.3 million while the turnover rose by 16% to £67.6 million. In order to continue further expansion in some of their key markets, the company has secured a £60m bank loan in May 2016.

Ian Macleod Distillers is known for its devotion to sherry casks to mature whisky and during the last year, it has spent 73% of its capital expenditure budget on these casks. Apart from Tamdhu and Glengoyne single malts, the company also acts as an independent bottler by releasing malts from other distilleries under the name of Dun Bheagan and The Chieftain's. Isle of Skye (with four different expressions) is a blended malt and there is also Smokehead, a peated single malt from Islay. A new addition to its portfolio in 2016 was Rocket Cat, a whisky infused with cinnamon and this was its first contribution to the growing range of flavoured whisky. In addition to this, it also produces gin and vodka, as well as selling bulk whisky to customers who wish to create their own brand, both within the UK and abroad.

Beam Suntory

When Suntory bought Beam Inc in May 2014 for $16bn, a new company called Beam Suntory was formed. It is now the third largest drinks group in the world after Diageo and Pernod Ricard. The new company is owned by Suntory Holdings. Before the merger, Suntory's portfolio included Japanese brands such as Yamazaki, Hakushu, Hibiki and Kakubin. With the deal, a range of other spirit brands have been added to the list; Jim Beam bourbon, Teacher's blended Scotch, the two single malts Laphroaig and Ardmore, as well as Canadian Club and Courvoisier cognac.

Its first year of full results after the formation of the new company, saw an increase in sales by 23% to £6.3 billion. The strong demand for bourbon was one of the main driving forces behind the increase. In Japan alone, sales of Jim Beam went up by 62% and global volumes for the brand are now 89 million bottles. Laphroaig single malt also performed well with sales going up by 10% to 3.5 million bottles, while the sales of Teacher's blend decreased by 5%.

The merger of the two companies hasn't been problem free. Suntory is struggling with a debt of $15 billion and handling two very different corporate cultures (the Japanese and the American) within one company, has been a tremendous challenge. Takeshi Niinami, the president and CEO of Suntory Holdings, noted that while Japanese employees generally don't leave the company, Americans have a three-to-five-year horizon. Compensation systems in the two countries also differ. Niinami also said that "I don't have a solution yet in my hand, but at first we have to recognize differences like that."

Brown Forman

Brown Forman's purchase of the BenRiach Distillery Company in spring 2016, meant that, for the first time since 2004 when it sold off its minority share in Glenmorangie Co., is involved in the Scotch whisky business. This allows Brown Forman to be included in this chapter of the Malt Whisky Yearbook.

The backbone of Brown Forman's business is, of course, Jack Daniel's – the most sold American whiskey in the world and is in sixth place of all whiskies that are produced. No less than 146 million bottles were sold in 2015! The company has other brands in the portfolio such as Finlandia vodka, Woodford Reserve bourbon and El Jimador tequila, but more than half of the volumes sold last year were made up of Jack Daniel's. The company was started in 1870 when George Garvin Brown formed J.T.S. Brown and Bros. and twenty years later he had joined George Forman and the company was changed. Jack Daniel's as a brand was established in the late 1800s and Brown Forman acquired it and the associated distillery in 1956. Over the years, the company had also entered into the wine business and produced Southern Comfort for many years until it was sold to Sazerac in 2016.

The financial report for 2015 showed a decrease in net sales by 2% to $4 billion, while net profits were up by 56% to $1.1 billion. A large contribution to the astounding increase in profits was generated by the sale of Southern Comfort. Volumes of Jack Daniel's were up by 4% and values by 6%. Finlandia vodka, on the other hand, has not experienced the same joy. The decline in recent years has continued in 2015 when the brand was down by 5%. According to Forbes Magazine, the Brown family, who owns 51% of Brown Forman, is the 20th richest family in the USA.

Inver House Distillers

Inver House Distillers is a part of International Beverage Holdings which is the international arm of ThaiBev. The business of Inver House rests on three pillars; single malts, blended Scotch and sales of whisky to third parties. The two biggest sellers of the single malts are Speyburn and Old Pulteney, followed by anCnoc and Balblair. There are no official bottlings from the fifth distillery, Balmenach, but it is here where its successful prestige gin Caorunn is produced. The last financial statement which was available at the time of going to press, is 2014, the year when the company celebrated its 50th anniversary with a very favourable report. Net sales were up by 3% to £79.2m, while net profits had jumped by 22% to £9.1. The single malts contribution was also significant; Old Pulteney (values +8%), Speyburn (+28%) and anCnoc (+12%). Their biggest blend, Hankey Bannister, had climbed 4.5%.

The company has invested heavily in the last couple of years, both in producion capacity at Speyburn and in maturation capacity with 12 new warehouses being built. With this in place, Inver House is now targeting new markets in Kazakhstan, Poland and India.

BenRiach Distillery Co.

The financial report for the last full year, before Brown Forman took over, sees a slight decline by 1.4% in turnover to £41 million and pre-tax profits also slipped by 4% to £10.7 million. The reason for this, the owners say, is the result of a decision taken the previous year to reduce sales of new-fill spirit. The owner, Billy Walker, comments that "...the market outlook for 2016 continues to be extremely buoyant." In June 2016, the take-over by Brown Forman was concluded. The American drinks company paid £280 million for the company, which includes brands, three distilleries (BenRiach, GlenDronach and Glenglassaugh), as well as a bottling plant.

The big brands

The most sold whisky in the world comes, unsurprisingly, from India. For the fourth year in a row, Officer´s Choice with 416 million bottles sold, occupies the top spot. The volume is more than the Top 4 Scotch whiskies put together. In 2015 it also managed to surpass the Philippine rum Emperador and is now the second most sold spirits brand in the world, with the Japanese soju Jinro still maintaining the number one spot (with an incredible 885 million bottles).

But Officer´s Choice is not the only top selling Indian whisky, to the contrary. Of the 10 most sold whiskies in

2015, seven come from India and it's only Johnnie Walker, Jack Daniels and Jim Beam that have managed to ensure total domination. Actually, the surprise this year is that as many as three non-Indian brands are in the Top 10. Jim Beam managed, for the first time, to secure a place amongst the giants, at the expense of the Indian Hayward´s Fine, which has lost no less than 37% during the past year.

If we look at the Top 30 whisky brands, the list contains 13 brands from India, 10 from Scotland, two from America, two from Canada, two from Japan and one from Ireland.

Blended Scotch

The unchallenged category leader, Johnnie Walker, managed to bounce back in 2015 after a weak 2014 where it had shown declining sales. According to Drinks International 226 million bottles were sold, while figures from the IWSR state that 219 million bottles were sold. Either way, this means that Johnnie Walker is still the third biggest whisky in the world after two Indian brands. While sales in Asia (and to a certain extent in the USA) still continue to decline, the turn-around this year can be attributed to increasing sales of the luxury range from Gold Label and upwards (especially in travel retail) but also from strong performance in Latin America.

Just as expected, as Johnnie Walker occupies the number one spot, Ballantine´s is still holding on to second place, a position it has maintained since 2007. A total of 75 million bottles were sold during 2015 and this reflects an increase of 5%. Depending on which statistic one reads, it's either Chivas Regal or Grants that occupies third place. Both have sales of about 53 million bottles with Grants showing roughly the same figures as last year, while Chivas Regal has declined by 4%. If Grants is in third spot it would mean that this would be their highest placing since 2011. After having had downturns every year for more than a decade, it does seem surprising that J&B is ranked as high as fifth place with 43 million bottles. The reason for this is that the decline has started at a level of sales so high that the brand challenged Johnnie Walker for the top spot towards the end of the 1990s when they were selling 75 million bottles per year. The question that begs is if this year´s number six contender, William Lawson's, will have the ability to surpass J&B next year. Two years ago the difference between the two brands was 12 million bottles and now it is down to 6 million. William Lawson's is the biggest climber the past decade, showing an increase in volume of 180% which in 2013 took the brand past Dewar's, Bacardi's other big Scotch. In seventh place with 35 million bottles sold in 2015 you find Famous Grouse which hasn't experienced any major growth since 2007. This is not the situation for William Peel, owned by the French company Belvédère and currently lies in eighth place. Together with Label 5 and Sir Edward´s (both owned by Martiniquaise) they make up a trio of blends that are very strong, especially on the huge French market. William Peel sold 34 million bottles in 2015, followed by Dewar´s with 31 million and Label 5 in tenth place with 28 million.

Single Malt Scotch

The first single malt to be actively promoted and marketed was Glenfiddich. It started in 1963 with their Straight Malt and ever since, Glenfiddich has been the world´s best selling single malt. Its track record ended in 2014 when Glenlivet had eclipsed it by a whisker. The difference was just 192,000 bottles which isn´t much when we are talking about a total of nearly 13 million bottles. But the joy for Chivas Brothers was short lived. As soon as 2015, Glenfiddich had regained its top position according to figures released by IWSR. The difference this time was even more negligible. Glenfiddich had sold 13,116,000 bottles compared to Glenlivet´s 12,973,000! Ever since 2010, sales of Glenfiddich have increased by 13% while Glenlivet´s volumes have gone up by a whopping 59%. Together, the two accounts for one quarter of all Scotch single malt sold globally.

Macallan, which occupies third place, saw sales declining marginally with a total volume of 9.5 million bottles. Glenmorangie, on the other hand, reflected a 3.7% sales growth and currently occupies fourth place with 6.1 million bottles. The brand has had a few difficult years between 2005 and 2010 but, since then, sales have increased by 57%. In fifth place we have a brand which actually is made up of three sub-brands – The Singleton – which can come from either Glen Ord, Dufftown or Glendullan distilleries. Since its launch 10 years ago, it has shown phenomenal growth, but Diageo will, nevertheless, not settle for that. In November 2015 their plan was revealed, to take The Singleton to the very top and to become the world´s most sold single malt. One part of the strategy was to make all three expressions available globally. Until now, Glen Ord has only been available in Asia, Dufftown in Europe and Glendullan in the USA. The Singleton has sold 5.8 million bottles in 2015 which means an increase of 19%. Aberlour, a big seller in France, has shown the same growth rate over the last five years as Glenlivet and Glenmorangie (53%) and during 2015 the sales were 3.8 million bottles. The world´s best selling Islay malt, and the only one in the Top 10, comes in at place number

seven. Laphroaig had a few tough years up until 2010 when the stock of mature whisky wasn't enough. Ever since, its growth has been positive and since 2010, the brand has increased its sales by 54% and has sold almost 3.5 million bottles in 2015. Glen Grant, which only ten years ago was in fourth place, has lost ground and is now parked in eighth place with 3.4 million bottles and that is roughly the same volume as in 2010. The brand is actually doing very well in many markets around the world, but it hasn't been able to fully compensate for the extended decline in Italy. Balvenie which features in ninth place delivers a steady growth year after year and managed to sell 3.2 million bottles in 2015. Last year, Talisker made it into the Top 10, a goal that the owners, Diageo, have envisaged for some time. Still in tenth place this year and with a growth of 83% since 2010, the brand has sold 2.4 million bottles. As a combined total, the Top 10 malts accounted for 60% of the global sales of single malt.

Finally, let´s have a look at the top whiskies in North America, India and Ireland.

In North America, Jack Daniel´s is the undisputed leader and the sixth most sold whisky in the world with 146 million bottles, followed by the bourbon Jim Beam (89 million), the Canadian Crown Royal (64 million), Black Velvet, also from Canada (26 million). In fifth place, we have a tie between the blended American whiskey Seagram´s 7 Crown and the bourbon Evan Williams with 25 million bottles each.

India is always an exciting read. They have the biggest whisky brands in the world, but a rollercoaster market have resulted in that the individual brands show huge changes from year to year. For 2015, Officer´s Choice still reigns supreme (the best selling whisky in the world for four years in a row) with 416 million bottles (+15%), followed by McDowell´s No. 1 (299 million, -1%), Imperial Blue (210 million, +25%), Royal Stag (208 million, +10%) and Old Tavern (143 million, +6%).

The Irish whiskey industry is dominated by three big brands with Jameson in top spot with 64 million bottles and a growth since last year of 13%. This is followed by Tullamore Dew (11.6 million) and Bushmill´s (9.6 million).

Changes in ownership

Since 2013 there have been several changes in ownership in the Scotch whisky business with companies from such diverse corners of the world as Japan, South Africa, The Philippines and USA either wanting to add to their existing Scotch whisky business or entering into this category. In 2013 Diageo started their take-over of United Spirits and this was completed by 2014. At the same time, South African drinks giant, Distell, bought Burn Stewart, including Bunnahabhain, Deanston and Tobermory. At the beginning of 2014, Suntory and Beam joined forces and became the third biggest spirits company in the world with single malts such as Laphroaig and Bowmore. But that was not the only merger in 2014. A few months later, the world's largest brandy producer, Emperador from the Philippines, took over Whyte & Mackay from Diageo and, in so

Glenfiddich is back in the top spot

Billy Walker sold The BenRiach Distillery Company to Brown Forman for £285 million

doing, acquired ownership of Dalmore and Jura. Apart from these four major deals, two smaller distilleries changed hands when BenRiach bought Glenglassaugh distillery in 2013 and Australian businessman, David Prior, acquired the liquidated Bladnoch distillery in 2015 with a view to starting production again in 2017.

An exciting start was made to 2016 when one of the biggest players in the whisky industry, the American company Brown Forman, announced that it had placed a bid for BenRiach Distillers – owners of BenRiach, GlenDronach and Glenglassaugh. The company had a previous involvement in the Scotch whisky business when it owned 10% of Glenmorangie, but those shares were sold off way back in 2004. Brown-Forman was founded in the late 1800s and the crown jewel in the company´s portfolio is Jack Daniel´s – the most sold American whiskey. Other brands include Finlandia vodka, Woodford Reserve bourbon and El Jimador tequila. The £285 million acquisition of BenRiach Distillery Company gives the company three distilleries and brands, as well as a bottling plant.

Billy Walker, together with South African business partners Geoff Bell and Wayne Kieswetter, bough BenRiach distillery in 2004 for £5.4 million. Four years later they acquired GlenDronach at an estimated cost of £15 million and finally in 2013, Glenglassaugh became a part of the company for an undisclosed amount. In the deal with Brown Forman, the Walker family´s stake in the firm is worth £95 million. Billy Walker will remain in the company as master distiller and blender while his son, Alistair, will continue as key sales executive.

New distilleries

Scotland

Given the ongoing expansions of distilleries that are already operative (like Macallan, Glenlivet and Glenfiddich), there are now more than 30 distilleries that are either being built or being planned in Scotland! The vast number of them is considerably smaller in size than the three afore-mentioned, ranging from 30,000 litres per year up to 500,000 litres. There is one exception though and that is Inchdairnie distillery which was opened in May 2016 near Glenrothes in Fife. The distillery will be able to distil 2 million litres per year with a possibility to expand to 4 million litres. Read more about Inchdairnie on page 176 and three more distilleries that have opened since last year - Arbikie (page 182), Lone Wolf (page 181) and Dornoch (page 182).

The idea to build a second distillery on Skye (with Talisker being the first) was presented several years ago by the late Sir Iain Noble. He had chosen a listed farm building near Torabhaig on the southeast coast as a suitable location, but the plans were never realized until Sir Iain died in 2010. A new company, Mossburn Distillers, has now taken over the plans and after a planning consent was granted, the first phase of restoration was completed in December 2014. By June 2016, two copper pot stills, as well as eight washbacks had been installed and the plan is to start production in October and to open the distillery to the public in spring 2017. The Torabhaig distillery will have a capacity of producing 500,000 litres of alcohol and the cost is estimated at £5m. Mossburn Distillers already produces three million bottles of wine, vodka and rum from sites in Russia, Poland and France and it is owned by the Swedish company, Haydn Holdings.

Jean Donnay, the owner of Glann ar Mor distillery in Brittany, France, has initiated a project to build the ninth distillery on Islay. Gartbreck Distillery will be situated at Saltpan Point on the shore of Loch Indaal, just south of Bowmore distillery and overlooks Port Charlotte which is situated on the other side of the bay. An old farm will be transformed into a traditional distillery equipped with a one ton mashtun, six washbacks made of Oregon pine and one pair of directly fired stills connected to a wormtub. The total capacity will be 55,000 litres of pure alcohol per year.

The artist´s impression of the future Ardnahoe Distillery on Islay

Construction work has been delayed on several occasions and will probably not commence until sometime in 2016 or 2017.

In January 2016 it became known that the independent bottler, Hunter Laing, plans to build a distillery on the northeast coast of Islay near Bunnahabhain. A planning application has been filed and the company is awaiting a decision. The estimated cost for the project is £8m and if everything goes according to plan, Ardnahoe distillery could be up and running by the end of 2017. It will have an annual capacity of 500,000 litres of alcohol, although 200,000 litres will be the target for the owners initially.

There have also been talks about yet another Islay distillery, this time on the Kildalton coast, just outside Port Ellen. The name is supposed to be Farkin distillery and rumours have it that Sukhinder Singh from the Whisky Exchange could be involved. A company named Farkin Distillery Limited was incorporated in May 2016 with an address in Campbeltown.

Tim Morrison, owner of the independent bottler AD Rattray and formerly of Morrison Bowmore Distillers (owners of Bowmore, Auchentoshan and Glen Garioch, now Suntory Beam) is building a single malt distillery on the banks of the river Clyde, in Glasgow. The distillery, which will be situated at the old Queens dock, will include an interactive visitor experience, as well as a café that will be housed in the old Pumphouse building which was built by Morrison´s great grandfather in 1877. Construction was supposed to have started in November 2015 but was delayed until July 2016 and the expectation is to have it ready for distillation by summer 2017. The distillery will be equipped with one mash tun, eight washbacks and one pair of stills with a total capacity of 500,000 litres.

Another delegation of the Morrison family represented by Tim´s brother, Brian, and his son, Jamie, is looking at building a distillery and bottling plant near the hamlet of Aberargie in Perthshire. The Morrison's, together with the Mackay family, own and operate Scottish Liqueur Centre which is situated in Bankfoot, 5 miles north of Perth. In January 2015, Morrison 6 MacKay received £430,000 from the Scottish Government and their planning application was approved in May 2016. The distillery will be equipped with one pair of stills and four washbacks with a possibility of expanding to eight washbacks.

In 2010, Alasdair Day launched a new blended Scotch whisky by the name of The Tweeddale. To be entirely accurate, it wasn´t a new whisky, but a recreation of a whisky manufactured in the 19th century. A company called J & A Davidson launched the brand and in 1895, Alasdair´s great grandfather, Richard Day, joined the company and eventually took over the business. When Richard Day retired after World War II, the business ceased to trade and the brand fell into oblivion. Alasdair inherited the old company´s cellar book and based on the recipes noted there, he was able to recreate the whisky. Alasdair soon began planning a distillery of his own and decided it should be situated in the Scottish Borders south of Edinburgh. The funding, however, was an issue but that problem seems to have been resolved when Alasdair teamed up with Bill Dobbie, entrepreneur and co-founder of online dating site, Cupid. A company, R&B Distillers, was formed, and yet another plan for a new distillery took shape. This will be built on the small Isle of Raasay, off the Isle of Skye. A derelict Victorian hotel will be turned into a distillery and a planning approval was given by the Highland Council in February 2016. The distillery will be equipped with two copper pot stills made by Frilli in Italy with a capacity of producing 150,000 bottles annually. If everything goes according to plan the Raasay distillery should be up and running by April 2017. The owners also decided that the project in the Borders should be put on hold until the distillery on Raasay had been built. Meanwhile, R&B Distillers are asking whisky lovers around the world to help choose a location for its second distillery.

Apart from the R&B project, there are two proposed distillery projects for the Borders. No matter who opens up their doors first, it will undoubtedly be the first distillery in the area since 1837. In 2014, Mossburn Distillers (who are currently involved in building a whisky distillery on Skye), have revealed their plans to build a considerably larger distillery near the former Jedforest Hotel at Camptown. The Mossburn distillery will be a combined malt and grain distillery with a total capacity of no less than 2,5 million litres of alcohol. The budget for the construction amounts to a staggering £35-40m! The plans also involve a bottling hall, maturation facilities and the largest whisky shop in Scotland. A planning permission form has been submitted to the Scottish Borders council and the company is hoping for a positive decision in autumn 2016.

The third proposed distillery in the area is one which will be built in Hawick by The Three Stills Company, a company incorporated in 2013 and spearheaded by former William Grant executive, John Fordyce. In November 2015, TTSC had secured £10 million through a group of private investors. The idea is to transform the former site of Turnbull & Scott Engineers on Commercial Road in Hawick into a distillery with two pairs of stills and eight washbacks. A planning application was approved in July 2016. The company has also released a blended Scotch called Clan Fraser made from sourced whiskies.

Plans to build a distillery in the Shetlands were announced in 2002 by a company called Blackwood Distillers. After a few years, it became abundantly clear that the plans would never materialise. The issue regarding a distillery was resuscitated in 2013 by the whisky consultant, Stuart Nickerson, former distillery manager at Highland Park and Glenglassaugh. The idea was to build it at Saxa Vord on Unst, the most northerly of the islands. The first stage, a gin distillery producing Shetland Reel Gin, came to fruition in summer 2014. In autumn 2015, four cask strength single malts, distilled at the Glenglassaugh distillery but bottled on Unst by The Shetland Distillery Co, were released, as well as a blended malt. A timeline for the whisky distillery has, as yet, not been announced, but the latest news from the company is that construction may be starting towards the end of 2016.

The famous, first written record of whisky was a letter to Friar John Cor, a monk at the Abbey of Lindores, dated 1494 where, by order of King James IV, he was instructed to make "aqua vitae, VIII bolls of malt". Five hundred and twenty years later, there are plans to revive whisky production at Lindores Abbey. Drew McKenzie Smith, whose family has owned the land on which the derelict abbey has stood for a century, has attracted investors in order to build a distillery on farmland near the abbey. To assist him is the well-known whisky consultant, Dr. Jim Swan, and if everything goes according to plan, construction of the £10m distillery could start in 2016 with a possible production starting late in 2017.

Plans for a new distillery in Falkirk were announced in 2008 and in May 2010, the project got the final approval. Little news has come from the initiators, Fiona and Alan Stewart since then, but in June 2013 the owners were awarded a grant of £444,000 by the Scottish Government. In August 2015, the company announced that stills and washbacks were in place. The distillery is located at Cadger's Brae, Polmont and the projected cost is estimated at £5m.

Another project which we have heard about for some time now is a distillery on the Isle of Barra. Future casks have been sold to the public since early 2008 and most of the plans regarding building and construction are ready. In July 2010, Peter Brown bought all the shares owned by Andrew Currie (of Arran Distillery fame) who had been part of the project since its inception. The original idea was to start building in autumn of 2009, but the economic climate has made funding difficult and the future of the distillery is now uncertain. The proposed site is Borve, which is situated on the west side of the island.

In 2007, independent bottler Duncan Taylor acquired an old granary which was built in 1899 just outside Huntly with the express purpose of transforming it into a distillery. Following the financial crisis in 2008/2009, the plans were put on hold. In summer 2013, however, the work on the distillery began with contractors paving a new road for the diggers and trucks. The plan is to dismantle the old building brick by brick, then to install the distilling equipment and finally to reassemble the building. The latest report is that the original building had been demolished and the site had been cleared, ready for the foundations to be laid. The owners are planning for a distillery with a capacity of 1,1 million litres.

And so, the first malt whisky distillery in Edinburgh in over 90 years (Glen Sciennes having closed in 1925) could become a reality within a couple of years. David Robertson, who has been working for Macallan and Whyte & Mackay for many years, has plans to convert the old Engine Shed building near Holyrood Park into a micro distillery, complete with a visitor centre and restaurant. A planning application was approved in August 2016. The distillery will be able to produce 100,000 litres of alcohol annually and the estimated cost of the project is £3.6 million.

When Sandy Bulloch sold his company in 2014, which included Loch Lomond and Glen Scotia, there was a lot of talk about the fact that he already had plans for a quick comeback into the whisky business. Sure enough, news had surfaced about a distillery project in Pollphail Village at Portavadie near Tighnabruaich. This happens to be the site where Bulloch owns a house near the shores of Loch Fyne. After a while, it all went quiet about the project and it didn't seem like it would materialise. In spring 2016, reports were bandied about a distillery to be built in the former Rolls Royce factory in East Kilbride, just south of Glasgow. The company involved is Campbell Meyer & Co – blenders, bottlers and exporters of whisky. The company was already founded in 1990 with Sandy Bulloch being one of the directors until 2005. The head of Campbell Meyer today is Colin Barclay, a nephew of Sandy Bulloch and Barclay is also the only director in a newly incorporated company called A Bulloch & Co Ltd. All in all, it does seem possible that the whisky tycoon, Sandy Bulloch, could indeed be back in the whisky production business. With the help of experienced whisky consultant, Harry Riffkin, Burnbrae distillery will be equipped with a full lauter mash tun, temperature controlled washbacks and one pair of stills.

Drimnin Estate, which overlooks the Isle of Mull in the west, is located on the Morvern peninsula in the Western Highlands. The 7,000 acre estate was bought by Derek and Louise Lewis in 2001 and a couple of years ago they started planning for a distillery on the estate. In early 2016, they received a £513,000 grant from the Scottish government and construction work began. The plan is to have the distillery commissioned in spring 2017. The distillery, which will be equipped with one pair of stills and four washbacks, will be one of the remotest distilleries in Scotland once it is finished, competing with Ardnamurchan which isn't far away, but on the opposite side of Loch Sunart.

Local farmer and helicopter pilot, John McKenzie has initiated the building of Scotland's very first community owned whisky distillery. The land that is earmarked is situated in Dingwall, north of Inverness, which is located towards the inner part of Cromarty Firth. This is classic whisky land. Just east of Dingwall, the oldest recorded whisky distillery in Scotland, namely Ferintosh, was established in 1690 and the town itself had a distillery until 1926 when Ben Wyvis closed. A planning application was submitted in March 2016 and by June more than £1.5 million had been raised via a community share offer. The Glen Wyvis distillery will be equipped with one pair of stills and eight washbacks with a capacity of producing up to 200,000 litres of pure alcohol. The expectation is that production will commence during the first half of 2017.

A new farm distillery is also planned in Lochlea, Ayrshire just south of Kilmarnock. The man behind it, Neil McGeoch, had his planning application approved by the local council in autumn 2015. The farm is located on the Robert Burns visitor trail and in his marketing, McGeoch is planning to use the famous bard's strong links with the neighbourhood. Burns came to Lochlea as an eighteen year old in 1777 and lived there for seven years, during which time he had founded the famous Bachelor's Club.

Bladnoch distillery in Wigtown might soon get a distillery neighbour situated just 20 kilometres to the north in Newton Stewart. Local businessman, Graham Taylor, managing director of Crafty Scottish Distillers, is planning to build a combined gin, vodka and whisky distillery. The planning application was approved in January 2016 and construction work began in April.

The surroundings of Loch Eriboll in the northwest corner of the Highlands are one of the remotest parts of Scotland and subsequently have the lowest population density in the UK. This is now the most unlikely scene of not one, but two distillery projects just a mile apart. Construction tycoon, David Morrison, is the driving force behind one of the projects and he incorporated Loch Eriboll Distillery Ltd in March 2015. His plan is to build a whisky/gin/vodka distillery, as well as a micro brewery. The other project has been initiated by a community group called Durness Development Group and, according to a spokesperson, they "want to copy the Harris distillery but on a smaller scale." At the time of writing, no planning application for either project had been submitted.

Other distillery projects that are at an early stage of development are the Port of Leith Distillery in Edinburgh and possibly distilleries on Benbecula in the Western Isles, in Fort William in the west and one near Dunrobin Castle on the east coast.

Ireland & Northern Ireland

Since the latest edition of the Malt Whisky Yearbook, another six distilleries have opened in Ireland and Northern Ireland and have therefore been moved from this chapter to "Distilleries around the world". A total of nineteen distilleries are producing at the moment compared to three just ten years ago. Another twenty are either under construction or in a planning stage. Theoretically, provided of course that all the projects are successful this could mean around 40 working distilleries in just a few years' time – an astonishing development!

One distillery, amongst the current projects, that could be the first to produce is Slane Castle distillery, just north of Dublin. The owners of the estate, the Conyngham family, established a whiskey brand a few years ago which has since become popular in the USA. Until recently, the whiskey has been produced at the Cooley Distillery but, when Beam Inc. took over the distillery in 2012, they also stopped selling whiskey to independent bottlers. This prompted the Conyngham family to plan for a distillery of their own on the estate. They partnered with Camus Wine & Spirits to begin the construction but, eventually, Camus withdrew from the project. In June 2015, however, Brown-Forman, one of the biggest companies in the industry, announced that they were buying Slane Castle Irish Whiskey Ltd. for $50m, with the hope of having a distillery with a one million litre capacity ready by the end of 2016. The plan is to produce a range of blended, pot still and single grain whiskey.

A slightly smaller distillery but still big in comparison to most craft distilleries (with a capacity of 500,000 litres) is being built in County Mayo in western Ireland. Paul Davis and Mark Quick are two of the men behind Nephin distillery which hasn't started producing yet, but a cooperage has been opened. At the moment they are securing funds for the project which is estimated to cost €5 million. Unlike many other new distillers, Nephin will not source whiskey from other producers to sell under its own name, but prefers to wait until its own whiskey is ready to be bottled.

While still on the west coast, we can report on a few more projects. Irish Fiddler Whiskey Company, with Colm Regan at the helm, has launched a range of whiskys sourced from other distilleries. They are now looking at building their own distillery in County Galway. Planning permission has also been approved for Burren Distillers to build a distillery in the coastal village, Ballyvaugn. The planned capacity is 100,000 litres. Software developer, David Raethorne, has recently bought Hazelwood House in Co. Sligo and plans to restore the mansion which was built in the early 1700s. Adjacent to the house lays a factory where Raethorne will establish a craft distillery called Lough Gill, as well as a visitor's centre. Sliabh Liag Distillery in south west Donegal, is still awaiting an approval on the planning application which was submitted in April 2016. Meanwhile, a sourced blended whiskey named Silkie was released by the owners in summer 2016.

Moving down to the southeast in Co. Cork and Co. Waterford, there are at least four distilleries which are being planned, two of which are in the same town. Gortinore distillery, with Denis and Aidan Mehigan, has acquired The Old Mill in Kilmacthomas and plans to turn it into a distillery with three pot stills. In the meanwhile, Stephen

Alex Conyngham, the Earl of Mount Charles, in front of Slane Castle and Mark Quick, one of the founders of Nephin Irish Whiskey

Keating and Niall Barry have set up a company called Kilmacthomas Whiskey Distillery with the aim to open up a distillery in the same town. There are currently two projects in Scotland where local communities have taken the initiative to build distilleries. It now appears that it may also be the turn of Ireland to follow suit. The island co-op at Cape Clear, six kilometres off the Cork coast, has submitted a planning application to build a distillery on the island. No decision has been taken yet, but the cost for the application which includes numerous studies on the impact that the distillery may have on the island, has already reached €200,000. Peter Mulryan has made greater progress with his Blackwater Distillery in Cappoquin in West Waterford. A distillery is already producing but, so far, it has only been gin and vodka. Mulryan is now planning an expansion with more stills in order to produce whiskey.

Tipperary Boutique Distillery was founded more than a year ago but a distillery has yet to be built. Local farmer, Liam Ahearn, and his fiancée, Jennifer Nickerson, have chosen the Ahearn Family farm between Clonmel and Tipperary as the designated spot for their distillery. In addition to this, they have also included Jennifer´s father in the business. Stuart Nickerson is well-known to lovers of Scotch after having been the distillery manager at Glenmorangie and the mastermind behind the resurrection of Glenglassaugh. In March 2016, the company released a sourced 11 year old Irish single malt under the name The Rising.

In Dublin things are heating up. In 2015, Jack and Stephen Teeling opened up the first new whiskey distillery in the city in 125 years. Now there are at least another three proposed distilleries in the pipeline. Dublin Whiskey Company was founded in 2012 with plans to rebuild a former mill in Dublin´s Liberties less than 500 metres from St Patrick´s Cathedral and converting it into a whiskey distillery. The project came to a temporary halt in April 2014 when the City Council asked the company to make a number of revisions to its plans, but in summer 2014, DWC were finally given planning permission. Not much has hap-

pened since, but in March 2016, the company was bought by the UK-based drinks group, Quintessential Brands, and the project is ready to go forward with the aim of having a distillery ready for production by the end of summer 2017. Quintessential´s first appearance in the Irish whiskey business, came in 2014 when they acquired First Ireland Spirits Company, including its consignment of Irish creams and liqueurs, as well as its production facility at Abbeyleix, Co Laois. Another company with a similar name, Dublin Whiskey Distillery Company Ltd, was founded in 2014 and more than €500,000 has been invested in the company by a number of businessmen including the former Diageo executive, Lorcan Rossi. Whether or not they will actually go ahead and build a distillery has not yet been decided. As Lorcan Rossi says;"Owning a distillery is not a prerequisite for making a great whiskey." The third proposed distillery in Dublin will be built by the American company, Alltech. They already have a brewing and distilling business in Kentucky and in 2012, they started a small distilling operation in collaboration with a brewery in County Carlow. Two years later, they bought an abandoned church in St. James´ Street in Dublin with the express purpose of turning it into a whiskey distillery. The plan is to start producing in spring 2017 and the distillery will be named after the founder and owner of Alltech, Dr. Pearse Lyons. The Lyons family has strong connections with St James´ Church. His father was born near the church and his grandfather was one of the last people buried in the graveyard.

South of Dublin in Enniskerry, Co. Wicklow, lays the Powerscourt Estate and Gardens, a popular tourist attraction with 500,000 visitors per year and owned by the Slazenger family. Two local entrepreneurs, Gerry Ginty and Ashley Gardiner, have now teamed up with the family to build a distillery on the estate. The whole investment will cost €10m and once at full production, the distillery will have the capacity of producing 1 million bottles per year. The planning application was approved in March 2016 and the plan is to have the distillery ready by early 2018.

Finally, in Northern Ireland, there are currently three distilleries which are producing - the giant Bushmill's and the two considerably smaller ones, Echlinville and Rademon Estate. In addition to that, there are another four proposed distilleries. In Derry, the producer of cream liqueurs, Niche Drinks, has been granted a permission to build a distillery in Ebrington Square. The total investment will amount to £15m with a capacity of 1 million litres per year and construction is scheduled to begin in 2016. In anticipation of its own whiskey, the company has released a blend called The Quiet Man based on whiskies from other sources. Another company that recently submitted an application to build a distillery in Ebrington Square is the Derry Craft Distillery which, apart from whiskey plans to produce poteen, as well as vodka and gin.

Peter Lavery, lottery millionaire and founder of The Belfast Distillery Company, has started to transform the former Crumlin Road jail into a whiskey distillery. Three stills have been ordered from Forsyth's in Rothes and its capacity will be 300,000 litres of alcohol. The whole investment is expected to be £6.8m, but construction came to a temporary halt in spring 2016 when it was discovered that additional repairs to the old building had to be undertaken. The company is already selling whiskey which has been produced by other distilleries under the brand names Danny Boy, Titanic and McConnell's.

Joe McGirr is the mastermind behind Boatyard Distillery in Enniskillen and he has taken on Darren Rook as his right hand, who's known as the founder and owner of London Distillery Company. The company received its planning permission in December 2015 and in spring of the ensuing year, the first still (of 250 litres) was installed. The beginning of May marked the first distillation and initially gin and potato vodka will be produced with whiskey to follow at a later stage.

Bottling grapevine

Now I could be wrong, but going through the new releases of the past year, it seems as if we have more bottlings with age statements than the previous year. Even more fascinating is the fact that these have come from producers of whom you would least have expected it. Have the producers finally listened to all and sundry who dislike NAS expressions? Do we actually see a new trend here? The answer is, I'm afraid, definitely not in the affirmative. I'm convinced that NAS is here to stay, at least for quite a few years to come, but it is interesting to note that fewer distillers have abandoned age statements this year than in the previous couple of years.

But let's begin the run-through with some old bottlings, wearing their age with pride. Glenfarclas is always a good start when it comes to aged malts. The Generations Range came to an end in 2016 with four rarities – a 50 year old matured in oloroso casks, a 1981 matured in port pipes, a 1986 cask strength and a 40 year old from 1976. From Glenlivet came its second edition of the 50 year old from the Alan Winchester Collection, Tullibardine launched a Vintage 1970, Tomatin presented a 44 year old and Tomintoul a 40 year old. Finally from Macallan came – the oldest one this year – The Peerless Spirit, a 65 year old. This was the final release in the Six Pillars Collection which was introduced in 2005.

Some producers made a revamp of their current ranges, like Glen Grant for instance. The 16 year old was removed and in its place came a 12 year old, as well as an 18 year old. Simultaneously, all their bottles and labels were given a new look. The Tomatin range also got a make-over and at the same time two new vintages in their peated range, Cù Bòcan 1988 and 2005, were released. And then, one day before printing, I received a press release about a range of Tomatin's destined for travel retail. This means you won't be reading about them on page 166 because that one had just been printed (the life of a Yearbook editor!). Anyway, the range comprises of an 8 year old (40%), a 15 year old (46%) and a 40 year old (43%)

The people at Highland Park have been industrious during the past year. Two new additions to the travel retail series, The Warriors, in the shape of Ingvar destined for the Taiwanese market, as well as the very limited King Christian I. These were complemented by the 17 year old Ice Edition and, later in 2016, Hobbister, the first in a series based on the distillery's five keystones – in this case the peat. The final four expressions will appear in 2017. At Glencadam, they were not idle either. No fewer than six new bottlings saw the light of day during 2015/2016; Origin 1825 without age statement, a 17 year old port finish, a 19 year old oloroso finish, an 18 year old, a 25 year old and a 33 year old single cask.

Being experts on wood finishes, Dalmore released three new exclusives for travel retail and all with a second maturation in various sherry casks – Regalis, Luceo and Dominium. Two exclusives, a 35 year old and the Quintessence with a finish in five different red wine casks were also released. Ardbeg's special bottling for this year's Ardbeg Day was Dark Cove. As usual, it came in two versions; a committee version bottled at 55% and a general release at 46%. But Ardbeg fans had one more reason to rejoice when a 21 year old was launched in autumn 2016.

While still staying on Islay, Lagavulin celebrated its 200th anniversary in 2016. The first bottling to appear was surprisingly young, an 8 year old, and it was followed up by a sherry matured 25 year old a few months later. From Laphroaig came a 30 year old, while at the same time it was announced that the 18 year old was to be discontinued. Its replacement came to light in spring 2016 when Lore, without age statement and matured in first fill bourbon barrels, quarter casks and oloroso hogsheads, was launched.

Kilkerran from Glengyle distillery came of age and the first 12 year old was launched. Tomintoul got a new introduction malt to their core range with Tlàth and Tullibardine released The Murray, the first cask strength version from the distillery that was distilled this century. The range from Glen Moray keeps growing and, while Classic Chardonnay Finish and Classic Sherry Finish were released, they also replaced the 10 and 16 year olds with a 15 and an 18 year old.

Glenrothes added Peated Cask Reserve, with additional maturation in casks that have formerly held Islay malt, to its range and Jura came out with a 22 year old pinot noir finish to honour the distillery manager, Willie Cochrane, who retired after having been at the distillery for 39 years. In 2016 we also saw the return of Springbank Local Barley.

This time it was in the form of a 16 year old, the first in a series of five to be released during the coming years.

The owners of BenRiach launched a Cask Strength and Peated Quarter Cask, as well as batch 13 of their popular single casks. The other two distilleries in the group also had something new to show off. GlenDronach released its first peated expression, as well as Octaves Classic with seven years of full maturation in smaller casks. And from Glenglassaugh came Octaves Classic and Octaves Peated, also from smaller casks. It´s been many years since we last saw an official bottling from Tamnavulin but in autumn 2016, the Double Cask with a sherry finish was launched to celebrate the distillery´s 50th anniversary.

Macallan surprised many with a lightly peated version for travel retail, the Rare Cask Black and in spring 2016, it also released a new core expression (in Taiwan and the USA at first) – the 12 year old Double Cask. Glenfiddich has introduced the Experimental Series with space for some new innovations. The IPA Experiment had received a finish in IPA beer casks and the casks for Project XX had been selected by 20 brand ambassadors. Talisker released a new bottling for travel retail, Neist Point, which joins Dark Storm, while Bruichladdich launched three new items for duty free – The Laddie Eight, Octomore 7.4 and Port Charlotte 2007 CC:01.

Bowmore released two bottlings with age statements. This includes a 9 year old for the core range and a 10 year old for travel retail, while it has also started a new range where the first expression, Bowmore Vault Edit1on (yes, the spelling is correct), highlights the effect from its Vault No. 1 warehouse on the spirit. Every year in February there is a new expression of Glenmorangie´s Private Edition. This year it was Milsean, matured in ex-bourbon casks and finished in re-toasted wine casks. The distillery also relea-sed two more bottlings in the expanding duty free range; Tayne, finished in amontillado sherry casks and Tarlogan

with a maturation in both virgin oak and ex-bourbon casks.

Deanston finally released its long awaited Organic Dean-ston, as well as an 18 year old, while Kilchoman added Sanaig, matured in both bourbon and sherry casks, to its core range. Glenturret, for so long hidden away in the Famous Grouse blend, was given a chance to shine when the 32 year old James Fairlie was launched and, a few months later, the 16 year old Fly´s 16 Masters made its appearance. The big seller in the Inver House stable of distilleries, Speyburn, has released Arranta Casks as an exclusive to the American market and its other top brand, Old Pulteney, was blessed with a Vintage 1989 and the second release of the 35 year old.

The owners of Benromach, Gordon & MacPhail, are known for their stock of old whiskies and this year they wanted to showcase it in their distillery range as well when a 35 year old and a 1974 single cask were released. Even older, at 43 years, was the very limited, official Craggan-more bottling that was released in Dubai in autumn 2015. That was the oldest ever from the distillery! For many years, W Grant´s Kininvie distillery was used only to pro-duce malts for blends. However, a few years ago, the first official bottlings of the single malt appeared and in 2016, a 23 year signature bottling was released.

Finally, and I´m writing this 24 hours before we start printing, I received the official clearance from Diageo about the Special Releases. Pictures of labels have been floating around on the internet for a few months now but here´s the official list; a 25 year old Auchroisk (51.2%), a 24 year old Glenkinchie (57.2%), a 37 year old Linkwood (50.3%), a 25 year old Mannochmore (53.4%) and a 40 year old Cambus single grain (52.7%). Finally, we can add what we sometimes call "the usual suspects"; a 12 year old Lagavulin (57.7%), an unpeated 15 year old Caol Ila (61.5%), a 38 year old Brora (48.6%) and 37 year old Port Ellen (55.2%).

King Christian I, Tomatin 40 years old, Tullibardine 1970, Ailsa Bay and Jura "One For The Road", 22 years old

Independent
bottlers

The independent bottlers play an important role
in the whisky business. With their innovative bottlings, they increase
diversity. Single malts from distilleries where the owners' themselves
decide not to bottle also get a chance through the independents.
The following are a selection of the major companies.
All tasting notes have been prepared by Suzanne Redmond.

Gordon & MacPhail

www.gordonandmacphail.com

Established in 1895 the company, which is owned by the Urquhart family, still occupies the same premises in Elgin. Apart from being an independent bottler, there is also a legendary store in Elgin and, since 1993, an own distillery, Benromach. There is a wide variety of bottlings, for example Connoisseurs Choice (single malts bottled at either 43 or 46%), Private Collection (single malts, some dating back to the 1950s, usually bottled at 45%), MacPhail's Collection (single malts bottled at 43%), Distillery Labels (a relic from a time when Gordon & MacPhail released more or less official bottlings for several producers. Currently 10 distilleries are represented in the range and the whisky is bottled at either 40 or 43%), Rare Old (exclusive whiskies from distilleries that are closed and sometimes even demolished, for example Glenugie, Glenury Royal, Coleburn, Glenesk and Glenlochy), Secret Stills (single malts from 1966 to 2000 where the distillery name in not disclosed, bottled at 45%), Cask Strength (a range of single malts bottled at cask strength), Rare Vintage (single malts, including several Glen Grant and Glenlivet bottlings going back to the 1940s) and Speymalt (a series of single malts from Macallan from 1938 and onwards).

In 2010, a new range was launched under the name Generations. To say that these are rare and old whiskies is an understatement. The first release was a Mortlach 70 year old, which was followed the year after by a Glenlivet 70 year old. In September 2015, it was time for the third instalment in the series - a Mortlach 75 years old. This is the oldest single malt ever bottled and only 100 bottles were released. Amazing bottles were also released in autumn 2014 when Private Collection Ultra was launched. To celebrate the transition of the family-owned business to the next generation, four extremely rare whiskies were presented; Linkwood 1953 61 years old, Glenlivet 1952 62 years old, Mortlach 1951 63 years old and Strathisla 1957 57 years old. The whiskies were chosen by members of the third and fourth generations of the Urquhart family.

Gordon & MacPhail rarely buy matured whisky from other producers. Instead, around 95% is bought as new make spirit and filled by the company. Some 7,000 casks are maturing in one racked and one dunnage warehouse in Elgin, another 7,000 casks are found at various distillers around Scotland and 20,000 casks are located in the warehouses at Benromach.

Glen Grant 1954, 40%
Nose: Deep and intoxicating, with wet earthy aromas, along with damp wood and vegetal forest floor.
Palate: Smooth velvet with chunky toffee, with light spice, toasted nuts and a seductive tea quality.
Finish: A dram that keeps giving.

Mortlach 1954, 43%
Nose: Notes of wilted roses, over-ripe sultanas, ginger, Christmas cake, earthy tones, forest floor.
Palate: Quite spicy, with crushed cloves and ginger dominating; add some teacake, with a hint of aged pastrami.
Finish: Warm, spicy length.

Berry Bros. & Rudd

www.bbr.com

Britain's oldest wine and spirit merchant, founded in 1698 has been selling their own world famous blend, Cutty Sark, since 1923. Berry Brothers had been offering their customers private bottlings of malt whisky for years, but it was not until 2002 that they launched Berry's Own Selection of single malt whiskies. Under the supervision of Spirits Manager, Doug McIvor, some 30 expressions are on offer every year. Bottling is usually at 46% but expressions bottled at cask strength are also available. The super premium blended malt, Blue Hanger, is also included in the range. So far, eleven different releases have been made, each different from the other. The sixth edition sets itself apart from the rest as it combines both sherried malts from Speyside and peated Islay whisky. The ninth release, based on whiskies from Clynelish, Glen Elgin and Bunnahabhain, also showed some peaty notes as did the 11th and latest edition, which was released in late 2014. In autumn 2014 the Exceptional Casks Collection was launched. Handpicked by Doug McIvor a 50 year old North British single grain, two single casks of Glenlivet 1972 and a Jamaican rum from 1977 were the first bottles in the new range. In 2010, BBR sold Cutty Sark blended Scotch to Edrington and obtained The Glenrothes single malt in exchange.

A visit to Berry Bros. & Rudd at 3 St James's Street in London is an extraordinary experience. The business was established in 1698 by the Widow Bourne and the company has traded from the same shop for over 300 years! Originally selling coffee, the company soon expanded into wine and started supplying the Royal Family during the reign of King George III and still continues to do so today.

Glenlossie 1992 21 year old, 46%
Nose: Fresh baled hay, with leafy notes and hints of gooseberry and wild elderflower.
Palate: The aromas from the nose pop with a toffee edge, along with barley sugar and lime.
Finish: Long, with lemongrass and lime.

North British 1962 50 years old, 58.9%
Nose: Toasted honeycomb and caramelized nuts; spiced mandarin zest with developing woody notes.
Palate: The toasted nuts and spiced mandarin pop immediately with hints of clove, nutmeg, cocoa and wood chippings.
Finish: Medium dry, lengthy.

Signatory

Founded in 1998 by Andrew and Brian Symington, Signatory Vintage Scotch Whisky lists at least 50 single malts at any one occasion. The most widely distributed range is Cask Strength Collection which sometimes contains spectacular bottlings from distilleries which have long since disappeared. One of the most recent additions to the range in 2014 was a rare Glencraig 1976, 38 years old. Another range is The Un-chill Filtered Collection bottled at 46%. Some of the latest bottlings released are also spectacular; Craigduff 1973 (an extremely rare, peated Strathisla), Mosstowie 1979 and Glen Mhor 1982. Andrew Symington bought Edradour Distillery from Pernod Ricard in 2002

Ian Macleod Distillers

www.ianmacleod.com

The company was founded in 1933 and is one of the largest independent family-owned companies within the spirits industry. Gin, rum, vodka and liqueurs, apart from whisky, are found within the range and they also own Glengoyne and Tamdhu distilleries. In total 15 million bottles of spirit are sold per year. Their single malt ranges are single casks either bottled at cask strength or (more often) at reduced strength, always natural colour and un chill-filtered. The Chieftain's cover a range of whiskies from 10 to 50 years old while Dun Bheagan is divided into two series – Regional Malts, 8 year old single malts expressing the character from 4 whisky regions in Scotland and Rare Vintage Single Malts, a selection of single cask bottlings from various distilleries. There are two As We Get It single malt expressions – Highland and Islay, both 8 year olds and bottled at cask strength. The Six Isles blended malt contains whisky from all the whisky-producing islands and is bottled at 43%. One of the top sellers is the blended malt Isle of Skye with five domestic expressions – 8, 12, 18, 21 and 50 years old

as well as Isle of Skye Elgol, exclusive to travel retail. Finally, Smokehead, a heavily, peated single malt from Islay introduced in 2006, has become a huge success. There is also a Smokehead Extra Black 18 years old, Smokehead Extra Rare (which basically is a 1 litre duty free bottling of the 12 year old) and the limited Smokehead Rock Edition. The company also has a blended Scotch portfolio which includes its biggest seller, King Robert II as well as Langs Supreme (5 years old) and Langs Select (12 years old). New additions to the portfolio in 2016 were Shieldaig Speyside single malt for duty free and Rocket Cat, a cinnamon flavoured spirit based on whisky.

'As We Get It' Highland Single Malt, 65.8%
Nose: Over-ripe apricots and crab apples, along with fresh marmalade with a hint of clover and leather.
Palate: The juicy apricots are alive with spice and soft orange. The fruit and wood spice mingle gently with autumnal soft fruits.
Finish: Long juicy and fruity.

'As We Get It' Islay Single Malt, 61.3%
Nose: Salty sea air with lemons and limes, sea-salted caramel, coconut shell and mineral smoky note.
Palate: Cactus, royal icing, warm grapefruit, salted caramel and a peaty tone.
Finish: Long and inviting.

Blackadder International

www.blackadder.se

Blackadder is owned by Robin Tucek, one of the authors of The Malt Whisky File. Apart from the Blackadder and Blackadder Raw Cask, there are also a number of other ranges – Smoking Islay, Peat Reek, Aberdeen Distillers, Clydesdale Original and Caledonian Connections. One of the latest brands in the Blackadder family is Riverstown which is especially earmarked for the Asian market. The company has also been known for bottling unusual expressions of Amrut single malt. All bottlings are single cask, uncoloured and un chill-filtered. Most of the bottlings are diluted to 43-46% but Raw Cask is always bottled at cask strength. Around 100 different bottlings are launched each year.

Duncan Taylor

www.duncantaylor.com

Duncan Taylor was founded in Glasgow in 1938 as a cask broker and trading company. Over the decades, the company built strong ties with distillers over Scotland, with the company bringing their own casks to the distilleries to be filled with new make spirit. This resulted in a collection of exceptionally rare casks, many from distilleries which are now closed. Duncan Taylor was acquired by Euan Shand in 2001 and operations were moved to Huntly.

Duncan Taylor's flagship brand is the blended Scotch Black Bull, a brand with a history going back to 1864. The brand was trade-marked in the US on the repeal of prohibition in 1933 and was re-branded in 2009 by Duncan Taylor. The range consists of three core releases – Kyloe, a 12 year old and a 21 year old. There are also three limited versions, 30 year old, 40 year old and Special Reserve. The Black Bull brand is complimented by Smokin' which is a blend of peated Speyside, Islay and grain whisky from the Lowlands.

The portfolio also includes Rarest (single cask, cask strength whiskies of great age from demolished distilleries), Dimensions (a collection of single malts and single grains aged up to 39 years and bottled either at cask strength or at 46%), The Octave (single malt whiskies matured or 'Octavised' for a further period in small, 50 litre ex-sherry octave casks), Rare Auld (single malts and, not least, single grains of an exceptional age), The Tantalus (a selection of whiskies all aged in their 40s) and The Duncan Taylor Single Range (whiskies aged 30 years or more from closed distilleries). The blended malt category is represented by Big Smoke, a young peated whisky available in two strengths, 40% and 60%.

In 2014, a new bottling plant with additional warehousing was opened in Huntly. Since 2007, the owners have also had plans to build their own distillery. Construction work has began but no final date for the production start has been given.

Black Bull 40 year old, 47.6%

Nose: Honey and sherried tones pop alongside apricots, but tercups and butterscotch.

Palate: Notes of honeycomb, ginger, straw, chewy over-ripe Golden Delicious apples and spiced apricots.

Finish: Long and smooth with a kiss of orange.

Cambus 1991 24 years old, 55.2%

Nose: Springtime freshness with cut grass mingling with notes of grapefruit, limes, kiwi and elderflower.

Palate: Juicy and fruity, with fresh lemongrass, limes, meadow honey, lightly toasted nuts, nutmeg, dried tobacco leaf and a touch of caramel.

Finish: Long, fresh lightly honeyed

Scotch Malt Whisky Society

www.smws.com

The Scotch Malt Whisky Society, established in the mid 1980s and owned by Glenmorangie Co since 2003, has more than 25,000 members worldwide and apart from UK, there are 17 chapters around the world. The idea from the very beginning was to buy casks of single malts from the producers and bottle them at cask strength without colouring or chill filtration. The labels do not reveal the name of the distillery. Instead there is a number but also a short description which will give you a clue to which distillery it is. A Tasting Panel selects and bottles around twenty new casks the first Friday of every month. The SMWS also arranges tastings at their different venues but also at other locations. In recent years, the range has been expanded to also include single grain, whiskies from other countries as well as rum. In April 2015, Glenmorangie sold the SMWS to the HotHouse Club and a group of the managers. A spokesperson for the new owners revealed in spring 2016 that £5 million had been invested in whisky stock since the take over.

Compass Box Whisky Co

www.compassboxwhisky.com

Most people within the whisky industry acknowledge the fact that the cask has the greatest influence on the flavour of whisky, but none more so than the founder and owner of Compass Box, John Glaser. His philosophy is strongly influenced by meticulous selection of oak for the casks, clearly inspired by his time in the wine business. But he also has a lust for experimenting and innovation to test the limits, which was clearly shown when Spice Tree was launched in 2005. For an additional maturation, Glaser filled malt whisky in casks prepared with extra staves of toasted French oak suspended within the cask. In spring 2016, Compass Box launched a campaign for more transparency in the Scotch whisky industry where a producer would be allowed to give "complete, unbiased and clear" information on the components of their whiskies. Today, under EU law, a producer is only allowed to disclose the age of the youngest whisky in a blend. Glaser wants to have a change where it is optional (but not compulsory) for a producer to give as much information as they desire.

The company divides its ranges into a Signature Range and a Limited Range. Spice Tree (a blended malt), The Peat Monster (a combination of peated islay whiskies and Highland malts), Oak

Cross (American oak casks fitted with heads of French oak), Asyla (a blended whisky matured in first-fill ex-bourbon American oak) and Hedonism (a vatted grain whisky) are included in the former.

In the Limited range, whiskies are regularly replaced and at times only to resurface a couple of years later in new variations. In 2011 it became illegal to use the term vatted malt. Instead the term blended malt must be used. To mark this change of terminology, which was heavily debated, Compass Box released two expressions in the Limited range – The Last Vatted Malt (a vatting of 36 year old Glenallachie and 26 year old Caol Ila) and The Last Vatted Grain (with whiskies from Invergordon, Cameron Bridge and the two closed distilleries Carsebridge and Port Dundas). The first new bottling in 2015 was a cask strength version of Peat Monster which was sold in magnum bottles. This was followed up by 15th anniversary expressions of Hedonism and Flaming Heart and, later, This Is Not A Luxury Whisky - a blend of 19 year old Glen Ord and 40 year old grain from Strathclyde and Girvan. Two limited releases were made in summer 2016; Enlightenment, which is a blend of four different single malts and bottled at 46% and Circus, an unusual vatting of two blended malts, a blended grain and Benrinnes single malt - all matured in sherry casks and bottled at 49%.

A third range was added in summer of 2011 when Great King Street was launched. The range will offer blended Scotch with a 50% proportion of malt whisky and using new French oak for complexity. The first expression was called Artist's Blend and in autumn 2014 Glasgow Blend was released.

In autumn 2014, Compass Box made a long-term agreement with John Dewar & Sons where the Bacardi-owned company would supply Compass Box with stocks of whisky for future bottlings. In spring 2015 it was further announced that Bacardi had aqcuired a minority share of the independent bottler. Both parties confirm that Compass Box will be run as a separate entity from Bacardi also in the future with John Glaser continuing to lead and run the business..

The Circus, 49%

Nose: Spicy, with orchard fruits popping up alongside lightly toasted hazelnuts and orange peel.

Palate: The orange peel is kicked up a notch with spice and a lick of liquorice and coconut.

Finish: Warm and lengthy.

Enlightenment, 46%

Nose: A twist of lemon and lime, along with aromas of woodruff, fresh daisies and peanuts.

Palate: Fresh cut grass with peanuts, limes and dandelions. Soft, yet dry.

Finish: Long and heated, with a citrus freshness.

Creative Whisky Company

www.creativewhisky.co.uk

David Stirk started the Creative Whisky Co in 2005 and the company exclusively bottles single casks, divided into three series: The Exclusive Malts are bottled at cask strength and vary in age between 8 and 40 years. Around 20 bottlings are made annually. This is followed by the Exclusive Range which comprises of somewhat younger whiskies, between 8 and 16 years, bottled at either 45% or 45.8%. Finally, Exclusive Casks are single casks, which have been 'finished' for three months in another type of cask, e. g. Madeira, Sherry, Port or different kinds of virgin oak. In 2015, the company's 10th anniversary was celebrated with a range of 7 new bottlings and this was followed up by The Exclusive Malts Ireland – a 13 year old single cask from Cooley. In 2016, a new range was added where the distillery is undisclosed. The first three bottlings were Speyside Over 8 Years Old, Peated Highland Over 8 Years Old and Grain Over 10 Years Old.

Master of Malt

www.masterofmalt.com

Master of Malt is one of the biggest and most innovative whisky retailers in the UK. The company also has ranges of its own bottled single malts. One range is called the Secret Bottlings Series, where no distillery names appear on the labels. It's split between well-aged releases (30, 40, 50 & 60 year olds from Speyside) and a range of no age statement regional bottlings at 40% (Highland, Speyside, Lowland, Islay and Island). They also bottle single casks at natural cask strength from various distilleries in their Single Cask Series. Some of the latest are a 12 year old Ardbeg, a 33 year old Bunnahabhain, a 29 year old Macallan and a 3 year old Slyrs from Germany. You can also Blend Your Own whisky on the site. Another feature is that they stock thousands of Drinks by the Dram's 30ml bottles, available for sale individually from the full product pages of the website, as well as allowing customers to personalise the contents of Drinks by the Dram Tasting Sets and spirits-filled Advent Calendars as they order.

Bunnahabhain 1982 33 years old, 48.6%

Nose:	Quite fruity, with notes of pineapple, lemons, dried orange and salted caramel.
Palate:	Warmed caramel sponge pudding with flickers of orange, lemon and lime zest. Walnuts, sherried sultanas and leather towards the end.
Finish:	Long luscious length.

Atom Brands

Part of the same ATOM group as retailer Master of Malt, ATOM Brands includes a number of independent bottlers. They're distributed by Maverick Drinks who also import many American craft whiskeys from the likes of St. George Spirits and FEW Spirits.

That Boutique-y Whisky Company

www.thatboutiqueywhiskycompany.com

2016 saw That Boutique-y Whisky Company (who launched in 2012 and have, to date, offered only a NAS range of whiskies) introduce age statements for all their new releases. Previously, the age difference between the whiskies in a single batch had been as much as 30 years, but this is less the case now. The company has made it clear that they believe flavour is still the most important thing when it comes to whisky, but are aware that customers are nonetheless interested in ages of the constituent parts. TBWC has also offered their support to the Campaign for Scotch Whisky Transparency launched by John Glaser of Compass Box in early 2016.

The whiskies continue to be a success and over 150 different bottlings have now been released from over 70 different distilleries including Springbank, Ardbeg, Macallan, Overeem and Paul John. The range also includes a handful of blended malts, blends, single grains and even a couple of bourbons.

Mortlach 27 year old, 52.6%

Nose:	Zippy, with lime, lemongrass and fresh hay. Add hedgerow flowers and green apples to give it a twist.
Palate:	Elegant with a touch of sweetness. Smooth body with hints of pineapple, green olive, pine and pistachio.
Finish:	Great length that continues to develop.

The Blended Whisky Company

www.theblendedwhiskycompany.com

The Blended Whisky Company, founded in 2012, produces The Lost Distilleries Blend (World's Best Blend at the World Whiskies Awards 2014) and The Golden Age Blend (Best Scotch Blend WWA 2016). The former is made exclusively from whiskies produced at now closed distilleries. The seventh batch contains Port Ellen, Caperdonich, Mosstowie, Glenisla, Glenlochy and Imperial malts with the grain coming from Port Dundas. The Golden Age Blend, meanwhile, harks back to the early 1960s to mid 1970s and is made exclusively with whiskies that are at least 40 years old. Malts from Macallan, Glenrothes and Tamdhu are used as well as a little peated Bunnahabhain. An extremely old grain from North British was selected to complete the blend and bring the different components together (with a ratio of four parts malt to just one part grain).

The Golden Age Blend, 44.3%

Nose:	Spicy, dried yellow fruits, burnt sugar and apricots.
Palate:	Citrus zest dominates, with floral notes popping in with a toffee apples giving slightly sugared edge.
Finish:	Medium to long length with fresh orange.

Darkness!

www.darknesswhisky.com

The first whiskies from Darkness! were released in spring 2014 and the key words for these expressions are dark and heavily sherried. To create the character, single malts are filled into specially commissioned 50 litre first fill Sherry casks where they are finished for more than 3 months. Pedro Ximénez, Oloroso or Palo Cortado Sherry casks are used (specified on each bottling) as well as hybrid PX and Oloroso casks made up with staves from each. Recent releases include a 26 year old Tullibardine finished in an PX cask and a 6 year old Port Charlotte finished in one of the hybrid casks.

Glenrothes 26 years oloroso finish, 52%

Nose:	Enticing, with crab apple, spice and dried apricots, with a kick of mandarin blossom.
Palate:	Drying yet juicy with notes of pineapple, fresh ginger, fresh parsley, and sherried yellow fruits.
Finish:	Long and spicy, with a touch of toffee.

Reference Series

www.referenceserieswhisky.com

Reference Series is a range of educational blended malts that goes vertically from I, to II, to III, each made with the same four whiskies but with III being made with a far greater proportion of the older, more complex malts compared to I, which is more youthful and clean. The range then continues horizontally, if you will, with .1 (additional PX finish), .2 (includes 10% heavily peated Islay malt) and .3 (containing e150a caramel colouring) editions. Comparisons can then be made throughout the range to help drinkers understand how composition and maturity can affect the final whisky. Reference Series III.2 was named World's Best Blended Malt at the World Whiskies Awards 2016. The blend was made up of more than 50% very old whisky with an addition of 10% heavily peated Islay whisky.

Reference Series III.2, 47.5%.
Nose: A hit of fresh orange peel, spice and a hint of coconut. Add some honeyed walnuts, dandelions and a light earthy tone.
Palate: Smooth, with a spicy coconut kick. Some dried mango and a touch of autumnal leaves give an interesting palate.
Finish: Long, with persistent mango.

A Dewar Rattray Ltd

www.adrattray.com

This company was founded by Andrew Dewar Rattray in 1868. In 2004 the company was revived by Tim Morrison, previously of Morrison Bowmore Distillers and fourth generation descendent of Andrew Dewar, with a view to bottling single cask malts from different regions in Scotland. One of its best-sellers is a single malt named Stronachie. It is named after a distillery that closed in the 1930s. Tim Morrison bought one of the few remaining bottles of Stronachie and found a distillery, Benrinnes, that could reproduce its character. Each Stronachie bottling is a batch of 6-10 casks and there are currently two expressions - 10 and 18 year old. A peated, blended malt, Cask Islay, became available in 2011 and released again in 2013 but this time as a single malt. In 2012 a new, 5 year old blend was launched under the name Bank Note. The AD Rattray´s Cask Collection is a range of single cask whiskies bottled at cask strength and without colouring or chill-filtration. This range was recently complemented by Vintage Cask Collection, including rare and older whiskies.

In 2011, the company opened A Dewar Rattray´s Whisky Experience & Shop in Kirkoswald, South Ayrshire. Apart from having a large choice of whiskies for sale, there is a sample room, as well as a cask room. All the products in the shop, including personalised own label single cask bottlings, are also available on-line from thewhiskyangel.com.

Stronachie 18 years old, 46%
Nose: Notes of honey, caramel, and nutmeg with a hint of orange zest.
Palate: Robust, with the citrus notes mingling gently with spice and woody tones.
Finish: Good length of yellow autumnal fruits, with a hint of vanilla.

A D Rattrays´s Whisky Experience - Strathclyde 1990, 56.3%
Nose: Fresh cotton, hints of beeswax, lime leaf, meadow flowers and gentle hints of white peach and sherry.
Palate: White peaches mingle with meadow honey; a viscous mouthfeel. Sherry hits as it opens up with gently toasted walnuts and lightly spiced apricots.
Finish: Long and nutty, with a kick of lime.

The Whisky Agency

www.whiskyagency.de

The man behind this company is Carsten Ehrlich, to many whisky aficionados known as one of the founders of the annual Whisky Fair in Limburg, Germany. His experience from sourcing casks for limited Whisky Fair bottlings led him to start as an independent bottler in 2008 under the name The Whisky Agency. There are several ranges including The Whisky Agency with 12 series of whiskies released so far, The Perfect Dram (at least 40 expressions so far) and Specials with some un-usual bottlings. One of the latest ranges is Good Vibes including both old expressions (Speyside region 40 and 43 years old) as well as younger bottlings (Caol Ila 8 years old).

Douglas Laing & Co

www.douglaslaing.com

Established in 1948 by Douglas Laing, this firm was run for many years by his two sons, Fred and Stewart. In May 2013, the brothers decided to go their separate ways. Douglas Laing & Co is now run by Fred Laing and his daughter, Cara. The other side of the business, run by Stewart and his sons, Scott and Andrew, is called Hunter Laing. Douglas Laing has the following brands in their portfolio; Provenance (single casks typically aged between 8 and 20 years and bottled at 46%), Director´s Cut (old and rare single malts bottled at cask strength), Premier Barrel (single malts in ceramic decanters bottled at 46%), Clan Denny (two blended malts and a selection of old single grains), Double Barrel (two malts vatted together and bottled at 46%), Big Peat (a vatting of selected Islay malts) and Old Particular, a range of single malts and grains. During the Feis Ile 2016 on Islay, the company for the first time presented two special festival bottlings - a Big Peat bottled at 48% and Old Particular Bowmore 1999.

New releases in the last years include Scallywag, a blended malt influenced by sherried whiskies from Speyside and recently complemented by the limited Scallywag Cask Strength Edition, Timorous Beastie, a blended Highland malt with a limited 40 year old bottled at cask strength launched in September 2016 and Rock Oyster, a blended malt (available also at cask strength) combining malts from Islay, Arran, Orkney and Jura. Together with Big Peat, they are now all promoted under the name Regional Malts. In April 2016, a fifth region was added when The Epicurean, a blended Lowland malt was released. In October 2015, the first chapter of three in a limited range called Yula was released. This is a blended Islay malt and the first bottling was a 20 year old.

The Epicurean, 46.2%
Nose: Quite aromatic, with aromas of thyme, elderflower, white pepper and light lychee.
Palate: Juicy, with a candied sweetness of white blossom and pineapple, with some light grassy notes.
Finish: Medium length, with a touch of sweetened Granny Smith apples.

Scallywag cask strength, 54%
Nose: Vibrant spiced mandarins pop. Add vanilla and tobacco with a nutty tone.
Palate: Dry, with a hint of grapefruit and lemongrass, which moves to orange zest, spices, fruit cake, hazelnuts and cocoa.
Finish: Medium length, with a hint of burnt embers and spice.

Hunter Laing & Co

www.hunterlaing.com

This company was formed after the demerger between Fred and Stewart Laing in 2013 (see Douglas Laing). It is run by Stewart Laing and his two sons, Scott and Andrew. The relatively new company Edition Spirits, founded by the sons has also been absorbed into Hunter Laing with the range of single malts called The First Editions. In 2015, a sub-range of First Editions was introduced when the first bottlings in The Author's Series were launched with each single malt whisky linked to a world famous author.

From the demerger, the following ranges and brands ended up in the Hunter Laing portfolio; The Old Malt Cask (rare and old malts, bottled at 50%), The Old and Rare Selection (an exclusive range of old malts offered at cask strength), Douglas of Drumlanrig (single casks bottled at 46%) and Sovereign (a range of old and rare grain whiskies). A new range bearing the name Hepburn's Choice was launched in spring 2014. These single malts are younger than The Old Malt Cask expressions and bottled at 46%. A little later in the year, the blended malt Highland Journey was released. The portfolio also includes blended Scotch such as John Player Special, House of Peers and Langside.

In January 2016, the company announced their intentions of building a distillery on Islay. The company is still waiting for an approval of their planning application but if everything goes according to plans, Ardnahoe distillery near Bunnahabhain, could be producing end of 2017.

OMC Arran 1990, 50%
Nose: Quite aromatic, with light tropical fruits, beeswax, straw and mature lemon.
Palate: The nose slips onto the palate, with spiced pineapple, fresh almonds, cut grass and honey comb.
Finish: Medium length, with a lingering note of biscotti.

The Sovereign Girvan 1979, 51%
Nose: Banana peel, tropical fruits drizzled in honey, kaffir lime leaf and lightly spiced lemons.
Palate: Lightly toasted notes mingle with pineapple, meadow flowers, and baked lemons, plus a hint of thyme.
Finish: Long, soft length, with banana and hazelnuts.

Malts of Scotland

www.malts-of-scotland.com

Thomas Ewers from Germany, bought casks from Scottish distilleries and decided in the spring of 2009 to start releasing them as single casks bottled at cask strength and with no colouring or chill filtration. At the moment he has released more than 100 bottlings and apart from a large number of single casks, there are two special series, Amazing Casks and Angel's Choice, both dedicated to very special and superior casks. Recently, Ewers has also started bottling Irish malt whiskey, American whiskey and Indian whisky (Paul John).

Wemyss Malts

www.wemyssmalts.com

This family-owned company, a relatively newcomer to the whisky world, was founded in 2005. The family owns another two companies in the field of wine and gin and in November 2014 they opened up their own whisky distillery at Kingsbarns in Fife. Based in Edinburgh, Wemyss Malts takes advantage of Charles MacLean's experienced nose when choosing their casks. There are two ranges; one of which consists of single casks bottled at 46% or the occasional cask strength. The names of the whiskies reflect what they taste like although for some time now, the distillery name is also printed on the label. For instance, some of the most recent releases are called Nuts about Pears (1991 Blair Athol), Lemon Buttered Kippers (1997 Bunnahabhain) and Mocha Moment (Invergordon 1988). All whiskies are un chill-filtered and without colouring. The other range is made up of blended malts of which there are three at the moment – Spice King, Peat Chimney and The Hive. All three are un chill-filtered, bottled at 46% and are available without age statement and as 12 year olds. A limited addition to the range of blended malts, Kiln Embers, appeared in September 2015. This is a smokier version of Peat Chimney, bottled at 46% and without age statement. In 2012, the company released its first premium blended whisky based on a selection of malt and grain whiskies aged a minimum of 15 years. The whisky is named Lord Elcho after the eldest son of the 5th Earl of Wemyss. The Lord Elcho range has since then been expanded with a no age statement version.

Kiln Embers, 46%
Nose: Plenty of tropical fruit, with smoked pineapple, Caramac, fresh lemonade and chalky embers.
Palate: The fruit of lemon, lime and smoked pineapple carries over from the nose, within a smooth, smoky body.
Finish: Long, pleasing smoky citrus length.

Kingsbarns new make, 63.5%
Nose: Cut grass, unripe blueberries, menthol and medicinal qualities. Add to that some cucumber and mineral notes.
Palate: The menthol notes mingle with uncooked asparagus and nettles. It also has a sweet herbal tone which works well.
Finish: Soft, medium length.

Jewish Whisky Company

www.singlecasknation.com

A few years ago, Jason Johnstone-Yellin and Joshua Hatton, two well-known whisky bloggers, started, in alliance with Seth Klaskin, a new carer as independent bottlers. The idea with Single Cask Nation somewhat reminds you of Scotch Malt Whisky Society in the sense that you have to become a member of the nation in order to buy the bottlings. You can choose between three different cost levels which will give you various benefits, including one or more bottlings from the current range of whiskies. Some of the more recent bottlings include an 18 year old bourbon-matured Glen Elgin, a 13 year old Arran from an oloroso butt and a 13 year old Cooley, matured in refill sherry. Recently they have also included American and Indian whiskies in the range.

Among the latest releases are several bottlings from new American distilleries such as Westland, Koval, Catoctin Creek and FEW Spirits. Since 2013 the company also arranges popular whisky events around the USA under the name Whisky Jewbilee. The latest was held in September 2016 in Chicago.

Speciality Drinks

www.specialitydrinks.com

Sukhinder Singh, known by most for his very well-stocked shop in London, The Whisky Exchange, is behind this company. In the beginning of October every year, he is also hosting The Whisky Show in London, one of the best whisky festivals in the world. In 2005 he started as an independent bottler of malt whiskies operating under the brand name The Single Malts of Scotland. There are around 50 bottlings on offer at any time, either as single casks or as batches bottled at cask strength or at 46%. In 2009 a new range of Islay single malts under the name Port Askaig was introduced, starting with a cask strength, a 17 year old and a 25 year old. Over the years, a number of new releases have been made while others have been discontinued. In 2015, a 16, 30 and 45 year old were released as well as Port Askaig 100 proof, bottled without age statement, which will be available on a more regular basis. Elements of Islay, a series of cask strength single malts in which all Islay distilleries are, or will be, represented was introduced around the same time as Port Askaig. The list of the product range is cleverly constructed with periodical tables in mind in which each distillery has a two-letter acronym followed by a batch number, for example Ar_6 (Ardbeg) or Lp_7 (Laphroaig). Two of the new releases in 2016 were Ma_1 where Ma stands for Margadale indicating a heavily peated Bunnahabhain and Ln_1, Lochindaal, a medium peated Bruichladdich. In spring 2016, Elements of Islay Peat, the first blended malt version of the range, was launched.

Elements of Islay Peat (blended malt), 59.3%
Nose: Freshly-baled hay, limes, sea grass, light nutty tones and peaty smoky mineral notes.
Palate: The peaty notes infuse into the lemon grass; vanilla, dried tobacco leaf, lime and chewy toffee.
Finish: Long, smoky lime.

Port Askaig 100 proof, 57.1%
Nose: Soft and sweet, with barley and fragrant peat. Mild antispectic and emerging oranges and lemons.
Palate: Smooth and engaging, with big notes of earthy peat, seaweed and citrus fruit.
Finish: Long, with oily peat and lingering citrus.

Meadowside Blending

www.meadowsideblending.com

The company may be a newcomer to the family of independent bottlers but the founder certainly isn't. Donald Hart, a Keeper of the Quaich and co-founder of the well-known bottler Hart Brothers, runs the Glasgow company together with his son, Andrew. There are two sides to the business – blends sold under the name The Royal Thistle where the core expression is a 3 year old, as well as single malts labelled The Maltman.

The Vintage Malt Whisky Company

www.vintagemaltwhisky.com

Founded in 1992 by Brian Crook who previously had twenty years experience in the malt whisky industry. In recent years, Brian has been joined in the company by his son Andrew. The company also owns and operates a sister company called The Highlands & Islands Scotch Whisky Co. The most famous brands in the range are undoubtedly two single Islay malts called Finlaggan and The Ileach. The latter comes in two versions, bottled at 40% and 58%.

The Finlaggan range was recently repackaged and now consists of Old Reserve (40%), Eilean Mor (46%), Port Finish (46%), Sherry Finish (46%) and Cask Strength (56%). For the first time a special, limited version of Finlaggan bottled at 50% was released in connection with Feis Ile 2016. Another recent addition is the single malt Islay Storm. Other expressions include two blended malts, Glenalmond and Black Cuillin and, not least, a wide range of single cask single malts under the name The Cooper's Choice. They are bottled at 46% or at cask strength and are all non coloured and non chill-filtered. In 2012, the company launched a range extension called Cooper's Choice Golden Grains with a selection of old single grain whiskies from closed distilleries.

Finlaggan Sherry Finish, 46%
Nose: Exotic fruits such as guava and mango jump out, with a gentle smoky tone. Add some dried orange and apricots.
Palate: The juicy fruits are embodied in a smoky, ashy note with hints of sherried fruit cake towards the end.
Finish: Lovely long peaty length.

Finlaggan Port Finish, 46%
Nose: Deep red fruit and floral notes. Red roses, plums and orange mingle with a charred wood tone.
Palate: The fruit and floral notes are less dominant, with the peat taking front of stage with a final orange twang.
Finish: Long smooth warm length.

Svenska Eldvatten

www.eldvatten.se

Founded in 2011 by Tommy Andersen and Peter Sjögren. They both have extensive experience from whisky and other spirits, which they have gained from arranging tastings for many years. Since the start, more than 50 single casks, bottled at cask strength, have been released. The owners have also released their own blended malt, bottled at 50%, under the name Glenn (a humorous tip of the hat to their home town Gothenburg where Glenn is one of the most common names). In their range of spirits they also have aged tequila and rum from the famous and sadly closed Trinidadian distillery Caroni. They also recently launched their own rum, WeiRon Super Premium Aged Carribean Rum (both vatted and as a single cask), as well as gin and aquavit.

The Ultimate Whisky Company

www.ultimatewhisky.com

Founded in 1994 by Han van Wees and his son Maurice, this Dutch independent bottler has until now bottled more than 500 single malts. All whiskies are un chill-filtered, without colouring and bottled at either 46% or cask strength. Recent bottlings include older whiskies such as a 25 year old Longmorn and a 27 year old Balmenach but also younger malts (7-10 years) be found. The van Wees family also operate one of the finest spirits shops in Europe - Van Wees Whisky World in Amersfoort - with i.a. more than 1,000 different whiskies including more than 500 single malts.

Adelphi Distillery

www.adelphidistillery.com

Adelphi Distillery is named after a distillery which closed in 1902. The company is owned by Keith Falconer and Donald Houston, who recruited Alex Bruce from the wine trade to act as Managing

Director. Their whiskies are always bottled at cask strength, uncoloured and non chill-filtered. Adelphi bottles around 50 casks a year. Two of their recurrent brands are Fascadale (a Highland Park) and Liddesdale (a Bunnahabhain) which are in batches of approximately 1,500 bottles. They also have their own blended Scotch, Adelphi Private Stock, which is bottled at 40%. In October 2015, the first two bottlings of a new brand were launched. The Glover is a unique vatting of single malt from the closed Japanese distillery Hanyu and two Scottish single malts, Longmorn and Glen Garioch. A 14 and a 22 year old sold out almost instantaneously and they were followed in autumn 2016 by an 18 year old. The name of the whisky honours Thomas Blake Glover, an influential Scottish businessman working in Japan in the second half of the 19th century. Since 2014, Adelphi is also operating its own distillery in Glenbeg on the Ardnamurchan peninsula, a couple of miles from the company's office.

The Glover 18 years old, 48.6%
Nose: Fresh cut daisies, grapefruit, hints of lemon balm, digestive biscuits with butter and lemon and lime jelly.
Palate: Dry, yet with juicy baked limes with a salty edge. Walnuts, spice, oak and leather add to an interesting mix.
Finish: Long, with a hint of beeswax at the end.

Macaloney's Malt Whisky
www.vcaledonian.com/guest-whiskies/

Founded in 2016 by Graeme Macaloney as an extension to his Victoria Caledonian Distillery in Canada. Working with a number of Scotch distilleries around Scotland and contract bonded warehouses there, Macaloney and his fellow whisky makers Mike Nicolson and Dr. Jim Swan, have selected and created a range of vatted malt whiskies for an initial bottling. However, these same vattings will then be further finished is oak casks selected by Dr. Swan.

The Heritage Series, bottled at 46%, presently consists of Prince Dougal's Dram, a Sherry-influenced vatting including Blair Athol, Teaninich, Clynelish and Auchroisk distilleries, and Among the Heather, which is a lightly peated vatting including Blair Athol, Clynelish, Ardmore and Caol Ila. The Twa Cask Series is focused on cask strength and the initial bottlings will consist of two-distillery, regional pairings (hence Twa, Scots for Two), all matured in bourbon casks. These include a Speyside vatting of Benrinnes and Glenlossie, an Islay vatting of Caol Ila and Bunnahabhain, and a Highland vatting of Blair Athol and Macduff.

Wm Cadenhead & Co
www.wmcadenhead.com

This company was established in 1842 and is owned by J & A Mitchell (who also owns Springbank) since 1972. The single malts from Cadenheads are neither chill filtered nor coloured. In 2012, Mark Watt, who had been working for Duncan Taylor for several years, joined the company. His mission was to revamp the portfolio of whiskies and a number of new ranges were created. Today there is Authentic Collection (single cask cask strength whiskies, exclusively sold in their own shops), World Whiskies (single malts from non Scottish distillers as well as from Scottish grain distillers) and Small Batch, a range which can be divided into three separate ranges; Gold Label (single casks bottled at cask strength), Small Batch Cask Strength (2-4 casks of whisky from the same vintage, bottled at cask strength) and Small Batch 46% (same as the previous but diluted to 46%). A fourth range has recently been

introduced, William Cadenhead Range, which consists of blended whisky as well as single malts from undisclosed distilleries. Recent bottlings in this range are a 13 year old Irish single malt, a 7 year old Islay single malt and a 40 year old Speyside single malt. The company will be celebrating its 175th anniversary in 2017 and it has been announced that a number of special bottlings will be released throughout the year.

A chain of ten whisky shops working under the name Cadenhead´s can be found in the UK, Denmark, Germany, Austria, Italy and Switzerland.

Glen Garioch 26 years old, 44%
Nose: Fresh grassy notes hit with a waxy tone coming behind. Add some crisp Granny Smith apples drizzled in honey.
Palate: There is a creamy ashy tone mingling with the green apples and meadow honey, along with a gentle touch of leather.
Finish: Long and waxy, while the palate notes never end.

Blended Scotch Whisky 12 years old, 46%
Nose: Sherry and toffee apples leap from the nose with light spice and a faint hint of milk chocolate.
Palate: Rich with spice, fruit cake and toffee hitting first, then a flicker of chocolate powder and red currants.
Finish: Long in length, with lightly spiced milk chocolate drink.

Deerstalker Whisky Co
www.deerstalkerwhisky.com

The Deerstalker brand, which dates from 1880 was originally owned by J.G. Thomson & Co of Leith and subsequently Tennent Caledonian Breweries. It was purchased by Glasgow based Aberko Ltd in 1994 and is managed by former Tennent's Export Director Paul Aston. The Deerstalker range covers single cask as well as blended malt whiskies. The 12 year old single malt (46%, un chill-filtered, natural colour) is the best known and has sourced its malt from Balmenach distillery for over 35 years. More recent additions are 'Limited Release' single cask bottlings of Allt-a-Bhainne (18 year old), Braeval (19 year old) and Auchroisk (16 year old) at 48%. A Deerstalker Blended Malt (Highland Edition) was launched in 2014 and in autumn 2016 the Peated Edition of Deerstalker was released.

Deerstalker Blended Malt Peated Edition, 43%
Nose: Lemons and limes blend with peated saline aromas. The warm darkness of treacle and blood oranges are in the background.
Palate: Almost liquid peat, with dark molten chocolate cake and some fresh, wild blackberries giving a lovely soft fruity edge.
Finish: Long, with chocolate peaty tones.

Deerstalker Blended Malt Highland Edition, 43%
Nose: Sweet perfume hits with dried apricots, clover, dark roasted nuts, cloves and cinnamon.
Palate: The palate is darker than the nose with the spice mingling with spent coffee beans, a hint of ferns and dark leather.
Finish: Medium length, with crushed cloves and cinnamon.

Whisky
shops

AUSTRALIA

The Odd Whisky Coy
PO Box 2045
Glynde, SA, 5070
Phone: +61 (0)8 8365 4722
www.theoddwhiskycoy.com.au
Founded and owned by Graham Wright, this on-line whisky specialist has an impressive range. They are agents for famous brands such as Springbank, Benromach and Berry Brothers and arrange recurrent seminars on the subject.

World of Whisky
Shop G12, Cosmopolitan Centre
2-22 Knox Street
Double Bay NSW 2028
Phone: +61 (0)2 9363 4212
www.worldofwhisky.com.au
A whisky specialist which offers a range of 300 different expressions, most of them single malts. The shop is also organising and hosting regular tastings.

AUSTRIA

Potstill
Laudongasse 18
1080 Wien
Phone: +43 (0)664 118 85 41
www.potstill.org
Austria's premier whisky shop with over 1100 kinds of which c 900 are malts, including some real rarities. Arranges tastings and seminars and ships to several European countries. On-line ordering.

Cadenhead Austria
Alter Markt 1
5020 Salzburg
Phone: +43 (0)662 84 53 05
www.cadenhead.at
Number 8 in the famous Cadenhead's chain of whisky shops. At the moment they offer 350 different whiskies, mostly single malts and they also arrange monthly tastings.

BELGIUM

Whiskycorner
Kraaistraat 16
3530 Houthalen
Phone: +32 (0)89 386233
www.whiskycorner.be
A very large selection of single malts, no less than 1100 different! Also other whiskies, calvados and grappas. The site is in both French and English. Mail ordering, but not on-line. Shipping worldwide.

Jurgen´s Whiskyhuis
Gaverland 70
9620 Zottegem
Phone: +32 (0)9 336 51 06
www.whiskyhuis.be
An absolutely huge assortment of more than 2,000 different single malts with 700 in stock and the rest delivered within the week. Also 40 different grain whiskies and 120 bourbons. Worldwide shipping

Huis Crombé
Doenaertstraat 20
8510 Marke
Phone: +32 (0)56 21 19 87
www.crombewines.com
A wine retailer which also covers all kinds of spirits. The whisky range is very nice where a large assortment of Scotch is supplemented with whiskies from Japan, the USA and Ireland to mention a few.

Anverness
Grote Steenweg 74
2600 Berchem – Antwerpen
Phone: +32 (0)3 218 55 90
www.anverness.be
Peter de Decker has established himself as one of the best Belgian whisky retailers where, apart from an impressive range of whiskies, recurrent tastings and whisky dinners play an important role.

We Are Whisky
Avenue Rodolphe Gossia 33
1350 Orp-Jauche (Jauche)
Phone: +32 (0)471 134556
www.wearewhisky.com
A fairly new shop and on-line retailer with a range of more than 400 different whiskies. They also arrange 3-4 tasting every month.

Dram 242
Opwijksestraat 242
9280 Lebbeke
Phone: +32 (0)477 260993
www.dram242.be
Started in 2012 by Dirk Verleysen, this shop has a wide range of whiskies. Apart from the core official bottlings, Dirk has focused on rare, old expressions as well as whiskies from small, independent bottlers.

BRAZIL

Single Malt Brasil
Phone: +55 (21) 3566-0158
www.lojadewhisky.com.br
The biggest whisky specialist In Brazil (and one of few in the country) with a nice range of other spirits as well, especially cachaça. The sister site, singlemalt.com.

br, is a great, educational site about single malt whisky.

CANADA

Kensington Wine Market
1257 Kensington Road NW
Calgary
Alberta T2N 3P8
Phone: +1 403 283 8000
www.kensingtonwinemarket.com
With 400 different bottlings this is the largest single malt assortment in Canada. Also 2,500 different wines. Regular tastings in the shop.

DENMARK

Juul´s Vin & Spiritus
Værnedamsvej 15
1819 Frederiksberg
Phone: +45 33 31 13 29
www.juuls.dk
A very large range of wines, fortified wines and spirits. Around 500 single malts. Also a good selection of drinking glasses.

Cadenhead´s WhiskyShop Denmark
Kongensgade 69 F
5000 Odense C
Phone: +45 66 13 95 05
www.cadenheads.dk
Whisky specialist with a very good range, not least from Cadenhead's. Nice range of champagne, cognac and rum. Arranges whisky and beer tastings. On-line ordering with worldwide shipping.

Whisky.dk
Sjølund Gade 12
6093 Sjølund
Phone: +45 2081 3743
www.whisky.dk
Henrik Olsen and Ulrik Bertelsen are well-known in Denmark for their whisky shows but they also run an on-line spirits shop with an emphasis on whisky but also including an impressive stock of rums.

Kokkens Vinhus
Hovedvejen 102
2600 Glostrup
Phone: +45 44 97 02 30
Peter Bangs Vej 74
2000 Frederiksberg
Phone: +45 38 87 86 70
www.kokkensvinhus.dk
A shop with a complete assortment of wine, spirit, coffee, tea and delicatessen. More than 500 whiskies, mostly single malts. They are specialists in independent bottlings.

ENGLAND

The Whisky Exchange
2 Bedford Street, Covent Garden
London WC2E 9HH
Phone: +44 (0)20 7100 0088
www.thewhiskyexchange.com
An excellent whisky shop owned by
Sukhinder Singh. Started off as a mail
order business, run from a showroom in
Hanwell, but later opened up at Vinopolis
in downtown London. Recently the
shop was re-located to a new and bigger
location in Covent Garden. The assortment
is huge with well over 1000 single malts
to choose from. Some rarities which can
hardly be found anywhere else are offered
thanks to Singh's great interest for antique
whisky. There are also other types of
whisky and cognac, calvados, rum etc. On-
line ordering and ships all over the world.

The Whisky Shop
(See also Scotland, The Whisky Shop)
11 Coppergate Walk
York YO1 9NT
Phone: +44 (0)1904 640300

510 Brompton Walk
Lakeside Shopping Centre
Thurrock Grays, Essex RM20 2ZL
Phone: +44 (0)1708 866255

7 Turl Street
Oxford OX1 3DQ
Phone: +44 (0)1865 202279

3 Swan Lane
Norwich NR2 1HZ
Phone: +44 (0)1603 618284

70 Piccadilly
London W1J 8HP
Phone: +44 (0)207 499 6649

Unit 7 Queens Head Passage
Paternoster
London EC4M 7DZ
Phone: +44 (0)207 329 5117

3 Exchange St
Manchester M2 7EE
Phone: +44 (0)161 832 6110

25 Chapel Street
Guildford GU1 3UL
Phone: +44 (0)1483 450900

Unit 35 Great Western Arcade
Birmingham B2 5HU
Phone: +44 (0)121 212 1815

64 East Street
Brighton BN1 1HQ
Phone: +44 (0)1273 327 962

3 Cheapside
Nottingham NG1 2HU
Phone: +44 (0)115 958 7080

9-10 High Street
Bath BA1 5AQ
Phone: +44 (0)1225 423 535

Unit 1/9 Red Mall,
Intu Metro Centre
Gateshead NE11 9YP
Phone: +44 (0)191 460 3777
Unit 201 Trentham Gardens
Stoke on Trent ST4 8AX
Phone: +44 (0)1782 644 483
www.whiskyshop.com

The first shop opened in 1992 in
Edinburgh and this is now the UK's largest
specialist retailer of whiskies with 20
outlets (plus one in Paris). A large product
range with over 700 kinds, including 400
malt whiskies and 140 miniature bottles, as
well as accessories and books. They also
run The W Club, the leading whisky club
in the UK where the excellent Whiskeria
magazine is one of the member's benefits.
On-line ordering and shipping all over the
world except to the USA.

Royal Mile Whiskies
3 Bloomsbury Street
London WC1B 3QE
Phone: +44 (0)20 7436 4763
www.royalmilewhiskies.com
The London branch of Royal Mile
Whiskies. See also Scotland, Royal Mile
Whiskies.

Berry Bros. & Rudd
3 St James' Street
London SW1A 1EG
Phone: +44 (0)800 280 2440

The Warehouse Shop
Hamilton Close, Houndmills
Basingstoke RG21 6YB
Phone: +44 (0)800 280 2440
www.bbr.com/whisky
A legendary shop that has been situated
in the same place since 1698. One of
the world's most reputable wine shops
but with an exclusive selection of malt
whiskies. Also shops in Dublin and Hong
Kong.

The Wright Wine
and Whisky Company
The Old Smithy, Raikes Road, Skipton,
North Yorkshire BD23 1NP
Phone: +44 (0)1756 700886
www.wineandwhisky.co.uk
An eclectic selection of near to 1000
different whiskies. 'Tasting Cupboard' of
nearly 100 opened bottles for sampling
with regular hosted tasting evenings. Great
'Collector to Collector' selection of old
whiskies plus a fantastic choice of 1200+
wines, premium spirits and liqueurs.

Master of Malt
2 Leylands Manor
Tubwell Lane
Crowborough TN6 3RH
Phone: +44 (0)1892 888 376
www.masterofmalt.com
Independent bottler and online retailer
since 1985. A very impressive range of
more than 1,000 Scotch whiskies of which
800 are single malts. In addition to whisky
from other continents there is a wide selection of rum, cognac, Armagnac and tequila. The website is redesigned and contains
a wealth of information on the distilleries.
They have also launched "Drinks by the
Dram" where you can order 3cl samples
of more than 500 different whiskies to try
before you buy a full bottle.

Whiskys.co.uk
The Square, Stamford Bridge
York YO4 11AG
Phone: +44 (0)1759 371356
www.whiskys.co.uk

Good assortment with more than 600
different whiskies. Also a nice range of
armagnac, rum, calvados etc. On-line
ordering, ships outside of the UK. The
owners also have another website, www.
whiskymerchants.co.uk with a huge
amount of information on just about every
whisky distillery in the world.

The Wee Dram
5 Portland Square, Bakewell
Derbyshire DE45 1HA
Phone: +44 (0)1629 812235
www.weedram.co.uk
Large range of Scotch single malts (c
450) with whiskies from other parts of the
world and a good range of whisky books.
Run 'The Wee Drammers Whisky Club'
with tastings and seminars. End of October
they arrange the yearly Wee Dram Fest
whisky festival.

Hard To Find Whisky
1 Spencer Street
Birmingham B18 6DD
Phone: +44 (0)8456 803 489
www.htfw.com
As the name says, this family owned shop
specialises in rare, collectable and new
releases of single malt whisky. The range
is astounding - almost 3,000 different bottlings including no less than 263 different
Macallan. World wide shipping.

Nickolls & Perks
37 High Street, Stourbridge
West Midlands DY8 1TA
Phone: +44 (0)1384 394518
www.nickollsandperks.co.uk
Mostly known as wine merchants but
also has a good range of whiskies with c
300 different kinds including 200 single
malts. On-line ordering with shipping
also outside of UK. Since 2011, they also
organize the acclaimed Midlands Whisky
Festival, see www.whiskyfest.co.uk

Gauntleys of Nottingham
4 High Street
Nottingham NG1 2ET
Phone: +44 (0)115 9110555
www.gauntley-wine.co.uk
A fine wine merchant established in 1880.
The range of wines are among the best
in the UK. All kinds of spirits, not least
whisky, are taking up more and more
space and several rare malts can be found.
Mail order service available.

Hedonism Wines
3-7 Davies St.
London W1K 3LD
Phone: +44 (020) 729 078 70
www.hedonism.co.uk
Located in the heart of London's Mayfair,
this is a new temple for wine lovers but
also with an impressive range of whiskies
and other spirits. They have over 1,200
different bottlings from Scotland and the
rest of the world! The very elegant shop is
in itself well worth a visit.

The Wine Shop
22 Russell Street, Leek
Staffordshire ST13 5JF
Phone: +44 (0)1538 382408
www.wineandwhisky.com

In addition to wine there is a good range of 300 whiskies and also calvados, cognac, rum etc. They also stock a range of their own single malt bottlings under the name of 'The Queen of the Moorlands'. Mailorder within the UK.

The Lincoln Whisky Shop
87 Bailgate
Lincoln LN1 3AR
Phone: +44 (0)1522 537834
www.lincolnwhiskyshop.co.uk
Mainly specialising in whisky with more than 400 different whiskies but also 500 spirits and liqueurs and some 100 wines. Mailorder only within UK.

Milroys of Soho
3 Greek Street
London W1D 4NX
Phone: +44 (0)207 734 2277
www.milroys.co.uk
A classic whisky shop in Soho with a very good range with over 700 malts and a wide selection of whiskies from around the world. On-line ordering.

Arkwrights
114 The Dormers
Highworth
Wiltshire SN6 7PE
Phone: +44 (0)1793 765071
www.whiskyandwines.com
A good range of whiskies (over 700 in stock) as well as wine and other spirits. Regular tastings in the shop. On-line ordering with shipping all over the world except USA and Canada.

Edencroft Fine Wines
8-10 Hospital Street, Nantwich
Cheshire, CW5 5RJ
Phone: +44 (0)1270 629975
www.edencroft.co.uk
Family owned wine and spirits shop since 1994. Around 250 whiskies and also a nice range of gin, cognac and other spirits including cigars. Worldwide shipping.

Cadenhead´s Whisky Shop
26 Chiltern Street
London W1U 7QF
Phone: +44 (0)20 7935 6999
www.whiskytastingroom.com
One in a chain of shops owned by independent bottlers Cadenhead. Sells Cadenhead's product range and c. 200 other whiskies. Regular tastings.

Constantine Stores
30 Fore Street
Constantine, Falmouth
Cornwall TR11 5AB
Phone: +44 (0)1326 340226
www.drinkfinder.co.uk
A full-range wine and spirits dealer with a good selection of whiskies from the whole world (around 800 different, of which 600 are single malts). Worldwide shipping except for USA and Canada.

The Vintage House
42 Old Compton Street
London W1D 4LR
Phone: +44 (0)20 7437 5112
www.sohowhisky.com
A huge range of 1400 kinds of malt

whisky, many of them rare. Supplementing this is also a selection of fine wines.

Whisky On-line
Units 1-3 Concorde House, Charnley Road, Blackpool, Lancashire FY1 4PE
Phone: +44 (0)1253 620376
www.whisky-online.com
A good selection of whisky and also cognac, rum, port etc. On-line ordering with shipping all over the world.

FRANCE

La Maison du Whisky
20 rue d´Anjou
75008 Paris
Phone: +33 (0)1 42 65 03 16

6 carrefour d l´Odéon
75006 Paris
Phone: +33 (0)1 46 34 70 20

(2 shops outside France)
47 rue Jean Chatel
97400 Saint-Denis, La Réunion
Phone: +33 (0)2 62 21 31 19

The Pier at Robertson Quay
80 Mohamed Sultan Road, #01-10
Singapore 239013
Phone: +65 6733 0059
www.whisky.fr
France's largest whisky specialist with over 1200 whiskies in stock. Also a number of own-bottled single malts. La Maison du Whisky acts as a EU distributor for many whisky producers around the world. Four shops and on-line ordering.

The Whisky Shop
7 Place de la Madeleine
75008 Paris
Phone: +33 (0)1 45 22 29 77
The large chain of whisky shops in the UK has now opened up a store in Paris as well.

GERMANY

Celtic Whisk(e)y & Versand
Otto Steudel
Bulmannstrasse 26
90459 Nürnberg
Phone: +49 (0)911 45097430
www.whiskymania.de/celtic
A very impressive single malt range with well over 1000 different single malts and a good selection from other parts of the world. On-line ordering.

SCOMA
Am Bullhamm 17
26441 Jever
Phone: +49 (0)4461 912237
www.scoma.de
Very large range of c 750 Scottish malts and many from other countries. Holds regular seminars and tastings. The excellent, monthly whisky newsletter SCOMA News is produced and can be downloaded as a pdf-file from the website. On-line ordering.

The Whisky Store
Am Grundwassersee 4
82402 Seeshaupt
Phone: +49 (0)8801 30 20 000
www.whisky.de

A very large range comprising c 700 kinds of whisky of which 550 are malts. Also sells whisky liqueurs, books and accessories. The website is a goldmine of information. On-line ordering.

Cadenhead´s Whisky Market
Luxemburger Strasse 257
50939 Köln
Phone: +49 (0)221-2831834
www.cadenheads.de
Good range of malt whiskies (c 350 different kinds) with emphasis on Cadenhead's own bottlings. Other products include wine, cognac and rum etc. Arranges recurring tastings and also has an on-line shop.

Cadenhead´s Whisky Market
Mainzer Strasse 20
10247 Berlin-Friedrichshain
Phone: +49 (0)30-30831444
www.cadenhead-berlin.de
Excellent product range with more than 700 different kinds of whiskies with emphasis on Cadenhead's own bottlings as well as cognac and rum. Arranges recurrent tastings.

Malts and More
Hosegstieg 11
22880 Wedel
Phone: +49 (0)40-23620770
www.maltsandmore.de
Large assortment with over 800 different single malts as well as whiskies from many other countries. Also a nice selection of cognac, rum etc. On-line ordering.

Reifferscheid
Mainzer Strasse 186
53179 Bonn / Mehlem
Phone: +49 (0)228 9 53 80 70
www.whisky-bonn.de
A well-stocked shop with a large range of whiskies, wine, spirit, cigars and a delicatessen. Regular tastings.

Whisky-Doris
Germanenstrasse 38
14612 Falkensee
Phone: +49 (0)3322-219784
www.whisky-doris.de
Large range of over 300 whiskies and also sells own special bottlings. Orders via email. Shipping also outside Germany.

Finlays Whisky Shop
Friedrichstrasse 3
65779 Kelkheim
Phone: +49 (0)6195 9699510
www.finlayswhiskyshop.de
Whisky specialists with a large range of over 1,400 whiskies. Finlays also work as the importer to Germany of Douglas laing, James MacArthur and Wilson & Morgan. On-line ordering.

Weinquelle Lühmann
Lübeckerstrasse 145
22087 Hamburg
Phone: +49 (0)40-25 63 91
www.weinquelle.com
An impressive selection of both wines and spirits with over 1000 different whiskies of which 850 are malt whiskies. Also an impressive range of rums. On-line ordering.

The Whisky-Corner
Reichertsfeld 2
92278 Illschwang
Phone: +49 (0)9666-951213
www.whisky-corner.de
A small shop but large on mail order.
A very large assortment of over 1600
whiskies. Also sells blended and American
whiskies. The website is very informative
with features on, among others, whisky-
making, tasting and independent bottlers.
On-line ordering.

World Wide Spirits
Hauptstrasse 12
84576 Teising
Phone: +49 (0)8633 50 87 93
www.worldwidespirits.de
A nice range of c 500 whiskies with some
rarities from the twenties. Also large
selection of other spirits.

WhiskyKoch
Weinbergstrasse 2
64285 Darmstadt
Phone: +49 (0)6151 99 27 105
www.whiskykoch.de
A combination of a whisky shop and
restaurant. The shop has a nice selection
of single malts as well as other Scottish
products and the restaurant has specialised
in whisky dinners and tastings.

Kierzek
Weitlingstrasse 17
10317 Berlin
Phone: +49 (0)30 525 11 08
www.kierzek-berlin.de
Over 400 different whiskies in stock. In
the product range 50 kinds of rum and
450 wines from all over the world are
found among other products. Mail order
is available.

House of Whisky
Ackerbeeke 6
31683 Obernkirchen
Phone: +49 (0)5724-399420
www.houseofwhisky.de
Aside from over 1,200 different malts
also sells a large range of other spirits
(including over 100 kinds of rum).
On-line ordering.

World Wide Whisky (2 shops)
Eisenacher Strasse 64
10823 Berlin-Schöneberg
Phone: +49 (0)30-7845010
Hauptstrasse 58
10823 Berlin-Schöneberg
www.world-wide-whisky.de
Large range of 1,500 different whiskies.
Arranges tastings and seminars. Has a
large number of rarities. Orders via email.

HUNGARY
Whisky Net / Whisky Shop
Kovács Làszlò Street 21
2000 Szentendre

Veres Pálné utca 8.
1053 Budapest
Phone: +36 1 267-1588
www.whiskynet.hu
www.whiskyshop.hu
The largest selction of whisky in Hungary.

Agents for Arran, Benriach, Glenfarclas,
Gordon & MacPhail, Benromach, Douglas
Laing, Springbank, Angus Dundee, Ian
Macleod, Kilchoman among others. Also
mailorder.

INDIA
The Vault
World Whiskies & Fine Spirits
Mumbai
Phone: +91 22-22028811/22
www.vaultfinespirits.com
India´s first curated fine spirits platform,
opened in October 2013. An interesting
concept where personal assistance in choosing a gift or planning an event is also part
of the service. Expect many more brands
to be added in coming years.

IRELAND
Celtic Whiskey Shop
27-28 Dawson Street
Dublin 2
Phone: +353 (0)1 675 9744
www.celticwhiskeyshop.com
More than 70 kinds of Irish whiskeys but
also a good selection of Scotch, wines and
other spirits. World wide shipping.

ITALY
Whisky Shop
by Milano Whisky Festival
Via Cavaleri 6, Milano
Phone: +39 (0)2 48753039
www.whiskyshop.it
The team behind the excellent
Milano Whisky Festival also have an on-
line whiskyshop with almost 500 different
single malts including several special
festival bottlings.

Whisky Antique S.R.L.
Via Quattro Passi, 21/C
41043 Formigine (MO)
Phone: +39 (0)59 574278
www.whiskyantique.com
Long-time whisky enthusiast and collector
Massimo Righi owns this shop specialising
in rare and collectable spirits – not only
whisky but also cognac, rum, armagnac
etc. They are also the Italian importer for
brands like Jack Wiebers, The Whisky
Agency and Perfect Dram.

Whisky & Co.
Via Margutta, 29
00187 Rome
Phone: +39 (0)6 3265 0514
www.whiskyandco.it
A new and very elegant whiskyshop has
recently been opened in the heart of Rome
by Massimo Righi, knwon from Whisky
Antique in Modena.

Cadenhead's Whisky Bar
Via Poliziano, 3
20154 Milano
Phone: +39 (0)2 336 055 92
www.cadenhead.it
This is the newest addition in the Caden-
head´s chain of shops. Concentrating
mostly on the Cadenhead´s range but they
also stock whiskies from other producers.

JAPAN
Liquor Mountain Co.,Ltd.
4F Kyoto Kowa Bldg.
82 Tachiurinishi-Machi,
Takakura-Nishiiru,
Shijyo-Dori, Shimogyo-Ku,
Kyoto, 600-8007
Phone: +81 (0)75 213 8880
www.likaman.co.jp
The company has more than 150 shops
specialising in spirits, beer and food.
Around 20 of them are designated whisky
shops under the name Whisky Kingdom
(although they have a full range of other
spirits) with a range of 500 different whiskies. The three foremost shops are;

Rakzan Sanjyo Onmae
1-8, HigashiGekko-cho, Nishinokyo,
Nakagyo-ku, Kyoto-shi
Kyoto
Phone: +81 (0)75-842-5123

Nagakute
2-105, Ichigahora, Nagakute-shi
Aichi
Phone: +81 (0)561-64-3081

Kabukicho 1chome
1-2-16, Kabuki-cho, Shinjuku-ku
Tokyo
Phone: +81 (0)3-5287-2080

THE NETHERLANDS
Whiskyslijterij De Koning
Hinthamereinde 41
5211 PM 's Hertogenbosch
Phone: +31 (0)73-6143547
www.whiskykoning.nl
An enormous assortment with more than
1400 kinds of whisky including
c 800 single malts. Arranges recurring
tastings. On-line ordering. Shipping all
over the world.

Van Wees - Whiskyworld.nl
Leusderweg 260
3817 KH Amersfoort
Phone: +31 (0)33-461 53 19
www.whiskyworld.nl
A very large range of 1000 whiskies
including over 500 single malts. Also have
their own range of bottlings (The Ultimate
Whisky Company). On-line ordering.

Wijnhandel van Zuylen
Loosduinse Hoofdplein 201
2553 CP Loosduinen (Den Haag)
Phone: +31 (0)70-397 1400
www.whiskyvanzuylen.nl
Excellent range of whiskies (circa 1100)
and wines. Email orders with shipping to
some ten European countries.

Wijnwinkel-Slijterij
Ton Overmars
Hoofddorpplein 11
1059 CV Amsterdam
Phone: +31 (0)20-615 71 42
www.tonovermars.nl
A very large assortment of wines, spirits
and beer which includes more than 400
single malts. Arranges recurring tastings.
Orders via email.

Wijn & Whisky Schuur
Blankendalwei 4
8629 EH Scharnegoutem
Phone: +31 (0)515-520706
www.wijnwhiskyschuur.nl
Large assortment with 1000 different
whiskies and a good range of other spirits
as well. Arranges recurring tastings. On-
line ordering.

Versailles Dranken
Lange Hezelstraat 83
6511 Cl Nijmegen
Phone: +31 (0)24-3232008
www.versaillesdranken.nl
A very impressive range with more than
1500 different whiskies, most of them
from Scotland but also a surprisingly good
selection (more than 60) of Bourbon. Arranges recurring tastings. On-line ordering.

Alba Malts
Kloosterstraat 15
6981 CC Doesburg
Phone: +31 (0)65-4295905
www.albamalts.com
A new whisky shop situated in an old
chapel dating back to 1441. Marnix Okel
has a passion for Scotland and will focus
on Scotch single malt only, with a range of
400 whiskies to start with.

NEW ZEALAND
Whisky Galore
66 Victoria Street
Christchurch 8013
Phone: +64 (3) 377 6824
www.whiskygalore.co.nz
The best whisky shop in New Zealand with
550 different whiskies, approximately
350 which are single malts. There is also
online mail-order with shipping all over
the world except USA and Canada.

POLAND
George Ballantine´s
Krucza str 47 A, Warsaw
Phone: +48 22 625 48 32
Pulawska str 22, Warsaw
Phone: +48 22 542 86 22
Marynarska str 15, Warsaw
Phone: +48 22 395 51 60
Zygmunta Vogla str 62, Warsaw
Phone: +48 22 395 51 64
www.sklep-ballantines.pl
The biggest assortment in Poland with
more than 500 different single malts.
Apart from whisky there is a full range of
spirits and wines from all over the world.
Recurrent tastings and mailorder.

RUSSIA
Whisky World Shop
9, Tverskoy Boulevard
123104 Moscow
Phone: +7 495 787 9150
www.whiskyworld.ru
Huge assortment with more than 1,000
different single malts. The range is
supplemented with a nice range of cognac,
armagnac, calvados, grappa and wines.
Tastings are also arranged.

SCOTLAND
Gordon & MacPhail
58 - 60 South Street, Elgin
Moray IV30 1JY
Phone: +44 (0)1343 545110
www.gordonandmacphail.com
This legendary shop opened already in
1895 in Elgin. The owners are perhaps
the most well-known among independent
bottlers. The shop stocks more than 800
bottlings of whisky and more than 600
wines and there is also a delicatessen
counter with high-quality products.
Tastings are arranged in the shop and there
are shipping services within the UK and
overseas. The shop attracts visitors from
all over the world.

Royal Mile Whiskies (2 shops)
379 High Street, The Royal Mile
Edinburgh EH1 1PW
Phone: +44 (0)131 2253383

3 Bloomsbury Street
London WC1B 3QE
Phone: +44 (0)20 7436 4763
www.royalmilewhiskies.com
Royal Mile Whiskies is one of the most
well-known whisky retailers in the UK.
It was established in Edinburgh in 1991.
There is also a shop in London since 2002
and a cigar shop close to the Edinburgh
shop. The whisky range is outstanding
with many difficult to find elsewhere.
They have a comprehensive site regarding
information on regions, distilleries,
production, tasting etc. Royal Mile
Whiskies also arranges 'Whisky Fringe'
in Edinburgh, a two-day whisky festival
which takes place annually in mid August.
On-line ordering with worldwide shipping.

The Whisky Shop
(See also England, The Whisky Shop)
Unit L2-02 Buchanan Galleries
220 Buchanan Street
Glasgow G1 2GF
Phone: +44 (0)141 331 0022

17 Bridge Street
Inverness IV1 1HD
Phone: +44 (0)1463 710525

93 High Street
Fort William PH33 6DG
Phone: +44 (0)1397 706164

52 George Street
Oban PA34 5SD
Phone: +44 (0)1631 570896

Unit 23 Waverley Mall
Waverley Bridge
Edinburgh EH1 1BQ
Phone: +44 (0)131 558 7563

28 Victoria Street
Edinburgh EH1 2JW
Phone: +44 (0)131 225 4666
www.whiskyshop.com
The first shop opened in 1992 in
Edinburgh and this is now the United
Kingdom's largest specialist retailer
of whiskies with 20 outlets (plus one
in Paris). A large product range with
over 700 kinds, including 400 malt
whiskies and 140 miniature bottles, as
well as accessories and books. The own

range 'Glenkeir Treasures' is a special
assortment of selected malt whiskies.
The also run The W Club, the leading
whisky club in the UK where the excellent
Whiskeria magazine is one of the
member´s benefits. On-line ordering.

Loch Fyne Whiskies
Inveraray
Argyll PA32 8UD
Phone: +44 (0)1499 302 219
www.lfw.co.uk
A legendary shop! The range of malt
whiskies is large and they have their own
house blend, the prize-awarded Loch
Fyne, as well as their 'The Loch Fyne Whisky
Liqueur'. There is also a range of house
malts called 'The Inverarity'. On-line
ordering with worldwide shipping.

Single Malts Direct
36 Gordon Street
Huntly
Aberdeenshire AB54 8EQ
Phone: +44 (0) 845 606 6145
www.singlemaltsdirect.com
Owned by independent bottler Duncan
Taylor. In the assortment is of course the
whole Duncan Taylor range but also a
selection of their own single malt bottlings
called Whiskies of Scotland. A total of
almost 700 different expressions. On-line
shop with shipping worldwide.

The Whisky Shop Dufftown
1 Fife Street, Dufftown
Moray AB55 4AL
Phone: +44 (0)1340 821097
www.whiskyshopdufftown.co.uk
Whisky specialist in Dufftown in the heart
of Speyside, wellknown to many of the
Speyside festival visitors. More than 500
single malts as well as other whiskies.
Arranges tastings as well as special events
during the Festivals. On-line ordering.

Cadenhead's Whisky Shop
(Eaglesome)
30-32 Union Street
Campbeltown
Argyll PA28 6JA
Phone: +44 (0)1586 551710
www.wmcadenhead.com
One in a chain of shops owned by
independent bottlers Cadenhead. Sells
Cadenhead's products and other whiskies
with a good range of Springbank. On-line
ordering.

Cadenhead´s Whisky Shop
172 Canongate, Royal Mile
Edinburgh EH8 8BN
Phone: +44 (0)131 556 5864
www.wmcadenhead.com
The oldest shop in the chain owned by Cadenhead. Sells Cadenhead's product range
and a good selection of other whiskies
and spirits. Recurrent tastings. On-line
ordering.

The Good Spirits Co.
23 Bath Street,
Glasgow G2 1HW
Phone: +44 (0)141 258 8427
www.thegoodspiritsco.com
A newly opened specialist spirits store selling whisky, bourbon, rum, vodka, tequila,

gin, cognac and armagnac, liqueurs and other spirits. They also stock quality champagne, fortified wines and cigars.

The Scotch Whisky Experience

354 Castlehill, Royal Mile
Edinburgh EH1 2NE
Phone: +44 (0)131 220 0441
www.scotchwhiskyexperience.co.uk
The Scotch Whisky Experience is a must for whisky devotees visiting Edinburgh. An interactive visitor centre dedicated to the history of Scotch whisky. This five-star visitor attraction has an excellent whisky shop with almost 300 different whiskies in stock. Recently, after extensive refurbishment, a brand new and interactive shop was opened.

Whiski Shop

4 North Bank Street
Edinburgh EH1 2LP
Phone: +44 (0)131 225 1532
www.whiskishop.com
www.whiskirooms.co.uk
A new concept located near Edin-burgh Castle, combining a shop, a tasting room and a bistro. Also regular whisky tastings. Online mail order with worldwide delivery.

Robbie's Drams

3 Sandgate, Ayr
South Ayrshire KA7 1BG
Phone: +44 (0)1292 262 135
www.robbiesdrams.com
Over 600 whiskies available in store and over 900 available from their on-line shop. Specialists in single cask bottlings, closed distillery bottlings, rare malts, limited edition whisky and a nice range of their own bottlings. Worldwide shipping.

The Whisky Barrel

PO Box 23803, Edinburgh, EH6 7WW
Phone: +44 (0)845 2248 156
www.thewhiskybarrel.com
Online specialist whisky shop based in Edinburgh. They stock over 1,000 single malt and blended whiskies including Scotch, Japanese, Irish, Indian, Swedish and their own casks. Worldwide shipping.

The Scotch Malt Whisky Society

www.smws.com
A society with more than 20 000 members worldwide, specialised in own bottlings of single casks and release between 150 and 200 bottlings a year.

Drinkmonger

100 Atholl Road
Pitlochry PH16 5BL
Phone: +44 (0)1796 470133

11 Bruntsfield Place
Edinburgh EH10 4HN
Phone: +44 (0)131 229 2205
www.drinkmonger.com
Two new shops opened in 2011 by the well-known Royal Mile Whiskies. The idea is to have a 50:50 split between wine and specialist spiritswith the addition of a cigar assortment. The whisky range is a good cross-section with some rarities and a focus on local distilleries.

A.D. Rattray's Whisky Experience & Whisky Shop

32 Main Road
Kirkoswald
Ayrshire KA19 8HY
Phone: +44 (0) 1655 760308
www.adrattray.com
A combination of whisky shop, sample room and educational center owned by the independent bottler A D Rattray. Tasting menus with different themes are available.

Robert Graham Ltd (3 shops)

194 Rose Street
Edinburgh EH2 4AZ
Phone: +44 (0)131 226 1874

Robert Graham's Global Whisky Shop
111 West George Street
Glasgow G2 1QX
Phone: +44 (0)141 248 7283

Robert Graham's Treasurer 1874
254 Canongate
Royal Mile
Edinburgh EH8 8AA
Phone: +44 (0)131 556 2791
www.whisky-cigars.co.uk
Established in 1874 this company specialises in Scotch whisky and cigars. They have a nice assortment of malt whiskies and their range of cigars is impressive.

SOUTH AFRICA

Aficionados Premium Spirits Online

M5 Freeway Park
Cape Town
Phone: +27 21 511 7337
www.aficionados.co.za
An online liquor retailer specialising in single malt whisky. They claim to offer the widest of range of whiskies available in South Africa and hold regular tastings around the country. Shipping only within South Africa.

WhiskyBrother

Hyde Park Corner
(middle level inside shopping mall)
Johannesburg
Phone: +27 (0)11 325 6261
www.whiskybrother.com
A shop specialising in all things whisky - apart from 400 different bottlings they also sell glasses, books etc. Also sell whiskies bottled exclusively for the shop. Regular tastings and online shop.

SWITZERLAND

P. Ullrich AG

Schneidergasse 27
4051 Basel
Phone: +41 (0)61 338 90 91
Another two shops in Basel:
Laufenstrasse 16 & Unt. Rebgasse 18
and one in Talacker 30 in Zürich
www.ullrich.ch
A very large range of wines, spirits, beers, accessories and books. Over 800 kinds of whisky with almost 600 single malt. On-line ordering. Recently, they also founded a whisky club with regular tastings (www.whiskysinn.ch).

Eddie's Whiskies

Dorfgasse 27
8810 Horgen
Phone: +41 (0)43 244 63 00
www.eddies.ch
A whisky specialist with more than 700 different whiskies in stock with emphasis on single malts (more than 500 different). Also arranges tastings.

Scot & Scotch

Wohllebgasse 7
8001 Zürich
Phone: +41 44 211 90 60
www.scotandscotch.ch
A whisky specialist with a great selection including c 560 single malts. Mail orders, but no on-line ordering.

Angels Share Shop

Unterdorfstrasse 15
5036 Oberentfelden
Phone: +41 (0)62 724 83 74
www.angelsshare.ch
A combined restaurant and whisky shop. More than 400 different kinds of whisky as well as a good range of cigars. Scores extra points for short information and photos of all distilleries. On-line ordering.

UKRAINE

Good Wine

Illi Mechnykova 9
Kiev 01133
Phone: +38 (0)44 4911075
www.goodwine.ua
Wine Bureau Company is the largest importer of wine and spirits in Ukraine, with sales of 4 million bottles per year. They also operate a flagship store in Kiev called Good Wine. The impressive and large shop (2,500 sqm) has a range of more than 1000 different spirits including 400 single malts. The owners arrange weekly tastings and also produce their own magazine.

USA

Binny's Beverage Depot

5100 W. Dempster (Head Office)
Skokie, IL 60077
Phone:
Internet orders, 888-942-9463 (toll free)
Whiskey Hotline, 888-817-5898 (toll free)
www.binnys.com
A chain of no less than 34 stores in the Chicago area, covering everything within wine and spirits. Some of the stores also have a gourmet grocery, cheese shop and, for cigar lovers, a walk-in humidor. Also lots of regular events in the stores. The range is impressive with more than 1800 whisk(e)y (700 single malts, 260 bourbons, 110 Irish whiskeys) and more. Among other products almost 400 kinds of tequila and mezcal, 450 vodkas and almost 350 rums should be mentioned. And, on top of that more than 10,000 different wines! Online mail order service.

Statistics

The following pages have been made possible,
first and foremost thanks to kind cooperation from The IWSR.
Data has also been provided by Drinks International, The Scotch Whisky
Industry Review and the Scotch Whisky Association.

Whisk(e)y forecast (volume) by region and category 2014-2019

■ = positive volume growth ■ = negative volume growth

SW=Scotch Whisky, IW=Irish Whiskey, UW=US Whiskey, CW=Canadian Whisky, OW=Other Whisky, TOT=Total.
The figures show CAGR% (Compound Annual Growth Rate) i. e. year-over-year growth rate.

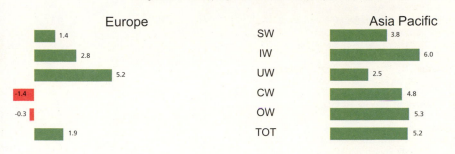

Europe

SW	1.4
IW	2.8
UW	5.2
CW	-1.4
OW	-0.3
TOT	1.9

Asia Pacific

SW	3.8
IW	6.0
UW	2.5
CW	4.8
OW	5.3
TOT	5.2

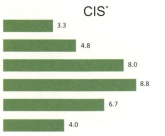

Americas

SW	2.4
IW	13.1
UW	4.1
CW	-0.2
OW	-3.3
TOT	2.7

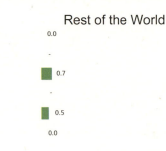

Africa & Middle East

SW	3.1
IW	6.1
UW	6.1
CW	- 3.3
OW	5.8
TOT	4.3

CIS*

SW	3.3
IW	4.8
UW	8.0
CW	8.8
OW	6.7
TOT	4.0

Rest of the World

SW	0.0
IW	-
UW	0.7
CW	-
OW	0.5
TOT	0.0

* Russia and other former Soviet Socialist Republic states

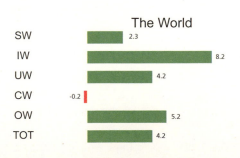

The World

SW	2.3
IW	8.2
UW	4.2
CW	-0.2
OW	5.2
TOT	4.2

Source: © The IWSR 2015

The Top 30 Whiskies of the World

Sales figures for 2015 (units in million 9-litre cases)

Officer's Choice (Allied Blenders & Distillers), Indian whisky — 34,7
McDowell's No. 1 (United Spirits), Indian whisky — 24,9
Johnnie Walker (Diageo), Scotch whisky — 18,8
Imperial Blue (Pernod Ricard), Indian whisky — 17,5
Royal Stag (Pernod Ricard), Indian whisky — 17,3
Jack Daniel's (Brown-Forman), Tennessee whiskey — 12,2
Old Tavern (United Spirits), Indian whisky — 11,9
Original Choice (John Distilleries), Indian whisky — 10,7
Bagpiper (United Spirits), Indian whisky — 8,0
Jim Beam (Beam Suntory), Bourbon — 7,4
Hayward's Fine (United Spirits), Indian whisky — 6,6
Ballantine's (Pernod Ricard), Scotch whisky — 6,2
Jameson (Pernod Ricard), Irish whiskey — 5,3
Crown Royal (Diageo), Canadian whisky — 5,3
Blenders Pride (Pernod Ricard), Indian whisky — 5,2
William Grant's (William Grant & Sons), Scotch whisky — 4,4
Chivas Regal (Pernod Ricard), Scotch whisky — 4,4
8PM (Radico Khaitan), Indian whisky — 4,1
Royal Challenge (United Spirits), Indian whisky — 3,8
Director's Special (United Spirits), Indian whisky — 3,7
J&B Rare (Diageo), Scotch whisky — 3,6
Kakubin (Suntory), Japanese whisky — 3,5
William Lawson's (Bacardi), Scotch whisky — 3,1
William Peel (Bélvedère), Scotch whisky — 2,9
Dewar's (Bacardi), Scotch whisky — 2,7
Label 5 (La Martiniquaise), Scotch whisky — 2,6
Director's Special Black (United Spirits), Indian whisky — 2,5
Black Nikka Clear (Asahi Breweries), Japanese whisky — 2,4
Black Velvet (Constellation Brands), Canadian whisky — 2,2
Bell's (Diageo), Scotch whisky — 2,2

Source: Drinks International, The Millionaires Club 2016

Global Exports of Scotch by Region

Volume (litres of pure alcohol)			chg	Value (£ Sterling)			chg
Region	2015	2014	%	Region	2015	2014	%
Africa	20,252,487	22,713,779	-11	Africa	193,676,818	219,338,371	-12
Asia	63,654,973	67,056,990	-5	Asia	772,386,515	800,622,978	- 4
Australasia	9,235,830	8,520,307	8	Australasia	97,559,266	92,719,463	5
C&S America	35,544,962	39,715,835	-11	C&S America	332,667,493	361,399,671	- 8
Eastern Europe	888,625	1,242,474	-28	Eastern Europe	9,776,958	14,754,642	-34
Europe (other)	6,653,246	6,106,119	9	Europe (other)	102,696,130	95,439,307	8
European Union	121,834,459	125,132,176	-3	European Union	1,198,212,215	1,243,456,295	- 4
Middle East	14,174,307	14,976,159	-5	Middle East	207,231,516	209,700,635	-1
North America	52,115,294	48,363,451	8	North America	941,136,341	913,583,180	3
Total	**324,354,183**	**333,827,290**	**-3**	**Total**	**3,855,343,252**	**3,951,014,542**	**- 2**

Source: Scotch Whisky Association

World Consumption of Blended Scotch

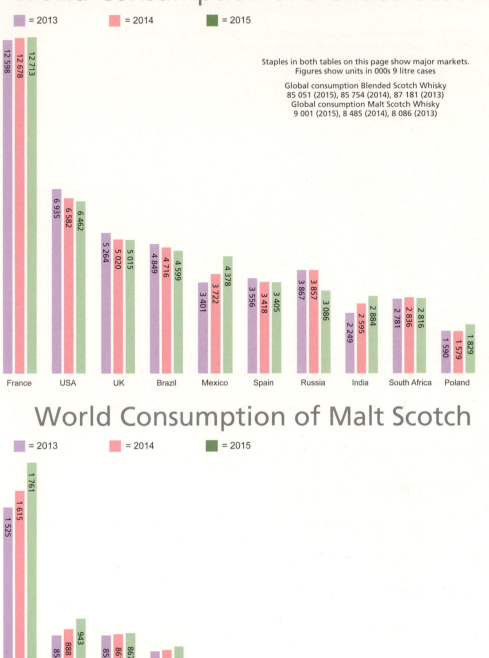

= 2013   = 2014   = 2015

Staples in both tables on this page show major markets.
Figures show units in 000s 9 litre cases

Global consumption Blended Scotch Whisky
85 051 (2015), 85 754 (2014), 87 181 (2013)
Global consumption Malt Scotch Whisky
9 001 (2015), 8 485 (2014), 8 086 (2013)

Country	2013	2014	2015
France	12 598	12 678	12 713
USA	6 935	6 582	6 462
UK	5 264	5 020	5 015
Brazil	4 849	4 716	4 599
Mexico	3 401	3 722	4 378
Spain	3 556	3 418	3 405
Russia	3 867	3 857	3 086
India	2 249	2 595	2 884
South Africa	2 781	2 836	2 816
Poland	1 590	1 579	1 829

Source: © The IWSR 2016

World Consumption of Malt Scotch

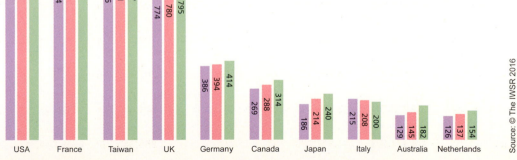

= 2013   = 2014   = 2015

Country	2013	2014	2015
USA	1 525	1 615	1 761
France	854	888	943
Taiwan	856	861	867
UK	774	780	795
Germany	386	394	414
Canada	269	288	314
Japan	186	214	240
Italy	215	208	200
Australia	129	145	182
Netherlands	126	137	154

Source: © The IWSR 2016

Top 10 Scotch Malt Whisky brands - world market share %

Brand	Year	Share
Glenfiddich	2015	12,1
	2014	12,1
	2013	12,9
The Glenlivet	2015	12,0
	2014	12,5
	2013	12,0
The Macallan	2015	8,8
	2014	9,4
	2013	9,8
Glenmorangie	2015	5,6
	2014	5,8
	2013	5,6
The Singleton Dufftown, Glendullan, Glen Ord	2015	5,4
	2014	4,8
	2013	4,2
Aberlour	2015	3,5
	2014	3,4
	2013	3,2
Laphroaig	2015	3,2
	2014	3,1
	2013	2,8
Glen Grant	2015	3,2
	2014	3,3
	2013	3,3
Balvenie	2015	3,0
	2014	2,8
	2013	2,8
Talisker	2015	2,2
	2014	2,2
	2013	2,1

Top 10 Scotch Blended Whisky brands - world market share %

Brand	Year	Share
Johnnie Walker	2015	21,5
	2014	21,3
	2013	21,3
Ballantine´s	2015	7,0
	2014	6,8
	2013	6,7
Chivas Regal	2015	5,3
	2014	5,4
	2013	5,4
Grant´s	2015	5,1
	2014	5,1
	2013	5,3
J&B	2015	4,1
	2014	4,2
	2013	4,2
William Lawson´s	2015	3,5
	2014	3,4
	2013	3,0
Famous Grouse	2015	3,4
	2014	3,6
	2013	3,5
William Peel	2015	3,3
	2014	3,1
	2013	3,0
Dewar´s	2015	3,1
	2014	3,2
	2013	3,4
Label 5	2015	2,8
	2014	2,7
	2013	2,6

Source: © The IWSR 2016

Distillery Capacity

Litres of pure alcohol - Scottish, active distilleries only

Distillery	Capacity	Distillery	Capacity	Distillery	Capacity
Glenfiddich	14 000 000	Bowmore	2 000 000	Springbank	750 000
Roseisle	12 500 000	Inchdairnie	2 000 000	Benromach	700 000
Ailsa Bay	12 000 000	Knockdhu	2 000 000	Kingsbarns	600 000
Glen Ord	11 000 000	Balblair	1 800 000	Speyside	600 000
Macallan	11 000 000	Pulteney	1 800 000	Annandale	500 000
Glenlivet	10 500 000	Bruichladdich	1 500 000	Ardnamurchan	500 000
Dalmunach	10 000 000	Bladnoch	1 500 000	Royal Lochnagar	500 000
Teaninich	9 800 000	Glendronach	1 400 000	Lone Wolf	450 000
Balvenie	6 800 000	Glen Spey	1 400 000	Glenturret	340 000
Caol Ila	6 500 000	Knockando	1 400 000	Harris	230 000
Glen Grant	6 200 000	Glen Garioch	1 370 000	Arbikie	200 000
Dufftown	6 000 000	Ardbeg	1 300 000	Glasgow	200 000
Glen Keith	6 000 000	Glencadam	1 300 000	Kilchoman	200 000
Glenmorangie	6 000 000	Scapa	1 300 000	Wolfburn	135 000
Mannochmore	6 000 000	Arran	1 200 000	Edradour	130 000
Auchroisk	5 900 000	Glenglassaugh	1 100 000	Ballindalloch	100 000
Miltonduff	5 800 000	Glengoyne	1 100 000	Eden Mill	80 000
Glen Moray	5 700 000	Tobermory	1 000 000	Daftmill	65 000
Glenrothes	5 600 000	Oban	870 000	Dornoch	30 000
Linkwood	5 600 000	Glen Scotia	800 000	Strathearn	30 000
Ardmore	5 550 000	Glengyle	750 000	Abhainn Dearg	20 000
Dailuaine	5 200 000				
Glendullan	5 000 000				
Loch Lomond	5 000 000				
Tomatin	5 000 000				
Clynelish	4 800 000				
Kininvie	4 800 000				
Longmorn	4 500 000				
Tormore	4 400 000				
Glenburgie	4 200 000				
Glentauchers	4 200 000				
Speyburn	4 200 000				
Craigellachie	4 100 000				
Allt-a-Bhainne	4 000 000				
Braeval	4 000 000				
Dalmore	4 000 000				
Glenallachie	4 000 000				
Royal Brackla	4 000 000				
Tamdhu	4 000 000				
Tamnavulin	4 000 000				
Aberlour	3 800 000				
Mortlach	3 800 000				
Glenlossie	3 700 000				
Aberfeldy	3 500 000				
Benrinnes	3 500 000				
Glenfarclas	3 500 000				
Cardhu	3 400 000				
Macduff	3 340 000				
Laphroaig	3 300 000				
Tomintoul	3 300 000				
Aultmore	3 200 000				
Fettercairn	3 200 000				
Inchgower	3 200 000				
Deanston	3 000 000				
Tullibardine	3 000 000				
Balmenach	2 800 000				
Benriach	2 800 000				
Blair Athol	2 800 000				
Bunnahabhain	2 700 000				
Glen Elgin	2 700 000				
Talisker	2 700 000				
Strathmill	2 600 000				
Glenkinchie	2 500 000				
Highland Park	2 500 000				
Lagavulin	2 450 000				
Strathisla	2 450 000				
Cragganmore	2 200 000				
Dalwhinnie	2 200 000				
Jura	2 200 000				
Auchentoshan	2 000 000				
Ben Nevis	2 000 000				

Summary of Malt Distillery Capacity by Owner

Owner (number of distilleries)	Litres of alcohol	% of Industry
Diageo (28)	120 210 000	31,8
Pernod Ricard (14)	69 150 000	18,3
William Grant (4)	37 600 000	10,0
Edrington Group (4)	19 440 000	5,2
Bacardi (John Dewar & Sons) (5)	18 140 000	4,8
Beam Suntory (5)	14 220 000	3,8
Emperador Inc (Whyte & Mackay) (4)	13 400 000	3,6
Pacific Spirits (Inver House) (5)	12 600 000	3,3
Moët Hennessy (Glenmorangie) (2)	7 300 000	1,9
Distell (Burn Stewart) (3)	6 700 000	1,8
Campari (Glen Grant) (1)	6 200 000	1,6
Loch Lomond Group (2)	5 800 000	1,5
La Martiniquaise (Glen Moray) (1)	5 700 000	1,5
Suntory (Morrison Bowmore) (3)	5 370 000	1,4
Benriach Distillery Co (3)	5 300 000	1,4
Ian Macleod Distillers (2)	5 100 000	1,4
Tomatin Distillery Co (1)	5 000 000	1,3
Angus Dundee (2)	4 600 000	1,2
J & G Grant (Glenfarclas) (1)	3 500 000	0,9
Picard (Tullibardine) (1)	3 000 000	0,8
John Fergus & Co. (1)	2 000 000	0,5
Nikka (Ben Nevis Distillery) (1)	2 000 000	0,5
Rémy Cointreau (Bruichladdich) (1)	1 500 000	< 0,5
J & A Mitchell (2)	1 500 000	< 0,5
David Prior (Bladnoch) (1)	1 500 000	< 0,5
Isle of Arran Distillers (1)	1 200 000	< 0,5
Gordon & MacPhail (Benromach) (1)	700 000	< 0,5
Wemyss Malts (Kingsbarns) (1)	600 000	< 0,5
Harvey´s of Edinburgh (Speyside) (1)	600 000	< 0,5
Adelphi Distillery (Ardnamurchan) (1)	500 000	< 0,5
Annandale Distillery Co. (1)	500 000	< 0,5
BrewDog plc (Lone wolf) (1)	450 000	< 0,5
Isle of Harris Distillers (1)	230 000	< 0,5
Glasgow Distillery Company (1)	200 000	< 0,5
Kilchoman Distillery Co (1)	200 000	< 0,5
Stirling family (Arbikie) (1)	200 000	< 0,5
Wolfburn Distillery (1)	135 000	< 0,5
Signatory Vintage (Edradour) (1)	130 000	< 0,5
Ballindalloch Estate (1)	100 000	< 0,5
Paul Miller (Eden Mill) (1)	80 000	< 0,5
Francis Cuthbert (Daftmill) (1)	65 000	< 0,5
Strathearn Distillery (1)	30 000	< 0,5
Thompson family (Dornoch) (1)	30 000	< 0,5
Mark Thayburn (Abhainn Dearg) (1)	20 000	< 0,5
Total	**377 430 000**	

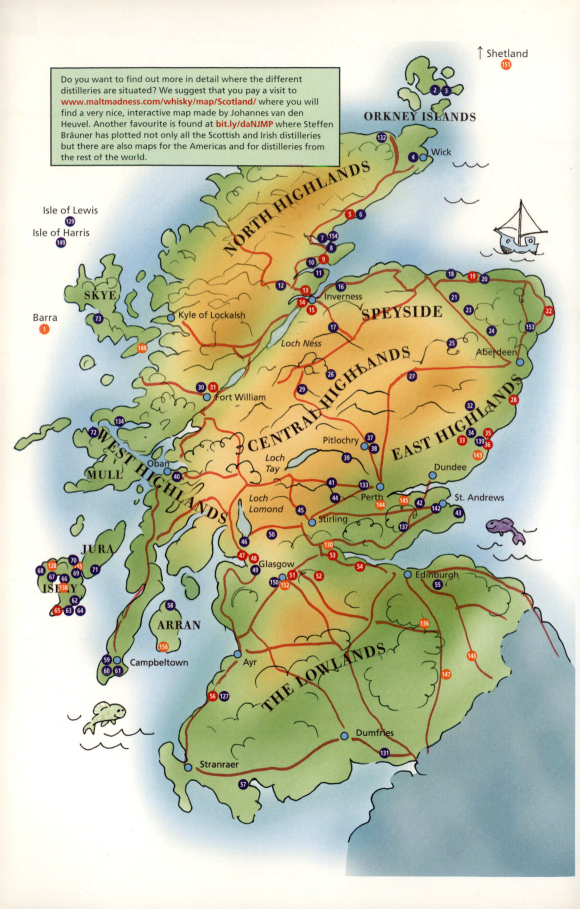

Do you want to find out more in detail where the different distilleries are situated? We suggest that you pay a visit to **www.maltmadness.com/whisky/map/Scotland/** where you will find a very nice, interactive map made by Johannes van den Heuvel. Another favourite is found at **bit.ly/daNJMP** where Steffen Bräuner has plotted not only all the Scottish and Irish distilleries but there are also maps for the Americas and for distilleries from the rest of the world.

Distilleries in red letters are Speyside ● **Active** ● **Closed, mothballed, dismantled or demolished** ● **Planned**

c = Closed, m = Mothballed, dm = Dismantled, d = Demolished

39 Aberfeldy	126 Duncan Taylor	100 Knockando	1 Barra	53 Rosebank (c)	105 Glenallachie
106 Aberlour	142 Eden Mill	21 Knockdhu	2 Highland Park	54 St Magdalene (dm)	106 Aberlour
129 Abhainn Dearg	38 Edradour	56 Ladyburn (dm)	3 Scapa	55 Glenkinchie	107 Macallan
127 Ailsa Bay	130 Falkirk	63 Lagavulin	4 Pulteney	56 Ladyburn (dm)	108 Craigellachie
119 Allt-a-Bhainne	32 Fettercairn	156 Lagg	5 Brora (c)	57 Bladnoch	109 Convalmore (dm)
143 Aniston Farms	138 Gartbreck	64 Laphroaig	6 Clynelish	58 Arran	110 Dufftown
131 Annandale	150 Glasgow Dist.	145 Lindores Abbey	7 Balblair	59 Springbank	111 Pittyvaich (d)
139 Arbikie	13 Glen Albyn (d)	79 Linkwood	8 Glenmorangie	60 Glengyle	112 Glenfiddich
62 Ardbeg	105 Glenallachie	48 Littlemill	9 Ben Wyvis (c)	61 Glen Scotia	113 Balvenie
25 Ardmore	76 Glenburgie	46 Loch Lomond	10 Teaninich	62 Ardbeg	114 Kininvie
155 Ardnahoe	34 Glencadam	36 Lochside (d)	11 Dalmore	63 Lagavulin	115 Mortlach
134 Ardnamurchan	23 Glendronach	153 Lone Wolf	12 Glen Ord	64 Laphroaig	116 Glendullan
58 Arran	116 Glendullan	84 Longmorn	13 Glen Albyn (d)	65 Port Ellen (dm)	117 Tormore
49 Auchentoshan	85 Glen Elgin	107 Macallan	14 Glen Mhor (d)	66 Bowmore	118 Cragganmore
92 Auchroisk	35 Glenesk (dm)	141 Macallan II	15 Millburn (dm)	67 Bruichladdich	119 Allt-a-Bhainne
94 Aultmore	101 Glenfarclas	81 Mannochmore	16 Royal Brackla	68 Kilchoman	120 Balmenach
7 Balblair	112 Glenfiddich	15 Millburn (dm)	17 Tomatin	69 Caol Ila	121 Tomintoul
135 Ballindalloch	52 Glen Flagler (d)	77 Miltonduff	18 Glenglassaugh	70 Bunnahabhain	122 Glenlivet
120 Balmenach	24 Glen Garioch	144 Morrison family	19 Banff (d)	71 Jura	123 Tamnavulin
113 Balvenie	18 Glenglassaugh	115 Mortlach	20 Macduff	72 Tobermory	124 Braeval
19 Banff (d)	50 Glengoyne	33 North Port (d)	21 Knockdhu	73 Talisker	125 Roseisle
1 Barra	87 Glen Grant	40 Oban	22 Glenugie (dm)	74 Benromach	126 Duncan Taylor
30 Ben Nevis	60 Glengyle	111 Pittyvaich (d)	23 Glendronach	75 Dallas Dhu (c)	127 Ailsa Bay
82 Benriach	96 Glen Keith	128 Port Charlotte	24 Glen Garioch	76 Glenburgie	128 Port Charlotte
104 Benrinnes	55 Glenkinchie	65 Port Ellen (dm)	25 Ardmore	77 Miltonduff	129 Abhainn Dearg
74 Benromach	122 Glenlivet	4 Pulteney	26 Speyside	78 Glen Moray	130 Falkirk
9 Ben Wyvis (c)	31 Glenlochy (d)	53 Rosebank (c)	27 Royal Lochnagar	79 Linkwood	131 Annandale
57 Bladnoch	83 Glenlossie	125 Roseisle	28 Glenury Royal (d)	80 Inchgower	132 Wolfburn
37 Blair Athol	14 Glen Mhor (d)	16 Royal Brackla	29 Dalwhinnie	81 Mannochmore	133 Strathearn
66 Bowmore	8 Glenmorangie	27 Royal Lochnagar	30 Ben Nevis	82 Benriach	134 Ardnamurchan
124 Braeval	78 Glen Moray	54 St Magdalene (dm)	31 Glenlochy (d)	83 Glenlossie	135 Ballindalloch
5 Brora (c)	12 Glen Ord	3 Scapa	32 Fettercairn	84 Longmorn	136 Tweeddale
67 Bruichladdich	89 Glenrothes	151 Shetland Dist.	33 North Port (d)	85 Glen Elgin	137 Inchdairnie
70 Bunnahabhain	61 Glen Scotia	88 Speyburn	34 Glencadam	86 Coleburn (dm)	138 Gartbreck
69 Caol Ila	91 Glenspey	26 Speyside	35 Glenesk (dm)	87 Glen Grant	139 Arbikie
90 Caperdonich (c)	93 Glentauchers	59 Springbank	36 Lochside (d)	88 Speyburn	140 Dalmunach
99 Cardhu	41 Glenturret	133 Strathearn	37 Blair Athol	89 Glenrothes	141 Macallan II
152 Clydeside Distillery	22 Glenugie (dm)	97 Strathisla	38 Edradour	90 Caperdonich (c)	142 Eden Mill
6 Clynelish	28 Glenury Royal (d)	95 Strathmill	39 Aberfeldy	91 Glenspey	143 Aniston Farms
86 Coleburn (dm)	149 Harris	73 Talisker	40 Oban	92 Auchroisk	144 Morrison
109 Convalmore (dm)	147 Hawick	98 Tamdhu	41 Glenturret	93 Glentauchers	145 Lindores Abbey
118 Cragganmore	2 Highland Park	123 Tamnavulin	42 Daftmill	94 Aultmore	146 Jedburgh
108 Craigellachie	137 Inchdairnie	10 Teaninich	43 Kingsbarns	95 Strathmill	147 Hawick
42 Daftmill	102 Imperial (d)	72 Tobermory	44 Tullibardine	96 Glen Keith	148 Torabhaig
103 Dailuaine	80 Inchgower	17 Tomatin	45 Deanston	97 Strathisla	149 Harris
75 Dallas Dhu (c)	47 Inverleven (d)	121 Tomintoul	46 Loch Lomond	98 Tamdhu	150 Glasgow Distillery
11 Dalmore	146 Jedburgh	148 Torabhaig	47 Inverleven (d)	99 Cardhu	151 Shetland
140 Dalmunach	71 Jura	117 Tormore	48 Littlemill (d)	100 Knockando	152 Clydeside Distillery
29 Dalwhinnie	68 Kilchoman	44 Tullibardine	49 Auchentoshan	101 Glenfarclas	153 Lone Wolf
45 Deanston	51 Kinclaith (d)	136 Tweeddale	50 Glengoyne	102 Imperial (d)	154 Dornoch
154 Dornoch	43 Kingsbarns	132 Wolfburn	51 Kinclaith (d)	103 Dailuaine	155 Ardnahoe
110 Dufftown	114 Kininvie		52 Glen Flagler (d)	104 Benrinnes	156 Lagg

Distillery Index